EIGHTH EDITION

Interpretations of AMERICAN HISTORY

Patterns and Perspectives

| VOLUME TWO | *Since Reconstruction*

Edited by

FRANCIS G. COUVARES
Amherst College

MARTHA SAXTON
Amherst College

GERALD N. GROB
Rutgers University

GEORGE ATHAN BILLIAS
Clark University

BEDFORD/ST. MARTIN'S

Boston • New York

To Gerald F. Linderman and Alexander Saxton, teachers and historians

For Bedford/St. Martin's

Executive Editor for History: Mary V. Dougherty
Executive Editor: William J. Lombardo
Director of Development for History: Jane Knetzger
Senior Editor: Sara Wise
Developmental Editor: Jim Strandberg
Editorial Assistant: Lynn Sternberger
Production Supervisor: Sarah Ulicny
Executive Marketing Manager: Jenna Bookin Barry
Text Design: Brian Salisbury
Project Management: Books By Design, Inc.
Index: Books By Design, Inc.
Cover Design: Sara Gates
Composition: Achorn International
Printing and Binding: RR Donnelley & Sons Company

President: Joan E. Feinberg
Editorial Director: Denise B. Wydra
Director of Marketing: Karen R. Soeltz
Director of Editing, Design, and Production: Marcia Cohen
Assistant Director of Editing, Design, and Production: Elise S. Kaiser
Manager, Publishing Services: Emily Berleth

Library of Congress Control Number: 2008923367

Manufactured in the United States of America.

3   2   1   0   9   8
f   e   d   c   b   a

For information, write: Bedford/St. Martin's, 75 Arlington Street, Boston, MA 02116   (617-399-4000)

ISBN-10: 0-312-48050-4
ISBN-13: 978-0-312-48050-9

Preface

We are very pleased to offer readers a thoroughly revised edition of *Interpretations of American History*, now published by Bedford/St. Martin's. First conceived by George Billias and Gerald Grob more than three decades ago, this collection has provided students of American history with a unique introduction to the major debates in American history, from the nature of the earliest settlements to contemporary conflicts. We intend this new edition of *Interpretations of American History* to provide students with selections of the best recent and classic works in American history, as well as updated historiographical essays that help them understand what is at stake when thoughtful historians disagree.

Interpretations of American History has long been a popular choice for both undergraduate and graduate historiography and methods courses, and a valued resource for historians. Based on positive feedback from reviewers, we have retained the general structure and format of the book. The book is again published as a two-volume paperback, with the chapter on Reconstruction appearing in both volumes. Each volume includes eleven chapters, and every chapter opens with a historiographical essay that tracks the major debates about the events or era covered in that chapter. Each chapter's historiographical essay is followed by two readings by outstanding scholars who offer differing viewpoints on — or approaches to — the general topic of that chapter. In many cases, we have chosen selections that overlap or complement each other to show students how historians build on the work of others to advance the field. By moving beyond a simple "either-or" format, we invite a deeper understanding of how historians work, why discourses take the shape they do, and how and why this changes over time.

New to This Edition

While the overall structure of the book remains the same, the eighth edition has been seriously revised and freshened. Each of the opening historiographical essays has been rewritten to reflect the most recent scholarship, with dozens of new books and articles discussed in the essays and hundreds of new historical works added to the extensive footnote citations. Volume One includes the newest scholarship on the struggles between Native Americans and colonists over the settlement of North America, the slave trade, the

Revolution, and the Constitution, as well as the Civil War and Reconstruction. Volume Two has been updated to reflect the latest interpretations of Progressivism and immigration and includes significantly revised coverage of the debates over the causes and consequences of the Cold War, the inclusivity of Second Wave feminism, and the evolution of the New Right. Beyond this crucial updating of our opening essays, fully half of the readings are new to this edition — Volume One includes twelve new readings, while eight new readings appear in Volume Two.

In the last decade, an explosion of historical writing has interpreted events in an international perspective. A rich and continuing harvest of comparative history has broadened the array of themes within which students must now consider our past. This dramatic development often challenges long held notions of American exceptionalism and, even more important, offers broader perspectives with which to judge the distinctive and common elements of historical experience across national and regional borders. Nearly every chapter of the eighth edition includes reference to this extensive new comparative, transnational scholarship. This new scholarship is reflected mostly in the historiographical essays but is not ignored in the new readings. For example, in Chapter 3 of Volume One, a new reading by Claudio Saunt analyzes the Choctaw-Cherokee conflict in the Old Southwest as a proxy war in the global struggle between the French and the British. In Volume Two, the new essay on the Cold War shows that even a field long committed to international perspectives has been transformed by new transnational approaches. The essay reviews older debates about the origins of the Cold War, most of which weighed the relative responsibility of the Soviet Union and the United States for the origins and evolution of conflict. Going beyond these debates, some contemporary historians increasingly take a "pericentric" approach that emphasizes the efficacy of nations that became independent after World War II, each with an agenda of its own, each tugging at the two superpowers. A new reading for the chapter by Odd Arne Westad shows that this new paradigm helps account for the duration and intensity of superpower conflict, even after many of the premises of a Euro-centered rivalry had outlived their purpose.

These volumes also emphasize even more than previous editions the centrality of race in American history. Work on the slave trade and the Black Atlantic provided early models for transnational history, while studies of race influenced later work on gender, ethnicity, and immigration — all fields that transcend nationality. In this edition, race figures importantly, not only with regard to obvious subjects such as the slave trade, slave culture, Reconstruction, and civil rights, but also in essays on Jacksonian politics, labor-capital conflict, immigration, Progressivism, Second Wave feminism, and the origins of the New Right.

In addition to the new scholarship that enlivens this edition, we also include classic arguments that have generated enduring debates within the discipline. For example, the first essay on the slave trade reaches back to Eric Williams, whose seminal 1944 book, *Capitalism and Slavery*, argued that slave traders acted out of a desire for profit, not racism, and that those profits propelled the Industrial Revolution in England and other capitalist countries. Economic historian David Eltis counters that Europeans targeted Africans for enslavement only because they considered them sufficiently "other" to be excluded from European notions of individual rights. The fast growing and conceptually adventurous historiography of the slave trade exemplifies both the centrality of slavery and race in U.S. history and the transnational turn in almost all fields of history today.

In Volume One, we have brought back a chapter on Jacksonian democracy to reflect recent scholarship that has reinvigorated study of that period. This revision's treatment of the Jacksonian era focuses on the Democratic Party's policies toward blacks and Native Americans. Sean Wilentz emphasizes the profound democratizing of politics that brought working men and farmers into the Jacksonian Democratic coalition. He defends the Democratic Party against proslavery charges, arguing that the diverse, sometimes antislavery northern Jacksonians of earlier years should not be confused with the more thoroughly proslavery party of the 1850s. In contrast, Lacy Ford insists that Jacksonian Democrats in the South widely and continuously supported slavery, reinforcing Alexander Saxton's demonstration that white workingmen's constructions of blackness and whiteness were fundamental to their ideas of democracy in the antebellum years and beyond.

While race is a central concern of these volumes, the chapter on the rise and possible fall of the New Right in Volume Two shows just how difficult it is to interpret late-twentieth-century politics through that lens. A new selection by Matthew Lassiter argues forcefully that the so-called Southern Strategy does not account for Republican victories in the last decades of the century. Rather, a Suburban Strategy linked middle-class Americans of all regions not only in resisting the politics of racial equality, but also in joining anti-crime, anti-tax, anti-abortion, and anti-busing movements. While many historians have explained the new conservatism as the southernization of the nation's politics, this new reading suggests that class concerns intermixed with racial ones in ways that transcended region.

We hope that this new edition of *Interpretations of American History* leads students to find in history what we and many others have discovered: an opportunity to explore the record of human thought and action with a commitment to accuracy, thoroughness, and imaginative sympathy.

Acknowledgments

For their important help in evaluating the seventh edition and helping us to identify which readings to keep or replace, we wish to thank the following reviewers: Steven J. Bucklin, University of South Dakota; William W. Cutler III, Temple University; Andrew Darien, Salem State College; Charles W. Eagles, University of Mississippi; Michael Frisch, University at Buffalo, The State University of New York; Larry G. Gerber, Auburn University; Kurt E. Leichtle, University of Wisconsin–River Falls; Lisa Levenstein, University of

North Carolina–Greensboro; Greg O'Brien, University of Southern Mississippi; Bradford Sample, Indiana Wesleyan University; and Matthew Avery Sutton, Washington State University.

We also wish to thank many people for their invaluable assistance on this project, including Mary Dougherty, Jane Knetzger, Sara Wise, Emily Berleth, Nancy Benjamin, Mary Sanger, Sybil Sosin, Jim Strandberg, Christopher Tullis, Rhea Cabin, Enrico Ferorelli, Betty Couvares, Eric Foner, Bruce Laurie, David Blight, Celso Castro-Alves, Joyce Avrech Berkman, and Gregory Call.

Contents

Introduction to U.S. Historiography

These volumes reflect our understanding that history is an act of interpretation. They also reflect the dramatic changes in the practice of history over the last four decades. Fifty years ago, historians primarily interpreted politics, diplomacy, and war. Since then, the civil rights, antiwar, and women's movements have dramatically opened up what historians and readers think of as history, while bringing into the profession women, African Americans, Hispanics, and Native Americans. Contemporary American historians write about nearly everything that has affected nearly everybody — from war to childbirth, agriculture to housework, illness to leisure, and banking systems to sewer systems. The expansive new history and the influx of new and diverse historians have linked the past more strongly to the present. Over a hundred years ago, the Italian philosopher Benedetto Croce observed, "Every true history is contemporary history."[1] He was trying to cast doubt on arguments of late-nineteenth-century historians (called "historicists" or "positivists") that history was a science and could recover objective truths if properly practiced. Croce insisted that the past "in itself" is unknowable and that history represents our collective effort to make sense of the world. Inviting into the practice of history groups previously excluded from the profession has demonstrated the validity of Croce's view in new ways. Views of the past vary not only with generations but also because of divergent experiences stemming from the historian's gender, ethnicity, class, and race. This does not mean that we cannot find out anything solid about the past. But it does mean that no account of the past is free of the perspectives, prejudices, and priorities of its author and that the more varied the range of historians, the more likely their collective output will achieve a balanced totality.

When we read history, we are reading a particular historian's encounter with the world. The historian is devoted to the "facts," spends years of his or her life combing through the archives, and believes that the story she or he comes away with represents reality. But in writing, the historian renders this material into a story. The design of a narrative reflects its author's

---

[1]Benedetto Croce, *History: Its Theory and Practice* (New York, 1921), develops ideas he first articulated in 1893; for a sampling of the work of Croce and other philosophers of history in the first half of the twentieth century, see Hans Meyerhoff, ed., *The Philosophy of History in Our Time* (New York, 1959); and Patrick Gardiner, ed., *Theories of History* (Glencoe, Ill., 1959). See also Fritz Stern, ed., *Varieties of History: From Voltaire to the Present* (Cleveland and New York, 1956). An excellent guide through these philosophical thickets, designed especially for students, is Michael Stanford, *A Companion to the Study of History* (Oxford, 1994).

circumstances, values, ideology, nationality, school of thought, or theoretical and methodological preference. One historian is, we say, a Jeffersonian liberal, another a neo-Marxist, another a progressive or a conservative, still another a feminist or postmodernist. We note that Perry Miller's account of the Puritans reflects his alienation from twentieth-century American liberalism, John Hope Franklin's or Eric Foner's account of Reconstruction is shaped by his engagement with the civil rights movement, Oscar Handlin's or George Sanchez's history of immigration reflects his own ethnic experience, or Kathryn Sklar's ideas about Progressivism are informed by her feminism. In doing so, we acknowledge that personal perspective influences the angle of vision and the character of illumination that the historian brings to the historical landscape.

If history is partly craft and partly personal perspective, however, it is also partly science. An error as common as thinking history is "just the facts" is thinking it is "just your story." Whereas the nineteenth-century positivists thought that scientific method could guarantee objective truth in history just as it does in physics, some present-day postmodern theorists maintain that history is inescapably opinion. Postmodern criticism has encouraged historians to be more attentive to the possible layers of meaning in their documents, to their unacknowledged theoretical commitments, and to their use of language in writing history. But those postmodernists who assert that historians cannot arrive at truth, or that history is no different than fiction, err like the positivists but in the opposite direction. However parallel some of the techniques of ideologue, novelist, and historian, the historian is constrained by the record in a way the other two are not. One literary critic has written that, like other writers of nonfiction, the historian's "allegiance is to fact."[2] Historians willingly acknowledge that no account is absolutely true and is certainly never final, but they also insist that some histories are better than others. Something other than the historian's political, moral, or esthetic preferences comes into play in judging one history better than another, something, for want of a better term, objective.

While committed to a particular interpretation, the historian remains faithful to the evidence and determined to test the accuracy and the adequacy of every historical account. History succeeds when it tells us how things were, yet at the same time reminds us that the only access we have to the past is through the imagination of a finite and very contemporary human being. A historian reveals the contours of a landscape from a distinct perspective, but he or she does not invent the landscape.[3] The British

---

[2]Sue Halpern, "The Awful Truth," *New York Review of Books* (September 25, 1997): 13.

[3]The most recent denial of history's truth claims is Peter Novick, *That Noble Dream: The "Objectivity Question" and the American Historical Profession* (Cambridge, 1988). Dorothy Ross, "Grand Narrative in American Historical Writing: From Romance to Uncertainty," *American Historical Review* 100 (June 1995): 651–77, offers brilliant critiques of historians' narrative strategies and somewhat elusive postmodernist suggestions about alternatives. Arguments for a middle ground between objectivism and Novick's relativism can be found in James T. Kloppenberg, "Objectivity and Historicism: A Century of American Historical Writing," *American*

historian Mary Fulbrook has recently affirmed convincingly that there are reasonable "criteria for preferring one historical approach or interpretation to another; and that these criteria need not be, as the postmodernists would have it, purely based on moral, political, or aesthetic considerations."[4] Fulbrook insists that, when theoretically alert, historians can deploy "empirical evidence and inter-subjective professional dialogue" to produce "progress" in historical knowledge.[5]

In practical terms, historians make progress and get closer to the truth by arguing with one another. And so history relies on historiography, the study of history and its changing interpretations.[6] Every historian begins work by immersing himself or herself in the subject and remains in dialogue with others interested in similar matters. Most books by serious historians include historiographical essays that locate the work within the context of related works. Historiography reminds us that history is not a closed book, not a collection of inarguable facts. There is always something to argue about in history, something that makes us think about the conduct of our contemporary lives. Thus, in a world of liberation movements and resurgent nationalism, it matters how we tell the story of the American Revolution or of the growth of America's overseas empire. In a society riven by conflicts over racism, sexual exploitation, and growing disparities between rich and poor, it matters how we narrate the history of labor, or the New Deal, or the rights movements of the 1960s and 1970s. Knowing that African American state governments during Reconstruction effectively delivered services while suffering only modest corruption makes it impossible to cast African American disfranchisement as a by-product of cleaning up government. It may also affect our judgments about contemporary liberals' confidence in elections as the road to equality and of conservatives' recent efforts to prevent "voter fraud." Similarly, knowing that some turn-of-the-century migrants to the United States returned to their homelands in great numbers might require us to adjust ideas about assimilation. It may also change the way we think about the dual loyalties of contemporary migrants.

Historical Review 94 (October 1989): 1011–30; Thomas L. Haskell, "Objectivity Is Not Neutrality: Rhetoric vs. Practice in Peter Novick's *That Noble Dream*," *History and Theory* 29 (1990): 129–57; David Hollinger, *In the American Province: Studies in the History and Historiography of Science* (Bloomington, Ind., 1985); and "*AHR* Forum: Peter Novick's *That Noble Dream*: The Objectivity Question and the Future of the Historical Profession," *American Historical Review* 96 (June 1991): 675–708, with contributions from Hollinger and others and with a reply from Novick. See also Joyce Appleby, Lynn Hunt, and Margaret Jacoby, *Telling the Truth about History* (New York, 1994); Alan B. Spitzer, *Historical Truth and Lies about the Past: Reflections on Dewey, Dreyfus, de Man, and Reagan* (Chapel Hill, N.C., 1996); and Richard J. Evans, *In Defense of History* (New York, 1999). A more conservative and alarmist defense of objectivity is Keith Windschuttle, *The Killing of History: How Literary Critics and Social Theorists Are Murdering Our Past* (New York, 1997).

[4] Mary Fulbrook, *Historical Theory* (London, 2002), ix–x.

[5] Ibid., 188, 30.

[6] J. H. Hexter defines historiography as "the craft of writing history" or the "rhetoric of history," in "The Rhetoric of History," originally published in the *International Encyclopedia of the Social Sciences*, vol. 6 (New York, 1968), 368–94, and republished in revised form in his *Doing History* (Bloomington, Ind., 1971), 15–76.

Historical scholarship is thus in continual flux. But for careful students of historiography, disagreement is more interesting than agreement could ever be, for it holds the key to a better understanding not just of the past but of the present and possibly the future as well.

What follows is a sketch of the evolution of American history as a discipline over the course of the last two centuries.[7] As with all attempts to fit diverse strands of thought and experience into a single story, ambiguities haunt this narration or are suppressed in the interest of a continuous story line. As much as possible, the following overview tries to balance human complexity with narrative simplicity.

Broadly speaking, the writing of American history has passed through four stages: the providential, the rationalist, the nationalist, and the professional. The ministers and magistrates of the seventeenth and eighteenth centuries, and most of the women who wrote history through the Civil War, wrote a form of providential history. The Puritan practitioners who originated this form wished to justify the ways of God to man, and vice versa. Their history was a holy chronicle, revealing his Providence toward his Chosen People and their efforts to build a New Canaan in the wilderness. The preeminent work in this tradition was William Bradford's *Of Plimoth Plantation*. Written during the 1630s and 1640s when Bradford was governor of the colony, the book recounts the fate of a tiny band of Puritans who fled England for Holland and then for the New World. They rested in the certainty that God's hand led them forward, that their disasters were his rebukes, their successes his merciful rewards. Governor John Winthrop of Massachusetts wrote such a history, as did Cotton Mather in the next century. Mary Rowlandson's eyewitness account of her own captivity employed the same providential themes. Well into the nineteenth century, male and female historians, including Mercy Otis Warren, Elizabeth Peabody, and Hannah Adams, viewed the story of America as an extension of the history of the Protestant Reformation. The Revolution became for them a triumph of reformed Christianity over paganism and Catholicism. And the United States as a whole took the place of New England as the model of Christian virtue for the corrupt Old World to emulate.[8]

In the late eighteenth century, as the European Enlightenment came to America, history took on a secular and naturalistic cast. A new class of intellectuals, influenced by Newton, Locke, and the French philosophes, had come to see history, like the physical universe, as subject to natural law. These rationalist historians flourished alongside and sometimes superseded the clerics who had once dominated the educated class in the colonies. The new story they told was of progress, reason — and, indeed, "the progress of reason" — in human affairs. Although a few Protestant ministers responded to the new intel-

---

[7]On the development of the historical profession in America, see John Higham, *History: Professional Scholarship in America* (New York, 1973). See also works cited in footnote 3.

[8]Nina Baym, *American Women Writers and the Work of History* (New Brunswick, N.J., 1995), particularly "History from a Divine Point of View," 46–66.

lectual currents,[9] most historians in the late eighteenth century were lawyer-politicians, planter-aristocrats, merchants, professionals, and, in the case of Judith Sargent Murray, the daughter and wife of a minister. Among the most prominent were Thomas Hutchinson, leading merchant and royal governor of Massachusetts; William Smith, physician, landowner, and prominent politician of New York; and Robert Beverley and William Byrd of Virginia, both planter-aristocrats and officeholders. These men possessed classical educations, fine private libraries, and the leisure time to use both. Their writing was more refined and allusive than the studiously plain prose of their Puritan predecessors. They wrote history for their own satisfaction, but also to explain to the enlightened world the success of men like themselves — free, bold, intelligent, and ambitious men who built fortunes and governed provinces that embodied a perfect balance between liberty and order.

Thomas Jefferson's *Notes on the State of Virginia* (written in the midst of revolutionary turmoil and finally published in 1785) is a highly evolved product of this rationalist tradition. America is for Jefferson, as it was for the Puritans, a model for the world, but natural law takes the place of divine providence in directing its affairs. Self-interest, not piety, motivates men; reason, not faith, allows them to discover and pursue their destiny. The fruits of liberty include not only astonishing material prosperity and advances in knowledge but moral progress as well. The new nation is destined to open the way toward a new era in human history not only because its natural resources are vast but also because free people are virtuous and possessed of the moral energy to change the world. Some evangelical Protestants called Jefferson a "confirmed infidel" and a "howling atheist" for his emphasis on human as opposed to divine agency. But Jefferson's most potent enemies were political: in the 1790s, he led the Republican opposition to the Federalist Party of Washington, Hamilton, and Adams. During the brutal presidential election campaigns of 1800 and 1804, both of which Jefferson won, Federalist writers combed the *Notes* to find ammunition against Jefferson the infidel, the apologist for slavery, the lover of French revolutionary excess. Their charges reveal, among other things, that history had already become politicized. History was a story about how wealth, power, rights, and wrongs came to be in this world — how causes produced effects, and how human actions could change those effects. But the story for the rationalists was no more open-ended than it was for the providentialists: it still pointed toward improvement. Through most of the nineteenth century and into the early twentieth, American history remained the story of the progress of the "Empire of Liberty."

As the nineteenth century wore on, historians began to temper their Enlightenment assurance about human beings' capacity for rational improvement. They increasingly believed that races possessed different inherent capacities and viewed the rise of America as the triumph of Anglo-Saxon

---

[9]See Edmund S. Morgan, *The Gentle Puritan: A Life of Ezra Stiles, 1727–1795* (New Haven, Conn., 1962).

people over inferior races. Similar strains of thinking in Europe helped to justify colonization. George Bancroft, the most distinguished American historian of the mid-nineteenth century, organized the history of America around three themes: progress, liberty, and Anglo-Saxon destiny. Bancroft deviated from his own rationalist background after studying in Germany, where he absorbed the romantic emphasis on the inborn virtues of the "folk." The idea that Teutonic peoples (who included Anglo-Saxons) were racially destined to spread freedom across the globe was central to this romantic nationalism. In twelve volumes published between 1834 and 1882, Bancroft chronicled the spread of Anglo-Saxon ideas of political freedom, their perfection in American democratic institutions, and their realization in Jacksonian democracy.[10]

Even women historians such as Hannah Adams, Susanna Rowson, Elizabeth Peabody, and Emma Willard, whose evangelical commitments made them political enemies of the Jacksonian Democratic Party, manifested romantic nationalist thinking not unlike Bancroft's. In her *Pioneer Women of the West* (1852), Elizabeth Ellet focused on conflict between white settlers and indigenous people. As Nina Baym put it in 1995, Ellet "is as close to a genocidal writer as one is likely to find."[11] Some women, however, did break the barriers of gender and nationalist history. Helen Hunt Jackson explored white-Indian relations in both fiction and history. Her *Century of Dishonor* (1881) — which she sent to every member of Congress — documented the American nation's shameful dealings with Indians. Intent on reaching a wider popular audience, she then published a novel, *Ramona*, that dramatized white appropriation of Indian lands and other cruelties. At the same time, white and Indian anthropologists began studying native cultures, some because they thought Indians were disappearing, others because they wished to counteract racist myths by displaying the vigor and richness of Indian cultures.[12] Unfortunately, neither criticism nor ethnographic knowledge seriously affected the trajectory of mainstream history. Not until the arrival of the inclusionary politics of the late twentieth century would the work of anthropologists and ethnographers find its way into the pages of historical scholarship.

By the 1870s, Bancroft's self-congratulatory epic history had become conventional wisdom. But changes were afoot in the discipline. The first change was in leadership: amateur writers increasingly gave way to professional historians. As college education became more common among middle-class Americans and as industrialization reinforced the value of technical and scientific knowledge, historians increasingly concerned themselves with specialized training, research methodology, and educational credentials. History became a profession like any other. This meant, among other things,

---

[10]On Bancroft and other romantic historians, see David Levin, *History as Romantic Art* (New York, 1963).

[11]Baym, *American Women Writers*, 219, 238; other enemies of Jackson, such as historians Francis Parkman and W. H. Prescott, wrote a similar kind of romantic-racial epic: see Levin, *History as Romantic Art.*

[12]See Volume One, Chapter 3.

that it would be practiced by the only people who had access to advanced education — white men. Many of them were trained in Germany, but in 1876 Johns Hopkins University became the first exclusively graduate research institution in the United States. Soon thereafter, graduate study spread to the midwestern land-grant universities and the Ivy League. The newly minted historians usually planned careers in the same university system that had trained them. They prided themselves on rigorous research and a capacity to distinguish scientifically verified truth from romantic notion. Reflecting on these developments in 1894, Henry Adams imagined this new professional historian "dreaming of the immortality that would be achieved by the man who should successfully apply Darwin's method to the facts of human history."[13]

Along with Frederick Jackson Turner, Adams exemplified the first generation of professional historians, which held sway from about 1870 to 1910. A scion of the great family that had produced presidents and statesmen, Adams might appear at first to be a throwback to the era of patrician amateurs. Politics was the career he had hoped for, while history seemed an avocation. But as his political hopes dimmed, his professional ambitions ignited. In 1870, he was invited to Harvard to teach the first seminar ever devoted to historical research at that institution. Adams taught the meticulous methods of German scholarship and insisted that history's goal was to develop knowledge every bit as sound as that in physics. His exhaustively researched nine-volume history of the Jefferson and Madison administrations represented the fruit of his commitment to the scientific method and remains a classic. Although he left Harvard after a few years, his career exemplified the new professionalism that would permanently transform the discipline.

Turner could not have been more different from Adams in background and personal circumstances. Born of modest means in a rural town in Wisconsin, he attended the University of Wisconsin, received a Ph.D. in history at Johns Hopkins, and went on to teach at Wisconsin and Harvard. While different from Adams in so many ways, Turner shared the belief that history should be a science. He fulfilled Adams's prophecy in using Darwin's evolutionary theory to explain the genesis of the American character. Just as one species surpassed another, he argued in his famous "The Significance of the Frontier in American History," so one frontier environment succeeded another in the course of American expansion. As successive frontiers grew more remote from European antecedents, they increasingly nurtured the distinctive American virtues of self-reliance, egalitarianism, tolerance, practicality, and realism.[14] Although he embodied the new scientific history, Turner's sweeping generalizations and his assumptions about the "progress of the

---

[13] Henry Adams, "The Tendency of History," *Annual Report of the American Historical Association for the Year 1894* (Washington, D.C., 1895), 19.

[14] Turner's essay, originally delivered as his presidential address to the American Historical Association in 1893, can be found in *The Frontier in American History* (New York, 1920). For more on Turner, see John Higham, *Writing American History: Essays on Modern Scholarship* (Bloomington, Ind., 1970), 118–29.

race" linked him to his nationalist predecessors. He conflated America with capitalism, democracy, and the heroic deeds of the pioneers.

Between 1910 and 1945, a second generation of professional scholars — the Progressive historians — rose to prominence. They were identified with the Progressive movement in politics, which worked to combat corporate and political corruption and the suffering of working families in early-twentieth-century America.[15] They observed that modernity — industrialization, urbanization, and class conflict — had fundamentally transformed the society. If democracy was to survive, people needed a materially based history of changing institutions and economic interests, not fables about the progress of liberty and justice. Progressives saw history as politics, not science or art. To be sure, science was needed to produce usable facts and art to persuade people to act on them, but Progressive historians wanted their history to provoke political action above all. Neither genteel amateurs nor morally neutral scientists, Progressives were muscular intellectuals — or, as they would have gladly called themselves, reformers.

In 1913, the most famous Progressive historian, Charles A. Beard, published *An Economic Interpretation of the Constitution,* one of the most influential books ever written in American history. It argued that the Constitution was the product not of wise men intent on balancing liberty and order, but of a clique of wealthy merchants and landowners who wanted a central government strong enough to defend their privileges against the unruly masses. A series of books culminating in *The Rise of American Civilization* (1927), which Beard wrote with his wife, Mary Ritter Beard, elaborated the thesis that American history was a succession of conflicts between economic interest groups. Although critics found flaws with his economic determinism and faith in Progressive reform, Beard managed to inspire a generation to look to history for answers to the questions that pressed most insistently on the democratic citizenry.

With a literary flair that exceeded that of either Turner or Beard, Vernon L. Parrington brought the Progressive interpretation to intellectual history in *Main Currents in American Thought.* His story was arrestingly simple: all of American history was shaped by the contest between Jeffersonian and Hamiltonian ways of thinking. Jefferson, champion of the people, represented decentralized agrarian democracy; Hamilton, tribune of the privileged, stood for centralized commercial aristocracy. From the moment the Revolution ended, these two ideas fought for control of American minds. In whatever guise — Federalist versus Republican, Whig versus Jacksonian, Conservative versus Progressive — all these conflicts reflected a continuous economic dynamic that animated American history. The function of history was to uncover the economic basis of political ideas and thereby to educate the citizenry. Parrington wanted his fellow citizens to take on the task of fighting reaction and pushing reform.

---

[15]See Chapter 6.

Progressive history challenged the profession in another way: it insisted that historical knowledge is relative. In an essay published in 1935 entitled "That Noble Dream," Charles Beard observed that one bar to objectivity is that the historian's documentation is always partial. More important, like Croce he insisted that the historian is never neutral and therefore must write an interpretation, not a scientific re-creation, of the past. The dream of objectivity must be discarded by the serious and honest historian. Acknowledging one's politics and prejudices does not weaken the value of the historian's work, Beard insisted, but rather strengthens it. An interpretation — which he defined as an "overarching hypothesis or conception employed to give coherence and structure to past events" — should be measured not by whether it is correct or incorrect but by whether it is useful to people who are trying to improve their world.[16] Carl L. Becker, a Progressive historian of early America, made the promotion of relativism one of the central purposes of his career. In his 1931 presidential address to the American Historical Association, "Everyman His Own Historian," and in other essays, Becker repeated that, however indispensable the scientific pursuit of facts, history meant nothing unless it was yoked to the political necessities of real people. History's obligation is not to the dead but to the living; its account of the past is "perhaps neither true nor false, but only the most convenient form of error."[17]

Female and African American scholars challenged the profession in still other ways, though historians were not yet ready to respond. Mary Ritter Beard, for example — who published many works with her husband and many books about women on her own, culminating in *Woman as a Force in History* in 1946 — achieved little or no recognition from the profession. She entered Columbia graduate school with her husband in 1902, but dropped out two years later and subsequently nurtured a hostility for academics and for college education for women. She chose to wear her amateur status like a crown in the face of a profession that refused to welcome her.[18] Other women in the Progressive Era who chose to write women's history similarly saw their work ignored by their male colleagues.[19]

African American historians fared little better. At the American Historical Association meeting in 1909, W. E. B. Du Bois, having earned a Ph.D. from Harvard, offered a startling reinterpretation of Reconstruction that focused on the lives of poor blacks and whites. In the face of a daunting tradition condemning Reconstruction, he argued that it had briefly

---

[16]Charles A. Beard, "That Noble Dream," *American Historical Review* 41 (October 1935): 74–87.

[17]This and related essays may be found in *Everyman His Own Historian* (New York, 1935). See also Phil L. Snyder, ed., *Detachment and the Writing of History: Essays and Letters of Carl L. Becker* (Ithaca, N.Y., 1958). For more on historical relativism, see Higham, *History*; a neo-relativist argument can be found in Novick, *That Noble Dream*, and other works cited in note 3, above. Still very useful as a philosophical guide is Jack W. Mieland, *Scepticism and Historical Knowledge* (New York, 1965).

[18]Ann J. Lane, *Mary Ritter Beard, A Sourcebook* (New York, 1977), 33, 53–54.

[19]Helen Sumner's *Women and Industry in the U.S.* and Edith Abbott's *Women in Industry*, both published in 1910, were barely noticed by the male profession.

provided the South with democratic government, public schools, and other needed social programs. Like other Progressives, Du Bois found economic causes underlying political events; unlike them, however, he included black people as legitimate historical subjects. This simple act of inclusion irrevocably altered his assessment of Reconstruction. Published in 1935, his book attracted many favorable reviews, but most historians ignored it. Du Bois's views did not enter the mainstream of the profession until John Hope Franklin's and Kenneth Stampp's revisionist interpretations appeared in the 1960s.[20]

The Progressives' economic determinism and their relativism both had an enormous impact on the history profession, but neither Beard nor Becker held the center stage exclusively or for long. Critics of both progressive and relativist assertions began to multiply. In part, the critics were responding to the rise of totalitarianism, which made faith in progress seem naive and relativism seem cowardly. The fact that Charles Beard quite conspicuously continued to oppose American involvement in World War II, at a time when most left-wing intellectuals were rapidly shifting from pacifism to intervention, seemed to many intellectuals to emphasize the narrow-mindedness of the Progressive point of view. In the face of Hitler and Stalin, and especially after the horrors of Auschwitz, Dresden, and Hiroshima, American historians asked themselves if Progressive history had ill-prepared them and their fellow citizens for the harrowing obligations of the twentieth century. But it was not just the weight of tragic events that shifted the historiographical terrain.

In the 1930s and into the 1950s, younger historians increasingly found the Progressive historians' psychology shallow, their social analysis predictable, and their moral judgments superficial. Like the philosophers and theologians who were criticizing liberalism for its facile optimism and obtuseness in the face of human tragedy, these critics charged that Progressive historians underestimated humankind's propensity for evil, overestimated its capacity for good, and turned history into a simple morality play. More important, they found the Progressive insistence on explaining most events as the product of conflict between rich and poor, East and West, reactionaries and reformers, and the like to be more hindrance than help in making sense of specific historical problems. More and more historians were insisting that, for better *and* worse, consensus rather than conflict marked American political history, that the absence of European-style class conflict had indelibly shaped American institutions and ideas. In Europe, the crises of depression and war led many historians in radical directions; here, under the influence of the Cold War, it led toward what came to be called "consensus history."

The caricature of consensus historians is that they asserted the unity and homogeneity of America's past, the stability of basic institutions, and the existence of a homogeneous national character. When they did acknowl-

---

[20]W. E. B. Du Bois, *Black Reconstruction in America, 1860–1880* (New York, 1992), vii–viii, xvi. For more on the historiography of Reconstruction, see Chapter 2.

edge that conflict occurred between sections, classes, and groups, the consensus historians insisted that contestants fought within a common liberal framework and never really disagreed over fundamentals. Moreover, this caricature continues, consensus historians doubted the value of social change and, having observed a world brutalized by fascism and communism, feared mass movements of any kind. In this reading, consensus historians trimmed the sails of history to the conservative and anti-Communist winds of the McCarthy era. In fact, so-called consensus historians were remarkably diverse, and many were liberals. Some were indeed "Cold War liberals" who believed that a defense of American values and institutions was more important than social criticism at a moment when totalitarianism threatened to take over the world. However, there was no simple correlation between Cold War attitudes and consensus historiography. Arthur M. Schlesinger Jr., who never departed from the Progressive camp, was the leading Cold War liberal in the history profession. On the other hand, the distinguished Columbia University historian Richard Hofstadter, who was called a consensus historian and was a sharp critic of Progressive historiography, was equally if not more critical of the consensus he found in American history.

Some consensus history did prove useful to cold warriors. In his influential *The Liberal Tradition in America,* Louis Hartz argued that because America lacked a feudal tradition, it escaped the struggles between reactionaries, liberals, and socialists that characterized the history of most European countries. The United States instead had a three-century-long tradition of liberal consensus, wherein all Americans subscribed to the Lockean tenets of individualism, private property, natural rights, and popular sovereignty. The differences among Americans, Hartz maintained, were over means rather than ends. And thus America had very little class conflict and little ground for the breeding of class-based ideologies. Socialism could mean little in America because nearly everyone had access to a middle-class way of life. Conservatism, too, could mean little because the only thing to conserve — the only continuous tradition — was liberalism.[21]

Another postwar consensus historian, Daniel Boorstin, wrote a three-volume epic story of settlement, westward migration, and community building. Although he echoed the Progressive Turner in many ways, Boorstin described characters who were largely uninterested in politics and ideology. Most of them were pragmatic, energetic, healthy-minded "Versatiles," ready to conquer a continent, invent the balloon-frame house, experiment with popular democracy, and in the process develop the freest and most prosperous society on earth. Boorstin's approach was social-historical. Like the more radical social historians who would soon transform the discipline,

---

[21]Louis Hartz, *The Liberal Tradition in America: An Interpretation of American Political Thought since the Revolution* (New York, 1955). A brilliant critique (and also appreciation) of Hartz can be found in James T. Kloppenberg, "From Hartz to Tocqueville: Shifting the Focus from Liberalism to Democracy in America," in Meg Jacobs, William J. Novak, and Julian E. Zelizer, eds., *The Democratic Experiment: New Directions in American Political History* (Princeton, N.J., 2003), 350–80.

Boorstin insisted that American society and culture were decisively shaped by millions of ordinary people, not by elites. But for Boorstin, those anonymous masses were middle class at heart and yearned for nothing so much as a house with a picket fence and a little room to breathe. Distinct from most of the other consensus historians, Boorstin preached a political message that might be called conservative populism.

If Hartz's insistence on ideological homogeneity and Boorstin's populist social history seemed to affirm a Cold War consensus, the political tonality of Richard Hofstadter's work proved harder to gauge. Beginning in 1948 with the publication of *The American Political Tradition and the Men Who Made It*, Hofstadter argued that the liberal tradition had failed to escape the acquisitive and individualistic assumptions that had shaped it. Supposed reformers such as the Populists and Progressives looked back with nostalgia to an era of self-made men, rather than facing up to the fundamental problems of an industrialized and corporate America. Even Franklin Delano Roosevelt, who did not share the nostalgia common to the Progressive tradition, was primarily a pragmatist whose strength lay in the force of his personality rather than in any consistent ideology or philosophy. In *The Age of Reform: From Bryan to F.D.R.*, Hofstadter exposed what he saw as the curious blend of racism, nativism, and provincialism that shaped the Populists and would later manifest itself in paranoid scares such as McCarthyism in the 1950s. All such movements meant "to restore the conditions prevailing before the development of industrialism and the commercialization of agriculture."[22] Hofstadter maintained that American political conflict reflected not the clash of economic interests but the search by different ethnic and religious groups for a secure status in society. By the latter third of the nineteenth century, the middle-class offspring of Anglo-Saxon Protestant families found themselves displaced from traditional positions of leadership by a nouveau-riche plutocracy, on the one hand, and urban immigrant political machines, on the other. Responding to this displacement, the elite launched a moral crusade to resuscitate older Protestant and individualistic values — the Progressive movement. In this campaign "to maintain a homogeneous Yankee civilization," Hofstadter wrote, "I have found much that was retrograde and delusive, a little that was vicious, and a good deal that was comic."[23]

Hofstadter emerged from within the Progressive historiographical tradition, briefly flirted with Marxism in the 1930s, and thereafter, though his sympathies remained on the left, considered himself effectively nonpolitical.[24] In a sense, his entire career can be seen as a lover's quarrel with liberalism, in the course of which he recognized its promise but relentlessly

---

[22]Richard Hofstadter, *The Age of Reform: From Bryan to F.D.R.* (New York, 1955), 62.

[23]Ibid., 11.

[24]For a brief assessment of the historian, see Eric Foner, "The Education of Richard Hofstadter," in *Who Owns History? Rethinking the Past in a Changing World* (New York, 2002), 25–46; other assessments are cited in his footnotes. For a fuller picture, see Richard S. Brown's fine biography, *Richard Hofstadter* (Chicago, 2006).

exposed its inadequacies, delusions, and failures. Despite his own leftist tendencies, Hofstadter resisted completely the temptation to find heroic victories for the people in what he saw as a depressing chronicle of consensus based on common cupidity. America was more illiberal than the Progressive historians would prefer; they wrote history that fostered the illusion of liberal reform, but he would not.

Hofstadter's powerful critique of American liberalism was shaped not only by his evolving political views, but also by his reading of twentieth-century social science research. Based on that reading, he began to address in new ways a familiar set of questions about American society. Who were American reformers, and what did they want? Hofstadter used the findings of social scientists to explain the significance of status in shaping social behavior. If abolitionists, Populists, and Progressives had not in fact democratized America, just what had they accomplished? Hofstadter looked to the sociology of bureaucracy and complex organizations, as well as research into the modernization of societies in the European and non-European world, to illuminate an era in which Americans were moving from small towns to big cities, from simple and homogeneous to complex and pluralistic social structures. To explain the reformers' passions, he employed social-psychological concepts such as projection, displacement, scapegoating, and the authoritarian personality.

If Hofstadter derived critical insights from social science, another consensus historian, Edmund S. Morgan, looked elsewhere. A student of Perry Miller, the distinguished Harvard historian of early American religion and culture, Morgan echoed his mentor's distrust of Progressive history and of liberalism generally. Liberalism, Miller had believed, possessed few intellectual resources with which to criticize the modern pursuit of individualism, self-expression, and material success. In the premodern and therefore preliberal Puritan world, Morgan (like Miller) found depths of wisdom that seemed lacking in the twentieth century. Wary of those who applied present-day assumptions to the task of understanding the past, Morgan refused to see Puritans as sexually repressed and obsessed with sin. And he refused to see colonial dissidents as anticipators or forerunners of latter-day democratic liberalism. Thus, in his earliest works, he portrayed Anne Hutchinson and Roger Williams not as progressive critics of Puritan oligarchy, but as self-righteous zealots, nihilists even. In contrast, Governor John Winthrop was not a repressive Puritan oligarch but a man striving to live responsibly in a deeply imperfect world that required order more than individual freedom for visionaries.[25]

If Progressives and Marxists insisted that economic interests and material forces shaped history, Morgan would follow his mentor Perry Miller in insisting that ideas mattered. Winthrop and his adversaries were obsessed with ideas, led by them, willing to suffer and even die for them. In 1967, in a striking demonstration of this belief, Morgan admitted that he had been wrong

---

[25]See especially Edmund S. Morgan, *The Puritan Dilemma: The Story of John Winthrop* (Boston, 1958).

about Roger Williams. In *Roger Williams: The Church and the State,* Morgan now acknowledged that Williams's ideas were momentous. Williams had understood that conscientious protest was an act "not so much of defiance as of discovery." What Williams discovered — what John Winthrop could not — was that separation of church and state was absolutely necessary, first, to preserve religion from being corrupted by the state and, second, to protect the state from becoming the engine of religious intolerance. Thus, the historian who began his career by rebuking modern liberals for misrepresenting the strange world of seventeenth-century Puritanism found himself in the 1960s affirming the connection between Puritanism and the tradition of civil-libertarian protest that became a hallmark of the later democratic republic.[26] Perhaps the America he and his students encountered in the 1960s forced this most scrupulous of historians to reflect on what Croce called the contemporaneous character of history.

Morgan's work spanned a great variety of subjects from Puritan thought, to the Revolution, to slavery. Although he never abandoned his faith in the power of ideas, by the late 1960s his research into the origins of slavery had plunged him deeply into social history, that is, into the realm of group experience and collective fate that seemed very far away from the world of intellectuals and political leaders that had once so occupied him. Executing a dazzling intellectual pirouette, Morgan came to insist that there was nothing incompatible between asserting that consensus dominated mainstream American political and intellectual history and insisting that the most egregious form of oppression — slavery — lay at the heart of the American social experience. Indeed, he claimed, it was precisely because white America relied on slavery to keep the lowest of the low under control, thereby minimizing class conflict among the free, that liberal democracy was able to flower in the late eighteenth and nineteenth centuries.

Morgan's *American Slavery, American Freedom* is the book named "most admired" more frequently than any other in a 1994 poll of American historians.[27] Morgan's complex argument cannot be summarized here, but its power can be attributed to its capacity to span the historiography wars that marked the history profession in the 1960s and for several decades thereafter. What historian John Higham called the "Cult of American Consensus" had made American history tame and predictable.[28] Within that consensus perspective, eighteenth-century America appeared to be the spawning ground for middle-class democracy; the Revolution was a largely intellectual movement; radicals, abolitionists, Reconstructionists, and socialists were maladjusted sufferers of status anxiety; and the Cold War was a noble (if reluctant) effort to save the world from totalitarianism. In the face of this antiseptic treatment of the past, dissenters predictably arose. A new

---

[26]Edmund S. Morgan, *Roger Williams: The Church and the State* (New York, 1967).

[27]Edmund S. Morgan, *American Slavery, American Freedom: The Ordeal of Colonial Virginia* (New York, 1975); the historians' poll and commentary on it can be found in *Journal of American History* 81 (December 1994).

[28]John Higham, "The Cult of 'American Consensus': Homogenizing Our History," *Commentary* 27 (February 1959): 93–100.

generation of neo-Progressives began to insist that conflict, not consensus, marked the American past.

The assault on consensus history reflected the erosion of political consensus in 1960s America. Already in the late 1950s, the emergence of the civil rights movement signaled the reemergence of the African American struggle against inequality and racism in American society. For a time, the movement could be subsumed under the rubric of liberal reform, welcomed as a perfection of liberal democracy rather than a fundamental challenge to it. But by the mid-1960s, the racial animosity and poverty that had once been invisible to whites, and for a time appeared readily curable, came to seem more endemic and intractable. Radical inequality would require radical measures — at least, some insisted, measures more radical than integration or voting rights. When New Left critics of American society looked for radical antecedents in prominent historical accounts, they found chronicles of consensus — but not for long. Increasingly, younger historians found in older Progressive historical works and in neo-Marxist scholarship from Europe the inspiration to rewrite American history as a chronicle of struggle — for working-class power, for racial equality, for women's rights, for ethnic identity, and for all forms of social justice. The Vietnam War added immense energy to this endeavor. As college campuses became centers of protest against the war, historians absorbed the growing suspicion that the U.S. foreign policy establishment served interests quite distinct from the national interest. They condemned all forms of concentrated power — corporations, political parties, government bureaucracies, professional organizations, and the like — that seemed to profit from inequality and promote injustice in the United States and around the world.

Methodological innovation involving the increased interaction of history with social science, comparative history, and quantitative methods only reinforced tendencies toward radical critique. While Hofstadter, Hartz, and other historians had already begun to pay attention to social science research and comparative approaches, the move to quantification was new. With the exception of economic historians, most historians had no acquaintance with the use of scientifically measurable historical data. One of the attractions of quantitative techniques was quite old-fashioned: like the positivists of the late-nineteenth and early-twentieth centuries, modern-day quantifiers sought the authority of science. They also wanted to strengthen their claim to the growing pools of research money available in the postwar United States from both government and private funders of social science research. At the same time, the urge to quantify drew energy from a democratic urge to capture the reality of ordinary lives through social history. Peasants, workers, slaves, migrants — whole categories of human beings — were invisible because they had been "inarticulate," that is, illiterate and ignored by those who left written documents. Quantitative history suggested a way to make them speak: through records that traced collective behavior and from which ideas, values, intentions, and beliefs might be inferred. Thus John Demos surprisingly could bring in view the interior lives of the earliest settlers of Plymouth colony through the analysis of wills, deeds, contracts, and probate records.[29] On a broader canvas, Paul Kleppner's quantitative analysis of voting records revealed the ethnic motives of voters in the nineteenth-century Midwest; and as a result of computer analysis of manuscript censuses and other data, Stephen Thernstrom discovered the astounding geographical (and limited social) mobility of working-class New Englanders in the industrial era.[30]

Quantitative historians drew inspiration not only from the social and behavioral sciences but also from the work of historians associated with the French journal *Annales*. Led by Lucien Febvre and Marc Bloch, who had begun using quantitative techniques in the 1930s and 1940s, these French historians strove for "total history" — a history that recorded the myriad experiences of masses of people, not just the dramatic events that featured prominent actors. In the hands of a leading figure in the *Annales* school, Fernand Braudel, history became a slow, majestic procession of material change — change in population, agricultural production, prices, trade, and so on — that created, unbeknownst to any individual, the true conditions of life in medieval and early modern Europe. This version of social history was "history with the politics left out," indeed, history with all the usual markers of individual consciousness left out.[31]

Others trying to write a new social history took a very different tack. For them, social history meant history from the bottom up. Though sometimes inspired by the quantifiers' capacity to occupy a distant perch and from there comprehend a vast historical terrain, these new social historians more closely observed institutional change and group action. They refused to believe that the masses were inaccessible to creative historical research. In fact, social historians began to find copious evidence of conscious thought and action among the lower orders. Slave narratives, diaries of farm wives and artisan workers, letters and articles in obscure newspapers, broadsides and pamphlets, court and police records, institutional memoranda and reports — these and many other sources began to give up their secrets. The new social historians were neo-progressives, in a way, but far more radical than Beard and Becker. Piecemeal political reform would not easily remake a society hideously distorted by racism and sexism, dominated by immense corporations, regulated by "therapeutic" bureaucracies, and dedicated to the systematic exploitation of the third world. Not Progressive reformers, but militant, even revolutionary activists — like the artisan revolutionaries in the 1770s, the abolitionists and radical Reconstructionists in the nineteenth

---

[29]John Demos, *A Little Commonwealth: Family Life in Plymouth Colony* (New York, 1970). See also Kenneth A. Lockridge, *A New England Town: The First Hundred Years* (New York, 1970); a later community study focusing on the Chesapeake is Darrett B. and Anita H. Rutman, *A Place in Time: Middlesex County, Virginia, 1650–1750* (New York, 1984).

[30]Paul Kleppner, *The Third Electoral System: 1853–1892: Parties, Voters, and Political Cultures* (Chapel Hill, N.C., 1979); Stephen Thernstrom, *Poverty and Progress: Social Mobility in a Nineteenth-Century City* (Cambridge, Mass., 1964), and *The Other Bostonians: Poverty and Progress in an American Metropolis* (Cambridge, Mass., 1973).

[31]Of Braudel's many works, perhaps the most accessible is *Capitalism and Material Life, 1400–1800* (New York, 1967).

century, and the most combative unionists in the 1930s — became models for latter-day radicals in the 1960s and 1970s.[32]

As Chapter 3 makes clear, among the first subjects to respond to this approach was labor history or, as it came increasingly to be called, working-class history. Inspired especially by the English neo-Marxist E. P. Thompson, new labor historians rewrote the history of unions and unionization but, more importantly, of working-class families and communities, working-class politics and culture. The people whom they studied, far from seeming to be either aspirants to middle-class status or alien radicals, came to seem at once both more militantly class-conscious and more deeply rooted in American society and culture. Other fields, such as immigration history, African American history, and women's history, similarly experienced a dramatic renaissance. Both white and black scholars helped turn the history of slavery into one of the most exciting and fruitful fields of history. Recovering the seminal scholarship of African American historians such as W. E. B. Du Bois and Eric Williams, and plunging into previously ignored archival sources, the historians of the 1960s found not passivity but agency among slaves, not imitation of white culture but cultural resistance and the endurance of African traditions and practices. They insisted that the Civil War had been fought to abolish slavery, that African Americans played a crucial part in its conduct and success, and that only force and betrayal — not the alleged cultural deprivation or political immaturity of blacks — had led to the failure of Reconstruction.[33]

Women's historians began to effect a similarly profound change in the standard narrative of American history. If women had been excluded from the conventionally male realms of power and privilege, they had no less been excluded from the pages of American history. Inspired by the women's liberation movement and the simultaneous arrival of history from the bottom up in the 1960s and 1970s, male and especially female historians began to hear the voices of women and transfer them to the pages of

---

[32]See, for example, Alfred F. Young, ed., *The American Revolution: Explorations in the History of American Radicalism* (DeKalb, Ill., 1976); John Hope Franklin, *Reconstruction: After the Civil War* (Chicago, 1961); Kenneth M. Stampp, *The Era of Reconstruction, 1865–1877* (New York, 1965); and Daniel J. Leab, ed., *The Labor History Reader* (Urbana, Ill., 1980), which includes classic essays published over a twenty-year period. A sweeping narrative (and celebration) of the rise of radical history can be found in Jonathan M. Wiener, "Radical Historians and the Crisis in American History, 1959–1980," *Journal of American History* 76 (September 1989): 399–434, part of a roundtable that includes criticism and commentary from a variety of historians and a response from Wiener.

[33]On slavery, see John W. Blassingame, *The Slave Community: Plantation Life in the Ante-Bellum South* (New York, 1972); George P. Rawick, *From Sundown to Sunup: The Making of the Black Community* (Westport, Conn., 1972); and Leslie Howard Owens, *This Species of Property: Slave Life and Culture in the Old South* (New York, 1976). On African Americans in the Civil War, the classic study is Benjamin Quarles, *The Negro in the Civil War* (Boston, 1953), which James M. McPherson built upon in *The Negro's Civil War: How American Negroes Felt and Acted during the War for the Union* (New York, 1965). On Reconstruction, the epic work is C. Vann Woodward, *Origins of the New South* (Baton Rouge, La., 1951); see also works by Franklin and Stampp cited in footnote 32 and others cited in Volume One, Chapters 4 and 9.

history.[34] In the suffrage movement and the labor movement; in the records of settlement houses and women's academies and colleges; in the records of births and marriages, of prostitution arrests and temperance campaigns; in the copious records of literary and moral reform publications, in which women argued both for equality and for recognition of their distinctive feminine gifts; and in many other sources, historians of women rewrote the story of America from its very beginnings up to the recent past. They did not merely give women a place in the existing narratives; rather, they reconceived whole fields of history. Thus, for example, the culture of slavery appears to be a realm not simply of *either* accommodation *or* resistance, but — when women are brought centrally into its historical reconstruction — a realm of endurance and cultural creativity.[35] Likewise, the history of progressive reform becomes the story of women, denied direct access to political office, asserting their rights to set the public agenda and to demand maternalist state action in the interest of reforming the social household.[36]

In these and many other ways, historians of women and of African Americans joined a broader wave of socially critical scholarship that had moved very far away from even the history of the most progressive men of earlier generations. Today it seems that every man and woman has become his and her own historian in a way even Carl Becker would have found surprising (and cheering). Considerable success in democratizing the academy in the wake of civil rights and women's rights movements has unseated dominant perspectives and opened the way for more diverse and more politically critical schools of interpretation in history and other disciplines. So unsettling have these developments been that by the 1980s many historians complained that both interpretive coherence and objectivity had vanished from the profession. They feared that fragmentation threatened to consign scholars to increasingly microscopic and specialized enclaves, making it impossible to communicate with one another, let alone with a broader public. To others, this lack of coherence seemed a healthy state of ferment and pluralistic openness: "Maybe drift and uncertainty," one such historian remarked, ". . . are preconditions for creativity."[37] It is probably true that coherence and fragmentation, harmony and polytonality, the pursuit of

---

[34]A few early works include Gerda Lerner, *The Woman in American History* (Menlo Park, Calif., 1971); William H. Chafe, *The American Woman: Her Changing Social, Economic and Political Roles, 1920–1970* (New York, 1972); and Nancy F. Cott, *The Bonds of Womanhood: "Woman's Sphere" in New England, 1780–1835* (New Haven, Conn., 1977). See also classic essays in Linda K. Kerber and Jane DeHart Matthews, eds., *Women's America: Refocusing the Past* (New York, 1982), and other works cited in Chapter 10.

[35]See Volume One, Chapter 9.

[36]See Chapter 6, and also Chapter 8 in Volume One.

[37]On the perils of fragmentation, see Thomas Bender, "Wholes and Parts: The Need for Synthesis in American History," *Journal of American History* 73 (June 1986): 120–36; see the ensuing debate on Bender's essay in "A Round Table: Synthesis in American History," *Journal of American History* 74 (June 1987): 107–30. See also John Higham, "The Future of American History," *Journal of American History* 80 (March 1994): 1289–1309. The quotation is from Jackson Lears, "Mastery and Drift," *Journal of American History* 84 (December 1997): 979–88.

the microscopic and the synthetic are parallel rather than alternative practices within the history profession. In the end, moreover, diversity of perspectives does not rule out a broadly synthetic multicultural history. The ambition to make sense of a complex past — to narrate a big story — should not be confused with an urge to drown difference in a wave of false or oppressive homogeneity.

The charge that history had descended into political partisanship gained more energy from forces outside the academy than from within. To be sure, historians as different as the Marxists Elizabeth Fox-Genovese and Eugene D. Genovese, the liberals Arthur Schlesinger Jr. and Diane Ravitch, and the conservative Gertrude Himmelfarb, to name a few, pilloried the profession for allowing social history to descend into what they considered tendentious, multiculturalist special pleading. Several of them helped organize a new professional organization, the Historical Society, which published a new journal designed to avoid the pitfalls of the "balkanized" history and restore dispassion and breadth of view to the profession.[38] Its founding manifesto announced the aim of "reorienting the historical profession toward an accessible, integrated history free from fragmentation and over-specialization." For the most part, however, despite manifestos, the new journal features articles that are mostly indistinguishable from those published in mainstream journals.[39] Moreover, the vigor of debate in professional journals and meetings belies the charge that conformity on ideological or methodological matters has stifled free inquiry.

In the realm of public history, however, the highly politicized claims about leftist bias in history have sparked real rancor. The controversy over the National History Standards in the mid-1990s generated much heat and throws a little light on the "history wars."[40] In 1994, spurred by Lynne Cheney, who headed the National Endowment for the Humanities under the first President Bush, and directed by the eminent historian of early America, Gary Nash, the project — after years of discussion, preparation,

---

[38] The *Journal of the Historical Society* began publication in 2000. On the Historical Society, see Elizabeth Fox-Genovese and Elisabeth Lasch-Quinn, eds., *Reconstructing History: The Emergence of a New Historical Society* (New York, 1999); it should be noted that the Historical Society's founders included liberals such as Sean Wilentz, who shared very few of his cofounders' views other than an allegiance to publicly accessible narrative history.

[39] See Elizabeth Fox-Genovese and Eugene D. Genovese, "The Political Crisis of Social History: A Marxist Perspective," in Peter N. Stearns, ed., *Expanding the Past* (New York, 1988): 16–32; Arthur Schlesinger Jr., *The Disuniting of America* (New York, 1992); Diane Ravitch's views have appeared mostly in occasional essays and articles, several of which are cited, along with a host of other works representing many views, in a special issue of the *Journal of Social History* 29 (1995) entitled "Social History and the American Political Climate — Problems and Strategies"; Gertrude Himmelfarb, *The New History and the Old: Critical Essays and Reappraisals* (Cambridge, Mass., 1987). See also "AHR Forum: The Old History and the New," *American Historical Review* 94 (June 1989), with contributions from Himmelfarb along with other historians of various persuasions.

[40] See Gary B. Nash, Charlotte Crabtree, and Ross E. Dunn, *History on Trial: Culture Wars and the Teaching of the Past* (New York, 1997), and Diane Ravitch, "The Controversy over the National History Standards," in Fox-Genovese and Lasch-Quinn, *Reconstructing History*, 242–52.

and consultation — published preliminary guidelines for the teaching of history in public schools. Critics exploded with outrage. Diane Ravitch and Arthur Schlesinger Jr. leveled measured critiques of the pedagogical strategies recommended by the drafters, but less temperate right-wing pundits blasted the standards as anti-American. Cheney herself, now "in opposition" to the Clinton administration, turned on the project she had helped spawn; and in early 1995 the U.S. Senate voted ninety-nine to one to condemn the standards. Although revised standards eventually won broad support, other battles in the history wars erupted around the same time and in similar ways. Most notoriously, several exhibitions at the Smithsonian Institution museums in Washington, D.C., evoked cries of anti-Americanism from conservative critics. In response to such criticism, the National History Museum removed "excessive" references to genocide from its exhibition "The American West," and the Air and Space Museum abandoned its Enola Gay exhibition when it could not find a way to both celebrate the patriotic struggle against Japan and take note of the horrors of nuclear destruction.[41]

The most important challenge to American historians in the twenty-first century comes not from those demanding more patriotic narratives but from those advocating the "internationalization" of American history. Sometimes advocating "global" or "transnational" or "postnational" history, these critics insist that Americans' "exceptionalism" distorts both the national record and the reality of historical change. In the modern and postmodern world, almost none of the important forces shaping events are nation-based, they argue. Wars and revolutions, racial hierarchies and forms of economic dominance and subordination, markets, migrations, and media, among other phenomena, all emerge and develop in response to forces well beyond state boundaries. Most historians seem to welcome the new effort, although disagreements arise as soon as they try to clarify what it means.

In a collection of essays entitled *Rethinking American History in a Global Age*, Thomas Bender celebrates the urge to "deprovincialize" and "defamiliarize" American history.[42] Another contributor to that volume, the eminent diplomatic historian Akira Iriye, proposes that international history means comparative history, an immersion into more than one national archive, usually requiring skill in more than one language. But he also insists that comparison must incorporate peoples, cultures, and non-state movements, not just states. The character and outlines of such an approach remain elusive, but Iriye believes that a more international approach will one day generate a truly global or transnational history of human affairs.[43] For other diplomatic historians, internationalizing means turning the tables on U.S.-centered,

[41]See Edward T. Linenthal and Tom Engelhardt, eds., *History Wars: The Enola Gay and Other Battles for the American Past* (New York, 1996). See also Mike Wallace, *Mickey Mouse History and Other Essays on American Memory* (Philadelphia, 1996).

[42]Thomas Bender, "Introduction: Historians, Nations, and the Plenitude of Narratives," in Bender, ed., *Rethinking American History in a Global Age* (Berkeley, Calif., 2002).

[43]Akira Iriye, "Internationalizing International History," in Bender, *Rethinking*, 47–62.

hegemonic renderings of history. While Louis A. Perez Jr. finds many of the goals of transnational history admirable, he spots a worm in the global apple. "A new historiography that celebrates the promise of borderlessness seems entirely congruent with the larger assumptions through which to validate the assumptions of globalization. Is the new international history the handmaiden to globalization?" He insists that the nation that sponsors and reaps the most immense rewards from globalization — the United States — must remain clearly in the historian's focus. Similarly, Marilyn Young warns historians to distinguish between "de-centering" U.S. history and creating "a world free of [America's] overwhelming military power"; she continues, "it is crucial to remember the difference" and to make sure that "the effort to de-center American history" does not "run the danger of obscuring what it means to illuminate."[44]

A different view of transnational history emerges from the work of historians of migration, gender, and race. For them, "diasporic" approaches offer the opportunity to comprehend the meaning of lives in motion, not primarily defined by nations but by the spaces created by capitalist markets, international political movements, and mass communication. Such approaches sometimes begin with the subnational — family economies, local religious cultures, regional environments — but proceed to link them to phenomena of the largest scale — capitalism, imperialism, patriarchy, and the like. When grounded in exhaustive archival and oral research, as in the work of Dirk Hoerder and Donna Gabaccia, such studies succeed in reframing what once seemed a simple story of immigrants reaching and assimilating into the Promised Land into a far more complex tale of migration, reverse migration, and the simultaneous construction of national, racial, and ethnic identities among both settlers and sojourners within many different national contexts.[45]

Felipe Fernandez-Armesto takes another approach to the challenge of transnational history, writing a history of the continent that highlights the starkly different fates of North America and America south of the Rio Grande. He treats the rise and fall of indigenous societies and colonization comparatively and then asks, Why did these two regions, similar for so long, diverge so dramatically in the nineteenth century? The south had conspicuously provided much of the wealth for the development of Western capitalism, but in the nineteenth century, Canada and the United States began exploiting their resources with unparalleled success while maintaining political stability. The reverse was true for the south. In light of this comparison,

---

[44]Louis A. Perez Jr., "We Are the World: Internationalizing the National, Nationalizing the International," *Journal of American History* 89 (September 2002): 564; Marilyn B. Young, "The Age of Global Power," in Bender, *Rethinking*, 291.

[45]See Dirk Hoerder, "From Euro- and Afro-Atlantic to Pacific Migration System: A Comparative Migration Approach to North American History," in Bender, *Rethinking*, 195–235; Donna R. Gabaccia, "When the Migrants Are Men: Italy's Women and Transnationalism as a Working-Class Way of Life," in Gabaccia and Vicki L. Ruiz, eds., *American Dreaming, Global Realities: Rethinking U.S. Immigration History* (Urbana, Ill., 2006), and other works cited therein and in Chapter 5.

Fernandez-Armesto identifies crucial conditions and resources that facilitated the remarkable economic growth and political stability of the north. He sees a constellation of these opportunities presently taking shape in the south and wonders if that region will be able to take advantage of them.[46]

In *The Theft of History*, Jack Goody radically reappraises most histories of the Western world since the sixteenth century, in which Europe and the United States were the measure of all other civilizations. This "provincial" perspective obviated careful studies of societies marked by significantly different forms of land tenure, market activity, and communal traditions. If provincialism deprived historians of models of social and cultural difference, it also blinded them to similarities. Thus, Goody asserts, abundant evidence shows that romantic love, freedom, and humanism, usually characterized as essentially European values, appeared elsewhere.[47] Thomas Bender's *A Nation among Nations* offers a different worldwide perspective on U.S. history. He sees in the age of discovery the beginning of global history, which, he emphasizes, began with the importation and exploitation of millions of Africans. He treats the American Revolution as one event in the long war between England and France that began in 1689 and continued until 1815. He connects the Civil War with the Europeans' revolutions of 1848, the failure of Reconstruction with European failures to realize the ideals of its revolutions. Similarly, for Bender the Spanish-American War makes sense only in the larger context of European imperialism; progressive reform only as one of many global responses to industrial capitalism. Although Bender uses comparative history explicitly to explain American developments, *A Nation among Nations* never becomes a triumphant tale of economic progress or political virtue.[48]

Despite the benefits of transnational history, some historians have raised cautionary flags. They worry that transnational insights claimed by American historians suggest an ironic reverse imperialism. Just as the United States appropriates resources, labor, and cultural space around the world, these critics imply, American historians appropriate the right to tell everybody's story.[49] In a very different way, some scholars qualify their endorsement of transnational approaches with reminders about the enduring significance of the nation as an idea and a reality in human history.[50] Ian Tyrell applauds the exploitation of "new, non-national records" to "suggest models of transnational processes," but insists that historians have long transcended narrow nationalism. He notes that nation-focused and transnational approaches will together be required to account adequately for the overwhelming power of the United States within the world. Recalling the com-

---

[46]Felipe Fernandez-Armesto, *The Americas, A Hemispheric History* (New York, 2003).

[47]Jack Goody, *The Theft of History* (New York, 2006), 1–8, 240, 246, 286.

[48]Thomas Bender, *A Nation among Nations: America's Place in World History* (New York, 2006), 3–9, 290–301.

[49]Doubts of this sort surface in essays by Ron Robin and a few others in Bender's *Rethinking*.

[50]See John Higham, "The Future of American History," *Journal of American History* 80 (March 1994): 1289–1307.

parative and global tendencies of historians often thought to be avatars of "American exceptionalism," from Frederick Jackson Turner to Louis Hartz, Tyrell, like Bender, advocates the enrichment and complication of American history, not its dissolution into the sea of transnationalism.[51]

However one reads the opportunities and challenges of the transnational turn in historiography, that turn cannot be ignored. This edition of *Interpretations of American History* pays greater attention to the global dimensions of the transatlantic economy, slave trade, and abolitionist movements. It addresses transnational approaches to the study of migration, to state-making and Progressive reform, to the role of multiple states and non-state actors, not just great powers, in shaping international relations during and after the Cold War, and to many other subjects. Yet it also heeds the words of several of the participants in the *Journal of American History*'s recent "Interchange," cited above, who affirm history's intense empirical focus and openness to different approaches and who warn that some kinds of "interdisciplinarity . . . narrow rather than widen inquiries." History's "eclecticism" has, as David Hollinger notes, always made it "easier for us to absorb and use a variety of theories and methods . . . without being captured by any." History's "methodological integrity," he goes on, remains a solid bottom on which to navigate the shifting seas of transnational and other approaches to the study of human affairs. As Joyce Appleby and others have noted, moreover, if people desire "to chart their lives by what they believe to be true," then they will turn to history, which "offers a variety of tools for effecting liberation from intrusive authority, outworn creeds, and counsels of despair."[52] In responding to that demand, historians will continue to write narratives both broad and narrow and to argue about them strenuously in the decades to come.

A final note about the way these chapters present competing interpretations of historical phenomena. While interpretive argument undoubtedly remains among the most common and necessary practices in the discipline, it is equally true that the either-or format can distort the true nature of historians' arguments. Indeed, burlesquing this format is a happy pastime common in graduate student lounges all over the country (Fat-Free Mozzarella: Noble Experiment or Tragic Error?). We have, in fact, tried wherever possible to offer differences in interpretation that are not polar or mutually exclusive, but rather partially overlapping and complementary.

---

[51]Ian Tyrell, "Making Nations/Making States: American Historians in the Context of Empire," *Journal of American History* 80 (March 1994): 1015–44; see also Richard White, "The Nationalization of Nature," *Journal of American History* 80 (March 1994): 976–86. On a more theoretical level, see Craig Calhoun, *Nations Matter: Culture, History, and the Cosmopolitan Dream* (London, 2007). On both traditional comparative approaches and the recent "transnational turn" (as well as cultural studies, subaltern studies, and approaches that focus on religion, gender, and race), see the enlightening "Interchange: The Practice of History," *Journal of American History* 90 (September 2003): 576–611. See also Michael Adas, "From Settler Colony to Global Hegemon: Integrating the Exceptionalist Narrative of the American Experience into World History," *American Historical Review* 106 (December 2001): 1692–1720.
[52]Appleby et al., *Telling the Truth about History*, 301, 308.

Sharp differences there are, and sometimes hot debate produces light. But historians usually do not differ by excluding each other's evidence or utterly demolishing each other's arguments. More often, they try to incorporate as much of the former and recast as much of the latter as possible in order to better explain a historical phenomenon. Thus, for example, whereas Progressive historians might have once portrayed the New Deal as a radical advance in liberal reform, and New Left historians as a triumph of corporate hegemony, the liberal William Leuchtenberg and the radical Alan Dawley in their essays in this volume acknowledge a good deal of common ground, even while clearly disagreeing over important points. Whether the New Deal was "radical within limits" or "conservative with radical implications" remains truly a matter of opinion, but the common ground shared by these two historians makes clear the cumulative and "objective" quality of scholarship on the subject. In coming to a judgment on this and other questions posed in the following chapters, we hope that students will find in the debates, and the historiographical essays that precede them, a pathway to understanding the world in which they live and an encouragement to change that world for the better.

The Reconstruction Era: How Large Its Scope?

To students of American history, the Civil War years stand in sharp contrast to those of the Reconstruction era. The war years represented a period of heroism and idealism; out of the travail of conflict, there emerged a new American nation. Although the cost in lives and money was frightful, the divisions that had plagued Americans for over half a century were eliminated in the ordeal. Henceforth America would stand as a united country, cleansed of slavery, destined to take its rightful place as one of the leading nations in the world.

Reconstruction, on the other hand, had to address the problems of putting the nation back together again. The federal government had to bring back the South into the Union on terms that permitted reconciliation, protect newly freed slaves from the wrath of angry whites, and construct a biracial society of free people. The era was marked by conflict, brutality, and corruption, and historians have not agreed in evaluating the results. Three schools of thought about Reconstruction succeeded one another: the Dunning school, the Progressives, and the revisionists. A fourth that sees Reconstruction exceeding its traditional geographic and temporal boundaries is emerging.

The first dominant view of Reconstruction, called the Dunning school after its founder, emerged from the widespread racism of both North and South in the years after the Civil War. It was reinforced by the worldwide European imperialism of the late nineteenth century and the racist ideology that intensified to justify it. These historians saw Reconstruction as a disaster, giving rights to freed people who were unprepared for them and were vulnerable to corruption. The best thing about it was that it ended, and whites reestablished political control of the South.[1]

By the 1920s, American historiography had come under the influence of the Progressive, or new history, school. Growing out of the dissatisfaction with the older scientific school of historians that emphasized the collection of impartial empirical data and eschewed "subjective" interpretations, this school borrowed heavily from the new social sciences. These historians sought to explain historical change by isolating underlying economic and social forces that transformed institutions and structures. In place of tradition and stability, it emphasized change and conflict. Liberal and democratic in their

---

[1]For example, William A. Dunning, *Reconstruction: Political and Economic, 1865–1877* (New York, 1907), and John W. Burgess, *Reconstruction and the Constitution, 1866–1876* (New York, 1902).

orientation, Progressives maintained that economic issues were basic in shaping this era. The real conflict was not between North and South or white and black; it was between industrial capitalism and agrarianism, with the former ultimately emerging victorious. The question of the status of black people in American society was simply a facade for the more basic conflicts that lay hidden beneath the surface. Reconstruction, they concluded, was the first phase in the emergence of the United States as a leading industrial and capitalist nation.

The revisionists, although owing much to the Progressives, were influenced by the egalitarianism of the period following World War II and the idealism and optimism of the civil rights movement. Providing equal rights for blacks, revisionists maintained, was complicated by economic and other factors but was, nevertheless, a potent issue in its own right. In a real sense, the fundamental problem of Reconstruction was on what terms freed people would participate economically and politically in the nation. Even though the Radical Republicans ultimately failed in achieving equality for African Americans, they left an enduring legacy in the forms of the Fourteenth and Fifteenth Amendments. These amendments took on a new meaning as they gave legal sanction to civil rights after 1945. This is a broad school and includes social historians whose work has been to broaden history to include the poor, blacks, other minorities, and women. In the wake of Eric Foner's stunning, definitive revisionist synthesis, *Reconstruction: America's Unfinished Revolution, 1863–1877*, historians are not so much challenging his interpretation as broadening the field of Reconstruction studies to include questions of intellectual history, gender, and culture, as well as literally broadening the field forward and backward to include the Mexican-American War through the Gilded Age and territories beyond the South, even other post-emancipation societies.[2]

In the 1890s, led by Professor William A. Dunning of Columbia University, who founded the school of Reconstruction historiography that still bears his name, the historical profession set out to prove that the years following the Civil War were marked by tragedy because men of good will were momentarily thrust out of power by the forces of evil. In this period, in the words of one historian, "The Southern [white, it went without saying] people literally were put to the torture."[3]

Dunning school historians assumed first that the South should have been restored to the Union quickly and without penalty. Most Southerners, they asserted, had accepted their military defeat gracefully and were prepared to pledge their loyalty to the Union. Second, white Southerners should have had political and economic responsibility for the freedmen, who as former slaves and blacks could never be integrated into American society on

---

[2] Eric Foner, *Reconstruction: America's Unfinished Revolution, 1863–1877* (New York, 1988). For differing new perspectives, see Thomas J. Brown, ed., *Reconstructions: New Perspectives on Postbellum America* (New York, 2006), 6–8; and Rebecca J. Scott, *Degrees of Freedom: Louisiana and Cuba after Slavery* (Cambridge, Mass., 2005).

[3] Claude G. Bowers, *The Tragic Era: The Revolution after Lincoln* (Cambridge, Mass., 1929), v–vi.

an equal plane with whites. Behind these assumptions were many others about antebellum society, among them that slavery was benign, that slave-holders were kindly patriarchs protecting their faithful but ignorant slaves, and that slavery was not very profitable.

According to the Dunning school, the Radical carpetbagger state governments that came into power were totally incompetent — in part because they included illiterate blacks who were unprepared for the responsibilities of self-government. Still worse, these governments were extraordinarily expensive because they were corrupt. Most of them, indeed, left nothing but a legacy of huge debts.[4] The decent whites in the South united out of sheer desperation to force the carpetbaggers, scalawags, and blacks from power. In one state after another, Radical rule was eventually overthrown and good government restored. Thus the tragic era of Reconstruction came to an end.

For nearly three decades after the turn of the century, the Dunning point of view largely dominated in the academy, and it persisted into the 1960s in northern high schools. In 1942, Albert B. Moore, in his presidential address at the Southern Historical Association, argued that Reconstruction had the effect of converting the South into a colonial appendage of the North. Moore found the enfranchisement of blacks, which laid the basis for carpet-bag government, perhaps the most incredible event of an incredible era. The South, he concluded, was still paying for the wrongs of Reconstruction.[5]

In the late 1920s, however, historians influenced by Progressive thinking, particularly its emphasis on the importance of economic considerations, changed the interpretive framework of the Reconstruction era. In 1939, Francis B. Simkins, a distinguished Southern historian (who with Robert Woody published one of the first Progressive studies of Reconstruction in 1932), summed up some of the findings of the school. He emphasized many of Radical Reconstruction's constructive achievements. Simkins denied that the Radical program was radical; indeed, the Radical Republicans failed because they did not provide freedmen with a secure economic base. Past historians, he concluded, had given a distorted picture of Reconstruction because they had assumed that blacks were racially inferior. Only by abandoning their biases could historians contribute to a more accurate understanding of the past.[6]

While the Progressives often disagreed among themselves, there were common areas of agreement. For example, most viewed the problem of corruption in American society during these years as national rather than sectional in scope. To single out the South in this regard was patently unfair and

---

[4]E. Merton Coulter, *The South during Reconstruction, 1865–1877* (Baton Rouge, La., 1947), 148.

[5]Albert B. Moore, "One Hundred Years of Reconstruction of the South," *Journal of Southern History* 9 (May 1943): 153–65.

[6]Francis B. Simkins, "New Viewpoints of Southern Reconstruction," *Journal of Southern History* 5 (February 1939): 49–61; Francis B. Simkins and Robert Hilliard Woody, *South Carolina during Reconstruction* (Chapel Hill, N.C., 1932).

ahistorical.[7] Progressives also denied that the Radical governments in the South were always dishonest, incompetent, and inefficient. On the contrary, they claimed, such governments accomplished much of enduring value. The new Reconstruction constitutions, written by black and white Republicans, represented a vast improvement over the older ones, bringing about many long-needed and lasting social reforms, including state-supported school systems for both blacks and whites and a revision of the judicial system. Above all, these governments operated — at least in theory — on the premise that all men, white and black alike, were entitled to equal political and civil liberties.

Second, the Progressives drew a sharply different portrait of blacks during Reconstruction. They denied that corruption and violence in the postwar South resulted from black participation in government or that the freedmen were illiterate, naive, and inexperienced. In no Southern state, they pointed out, did blacks control both houses of the legislature. Moreover, there were no black governors and only one black state supreme court justice. Only two blacks were elected to the U.S. Senate and fifteen to the House of Representatives. These numbers hardly supported the charge that the supposed excesses of Reconstruction were due to activities of black Americans.

Indeed, the Progressives maintained that blacks, as a group, were quite capable of understanding their own interests without disregarding the legitimate interests of others. The freedmen were able to participate at least as intelligently as other groups in the American political process. As Vernon L. Wharton concluded in his pioneering study of the Negro in Mississippi after the Civil War, there was "little difference . . . in the administration of . . . counties [having blacks on boards of supervisors] and that of counties under Democratic control. . . . Altogether, as governments go, that supplied by the Negro and white Republicans in Mississippi between 1870 and 1876 was not a bad government. . . . With their white Republican colleagues, they gave to the state a government of greatly expanded functions at a cost that was low in comparison with that of almost any other state."[8]

Progressives refuted the Dunning school contention that state governments were controlled by evil, power-hungry, profit-seeking carpetbaggers and renegade scalawags who used black votes to maintain themselves in power. The stereotype of the carpetbagger and scalawag, according to Progressives, was highly inaccurate. Carpetbaggers, for example, migrated to the South for a variety of reasons — including the lure of economic opportunities as well as a desire to serve the former slaves in some humanitarian capacity. Among them were former Southern unionists and Whigs, lower-

---

[7]For a progressive synthesis, see J. G. Randall and David Donald, *The Civil War and Reconstruction*, 2nd ed. (Boston, 1961). The first edition, written by Randall in 1937, was in the Dunning school tradition.

[8]Vernon L. Wharton, *The Negro in Mississippi, 1865–1890* (Chapel Hill, N.C., 1947), 172, 179–80. See also Willie Lee Rose, *Rehearsal for Reconstruction: The Port Royal Experiment* (New York, 1964), and Joel Williamson, *After Slavery: The Negro in South Carolina during Reconstruction, 1861–1877* (Chapel Hill, N.C., 1965).

class whites who sought to use the Republican Party as the vehicle for confiscating the property of the planter aristocrats, and businessmen attracted by the promise of industrialization. The Radical governments, then, had a wide base of indigenous support in most Southern states.[9]

Finally, the Progressives rejected the charge that the Radical governments were extraordinarily expensive and corrupt, or that they had saddled the South with a large public debt. State expenditures did rise sharply after the war, but for good reasons. The war's destruction required an infusion of public funds. Deferring regular appropriations during the war years also meant that a backlog of legitimate projects had accumulated. Most important of all, the South for the first time had to build schools and provide other facilities and services for blacks and whites that did not exist before the 1860s and for which public funds had never been expended.

The Progressives also found that the rise in state debts, in some instances, was more apparent than real. Grants to railroad promoters, which in certain states accounted for a large proportion of the increase in the debt, were secured by a mortgage on the railroad property. Thus the rise in the debt was backed by sound collateral. The amount of the debt chargeable to theft, the Progressives maintained, was negligible. Indeed, the restoration governments, which were dominated by supposedly honest Southerners, proved to be far more corrupt than the governments controlled by the Radicals.

Progressives shared the conviction that economic forces related to the growth of an industrializing nation played a major role during this period. Beneath the political and racial antagonisms of this era, some Progressives argued, lay economic rivalries. Eager to gain an advantage over their competitors, many business interests used politics as the vehicle to further their economic ambitions — especially since the South, like the North and West, was ardently courting businessmen. The result was that economic rivalries were translated into political struggles.[10]

Progressives identified racism as important in party affiliation but otherwise subordinate to economics in determining the rise and fall of Reconstruction. During Reconstruction, many former Whigs joined the Republican Party because of its pro-business economic policies. These well-to-do conservatives, at first, were willing to ally with blacks and guarantee their civil and political rights in return for their support at the polls. Within the Democratic Party, however, Progressives argued that lower-class whites, fearful of competition from blacks, insisted on white supremacy. Conservatives found their

---

[9]See Otto H. Olsen, "Reconsidering the Scalawags," *Civil War History* 12 (December 1966): 304–20, and Allen W. Trelease, "Who Were the Scalawags?" *Journal of Southern History* 29 (November 1963): 445–68.

[10]Recent historians have once again begun to study the importance of economic factors and rivalries in Reconstruction. See Mark W. Summers, *Railroads, Reconstruction, and the Gospel of Prosperity: Aid under the Radical Republicans, 1867–1877* (Princeton, N.J., 1984), and Terry L. Seip, *The South Returns to Congress: Men, Economic Measures, and International Relationships, 1868–1879* (Baton Rouge, La., 1983). See also Mark Summers, *The Era of Good Stealings* (New York, 1993), which argues that there was no more corruption in the South than in the North.

affiliation with the Republican Party increasingly uncomfortable, and they slowly began to drift back into the Democratic Party.

This changed alignment left Southern blacks politically without white allies, which later made it easy to eliminate them from political life. This move came at a time when Northerners, tired of conflict and turmoil, became reconciled to the idea of letting the South work out its own destiny — even if it meant sacrificing black people. Northern businessmen likewise became convinced that only Southern conservatives could restore order and stability and thus create a favorable environment for investment. Elite Southern Democrats deliberately polarized politics along racial lines, disguising their desire to dominate the region economically through appeals to white racism.

The end of Reconstruction, according to the Progressives, accompanied the triumph of business values and industrial capitalism. When the contested presidential election of 1876 resulted in an apparent deadlock between Rutherford B. Hayes, the Republican candidate, and Samuel J. Tilden, his Democratic opponent, some prominent Republicans saw an opportunity to rebuild their party in the South upon a new basis. Instead of basing their party upon propertyless former slaves, they hoped to attract well-to-do former Whigs who had been forced into the Democratic Party to fight against Reconstruction governments. To accomplish this goal, a group of powerful Republican leaders began to work secretly to bring about a political realignment. If Southern Democratic congressmen would not stand in the way of Hayes's election and would also provide enough votes to permit the Republicans to organize the House of Representatives, these leaders were willing to promise the South federal subsidies — primarily for railroads — to name a Southerner as postmaster general, and to abandon Radical Reconstruction. The Compromise of 1877, as this political deal was called, was not fully carried out, but the broad outline prevailed.

Perhaps the most important and initially the most overlooked Progressive was W. E. B. Du Bois who published *Black Reconstruction, 1860–1880*, in 1935. Du Bois, like the other Progressives, claimed that economics, not race, shaped Reconstruction and black-white relations. In his passionately argued volume, he insisted that Reconstruction involved an effort to unite Northern workers with Southern blacks. The attempt failed because Southern conservatives employed racial animosities to fragment working-class unity and thus maintain their own class hegemony. Racism, in this view, was a tool that upper-class whites used to their advantage, not an inherent, unchanging characteristic of poor whites, as most historians portrayed it. For Du Bois, Reconstruction was a valiant but short-lived attempt to establish true democracy in the South, an opportunity quickly foreclosed.

The *Journal of American History* ignored the book, and most professional historians disparaged it. One complaint was that Du Bois had based his work on secondary sources, not archival materials. This was true, but it was also true that during Du Bois's research, most Southern archives were closed to blacks. When blacks were allowed in, they had to hide themselves from view of the white scholars. C. Vann Woodward was one of the few professional historians who recognized the value of Du Bois's work at the time. He wrote Du

Bois in 1938 of his "indebtedness for the insight which your admirable book, *Black Reconstruction*, has provided me."[11]

Woodward, the historian who propounded the thesis of the Compromise of 1877, concluded that the bargain "did not restore the old order in the South, nor did it restore the South to parity with other sections. It did assure the dominant whites political autonomy and nonintervention in matters of race policy and promised them a share in the blessings of the new economic order. In return the South became, in effect, a satellite of the dominant region. So long as the Conservative Redeemers held control they scotched any tendency of the South to combine forces with the internal enemies of the new economy — laborites, Western agrarians, reformers. Under the regime of the Redeemers the South became a bulwark instead of a menace to the new order."[12]

After the early 1950s, a new school of Reconstruction historiography called the revisionist school emerged. Many of these historians had been affected by the racial injustice that the civil rights movement demonstrated. Generally speaking, while the revisionists accepted many findings of the Progressives, they rejected the idea of interpreting Reconstruction in strictly economic terms. The Republican Party, the revisionists maintained, was not united on a pro-business economic program; it included individuals and groups holding quite different social and economic views. The revisionists saw the factor of race as an issue that had profound moral implications and was as much of a motivating factor — both positively and negatively — as economics. One of the unresolved dilemmas after the Civil War, they insisted, was the exact role that blacks were to play in American society.[13]

Within the Republican Party, a number of factions each offered their solution to this question. Andrew Johnson, who had been nominated as Lincoln's running mate in 1864 on a Union Party ticket despite his Democratic Party affiliation, spoke for the conservatives, for whom blacks were incapable of self-government. Consequently, he favored the white state governments in the South that came back into the Union shortly after the end of the war. He went along with the black codes passed by Southern whites whose aims were to make black freedom as much like slavery as possible. Radical Republicans fiercely opposed Johnson. While the Dunning school had painted the Radicals as vindictive hypocrites eager for power, and the Progressives saw them as representing the interests of the industrial Northeast, the revisionists saw many of them joining the Republican Party for antislavery rather than economic reasons. After the war, they wanted blacks to have the same rights as white Americans, which brought them into conflict with President Johnson. Taking advantage of Johnson's growing unpopularity and motivated

---

[11]W. E. B. Du Bois, *Black Reconstruction, 1860–1880* (New York, 1992; originally published 1935), x, xvi.

[12]C. Vann Woodward, *Reunion and Reaction: The Compromise of 1877 and the End of Reconstruction* (Boston, 1951), 246.

[13]Robert Sharkey, *Money, Class, and Party: An Economic Study of Civil War and Reconstruction* (Baltimore, 1959), and Irwin Unger, *The Greenback Era: A Social and Political History of American Finance, 1865–1879* (Princeton, N.J., 1964).

by idealism, the Radicals set out to remake Southern society by transferring political power from the planter class to the freedmen.[14]

In 1965, Kenneth M. Stampp published an important synthesis that emphasized the moral dimension of the Reconstruction years, arguing that the central question of the postwar period was the place of the freedmen in American society. To argue that the Radicals had invidious and selfish motives does them a severe injustice and results in a distorted picture of the Reconstruction era. The Radicals, according to the revisionists, ultimately failed in their objectives. Most Americans, harboring conscious and unconscious racial antipathies, were not willing to accept blacks as equals. By the 1870s, the North was prepared to abandon blacks to the white South for three reasons: a wish to return to the amicable prewar relations between the sections, a desire to promote industrial investment in the South, and a growing conviction that the cause of black Americans was not worth further strife. Reconstruction's tragedy was in ending short of achieving the major goal sought by the Radicals.

The struggle over Reconstruction, nevertheless, had not been in vain. In addition to the many achievements of the Radical governments, the Radicals had succeeded in securing the adoption of the Fourteenth and Fifteenth Amendments. These amendments, in Stampp's words, "which could have been adopted only under the conditions of radical Reconstruction, make the blunders of that era, tragic though they were, dwindle into insignificance. For if it was worth four years of civil war to save the Union, it was worth a few years of radical Reconstruction to give the American Negro the ultimate promise of equal civil and political rights."[15]

During and after the 1970s, revisionist scholarship began to take a more pessimistic turn, while interest in Reconstruction remained strong. Pervasive inequality and racial friction after the civil rights movement seemed to reflect mockingly the failure of post–Civil War Americans to ensure that blacks would be integrated into the social and political framework of the Union.[16] Revisionist scholars identified various reasons for the failure of Reconstruction, covering ground similar to that the Progressives had tilled. In his study of the Ku Klux Klan, Allen W. Trelease argued that Radical Reconstruction failed because the seeds of biracial democracy fell on barren soil in the South, and the federal government's artificial nurture was ephemeral and quickly discontinued. George C. Rable emphasized the counterrevolutionary guerrilla warfare employed by white Southerners concerned with the destruction of the Republican Party in the South. Michael Perman insisted that in the

---

[14]This point of view was best expressed by Howard K. Beale, one of the fathers of the revisionist school, in *The Critical Year: A Study of Andrew Johnson and Reconstruction* (New York, 1930); see James H. McPherson, *The Struggle for Equality: Abolitionists and the Negro in the Civil War and Reconstruction* (Princeton, N.J., 1964), and Hans L. Trefousse, *The Radical Republicans: Lincoln's Vanguard for Racial Justice* (New York, 1969).

[15]Kenneth M. Stampp, *The Era of Reconstruction, 1865–1877* (New York, 1965), 215.

[16]For a descriptive analysis of black Americans after slavery that does not deal with Reconstruction as a political event, see Leon F. Litwack's important *Been in the Storm So Long: The Aftermath of Slavery* (New York, 1979).

context of the political tensions that prevailed in the immediate postwar era, the very moderation that marked presidential and congressional Reconstruction was doomed to fail; only a coercive policy could have succeeded. In a subsequent work, Perman emphasized the ways in which the center in both the Republican and Democratic parties proved unable to hold together, thus permitting color to become the political line. And in a broad study of national politics, William Gillette observed that Reconstruction was so easily reversed because it had always been "fragmentary and fragile."[17]

Interest in Andrew Johnson persisted. Michael Les Benedict, for example, insisted that Johnson was impeached because he seemed to be violating the principle of the separation of powers and because he failed to carry out some key provisions in legislation pertaining to Reconstruction. Hans Trefousse emphasized the degree to which Johnson thwarted Radical policies and strengthened conservative forces, thereby facilitating the latter's eventual triumph in the 1870s. Of three other studies of Johnson, two (by Patrick W. Riddleberger and James E. Sefton) emphasized his commitment to sometimes incompatible principles that rendered him impotent, and one (by Albert Castel) accentuated the degree to which his inordinate ambition and desire for power helped to destroy him.[18]

Robert J. Kaczorowski synthesized many themes that have resonated throughout Reconstruction historiography through the 1980s. The Thirteenth and Fourteenth Amendments represented a revolutionary change in American federalism, for citizenship was no longer within state jurisdiction. Consequently, Congress had authority to protect all citizens in their enjoyment of rights. This congressional Radical Republican theory of constitutionalism, however, Kaczorowski argued, was altered during the 1870s by a Supreme Court bent on permitting partisans of states' rights in the South to reestablish their domination over former slaves.[19]

The first to use comparative history better to evaluate Reconstruction, George M. Fredrickson compared it with the experiences of Jamaica and South Africa. He concluded that white Southerners were less able than

[17]Allen W. Trelease, *White Terror: The Ku Klux Klan Conspiracy and Southern Reconstruction* (New York, 1971); George C. Rable, *But There Was No Peace: The Role of Violence in the Politics of Reconstruction* (Athens, Ga., 1984); Michael Perman, *Reunion without Compromise: The South and Reconstruction, 1865–1868* (Cambridge, 1973), and *The Road to Redemption: Southern Politics, 1869–1879* (Chapel Hill, N.C., 1984); William Gillette, *Retreat from Reconstruction, 1869–1879* (Baton Rouge, La., 1979), 380.

[18]Michael Les Benedict, *The Impeachment and Trial of Andrew Johnson* (New York, 1973); Hans L. Trefousse, *Impeachment of a President: Andrew Johnson, the Blacks, and Reconstruction* (Knoxville, Tenn., 1975); Patrick W. Riddleberger, *1866: The Critical Year Revisited* (Carbondale, Ill., 1979); James E. Sefton, *Andrew Johnson and the Uses of Constitutional Power* (Boston, 1980); Albert Castel, *The Presidency of Andrew Johnson* (Lawrence, Kans., 1979). See also the following works: Michael Les Benedict, *A Compromise of Principle: Congressional Republicans and Reconstruction, 1863–1869* (New York, 1974), and *The Fruits of Victory: Alternatives in Restoring the Union, 1865–1877* (Philadelphia, 1975); Dan T. Carter, *When the War Was Over: The Failure of Self-Reconstruction in the South, 1865–1867* (Baton Rouge, La., 1985); and Richard N. Current, *Those Terrible Carpetbaggers: A Reinterpretation* (New York, 1988).

[19]Robert J. Kaczorowski, "To Begin the Nation Anew: Congress, Citizenship, and Civil Rights after the Civil War," *American Historical Review* 92 (February 1987): 45–68.

Jamaicans or South Africans to make even a limited adjustment to the concept of equality, resulting in a racist order in the United States that was not
exceeded until the formal adoption of apartheid in South Africa after 1948.
Historians are just beginning to work comparatively again, a method that
can powerfully illuminate the past by placing it in a broad perspective.[20]

At the same time that interest in national politics remained high, monographic studies dealing with single states continued to appear, identifying
circumstances unique within the larger pattern of Reconstruction. Jonathan
Wiener's study of postwar Alabama argued that Reconstruction might never
have happened for all the difference it made in the lives of black people.
White elites retained control of the land and forced blacks into a form of
tenant serfdom in which they were little better off than in slavery. In a novel
study of black political leadership in South Carolina that utilized quantitative techniques, Thomas Holt argued that black leaders were divided among
themselves by education and prewar status; their divisions contributed to
the fall of the Republican Party in the state. Holt's profile of black leadership demonstrated that most owned property and were literate, and 10 percent were professionally or college trained. Other scholars pursued this topic
of diversity among politically and economically active blacks, such as John
Rodrigue in his work on sugar growers in Louisiana.[21] And Barbara Fields,
focusing on the changing economy in her study of Maryland, argued for
eventual changes as the market slowly transformed the border state. But the
racist fallout from slavery persisted with such intensity that change came
painfully slowly when it came.[22]

The 1988 publication of Eric Foner's massive *Reconstruction: America's
Unfinished Revolution, 1863–1877*, excerpted below, restored cohesion to a
field long fragmented and summed it up definitively. Initially, he argued,
Reconstruction was a Radical attempt to destroy the South's antebellum
social structure. But by the 1870s, fear of class conflict in the North led that
section's industrial leaders to evince greater sympathy for the white South.
The result was a resurgence of white domination below the Mason-Dixon
line. Like W. E. B. Du Bois, Foner centered much of his analysis on class and
the political initiatives of newly freed black people. Unlike Du Bois, Foner

---

[20]George M. Frederickson, "After Emancipation: A Comparative Study of White Responses
to the New Order of Race Relations in the American South, Jamaica and the Cape Colony of
South Africa," in David G. Sansing, ed., *What Was Freedom's Price?* (Jackson, Miss., 1978).

[21]Jonathan Wiener, *Social Origins of the New South: Alabama, 1860–1885* (Baton Rouge, La.,
1978); John Rodrigue, "Black Agency after Slavery," in Brown, ed., *Reconstructions*, 40–65; John
Rodrigue, *Reconstruction in the Cane Fields: From Slavery to Free Labor in Louisiana's Sugar Parishes,
1862–1880* (Baton Rouge, La., 2001); see also Mark Wetherington, *Plain Folk's Fight: The Civil
War and Reconstruction in Piney Woods, Georgia* (Chapel Hill, N.C., 2005).

[22]Thomas Holt, *Black Over White: Negro Political Leadership in South Carolina during Recon-
struction* (Urbana, Ill., 1977); Barbara Fields, *Slavery and Freedom on the Middle Ground, Mary-
land, during the Nineteenth Century* (New Haven, Conn., 1985). See also Jerrell H. Shofner, *Nor
Is It Over Yet: Florida in the Era of Reconstruction, 1863–1877* (Gainesville, Fla., 1974); Joe Gray
Taylor, *Louisiana Reconstructed, 1863–1877* (Baton Rouge, La., 1974); William C. Harris, *The
Day of the Carpetbagger: Republican Reconstruction in Mississippi* (Baton Rouge, La., 1979); Ted
Tunnell, *Crucible of Reconstruction: War, Radicalism and Race in Louisiana, 1862–1877* (Baton
Rouge, La., 1984).

could and did make use of enormous archival material, providing his political and economic history with a deep base in vivid social history. Looking at the political and economic experience of freed people, Foner charted the demise by the 1870s of the free-labor ideology that had brought the Republican Party into existence. White concern to restrict the conditions of work and the political participation of blacks led to a virtual abandonment of the equal rights and free-labor ideology. Sharecropping emerged as the compromise between planters who dreamed of the days of gang slave labor and freed people who longed for land and economic and social self-sufficiency. Foner saw Reconstruction as a failure, but an immensely important one. Through the mechanisms of Radical Reconstruction, the joint activism of white and black Republicans had created, however fleetingly, an unprecedented, biracial democracy.

Foner's inquiries into the ideology of free labor and ideas of contract prompted various studies of those topics. Foner himself addressed the issue in "The Meaning of Freedom in the Age of Emancipation," as well as in the book that grew out of that article.[23] He wrote that "Reconstruction emerges as a decisive moment in fixing the dominant understanding of freedom as self-ownership and the right to compete in the labor market, rather than propertied independence." Subsequently, Foner expanded on the transformation during Reconstruction of the meaning of the Fourteenth Amendment. In his view, it came to mean the freedom to contract, not equality before the law. Legal scholar Peggy Cooper Davis came at the disappointment blacks experienced with postwar interpretations of the Fourteenth Amendment from a different tack. In *Neglected Stories: The Constitution and Family Values*, she re-created, through stories from slavery and Reconstruction, the problems the Fourteenth Amendment was attempting to address, particularly the complete absence of white respect for the rights of blacks to make and protect their families.[24]

Recent historians have not so much challenged Foner's synthesis as added new perspectives to it, among them gender, a broader geographic and temporal definition of the period, and a fresh look at African American political mobilization and activities.[25]

Several scholars have supplemented Foner's work with studies of women's activities and how constructions of gender contributed to the dynamics of Reconstruction. Nina Silber published *The Romance of Reunion* in 1992, a study of the way the South, while losing the war itself, managed to win the interpretation of it. In her analysis, in the face of rapid postwar industrialization and immigration, Northerners and Southerners looked to antebellum Southern myths of manliness and femininity to give order to a fragmenting

---

[23]Eric Foner, *Reconstruction: America's Unfinished Revolution, 1863–1877* (New York, 1988); Eric Foner, "The Meaning of Freedom in the Age of Emancipation," *Journal of American History* 81 (March 1995): 435–60; see also Eric Foner, *The Story of American Freedom* (New York, 2000).

[24]Peggy Cooper Davis, *Neglected Stories: The Constitution and Family Values* (New York, 1997).

[25]Brooks D. Simpson, *The Reconstruction Presidents* (Lawrence, Kans., 1998) ix; Michael Perman, *Struggle for Mastery: Disfranchisement in the South* (Chapel Hill, N.C., 2001); Nicholas Lemann, *Redemption: The Last Battle of the Civil War* (New York, 2006).

society. Romantic myths of prewar chivalry, delicate femininity, and interracial harmony blossomed in a period of labor agitation, the violent retaliation of industrialists, the arrivals of millions of foreign poor, and militant suffragist activity.[26]

In 1995, LeeAnn Whites interpreted the Civil War and Reconstruction through a crisis in gender in Augusta, Georgia. Whites studied the conflicts for Confederate women as the war took their men away and called upon them to increase their domestic activities to help supply the troops. Demobilization exacerbated the tension that even this circumscribed female empowerment had created between the sexes. In the aftermath of emancipation, white males could now legitimately dominate only their wives, who were less prepared to accept it. Women's associational life after the war to memorialize the Confederacy promised them a public role, but, with Reconstruction and redemption, men assumed these tasks and forced women back into domesticity. Drew Faust's study of elite Confederate women portrayed them as reluctantly and resentfully shouldering male responsibilities during the war, unwilling victims of a kind of liberation. They eagerly embraced the old arrangements when men returned home and rejected Northern ideas of women's emancipation. Jane Turner Censer instead detected enthusiasm for limited independence among younger postbellum women that would ultimately be crushed by the imposition of Jim Crow in the 1890s. In LeeAnn Whites's most recent collection of essays, she has worked to make gender visible and show its significance in shaping women's postwar role as restorers of white men's rightful position, as well as in justifying the racial violence that accompanied redemption in the name of controlling white women's sexuality.[27]

Laura Edwards's *Gendered Strife and Confusion*, a subtle study of gender in Granville County in postwar North Carolina, points out that domestic institutions, particularly marriage, and constructions of masculinity and femininity served new political and social uses because of the demise of slavery as a method of control. Appealing to constructions of maleness, femaleness, and family sanctity provided freed people and poor whites with some new options for themselves. Edwards also describes how conservative Democrats could and did use the tool of gender construction to bring about the expulsion of blacks from political life.[28]

Tera Hunter's *To 'Joy My Freedom* studied black women's lives in Atlanta after the war. In an innovative mix of social, urban, political, economic, and gender history, Hunter revealed women's widespread postwar labor agitation, particularly by African American laundresses, as well as the concerted

[26]Nina Silber, *The Romance of Reunion: Northerners and the South, 1865–1900* (Chapel Hill, N.C., 1993).

[27]LeeAnn Whites, *The Civil War as a Crisis in Gender: Augusta, Georgia, 1860–1890* (Athens, Ga., 1995); Drew Faust, *The Mothers of Invention: Women of the Slaveholding South in the American Civil War* (Chapel Hill, N.C., 1996); Jane Turner Censer, *The Reconstruction of White Southern Womanhood, 1865–1895* (Baton Rouge, La., 2003); LeeAnn Whites, *Gender Matters: Civil War, Reconstruction, and the Making of the New South* (New York, 2005).

[28]Laura Edwards, *Gendered Strife and Confusion: The Political Culture of Reconstruction* (Urbana, Ill., 1997).

action of the white community to break women's first strike in the South. She also showed how real estate developers and city officials planned the growth of Atlanta to be sure that urban blacks would get as few benefits, such as running water, as possible.[29]

In *Gendered Freedoms*, a study of the Mississippi Delta, Nancy Bercaw looked at African American women's wartime economic independence and postwar family tensions as planters, trying to curtail women's power, tried to enforce patriarchy on black families. Bercaw studied the changing strategies and ideologies of African American households, arguing that family form developed in accord with ideas about property rights and the meaning of free labor. The nuclear family, essential to cotton production, became dominant among rural people, while urban families often created other arrangements. The shape of black families was the result of negotiations among black men and women, but was also subject to unwelcome pressure from white planters.[30]

Contributing to scholarship on the direction of postwar women's reform, Carol Faulkner studied the women of the Freedmen's Aid Movement (*Women's Radical Reconstruction*), finding a significant continuation of the tradition of abolitionist-feminism, usually construed to have been fatally wounded by the postwar split in the suffrage movement. Faulkner's radical women who went south to serve the needs of free people preceded and prefigured the Progressives in seeing the federal government as the natural ally of the vulnerable and in trying to make the government accept that responsibility. Faulkner also found blindness among these women about their own biases. Consequently, some tried to coerce freed people into adopting middle-class habits and values.[31]

In 2003, Elliott West published a provocative essay, excerpted below, titled "Reconstructing Race." West called for a study of "greater Reconstruction" that would take a broader national perspective and include the West, and would begin as far back as the 1840s with the integration of this region into the expanding, industrializing nation. This approach would allow for exploration of parallel conflicts over the rights of people of Native American, Hispanic, Chinese, and African descent. Because of their "races," members of all groups were welcome in only low-status and low-paying jobs. The United States excluded some from the body politic and only included others on limited terms. "This greater Reconstruction was even more morally ambiguous

---

[29]Tera Hunter, *To 'Joy My Freedom, Southern Black Women's Lives and Labors after the Civil War* (Cambridge, Mass., 1997); see also Elsa Barkley Brown's "Negotiating and Transforming the Public Sphere: African American Political Life in the Transition from Slavery to Freedom," *Public Culture* 7 (Fall 1994): 107–46.

[30]Nancy Bercaw, *Gendered Freedoms: Race, Rights, and the Politics of Household in the Delta, 1861–1875* (Gainesville, Fla., 2003). See also Amy Dru Stanley, *From Bondage to Contract: Wage Labor, Marriage, and the Market in the Age of Slave Emancipation* (New York, 1998), for an exploration of contract in an age of increasingly limited freedom for free people and workers; and Julie Saville's monograph on South Carolina free people contesting the notion of freedom as subjection to landowners and market values: Julie Saville, *The Work of Reconstruction: From Slave to Wage Laborer in South Carolina, 1860–1870* (New York, 1994).

[31]Carol Faulkner, *Women's Radical Reconstruction: The Freedmen's Aid Movement* (Philadelphia, 2004).

than the lesser one. It included not one war but three — the Mexican War, the Civil War, and the War Against Indian America — and while it saw the emancipation of one nonwhite people, it was equally concerned with dominating the others."[32]

Although West did not expand his themes into a book, Heather Cox Richardson has written about Reconstruction as a nationwide political negotiation lasting through the Gilded Age. In Richardson's view, this negotiation produced an American consensus uniting the political center that, she argues, still holds true and even explains the results of the 2004 presidential election. She identifies growing middle-class worry about "special interests" in the postwar nineteenth century, concerns that strikingly echo those of historians and journalists today explaining the decline of the New Deal Democratic consensus. (See Chapter 11.) In her view, Reconstruction failed nationally because the Northern middle class lost its enthusiasm for freed people as well as for Northern workers when it seemed to them that both groups were trying to use government for legislation to further their own welfare, instead of applying themselves to their work and trusting in the free-labor ideology to make them rise economically. In contrast to West, she underplays the significance of racism in favor of an increasingly outmoded middle-class belief in the free labor promise.[33]

Picking up West's challenge to include the Chinese in the postwar national experience, Moon-Ho Jung's case study, *Coolies and Cane*, portrays the struggles of Chinese laborers in the Reconstruction of Louisiana's sugar industry. The immigrants' disputed and unstable identity as "coolies," or coerced Caribbean plantation laborers (shipped in U.S. boats) made them (the false) equivalent, in the eyes of many postwar white Americans, of emancipated slaves. This, in turn, was critical in persuading the general public to deny them the possibility of naturalized citizenship and, eventually, in excluding them in 1888. This carefully argued monograph expands the agony of Reconstruction to include "outlawing coolies at home," which "became an endless and indispensable exercise that resolved and reproduced contradictory aims — racial exclusion and legal inclusion, enslavement and emancipation, parochial nationalism and unbridled imperialism — of a nation deeply rooted in race, slavery, and empire."[34]

Rebecca Scott's *Degrees of Freedom* also looks to Louisiana, but farther afield to Cuba, another sugar growing region, to enlarge Reconstruction's scope. While slaves in Louisiana achieved freedom in 1865, Cuba underwent emancipation more gradually, pushed forward by a liberation struggle that combined the demand for freedom with the demand for independence from Spain, finally producing freedom in 1886 and liberation from Spain only

---

[32]Elliott West, "Reconstructing Race," *Western Historical Quarterly* 34 (Spring 2003): 11.

[33]Heather Cox Richardson, *The Death of Reconstruction: Race, Labor, and Politics in the Post–Civil War North, 1865–1901* (Cambridge, Mass., 2001), and *West from Appomattox: The Reconstruction of America after the Civil War* (New Haven, Conn., 2007); for a different interpretation of the postwar reshaping of classical liberal thought that evolved to protect capitalism, see Nancy Cohen, *The Reconstruction of American Liberalism, 1865–1914* (Chapel Hill, N.C., 2002).

[34]Moon-Ho Jung, *Coolies and Cane: Race, Labor, and Sugar in the Age of Emancipation* (Baltimore, 2006), 9.

when the United States invaded in 1898. Although Louisiana black and white laborers had some limited experience of working together to better their conditions, the Cuban working class had united in its idea of a nation, so racism, while present, never achieved the suffocating supremacy that it had in Louisiana "after forty years of struggle."[35] Scott teases out numerous insights on the consequences of the way freedom arrived in the southern United States and the limits that emerged on what it meant from comparing it to the more fluid and extended process of achieving and defining freedom in Cuba.[36]

Stephen Hahn's *A Nation under Our Feet: Black Political Struggles in the Rural South from Slavery to the Great Migration* made a sweeping and original contribution to the study of Reconstruction that evoked a neo-revisionist turn to culture in an effort to make politics more visible and more inclusive.[37] Hahn stretched the period of Reconstruction to include slavery, wartime, and the hard years after redemption in order to trace the creation and development of African American politics. In this groundbreaking study, Hahn not only enlarged the time frame, but also enlarged and enriched the definition of politics itself. He identified politics during slavery as growing from a nucleus of resistance to the potentially deadly personal dominance of the slave owner. He found extended kin systems, both blood and fictive, at the root of slave solidarities, with the wisest members of these solidarities, usually but not always men, emerging as leaders. Hahn's discussion of those years officially defined as Reconstruction pointed out the continuity from the antebellum years of violence as a southern companion to politics. After the war, white militias and terror groups emerged out of prewar slave patrols. Blacks readied themselves to participate in a politics that they learned to their sorrow would be "paramilitary."

Hahn's extraordinary ability to recognize political activity in unusual shapes and around nontraditional issues informs this important and imaginative volume. Its scope develops organically from Hahn's incisive investigation, beginning with the emergence of pre-political groups united by the experience of resistance and mutual aid. The politics become more visible as African Americans shake off slavery and reach for citizenship. When the government fails to protect the prerogatives of these new citizens, they reorganize to find a place where they hope to be able to practice a less desperate form of politics.

Edward J. Blum also looks to culture — in this case religion — for broad explanations for the postwar settlement. In *Reforging the White Republic*, Blum argues for the centrality of northern Protestantism as an active agent in removing blacks from the postwar reunification and permitting the white South to define the nation's attitude toward African Americans. He cites the

---

[35]Rebecca Scott, *Degrees of Freedom: Louisiana and Cuba after Slavery* (Cambridge, Mass., 2005), 262.

[36]For another comparative view by a long-time student of the era, see Stanley Engerman, *Slavery, Emancipation, and Freedom: Comparative Perspectives* (Baton Rouge, La., 2007).

[37]Stephen Hahn, *A Nation under Our Feet: Black Political Struggles in the Rural South from Slavery to the Great Migration* (Cambridge, Mass., 2003).

response to the yellow fever epidemic of 1878 of denying African Americans the medical care they needed; the WCTU's racial exclusivity, particularly under Frances Willard's leadership (Willard famously refused to condemn lynching) and its racist effect on the suffrage movement; and the great revivals led by Dwight Moody, encouraging a retreat from social reform movements, as important moments in uniting Northerners and Southerners in whiteness. Finally, he sees this flourishing nationalistic, militaristic Christianity as crucial for our acquisition of an overseas empire and devastating for "African Americans and people of color throughout the world."[38]

Through Reconstruction, historians continue to struggle with the most basic questions about the meanings of democracy, citizenship, and freedom in our country with its long and ignominious history of racial slavery. Reconstruction, longer or shorter, in the South, in the nation, or in the context of the wider world, forces us to confront the overturning of a courageous experiment in democracy. And its historiography tells us that for a century, many of us refused to see this experiment as anything but a travesty of misrule. Future studies will no doubt include more attempts to realize the nationwide impact of both Reconstruction and redemption, the former in explorations like Hahn's of the politics of the dispossessed that have not been visible to us before, and the latter in expansive works like the one Elliott West proposed that will let us see what our nineteenth-century nation-building cost the people who labored on its construction, the people who willingly sacrificed democracy for domination, and increasingly people in the rest of the world.

---

[38]Edward J. Blum, *Reforging the White Republic: Race, Religion, and American Nationalism, 1865–1898* (Baton Rouge, La., 2005), 18.

ERIC FONER

from Reconstruction: America's Unfinished Revolution, 1863–1877   [1988]

ERIC FONER (1943–) is the DeWitt Clinton Professor of History at Columbia University. He is the author of *Free Soil, Free Labor, Free Men* (1970), *Tom Paine and Revolutionary America* (1976), *Reconstruction: America's Unfinished Revolution*, winner of the Bancroft Prize and Francis Parkman Prize (1988), and *The Story of American Freedom* (1998).

Thus, in the words of W. E. B. Du Bois, "the slave went free; stood a brief moment in the sun; then moved back again toward slavery." The magnitude of the Redeemer counterrevolution underscored both the

---

scope of the transformation Reconstruction had assayed and the consequences of its failure. To be sure, the era of emancipation and Republican
rule did not lack enduring accomplishments. The tide of change rose and
then receded, but it left behind an altered landscape. The freedmen's
political and civil equality proved transitory, but the autonomous black
family and a network of religious and social institutions survived the end
of Reconstruction. Nor could the seeds of educational progress planted
then be entirely uprooted. While wholly inadequate for pupils of both
races, schooling under the Redeemers represented a distinct advance
over the days when blacks were excluded altogether from a share in public services.

If blacks failed to achieve the economic independence envisioned in
the aftermath of the Civil War, Reconstruction closed off even more oppressive alternatives than the Redeemers' New South. The post-Reconstruction
labor system embodied neither a return to the closely supervised gang
labor of antebellum days, nor the complete dispossession and immobiliza-
tion of the black labor force and coercive apprenticeship systems envisioned by white Southerners in 1865 and 1866. Nor were blacks, as in
twentieth-century South Africa, barred from citizenship, herded into
labor reserves, or prohibited by law from moving from one part of the
country to another. As illustrated by the small but growing number of
black landowners, businessmen, and professionals, the doors of economic
opportunity that had opened could never be completely closed. Without
Reconstruction, moreover, it is difficult to imagine the establishment of a
framework of legal rights enshrined in the Constitution that, while fla-
grantly violated after 1877, created a vehicle for future federal intervention in Southern affairs. As a result of this unprecedented redefinition of
the American body politic, the South's racial system remained regional
rather than national, an outcome of great importance when economic
opportunities at last opened in the North.

Nonetheless, whether measured by the dreams inspired by emancipation or the more limited goals of securing blacks' rights as citizens and
free laborers, and establishing an enduring Republican presence in the
South, Reconstruction can only be judged a failure. Among the host of
explanations for this outcome, a few seem especially significant. Events
far beyond the control of Southern Republicans — the nature of the
national credit and banking systems, the depression of the 1870s, the
stagnation of world demand for cotton — severely limited the prospects
for far-reaching economic change. The early rejection of federally sponsored land reform left in place a planter class far weaker and less affluent
than before the war, but still able to bring its prestige and experience to
bear against Reconstruction. Factionalism and corruption, although hardly
confined to Southern Republicans, undermined their claim to legitimacy
and made it difficult for them to respond effectively to attacks by resolute
opponents. The failure to develop an effective long-term appeal to white
voters made it increasingly difficult for Republicans to combat the racial
politics of the Redeemers. None of these factors, however, would have

proved decisive without the campaign of violence that turned the electoral tide in many parts of the South, and the weakening of Northern resolve, itself a consequence of social and political changes that undermined the free labor and egalitarian precepts at the heart of Reconstruction policy.

For historians, hindsight can be a treacherous ally. Enabling us to trace the hidden patterns of past events, it beguiles us with the mirage of inevitability, the assumption that different outcomes lay beyond the limits of the possible. Certainly, the history of other plantation societies offers little reason for optimism that emancipation could have given rise to a prosperous, egalitarian South, or even one that escaped a pattern of colonial underdevelopment. Nor do the prospects for the expansion of scalawag support — essential for Southern Republicanism's long-term survival — appear in retrospect to have been anything but bleak. Outside the mountains and other enclaves of wartime Unionism, the Civil War generation of white Southerners was always likely to view the Republican party as an alien embodiment of wartime defeat and black equality. And the nation lacked not simply the will but the modern bureaucratic machinery to oversee Southern affairs in any permanent way. Perhaps the remarkable thing about Reconstruction was not that it failed, but that it was attempted at all and survived as long as it did. Yet one can, I think, imagine alternative scenarios and modest successes: the Republican party establishing itself as a permanent fixture on the Southern landscape, the North summoning the resolve to insist that the Constitution must be respected. As the experiences of Readjuster Virginia and Populist-Republican North Carolina suggest, even Redemption did not entirely foreclose the possibility of biracial politics, thus raising the question of how Southern life might have been affected had Deep South blacks enjoyed genuine political freedoms when the Populist movement swept the white counties in the 1890s.

Here, however, we enter the realm of the purely speculative. What remains certain is that Reconstruction failed, and that for blacks its failure was a disaster whose magnitude cannot be obscured by the genuine accomplishments that did endure. For the nation as a whole, the collapse of Reconstruction was a tragedy that deeply affected the course of its future development. If racism contributed to the undoing of Reconstruction, by the same token Reconstruction's demise and the emergence of blacks as a disenfranchised class of dependent laborers greatly facilitated racism's further spread, until by the early twentieth century it had become more deeply embedded in the nation's culture and politics than at any time since the beginning of the antislavery crusade and perhaps in our entire history. The removal of a significant portion of the nation's laboring population from public life shifted the center of gravity of American politics to the right, complicating the tasks of reformers for generations to come. Long into the twentieth century, the South remained a one-party region under the control of a reactionary ruling elite who used the same violence and fraud that had helped defeat Reconstruction to stifle internal dissent. An enduring consequence of Reconstruction's failure, the Solid

South helped define the contours of American politics and weaken the prospects not simply of change in racial matters but of progressive legislation in many other realms.

The men and women who had spearheaded the effort to remake Southern society scattered down innumerable byways after the end of Reconstruction. Some relied on federal patronage to earn a livelihood. The unfortunate Marshall Twitchell, armless after his near-murder in 1876, was appointed U.S. consul at Kingston, Ontario, where he died in 1905. Some fifty relatives and friends of the Louisiana Returning Board that had helped make Hayes President received positions at the New Orleans Custom House, and Stephen Packard was awarded the consulship at Liverpool — compensation for surrendering his claim to the governorship. John Eaton, who coordinated freedmen's affairs for General Grant during the war and subsequently took an active role in Tennessee Reconstruction, served as federal commissioner of education from 1870 to 1886, and organized a public school system in Puerto Rico after the island's conquest in the Spanish-American War. Most carpetbaggers returned to the North, often finding there the financial success that had eluded them in the South. Davis Tillson, head of Georgia's Freedman's Bureau immediately after the war, earned a fortune in the Maine granite business. Former South Carolina Gov. Robert K. Scott returned to Napoleon, Ohio, where he became a successful real estate agent — "a most fitting occupation" in view of his involvement in land commission speculations. Less happy was the fate of his scalawag successor, Franklin J. Moses, Jr., who drifted north, served prison terms for petty crimes, and died in a Massachusetts rooming house in 1906.

Republican governors who had won reputations as moderates by courting white Democratic support and seeking to limit blacks' political influence found the Redeemer South remarkably forgiving. Henry C. Warmoth became a successful sugar planter and remained in Louisiana until his death in 1931. James L. Alcorn retired to his Mississippi plantation, "presiding over a Delta domain in a style befitting a prince" and holding various local offices. He remained a Republican, but told one Northern visitor that Democratic rule had produced "good fellowship" between the races. Even Rufus Bullock, who fled Georgia accused of every kind of venality, soon reentered Atlanta society, serving, among other things, as president of the city's chamber of commerce. Daniel H. Chamberlain left South Carolina in 1877 to launch a successful New York City law practice, but was well received on his numerous visits to the state. In retrospect, Chamberlain altered his opinion of Reconstruction: a "frightful experiment" that sought to "lift a backward or inferior race" to political equality, it had inevitably produced "shocking and unbearable misgovernment." "Governor Chamberlain," commented a Charleston newspaper, "has lived and learned."

Not all white Republicans, however, abandoned Reconstruction ideals. In 1890, a group of reformers, philanthropists, and religious leaders gathered at the Lake Mohonk Conference on the Negro Question, chaired by former President Hayes. Amid a chorus of advice that blacks eschew political involvement and concentrate on educational and economic progress and remedying their own character deficiencies, former North Carolina Judge Albion W. Tourgée, again living in the North, voiced the one discordant note. There was no "Negro problem," Tourgée observed, but rather a "white" one, since "the hate, the oppression, the injustice, are all on our side." The following year, Tourgée established the National Citizens' Rights Association, a short-lived forerunner of the National Association for the Advancement of Colored People, devoted to challenging the numerous injustices afflicting Southern blacks. Adelbert Ames, who left Mississippi in 1875 to join his father's Minnesota flour-milling business and who later settled in Massachusetts, continued to defend his Reconstruction record. In 1894 he chided Brown University President E. Benjamin Andrews for writing that Mississippi during his governorship had incurred a debt of $20 million. The actual figure, Ames pointed out, was less than 3 percent of that amount, and he found it difficult to understand how Andrews had made "a $19,500,000 error in a $20,000,000 statement." Ames lived to his ninety-eighth year, never abandoning the conviction that "caste is the curse of the world." Another Mississippi carpetbagger, Massachusetts-born teacher and legislator Henry Warren, published his autobiography in 1914, still hoping that one day, "possibly in the present century," America would live up to the ideal of "equal political rights for all without regard to race."

For some, the Reconstruction experience became a springboard to lifetimes of social reform. The white voters of Winn Parish in Louisiana's hill country expressed their enduring radicalism by supporting the Populists in the 1890s, Socialism in 1912, and later their native son Huey Long. Among the female veterans of freedmen's education, Cornelia Hancock founded Philadelphia's Children's Aid Society, Abby May became prominent in the Massachusetts women's suffrage movement, Ellen Collins turned her attention to New York City housing reform, and Josephine Shaw Lowell became a supporter of the labor movement and principal founder of New York's Consumer League. Louis F. Post, a New Jersey-born carpetbagger who took stenographic notes for South Carolina's legislature in the early 1870s, became a follower of Henry George, attended the founding meeting of the NAACP, and as Woodrow Wilson's Assistant Secretary of Labor, sought to mitigate the 1919 Red Scare and prevent the deportation of foreign-born radicals. And Texas scalawag editor Albert Parsons became a nationally known Chicago labor reformer and anarchist, whose speeches drew comparisons between the plight of Southern blacks and Northern industrial workers, and between the aristocracy resting on slavery the Civil War had destroyed and the new oligarchy based on the exploitation of industrial labor it had helped to create. Having survived the perils of Texas Reconstruction, Parsons met his death on the Illinois gallows after being wrongfully convicted of complicity in the Haymarket bombing of 1886.

Like their white counterparts, many black veterans of Reconstruction survived on federal patronage after the coming of "home rule." P. B. S.

Pinchback and Blanche K. Bruce held a series of such posts and later moved to Washington, D.C., where they entered the city's privileged black society. Richard T. Greener, during Reconstruction a professor at the University of South Carolina, combined a career in law, journalism, and education with various government appointments, including a stint as American commercial agent at Vladivostok. Long after the destruction of his low-country political machine by disenfranchisement, Robert Smalls served as customs collector for the port of Beaufort, dying there in 1915. Mifflin Gibbs held positions ranging from register of Little Rock's land office to American consul at Madagascar. Other black leaders left the political arena entirely to devote themselves to religious and educational work, emigration projects, or personal advancement. Robert G. Fitzgerald continued to teach in North Carolina until his death in 1919; Edward Shaw of Memphis concentrated on activities among black Masons and the AME Church; Richard H. Cain served as president of a black college in Waco, Texas; and Francis L. Cardozo went on to become principal of a Washington, D.C., high school. Aaron A. Bradley, the militant spokesman for Georgia's low-country freedmen, helped publicize the Kansas Exodus and died in St. Louis in 1881, while Henry M. Turner, ordained an AME bishop in 1880, emerged as the late nineteenth century's most prominent advocate of black emigration to Africa. Former Atlanta councilman William Finch prospered as a tailor. Alabama Congressman Jeremiah Haralson engaged in coal mining in Colorado, where he was reported "killed by wild beasts."

Other Reconstruction leaders found, in the words of a black lawyer, that "the tallest tree . . . suffers most in a storm." Former South Carolina Congressman and Lieut. Gov. Alonzo J. Ransier died in poverty in 1882, having been employed during his last years as a night watchman at the Charleston Custom House and as a city street sweeper. Robert B. Elliott, the state's most brilliant political organizer, found himself "utterly unable to earn a living owing to the severe ostracism and mean prejudice of my political opponents." He died in 1884 after moving to New Orleans and struggling to survive as a lawyer. James T. Rapier died penniless in 1883, having dispersed his considerable wealth among black schools, churches, and emigration organizations. Most local leaders sank into obscurity, disappearing entirely from the historical record. Although some of their children achieved distinction, none of Reconstruction's black officials created a family political dynasty — one indication of how Redemption aborted the development of the South's black political leadership. If their descendants moved ahead, it was through business, the arts, or the professions. T. Thomas Fortune, editor of the New York *Age*, was the son of Florida officeholder Emanuel Fortune; Harlem Renaissance writer Jean Toomer, the grandson of Pinchback; renowned jazz pianist Fletcher Henderson, the grandson of an official who had served in South Carolina's constitutional convention and legislature.

By the turn of the century, as soldiers from North and South joined to take up the "white man's burden" in the Spanish-American War, Reconstruction was widely viewed as little more than a regrettable detour on the road to reunion. To the bulk of the white South, it had become axiomatic that Reconstruction had been a time of "savage tyranny" that "accomplished not one useful result, and left behind it, not one pleasant recollection." Black suffrage, wrote Joseph Le Conte, who had fled South Carolina for a professorship at the University of California to avoid teaching black students, was now seen by "all thoughtful men" as "the greatest political crime ever perpetrated by any people." In more sober language, many Northerners, including surviving architects of Congressional policy, concurred in these judgments. "Years of thinking and observation" had convinced O. O. Howard "that the restoration of their lands to the planters provided for [a] future better for the negroes." John Sherman's recollections recorded a similar change of heart: "After this long lapse of time I am convinced that Mr. Johnson's scheme of reorganization was wise and judicious. . . . It is unfortunate that it had not the sanction of Congress."

This rewriting of Reconstruction's history was accorded scholarly legitimacy — to its everlasting shame — by the nation's fraternity of professional historians. Early in the twentieth century a group of young Southern scholars gathered at Columbia University to study the Reconstruction era under the guidance of Professors John W. Burgess and William A. Dunning. Blacks, their mentors taught, were "children" utterly incapable of appreciating the freedom that had been thrust upon them. The North did "a monstrous thing" in granting them suffrage, for "a black skin means membership in a race of men which has never of itself succeeded in subjecting passion to reason, has never, therefore, created any civilization of any kind." No political order could survive in the South unless founded on the principle of racial inequality. The students' works on individual Southern states echoed these sentiments. Reconstruction, concluded the study of North Carolina, was an attempt by "selfish politicians, backed by the federal government . . . to Africanize the State and deprive the people through misrule and oppression of most that life held dear." The views of the Dunning School shaped historical writing for generations, and achieved wide popularity through D. W. Griffith's film *Birth of a Nation* (which glorified the Ku Klux Klan and had its premiere at the White House during Woodrow Wilson's Presidency), James Ford Rhodes's popular multivolume chronicle of the Civil War era, and the national best-seller *The Tragic Era* by Claude G. Bowers. Southern whites, wrote Bowers, "literally were put to the torture" by "emissaries of hate" who inflamed "the negroes' egotism" and even inspired "lustful assaults" by blacks upon white womanhood.

Few interpretations of history have had such far-reaching consequences as this image of Reconstruction. As Francis B. Simkins, a South Carolina-born historian, noted during the 1930s, "the alleged horrors of Reconstruction" did much to freeze the mind of the white South in unalterable opposition to outside pressures for social change and to any thought of breaching Democratic ascendancy, eliminating segregation, or restoring suffrage to disenfranchised blacks. They also justified Northern indifference to the nullification of the Fourteenth and Fifteenth Amendments. Apart from a few white dissenters like Simkins, it was left to black writers to challenge the prevailing orthodoxy. In the early years of this century, none did so more tirelessly than former Mississippi Congressman John R. Lynch, then living in Chicago, who published a series of devastating critiques of the racial biases and historical errors of Rhodes and Bowers. "I do not hesitate to assert," he wrote, "that the Southern Reconstruction Governments were the best governments those States ever had." In 1917, Lynch voiced the hope that "a fair, just, and impartial historian will, some day, write a history covering the Reconstruction period, [giving] the actual facts of what took place."

Only in the family traditions and collective folk memories of the black community did a different version of Reconstruction survive. Growing up in the 1920s, Pauli Murray was "never allowed to forget" that she walked in "proud shoes" because her grandfather, Robert G. Fitzgerald, had "fought for freedom" in the Union Army and then enlisted as a teacher in the "second war" against the powerlessness and ignorance inherited from slavery. When the Works Progress Administration sent agents into the black belt during the Great Depression to interview former slaves, they found Reconstruction remembered for its disappointments and betrayals, but also as a time of hope, possibility, and accomplishment. Bitterness still lingered over the federal government's failure to distribute land or protect blacks' civil and political rights. "The Yankees helped free us, so they say," declared eighty-one-year-old former slave Thomas Hall, "but they let us be put back in slavery again." Yet coupled with this disillusionment were proud, vivid recollections of a time when "the colored-used to hold office." Some pulled from their shelves dusty scrapbooks of clippings from Reconstruction newspapers; others could still recount the names of local black leaders. "They made pretty fair officers," remarked one elderly freedman; "I thought them was good times in the country," said another. Younger blacks spoke of being taught by their parents "about the old times, mostly about the Reconstruction, and the Ku Klux." "I know folks think the books tell the truth, but they shore don't," one eighty-eight-year-old former slave told the WPA.

For some blacks, such memories helped to keep alive the aspirations of the Reconstruction era. "This here used to be a good county," said Arkansas freedman Boston Blackwell, "but I tell you it sure is tough now. I think it's wrong — exactly wrong that we can't vote now." "I does believe that the negro ought to be given more privileges in voting," echoed Taby Jones, born a slave in South Carolina in 1850, "because they went through the reconstruction period with banners flying." For others, Reconstruction inspired optimism that better times lay ahead. "The Bible says, 'What has been will be again'," said Alabama sharecropper Ned Cobb. Born in 1885, Cobb never cast a vote in his entire life, yet he never forgot that outsiders had once taken up the black cause — an indispensable source of hope for one conscious of his own weakness in the face of overwhelming and hostile local power. When radical Northerners ventured South in the 1930s to help organize black agricultural workers, Cobb seemed almost to have been waiting for them: "The whites came down to bring emancipation, and left before it was over. . . . Now they've come to finish the job." The legacy of Reconstruction affected the 1930s revival of black militancy in other ways as well. Two leaders of the Alabama Share Croppers Union, Ralph and Thomas Gray, claimed to be descended from a Reconstruction legislator. (Like many nineteenth-century predecessors, Ralph Gray paid with his life for challenging the South's social order — he was killed in a shootout with a posse while guarding a union meeting.)

Twenty more years elapsed before another generation of black Southerners launched the final challenge to the racial system of the New South. A few participants in the civil rights movement thought of themselves as following a path blazed after the Civil War. Discussing the reasons for his involvement, one black Mississippian spoke of the time when "a few Negroes was admitted into the government of the State of Mississippi and to the United States." Reconstruction's legacy was also evident in the actions of federal judge Frank Johnson, who fought a twelve-year battle for racial justice with Alabama Gov. George Wallace. Johnson hailed from Winston County, a center of Civil War Unionism, and his great-grandfather had served as a Republican sheriff during Reconstruction. By this time, however, the Reconstruction generation had passed from the scene and even within the black community, memories of the period had all but disappeared. Yet the institutions created or consolidated after the Civil War — the black family, school, and church — provided the base from which the modern civil rights revolution sprang. And for its legal strategy, the movement returned to the laws and amendments of Reconstruction.

"The river has its bend, and the longest road must terminate." Rev. Peter Randolph, a former slave, wrote these words as the dark night of injustice settled over the South. Nearly a century elapsed before the nation again attempted to come to terms with the implications of emancipation and the political and social agenda of Reconstruction. In many ways, it has yet to do so.

ELLIOTT WEST

from Reconstructing Race   [2003]

ELLIOTT WEST (1945–) is the Distinguished Professor of History at the University of Arkansas, Fayetteville. He is the author of five books including *Growing Up with the Country: Childhood on the Far Western Frontier* (1989) and *The Contested Plains: Indians, Gold Seekers, and the Rush to Colorado* (1998).

I would like to look again at race in America during the crucial middle years of the nineteenth century and wonder aloud what that story might look like if expanded to more of a continental perspective. Specifically, I

Elliott West, "Reconstructing Race," *Western Historical Quarterly* 34 (Spring 2003): 1–14. Copyright © by Western Historical Quarterly. Reprinted by permission of Western Historical Quarterly.

will bring the West more into the picture. If I have a general premise, it is that the acquisition of the Far West in the 1840s influenced, much more than we have credited, our racial history — how people have thought about race, how racial minorities have fared, and what policies our government adopted. In fact, since race is always a bellwether of larger forces, I think we need to consider that the great gulping of land in the 1840s had as much to do with shaping the course of our history as any event of that century, including the Civil War that dominates the story as we tell it today.

Taken together, the acquisitions of 1845–1848 comprised our greatest expansion. The annexations of Texas and Oregon and the Mexican Cession made the United States much larger and richer — and far more ethnically mixed. Languages are one crude measure. While the United States grew in area by about 66 percent, the number of languages spoken within it increased by more than 100 percent. That number would grow still more during the next few years as tens of thousands flooded into the California gold fields. In the 1850s, no nation on earth had a region with so rich an ethnic stew as the American West.

Expansion triggered an American racial crisis. We have always taught that to our students, of course, but we have missed at least half the point. The connection we make is between expansion and slavery. We say that new western lands, full of opportunity, made the question of black slavery dangerously concrete outside the South. That, in turn, set loose disputes that by 1861 would tip us over the edge of catastrophe. This sequence seems to give the West a prominent role in America's racial history, but the effect is ironic. Because race remains strictly a matter of black and white, and because its prime issue is African American slavery and its central event is the Civil War, western expansion is important only on eastern terms. Once the Mexican War does its mischief, the focus quickly swings back East and stays there. The West has its consequential moment, then remains at the edge of the action.

But that's nothing close to the whole story. Expansion was double trouble. It not only sped up the old conflict between North and South. By complicating so hugely America's ethnic character it raised new questions on the relation between race and nation. These questions centered on the West. . . .

The term for this era, Reconstruction, has always thrummed with racial implications, but when broadened to apply seriously from coast to coast, the term strengthens and its implications deepen. In the twenty years of tumult after 1846, attitudes and institutions of race were in fact being reconstructed, and more thoroughly than we have recognized. Listening to the clatter of opinions, not merely about black-white relations but also, in the color code of the day, about red, brown, and yellow, the range of possible outcomes seems to me a lot wider than we have allowed. When I shift my attention from the idealism of Reconstruction's radicals toward what was being said and done out West, and when I remember how rapidly that idealism would wither by the late 1870s, I wonder whether this nation flirted more seriously than we have admitted with a racial order far more rigid than what we finally got. I wonder what kind of America we might have seen if the headhunters and racial purists had carried the day. Frankly (to use a boyhood phrase) it gives me the shivers.

But of course something else happened. We turned away from the western tendency toward absolute racial divides, even as we compromised an eastern ideal of a fuller racial equality for former slaves. Among the theorists, the hard lines of scientific racism softened. Polygenesis, the teaching that races were born separate and could never merge, fell from favor. Racial distinctions were as strong as ever, and so was the trust in sorting them out by skull volume and the length of fingers, but now everyone once again was called part of one humanity. Races were unequal at the moment, but they were all moving along the same path of development. We seemed to be back around 1800, back to the Jeffersonian faith in turning Indians into whites. But there were two big differences. The new ideas about race were full of pretensions from the new science, especially evolutionary notions of social Darwinism. And now the government was expected to take charge of racial development as it never had before. The federal government, newly muscular after the Civil War, would act within its borders much as other imperial powers did in their distant colonies of Africa and Asia. Washington would claim the jurisdiction and the know-how to be a kind of racial master, part policeman, part doctor, part professor.

The key to understanding this . . . story is the powerful drive toward national consolidation. This theme — the integration of a divided America into a whole — is the one our textbooks tell us ruled the late nineteenth century. And so it did. Those texts, however, usually tell us that the sectional crisis and Civil War were the prime causes behind that drive, while, in fact, consolidation took its energy at least as much from the expansion of the 1840s. Acquiring the West stretched our distances, enriched our variety, and uncovered enormous wealth on our farthest edge. That, as much as secession, compelled us to think in terms of pulling it all together and keeping it that way. Making a firmer, tighter union meant resolving questions about differences within this nation, and close to the top of the list were questions about race. Here, too, westward expansion, as much as the conflict of North and South, had churned up matters and pushed us toward some resolution. It follows that if we want to understand what happened — in national consolidation, in American race, and in how the two wove together — we need to keep our eyes moving in both directions, toward both West and South.

Consolidation, racial or any other kind, means finding common ground. There must be standards to measure the parts of the nation and to decide what fits where. In bringing West and South and their peoples more tightly into the union, two standards were most important. The first was economic. From Virginia plantations to Nevada mines and Nebraska homesteads, the nation would be pulled together under the ideals of free labor and yeoman agriculture and through the realities of corporate capitalism. The second standard was a union of mores — custom, religion, language, and the rest of what we call, inadequately, "culture" — nurtured from Boston to Charleston to Tombstone. A national economy and a national culture — together they would provide the common ground of the new America. America's racial parts would have to find their place, if they had a place to find, on that ground and inside its boundaries. Watching the results, West and South, is a revelation, not just about our racial drama, but also about the entire process of expansion and the remaking of a nation.

The case of the Chinese was the most extreme. They were America's most anomalous people. In language, dress, foodways, religion, and customs they seemed beyond the pale, and with their vast predominance of men, they lacked what all other groups, however different, had in common: the family as their central social unit. Culturally, then, the Chinese were uniquely vulnerable. Economically, their potential was much more promising, but ironically that made them a special threat. From early in the 1850s, some had compared Chinese work gangs to black slavery and had suggested them as a solution to the Far West's chronic labor shortage. An editor predicted (and he meant it positively) that the Chinese will "be to California what the African has been to the South." After the Civil War, some raised the possibility of Chinese playing the African in the South itself. In 1869, businessmen met in Memphis to consider importing Asia's rural workers into their cotton fields and factories. They heard that the Chinese, "industrious, docile, and competent," could be shipped in five hundred at a time at $44.70 per head. Bitter opposition, however, came from opponents of slavery and, more effectively, from champions of free white labor. Close to the heart of the Chinese image as hopelessly alien was the notion that they were sheeplike, easily controlled, and utterly without the individual gumption to stand up to their bosses. This made them free labor's ultimate nightmare: a race of automatons used by monopolists and labor-bashers to undercut wages or cast out honest workers altogether. The most vicious assaults on Asians came from spokesmen for white workingmen like Henry George and in political movements like California's Workingmen's Party. In the end, the Chinese found themselves without either a cultural or economic base in the new nation and with virtually no natural constituency. They suffered the most excessive answer to America's racial question. As of 1882, they were excluded.

The case of Hispanics was the oddest. Their numbers were greatest in relation to whites in the Southwest, our least populous region with resources that were, for the moment, the least exploitable. This corner of the nation consequently was the last to be brought close and consolidated, which in turn lessened somewhat the pressure to resolve its racial issues. Mexican-Americans still carried the burden of the old rhetoric, the images of listless, unenlightened people, but they were not as alien as the Chinese. After all they were Christian, albeit Catholic, and were family-oriented farmers. And they fit the emerging economy. They did the grunt labor in mines, and they worked the land in a system of debt peonage strikingly similar to southern sharecropping. Hispanics, that is, posed little cultural threat and played useful economic roles. The upshot was partly to ignore the racial issues raised by expansion and partly to turn vices into virtues.

Mexican-Americans were either rendered invisible, segregated in cities and countryside, or they were reimagined as a bit of American exotica in a region we could afford to fantasize as an escape from fast-paced modern life. In the land of *poco tiempo*, these people of color became what was much tamer: people of local color.

That left African and Native Americans. Their case was most revealing of all. Since the 1840s, southern blacks and western Indians had been counterpoised in our racial thinking: insiders and outsiders, enslaved and free-roaming, the essences of South and West. Now they converged. They were brought together as events of the 1860s shattered older arrangements and assumptions. Emancipated blacks still were insiders — they were, in the fine phrase of Frederick Douglass, close under the arm of white America — but they were no longer controlled through slavery. While not as free-roaming as Indians, they were definitely on the loose. Indians, meanwhile, contrary to the claims of the 1840s and 1850s, were obviously not vanishing. In fact, their lands were being pulled into the national embrace far more quickly than anyone had guessed possible. Indians were not as enmeshed in white society as the freedmen, but they *were* being brought inside the house. Blacks and Indians found themselves suddenly moving from opposite directions into the national mainstream. Paradoxically, liberation and conquest were carrying them to the same place.

Where exactly they would end up, and how they would get there, would be the self-appointed job of the newly centralized government, and nothing in the history of Reconstruction is more illuminating as the programs that resulted. As usual, we have treated events in the West and South as if they rolled along utterly independent of each other, while in fact Washington's treatment of blacks and Indians ran as a stunning parallel. Official strategies were virtually the same. Economic integration for freedmen was to come through forty acres and a mule, or at least some measure of agrarian self-sufficiency; for Indians, the answer was to be allotment in severalty. For cultural integration, ex-slaves would be educated under the Freedmen's Bureau; for Indians, it would be agency and boarding schools. (And sometimes, most famously in the Hampton Institute, the two were schooled in the same places.) For both, Christian service and evangelism directed and suffused the entire enterprise, mixing religious verities with the virtues of free enterprise, patriotism, and Anglo American civilization.

The differences were not in the government's goals and methods but in the responses to them. Freedmen, as insiders, had worked within private agriculture for generations and had been sustained by their own Christian worship. They found the government's stated goals perfectly fine. The Sioux and Apaches and Nez Perces and others, as outsiders, had their own traditions and cosmologies and relations with the land. They replied differently. Some accepted the new order, but for others the government finally had to turn to its strong arm to impose what former slaves wanted all along.

It takes a little effort, I will admit, to see Freedmen's schools and the Little Big Horn as two sides of the same process, but blink a few times and it makes perfect sense, once you look at Reconstruction's racial policies, not on strictly southern terms, narrowly, as an outgrowth of Civil War, but rather as a culmination of a development that began in the 1840s. Its first stage began with the expansion of the nation, and with that physical growth we were unsettled profoundly in our sense of who we were and might be. This stage raised a series of new racial questions and aggravated older ones. The second stage, the Civil War, brought those questions to the sticking place. By ending slavery and bringing the West closer into the union, the war left the nation as mixed and uncertain in its racial identity as it ever had been or would be. By revolutionizing relations of power, the war also opened the way for a settlement of a sort. In the third stage, from 1865 to the early 1880s, the government used its confirmed authority to flesh out the particulars of a new racial arrangement. Some peoples it excluded, some it left on the edges, some it integrated on the terms and by the means of its choosing, including in some cases by conquest and coercion.

This Greater Reconstruction was even more morally ambiguous than the lesser one. It included not one war but three — the Mexican War, Civil War, and War against Indian America — and while it saw the emancipation of one non-white people, it was equally concerned with dominating others. It included the Civil Rights Acts and the 13th, 14th, and 15th Amendments, but it began with U.S. soldiers clashing with a Mexican patrol on disputed terrain along the Rio Grande in 1846. And it closed, practically, with the Chinese Exclusion Act of 1882 and symbolically, in 1877, with Oliver Howard — former head of the Freedman's Bureau who had risked his life and given his arm for emancipation — running to ground Chief Joseph and the Nez Perces along our northern border, forty miles shy of freedom. Always the Greater Reconstruction was as much about control as liberation, as much about unity and power as about equality. Indians were given roles they mostly didn't want, and freedmen were offered roles they mostly did, but both were being told that these were the roles they *would* play, like it or not. There has always been a darker side to *e pluribus unum,* and when we look at the parallel policies toward Indians and blacks, we can see it in its full breathtaking arrogance. When the Lake Mohonk Conference of Friends of the Indians turned from its usual concerns to devote two annual meetings to answering the so-called "Negro Question," one of its members, Lyman Abbott, was asked why no African Americans would be attending. He answered: "A patient is not invited to the consultation of the doctors in his case."

I hope no one takes from what I have written any intent to lessen the enormity of southern slavery in our history or to devalue in the slightest its human costs. My southern friends, especially, might argue that the way I am telling the story neglects the sheer weight of black-white relations in our national consciousness and the scale of the calamities spun off by slavery. They might tell me also that my version misses the genuine idealism generated from abolition and the Civil War. They might say all that and more, and if they do I will admit that they might be right.

But there are a few things I know. I know we should put our foot down and not allow the Civil War to continue behaving as it does now in our texts and histories, sitting there like a gravity field, drawing to itself everything around it and bending all meanings to fit its own shape. I am certain that, while we call the mid-nineteenth century the Civil War Era, acquiring the West had at least as much to do with remaking America as the conflict between North and South. I know that race is essential to understanding what happened during those years, and I know that the conquest and integration of the West is essential to understanding race. I am sure that we will never grasp the racial ideas of that time without recognizing that they took their twisting shapes partly from exchanges between West and South — a vigorous, strange dialogue that included not only slavery apologists and the familiar tropes about black inferiority but also rhetorical flights on opium smoking, color-coded *Zeitgeists*, and headhunters and bodysnatchers in caps and gowns. And I am confident that when we bring the West more into the story, when we end the isolation of episodes like the California gold rush and the Indian wars and make them part of a genuinely coast-to-coast history of race in America, we will have learned a lot.

The lessons will teach us again how western history has plenty to say about America today. In the 1960s, movements for the rights of black Americans encouraged us to look back with new care at slavery, emancipation, and reconstruction. The situation today — when Hispanic Americans are our largest minority and Asian Americans are arriving in unprecedented numbers, when Pat Buchanan is fanning fears about brown and yellow hordes, when the fastest growing minority in southern cities is American Indians, and when I read in my local newspaper about rallies by an Arkansas anti-Hispanic group with the unintentionally ironic acronym of AIM (Americans for Immigration Moratorium) — this situation should encourage us to look yet again at those middle years of the nineteenth century, this time in search of the roots of racial thinking that goes beyond the simpler divisions of black and white.

The larger point, of course, is a broader awareness of the most troubling theme of our past. For many of us that awareness will mean a more intimate implication, especially if we live outside the South, or like me along its edges. Race is not the burden of southern history. Race is the burden of American history. Its questions speak to all of us, whichever region we call home, and press us all to ask where and how far we have fallen short in keeping promises we have made to ourselves. In 1869, near the end of the Great Reconstruction, the reformer and spiritualist Cora Tappan took this continental perspective when she offered her audience an observation that, in its essence, is still worth making today:

> A government that has for nearly a century enslaved one race (African), that proscribes another (Chinese), proposes to exterminate another (Indians), and persistently refuses to recognize the rights of one-half of its citizens (women), cannot justly be called perfect.

The Triumph of Capitalism: Efficiency or Class War?

3

"The old nations of the earth," Andrew Carnegie observed in 1886, "creep on at a snail's pace; the Republic thunders past with the rush of the express. The United States, [in] the growth of a single century, has already reached the foremost rank among nations, and is destined soon to outdistance all others in the race. In population, in wealth, in annual savings, and in public credit; in freedom from debt, in agriculture, and in manufactures, America already leads the civilized world."[1] This is the true voice of American triumphalism; having long congratulated itself on being the freest place in the world, America at the turn of the century looked around and noticed it had (or was about to) become the most powerful industrial economy on the face of the earth.

While Carnegie caught the dominant note of public self-congratulation, other Americans detested the greed and ugliness that accompanied the industrial transformation. Walt Whitman, in "Democratic Vistas," summed up this sort of criticism: "The depravity of the business classes of our country is not less than has been supposed but infinitely greater. . . . The great cities reek with respectable as much as nonrespectable robbery and scoundrelism. . . . I say that our New World democracy, however great a success . . . in materialistic development . . . is, so far, an almost complete failure in its social aspects, and in really grand religious, moral, literary, and esthetic results."[2] But even at their most pessimistic or radical such critics could never capture the quality of pain, bewilderment, and outrage inflecting the voices of workers, farmers, and other lower-class Americans who felt themselves to be victims of triumphant capitalism. A skilled iron molder, one of the supposed "aristocrats of labor," wrote in his diary during a serious depression in 1876: "No money, rent due. . . . Coal nearly out. Little food in the house. And, worst of all, no prospects ahead either to pay what is due or to replace what is nearly out. Even if I got a job, it would be a month before I could have any money. God only knows what I will or can do under such circumstances."[3] Reflecting both misery and a crushing sense of humiliation, a midwestern farmer wrote to a Populist editor in 1891: "I am one of those Poor

---

[1]Andrew Carnegie, *Triumphant Democracy* (New York, 1886), 1.

[2]Walt Whitman, "Democratic Vistas," in Floyd Stovall, ed., *Prose Works 1892*, 2 vols. (New York, 1963–1964), vol. 2, 370.

[3]Neil L. Shumsky, "Frank Roney's San Francisco — His Diary: April, 1875–March, 1876," *Labor History* 17 (Spring 1976): 258. A survey of the history of unemployment in one state is Alexander Keyssar, *Out of Work: The First Century of Unemployment in Massachusetts* (New York, 1986).

55

and unprotected. . . . I settled on this Land in good Faith . . . Spent years of hard labor in grubing fencing and Improving are they going to drive us out like trespassers . . . and give us away to the Corporations . . . we are robbed of our means . . . We are Loyal Citicens . . . We love our wife and children . . . But how can we protect them give them education as they should wen we are driven from sea to sea."[4]

The promise of freedom and prosperity seemed to have been revoked for those who labored, as opposed to those who owned and managed the nation's resources and industrial enterprises. Fundamental decisions about their lives — from whether they worked and for how much, to whose influence would shape politics and government on the local level and beyond — were no longer in their control. Pain and bewilderment led to outrage and action. Unionizing workers called for "industrial democracy," Populist farmers for a "cooperative commonwealth." Indeed, if corporate capitalists saw themselves as champions of a free market version of American democracy, organized labor and other advocates for the poor and dispossessed saw themselves as vindicating an egalitarian version of that same democracy.

Americans have continued to debate the merits of industrialization since its onset. They have argued about facts: How was wealth produced? How evenly was it distributed? How much social mobility took place between classes? And they argued about interpretations: Was the impoverishment of certain groups of laborers exceptional or endemic to industrial capitalism? Did labor unions and regulatory legislation represent a democratic restraint on capital or an anticompetitive and clumsy way to buy off radical protest? Was class conflict an aberration produced by greed and bad policy or a permanent feature of industrial capitalism? Was corporate capitalism an achievement or a betrayal of American democracy (or most painful to contemplate, perhaps both)? On these questions, historians of industrialization have been no less divided than journalists, politicians, and other citizens. Not all of their differences can be explored here, but it is possible to focus on two prominent areas of scholarly attention and debate: the character of the modern American corporation and the character of the American labor movement.

The first attempts to evaluate critically the achievements of the "captains of industry" who built the great corporations occurred at the beginning of the twentieth century. Against the prevailing triumphalism, Washington Gladden, Henry George, Henry Demarest Lloyd, and others agitated against the "robber barons." For Gladden, a Protestant minister who preached the Social Gospel, capitalist competition was warfare and its antidote a social welfare policy based on Christian brotherhood. For George, author of *Progress and Poverty* (1879), all the inequities of capitalist society derived from the monopolization of the land and its resources by a handful of lucky speculators; a single tax on their entirely unearned landed wealth thus represented the

---

[4]Quoted in Norman Pollack, ed., *The Populist Mind* (Indianapolis and New York, 1967), 33–34, variant spelling and punctuation in the original. On Populism, see Chapter 6.

crucial antidote to inequality. A journalist and a scholar, Lloyd, until his death in 1903, insisted that the American people were confronted with a choice between reform or revolution. In *Wealth against Commonwealth* (1894), which anticipated the writings of later muckrakers and reformers, Lloyd insisted that public ownership of monopolies and regulation of the economy were absolutely necessary to avoid the "misery, plagues, hatreds, [and] national enervation" that had wracked other nations in the industrialized world.[5] Within a general critique of industrial capitalism, Lloyd focused specifically on John D. Rockefeller's attempt to monopolize the petroleum industry. Rockefeller, wrote Lloyd, paid lip service to the ideal of competition, but actually aimed to achieve a form of monopolistic power that harkened back to feudalism. Like Lloyd, other critics of capitalism tended to personalize their critiques. Focusing on the unbridled selfishness of the captains of industry permitted critics to mobilize a language of moral and religious condemnation that resonated with many Christian Americans. And focusing on the robber baron's lust for power allowed the critics to mobilize an even more resonant language of democratic equality.

While critics etched the negative image of robber barons in the public's imagination, and the Progressive reform movement sought to restrain the power of the corporation, historians began to inquire into the economic realities of capitalism. The greatest of these, the Progressive historians Charles and Mary Beard and Vernon L. Parrington, compared the industrialists to the feudal barons of the medieval past.[6] Parrington's *Main Currents in American Thought* issued the severest judgment. Placing himself squarely within the tradition of Jeffersonian liberalism, Parrington portrayed the industrialists as predatory and materialistic, their bloated corporations as threats to republican virtue and democratic equality. Business tycoons had turned modern America, with "its standardized life, its machine culture, its mass-psychology," into a place in which "Jefferson and Jackson and Lincoln would be strangers." The giants of industry, Parrington thundered, "were primitive souls, ruthless, predatory, capable; single-minded men; rogues and rascals often, but never feeble, never hindered by petty scruple, never given to puling or whining — the raw materials of a race of capitalistic buccaneers."[7]

The 1930s provided a favorable climate for the critique of the robber baron. For decades the business community had asserted that the nation's greatness rested on the achievements of ambitious and energetic entrepreneurs. They applauded President Calvin Coolidge's dictum: "The business of America is business." Having taken credit for the apparent prosperity of the 1920s, however, they had to accept responsibility for the catastrophic depression of the 1930s. As unemployment, bankruptcy, and even starvation

---

[5]Henry Demarest Lloyd, *Wealth against Commonwealth* (New York, 1894), 517.
[6]Charles and Mary Beard, *The Rise of American Civilization*, 2 vols. (New York, 1927), vol. 2, 177.
[7]Vernon L. Parrington, *Main Currents in American Thought*, 3 vols. (New York, 1927–1930), vol. 3, 12, 26.

afflicted millions of Americans, the businessman's time-honored cliché — that wealth was the product of ambition, talent, and moral uprightness — seemed an obscene joke. Perhaps free enterprise capitalism had come to the end of the road, many now boldly suggested; new approaches were required to meet the needs of a complex, modern, industrial society.

Dedicating his 1934 book, *The Robber Barons: The Great American Capitalists 1861–1901*, to Charles and Mary Beard, Matthew Josephson developed the Beard-Parrington view of business into a full-scale historical critique. "This book," he began, "attempts the history of a small class of men who arose at the time of our Civil War and suddenly swept into power. . . . Under their hands the renovation of our economic life proceeded relentlessly: large-scale production replaced the scattered, decentralized mode of production, industrial enterprises became more concentrated, more 'efficient' techni-cally. . . . But all this revolutionizing effort is branded with the motive of pri-vate gain on the part of the new captains of industry. To organize and exploit the resources of a nation upon a gigantic scale, to regiment its farmers and workers into harmonious corps of producers, and to do this only in the name of an uncontrolled appetite for private profit — here surely is the great inherent contradiction whence so much disaster, outrage, and misery has flowed."[8]

Just as the robber baron concept reached maturity, another school of thought emerged: business history. The foundations of business history were laid in the 1930s by scholars at the Harvard Graduate School of Business Administration, as well as by sympathetic biographers of individual busi-ness leaders. Rejecting the robber baron view of industrial history, these scholars represented a distinctively new approach to the study of American economic history. By the 1950s business historians had created their own professional organization, developed a new vocabulary and research tech-niques, published their own journal, and in some cases even founded new departments within the university.

Business historians pictured industrialists as far more complex figures than had earlier scholars. Allan Nevins, who published major revisionist biographies of John D. Rockefeller in 1940 and 1953, argued that much of the blame heaped on this captain of industry was unwarranted. While con-ceding that Rockefeller used ethically dubious methods, Nevins depicted Rockefeller's Standard Oil monopoly as a natural response to cutthroat com-petition, which paralleled trends toward business consolidation in all indus-trial nations. No robber baron, but rather an "innovator, thinker, planner, bold entrepreneur," Rockefeller imposed upon American industry "a more rational and efficient pattern," while also creating a model of philanthropy for all to follow. Had it not been for the great men who consolidated the steel, oil, textile, chemical, electrical, and automotive industries, "the free

---

[8]Matthew Josephson, *The Robber Barons: The Great American Capitalists 1861–1901* (New York, 1934), vii–viii. See also Hal Bridges, "The Robber Baron Concept in America History," *Business History Review* 32 (Spring 1958): 1–13.

world might have lost the First World War and most certainly would have lost the Second."[9]

Like scholars in the robber baron tradition, business historians' assumptions influenced their approach to the subject. Relatively conservative politically, they believed that, in an era of war and Cold War, American economic and political institutions deserved to be admired, emulated, and defended. They insisted that the costs of industrialization were far lower, less degrading to the mass of Americans, and less threatening to liberal democracy than antibusiness writers asserted. They criticized Progressive historians for exaggerating the tension between democracy and corporate power and for employing historical analysis as an ideological weapon against capitalism. That they themselves were occupying an ideological position seemed not to occur to them. In any event, the Cold War certainly reinforced the tendency of business historians (and others) to find consensus, not conflict, over values and institutions in American society.

A more sophisticated development in business history emerged in the 1960s in the work of Alfred D. Chandler Jr. Unlike Nevins, Chandler had no interest in vindicating or otherwise morally assessing the career of any individual or group of individuals. He was rather absorbed in analyzing the impersonal processes whereby new business forms, methods, and structures came into being in the late nineteenth and twentieth centuries. Borrowing from social science theories and methods, Chandler identified four stages in the development of large industrial enterprises. First came a period of expansion and accumulation of resources, and then a period in which these resources were "rationalized." In the third phase, the organization expanded its operations to include new products. In the final phase, new structures emerged to promote effective use of resources and to manage long-term adaptation to market conditions. "Strategic growth," he noted, "resulted from an awareness of the opportunities and needs — created by changing population, income, and technology — to employ existing or expanding resources more profitably."[10]

Eschewing individual biography, Chandler had in essence written the collective biography of a social institution: the large multidivisional corporation. In his subsequent Pulitzer Prize–winning book, *The Visible Hand*, Chandler analyzed how the large-scale corporation altered the American economy between the Civil War and the depression of the 1930s.[11] Here he emphasized

---

[9] Allan Nevins, *John D. Rockefeller: The Heroic Age of American Enterprise*, 2 vols. (New York, 1940), vol. 2, 707–14; and *Study in Power: John D. Rockefeller, Industrialist and Philanthropist*, 2 vols. (New York, 1953), vol. 1, viii–ix; vol. 2, 436. For a direct confrontation of views, see "Should American History Be Rewritten? A Debate between Allan Nevins and Matthew Josephson," *Saturday Review* 37 (February 6, 1954): 7–10, 44–49.

[10] Alfred D. Chandler Jr., *Strategy and Structure: Chapters in the History of the Industrial Enterprise* (Cambridge, Mass., 1962), 15. A revised edition of this work appeared in 1990.

[11] Alfred D. Chandler Jr., *The Visible Hand: The Managerial Revolution in American Business* (Cambridge, Mass., 1977). For a summary of the findings of business historians, see Glenn Porter, *The Rise of Big Business, 1860–1910* (New York, 1973).

the crucial role of management and business executives in guiding these changes (especially in adopting new technology) and rejected forcefully laissez-faire notions of a self-realizing and self-correcting market. The first selection in this chapter is an article by Chandler on the role of business and businessmen in American society.[12]

Not all business or economic historians were content to analyze the corporation in structural and functional terms. In the late 1950s and 1960s, a younger cohort of scholars revived the Progressive insight that huge economic conglomerations were a threat to democratic institutions and egalitarian social relations. Typical of these was Carl Kaysen, an economist who noted that large corporations accumulated not just economic power but political and social power as well. American society possessed three alternative ways of controlling that business power: the promotion of competitive markets, regulation by agencies external to business, and self-regulation by the socially responsible corporation. Traditionally the United States relied on the first in the form of antitrust legislation, although far more could have been done along this line. As to government regulation and corporate self-regulation, the American experience was minimalist; effective control of business power remained an unfinished task, Kaysen concluded.[13] Kaysen consciously drew inspiration from Progressive-era antitrust crusaders, who sought to perfect American society by breaking up anticompetitive distortions in the economy. By the early 1960s, however, a small but growing number of scholars in a variety of disciplines proposed that American society was fundamentally malformed and required radical change.

New Left historians in the 1960s argued that war, poverty, and racism were direct outgrowths of American capitalism and that only the abolition of capitalism could usher in a just and peaceful society. They rejected scholarship that defended business as well as that which proposed to reform and regulate it. One of the first such monographs was Gabriel Kolko's *The Triumph of Conservatism* (1963). Kolko argued that the most distinctive feature of modern American society — which he designated political capitalism — dated only from the first two decades of the twentieth century. Denying the inevitability of the giant corporation, Kolko saw competition actually increasing at the turn of the century. Even the merger movement, which generated new combinations on an unprecedented scale, failed to stem the tide of competition. However vast their ambition and long their reach, that is, men like Rockefeller and J. P. Morgan could not squeeze the competitive unpredict-

---

[12]Other historians have emphasized the personal efficacy of businessmen in shaping business history: Harold C. Livesay, "Entrepreneurial Persistence through the Bureaucratic Age," *Business History Review* 51 (Winter 1977): 415–43; see also his *Andrew Carnegie and the Rise of Big Business* (Boston, 1975). More recently see H. W. Brands, *Masters of Enterprise: Giants of American Business from John Jacob Astor and J. P. Morgan to Bill Gates and Oprah Winfrey* (New York, 1999); Jean Strouse, *Morgan: American Financier* (New York, 1999); David Nasaw, *Andrew Carnegie* (New York, 2006); Charles R. Morris, *The Tycoons: How Andrew Carnegie, John D. Rockefeller, Jay Gould, and J. P. Morgan Invented the American Supereconomy* (New York, 2005).

[13]Carl Kaysen, "The Corporation: How Much Power? What Scope?" in Edward S. Mason, ed., *The Corporation in Modern Society* (Cambridge, Mass., 1959), Chapter 5.

ability out of the American economy or turn gigantic corporations into models of efficiency. In contrast to Chandler, Kolko believed that corporations turned to government regulation precisely because of their inefficiency and inability to control boom-and-bust swings in the economy.

as seen during Progressive era

Failure to control market swings not only meant economic losses for investors; Kolko showed that it raised also the specter of outraged masses using their democratic franchise to impose political solutions on business. In an era of labor radicalism, Populism, and a growing socialist movement, therefore, big business turned to government to control competition, while dampening the possibility that democratic politics might lead to a redistribution of wealth. The result was a synthesis of business and government: Progressivism. Unlike Populism or Socialism, Kolko concluded, this business-led movement equated the general welfare with corporate well-being. All those reformers who thought government regulation meant democratic control over robber barons had been duped. The men who wrote the legislation and staffed the regulatory commissions set about rationalizing the economy by confirming the rule of finance capitalists.[14]

Many scholars rejected Kolko's ideological assumptions and his conclusions. Edward A. Purcell Jr. discovered that, during the passage of the Interstate Commerce Act of 1887, entrepreneurs and managers adhered to no coherent body of thought. They improvised a political strategy to solve particular problems at the level of the firm or the sector of industry. Some fought over alternative models of regulation; others opposed it altogether. Purcell concluded that diverse economic groups, threatened by the new national economy, turned to the federal government without a general political strategy but rather hoping to protect their own interests.[15] However powerful Kolko's insights into the ideological and strategic ambitions of a small class of finance capitalists, his top-down assumptions about how politics worked could not comprehend the social and economic complexity of turn-of-the-century America.

Another new turn in the history of American capitalism has come in the last several decades as a result of the intersection of economic history with the history of technology. That intersection generated difficult questions: What are the economic, as well as social and political, causes and consequences of technological innovation? Does technology shape or respond to the social and economic organization of modern society? Chandler gave technology an increasingly important place in his interpretation of the origins and development of big business. Some businessmen, in this view, used new machinery in creative ways to promote efficiency and business success; others failed to understand the inevitable force of new technology

---

[14]Gabriel Kolko, *The Triumph of Conservation: A Reinterpretation of American History, 1900–1916* (New York, 1963); see also his *Railroads and Regulation 1877–1916* (Princeton, N. J., 1965).

[15]Edward A. Purcell Jr., "Ideas and Interests: Businessmen and the Interstate Commerce Act," *Journal of American History* 54 (December 1967): 561–78. See also Albro Martin, *Enterprise Denied: Origins of the Decline of American Railroads 1897–1917* (New York, 1971); and Thomas K. McGraw, ed., *Regulation in Perspective: Historical Essays* (Cambridge, Mass., 1981).

and consequently fell behind in the race for strategic advantage.[16] The disruptive consequences of technological change are, in this view, unfortunate but inevitable; and, in any event, in the long run consumers (and even workers) profit from increased productivity.

Other historians have come to very different conclusions. The economic historian Hugh G. J. Aitken's remarkable *Taylorism at Watertown Arsenal*, one of the founding studies in the history of technology as a subfield, went well beyond available business history models of scholarship. Aitken had read deeply in social history and displayed a sympathetic understanding of the men who labored in, not just those who managed, the business enterprise. Insisting that "the historian must have not one point of view but many," Aitken demonstrated that the "technological innovation" of scientific management was also a highly complex social change that revealed "all the stresses of an industrial society exposed to constant revolution in technology and organization." He showed that technical managerial strategies were not the only (or sometimes even the most important) element in the evolution of the industrial corporation.[17]

The radical historian David F. Noble went much further than Aitken in turning business history into antibusiness history. In *America by Design*, he argued that machines and technology are never by themselves "the decisive forces of production." At every point managers control technology and seek unchallenged power over their enterprises and workers, guided by "institutional fantasies of progress" that persuade them that they are the driving force in modern history. Noble further argued that when engineers failed to develop professional independence they ceased being agents of efficiency, becoming instead the uncritical servants of capitalists' thirst for control. Implicit in Noble's work was a political point: that social relations rather than technological change determined the rise of corporate power and that only a movement from below could shift the balance of power from machines to human beings.[18]

Historian James Livingston also suggested that neither structural nor technological forces determine economic development. Like Noble, employing neo-Marxist categories and borrowing from the new social and economic history, he insisted that the victory of corporate capitalism was neither inevitable nor easy. Neither powerless nor irrational, the working class conceived and carried out collective action that often won concessions from big business. Whenever prices declined and managers tried to restore profits by cutting wages, workers organized and mounted strikes. Businessmen's efforts to regulate output and market shares — that is, to impose order either through banker-led consolidation or through political capitalism — failed to control

---

[16]See Louis Galambos, "Technology, Political Economy, and Professionalization: Central Themes of the Organizational Synthesis," *Business History Review* 57 (Winter 1983): 472–78.

[17]Hugh G. J. Aitken, *Taylorism at Watertown Arsenal: Scientific Management in Action, 1908–1915* (Cambridge, Mass., 1960), 12.

[18]David F. Noble, *America by Design: Science, Technology, and the Rise of Corporate Capitalism* (New York, 1977); see also his *Forces of Production: A Social History of Industrial Automation* (New York, 1984).

competition and often led to acrimonious conflict among them. In the end, businessmen employed different tactics at different times (and sometimes simultaneously): consolidation designed to weed out weak enterprises and thereby restrain ruinous competition; reorganization of the workplace to cut labor costs and to shift control of the labor process from workers to employers; and creation of a new class of professionalized corporate managers. The rise of corporate capitalism, then, represented a medley of improvised economic solutions to a complex and unstable social stalemate.[19]

The evolution of business history — from the highly personalized tales of industrial statesmen or robber barons (depending on one's point of view), to the highly impersonal account of structural responses to market forces and technology, and finally to more complex narratives that connect the rise of corporations to broad social and political contexts — intersected with another kind of history that was evolving at the same time but in very different ways: labor history. Like business history, labor history after World War II developed its own professional organization and journal. Inspired and supported by the New Deal and the great mobilization of industrial workers by the Congress of Industrial Workers (CIO) in the 1930s, labor history became an important subfield in most major history departments by the 1960s. As with business historians, labor historians' political leanings were quite evident — situating them usually on the left wing of American politics. Likely to think of businessmen as robber barons, labor historians portrayed labor leaders as democratic heroes. But labor history intrinsically tended toward social history and tales of collective, rather than individual, struggle.

Well before World War II, John R. Commons and his "Wisconsin School" of labor economics had laid the groundwork for the emergence of labor history. With his colleagues at the University of Wisconsin, Commons published a massive four-volume *History of Labor in the United States* (1918–1935) that set the terms of scholarly research for several generations. Distilled in the work of Selig Perlman,[20] Commons's most astute disciple and later his collaborator, the narrative of American labor history contained several key elements. First, it was institutional: the unit of study was the labor union and the central question was how and why the modern "pure-and-simple" (or "bread-and-butter") trade union emerged, as opposed to a broad socialist movement for the fundamental reform of capitalism. Second, it was workplace-oriented: the subject of study was the evolution of wages and working conditions; except for labor's piecemeal efforts to influence politics, little of the world outside the workplace mattered to Commons and his followers. Third, it was progressive in two senses. It was politically progressive in that it was pro-labor, endorsing the right of workers to collective bargaining and the responsibility of government for regulation of economic relations. And it was theoretically progressive[21] in that it saw labor history as a maturation

---

[19] James Livingston, "The Social Analysis of Economic History and Theory: Conjectures on Late Nineteenth-Century American Development," *American Historical Review* 92 (February 1987): 69–97.

[20] Selig Perlman, *Theory of the Labor Movement* (New York, 1928).

[21] Ibid., Chapter 1.

from confused nineteenth-century attempts at utopian reform to sensible trade unionism in the early twentieth century. The latter trait made Wisconsin School labor history sometimes predictable. For the historians who adopted this approach, American realities overcame ideology: the grand socialist strategies that some immigrants brought with them from Europe, like the Jacksonian and Populist fantasies harbored by some American-born workers, were no match for the promise of middle-class prosperity and the likelihood of cumulative piecemeal gains at the bargaining table and the ballot box.[22]

Whatever its drawbacks, the Wisconsin School spawned a host of carefully wrought studies of labor relations and unionization in a wide variety of industries.[23] By the 1960s, these institutional studies reached a very high level of professional polish and intellectual richness.[24] They showed how changes in technology and the national economy, along with workforce recruitment and composition, determined the evolution of union structure and leadership.[25] However, the pathbreaking book that took the study of unions beyond the workplace was David Brody's *Steelworkers in America: The Nonunion Era* (1960). With admirable economy and graceful prose, Brody told the story of the achievements and failures of the iron- and steelworkers union, but his narrative encompassed much more: the immigrant experience, the cultural world of the skilled industrial artisan, the allure of new technology to managers and its threat to workers, the meaning of politics (from local to national) for workers in company towns and big cities, in eras of depression, expansion, and world war. It was a remarkable achievement, but it was not alone.

The most influential of the new labor historians were David Montgomery and Herbert Gutman. With the work of these two scholars, a "New Labor History" had clearly arrived, but it did so by an indirect route that is worth briefly tracing. Even in the heyday of the institutional approach to labor history, a few American historians had been telling a different story. Norman

---

[22]The Marxist historian Philip S. Foner produced an even more massive survey of labor history in six volumes, *History of the Labor Movement in the United States* (New York, 1947–1983). Ironically, it is no less institutional or progressive than that of Commons, merely reversing the latter's interpretive judgments: early "utopians" are here judged to be proto-revolutionary; narrowly job-conscious workers with middle-class aspirations appear deluded, not sensible; the truly progressive adaptation to modern industrial conditions is socialism not reformist capitalism, etc.

[23]For a fine overview of the historiography of the Commons School and the "New Labor History," see David Brody, "The Old Labor History and the New: In Search of an American Working Class," *Labor History* 20 (Winter 1979): 511–26; David Montgomery, "To Study the People: The American Working Class," *Labor History* 21 (Fall 1980): 485–512. See also Melvyn Dubofsky, *Industrialism and the American Worker, 1860–1925* (2nd ed., Arlington Heights, Ill., 1985).

[24]See, for example, Robert A. Christie, *Empire in Wood: A History of the United Brotherhood of Carpenters and Joiners of America* (Ithaca, N.Y., 1956), and Robert Ozanne, *A Century of Labor-Management Relations at McCormick and International Harvester* (Madison, Wis., 1967).

[25]An unusual work in the Wisconsin tradition is Gerald Grob, *Workers and Utopia: A Study of Ideological Conflict in the American Labor Movement, 1865–1900* (Evanston, Ill., 1961). Although Grob adhered to the Commons thesis, his attention to the intellectual history of the labor movement proved fruitful in connecting institutional history to the wider currents of politics and culture in nineteenth-century America.

Ware most notably departed from the Commons-Perlman narrative. For Ware, the industrial revolution was a "social revolution in which sovereignty in economic affairs passed from the community as a whole into the keeping of a special class." He depicted workers as not just wage earners, but citizens who valued their "status and independence."[26] Ware's work vivified Marx's original contribution to history: his explanation of the significance of class conflict in shaping the entire range of human experience, particularly during the era of industrial capitalism. It was precisely this insight which came rushing into American labor history from across the Atlantic in the 1960s.

The development of British neo-Marxist social history may be one of the signal events in modern historiography. In the work of historians Eric Hobsbawm, George Rude, Brian Harrison, and Gareth Stedman-Jones (and the literary historian Raymond Williams), but most momentously in E. P. Thompson's *The Making of the English Working Class* (1963), Marxist analysis of history evolved to encompass the lives of human beings imbedded in webs of culture and society. Never static, impenetrable, or finished, Thompson's story told of the "making" and "remaking" of class experience and class consciousness in the face of changing economic compulsions, political opportunities, cultural traditions, local developments, even individual imagination and heroism. From such a perspective, the building of labor unions was only one important feature of working-class lives caught up in the industrial revolution. It was precisely in changing the subject from the history of unions to the history of the industrial working class that the historiographical equivalent of "the British invasion" had its greatest impact in the United States.

Inspired by the English neo-Marxists and a few native scholars, American labor history took off in the 1960s. The New Labor History also drew energy from the contemporaneous New Left critique of American inequality and from a wave of labor militancy that sprang up in American factories, fueled in part by the rebellious energies of the baby boom generation of workers. Works of labor history became studies of urban development, ethnic conflict, political culture, family organization, and popular culture as much as studies of labor organization and workplace struggle. Thus, in David Montgomery's seminal *Beyond Equality*, working-class radicals appear on the page of history already deeply engaged in the struggle for equality. Inheritors of the American republican tradition of self-government, they were born political. Workers who fought politically against ascendant capitalism were not romantic and immature utopians. They were perfectly capable of acting like "pure-and-simple" craft unionists, fighting for better wages and benefits, but at the same time they could assume the mantle of "utopian reformers," opposing the National Bank, campaigning in favor of the Homestead Act, or organizing to build a "cooperative commonwealth." Fully engaged citizens, such

---

[26]Norman Ware, *The Industrial Worker, 1840–1860* (Boston, 1924), x–xi; see also *The Labor Movement in the United States, 1860–1895* (New York, 1929). Another historian who departed somewhat from the Commons-Perlman approach to create an original interpretation of the earliest years of American labor was Richard B. Morris in *Government and Labor in Early America* (New York, 1946).

reform-minded unionists sought "to impart to the emerging industrial order some values other than purely commercial ones, to impose moral order on the market economy."[27] Montgomery's book connected the early history of the trade union movement to the legacy of Revolutionary republicanism and to the "new birth of freedom" that was the deepest meaning of the Civil War. In so doing, *Beyond Equality* planted labor history squarely in the center of the historical map.

In a different way, Herbert Gutman opened broad new avenues of study for labor history, or the "history of the working class," as it was coming to be called.[28] Gutman's findings appeared in bits and pieces, but cumulatively they proved an impressive achievement.[29] His most important early essay, "The Workers' Search for Power,"[30] insisted that workers had never thought of themselves simply as wage earners but also as "locals" who sustained ties of kinship and community with neighboring farmers, shopkeepers, professionals, or small businessmen. Thus, workers' broad and fuzzy conception of class was not, as Commons thought, a sign of immaturity or delusion, but a useful way to understand a world in which they forged bonds of interest and fellowship both within and beyond the workplace. In the early industrial era, indeed, the fight against monopoly often became a community affair, with nonworkers supporting strikes and joining political movements to curb corporate power. Of course, at other times and in other places, the bonds of community could prove insidious. Local workers and their neighbors sometimes united against foreigners or blacks brought in to work (often to break strikes) in mines and factories, using vigilante tactics to restore temporarily the aggrieved community's sense of economic justice.[31]

In his most synthetic essay, "Work Culture and Society in Industrializing America," published in 1973, Gutman made a bid to turn the history of the working class into the history of America, indeed, of the modern world. Both the successes and failures of that essay marked a turning point in the evolution of labor history. Gutman's story chronicled the transformation of preindustrial people into industrial men and women and of their cultures into industrial cultures. Preindustrial people lived in a world, as E. P. Thompson had shown, marked by flexible notions of time and personal relationships within small communal boundaries. Industrialization imposed clock-time and repetitive routines on workers, who now sustained connections to their work and to one another that were impersonal, functional, and governed by the cash nexus. Ripped from their traditional settings, they careened across the

---

[27]David Montgomery, *Beyond Equality: Labor and the Radical Republicans, 1862–1872* (New York, 1967), 445.

[28]The appearance in the mid-1970s of a new journal, *International Labor and Working-Class History*, confirmed this new ambition, as well as a transnational turn, to be discussed below.

[29]Some of these are collected in *Work, Culture, and Society in Industrializing America* (New York, 1977).

[30]Herbert G. Gutman, "The Workers' Search for Power," originally published in 1970, can be found in his *Power and Culture: Essays on the American Working Class* (New York, 1987).

[31]This tendency erupted into virulent racism in California, as documented in Alexander Saxton's *The Indispensable Enemy: Labor and the Anti-Chinese Movement in California* (Berkeley, Calif., 1971).

countryside, around the globe, and, indeed, through the pages of history. While Thompson described the process in England as complex but of limited duration, Gutman portrayed American industrialization as a rolling and overlapping series of encounters, conflicts, and transformations, from the early nineteenth to the twentieth century, involving one ethnic group after another.

Dozens of young historians from the 1960s onward felt the power of Gutman's and Montgomery's work. Bruce Laurie showed how class, ethnicity, and religion intersected to shape the possibilities of labor power in antebellum Philadelphia. Alan Dawley and Paul Faler studied the fate of artisan shoeworkers and their community in Lynn, Massachusetts, under the assault of mechanization and industrial consolidation. Roy Rosenzweig and Francis G. Couvares explored the ways in which an evolving mass culture interacted with ethnic and workplace conflicts to shape class consciousness and class relations in Worcester, Massachusetts, and Pittsburgh, respectively. Thomas Dublin on Lowell, Massachusetts, and Christine Stansell on New York City, showed not only that female labor was central to the history of industrialization and unionization, but more generally that women's history, no less than the history of race, ethnicity, politics, and popular culture, was indispensable to a proper understanding of class formation and class conflict in the United States.[32]

These and a host of other works usually focused on single communities over a fairly limited span of years, making generalization across cases difficult. While many labor and social historians eschewed calls for synthesis, increasing numbers of them acknowledged the need to develop connections among their numerous findings and with the works of political, intellectual, and other historians.[33] Some began to question the only available rubric for synthesis — the Thompson-Gutman narrative of transformation from preindustrial to industrial culture. In an incisive critique, Daniel T. Rodgers suggested that this narrative oversimplified both the nature of capitalism and the complexity of culture.[34] When stripped of its Marxist touches, Rodgers argued, "the hypothesis of initial shock and gradual acculturation" that is at the heart of Gutman's story looks very much like the "modernization" thesis

---

[32]Bruce Laurie, *Working People of Philadelphia, 1800–1850* (Philadelphia, 1980); Alan Dawley, *Class and Community: The Industrial Revolution in Lynn* (Cambridge, Mass., 1976); Paul G. Faler, *Mechanics and Manufacturers in the Early Industrial Revolution: Lynn, Massachusetts, 1780–1860* (Albany, N.Y., 1981); Roy Rosenzweig, *Eight Hours for What We Will: Workers and Leisure in an Industrial City, 1870–1920* (New York, 1983); Francis G. Couvares, *The Remaking of Pittsburgh: Class and Culture in an Industrializing City, 1877–1919* (Albany, N.Y., 1984); Thomas Dublin, *Women and Work: The Transformation of Work and Community in Lowell, Massachusetts, 1826–1860* (New York, 1979); Christine Stansell, *City of Women: Sex and Class in New York, 1789–1860* (New York, 1986). See also Michael H. Frisch and Daniel J. Walkowitz, eds., *Working-Class America: Essays on Labor, Community, and American Society* (Urbana, Ill., 1983); Daniel J. Leab, ed., *The Labor History Reader* (Urbana, Ill., 1985); and Herbert G. Gutman and Donald H. Bell, *The New England Working Class and the New Labor History* (Urbana, Ill., 1987).

[33]One attempt to write a popular (and populist) narrative based on the new labor history is Bruce Levine et al., eds., *Who Built America? Working People and the Nation's Economy, Politics, Culture, and Society* (New York, 1989), published under the auspices of the American Social History Project, which was directed by Gutman until his death in 1985.

[34]Daniel T. Rodgers, "Tradition, Modernity, and the American Industrial Workers: Reflections and a Critique," *Journal of Interdisciplinary History* 7 (1977): 655–81.

that liberal and conservative social scientists have employed for decades, and not unlike the progressive tale of the Wisconsin School. Rodgers reminded readers that "all men in all cultures are born premodern," and that "working-class cultures are not made once and set in motion but must be refashioned with each generation." In the end, therefore, "traditional-to-modern," "pre-industrial-to-industrial," however attractive a rubric, overgeneralizes the past and cannot in itself become the basis of a new synthesis of American history.

A number of historians in the 1980s and 1990s found other ways to connect local studies with broad themes in American history. In *Chants Democratic*, Sean Wilentz turned the history of labor in New York City from 1788 to 1850 into an interpretation of the fate of the republican heritage in the Jacksonian era. Exploring similar themes, Leon Fink showed that the Knights of Labor struggled to adapt the republican heritage to the class realities of post–Civil War America.[35] For the twentieth century, Ronald Edsforth and Lizabeth Cohen showed that working-class Americans in Flint, Michigan, and Chicago, respectively, were both militant unionists *and* job-conscious employees, both advocates of the reform of unbridled capitalism *and* ardent consumers, both "ethnics" *and* "Americans."[36] Biography also bloomed as another way to make particular stories speak to larger themes in American history. Nick Salvatore brilliantly narrated the life of Eugene V. Debs, whose indisputably middle-American roots gave issue to a class-conscious "Citizen and Socialist." Nelson Lichtenstein made the life of Walter Reuther, perhaps the greatest labor leader of the period from the late 1930s through the 1960s, speak to every important issue that faced the United States through the depression, World War II, Cold War, and civil rights eras.[37]

In works published in the 1990s, Bruce Laurie and Walter Licht took up the challenge of writing historical syntheses that spanned the whole nineteenth-century experience of industrialization. Among its other virtues, Laurie's book offered a convincing explanation of the emergence of what he dubbed "prudential unionism." Not quite the progressive achievement that Commons would have considered it, but neither the sell-out that radical historians of the 1960s sometimes made it seem, Sam Gompers's trade union movement was limited by many factors, internal and external, but among the most important was the repressive power of American corporations and business-oriented state and federal governments. These powers never hesitated to use force to keep unions from becoming anything other than "pure-and-simple" collective bargaining institutions, that is, from evolving into broader

---

[35]Sean Wilentz, *Chants Democratic: New York City and the Rise of the American Working Class, 1788–1850* (New York, 1984); Leon Fink, *Workingmen's Democracy: The Knights of Labor and American Politics* (Urbana, Ill., 1983).

[36]Ronald Edsforth, *Class Conflict and Cultural Consensus: The Making of a Mass Consumer Society in Flint, Michigan* (New Brunswick, N.J., 1987); Lizabeth Cohen, *Making a New Deal: Industrial Workers in Chicago, 1919–1939* (Cambridge, Mass., 1990).

[37]Nick Salvatore, *Eugene V. Debs: Citizen and Socialist* (Urbana, Ill., 1972); Nelson Lichtenstein, *The Most Dangerous Man in Detroit: Walter Reuther and the Fate of American Labor* (New York, 1995); see also Melvin Dubofsky and Warren Van Tine, *John L. Lewis: A Biography* (Ann Arbor, Mich., 1969).

class-based or populist movements. Licht's work, from which the second reading in this chapter is drawn, similarly makes clear that the tremendous power wielded by capital, including the power of violence, significantly shaped the labor union (and working-class life more generally) throughout the nineteenth and into the twentieth century.[38]

The intersection of women's history and labor history provided another opportunity for historians to reconceive the narrative of industrial history. While monographic studies of women workers in particular industries proliferated in the last several decades,[39] in 1982 Alice Kessler-Harris encompassed the entire span of American history in *Out to Work*. She took as her theme the process whereby "wage work simultaneously sustained the patriarchal family and set in motion the tensions that seem now to be breaking it down."[40] Women workers also appear crucial to the history of politics and consumer culture. Kathy Peiss's groundbreaking *Cheap Amusements*, and more recently Nan Enstad's *Ladies of Labor, Girls of Adventure*, trace the shaping of working-class women by popular culture — and vice versa. Meg Jacobs's *Pocketbook Politics* connects consumerism to state-making, arguing not that mass culture distracted or co-opted women workers but, to the contrary, that it empowered them to assume "economic citizenship." These historians confirm that the history of women and the history of labor (as, also, the history of race, ethnicity, and politics) are inextricably intertwined and indispensable to understanding the major problems in American history.[41]

To some young historians in the 1990s, labor history seemed to position class as the most important unit of analysis and white male workers as the most important subject of study. Some of these historians looked to an approach that bid to become a new synthesis of labor and race history, under

---

[38]Bruce Laurie, *Artisans into Workers: Labor in Nineteenth-Century America* (New York, 1989); Walter Licht, *Industrializing America: The Nineteenth Century* (Baltimore, 1995).

[39]Excellent case studies include Susan Porter Benson, *Counter Cultures: Saleswomen, Managers and Customers in American Department Stores, 1890–1940* (Urbana, Ill., 1986); Nancy Schrom Dye, *As Equals and as Sisters: Feminism, the Labor Movement, and the Women's Trade Union League of New York* (New York, 1980); and Vicki L. Ruiz, *Cannery Women, Cannery Lives: Mexican Women, Unionization, and the California Food Processing Industry, 1930–1950* (Albuquerque, 1987). See also Ruth Milkman, ed., *Women, Work and Protest: A Century of U.S. Women's Labor History* (Boston, 1985); and Ava Baron, "Gender and Labor History: Learning from the Past, Looking to the Future," in her *Work Engendered: Toward a New History of American Labor* (Ithaca, N.Y., 1991).

[40]Alice Kessler-Harris, *Out to Work: A History of Wage-Earning Women in the United States* (New York, 1982), ix. See Elizabeth H. Pleck, "Two Worlds in One: Work and Family," *Journal of Social History* 10 (Winter 1976): 178–89, on the cross-fertilization of labor history and family history; also Tamara K. Hareven, *Family Time and Industrial Time: The Relationship between Family and Work in a New England Industrial Community* (Cambridge, Mass., 1982); Jacqueline Jones, *Labor of Love, Labor of Sorrow: Black Women, Work, and the Family from Slavery to the Present* (New York, 1985); and Jacqueline Dowd Hall et al., *Like a Family: The Making of a Southern Cotton Mill World* (Chapel Hill, N.C., 1987).

[41]Kathy Peiss, *Cheap Amusements: Working Women and Leisure in Turn-of-the-Century New York* (Philadelphia, 1986); Nan Enstad, *Ladies of Labor, Girls of Adventure: Working Women, Popular Culture, and Labor Politics at the Turn of the Twentieth Century* (New York, 1999); Meg Jacobs, *Pocketbook Politics: Economic Citizenship in Twentieth-Century America* (Princeton, N.J., 2005); see also essays in Linda K. Kerber et al., eds., *U.S. History as Women's History: New Feminist Essays* (Chapel Hill, N.C., 1995).

the rubric of "whiteness studies." In *The Wages of Whiteness*, David Roediger argued that the American labor movement was fundamentally shaped by racism. The trade union, among other institutions, awarded modest benefits to white working-class Americans who reinforced the racial dividing line. The trade union's most time-honored values and practices — that is, seniority and solidarity — reinforced the privileges of whites (and of men). Thus, "first hired, last fired" clauses in contracts protected white, male jobs and sacrificed black and female ones; and defending the union against strikebreakers became a way to keep white men employed and blacks and females unemployed. Even the hallowed heritage of republicanism, which many historians had sought to claim as labor's own, was basically a legacy of white men's democracy.[42]

Labor historians have taken sharp issue with many of the claims of whiteness studies. A symposium in *International Labor and Working-Class History* in 2001 aired the criticisms and drew a range of responses. Eric Arnesen noted the conceptual imprecision of the term *whiteness* and challenged the assertion that white workers achieved solidarity primarily by embracing white supremacy. Arnesen doubted that southern and eastern European immigrants had been treated as nonwhite or "not-quite-white." If whiteness is merely a metaphor for class and social power, Arnesen argued, then its descriptive and explanatory power is weak and its application to so many subjects in so many different contexts contributes to confusion. Since immigrants possessed the right to marry, own property, operate businesses, enroll children in the public schools, attain citizenship, vote, run for office, serve on juries, and so on, what stands out in the record of assimilation is not the experience of Europeans, who were never seriously or long considered nonwhite, but rather the record of Chinese exclusion, of Mexican deportations, of Japanese internment, of the continual assignment of African and Afro-Caribbean immigrants to the status of blackness and, therefore, second-class citizenship. Similarly, Barbara Fields doubted whether whiteness improves on explanations that note the influence of racism, but which incorporate detailed analyses of class, gender, religious, regional, national, and international influences that made events happen in the way they did. Despite such doubts about its explanatory adequacy, whiteness studies have succeeded in linking the history of class with that of immigration, ethnicity, race, nationalism, and imperialism. Moreover, as a result of whiteness studies, historians will never again be able to evade the evidence of racism within the white working class. Nor can they deny that, as David Brody put it, "working-class formation in America is entangled in white racial identity."[43]

---

[42]David Roediger, *The Wages of Whiteness: Race and the Making of the American Working Class* (3rd rev. ed., New York, 2007; orig. ed. 1991).

[43]Eric Arnesen, "Whiteness and the Historians' Imagination," part of "Scholarly Controversy: Whiteness and the Historians' Imagination," *International Labor and Working-Class History* 60 (Fall 2001): 20; Barbara J. Fields, "Whiteness, Racism, and Identity," *International Labor and Working-Class History* 60 (Fall 2001): 48–56; David Brody, "Charismatic History: Pros and Cons," *International Labor and Working-Class History* 60 (Fall 2001): 44.

Finally, the transnational turn in labor history should be acknowledged. Recent scholarship compares U.S. class formation (including its gendered and ethno-racial construction), unionization, labor politics, and state-making with similar phenomena in other countries.[44] This work seeks to connect features of capitalist development in "advanced" societies such as the United States — e.g., industrialization, technological change, immigration, urbanization, deindustrialization, and suburbanization — with events in less developed societies — e.g., agricultural consolidation, labor recruitment, emigration, and revolution. Thus Jefferson Cowie showed how RCA spent seven decades pursuing profit, first in Camden, New Jersey, later in Bloomington, Indiana, and Memphis, Tennessee, and finally in Ciudad Juárez, Mexico. In telling this tale, Cowie carefully described the ways in which workers' gender and ethnicity shaped both labor recruitment and labor organization. He explored the crucial power of place to anchor workers in community and strengthen their sense of solidarity. But he also noted the limits of such solidarity in the face of globalization, which stimulates both the export of capital and the importation of labor. In the end, he offered an example of labor history for the twenty-first century, what he called "a comparative social history of industrial relocation that explores community life, gender, and labor organization across time and space."[45] What Cowie and others have recognized — the international reach, myriad causes, and far-reaching and varied consequences of industrialization — has long required historians to study comparatively a range of subjects, including agricultural and commercial revolution, the rise of factories, rural-to-urban migration, class politics, and state-making. In the era of globalization, they will do so even more explicitly, intently, and frequently.[46]

At the beginning of the twenty-first century, few young historians identify themselves as labor historians, as opposed to social historians, economic historians, historians of industrialization, or historians of race and gender, among other subfields. Their reluctance may in fact be a tribute to a field that has always insisted that the history of the industrial revolution and its

---

[44]See, for example, Gerald Friedman, *State-Making and Labor Movements: France and the United States, 1876–1914* (Ithaca, N.Y., 1998); Karin Hofmeester, *Jewish Workers and the Labour Movement: A Comparative Study of Amsterdam, London and Paris (1870–1914)*, translated by Lee Mitzman (Burlington, Vt., 2004).

[45]Jefferson Cowie, *Capital Moves: RCA's Seventy-Year Quest for Cheap Labor*, 2nd ed. with new epilogue (New York, 2001), 2. See also Gigi Peterson, "'A Dangerous Demagogue': Containing the Influence of the Mexican Labor-Left and Its United States Allies," in Richard W. Cherny et al., eds., *American Labor and the Cold War: Grassroots Politics and Postwar Political Culture* (New Brunswick, N.J., 2004), 245–76.

[46]See Lowell Turner and Daniel B. Cornfield, eds., *Labor in the New Urban Battlegrounds: Local Solidarity in a Global Economy* (Ithaca, N.Y., 2007); Marcel van der Linden, *Transnational Labour History: Explorations* (Burlington, Vt., 2003). The study of industrial relations, which blends labor and business history with elements of organizational psychology, sociology, and management science, has long been comparative: two examples are Reinhard Bendix, *Work and Authority in Industry: Managerial Ideologies in the Course of Industrialization* (New Brunswick, N.J., 2001), and Bruce Nissen, ed., *Unions in a Globalized Environment: Changing Borders, Organizational Boundaries, and Social Roles* (Armonk, N.Y., 2002).

human consequences is the central story of the modern world. In similar, though possibly less dramatic ways, business history has stretched to include the history of technology, managerial and workplace cultures, and the rise and global expansion of corporate capitalism. Both business history and labor history have broadened to address the most challenging questions about the nature of modern industrial society. These include the sources of innovation and prosperity; the tension between profit and efficiency and more egalitarian ends; the interconnection of class inequality with racial, ethnic, and gender inequalities; and the strategies that promote not just growth and wealth, but equality and justice, within a globalized economy. These and similar questions will continue to be asked by labor and business historians, as well as by other historians who have been influenced by their best work over the last several decades.

ALFRED D. CHANDLER JR.

from The Role of Business in the United States: A Historical Survey   [1969]

ALFRED D. CHANDLER JR. (1918–2007) was Straus Professor of Business History at the Harvard Graduate School of Business Administration. He wrote a number of books in American business history, including *Henry Varnum Poor* (1956), *Strategy and Structure* (1969), and the Pulitzer Prize–winning *The Visible Hand* (1977).

For a paper on the historical role of business in America to provide a solid foundation for discussions of the present and future, it must examine a number of questions: Who were the American businessmen? How did they come to go into business? How were they trained? How broad was their outlook? And, of even more importance, what did they do? How did they carry out the basic economic functions of production, distribution, transportation, and finance? How was the work of these businessmen coordinated so that the American economic system operated as an integrated whole? Finally, how did these men and the system within which they worked adapt to fundamental changes in population, to the opening of new lands, resources, and markets, and to technological developments that transformed markets, sources of supply, and means of production and distribution? The answers to these questions, as limited as they may be, should help to make more understandable the present activities and future capabilities of American business.

Alfred D. Chandler Jr., "The Role of Business in the United States: A Historical Survey," *Daedalus* 98 (Winter 1969): 23–40. Reprinted by permission of MIT Press.

The Colonial Merchant

The merchant dominated the simple rural economy of the colonial period. By the eighteenth century he considered himself and was considered by others to be a businessman. His economic functions differentiated him from the farmers who produced crops and the artisans who made goods. Although the farmers and artisans occasionally carried on business transactions, they spent most of their time working on the land or in the shop. The merchant, on the other hand, spent nearly all his time in handling transactions involved in carrying goods through the process of production and distribution, including their transportation and finance.

The colonial merchant was an all-purpose, non-specialized man of business. He was a wholesaler and a retailer, an importer and an exporter. In association with other merchants he built and owned the ships that carried goods to and from his town. He financed and insured the transportation and distribution of these goods. At the same time, he provided the funds needed by the planter and the artisan to finance the production of crops and goods. The merchant, operating on local, inter-regional, and international levels, adapted the economy to the relatively small population and technological changes of the day and to shifts in supply and demand resulting from international tensions.

These men of business tended to recruit their successors from their own family and kinship group. Family loyalties were important, indeed essential, in carrying on business in distant areas during a period when communication between ports was so slow and uncertain. Able young clerks or sea captains might be brought into the family firm, but sons and sons-in-law were preferred. Trading internationally as well as locally, the merchants acquired broader horizons than the farmer, artisan, and day laborer. Only a few of the great landowners and leading lawyers knew the larger world. It was the colonial merchants who, allied with lawyers from the seaport towns and with the Virginia planters, encouraged the Revolution, brought about the ratification of the Constitution, and then set up the new government in the last decade of the eighteenth century.

The Rise of the Wholesaler, 1800–1850

During the first half of the nineteenth century, although the American economy remained primarily agrarian and commercial, it grew vigorously. The scope of the economy expanded as the nation moved westward into the rich Mississippi Valley, and as increasing migration from Europe still further enlarged its population. Even more important to American economic expansion were the technological innovations that occurred in manufacturing in Great Britain. Without the new machines of the Industrial Revolution, the westward movement in the United States and the migration to its shores would have been slower. These innovations reshaped the British textile industry, creating a new demand for cotton from the United

States. Before the invention of the water frame, the spinning jenny, the mule, and then the power loom, cotton had never been grown commercially in the United States, but by 1800 it had become the country's major export. The new plantations in turn provided markets for food grown on the smaller farms in both the Northwest and Southwest. The growth of eastern commercial cities and the development of the textile industry in New England and the middle states enlarged that market still further. The titanic struggle between Great Britain and Napoleon obscured the significance of these economic developments, but shortly after 1815 the economy's new orientation became clear.

The merchants who continued to act as economic integrators had the largest hand in building this new high-volume, regionally specialized, agrarian-commercial system. The merchants of Philadelphia, Baltimore, and New York took over the task of exporting cotton, lumber, and foodstuffs and of importing textiles, hardware, drugs, and other goods from Great Britain and the Continent. Those in the southern coastal and river ports played the same role in exporting cotton and importing finished goods to and from the eastern entrepôts; those in the growing western towns sent out local crops and brought in manufactured goods in a similar way. At first the western trade went via rivers of the Mississippi Valley and New Orleans. Later it began to be transported east and west through the Erie Canal and along the Great Lakes. To meet the needs of the expanding trade, the merchants, particularly those of the larger eastern cities, developed new forms of commercial banking to finance the movement of crops, set up packet lines on "the Atlantic Shuttle" between New York and Liverpool to speed the movement of news and imports, founded specialized insurance companies, and helped to organize and finance the new canals and turnpikes that improved transportation between them and their customers.

These innovations enabled the merchants to handle still more business, and the high-volume trade in turn forced the merchants to alter their functions and, indeed, their whole way of life. They began to specialize, becoming primarily wholesalers or retailers, importers or exporters. They came to concentrate on a single line of goods — dry goods, wet goods, hardware, iron, drugs, groceries or cotton, wheat or produce. Some became specialists in banking and insurance and spent their time acting as managers for these new financial corporations.

Of the new specialists, the wholesalers played the most influential role, taking the place of the colonial merchants as the primary integrators and adaptors of the economy. More than the farmers or the retailers, the wholesalers were responsible for directing the flow of cotton, corn, wheat, and lumber from the West to the East and to Europe. More than the manufacturers, they handled the marketing of finished goods that went from eastern and European industrial centers to the southern and western states.

Moreover, the wholesalers financed the long-term growth of the economy. Enthusiastic promoters of canals, turnpikes, and then railroads, they provided most of the local capital for these undertakings. They pressured the state and municipal legislatures and councils (on which they or their legally trained associates often sat) to issue bonds or to guarantee bonds of private corporations building transportation enterprises. At times they even persuaded the state to build and operate transport facilities.

The wholesalers also encouraged the adoption of the new technology in manufacturing. In Boston, the Appletons, the Jacksons, and the Cabots financed the new textile mills of Lowell and Lawrence. In New York, the Phelps and the Dodges started the brass industry in the Connecticut Valley, while in Philadelphia and Baltimore wholesalers like Nathan Trotter and Enoch Pratt financed the growing Pennsylvania iron industry. They not only raised the funds for plants and machinery, but also supplied a large amount of the cash and credit that the new manufacturers needed as working capital to pay for supplies and labor.

Although the wholesalers made important contributions to early-nineteenth-century economic life, they played a less dominant role in the economy than had the colonial merchant of the eighteenth century. The economic system had become too complex — involving too many units of production, distribution, transportation, and finance — for one group to supervise local, inter-regional, and international flows. Nonetheless, the wholesalers had more influence in setting prices, managing the flow of goods, and determining the amount and direction of investment than had other groups — the farmers, manufacturers, retailers, and bankers.

As the economy expanded, the recruitment of businessmen became more open than it had been in the colonial period. At the same time, the outlook of even the most broad-gauged businessmen grew narrower. Family and family ties became less essential, although they could still be a useful source of capital. Businessmen began to place more value on personal qualities, such as aggressiveness, drive, and self-reliance. Nor did one need any lengthy training or education to set up a shop as a wholesaler. Because of their increasing functional specialization, this new breed of wholesalers rarely had the international outlook of the colonial merchants. Not surprisingly, they and the lawyers and politicians who represented them saw their needs in sectional rather than national terms — as did so many Americans in the years immediately prior to the Civil War.

The Rise of the Manufacturer before 1900

By mid-century the American agrarian and commercial economy had begun to be transformed into the most productive industrial system in the world. The migration of Americans into cities became more significant in this transformation than the final settling of the western frontier. Immigration from Europe reached new heights, with most of the new arrivals staying in the cities of the East and the old Northwest. By 1900, therefore, the rate of growth of the rural areas had leveled off. From then on, the nation's population growth would come almost wholly in its cities.

The second half of the nineteenth century was a time of great technological change — the age of steam and iron, the factory and the railroad.

The steam railroad and the steamship came quickly to dominate transportation. In 1849 the United States had only six thousand miles of railroad and even fewer miles of canals, but by 1884 its railroad corporations operated 202,000 miles of track, or 43 per cent of the total mileage in the world. In 1850 the factory — with its power-driven machinery and its permanent working force — was a rarity outside the textile and iron industries, but by 1880 the Bureau of the Census reported that 80 per cent of the three million workers in mechanized industry labored in factories. And nearly all these new plants were powered by steam rather than by water.

America's factories made a vital contribution to the nation's economic growth. By 1894 the value of the output of American industry equalled that of the combined output of the United Kingdom, France, and Germany. In the next twenty years American production tripled, and by the outbreak of World War I the United States was producing more than a third of the world's industrial goods.

As manufacturing expanded, the wholesaler continued for many years to play a significant role in the economy. The period up to 1873 was one of increasing demand and rising prices. The manufacturers, concentrating on building or expanding their new factories, were more than happy to have the wholesalers supply them with their raw and semifinished materials and to market their finished goods. In addition, wholesalers continued to provide manufacturers with capital for building plants, purchasing equipment and supplies, and paying wages.

After the recession of 1873, however, the manufacturers began to replace the wholesaler as the man who had the most to say about coordinating the flow of goods through the economy and about adapting the economy to population and technological changes. The shift came for three reasons. First, the existing wholesale network of hundreds of thousands of small firms had difficulty in handling efficiently the growing output of the factories. Secondly, the manufacturer no longer needed the wholesaler as a source of capital. After a generation of production, he was able to finance plant and equipment out of retained profits. Moreover, until 1850 the commercial banking system had been almost wholly involved in financing the movement of agricultural products, but about mid-century it began to provide working capital for the industrialist. Commercial banks also began to provide funds for plant and equipment, particularly to new manufacturing enterprises.

The third and most pervasive reason why the manufacturer came to a position of dominance resulted from the nature of factory production itself. This much more efficient form of manufacturing so swiftly increased the output of goods that supply soon outran demand. From the mid-1870's to the mid-1890's, prices fell sharply. Moreover, the large investment required to build a factory made it costly to shut down and even more expensive to move into other forms of business activity. As prices fell, the manufacturers organized to control prices and the flow of goods within their industries. If the wholesalers would and could help them in achieving such control, the manufacturers welcomed their cooperation. If not, they did it themselves. In most cases, the industrialist came to play a larger role than the wholesalers in integrating the economy.

The wholesaler was pushed aside in transportation before he was in manufacturing. Railroad construction costs were high, and after 1849 when railroad expansion began on a large scale, the local merchants simply could not supply the necessary capital. Modern Wall Street came into being during the 1850's to meet the need for funds. By 1860 the investment banker had replaced the wholesaler as the primary supplier of funds to American railroads.

In the 1850's and 1860's the railroads also captured many of the merchant's functions. They took over freight forwarding in large towns and eliminated the merchant by handling through traffic in many commercial centers along the main routes west and south. Indeed, during the 1860's the railroads had absorbed most of the fast freight and express companies developed earlier by the wholesalers in order to use the new rail transportation. By the 1870's the coordination of the flow of most inter-regional transportation in the United States had come under the direction of the traffic departments of a few large railroads.

The first manufacturers to move into the wholesalers' domain were those who found that the wholesaler could not meet their special needs. These were of two types. The makers of new technologically complex and relatively expensive durable products quickly realized that wholesalers were unable to handle the initial demonstration to the consumer, provide consumer credit, or ensure the repair and servicing of the products sold. Thus manufacturers of agricultural implements, sewing machines, typewriters, cash registers, carriages, bicycles, or, most important of all, electrical machinery and equipment created national and even international marketing organizations well before the turn of the century. So did the second type, the processors of perishable goods requiring refrigeration, quick transportation, and careful storage for their distribution — fresh meat, beer, bananas, and cigarettes.

Once the pioneers of both types of enterprises — the McCormicks, the Remingtons, George Westinghouse and Charles Coffin, the Swifts and Armours, the Pabsts and Schlitzes, Andrew Preston and James B. Duke — had created their widespread distribution networks, they began again to eliminate the wholesaler by doing their own purchasing. They could not run the risk of stopping complex fabricating or assembling processes because they lacked critical parts or materials. Some integrated backwards even further, doing their own purchasing by building or buying factories to manufacture parts, controlling their own iron, steel, or lumber, or obtaining their own refrigerated cars and ships.

The manufacturers who produced standard commodities that might be distributed easily through the existing wholesaler network were slower to move into wholesaling. Even though the pioneering firms were demonstrating the economies resulting from a combination of mass production and mass distribution, most manufacturers had to be pushed rather than enticed into a strategy of vertical integration. They did so only after they failed to meet the oppressive pressure of falling prices by the more obvious methods of price control through trade associations, cartels, and other loose combinations.

The railroads pioneered in developing ways to control prices in the face of excess capacity and heavy fixed costs. During the 1870's, the railroads formed regional associations, of which the Eastern Trunk Line Association was the most powerful. By the 1880's, however, the railroad presidents and traffic managers admitted defeat. The associations could only be effective if their rulings were enforced in courts of law, but their pleas for legalized pooling went unheard. Indeed, the Interstate Commerce Act of 1887 specifically declared pooling illegal. As a result, the American railroad network became consolidated into large "self-sustaining," centrally managed regional systems. By 1900 most of American land transportation was handled by about twenty-five great systems informally allied in six groupings.

Where the railroads had hoped for legalized pooling, the manufacturers sought other ways of obtaining firmer legal control over the factories in their industries. They began personally to purchase stock in one another's companies. After 1882 when the Standard Oil Company devised the trust as a way of acquiring legal control of an industry, companies began to adopt that device. The holding company quickly superseded the trust as a more effective and inexpensive way of controlling price and production after 1889, when New Jersey passed a general incorporation law that permitted one company to hold stock in many others. The Supreme Court's interpretations of the Sherman Antitrust Act (1890) encouraged further consolidation in manufacturing. Court decisions discouraged loose combinations of manufacturers (or railroads) in any form, but (at least until 1911) appeared to permit consolidation of competing firms through a holding company if that company came to administer its activities under a single centralized management.

In many cases these new consolidations embarked on a strategy of vertical integration. Where the railroads formed "self-sustaining" systems to assure control of traffic over primary commercial routes, the manufacturers attempted to assure the uninterrupted flow of goods into and out of their production and processing plants. John D. Rockefeller and his associates at Standard Oil were the first of the combinations to adopt this strategy. The Standard Oil Trust had been formed after associations in the petroleum industry had proven to be, in Rockefeller's words, "ropes of sand." Legal control of the industry was followed by administrative consolidation of its refineries under a single centralized management. In the mid-1880's the trust began to build its own distribution network of tank farms and wholesaling offices. Finally, after enlarging its buying organization, it moved in the late-1880's into the taking of crude oil out of the ground.

The examples of Standard Oil, the Swifts, the McCormicks, and others who had by-passed the wholesaler, the rulings of the Supreme Court, the memories of twenty years of declining prices resulted between 1898 and 1902 in the greatest merger movement in American history. Combinations, usually in the form of holding companies, occurred in nearly all major American industries. Holding companies then were often transformed into operating companies. After manufacturing facilities were centralized under a single management, the new consolidated enterprise integrated forwards and backwards.

At the same time, retailers who began to appreciate the potential of mass markets and economies of scale also moved to eliminate the wholesalers — although they did so in a more restricted way than the manufacturers. The mail order houses (Sears, Roebuck and Montgomery Ward), which turned to the rural markets, and the department and chain stores, which looked to the growing cities, began to buy directly from the manufacturers. By the turn of the century, some large retailers had even bought into manufacturing firms. As a result, wholesalers' decisions were of less significance to the operation of the economy than they had been fifty years earlier. Far more important were the decisions of the manufacturers who had combined, consolidated, and integrated their operations and the few giant retailers who had adopted somewhat the same strategy.

As manufacturers replaced wholesalers as key coordinators in the national economy, they became the popular symbol of American business enterprise. The industrialists and the railroad leaders were indeed the reality as well as the symbol of business power in the Gilded Age. The recruitment of this new dominant business group remained open, at least for a generation. As had been true earlier for the wholesaler, aggressiveness, drive, and access to capital or credit were prerequisites for success. Lineage or specialized learning were less important, but some technological knowledge was an advantage. Although the manufacturers' horizons were more national and less regional than the wholesalers', they came to view the national scene from the perspective of their particular industry. They and their representatives in Washington tended to take positions on the major issues of the day — tariff, currency, immigration, and the regulation of business — from an industrial rather than a sectional or regional viewpoint.

It was not long, however, before the needs of the manufacturers and their response to these needs altered the recruitment and training of the nation's most powerful businessmen. The increasingly high investment required for large-scale production made the entry of new men and firms more difficult. The emergence of the vertically integrated enterprise limited opportunities still further. By 1900 it was becoming easier to rise to positions of business influence by moving through the new centralized managements than by starting a business enterprise of one's own. This pattern was already clear in the railroads, the nation's first modern business bureaucracies.

The Dominance of the Manager since 1900

Although the twentieth century was to become the age of the manager, the growing significance of the manager's role in the operation of the American economy was not immediately apparent. Until the 1920's manufacturers and their assistants concentrated on rounding out their integrated enterprises, creating the internal structures and methods necessary to operate these business empires, and employing the managers necessary to staff them.

At first, external conditions did not seriously challenge the new enterprises. Population trends continued, and heavy migration from abroad sustained urban growth until the outbreak of World War I. During the war, migration from the rural areas to the cities increased. At the same time, impressive technological innovations, particularly those involved with the generating of power by electricity and the internal combustion engine created new industries and helped transform older ones. The continuing growth of the city, the expansion of the whole electrical sector, and the coming of the automobile and auxiliary industries made the first decades of the twentieth century ones of increasing demand and rapid economic growth.

The initial task of the men who fashioned the first integrated giants at the beginning of this century was to build internal organizational structures that would assure the efficient coordination of the flow of goods through their enterprises and permit the rational allocation of the financial, human, and technological resources at their command. First came the formation of functional departments — sales, production, purchasing, finance, engineering, and research and development. At the same time, central offices were organized, usually in the form of an executive committee consisting of the heads of the functional departments. These offices supervised, appraised, and coordinated the work of the departments and planned long-term expenditures.

By the late-1920's the pioneer organization-builders at du Pont, General Motors, General Electric, Standard Oil of New Jersey, and Sears, Roebuck had developed new and sophisticated techniques to perform the vital coordinating and adaptive activities. They based both long- and short-term coordination and planning on a forecast of market conditions. On the basis of annual forecasts, revised monthly and adjusted every ten days, the companies set production schedules, purchases of supplies and semifinished products, employment and wage rolls, working capital requirements, and prices. Prices were determined by costs, which in turn closely reflected estimated volume of output. The annual forecasts took into consideration estimates of national income, the business cycle, seasonal fluctuations, and the company's normal share of the market. Long-term allocations were based on still broader estimates of demand. After 1920, the managers of many large corporations began to include in these allocations the funds and personnel needed to develop new products and processes through technological innovation. From that time on, the integrated firm began to diversify. The Depression and World War II helped to spread these methods, so that by mid-century most of the key industries in the United States were dominated by a few giant firms administered in much the same way.

Their managers considered themselves leaders in the business community and were so considered by others. Yet they differed greatly from the older types of dominant businessmen — the merchants, the wholesalers, and the manufacturers. They were not owners; they held only a tiny portion of their company's stock; they neither founded the enterprise nor were born into it; and most of them had worked their way up the new bureaucratic ladders.

Even to get on a ladder they were expected to have attended college. Studies of business executives in large corporations show that by 1950 the large majority had been to college — an advantage that was shared by few Americans of their age group. Like most of those who did receive higher education, these managers came primarily from white Anglo-Saxon Protestant stock. Once the college man with his WASP background started up the managerial ladder, he usually remained in one industry and more often than not in a single company. That company became his career, his way of life.

As he rose up the ranks, his horizon broadened to national and international levels. Where his firm diversified, his interests and concerns spread over several industries. Indeed, in some ways his perspectives were wider in the 1950's than those of most Americans; nevertheless, because of his specialized training, he had little opportunity to become aware of the values, ideas, ambitions, and goals of other groups of Americans. He had even fewer direct contacts with farmers, workers, and other types of businessmen than had the wholesaler and the manufacturer.

The dominance of the large integrated enterprise did not, of course, mean the disappearance of the older types of businessmen. Small business remained a basic and essential part of the American economy. The small non-integrated manufacturer, the wholesaler, and retailer have all continued to be active throughout the twentieth century. The number of small businesses has continued to grow with the rapid expansion of the service industries (such as laundries and dry cleaners, service and repair shops not directly tied to the large firm); with the spread of real-estate dealers, insurance agencies, and stock brokerage firms; and with the continuing expansion of the building and construction industries. Throughout the century small businessmen have greatly outnumbered the managers of big business. The former were, therefore, often more politically powerful, particularly in the local politics, than the latter. Economically, however, the managers of the large integrated and often diversified enterprises remained the dominant decision-makers in the urban, industrial, and technologically sophisticated economy of the twentieth century. Their critically significant position has been repeatedly and properly pointed out by economists ever since Adolf A. Berle and Gardner C. Means wrote the first analysis of the role and functions of the modern corporation in 1932.

In many ways, the managers were more of an elite than the earlier businessmen had been. Even though this elite was based on performance rather than birth and played a critically constructive role in building and operating the world's most productive economy, its existence seemed to violate basic American democratic values. At the same time, its control of the central sector of the American economy challenged powerful economic concepts about the efficacy of a free market. After 1930, the managers came to share some of their economic power with others, particularly the federal government. Nevertheless, they were forced to do so *not* because of ideological reasons, but because they failed by themselves to assure the coordination and growth of the economy, the basic activities they had undertaken after 1900.

Until the Depression, the government had played a minimal part in the management of the American economy. The merchants had used the government to assist in financing internal improvements that they found too costly or risky to undertake themselves, and the manufacturers had called upon the government to protect them from foreign competition. Small businessmen — wholesalers and retailers — had joined farmers and workers to use the government to regulate the large corporation, but such regulation did not deter the growth of big business nor significantly alter the activities of the managers. Before the Depression, the government had developed few means to influence consciously the over-all performance of the American economy, the major exception being the creation of a central banking system in 1913.

The Depression clearly demonstrated that the corporation managers alone were unable to provide the coordination and adaptation necessary to sustain a complex, highly differentiated, mass-production, mass-distribution economy. The coming of the Depression itself reflected population and technological developments. Legislation in the 1920's cut immigration from abroad to a tiny flow. After World War I, migration from country to city slowed. Meanwhile, new industries, particularly the electric and automobile industries, reached the limit of demand for their output permitted by the existing size and distribution of the national income. At the same time, improved machinery as well as the more efficient management of production and distribution meant that in still other industries potential supply was becoming greater than existing demand. By the mid-1920's prices had begun to decline. Only the existence of credit helped maintain the economy's momentum until 1929.

Corporate giants, like General Motors, General Electric, and du Pont, fully realized that the demand was leveling off in the 1920's, but they could do little more than maintain production at the existing rate or even cut back a bit. When the 1929 crash dried up credit and reduced demand, they could only roll with the punch. As demand fell, they cut production, laid off men, and canceled orders for supplies and materials. Such actions further reduced purchasing power and demand and led to more cuts in production and more layoffs. The downward pressure continued relentlessly. In less than four years, the national income was slashed in half. The forecasts at General Motors and General Electric for 1932 indicated that, at best, the firms would operate at about 25 per cent capacity.

The only institution capable of stopping this economic descent appeared to be the federal government. During the 1930's it undertook this role, but with great reluctance. Until the recession of 1937, Franklin D. Roosevelt and his Secretary of the Treasury still expected to balance the budget and to bring the end to government intervention in the economy. Roosevelt and his Cabinet considered large-scale government spending and employment only temporary. When Roosevelt decided in 1936 that the Depression was over despite high unemployment, he sharply reduced government expenditures. National income, production, and demand immediately plummeted in 1937. The nation then began to understand more clearly the relationship between government spending and the level of economic activity, although acceptance of the government's role in maintaining economic growth and stability was a decade away.

World War II taught other lessons. The government spent far more than the most enthusiastic New Dealer had ever proposed. Most of the output of these expenditures was destroyed or left on the battlefields of Europe and Asia. But the resulting increased demand sent the nation into a period of prosperity the like of which had never before been seen. Moreover, the supplying of huge armies and navies fighting the most massive war of all time required a tight, centralized control of the national economy. This effort brought corporate managers to Washington to carry out one of the most complex pieces of economic planning in history. That experience lessened the ideological fears over the government's role in stabilizing the economy. This new attitude, embodied in legislation by the Employment Act of 1946, continued to be endorsed by Eisenhower's Republican Administration in the 1950's.

The federal government is now committed to ensuring the revival of investment and demand if, and only if, private enterprise is unable to maintain full employment. In 1949 and again in 1953, 1957, and 1960, the government carried out this role by adjusting its monetary and fiscal policies, building roads, and shifting defense contracts. The continuing Cold War made the task relatively easy by assuring the government ample funds. The new role has been defined so that it meets the needs of the corporate managers. The federal government takes action only if the managers are unable to maintain a high level of aggregate demand; it has not replaced the managers as the major coordinators in the economy, but acts only as a coordinator of last resort.

The Depression helped bring the federal government into the economy in another way. During the late-nineteenth and twentieth centuries, workers, farmers, and (to some extent) retailers, wholesalers, and other small businessmen had formed organizations to help them share in making the economic decisions that most intimately affected their well-being. During the 1930's, when the managers were having difficulties in maintaining economic stability, these numerically larger and more politically influential groups were able to get the federal and state governments to support their claims. Through government intervention many workers acquired a say in determining policies in wages, hours, working rules, promotions, and layoffs; farmers gained control over the prices of several basic commodities; and retailers and wholesalers increased their voice in the pricing of certain goods they sold. Nevertheless, the Wagner Act, the Agricultural Adjustment Acts, the Robinson-Patman Act, and the "fair trading" laws did not seriously infringe on the manager's ability to determine current output and to allocate resources for present and future economic activities.

The growth of organized labor during the twentieth century indicates much about the economic power of the large corporation, for this politically powerful group has been able to impress its will on the decisions of corporate managers only in a limited way. Until the Depression, labor unions had little success in organizing key industries dominated by large, managerially operated enterprises. Even during its first major period of growth at the turn of the century, the American Federation of Labor was not successful in the manufacturing industries. From the start, organized labor's strength lay in mining, transportation, and the building and construction trades. In the manufacturing sector, the Federation's gains came not in factory but small-shop industries, such as cigar, garment, hat, and stove-making and ship-building. During the first quarter of the twentieth century, organized labor acquired its members in those industries where skilled workers achieved their goals by bargaining with many small employers. (The railroads were the exception.) The geographically oriented operating structure developed by the American Federation of Labor unions was admirably suited to this purpose.

Precisely because the craft union had grown up in industries where the factory and the large integrated enterprise had never been dominant, the American Federation of Labor found itself in the 1930's unable to organize, even with strong government support, the mass-production, mass-distribution industries so basic to the operation of the modern economy. To unionize these industries required the creation of a structure to parallel the structure of the large integrated enterprise and a program that appealed to semiskilled rather than skilled workers. The AF of L failed to meet this challenge. Only after "a civil war" within the ranks of labor and the creation of a new national labor organization, the CIO, did the automobile, iron and steel, nonferrous metal, rubber, electrical machinery, and other key industries become fully unionized.

During the great organizing drives of the late-1930's and immediately after World War II, union leaders rarely, if ever, sought to gain more than a voice in the determination of wages and hours, working rules, and hiring as well as promotion and layoff policies. Even when they asked (unsuccessfully) for an opportunity "to look at the company's books," union spokesmen did so primarily with the hope of assuring themselves that they were obtaining what they considered a fair share of the income generated by the firm. The critical issue over which management and labor fought in the years immediately following World War II was whether the managers or the union would control the hiring of workers. The unions almost never asked to take part in decisions about output, pricing, or resources allocation. With the passage of the Taft-Hartley Act of 1947, the managers obtained a control over hiring which has never been seriously challenged. Nor have any further inroads into "management's prerogatives" been seriously proposed.

Since 1950, business managers have continued to make the decisions that most vitally affect the coordination of the economy and the pace of its growth. They have also continued to have a major say in how the economy adapts to external forces generated by population movements and technological change.

Population movements in the 1960's present a different challenge than they did before the 1930's. Migration from abroad has remained only a trickle and that from the country to the city has continued to drop. The move to the suburbs, the most significant post-Depression development, has expanded the urban sprawl and undermined the viability of the central city. The resulting problems are, however, more political and social than economic. Whether government officials are better trained than corporate managers to handle these new problems is open to question. If the business managers fail to meet these new challenges, the government will obviously have to do so.

Meanwhile, technological change has maintained a revolutionary pace. Through their concentration on research and development of new products and new methods of production and distribution, corporate managers have been trained to handle the processes and procedures of technological innovation. The large corporation had so "internalized" the process of innovation that this type of change is no longer simply an outside force to which businessmen and others in the economy adjust. Here the expertise of the business manager covers a broader field than that of governmental or military managers. In most of the costly government programs involving a complex technology, the development and production of new products have been turned over to the large corporations through the contracting process. The federal government does, however, supply the largest share of funds for research and development. Thus, even though the business manager continues to play a critical part in adapting the economy to technological change, government officials are in a position to determine the direction and the areas in which research and development will be concentrated.

This brief history of the role of business in the operation of the American economy suggests several tentative conclusions. From the beginning, it seems, businessmen have run the American economy. They can take the credit and the blame for many of its achievements and failures. They, more than [any] other group in the economy, have managed the production, transportation, and distribution of goods and services. No other group — farmers, blue-collar workers, or white-collar workers — has ever had much to do with the over-all coordination of the economic system or its adaptation to basic changes in population and technology.

Over the two centuries, however, the businessman who ran the economy has changed radically. Dominance has passed from the merchant to the wholesaler, from the wholesaler to the manufacturer, and from the manufacturer to the manager. In the last generation, businessmen have had to share their authority with others, largely with the federal government. Even so, the government's peace-time role still remains essentially a supplementary one, as coordinator of last resort and as a supplier of funds for technological innovation.

In the past, businessmen have devoted their energies to economic affairs, giving far less attention to cultural, social, or even political matters. Precisely because they have created an enormously productive economy and the most affluent society in the world, the noneconomic challenges are now becoming more critical than the economic ones. There is little in the recruitment, training, and experience of the present business leaders — the corporate managers — to prepare them for handling the difficult new problems, but unless they do learn to cope with this new situation, they may lose their dominant position in the economy. As was not true of the merchant, wholesaler, or manufacturer, the corporate managers could be replaced by men who are not businessmen. To suggest how and in what way the managers will respond to the current challenges is, fortunately, not the task of the historian. Such analyses are properly left to social scientists and businessmen.

WALTER LICHT

from Industrializing America   [1995]

WALTER LICHT (1946–) is Walter H. Annenberg Professor of History at the University of Pennsylvania. He is the author of several works including *Working for the Railroad: The Organization of Work in the Nineteenth Century* (1983) and *Getting Work: Philadelphia, 1840–1950* (1992).

MONDAY, JULY 16, 1877. Martinsburg, West Virginia. A date and place emblazoned neither in history books nor in the historical consciousness of the American people. Yet, on that day and in that location, the people of the United States stepped precipitously into the future.

On July 16, 1877, railway workers in Martinsburg, employees of the Baltimore & Ohio Railroad, refused to handle rail traffic or let trains pass through the town. They were protesting the implementation of a 10 percent cut in wages that had been announced simultaneously a few weeks earlier by railway executives of the major rail lines in the country. The concerted nature of the announcement would be an important element in the story to unfold. In response to the job action, the president of the B&O persuaded the governor of West Virginia to send regiments of the state militia to Martinsburg to see to the safe movement of trains. The easy access of corporate leaders to the levers of government power would

Walter Licht, *Industrializing America*, pp. 166–68, 174–81. Copyright © 1995 The Johns Hopkins University Press. Reprinted with permission of The Johns Hopkins University Press.

be an additional ingredient in the saga. To the dismay of B&O officials, however, the troops who arrived on the sixteenth initially fraternized with townspeople. Later that day a melee did erupt, and in the ensuing fracas a striking railwayman guarding a track switch was shot and killed. That proved to be the spark that ignited a nationwide conflagration.

Word soon spread along the tracks of the B&O, and work and traffic on the entire line ground to a halt. On Wednesday evening, angry railwaymen and their supporters gathered in Baltimore to protest directly to B&O officials. Protest turned to riot; and by night's end, 10 people were dead, 16 injured, and 250 arrested through confrontations between demonstrators and city police. Shocked by the insurrection, the governor of Maryland prevailed on the president of the United States, Rutherford B. Hayes, to send federal troops to Baltimore to quell the disturbance — the first time in American history that federal forces were employed to suppress labor unrest.

The fire then spread to other communities in the country. Following the example of B&O workers in refusing to accept wage cuts, railwaymen from other lines walked off their jobs and were joined by fellow townspeople in demonstrations. Protests soon emerged in such places as Hornelsville and Buffalo, New York, and Reading, Harrisburg, and Altoona, Pennsylvania. The greatest explosion, however, was to occur in Pittsburgh. On Thursday, July 19, railwaymen from the Pennsylvania Railroad stopped rail traffic in the city. On Friday, state militia from the area were called in at the request and insistence of Thomas Scott, influential president of the road, with the aim of restoring train service. The local guardsmen, however, refused to take up their posts. Troops then had to be sent in from other parts of the state — a move that residents of Pittsburgh perceived as an invasion — and this set the stage for a brutal confrontation on Saturday. Pennsylvania Railroad executives were determined to renew freight traffic, and they arranged for troops to be stationed on the trains. As the first guarded train moved through the city, crowds gathered to block its progress. Troops then fired into the crowd of demonstrators, killing an estimated twenty people and wounding more than seventy more. Word of the massacre quickly spread, and the people of Pittsburgh took to the streets, attacking militiamen, looting stores, and setting fires to the property of the Pennsylvania Railroad. By late evening of Saturday, July 21, 1877, a red glow lit up the city, and daybreak revealed the stations and shops of the Pennsylvania reduced to embers.

Sunday did not prove to be a day of rest. Crowds continued to roam the streets, and a semblance of order would not be restored in the city until Tuesday. Over the weekend, more than two score lives had been lost, 104 locomotives and 2,153 railcars had been destroyed, and few buildings of the Pennsylvania Railroad remained standing.

Chicago was next. Three days of serious disturbances began in that city on Monday, the twenty-third, and confrontations between protestors and police would lead to eighteen dead. The railroad strikes in Chicago evolved into a general strike as workers across trades in the city walked off their

jobs in sympathy. Order was restored only with the arrival of Illinois guardsmen from other parts of the state and a contingent of federal troops just
fresh from fighting Native Americans on the Plains. After Chicago, the
contagion spread further west to St. Louis, Kansas City, Galveston, and even
San Francisco. Only two weeks after its onset did the fever run its course.
Trains first rolled again on a normal basis through Martinsburg on July
27, through Pittsburgh on July 29, and through Chicago on August 3.

The events of July 1877 shocked the nation, and the toll was enormous.
The nation's commerce had been effectively stilled; railroad companies
lost more than $30 million in lost property and business; railwaymen went
without pay during the strikes, and many returned to work only to be dis-
charged for their protests and blackballed from further employment in
the trade; thousands had also been jailed, hundreds wounded, and at least
fifty killed.

From the last two decades of the nineteenth century through World
War II, ongoing and vexing conflict between capital and labor marked
the American experience. The great railroad strikes of July 1877 represent
the formal and abrupt beginning to this history. In the immediate years
following the unrest of that month and until the turn of the new century,
industrial strife was particularly intense and violent. The severity of the
unrest can only be understood as a twofold response: while economic insecurity, not hardship per se, definitely spurred revolt, Americans from different walks of life also took to the streets to support striking workers in
the period to challenge the growing, encroaching political and economic
power of concentrated capital and the threat the corporation posed to
cherished democratic republican values and practices.

During the last two decades of the nineteenth century, the country was
also rocked by other kinds of explosions. Most notably, the period witnessed
evolving and escalating protest by American farmers. Various social critics
and reformers also came to the fore to question contemporary developments, galvanize public opinion, and suggest changes in economic and
political practices. The economic instabilities of the times and the sway of
the new corporations figured significantly in the complaints of farmers
and intellectuals as well.

Unrest during the last decades of the nineteenth century would lead to
a restructuring of American institutions and the creation of a new American political economic order. This remaking, however, occurred slowly
over a fifty-year period, in stages and unsystematically, and would involve
no single set of actors. Various groups would emerge and, often with
cross-purposes and differing motives, contribute to the same building of a
new United States. What is of interest is the *convergence* of efforts. What
was sought in common was greater security and a more administered
economy and polity. . . .

Despite the clear advantages held by business managers in countering
the job actions of workers — access to the policing powers of government,
the ability to hire strikebreakers in great numbers, especially with immigrants

and African Americans in desperate search of work — the deck obviously was not completely stacked against the strikers. One important weapon they had at their disposal was community support. An interesting statistic compiled by labor bureau officials speaks to this point. Strikes were recorded as ordered or not ordered by established unions. In the early 1880s, more than 50 percent of all strikes did not involve a formal trade union organization. The proportion of work stoppages orchestrated by unions rose over the next two decades, but by 1900, one-third of all strikes were still waged without union intervention.

The absolute grassroots insurgent nature of many late-nineteenth-century strikes has to be appreciated. State and federal investigative commissions established to determine the causes of the unrest of the period often searched in vain to find leaders or organizations to which responsibility could be assigned. The strikes also appeared to be as much community uprisings as work stoppages. Investigators found and local newspapers reported ample evidence of widespread support for strikers. Workers from trades not directly involved walked off their jobs in sympathy; local shopkeepers offered food and extended credit to families of strikers; editors of community newspapers blasted company officials for not dealing fairly with their employees; townsmen called up for service in state militia fraternized with their neighbors who were on strike and failed to take up positions in guarding business properties. Community members also took to the streets in protest with strikers. Arrest records for the period reveal people from all walks of life incarcerated for rioting, arson, and attacks on police forces during labor upheavals. Women participated in demonstrations as visibly as men. During railroad strikes, brigades of women greased and soaped tracks to impede the passage of trains.

Why did people who were not directly involved in labor disputes join in protest with striking workers in large numbers? Economic bad times is a contributing factor. Community uprisings accompanying strikes generally occurred during years of economic depression. Yet, material grievance alone cannot explain local insurgencies. The target of community aggression was corporate enterprise. During disputes, corporate property was attacked, not the businesses of local entrepreneurs. Tension exploded to riot when troops sent at the behest of corporate leaders entered the local scene. Reporters covering the disturbances discovered local shopkeepers sympathizing with striking workers and joining protest because the national based corporations threatened their existence; in the case of the railroads, proprietors were angered both at the physical incursions of the carriers and the seemingly unjust rates charged them for shipping goods. The very livelihoods and the autonomy of members of communities appeared challenged by the impersonal decisions made by executives in remote and unapproachable corporate headquarters.

The distrust of the first generation of Americans to be faced with the corporation is explicable; less easy to fathom is the violence. Protestors picked up bricks and rifles to defend their communities and republican ideals. The common ownership of guns in a nation where the right to bear arms was constitutionally protected is part of the explanation for the dramatic loss of life and limb in labor uprisings. The frontier also played somewhat of a role. Not every American community witnessed death and destruction during the labor upheavals. However, historians have been unable to discern patterns of insurgency; labor insurrection occurred in both metropolitan areas and small towns. Unrest unfolded in medium-sized cities as well, but notably in newly developed industrial communities — common to the Midwest — without established elites or ways. Finally, and crucially, the determination of American corporate executives to suppress strikes and unions at all cost and to employ public and private police forces to silence protest was also a key ingredient in the remarkably fierce battles that transpired. Fire was fought with fire.

Spontaneity and community support notably marked labor protest, but over the course of the last decades of the century, trade unions assumed a greater presence and importance in strikes. A trade union revival had first occurred in the 1850s. With economic recovery after the depression of the late 1830s and early 1840s, skilled workers on the local level reestablished their antebellum craft societies and then joined with workers from other localities to found national organizations. The arrival of skilled German and British workers, who were highly politicized and had trade union experience, fueled the rebirth; and vast improvements in transportation and communications during the 1850s allowed for (and demanded) greater cooperation across geographical boundaries.

The revival of trade unionism in the 1850s was followed by increased labor organization and strikes during the Civil War, especially as workers attempted to keep their wages in line with rising wartime prices. In another kind of labor protest, white workers in the North during the war took to the streets to protest the inequities of the military draft system, taking their wrath out on recruitment officers and, tragically, often on African Americans as well.

An expansion of trade union activity and membership during the Civil War led to the formation of the National Labor Union in 1866, the nation's first national federation of unions. Under the leadership of William Sylvis, an articulate iron molder, the NLU convened yearly conventions where trade unionists and various labor sympathizers discussed issues of the day. Delegates supported motions in favor of the eight-hour day, government monetary policies that favored debtors, federal land distribution programs for working people, increased efforts at labor organizing, and most notably, the building of so-called producers' cooperatives (if yeoman producership was increasingly untenable with rapid industrialization, then republican principles could be sustained with yeoman cooperatives). The NLU maintained a visible presence for five years, with some strike and legislative success, but the movement then dissipated and passed from the scene. The organization failed to survive the depression of 1873 and was further incapacitated by internal divisions over economic policy, political activism, and gender and racial issues. From the ashes of the NLU, however, rose another trade union federation, drawing upon and extending many of its predecessor's ideals, but having a much greater impact. This organization was the Knights of Labor.

Uriah Stephens and James Wright, skilled garment cutters, founded the Noble and Holy Order of the Knights of Labor in Philadelphia in 1869 as a secret organization. Little is known about the society in its early years, though it did survive the depression of 1873 and included some 500 lodges and 6,000 members by 1877. In 1878, the order went public (although a good many of the rituals of the original clandestine organization were maintained), and under the leadership of Terrence Powderly, a machinist by trade, members of the "producing classes," regardless of occupation, nationality, race, religion, or sex, were encouraged to join a movement bent on achieving better working conditions and a new social order based on equality and cooperation. Explicitly barred from membership were bankers, stockbrokers, lawyers, liquor dealers (temperance remained a guiding principle of the organization), and gamblers.

In the early 1880s, the society grew and spread throughout the country; recent analyses of the organization's surviving documents reveal lodges established in every state and county of the nation. In 1885, striking Knights railwaymen in the West won their spectacular victory over the powerful Jay Gould, boosting the organization's fortunes and membership to 750,000. The year 1886 saw the order at its peak of prominence as Knights of Labor members rushed into political activity, launching successful independent party ventures throughout the United States. From this zenith of visibility and impact, however, the Knights of Labor declined precipitously under the force of increased employer resistance to Knights-led strikes, internal divisions, and the defection of craft unionists from the cause. By the mid-1890s, few traces of the order remained.

An overview of the history of the Knights can thus be rendered, but understanding the Knights phenomenon has always provided difficulties for historians. For one thing, the activities of the federation varied from year to year and place to place. The organization itself was a crazy quilt of local assemblies of individuals, neighborhood groups, reform associations, existing craft unions, and workers variously organized by factory, trade, and geographical locale, and wider city, district, and state assemblies. The order stood for the enrollment of all workers — upholding the principle of so-called industrial unionism — yet craft unions joined the federation and maintained their autonomy and identities. The order made unprecedented strides in organizing women and African American workers though gender and racial divisions still marked its history. Knights activists moved into independent political party activity with a vengeance in 1886, yet an ambivalence toward politics, politicians, and the role of government — stemming from the republican and antistatist sentiments and ideals of those drawn into the movements — blunted the

Knights' political initiatives once Knights candidates found themselves actually elected to office. Temperance and chivalric behavior were hallmarks of the order, yet a number of Knights officials were involved in swindles and intrigues that rivaled the worst corruptions of the age. The organization stood officially for the abandonment of the wage labor system, but with the exception of support for public ownership of financial and transportation institutions, Knights leaders openly repudiated socialism. Knights officials upheld the building of producers' cooperatives as a principal goal and ideal, yet their actual record on establishing cooperative ventures was poor. Finally, and most notably, while the organization's leadership formally renounced strikes and espoused harmonious relations with fair-minded, hard-working employers and arbitration in the case of disputes, its members nonetheless participated fervently in hundreds of strikes under the Knights banner.

The Knights of Labor thus defies simple characterization. Can it be deemed a backward-looking movement aimed at recreating a mythical yeoman producer past, as some historians have suggested? Not really. Knights leaders and followers harked back to a more harmonious time, yet they were permanent wage laborers, decidedly immersed in modern issues like arbitration proceedings, challenging traditional mainstream politics, and struggling to find new forms of relationships. Was the organization instead a typical reform movement merely bent on extending the benefits of capitalism to the yet unbenefitted? Not really, again. The Knights were ambivalent about the capitalist system, definitely antagonistic to corporate or monopoly capitalism, and certainly not boosters of capitalism in general.

Was the organization an alternative movement looking forward to the building of a "cooperative commonwealth" (a frequently invoked phrase) to replace the bureaucratic and corporate future that loomed ahead? There is evidence to substantiate this interpretation, but how widely this vision was held by those enrolled is unclear. Was it, as other historians have suggested, a democratic movement at heart, an attempt to significantly widen political participation? Ample proof exists for this contention as well, though the notion hardly provides a comprehensive understanding. Was it simply a trade union effort? Certainly not.

Perhaps the only solution is to term the Knights of Labor an amorphous social movement of laboring people; the extent to which hundreds of thousands of American working men and women were enlisted, educated, and politicized in the 1870s and 1880s is what is to be ultimately appreciated. Recognition of the mobilization is apparent from studies of local Knights' activity and the countless meetings, lectures, parades, and picnics attended by those moved to join. If historians have to remain unsure in their estimations of the Knights, the Knights of Labor moment in American history nonetheless continues to fascinate.

Some trade unionists of the era, however, viewed the Knights venture as just pure folly. Leaders of the so-called brotherhoods of railway workers, for example, expressly forbade their members from joining the Knights;

the brotherhoods, in fact, avoided participation in all of the great uprisings of the day. Leaders of most craft unions similarly viewed the Knights with a jaundiced eye. Among detractors of the Knights, the key and historically critical figure was Samuel Gompers.

Samuel Gompers was born in England in 1850 and immigrated to New York City at the age of thirteen. Entering the cigar-making trade, he found himself immersed in a community of skilled English and German immigrant workers who ate, drank, and breathed Marxism and socialism. Gompers thus received lessons about the seeming hard truths of capitalism: a permanent proletariat had been formed; capital was concentrating and gaining overwhelming economic and political power; realism was in order; focused and well-organized trade unions had to be established to achieve gains for workers.

Despite this sober perspective, Gompers and his fellow craft trade unionists were swept into the Knights crusade. Having risen to the leadership of the Cigar Makers' International Union, he joined with other skilled men in 1881 in founding the Federation of Organized Trades and Labor Unions, which allied with the Knights. Over the next five years, however, Gompers and his associates became increasingly disenchanted with the movement. They resented Terrence Powderly's attempt to dictate policy, found themselves engaged in various jurisdictional disputes (what constituted a local or an assembly of the Knights organization remained a fuzzy and disputed matter), deemed most Knights pronouncements as naive and Knights-sponsored strikes as quixotic, and saw the sudden move of Knights members into independent party politics as misguided and wasteful of valuable time and energy. In 1886, Gompers thus led numerous craft unions out of the Knights of Labor and into his newly formed American Federation of Labor. The absolute loss in membership and the defection of the best-organized of the Knights' members contributed greatly to that order's subsequent demise.

Under Samuel Gompers' leadership, both the constituent unions of the AFL and the offices of the federation grew in strength and permanence. Gompers himself became the most important labor leader in the country, listened to by politicians, businessmen, and the press. Until his death in 1924, he was arguably the chief spokesman for the working people of the United States. This all occurred, however, because Gompers forged a limited agenda.

Gompers' strategy for the AFL included the following:

1. Organize the organizable — that is, skilled workers who possessed leverage in the workplace and who could win victories.
2. Do not pour energies into enrolling less skilled, easily replaced workers. In practice, this meant ignoring women, blacks, and most immigrants.
3. Build strong organizations with high dues, well-paid officers, and strike funds and other benefits that would engender the great loyalty of members.

4. Fight for what can be gained — "bread and butter" issues — meaning higher wages within reason, shorter hours, and work rules that curtailed the arbitrary decision making of firm managers.

5. Do not become involved and waste time and money in independent political action, much less radical political activity. Work within the system, in other words.

6. Support mainstream politicians of any party who favor prolabor legislation.

Gompers' strategy proved successful — in many ways it was programmed to be — and with each victory for AFL men, Gompers could upbraid his many detractors in the labor movement and point to the wisdom of his stance.

The history of Samuel Gompers and the AFL in the late nineteenth century, like that of the Knights of Labor, is not without its inconsistencies. Gompers developed his strategy over time and with experience, not presciently or at once. He fashioned his approach to trade unionism after his experiences with the Knights, through watching corporate capital become entrenched and powerful, after disastrous defeats for labor at Homestead and Pullman, in light of increasing judicial assaults on trade union activity and conservative court rulings against the government regulation of working conditions, after turning back significant challenges to his leadership by militants from within the AFL, and after seeing the efficacy of ingratiating himself to business leaders (as he warned, if they did not deal with him and the skilled workers he represented, they would have to deal with more radical groups within the laboring community). Gompers also asserted himself as a visible spokesman, but he insisted that the AFL be as decentralized as possible and that constituent unions be afforded maximum autonomy (the example of Powderly glared in his mind). Gompers also upheld the principle of craft unionism, yet the AFL included so-called federal unions, such as the United Mine Workers, which organized workers across skill levels. While in practice the AFL rendered little assistance to women and African American workers who struggled to form unions, Gompers himself spoke against racial and sexual prejudice, opposed segregated unions, and warned that without outreach, strikes would be lost through the employment of strikebreakers who remained antagonistic to the exclusive craft unions. Gompers similarly argued for labor to be nonpartisan and nonreliant on politicians (he espoused "voluntarism"), yet he would ultimately hitch the fortunes of the AFL to the Democratic Party. Finally, Gompers placed a definite conservative stamp on the American trade union movement, yet as noted, he constantly faced challenges from groups within the AFL who mobilized to see the federation adopt a much more militant, socialistic, and inclusive posture.

There are a number of great ironies in the story of the Knights of Labor, the American Federation of Labor, and other labor campaigns in the last decades of the nineteenth century. Samuel Gompers, schooled in

Marxism, became a force for moderation and acceptance of the powers that be. Eugene Victor Debs, on the other hand, born in small-town America, steeped in American republican traditions, would emerge a socialist after defeat at the hands of the powerful Pullman Company and the U.S. government. In launching effective strikes Gompers and his associates challenged capital head on, but not the capitalist system. The Knights, conversely, in raising on high the notion of a cooperative commonwealth and in their spontaneous protests, challenged the capitalist order but not, effectively, capital.

Egging on labor revolt during the late nineteenth century were also a host of socialists, anarchists, and other radicals, operating in such organizations as the Socialist Labor Party. During the great railroad strikes of July 1877, for example, leaders of the socialist Workingmen's Party assumed a key role in mobilizing protest in the city of St. Louis, one of the only instances during the nationwide stoppage where there is clear evidence of leadership and organization. Individuals and groups — whether craft unionists, Knights, or radicals — thus contributed to the labor upheavals of the period. Ultimately, however, a lesser role has to be assigned to all of them, for the unrest is only partially explicable in terms of formal organization and agitation. General resentment among working people and often among their middle-class neighbors against the emerging power of the corporation played a larger role. So, too, did anger about economic hard times.

American Imperialism: Economic Expansion or Ideological Crusade?

Around the turn of the twentieth century, the United States emerged as a great power. Having defeated Spain in war in 1898, it acquired Puerto Rico, the Philippines, and part of the Samoan archipelago, thereby coming to dominate the Caribbean and exert enormous influence in the Pacific. This acquisition of an overseas empire seemed sudden to many, but the United States had been tending toward such an outcome for years (it had annexed the Hawaiian Islands in 1893). Even before this time, its continental expanse, industrial and agricultural productivity, extensive trade, and growing population had made it a rising economic power. The construction of a modern navy was the final element required for the United States to set the course toward empire.

Many Americans were ambivalent about their country's new role. Some feared that America's democratic institutions were incompatible with an overseas empire and the large military establishment that would be required to sustain it. Others rejected empire because it implied bringing under the American flag groups they regarded as racial or social inferiors. Some Americans, on the other hand, favored the entry of the United States into world affairs either because of a crusading zeal to spread American institutions and values or a desire to find new economic markets. These divisions over foreign policy had their counterpart in the works of diplomatic historians. Just as Americans debated the wisdom of particular policies, so historians disagreed about interpretations of past events. The historical debate was never confined simply to an analysis of the past; implicit in each interpretation of diplomatic history was a vision of what America ought to be. Those who argued that the United States had traditionally been a champion of democracy were likely to take an interventionist position in debates about current-day policies toward "emerging nations." Similarly, those who recounted the imposition of American economic and military power on other countries tended to criticize the imperialist character of contemporary foreign policy.

The historical literature dealing with the decade of the 1890s, which culminated in the Spanish-American War, is a central case in point. Charles and Mary Beard, whose *Rise of American Civilization* was a landmark in the Progressive school of American historiography,[1] argued that the pursuit of economic interests led President William McKinley to seek war with Spain. Neither sympathy for Cubans, nor anticolonial impulse, nor any other dem-

---

[1]On the Progressive school of history, see Chapter 1.

ocratic ideal led to war fever. The Spanish government, after all, had practically acceded to most of McKinley's demands. McKinley, the Beards insisted, revised President Cleveland's policy of neutrality because American businessmen made him understand that Spanish policy threatened their investments in and trade with Cuba. The ensuing acquisition of overseas territory provided further proof of the Beards's charge that the business community played an important role in determining the country's foreign policy. Although the Beardian thesis was presented in somewhat qualified form, it clearly implied the primacy of economic forces in shaping foreign policy.[2]

Relatively few scholars, however, followed the Beards's interpretation. To Samuel Flagg Bemis, whose synthesis of American diplomatic history appeared in 1936, the acquisition of an overseas empire represented a "great aberration." Before the war, Bemis noted, "there had not been the slightest demand for the acquisition of the Philippine Islands." Military victory, however, fanned a jingoist tide that McKinley proved unable to resist. In demanding the Philippine Islands in the course of peace negotiations, the president demonstrated "adolescent irresponsibility." McKinley's decision, concluded Bemis, was unplanned and an indication of his weakness and folly. It was definitely not in accord with the traditional American aversion to colonial empire.[3]

Another anti-Beardian interpretation of the causes of war appeared at almost the same moment as Bemis's influential textbook. In *Expansionists of 1898*, Julius W. Pratt suggested that intellectual and emotional factors were responsible for the new expansionism. The emergence of social Darwinism provided some people with an intellectual justification for expanding America's sphere of influence. In this view, nations, like individuals, were engaged in a remorseless test of their fitness to survive. The criterion of success was dominion over others; failure to expand meant stagnation and decline. Other expansionist-minded individuals recruited religious and humanitarian zeal to the task of bringing American civilization to less advanced peoples. A small group of strategic thinkers adopted the doctrines of Captain Alfred Thayer Mahan, who declared sea power to be the key to a nation's greatness and overseas naval bases the key to sea power. These ideological factors, not economic interest, drove expansionist policies, Pratt insisted. Indeed, he noted that the business community, which was still recovering from the depression that began in 1893, opposed intervention in Cuba for fear that it might block the road to economic recovery. It was only after Admiral George Dewey's dramatic victory in the Philippines that American businessmen were converted to the expansionist cause by the alluring prospect of the potentially enormous Chinese market. Businessmen eventually found it just as easy to apply the same rationale to the Caribbean. The reasons why the United States went to war, therefore, were quite different from the reasons that led it to

---

[2]Charles A. Beard and Mary R. Beard, *The Rise of American Civilization*, 2 vols. (New York, 1927), vol. 2, 369–82.

[3]Samuel Flagg Bemis, *A Diplomatic History of the United States* (4th ed., New York, 1955), 463–75.

acquire an overseas empire. American imperialism, Pratt concluded, was born in ideological impulse but matured in economic ambition.[4]

After the publication of Pratt's work in 1936 scholarly interest in the early years of American imperialism waned. Between the 1930s and 1950s diplomatic historians focused primarily on the causes and consequences of the First and Second World Wars. But in 1959 William Appleman Williams published one of the most influential books ever written about American foreign policy, *The Tragedy of American Diplomacy*.[5] Called by one historian America's "preeminent critic of empire,"[6] Williams could never easily be categorized as New Left. Nevertheless, his writings were seized upon and extended by New Left and revisionist historians of all kinds. What Williams offered was a provocative set of hypotheses to explain the entire historical record of American diplomacy. First of all, he insisted, foreign policies were never just "reactions" to external events; they were always intimately related to domestic concerns. Conflicts over interests among different sectors of the economy, different regions, different classes, different political coalitions — these were the motivators of foreign policy.

Given this primary assumption, Williams continued, U.S. foreign policy revealed itself to have been expansionist from its very beginnings. Even before gaining independence, Americans had striven to achieve economic self-sufficiency within the British empire. Only independent control over their own economy could guarantee colonial elites continued dominance over contentious masses, who demanded land and other resources needed to realize their "American dream." Once independence had been won, the United States determined to meet such demands by developing ever-expanding markets for its products, that is, by pursuing an American empire. Until the 1890s, that empire lay mostly in the western regions of the American continent, but once the frontier was gone the search for markets continued overseas. During the depressions of the 1880s and 1890s, Williams specifically argues, the American business community concluded that, since economic depression resulted from America's tendency to produce more goods than its people could consume, foreign markets were needed to absorb growing productive capacity.

Despite the controversy between imperialists and anti-imperialists around the turn of the twentieth century, both groups agreed that economic expansion overseas was vital to the nation's prosperity and stability. The debate was over means rather than ends. Imperialists believed that formal acquisition of colonies was necessary to insure strategic security and market control; anti-imperialists, on the other hand, believed that security and economic expansion could be achieved without the material expense of maintaining

---

[4] Julius W. Pratt, *Expansionists of 1898* (Baltimore, 1936), and *America's Colonial Experiment: How the United States Gained, Governed, and in Part Gave Away a Colonial Empire* (New York, 1950).

[5] William Appleman Williams, *The Tragedy of American Diplomacy* (2nd ed., New York, 1972); this was followed by *The Contours of American History* (Cleveland, 1961) and *The Roots of the Modern American Empire* (New York, 1969).

[6] Paul Buhle, "William Appleman Williams: Grassroots against Empire," in Allen Hunter, ed., *Rethinking the Cold War* (Philadelphia, 1998), 289–306.

a colonial empire or the ideological expense of betraying the nation's anti-colonial heritage. The Open Door policy, according to Williams, resolved the dilemma and ultimately became the basis for America's future foreign policy. It sought to achieve all the advantages of economic expansion without the disadvantages of maintaining a colonial empire. It demanded that each nation maintain an open door for trade with all other countries on a most-favored-nation basis. By requiring all other nations to compete with the exuberant American economy, Open Door strategists believed, the United States would come out ahead in the scramble for trade advantages. Although formulated originally to apply to China, the policy was expanded to cover the entire globe and to include American investments as well as trade.[7]

Williams proclaimed the consequences of this continuous imperial policy to be disastrous. First of all, it was a betrayal and corruption of American democracy. Even worse were the consequences for people outside the United States. Armored with the "posture of moral and ideological superiority," American policymakers over the twentieth century proceeded to penetrate and dominate one underdeveloped nation after another, proclaiming their good intentions while reaping immense material rewards. They hoped to control markets and raw materials without having to resort to direct political or military intervention, but economic hegemony almost always required political hegemony. Cuba, the first case in point, set the pattern for others. The United States "dominated the economic life of the island by controlling, directly or indirectly, the sugar industry, and by overtly and covertly preventing any dynamic modification of the island's one-crop economy. It defined clear and narrow limits on the island's political system. It tolerated the use of torture and terror, of fraud and farce, by Cuba's rulers. But it intervened with economic and diplomatic pressure and with force of arms when Cubans threatened to transgress the economic and political restrictions established by American leaders."[8]

In 1963 Walter LaFeber published a prize-winning volume on American expansionism from 1860 to 1898 that lent strong support to the Williams thesis. The Civil War, LaFeber noted, marked an important dividing line in America's expansionist policies. Before 1860 expansionism was confined to the American continent; it reflected the desire of an agrarian society to find new and fertile lands. Post–Civil War expansionism, on the other hand, was motivated by the belief that foreign markets were vital to America's well-being. By the 1890s the American business community had concluded that additional foreign markets "would solve the economic, social, and political problems created by the industrial revolution." They found a coterie of new strategic thinkers, centered about Theodore Roosevelt, to lead the imperialist charge. Given Europe's imperialist penetration into many regions of

---

[7]For a revisionist account of the role of the mythic "China trade" in shaping U.S. foreign policy, see Thomas J. McCormick, *The China Market: America's Quest for Informal Empire, 1893–1901* (Chicago, 1967), and "Insular Imperialism and the Open Door: The China Market and the Spanish American War," *Pacific Historical Review* 32 (1963): 155–69.

[8]Williams, *Tragedy of American Diplomacy*, 2, 59.

the world, this line of strategic thought concluded, the United States needed strategic bases if it were to compete successfully. The diplomacy of the 1890s and the Spanish-American War grew out of these concerns. Debate between the imperialists and anti-imperialists during this decade was over the tactical means needed to attain common objectives. Whether they believed that the Open Door could operate entirely free of traditional colonialism, or that some formal colonization was necessary, Americans had come to accept the larger reality. "By 1899," concluded LaFeber, "the United States had forged a new empire."[9] LaFeber's classic expression of this argument is included as the first reading in this chapter.

The Williams-LaFeber interpretation of the origins of modern American foreign policy was enormously influential within the history profession.[10] It also had a wider appeal during the 1960s and 1970s as disillusionment with American policy grew during the Vietnam conflict. The argument that the nation's diplomacy was based less on democratic idealism and more on a desire to safeguard an international order that made possible America's economic supremacy seemed to resonate among scholars and citizens. The Cold War, for example, rather than resting on a moral foundation that pitted freedom against communism, was seen as a product of America's continued insistence on structuring a world order along lines that preserved its liberal capitalist hegemony. Thus American foreign policy, which grew out of domestic institutions and developments, was allegedly responsible in large measure for initiating and perpetuating the Cold War and causing the Vietnam conflict.[11]

The Williams thesis, however, did not gain universal acceptance in historical circles. Even scholars who shared its leftist tone and its assumptions about the domestic sources of foreign policy found a much more complex range of motives for American expansionism. Reflecting the surge of interest in social and cultural history, for example, John Higham and Christopher Lasch located motivation for imperialism in developments within the inner life of the American middle and upper classes. As professionalism and bureaucracy transformed the meaning of success in modernizing America, and as immigration and urbanization created a more polyglot and complex social order, white men found a way to reassert their individualism — and their masculine and racial supremacy — through the "strenuous life." What this meant was the way of life embodied by America's first politician-celebrity, Theodore Roosevelt, a life of continual exertion: challenging nature, playing

---

[9]Walter LaFeber, *The New Empire: An Interpretation of American Expansionism, 1860–1898* (Ithaca, N.Y., 1963).

[10]See Thomas J. McCormick's attempt to develop a general strategy for diplomatic history based on the Williams thesis: "Drift or Mastery? A Corporate Synthesis for American Diplomatic History," *Reviews in American History* 4 (December 1982): 318–30. See also Lloyd C. Gardner, "American Foreign Policy 1900–1921: A Second Look at the Realist Critique of American Diplomacy," in Barton J. Bernstein, ed., *Towards a New Past: Dissenting Essays in American History* (New York, 1968), 202–31; Ernest N. Paolino, *The Foundations of American Empire: William Henry Seward and U.S. Foreign Policy* (Ithaca, N.Y., 1973); Charles S. Campbell, *The Transformation of American Foreign Relations, 1865–1900* (New York, 1976).

[11]On Cold War historiography, see Chapter 8.

organized sports, cleaning up urban corruption, busting the trusts, and waving the imperial "big-stick."[12]

Other scholars departed altogether from the Williams school, denying its fundamental assumptions. They disputed its assessment of the relative importance of domestic factors in the determination of foreign policy. They denied in particular that one domestic factor — the expansive needs of capitalism — played the preponderant role in determining the character and direction of American society and therefore of its foreign policy. Some of these especially accused Williams and his followers of ignoring or trivializing the efficacy of other nations in shaping international relations. A more balanced approach, they argued, called not only for an understanding of the behavior of other governments, but more broadly for a recognition of the inherently multinational character of all diplomacy. For the historian this implied a multi-archival approach to research and a multi-perspectival approach to narration. A more critical examination of a wider range of sources and a renewed attention to noneconomic influences on policymaking, these critics of the Williams's thesis argued, led to a rejection of the idea that the United States was omnipotent in world affairs.

Typical of this approach was Ernest R. May's *Imperial Democracy*, published in 1961. May argued that in the 1890s the United States had not sought to play a new role in world affairs. On the contrary diplomatic problems concerning Hawaii, China, Venezuela, and Cuba had intruded upon the consciousness of political leaders who were preoccupied with domestic issues. "Some nations," May observed, "achieve greatness; the United States had greatness thrust upon it." President McKinley was not the harbinger of imperialism but rather a leader trying to keep his nation out of war in the face of a fractious Congress and a public inflamed by press accounts of Spanish atrocities in Cuba. When presidential intermediation designed to grant Cuba autonomy under Spain failed, McKinley faced a crucial choice. He could embark upon a war that he did not want or he could defy public opinion and thereby risk unseating Republican majorities in both houses of Congress. "When public opinion reached the point of hysteria, he succumbed," said May. "Neither the President nor the public had any aim beyond war itself." Coming as it did at a moment when depression, labor unrest, huge new inflows of immigration, and corruption scandals were shaking the political equanimity of many Americans, the Cuban crisis became a sort of psychic obsession. "In some irrational way, all these influences and anxieties translated themselves into concern for suffering Cuba. For the people as for the government, war with monarchical Catholic, Latin Spain had no purpose except to relieve emotion."[13]

---

[12] John Higham, "The Reorientation of American Culture in the 1890s," in *Writing American History: Essays on Modern Scholarship* (Bloomington, Ind., 1970), 73–102; Christopher Lasch, "The Moral and Intellectual Rehabilitation of the Ruling Class," in *The World of Nations: Reflections on American History, Politics, and Culture* (New York, 1974), 80–99.

[13] Ernest R. May, *Imperial Democracy: The Emergence of America as a Great Power* (New York, 1961), 268–70.

May's thesis was anticipated a decade earlier by Richard Hofstadter. Hofstadter's work in the 1940s and 1950s contributed to the emerging rejection of the basic tenets of the Progressive school of American historiography. In his eyes, modern American liberalism reflected less a concern for the welfare of the masses and more the inner feelings of Protestant, middle-class Americans who, buffeted by economic and technological change, feared a decline in their social status. In 1952 Hofstadter published an article that rejected an economic explanation of American diplomacy in the 1890s and suggested instead that the hysteria and jingoism of this decade grew out of the anxieties of just such people.[14] May's diplomatic history borrowed some of Hofstadter's insights into these irrational and noneconomic influences, as well as his use of social science theory and his interest in comparative history. In regard to the last, May's scholarship was especially suggestive. The forging of a new imperialist consensus at the turn of the century, May argued, owed much to European, and especially British, influence on American elites. Moreover, the eventual shift in opinion away from imperialism reflected not only a resurgence of traditional anticolonial sentiment but an awareness (especially in an era of vastly expanded newspaper readership) of the difficulties faced by the British during the Boer War in South Africa and the growth of an anti-imperialist movement in Britain. May concluded that the American debate between imperialist and anti-imperialist could be understood only in the context of a much broader Atlantic civilization.[15]

Gerald F. Linderman, who authored the second reading in this chapter, agreed fully with Williams and his followers that foreign policy emerged out of domestic concerns, but he focused on elites less than broader publics. Linderman described a society caught up in the drama of the Cuban struggle. Like Hofstadter, Linderman saw the war less as a proclamation of capitalist expansionism than as a "twilight expression" of a perishing nineteenth-century way of life. People of small towns and limited vision, Americans read the conflict through the lens of their traditional prejudices — at first seeing perfidious Spaniards versus Cuban freedom-fighters; later seeing white Europeans against black primitives. The new yellow press played an enormous role in deploying and manipulating these changing "images of enemy and ally," even as the president struggled to forge a modern executive office capable

---

[14]Richard Hofstadter, "Manifest Destiny and the Philippines," in Daniel Aaron, ed., *America in Crisis: Fourteen Crucial Episodes in American History* (New York, 1952), 173–200; republished in Hofstadter's *The Paranoid Style in American Politics and Other Essays* (New York, 1965), 145–87. Hofstadter proposed a comparable explanation of the roots of the 1950s anticommunist hysteria known as McCarthyism; for more on Hofstadter's career and influence, see Chapters 1 and 11.

[15]Ernest R. May, "American Imperialism: A Reinterpretation," *Perspectives in American History* 1 (1967): 123–283; also published as *American Imperialism: A Speculative Essay* (New York, 1968). On the anti-imperialists see Robert L. Beisner, *Twelve against Empire* (1968; rev. ed. 1985), and Christopher Lasch, "The Anti-Imperialists, the Philippines, and the Inequality of Man," in *The World of Nations: Reflections on American History, Politics, and Culture* (New York, 1974), 70–79. For international perspectives see Philip Darby, *Three Faces of Imperialism: British and American Approaches to Asia and Africa, 1870–1970* (New Haven, Conn., 1987), and Paul Kennedy, *The Rise and Fall of the Great Powers* (New York, 1987).

of managing foreign crises. The nation that went to war with Spain and became a great power did so in the process of grappling with the turbulence and uncertainty of modernization. The United States moved without clear purpose into the age of empire.[16]

A more vehement attack on the Williams thesis came from James A. Field Jr. He argued that nearly all accounts of American foreign policy in the 1890s suffered from serious faults: the adoption of a strictly rational explanation of events and a rejection of chance; the use of overly broad terms to describe complex situations; an American-centered, ethnocentric treatment of diplomacy; and inattention to factors crucial in determining foreign policy, including "time, distance, costs, [and] technological feasibility." Rather than grapple with such difficulties, Field charged, the Williams school preferred to begin with perceptions of American immorality in the twentieth century and then read them back into the past with "false continuities and imputations of sin." Field rejected such explanations of American imperialism, as well as those based on the influence of Darwinian theory (à la May), the psychic or cultural crisis of the 1890s (à la Hofstadter and Linderman), the rise of grand strategic theory (à la LaFeber), and the importance of the China market (à la McCormick). In their place Field proposed his own set of hypotheses. The new American navy that came into existence in the late nineteenth century was a defensive answer to European developments. The search for bases was a response to the strategic problems of the proposed canal linking the Atlantic and Pacific oceans. The rapid deployment of the American navy headed by Admiral Dewey in the Pacific was largely a result of the rapidity of communication made possible by new cables linking nations and continents. Democratic sympathy for the Cubans may have aroused Americans to confront Spain, but it was Dewey's victory that focused public attention on the Far East; only then did an avalanche of publicity for the advantages of empire descend upon the American people. "Imperialism," according to Field, "was the product of Dewey's victory."[17]

Other critics of the Williams–LaFeber interpretation of the origins of American imperialism added to these arguments. Paul A. Varg, for example, determined that China was not of major importance to the American policy officials whom he studied. Even Caribbean policy, which did occupy the attention of these officials, was never pursued solely for economic considerations. Moreover, whatever interests — economic, strategic, ideological — drove policy, most policymakers were, like most Americans, fairly insular; few ever believed that the nation's welfare hinged on developments in other parts of the world. And finally, every American intervention, actual or proposed, elicited strong opposition from other elites in business, politics, and

---

[16]Gerald F. Linderman, *The Mirror of War: American Society and the Spanish American War* (Ann Arbor, Mich., 1974).

[17]James A. Field Jr., "American Imperialism: The Worst Chapter in Almost Any Book," *American Historical Review* 83 (June 1978): 644–83, which includes rejoinders from Walter LaFeber and Robert L. Beisner. For a somewhat different rejection of the Williams school, see Richard E. Welch Jr., *Response to Imperialism: The United States and the Philippine-American War, 1899–1902* (Chapel Hill, N.C., 1979).

the press, and even occasionally from the broader public. Although the United States did become a world power it was not because of any master plan designed to control the destiny of other nations.[18]

Some historians challenged the very idea that imperialism necessarily inflicted harm. Stanley Lebergott, after noting the relative insignificance of American foreign investment in Latin America from 1890 to 1929, denied that it worked to the detriment of either workers or landowners in the nations that were affected. Indeed, American foreign investments increased the income of workers and peasants by expanding the need for labor, and improved land values by opening American markets to native products. Lebergott conceded that American business enterprise sometimes threatened the vested interests of native businesses and sometimes created rivalries among entrepreneurial groups. But this sort of conflict was not a struggle between U.S. imperialism and Latin American freedom-fighters. It was rather between two capitalist groups, one native and the other foreign, each fighting over the spoils of progress.[19]

Lebergott's effort to acquit imperialism of the most grievous charges against it runs into great difficulty. While critics of the Williams-LaFeber thesis mount strong arguments for the salience of noneconomic influences on the shaping of foreign policy, those who deny the baneful consequences of imperial interventions strain credibility. By the 1980s, some scholars managed to endorse arguments for broad sociocultural causes of the war with Spain, such as that of Linderman, with a sharp acknowledgment of the horrors of imperial domination. Thus Stuart Creighton Miller carefully narrated the entry of U.S. forces into the Philippines and their awful transformation into an army of occupation and conquest. Although cautious about exaggerating the "tragic parallels" between the Philippine and Vietnam wars, Miller insists that a fateful line of descent connects Cuba and the Philippines in the 1890s to Vietnam in the 1960s.[20] Similarly, Walter LaFeber assembled much evidence to support the argument that the foreign policy forged in the 1890s continued throughout the twentieth century to shape American policy in Central America and the Caribbean. Although he tells a complex story, by the end few readers can doubt that over the course of the century the United States wreaked great havoc among its neighbors to the south.[21]

In the 1980s and 1990s, historians placed new emphasis on ideological and cultural — especially racial — determinants of foreign policy. Recalling

[18]Paul A. Varg, "The United States as a World Power, 1900–1917: Myth or Reality?" in John Braeman, Robert H. Bremner, and David Brody, eds., *Twentieth-Century American Foreign Policy* (Columbus, Ohio, 1971), and *The Making of a Myth: The United States and China, 1897–1912* (East Lansing, Mich., 1968). An early work in this line is Howard K. Beale, *Theodore Roosevelt and the Rise of America to World Power* (Baltimore, 1956).

[19]Stanley Lebergott, "The Returns to U.S. Imperialism, 1890–1929," *Journal of Economic History* 40 (June 1980): 229–49; a level-headed review of some of these issues is David M. Pletcher, "Rhetoric and Results: A Pragmatic View of Economic Expansionism, 1865–1898," *Diplomatic History* 5 (Spring 1981): 93–104.

[20]Stuart Creighton Miller, *"Benevolent Assimilation": The American Conquest of the Philippines, 1899–1903* (New Haven, Conn., 1982).

[21]Walter LaFeber, *Inevitable Revolutions: The United States in Central America* (New York, 1983).

Linderman's discussion of "images of enemy and ally," Michael Hunt argues that racial supremacy has been a "core idea," inextricably intertwined with the idea of "national greatness," and strongly determinative of American foreign policy since the nineteenth century.[22] Focusing on the cultural components of imperial domination, Emily S. Rosenberg has argued that the ideology of "liberal-developmentalism" underlay a century of efforts to spread the "American dream of high technology and mass consumption." However rationalized in terms of "open doors" and "free markets," the policy that grew out of this ideology was really about "privately owned" — and distinctly American owned — markets.[23] Finally, a few historians have brought gender analysis to the interpretation of American imperialism. Mary A. Renda, for example, has shown that habits and ideologies of racial and gender dominance shaped American policies, and even more practices, in occupied Haiti. She also suggests that experience in Haiti challenged and subtly changed some American attitudes.[24] Kristin L. Hoganson shows that the "coercive power of gender" pushed leaders and citizens into a war for American "masculinity."[25]

These revisionist historians depart in significant ways from Williams's original thesis, but they reinforce the more general conclusion of his work that the United States was — and is — an expansive power, seeking advantage and even hegemony in the world of great-power competition. Although they have learned from Williams's critics, they in no way portray the United States as a reluctant crusader for liberal democracy in a violent and alien world. Especially those who approach the history of American expansion from the perspective of foreign nations tell a tale of aggression, domination, and exploitation. That tale appears, for example, in the work of Louis A. Perez Jr. not so much as a history of U.S. policy but as a history of Cuba and the Caribbean trying to live within the orbit of U.S. hegemony. Thus, in Perez's provocative interpretation, the United States intervened in 1898 not to support the Cuban independence movement but to defeat it. Having accomplished that, the United States turned Cuba into a compliant plantation (and later vacation) colony.[26]

---

[22]Michael H. Hunt, *Ideology and U.S. Foreign Policy* (New Haven, Conn., 1987).

[23]Emily S. Rosenberg, *Spreading the American Dream: American Economic and Cultural Expansion, 1890–1945* (New York, 1982); see also Daniel F. Headrick, *The Tentacles of Progress: Technology Transfer in the Age of Imperialism* (1988), and Robert W. Rydell, *All the World's a Fair: Visions of Empire at American International Expositions, 1876–1916* (Chicago, 1984).

[24]Mary A. Renda, *Taking Haiti: Military Intervention and the Culture of U.S. Imperialism, 1915–1940* (Chapel Hill, N.C., 2000).

[25]Kristin L. Hoganson, *Fighting for American Manhood: How Gender Politics Provoked the Spanish-American and Philippine-American Wars* (New Haven, Conn., 1998). See also Sarah Watts, *Rough Rider in the White House: Theodore Roosevelt and the Politics of Desire* (Chicago, 2003); a provocative look at competing masculinities in U.S. imperial encounters is Michelle Ann Stephens, *Black Empire: The Masculine Global Imaginary of Caribbean Intellectuals, 1914–1962* (Durham, N.C., 2005).

[26]Louis A. Perez Jr., *Cuba between Empires* (Pittsburgh, Pa., 1982); *Cuba under the Platt Amendment, 1902–1934* (Pittsburgh, Pa., 1986); *Cuba and the United States: Ties of Singular Intimacy* (Athens, Ga., 1990); *The War of 1898: The United States and Cuba in History and Historiography* (Chapel Hill, N.C., 1998). See also his "Intervention, Hegemony, and Dependency: The United States in the Circum-Caribbean, 1898–1980," *Pacific Historical Review* 51 (May 1982): 165–94.

More recently, scholars who specialize in fields other than U.S. history, or who adopt an explicitly transnational approach, have shown even more persuasively how American imperial ventures affect the colonized and are affected by them. They insist that America's democratic pretensions sometimes camouflaged, sometimes intermixed with a complex of economic and ideological motives. According to Julian Go, there was nothing distinctively American or democratic about imperial administrations in the Caribbean and the Pacific. Rather, Americans reacted pragmatically to local circumstances, avoiding like other colonizers the more expensive options of direct rule and force whenever possible. Even in formal colonies, success required understanding and partially accommodating local demands. Thus, in the Philippines and Puerto Rico, where "westernized" elites already deployed the discourses of constitutionalism and rights, imperial rule meant "tutelage" in democracy; in Guam and Samoa (and also in the Muslim provinces of the Philippines), where traditional leaders held sway, accommodating to undemocratic forms of governance seemed best.[27] Alongside resistance from below, Go posits that a "chain of empire" linked and influenced both colonized with colonizer. It linked administrator with superiors back home, metropolitan political leaders with constituents who asserted a range of economic, ideological, and religious interests in the colony. Pulled and pushed in many directions, from above, below, and from all sides, colonial administrators enacted no grand strategy, no tutelary democratic script, no civilizing mission.[28]

U.S. relations with Mexico reveal a similar record of democratic ideology meeting the seductions, as well as the trials and errors, of imperial control. In the case of Mexico, American intervention encountered one of the great revolutions of the twentieth century. In the process, according to historian John Mason Hart, policymakers set the course for U.S. relations with non-Western nations over the next century. They tested tactics such as "partnerships with local elites, cooperative arrangements among multinationals, particularly in the area of finance, and interventions ranging from covert operations . . . to outright invasions. . . ." Because U.S. behavior toward Mexico was governed by economic and policy elites for whom "access to strategic resources" always trumped democratic ideology, experience in Mexico taught policymakers to tolerate "oppressive tyrants" in the name of an alternative ideology of capitalist development. Because local elites enriched themselves at the American trough, sometimes at the expense of their fellow citizens, Mexican political history has been marked by a series

---

[27]Julian Go, "The Provinciality of American Empire: 'Liberal Exceptionalism' and U.S. Colonial Rule, 1898–1912," *Comparative Studies in Society and History* 49 (2007): 74–108; see also Lanny Thompson, "The Imperial Republic: A Comparison of Insular Territories under U.S. Dominion after 1898," *Pacific Historical Review* 71 (2002): 535–74.

[28]Julian Go, "Chains of Empire, Projects of State: Political Education and U.S. Colonial Rule in Puerto Rico and the Philippines," *Comparative Studies in Society and History* 42 (2000): 333–62. A recent full-scale study of American rule in the Philippines is Paul A. Kramer, *The Blood of Government: Race, Empire, the United States, and the Philippines* (Chapel Hill, N.C., 2006). Other scholars note the exceptionality of "liberal empire," without underestimating the misery it wrought: on Latin America, for example, see Greg Grandin, *Empire's Workshop: Latin America, the United States, and the Rise of Imperialism* (New York, 2006).

of crises pitting elites against poorer masses still inspired by their revolutionary past. In the end, the methods of U.S. imperial control never proved permanently effective, always required correction and improvisation, and often encountered resistance both at home and abroad.[29]

Several recent books about U.S.-Mexico relations focus less on U.S. imperial impulses and more on the competitive and revolutionary dynamics of the early-twentieth-century international system. Friedrich Katz places U.S.-Mexico relations in the context of great-power strategy in the era of World War I. Just as the United States sought advantage in Mexico, he argues, so did Germany and Britain try to limit upheaval or profit from it in revolutionary Ireland and India, the Hapsburg and Turkish empires, and in late Czarist and Bolshevik Russia.[30] Daniela Spenser exploited archives in the former Soviet Union, Mexico, and the United States to show that Mexican governments allowed both Germany and revolutionary Russia to woo them, mostly to acquire leverage against their northern neighbor. She also shows that despite their mutual revolutionary and anti-imperialist credentials, the Russians alienated Mexico because they never considered Mexicans true revolutionaries, and also because they spurred Mexican Communists to destabilize the country. By the end of the 1920s, with a conservative government in Mexico City, the Bolsheviks were out and the United States was supplying arms to help the government put down rebels. While the economic power of the United States continued to weigh heavily, Mexican nationalism made the intrusion of American power always dangerous and the negotiation of bilateral policies always tricky.[31]

In studying the origins of American empire, scholars will continue to raise many of the same questions asked by their predecessors for over three-quarters of a century. Did the United States go to war with Spain to resolve basic contradictions within its economic and social systems? Was the acquisition of an overseas empire a cause or a consequence of war? To what degree did moral, religious, and humanitarian sentiments play a role in the diplomacy of the 1890s and in the creation of a "liberal empire" thereafter? To what extent was American foreign policy a response to the diplomacy of other nations and events beyond its control? Did business and strategic thinkers direct the U.S. thrust toward world power status or did the nation stumble into its new status without plan or conscious purpose? Even if American intentions were benign, mixed, or confused, to what extent were the consequences of American policy harmful to those who experienced it not as expansion but as intrusion? As long as Americans continue to debate the proper role of their nation in world affairs, the events of the 1890s and the early years of the twentieth century will continue to occupy the attention of historians and citizens.

---

[29] John Mason Hart, *Empire and Revolution: The Americans in Mexico since the Civil War* (Berkeley, Calif., 2002), 5, 502.

[30] Friedrich Katz, *The Secret War in Mexico: Europe, the United States, and the Mexican Revolution* (Chicago, 1981).

[31] Daniela Spenser, *The Impossible Triangle: Mexico, Soviet Russia, and the United States in the 1920s* (Durham, N.C., 1999).

WALTER LAFEBER

from That "Splendid Little War" in Historical Perspective   [1968]

WALTER LAFEBER (1933–) retired in 2006 as Marie Underhill Noll Professor and Steven Wiesse Presidential Teaching Fellow at Cornell University. He is the author of *The New Empire: An Interpretation of American Expansionism, 1860–1898* (1963), *Inevitable Revolutions: The United States in Central America* (2nd ed., 1993), *America, Russia, and the Cold War, 1945–1966* (8th ed., 1997), and *The Clash: A History of U.S.–Japan Relations* (1997).

The "Splendid Little War" of 1898, as Secretary of State John Hay termed it at the time, is rapidly losing its splendor for those concerned with American foreign policy. . . . Over the past decade few issues in the country's diplomatic history have aroused academics more than the causes of the Spanish-American War, and in the last several years the argument has become not merely academic, but a starting point in the debate over how the United States evolved into a great power, and more particularly how Americans got involved in the maelstrom of Asian nationalism. The line from the conquest of the Philippines in 1898 to the attempted pacification of Vietnam in 1968 is not straight, but it is quite traceable, and if Frederick Jackson Turner was correct when he observed in the 1890s that "The aim of history, then, is to know the elements of the present by understanding what came into the present from the past," the causes of the war in 1898 demand analysis from our present viewpoint.

Historians have offered four general interpretations to explain these causes. First, the war has been traced to a general impulse for war on the part of American public opinion. This interpretation has been illustrated in a famous cartoon showing President William McKinley, in the bonnet and dress of a little old lady, trying to sweep back huge waves marked "Congress" and "public opinion," with a very small broom. The "yellow journalism" generated by the Hearst-Pulitzer rivalry supposedly both created and reflected this sentiment for war. A sophisticated and useful version of this interpretation has been advanced by Richard Hofstadter. Granting the importance of the Hearst-Pulitzer struggle, he has asked why these newspaper titans were able to exploit public opinion. Hofstadter has concluded that psychological dilemmas arising out of the depression of the 1890s made Americans react somewhat irrationally because they were uncertain, frightened, and consequently open to exploitation by men who would show them how to cure their frustrations through overseas adventures. In other words, the giddy minds of the 1890s could be quieted by foreign quarrels.

"That 'Splendid Little War' in Historical Perspective," by Walter LaFeber, from *Texas Quarterly* 11, no. 4 (1968): 89–98. Copyright © by the University of Texas Press. All rights reserved.

A second interpretation argues that the United States went to war for humanitarian reasons, that is, to free the Cubans from the horrors of Spanish policies and to give the Cubans democratic institutions. That this initial impulse resulted within ten months in an American protectorate over Cuba and Puerto Rico, annexation of the Philippines, and American participation in quarrels on the mainland of Asia itself, is explained as accidental, or, more familiarly, as done in a moment of "aberration" on the part of American policy-makers.

A third interpretation emphasizes the role of several Washington officials who advocated a "Large Policy" of conquering a vast colonial empire in the Caribbean and Western Pacific. By shrewd maneuvering, these few imperialists pushed the vacillating McKinley and a confused nation into war. Senator Henry Cabot Lodge, of Massachusetts, Captain Alfred Thayer Mahan, of the U.S. Navy, and Theodore Roosevelt, assistant Secretary of the Navy in 1897–1898, are usually named as the leaders of the "Large Policy" contingent.

A fourth interpretation believes the economic drive carried the nation into war. This drive emanated from the rapid industrialization which characterized American society after the 1840s. The immediate link between this industrialization and the war of 1898 was the economic depression which afflicted the nation in the quarter-century after 1873. Particularly important were the 1893–1897 years when Americans endured the worst of the plunge. Government and business leaders, who were both intelligent and rational, believed an oversupply of goods created the depression. They finally accepted war as a means of opening overseas markets in order to alleviate domestic distress caused by the overproduction. For thirty years the economic interpretation dominated historians' views of the war, but in 1936 Professor Julius Pratt conclusively demonstrated that business journals did not want war in the early months of 1898. He argued instead the "Large Policy" explanation, and from that time to the present, Professor Pratt's interpretation has been pre-eminent in explaining the causes of the conflict.

As I shall argue in a moment, the absence of economic factors in causing the war has been considerably exaggerated. At this point, however, a common theme which unites the first three interpretations should be emphasized. Each of the three deals with a superficial aspect of American life; each is peculiar to 1898, and none is rooted in the structure, the bedrock, of the nation's history. This theme is important, for it means that if the results of the war were distasteful and disadvantageous (and on this historians do largely agree because of the divisive problems which soon arose in the Philippines and Cuba), those misfortunes were endemic to episodes unique to 1898. The peculiarities of public sentiment or the Hearst-Pulitzer rivalry, for example, have not reoccurred; the wide-spread humanitarian desire to help Cubans has been confined to 1898 and the banding together of Lodge, Mahan, and Roosevelt to fight for "Large Policies" of the late 1890s was never repeated by the three men. Conspiracy theories, moreover, seldom explain history satisfactorily.

The fourth interpretation has different implications. It argues that if the economic was the primary drive toward war, criticism of that war must begin not with irrational factors or flights of humanitarianism or a few stereotyped figures, but with the basic structure of the American system.

United States foreign policy, after all, is concerned primarily with the nation's domestic system and only secondarily with the systems of other nations. American diplomatic history might be defined as the study of how United States relations with other nations are used to insure the survival and increasing prosperity of the American system. . . .

When viewed within this matrix, the diplomatic events of the 1890s are no longer aberrations or the results of conspiracies and drift; American policymakers indeed grabbed greatness with both hands. As for accident or chance, they certainly exist in history, but become more meaningful when one begins with J. B. Bury's definition of "chance": "The valuable collision of two or more independent chains of causes." The most fruitful approach to the war of 1898 might be from the inside out (from the domestic to the foreign), and by remembering that chance is "the valuable collision of two or more independent chains of causes."

Three of these "chains" can be identified: the economic crisis of the 1890s which caused extensive and dangerous maladjustments in American society; the opportunities which suddenly opened in Asia after 1895 and in the Caribbean and the Pacific in 1898, opportunities which officials began to view as poultices, if not cure-alls, for the illnesses at home; and a growing partnership between business and government which reached its nineteenth-century culmination in the person of William McKinley. In April 1898, these "chains" had a "valuable collision" and war resulted.

The formation of the first chain is the great success story of American history. Between 1850 and 1910 the average manufacturing plant in the country multiplied its capital thirty-nine times, its number of wage-earners nearly seven times, and the value of its output by more than nineteen times. . . . The United States traded more in international markets than any nation except Great Britain.

But the most accelerated period of this development, 1873–1898, was actually twenty-five years of boom hidden in twenty-five years of bust. That quarter-century endured the longest and worst depression in the nation's history. After brief and unsatisfactory recoveries in the mid-1880s and early 1890s, the economy reached bottom in 1893. Unparalleled social and economic disasters struck. One out of every six laborers was unemployed, with most of the remainder existing on substandard wages; not only weak firms but many companies with the best credit ratings were forced to close their doors; the unemployed slept in the streets; riots erupted in Brooklyn, California, and points in between, as in the calamitous Pullman Strike in Chicago; Coxey's Army of broken farmers and unemployed laborers made their famous march on Washington; and the Secretary of State, Walter Quentin Gresham, remarked privately in 1894 that he saw "symptoms of revolution" appearing. Federal troops were dispatched to Chicago and other urban areas, including a cordon which guarded the Federal Treasury building in New York City.

Faced with the prospect of revolution and confronted with an economy that had almost ground to a stop, American businessmen and political officials faced alternative policies: they could attempt to re-examine and reorient the economic system, making radical modifications in the means of distribution and particularly the distribution of wealth; or they could look for new physical frontiers, following the historic tendency to increase production and then ferreting out new markets so the surplus, which the nation supposedly was unable to consume, could be sold elsewhere and Americans then put back to work on the production lines. . . .

Some business firms tried to find such security by squashing competitors. Extremely few, however, searched for such policies as a federal income tax. Although such a tax narrowly passed through Congress in 1894, the Supreme Court declared it unconstitutional within a year and the issue would not be resurrected for another seventeen years. As a result, business and political leaders accepted the solution which was traditional, least threatening to their own power, and (apparently) required the least risk: new markets. . . .

This consensus included farmers and the labor movement among others, for these interests were no more ingenious in discovering new solutions than were businessmen. . . . The agrarians acted out of a long and successful tradition, for they had sought overseas customers since the first tobacco surplus in Virginia three hundred and fifty years before. Farmers initially framed the expansionist arguments and over three centuries created the context for the growing consensus on the desirability of foreign markets, a consensus which businessmen and others would utilize in the 1890s. . . .

Industrialists observed that export charts demonstrated the American economy to be depending more upon industrial than agrarian exports. To allow industrial goods to be fully competitive in the world market, however, labor costs would have to be minimal, and cheap bread meant sacrificing the farmers. Fully comprehending this argument, agrarians reacted bitterly. They nevertheless continued searching for their own overseas markets, agreeing with the industrialist that the traditional method of discovering new outlets provided the key to prosperity, individualism, and status. . . .

The political conflict which shattered the 1890s revolved less around the question of whether conservatives could carry out a class solution than the question of which class would succeed in carrying out a conservative solution. This generalization remains valid even when the American labor movement is examined for its response to the alternatives posed. This movement, primarily comprised of the newly-formed American Federation of Labor, employed less than 3 percent of the total number of employed workers in nonfarm occupations. In its own small sphere of influence, its membership largely consisted of skilled workers living in the

East. The AFL was not important in the West or South, where the major discontent seethed. Although Samuel Gompers was known by some of the more faint-hearted as a "socialist," the AFL's founder never dramatized any radical solutions for the restructuring of the economy. He was concerned with obtaining more money, better hours, and improved working conditions for the Federation's members. Gompers refused, moreover, to use direct political action to obtain these benefits, content to negotiate within the corporate structure which the businessman had created. The AFL simply wanted more, and when overseas markets seemed to be a primary source of benefits, Gompers did not complain. . . .

The first "chain of causes" was marked by a consensus on the need to find markets overseas. Fortunately for the advocates of this policy, another "chain," quite complementary to the first, began to form beyond American borders. By the mid-1890s, American merchants, missionaries, and ship captains had been profiting from Asian markets for more than a century. Between 1895 and 1900, however, the United States for the first time became a mover-and-pusher in Asian affairs.

In 1895 Japan defeated China in a brief struggle that now appears to be one of the most momentous episodes in the nineteenth century. The Japanese emerged as the major Asian power, the Chinese suddenly seemed to be incapable of defending their honor or existence, Chinese nationalism began its peculiar path to the 1960s, and European powers which had long lusted after Asian markets now seized a golden opportunity. Russia, Germany, France, and ultimately Great Britain initiated policies designed to carve China and Manchuria into spheres of influence. Within a period of months, the Asian mainland suddenly became the scene of international power politics at its worst and most explosive.

The American reaction to these events has been summarized recently by Professor Thomas McCormick: "The conclusion of the Sino-Japanese War left Pandora's box wide open, but many Americans mistook it for the Horn of Plenty." . . . Now, just at the moment when key interest groups agreed that overseas markets could be the salvation of the 1890s crisis, China was almost miraculously opening its doors to the glutted American factories and farms. United States trade with China jumped significantly after 1895, particularly in the critical area of manufactures; by 1899 manufactured products accounted for more than 90 per cent of the nation's exports to the Chinese, a quadrupling of the amount sent in 1895. In their moment of need, Americans had apparently discovered a Horn of Plenty.

But, of course, it was Pandora's box. The ills which escaped from the box were threefold. Least important for the 1890s, a nascent Chinese nationalism appeared. During the next quarter-century, the United States attempted to minimize the effects of this nationalism either by cooperating with Japan or European powers to isolate and weaken the Chinese, or by siding with the most conservative groups within the nationalist movement. Americans also faced the competition of European and Japanese products, but they were nevertheless confident in the power of their newly-tooled industrial powerhouse. Given a "fair field and no favor," as the Secretary of State phrased the wish in 1900, Americans would undersell and defeat any competitors. But could fair fields and no favors be guaranteed? Within their recently-created spheres of influence European powers began to grant themselves trade preferences, thus effectively shutting out American competition. In 1897, the American business community and the newly-installed administration of William McKinley began to counter these threats.

The partnership between businessmen and politicians, in this case the McKinley administration, deserves emphasis, for if the businessman hoped to exploit Asian markets he required the aid of the politician. Americans could compete against British or Russian manufacturers in Asia, but they could not compete against, say, a Russian manufacturer who could turn to his government and through pressure exerted by that government on Chinese officials receive a prize railroad contract or banking concession. United States businessmen could only compete against such business-government coalitions if Washington officials helped. Only then would the field be fair and the favors equalized. To talk of utilizing American "rugged individualism" and a free enterprise philosophy in the race for the China market in the 1890s was silly. There consequently emerged in American policy-making a classic example of the business community and the government grasping hands and, marching shoulder to shoulder, leading the United States to its destiny of being a major power on a far-Eastern frontier. As one high Republican official remarked in the mid-1890s: "diplomacy is the management of international business."

William McKinley fully understood the need for such a partnership. He had grown to political maturity during the 1870s when, as one Congressman remarked, "The House of Representatives was like an auction room where more valuable considerations were disposed of under the speaker's hammer than in any other place on earth." . . . The new Chief Executive believed there was nothing necessarily manifest about Manifest Destiny in American history, and his administration was the first in modern American history which so systematically and completely committed itself to helping businessmen, farmers, laborers, and missionaries in solving their problems in an industrializing, supposedly frontierless America. . . .

Often characterized as a creature of his campaign manager Mark Hanna, or as having, in the famous but severely unjust words of Theodore Roosevelt, the backbone of a chocolate eclair, McKinley was, as Henry Adams and others fully understood, a master of men. McKinley was never pushed into a policy he did not want to accept. Elihu Root, probably the best mind and most acute observer who served in the McKinley cabinets, commented that on most important matters the President had his ideas fixed, but would convene the Cabinet, direct the members toward his own conclusions, and thereby allow the Cabinet to think it had formulated the policy. In responding to the problems and opportunities in China, however, McKinley's power to exploit that situation was limited by events in the Caribbean.

In 1895 revolution had broken out in Cuba. By 1897 Americans were becoming increasingly belligerent on this issue for several reasons: more than $50,000,000 of United States investments on the island were endangered; Spaniards were treating some Cubans inhumanely; the best traditions of the Monroe Doctrine had long dictated that a European in the Caribbean was a sty in the eye of any red-blooded American; and, finally, a number of Americans, not only Lodge, Roosevelt, and Mahan, understood the strategic and political relationship of Cuba to a proposed isthmian canal. Such a canal would provide a short-cut to the west coast of Latin America as well as to the promised markets of Asia. Within six months after assuming office, McKinley demanded that the island be pacified or the United States would take a "course of action which the time and the transcendent emergency may demand." Some Spanish reforms followed, but in January 1898, new revolts wracked Havana and a month later the "Maine" dramatically sank to the bottom of Havana harbor.

McKinley confronted the prospect of immediate war. Only two restraints appeared. First, a war might lead to the annexation of Cuba, and the multitude of problems (including racial) which had destroyed Spanish authority would be dumped on the United States. Neither the President nor his close advisers wanted to leap into the quicksands of noncontiguous, colonial empire. The business community comprised a second restraining influence. By mid-1897 increased exports, which removed part of the agricultural and industrial glut, began to extricate the country from its quarter-century of turmoil. Finally seeing light at the end of a long and treacherous tunnel, businessmen did not want the requirements of a war economy to jeopardize the growing prosperity.

These two restraints explain why the United States did not go to war in 1897, and the removal of these restraints indicates why war occurred in April 1898. The first problem disappeared because McKinley and his advisers entertained no ideas of warring for colonial empire in the Caribbean. After the war Cuba would be freed from Spain and then ostensibly returned to the Cubans to govern. The United States would retain a veto power over the more important policy decisions made on the island. McKinley discovered a classic solution in which the United States enjoyed the power over, but supposedly little of the responsibility for, the Cubans.

The second restraint disappeared in late March 1898, exactly at the time of McKinley's decision to send the final ultimatum to Madrid. The timing is crucial. Professor Pratt observed in 1936 that the business periodicals began to change their antiwar views in mid-March 1898, but he did not elaborate upon this point. The change is significant and confirms the advice McKinley received from a trusted political adviser in New York City who cabled on March 23 that the larger corporations would welcome war. The business journal and their readers were beginning to realize that the bloody struggle in Cuba and the resulting inability of the United States to operate at full-speed in Asian affairs more greatly endangered economic recovery than would a war.

McKinley's policies in late March manifested these changes. This does not mean that the business community manipulated the President, or that he was repaying those businessmen who had played vital roles in his election in 1896. Nor does it mean that McKinley thought the business community was forcing his hand or circumscribing his policies in late March. The opinions and policies of the President and the business community had been hammered out in the furnace of a terrible depression and the ominous changes in Asia. McKinley and pivotal businessmen emerged from these unforgettable experiences sharing a common conclusion: the nation's economy increasingly depended upon overseas markets, including the whole of China; that to develop these markets not only a business-government partnership but also tranquillity was required; and, finally, however paradoxical it might seem, tranquillity could be insured only through war against Spain. Not for the first or last time, Americans believed that to have peace they would have to wage war. Some, including McKinley, moved on to a final point. War, if properly conducted, could result in a few select strategic bases in the Pacific (such as Hawaii, Guam, and Manila) which would provide the United States with potent starting-blocks in the race for Asian markets. McKinley sharply distinguished between controlling such bases and trying to rule formally over an extensive territorial empire. In the development of the "chains of causes" the dominant theme was the economic, although not economic in the narrow sense. As discussed in the 1890s, business recovery carried most critical political and social implications.

Some historians argue that McKinley entered the war in confusion and annexed the Philippines in a moment of aberration. They delight in quoting the President's announcement to a group of Methodist missionaries that he decided to annex the Philippines one night when after praying he heard a mysterious voice. Most interesting, however, is not that the President heard a reassuring voice, but how the voice phrased its advice. The voice evidently outlined the points to be considered; in any case, McKinley numbered them in order, demonstrating, perhaps, that either he, the voice, or both had given some thought to putting the policy factors in neat and logical order. The second point is of particular importance: "that we could not turn them [the Philippines] over to France or Germany — our commercial rivals in the Orient — that would be bad business and discreditable. . . . " Apparently everyone who had been through the 1890s knew the dangers of "bad business." Even voices.

Interpretations which depend upon mass opinion, humanitarianism, and "Large Policy" advocates do not satisfactorily explain the causes of the war. Neither, however, does Mr. Dooley's famous one-sentence definition of American imperialism in 1898: "Hands acrost th' sea an' into somewan's pocket." The problem of American expansion is more complicated and historically rooted than that flippancy indicates. George Eliot once observed, "The happiest nations, like the happiest women, have no history." The United States, however, endured in the nineteenth century a history of growing industrialism, supposedly closing physical frontiers, rapid urbanization, unequal distribution of wealth, and an over-dependence upon export trade. These historical currents clashed in the 1890s. The result was chaos and fear, then war and empire.

In 1898 McKinley and the business community wanted peace, but they also sought benefits which only a war could provide. Viewed from the per-spective of the 1960s, the Spanish-American conflict can no longer be viewed as only a "splendid little war." It was a war to preserve the Ameri-can system.

GERALD F. LINDERMAN

from The Image of Enemy and Ally   [1974]

GERALD F. LINDERMAN (1934–) is professor of history emeritus at the Uni-versity of Michigan. He is the author of *Mirror of War: American Society and the Spanish-American War* (1974), *Embattled Courage: The Experience of Combat in the American Civil War* (1987), and *The World within War: America's Combat Experience in World War II* (1997).

In nineteenth-century America . . . [n]o people fared worse in the schoolbooks than the Spanish. In the American view, Spanish history was a syllabus of barbarism that left both participants and their progeny morally misshapen. Such an image, moreover, did not exist only as an intellectual abstraction. With so few alternative sources of information available, it often set the lines of political debate. In the prelude to the Spanish-American War those who wished to resist American intervention in Cuba were handicapped by their inability to say anything in defense of the Spanish character. Those who urged American participation had the easier task of demonstrating that Spanish behavior was the simple exten-sion of that Spanish history every American had memorized from his reader.

Americans at first hardly distinguished the image of the Cuban from that of the Spaniard. As anger against Spain mounted, however, it became necessary for them to differentiate, to convert to ally the enemy of their enemy. This was accomplished, but not through any objective examination of the conditions or attributes of the Cuban people. Instead, Americans of public consequence employed various and often contradictory histori-cal analogies which, with scant reference to the Cubans themselves, had by 1898 persuaded most Americans that the Cubans were a moral, en-lightened, and kindred race. The first physical contacts of American with Cuban and Spaniard would test these images of good and evil.

In mid-December 1895 President Grover Cleveland and Secretary of State Richard Olney precipitated a diplomatic crisis over a fifty-year-old boundary dispute between Venezuela and Great Britain's colony of Guiana. Angry at London's rejection of earlier Washington suggestions that the controversy be submitted to arbitration, the president announced to Congress on December 17 his decision to appoint an American commission to determine the "true divisional line" between the two territories. Once the boundary was set, Cleveland warned, "it will . . . be the duty of the United States to resist, by every means in its power, as a willful aggression upon its rights and interests, the appropriation by Great Britain of any lands or the exercise of governmental jurisdiction over any territory which . . . we have determined of right belongs to Venezuela." The United States, charging Britain with violating the Monroe Doctrine, threatened war. . . .

Of special concern here are the terms employed by Americans in debating the meaning of Britain's behavior.

Joseph Pulitzer — in 1864 an emaciated German-Hungarian immigrant without resources save for his own will to succeed, thirty years later the powerful publisher of the New York *World* whose extraordinary energies had already cracked the frail shell of his body — was one of those who led public opposition to Cleveland's policy. The president's bludgeon diplomacy, he told the *World*'s half-million readers, was "a grave blunder"; an Anglo-American war would be unpardonable folly. Into his antiwar editorials Pulitzer wove three themes. There was in the Venezuelan dispute, he insisted, no possible menace to the United States. He further denied Cleveland's contention that the controversy challenged, or that its outcome could affect, the validity of the Monroe Doctrine. Finally, he cautioned against what he judged to be the nation's state: "Let the war idea once dominate the minds of the American people and war will come whether there is cause for it or not" — an interesting hypothesis that Pulitzer himself did much to verify two years later.

Laced through these arguments were the lineaments of an image of a Britain benevolently disposed to American interests, of an admirable people[,] friend rather than foe. England was a "friendly and kindred nation," "the great naval and commercial and banking nation of the world" whose political system was "essentially . . . of the people, more quickly and completely responsible to the popular will as expressed in the elections than our government is." . . .

In short, who the English were determined what the English did. By definition, kindred peoples would not harm one another's vital interests in Venezuela or anywhere else. War was incomprehensible when Anglo-American ties meant that it must be a species of civil war.

Supporters of the Cleveland-Olney ultimatum wove into their attack on the English a very different image. Henry Cabot Lodge charged that the British government, having already hemmed in the United States with a fortified line in the Pacific, was forging another ring in the Caribbean. London had recently fortified Santa Lucia, Trinidad, and Jamaica. The

South American mainland was the next, but not the final, link. "If . . . [Britain] can do it successfully in Venezuela she can do it in Mexico or Cuba; if she can do it other nations can also."

Lodge found nothing remarkable in such notions of British conspiracy. It was the thing to expect of a people no less treacherous and hostile to American interests than any other people. As he earlier told the Senate, "Since we parted from England her statesmen have never failed to recognize that in men speaking her language, and of her own race she was to find her most formidable rivals. She has always opposed, thwarted, and sought to injure us." . . .

Did England's behavior constitute a threat to the United States? One's answer had less to do with London's behavior in this particular controversy, still less with what was transpiring on the banks of the Orinoco, than on the image of England that Cleveland's message summoned to mind. The availability of alternative images set the lines of the American debate.

In a valuable study Ruth Miller Elson has suggested the influence of the stereotyped figures of foreign nationalities so prominent in the grammar-school readers one hundred years ago. The belief that specific personality traits inhere in all members of designated nationality groups is still today a part of our intellectual baggage, but several factors added to the tyranny of nineteenth-century national images. Children, spending on average far fewer years in school, were deeply stamped by the long passages they were compelled to memorize. Moreover, American small-town life offered few of the experiences that today render rigid national stereotypes vulnerable to a more complex reality. Only the rich traveled abroad. Few European tourists or cultural organizations visited this country. . . .

A people buoyed by a sense of its own uniqueness, requiring no continuous relationships with other nationalities, and lacking bridges between its own and other cultures, was likely to find authoritative the lessons of the reader, "that first and only formal presentation of other nations."

The world of the nineteenth-century schoolbook was almost static. Authors precipitated from each nation's history certain men and events on which they pronounced moral judgment and then offered the reader as the embodiment of a collective personality. The character traits thus extracted were often more censorious than complimentary, but almost every characterization combined the two categories. The English, as the rhetoric of the Venezuelan crisis made clear, could be both exemplar and oppressor, a parent solicitous, neglectful, or cruel. . . .

By contrast, schoolbooks found almost nothing to praise in the Spanish. . . . Characteristics that drew American attention (though not necessarily praise) at midcentury — Spanish dignity, honor, military prowess — were subject to slow dilution, it seemed, as Spain disintegrated. That was nothing worthy, and much that was repugnant to Americans, in a conqueror grown indolent. . . .

"No single good thing in law, or science, or art, or literature . . . has resulted to the race of men . . . from Spanish domination in America. . . . I have tried to think of one in vain," announced Charles Francis Adams in 1897. The same theme received scholarly treatment six months later when the president of the University of Wisconsin asked graduating seniors: "What has Spain ever done for civilization? What books, what inventions have come from Spain? What discoveries in the laboratory or in scientific fields?" His own answer was brief: "So few have they been that they are scarcely worth mentioning." He then returned in the climax of his address to the central American perception of Spain — changeless cruelty. "Examination of the Spanish character shows it to be the same as it was centuries ago. Wherever the Spaniard has endeavored to rule he has shown an unrivaled incapacity for government. And the incapacity was such and the cruelty was such that all their colonies and provinces have slipped away." . . .

The image's ability to distort reality, to obscure the logic of particular situations, was most pronounced at the time of the *Maine*'s destruction. Today, though neither proven nor disproven, official Spanish culpability seems unlikely: Spain had nothing to gain, and much to lose, by sinking the vessel. Today the American rush to condemn Spain appears a psychic aberration, a lapse into irrationality. At the time, however, the image of the Spaniard made any *other* explanation appear illogical. A sneak bombing against a background of treacherous assurances of Spanish goodwill; sleeping men plunged to watery graves — it was Spanish history come alive, this time with young Americans as its victims. Rough-shaped pieces of fact could be made to fit. When the Havana command offered the American survivors expressions of regret and every appropriate aid, Henry Watterson concluded that, while Cuban sadness was genuine, Spanish sympathy, so "ostentatious," must conceal an inward festiveness. . . .

If there was near unanimity on the nature of the enemy, there remained considerable uncertainty regarding his capacity. The Spaniard was malevolent, all agreed, but what danger did he pose for Americans? On this point the image was ambiguous. Henry Cabot Lodge had spoken of Spain as "mediaeval, cruel, dying." How rapid was her decline? How much harm was she still capable of inflicting on others?

These questions produced speculation and considerable anxiety. Since there could be no definitive answers short of a test of arms, Americans anticipated war with ambivalent emotions. Those who often voiced the fear that the Spanish would not stand and fight could not always suppress the fear that they would. When Henry Watterson complained that Spanish courage was not the courage of "cool tenacity and hope," but that of desperation, others sensed the unspoken corollary: desperate men could exact a high toll from their enemies.

No one caught better than Sherwood Anderson the American vacillation in definitions of Spanish prowess. At one moment he was confident war would be "a kind of glorious national picnic." He could even indulge in a thin guilt that the job would be so easy, "like robbing an old gypsy woman in a vacant lot at night after a fair." In other moments, however, the Spaniard as cyclonic evil seemed very near: "Dark cruel eyes, dark swaggering men in one's fancy." Anderson dreamed of grappling with a

Spanish commandant who, half drunk and surrounded by his concubines, plunged his sword into a serving-boy who had spilled the wine. Americans like Sherwood Anderson, conceiving of themselves as moral vindicators, were given pause: was the Spaniard a still vigorous and thus dangerous evil-doer or only an unrepentant invalid?

This uncertainty may have had some bearing on the undulation of public emotion before and during the Spanish-American War. So often the objective situation seemed insufficient explanation for those roller coaster spurts up and down emotional inclines and through the curves. . . .

Public tension before battles, public jubilation afterward, seems inordinate. The unprecedented celebration of Dewey's victory at Manila Bay suggests relief from the fear of disaster, disaster overtaking Americans in distant islands so exotic and unfamiliar. Dewey was deified. In the Caribbean campaign too there were wide swings of emotion. General Shafter, vacillating between the enemy as destroyer and as invalid, was never able to gauge clearly the danger that the Spanish Army posed for his own forces. Indecisive, he tried in the aftermath of the battle of San Juan to act so as to encompass both images. At the same moment that he telegraphed Washington that his Army was in such extreme danger that he was preparing to retreat, he sent an ultimatum to his opponent demanding the immediate surrender of Santiago. Americans certain of Spanish malevolence but unsure of Spanish power swung rapidly back and forth between an almost swaggering confidence and a deep-seated dread, between excessive celebration and excessive fear.

The image of the Cuban had at first none of the compelling emotional quality of the Spaniard. Indeed, since few Americans prior to 1895 counted the Cubans a distinct people, the image of the ally required simultaneously both separation from the image of the enemy and a delineation of its own.

The crafting of distinctions between Cuban and Spaniard did not begin with the arrival of the news of the Cuban revolt. Americans convinced of Spanish immorality assumed, correctly, that there had been considerable racial mixture in Cuba; Cubans must have thereby inherited every unlovely Spanish trait. Learning of the Cuban insurrection, Americans did not rush to embrace Cubans as kindred. There was no automatic assumption of Cuban virtue as there was of Spanish wrongdoing. Initial statements reveal both denunciation of the Spaniards *and* a deprecation of the *insurrectos* that hewed to Madrid's line. The Cubans were insignificant black rioters or bandits who would be easily dispersed. Richard Franklin Pettigrew, a South Dakota senator who wished war because he thought it would remonetize silver, cared nothing for Spaniard or Cuban: the best idea was to sink the island for twenty-four hours "to get rid of its present population." A prominent Methodist clergyman thought the Cubans "indolent, seditious, ignorant, superstitious and greatly useless." Somewhat less genteel was William Allen White: the Cubans were "Mongrels with no capacity for self government . . . a yellow-legged, knife-sticking, treacherous outfit." Speaker of the House Reed called them "yellow-bellies."

No evidence suggests that Reed, with McKinley a last-ditch opponent of the war, ever changed his mind about Cuban deficiencies. There is, however, ample evidence for the assertion that in the period 1895–97 the majority of Americans began to view Cubans in a favorable, or at least a different, way. It became increasingly difficult to deny sympathy to an enemy of *the* enemy. How could the Spaniards so richly deserve chastisement if the Cubans were undeserving of freedom? How could American strength secure justice for the weak if the weak were themselves malicious? . . .

To some Americans the Cuban rising became a latter-day American Revolution. Richard Harding Davis, watching a Spanish firing squad execute an "erect and soldierly" Cuban youth named Rodriquez, invoked for his many readers the death of Nathan Hale. Governor John P. Altgeld of Illinois declared in public address that the Cubans' struggle was their American Revolution, and Senator George G. Vest of Missouri drew out the moral: the insurrectionists deserved American support because they were emulating the American experience. Senator William E. Mason of Illinois claimed a more substantial connection. Cuban boys had come to our colleges, learned about George Washington and returned home to tell their compatriots. Revolution was an inevitable result. These judgments were based on a widespread but erroneous assumption that the Cubans had revolted to secure, not their own government, but good government on the American model.

Another prominent analogy was that of the Cuban as Southerner. Many former Confederates discovered in Spanish oppression echoes of the North's military occupation of the South during Reconstruction. Joseph Bailey's biographer assigns nine-tenths of the Texan's sympathy to empathy with those whom he thought resisting the same sort of military despotism he had opposed three decades before. . . . Racist and racial liberal thus moved from opposite poles to join hands in support of the Cuban.

Other groups looked to European history for images to unlock the meaning of events in the Caribbean. To staunch Protestants, especially the clergy, the Cubans were another in a series of peoples who had risen against Catholic oppression. (Anti-clericalism was an insignificant factor in the revolt of the Cubans. It was prominent in the Philippines, but few Americans had heard that there was a simultaneous Filipino uprising.) American Catholic publications, unable to support either "brigands" or a revolt advertised by Protestants as anti-Catholic, found a quite different analogy: Cuba was suffering Spanish tyranny as Ireland endured English tyranny. Its persuasiveness lay in the suggestion that the Cubans, like the Irish, were oppressed *because* of their religion, the faithful persecuted for their beliefs. Its weakness lay in the necessity to overlook the Catholicism of the Spaniards. . . .

However confusing and contradictory, the various roles which Americans imposed on the Cuban had one element in common: support for American intervention on behalf of the Cuban. However divided at home on political, economic, or religious grounds, Americans found an appropriate interventionist argument in the grab bag of history. . . .

White Americans of the 1890s were all but unanimous in their belief in black inferiority and the necessity of the social separation of the races. For prominent Americans to champion the aspirations of a mixed people — for a Joseph Wheeler, for example, to wage a viciously negrophobic campaign for the House of Representatives and then refer to Cubans as "our brethren" — required reappraisal of Cuban color and temperament. One avenue . . . involved the bleaching of the Cuban.

In his influential Senate speech of March 17, 1898, Vermont's Redfield Proctor assured his countrymen that better than three of four Cubans were "like the Spaniards, dark in complexion, but oftener light or blond." The figure whom Americans came to accept as the prototypical victim of Spanish inhumanity, William Randolph Hearst's most successful promotion, the rescued maiden Evangelina Cisneros, was described as possessing "a white face, young, pure and beautiful." The Kansas soldier of fortune Frederick Funston, a volunteer smuggled to the island along underground routes maintained by the Cuban Junta's New York headquarters, wrote that "fully nine-tenths [of the insurrectionists] were white men." General Gomez was himself "of pure Spanish descent." Most Cuban officers were former planters, stockmen, farmers, professionals, and businessmen — "the best men." Later, when Gomez ordered General Garcia to join forces, Funston noted an important difference: rebel units from eastern Cuba contained a much higher proportion of Negroes. Few other Americans were aware of the distinction. Correspondents, almost all of them strongly interventionist, made their way into rebel territory by working east from Havana. Few penetrated easternmost Santiago Province where black Cubans were most numerous. Their reports, like Funston's first letters, conveyed the impression that the Cuban Army was almost entirely white. This misconception would be corrected with abrupt and calamitous results when the Fifth Corps landed only thirty miles from the city of Santiago.

Another theme, Americanization, accompanied the stress on Cuban whiteness. This enlarged the basis of Cuban–American cooperation beyond bonds of color to include temperamental similarities. After a visit to rebel territory, Grover Flint wrote *McClure's Magazine* that Gomez had shown an "Anglo-Saxon tenacity of purpose." The general's staff was "business-like." When Flint and others then praised the Cuban Army for its self-respect, determination, discipline, and concern for its wounded, the insurrectionary forces seemed an organization very similar to the United States Army. A plausible extension would suggest comparable fighting capacities. Here again Americans built unrealistic expectations. In fact they understood neither the Cuban Army nor the nature of the war it was fighting. . . .

Images of ally and enemy reversed rapidly, though not simultaneously. Members of the Fifth Corps reappraised the Cuban almost as they touched the beaches. The Cuban *insurrectos* who greeted them did not *look* like soldiers. Their clothes were in tatters, their weapons a strange assortment, their equipment woefully incomplete — "a crew," thought Theodore Roosevelt, "as utter tatterdemalions as human eyes ever looked on." . . .

Personal contact converted admiration to disgust. The English correspondent John Black Atkins, noting that the insurgents looked "incredibly tattered and peaked and forlorn," thought "by far the most notable thing" about the American volunteers' reaction "was their sudden, open disavowel of friendliness toward the Cubans." Unaware of the true nature of the Cubans' war, Americans were quick to generalize from appearance to fighting ability. Roosevelt immediately concluded that the Cubans would be useless in "serious fighting." Captain John Bigelow's professional eye caught little more: "Bands of Cubans in ragged and dirty white linen, barefooted, and variously armed, marched past us, carrying Cuban and American flags. . . . The Cubans were evidently undisciplined. I thought from their appearance that they would probably prove useful as guides and scouts, but that we would have to do practically all the fighting." George Kennan of the Red Cross, perhaps the most judicious observer of events in Cuba, found himself struggling to reconcile his preconception of Cuban military prowess with an appearance that seemed to preclude fighting qualities. The *insurrectos* "may have been brave men and good soldiers," but "if their rifles and cartridge belts had been taken away . . . they would have looked like a horde of dirty Cuban beggars and ragamuffins on the tramp."

If before white Americans had imagined Cuban complexions as pale as their own, now the darker shades seemed ubiquitous. Roosevelt thought Cuban soldiers "almost all blacks and mulattoes." In a later letter to Secretary of War Alger, Leonard Wood elaborated the significance of color: the Cuban Army "is made up very considerably of black people, only partially civilized, in whom the old spirit of savagery has been more or less aroused by years of warfare, during which time they have reverted more or less to the condition of men taking what they need and living by plunder." . . .

Cuban behavior soon joined appearance as the next item in a lengthening indictment of the ally. American soldiers had accepted earnestly public declarations of their country's unselfishness in entering the war; they did, nevertheless, expect a return. Implicit in the dominant concept of the war — the disinterested relief of suffering Cubans — was the confidence that Cubans would view themselves as victims delivered from oppression and would be grateful. In reality, there was little Cuban gratitude. No cheering greeted the American landings. The *insurrecto* accepted gifts of American rations but, thought Stephen Crane, "with the impenetrable indifference or ignorance of the greater part of the people in an ordinary slum." "We feed him and he expresses no joy." The volunteers could not miss Cuban stolidity. At first surprised, they became resentful and then angry.

Additional disillusionment was to come. Sharing his rations in what he thought an act of charity, the volunteer who went unthanked was not likely to repeat the gesture, especially when it was already obvious that the Army commissariat could not keep his own stomach full. The hungry *insurrecto*, however, contrasting the supply bonanza on the beach with his own meager resources, concluded that the Americans would hardly miss what would suffice to feed him. He returned several times to his original benefactors, who were perplexed and then indignant at the conversion of charity at lunch-time to obligation by the dinner hour. When the Cubans found that this method produced diminishing results, they began pilfering from food stocks and picking up discarded items of equipment. With each episode American contempt grew.

Other Cuban behavior antagonized the volunteers. The principal charge here, precisely that against the Spaniard, was cruelty. Atkins reported the disgust of Americans watching Cubans stab a bull to death and, later, decapitating a Spaniard caught spying out American positions. After the battle of Santiago Bay, Captain Robley Evans, USN, was shocked by Cubans shooting at Spanish sailors swimming ashore to escape their burning vessels. . . .

Angry at what Cubans did, Americans were equally perturbed by what they would not do — act as labor forces for American fighting units. The Cubans "while loitering in the rear" — half of them feigning illness or simply lazing about, it was reported — refused to aid in building roads or cutting litter poles for the American wounded. They would not act in mere logistical support of American units whose anxiety to close with the enemy would in any case have left little substantial role for the Cubans. . . .

The first trial of Cuban-American cooperation came at Guantanamo where just prior to the main landings a Cuban detachment assisted a unit of Marines under Lieutenant Colonel Robert W. Huntington. The Cubans, cabled Admiral Sampson to the president, were "of great assistance" in securing the beachhead and repulsing Spanish attacks. Stephen Crane, one of the few Americans to see the landings at both Guantanamo and Daiquiri, was less complimentary. Conceding that the Cubans were at first efficient in supporting Huntington, he insisted that they soon traded the fight for food and a nap. Americans "came down here expecting to fight side by side with an ally, but this ally has done little but stay in the rear and eat Army rations, manifesting an indifference to the cause of Cuban liberty which could not be exceeded by some one who had never heard of it." . . .

A short time later Shafter decided to exclude all *insurrectos* from the ceremony marking Santiago's surrender and to maintain largely intact the city's Spanish administration: "This war," he told Garcia, ". . . is between the United States of America and the Kingdom of Spain, and . . . the surrender . . . was made solely to the American Army." . . .

Disillusionment with America's ally reached those at home very quickly. Correspondents, often busier as participants than as observers, shared the soldiers' bitterness toward the Cuban. Confident of their objectivity and immune to appeals to higher statecraft, they filled their stories with their anger. Just as important was the informal communications network. Visitors

returning home from the war zone and uncensored letters published by
the hundreds in hometown newspapers spread the news of Cuban villainy.
The speed of the reversal was impressive. On June 30, 1898, an editorial in
the Clyde *Enterprise* referred to the Cuban Army, old style, as "a large and
effective fighting force of intelligent soldiers, who have already been
repeatedly complimented for bravery by the generals of the invading
[American] Army. Before this war is over it will be found that the people
who for three years have been opposing Spanish tyranny . . . are as brave
as any who wear the blue." It was the last such reference. On July 21 the
Enterprise announced that the Cubans were "worthless allies." . . .

American soldiers concluded shortly after landing that Cubans were
no better than Spaniards. The next revelation was equally unexpected:
Spaniards were superior to Cubans. . . .

El Caney was a small crossroads hamlet of thatched huts and tileroof
buildings dominated by a stone church. On the morning of July 1 Shafter
sent units totaling six thousand men under the command of General
Henry W. Lawton to seize the town. The resistance was much stiffer than
the Americans had expected. Despite the fatalism of the Spanish high
command, middle-grade officers and their men, conceding nothing,
resisted stubbornly. The fighting lasted into the afternoon. When the
church and a nearby fort were at last reduced, almost four hundred of
the six hundred defenders were dead, wounded, or captured. The attack-
ers suffered four hundred and forty-one casualties, including eighty-one
dead.

At El Caney the stereotyped Spaniard dissolved. As soon as his men
overran the final Spanish bastion, General Chaffee advanced to shake the
hand of the Spanish lieutenant in charge. In turn, a Spanish officer praised
the courage of the Americans who had thrown themselves at Caney's
trenches. George Kennan was sure that the "moral effect of this battle was
to give each of the combatants a feeling of sincere respect for the bravery
of the other." A second battle that day on the San Juan ridges enlarged
the volunteers' regard for Spanish valor. Americans whose commander
calculated that they would sustain four hundred wounded suffered three
times that number. When the crests were finally in American hands,
Theodore Roosevelt felt a new esteem for a tenacious enemy. "No men of
any nationality could have done better." The Spaniards were "brave foes."

There was a similar, though not identical, turn in the war at sea. When
Admiral Sampson hit on a scheme to block the channel from Santiago
harbor by sinking the collier *Merrimac* in its midpassage, Lieutenant
Richmond Pearson Hobson accepted the assignment. Enemy fire, however,
disrupted the plan. Hobson and his crew were unable to scuttle the vessel
at the critical spot or make their way to rescue craft. The next day, just as
Americans were beginning to despair of Hobson's fate, Admiral Cervera
sent a message to his blockaders: he had captured Hobson and his men
and now offered assurances of their well-being. American officers were
impressed. There was, said Captain Robley Evans, "never a more courte-
ous thing done in war."

A reconsideration of the enemy begun with Cervera's note ended with the destruction of the Spanish fleet. American naval officers who on July 4 inflicted terrible destruction on the Spaniards immediately felt a sympathy for foes crushed so decisively. Evans was sorry for Cervera, who was hauled from the water and then received with military honors and champagne. There was an even greater measure of sympathy and respect when Americans soon discovered the abominable physical condition of the vessels in which the Spaniards had tried to fight them. The ties of professional standards were cemented; with wretched resources, the Spaniards had played the game honorably. . . . For many Americans the ally of early 1898 had become enemy and the enemy, ally.

In a 1912 article entitled "The Passing of San Juan Hill," Richard Harding Davis reported that on a return visit to Cuba he had found changes "startling and confusing." The course of the San Juan River had altered and obliterated the Bloody Bend of such moment to the battle. More troubling was the Cuban view of what had happened on that terrain fourteen years earlier. The battlefield guide insisted that American forces, arriving just as the Cubans were about to conquer the Spaniards, had by luck alone received all the credit. He further reported that Cubans now ranked the fighting qualities of their Spanish foes much higher than those of their American allies.

Immigration: American Assimilation or Transnational Race-Making?

"We are all immigrants." For many Americans, this statement sums up a relatively uncomplicated affirmation of inclusive nationalism. In their view, America is an idea more than a nation in the European sense. Rather than affiliations of blood and tradition, Americans sustain consensual ties of citizenship based on common devotion to core principles of liberty, equality, and tolerance. In the words of former New York governor Mario M. Cuomo, ours is a "politics of inclusion"[1] and, while the struggle to realize this ideal never ends, the trajectory is clear. Unity will come from Diversity, the One from the Many.

As an ideal there is much to be said for this formulation, though some would argue whether unity or diversity should be more highly valued, and many resist the self-congratulatory tone of such pronouncements. Aside from such normative questions, however, historians ask whether the stirring tale of immigrant struggle and successful inclusion adequately captures either the reality or the significance of the immigration experience over several centuries. Why did certain people at certain times leave their homelands? Why did they go to certain destinations? Were they sojourners intending to return to old worlds, or refugees from poverty and injustice intent on permanently residing in new worlds? How did they settle — in large groups, in family units, as individuals? How did they build new lives — what work did they find, where did they reside, what sort of cultural institutions did they reproduce or create? To what extent did they retain old world customs, gender relations, and family values, and to what extent did they merge into the host culture? What sort of ethnic identity did they develop as an outcome of this process? With what degree of welcome or hostility were they treated by their American hosts? What was the character of that host culture — was it Anglo-Saxon, or a diverse mix of subcultures, or some sort of amalgam? What impact did the immigrants have on the society they entered, on local or national politics, on gender and racial practices, on intellectual and cultural developments, and on the very definition of *American*?

In recent years, some historians have raised new questions about the fate of immigrants. Most importantly, they have insisted that the immigrant assimilation narrative and the "Ellis Island Myth" occlude the real story of ethnic and racial inequality in the United States. They note, first, the presence of

---

[1]Mario M. Cuomo, "The American Dream and the Politics of Inclusion," *Psychology Today* (July 1986): 54–56.

groups other than immigrants within the American ethno-racial mix. Indians were not immigrants but native inhabitants who were driven back and, in many cases, exterminated by European immigrants. Second, Africans migrated involuntarily and were forced into slavery for hundreds of years. Third, native Mexicans in what became the American Southwest, like Indians, were invaded by, not received into, America; along with Latino and Asian immigrants, these non-Europeans entered American society and polity under a "mark of Cain," racially distinguished from the European newcomers who might be awarded, even if grudgingly, the true badge of assimilation, "whiteness." Although the story remains complex in these newer narratives, the making of race — white, black, red, yellow, brown — dominates the tale. Locating the peopling of America in a multi-century process of capitalist expansion, some of these new histories insist that colonialism accounts for the making of modern racial differences. The power of expansive capitalist nations to subordinate non-European populations for the purpose of exploiting their labor and resources created the modern dynamics of ethnic inclusion and exclusion.

Still, this essay begins with the assimilation model both because it dominates popular consciousness and, more important, as argued below, retains value in explaining important historical phenomena. The tale of immigrant assimilation is certainly venerable. Crèvecoeur announced even before the American Revolution had run its course that the new world immigrant had become a "new man," one who sloughed off his old world skin and set forth toward a new destiny: "Here individuals of all nations are melted into a new race of men, whose labours and posterity will one day cause great changes in the world."[2] With a minimum of anxiety and full confidence in the future that opened before him, this new man was a creature of his environment, imbibing entirely new ideas, principles, and habits from the salubrious air of freedom all around him. To many Europeans who had for centuries witnessed the oppression of religious minorities within states, as well as bloody religious wars among states, the American social fabric appeared something of a miracle. It seemed to have harmoniously woven together English and French Catholics, Dutch Calvinists, German and Scandinavian Lutherans, Moravian pietists, Scots Presbyterians, English Congregationalists and Anglicans, as well as a Baptists, Quakers, Methodists, and a dizzying proliferation of breakaway Protestant denominations and nearly irreligious Deists and freethinkers. Although the term was not yet in use, *pluralism* was practiced in the United States to a significant and noteworthy extent.[3] But it was a

---

[2] J. Hector St. John de Crèvecoeur, *Letters of an American Farmer* (1782; New York, 1963), 70. Although Crèvecoeur pioneered use of the metaphor, the term *melting pot* did not come into general use until the twentieth century, especially after the publication of Israel Zangwill's play, *The Melting-Pot* (1908); see Arthur Mann, *The One and the Many: Reflections on the American Identity* (Chicago, 1979), Chapter 5. The term *pluralism*, employed most assertively in 1915 by Horace Kallen, who is discussed below, came into use somewhat later; see Ibid., Chapter 6.

[3] On Pennsylvania, see Sally Schwartz, *"A Mixed Multitude": The Struggle for Toleration in Colonial Pennsylvania* (New York, 1987); J. William Frost, *A Perfect Freedom: Religious Liberty in Pennsylvania* (Cambridge, Mass., 1990); on Rhode Island, Carla Gardina Pestana, *Liberty of Conscience and the Growth of Religious Diversity in Early America, 1636–1786* (Providence, 1986).

pluralism that was understood to be temporary — eventually the melting pot of America would assimilate these different subgroups into a common "new man" culture.

Although a few dissenting voices could be heard in the century after Crèvecoeur wrote, most American writers and orators continued to sound the confident note of transformation that was the hallmark of the new man theory of Americanization. Certainly, the brief anti-alien campaign of the 1790s and the more substantial Know-Nothing movement of the 1850s marked moments in which confidence in the assimilative capacity of the American republic (as well as the assimilative intentions of the newcomers) dimmed considerably. More troubling to proponents of the melting pot thesis, white Americans almost never entertained the idea of equal coexistence, let alone amalgamation, with the red and black inhabitants of the continent. When forced to consider the unthinkable by a minority of abolitionists or advocates of Indian rights, most Americans declined to extend their pluralistic ideals to any but fellow descendants of Europeans. Nevertheless, it was not until the simultaneous arrival of both labor radicalism and millions of new immigrants in the late nineteenth century that large numbers of Americans came seriously to doubt the new man myth.

To understand the significance of immigration in American history it is useful to consider the scale of the phenomenon. According to one estimate, approximately 100 million people emigrated from a myriad of homelands between the mid-sixteenth and the mid-twentieth centuries.[4] At least 45 million, that is, almost half of the total, headed for the United States or the colonies that preceded it, and most of them — around 38 million — ended up staying in America.[5] Moreover, around 10 million Africans arrived as slaves.[6] By any measure, this immense migration is a major event in the history of the modern world and especially of the United States. Even in the eighteenth and early nineteenth centuries, the immigrants were diverse, including not only English but very large numbers of Scottish, Irish, and German migrants, as well as smaller numbers of other western Europeans. By the late nineteenth and early twentieth centuries, however, the composition of the influx changed significantly. Continuing streams of British, Irish, and Germans were accompanied by larger streams of southern and eastern Europeans, and small but sharply increased numbers of Asian and Mexican immigrants. These new immigrants, especially the Italians, Jews, and Slavs who together became majorities in many big and small industrial towns throughout America, generated fear, anger, and perplexity among millions of older-stock Americans.

From the start these migrants were pushed by need and pulled by opportunity. At first, American historians focused on the latter, assuming that "the land of opportunity" was itself an irresistible argument for migration.

---

[4]Virginia Yans-McLaughlin, ed., *Immigration Reconsidered: History, Sociology, and Politics* (New York, 1990), 3.

[5]Stephen Thernstrom, ed., *The Harvard Encyclopedia of American Ethnic Groups* (Cambridge, Mass., 1980), 476.

[6]On the slave trade, see Volume One, Chapter 4.

Although historians referred to "religious oppression" or "economic up-heaval" in Europe as a cause of emigration, this dark background (sometimes luridly, but always briefly, sketched) only served to set off the glory of America, which shone forth in the bright foreground. In whatever form, the re-demptive tale of immigration achieved the status of folk legend or religious epic, which historians continued to invoke in the twentieth century. The Harvard historian Albert Bushnell Hart expostulated in 1907: "O Marvellous Constitution! Magic Parchment! Transforming Word! Maker, Monitor, Guard-ian of Mankind! Thou hath gathered to thy impartial bosom the peoples of the earth, Columbia, and called them equal."[7] The far more restrained Frederick Jackson Turner, in his famous 1893 essay, "The Significance of the Frontier in American History," declared: "In the crucible of the fron-tier, the immigrants were Americanized, liberated, and fused into a mixed race, English in neither nationality nor characteristics."[8] Whatever we make of these pronouncements today, it should be noted that such melting pot rhetoric could have a progressive political function at the beginning of the twentieth century. At a time when many old-stock Americans were lament-ing "the passing of the great race" and the mongrelization of America, writ-ers who idealized assimilation were suggesting that America's traditional welcome to the refugees of the world, and the new man myth that under-lay it, deserved to be extended indefinitely.

In the twentieth century such views came to be supported not only by folk legend but also by social science. Especially in the Chicago School of sociology, historians had access to a persuasive account of assimilation in stages. As described in the so-called race relations cycle,[9] immigrants under-went a general and straight-line development from peasants to moderns. The process began with the formation of ethnic communities within a com-petitive social environment; it proceeded through conflict, accommodation, and assimilation, at which point former outsiders had sloughed off immigrant identities and emerged as fully Americanized moderns.[10] What distinguished the sociological from the mythic tale, however, was the capacity of the for-mer to acknowledge not only the success of assimilation, but also its costs. And in the years following World War II, a new generation of historians was ready to weigh those costs in narrating the story of immigration.

Not incidentally, the revised story of immigration arrived in the academy after World War II simultaneously with the descendants of those new immi-grants who had come to the United States around the turn of the twentieth century. Even when these social scientists and historians celebrated the trans-

---

[7]Quoted in Mann, *The One and the Many*, 63.

[8]Reprinted in *The Frontier in American History* (New York, 1920), 22–23.

[9]It should be noted that, around the turn of the twentieth century, the word *race* occupied much of the ground we now allocate to *ethnicity*. Phrases such as *the Anglo-Saxon race* and *the Slavic race* seemed just as natural as *Negro race* and *Mongolian race*.

[10]See Robert E. Park and Ernest W. Burgess, *Introduction to the Science of Sociology* (2nd ed., Chicago, 1924); Robert E. Park and Herbert A. Miller, *Old World Traits Transplanted* (New York, 1921); and William I. Thomas and Florian Znaniecki, *The Polish Peasant in Europe and America: Monograph of an Immigrant Group*, 5 vols. (Boston, 1918–1920).

formative and redemptive power of America, they tended to linger more intently than had earlier scholars on the sufferings required of immigrants striving to realize the American dream. The greatest of the new historians of immigration was Oscar Handlin. His *The Uprooted*, published in 1951, took the form of an epic, the trajectory of which — from "uprooting" to "acculturation" — was faithful to both new man legend and Chicago School theory. What distinguished Handlin's account from that of all his predecessors was his determination to give a dramatic and detailed account of the high costs of the immigration experience. Clearly, the immigrants whose experience Handlin traced were *his* ancestors, not some mass of anonymous foreigners ready for the melting pot.

Ten years earlier, in *Boston's Immigrants*, Handlin had already shown how sympathetic identification with the travails of the immigrants could generate convincing social history.[11] In that book, however, he tentatively suggested that ethnic identity might endure for a long time alongside the inevitable process of "adjustment" to the host society. In *The Uprooted* he downplayed suggestions of ethnic resilience, while generalizing the story of adjustment to cover the experience of millions. With characteristic grandeur, he identified the immigrant experience with the American experience: "The newcomers were on the way toward being Americans almost before they stepped off the boat, because their own experience of displacement had already introduced them to what was essential in the situation of Americans," that is, fluidity of social role, acceptance of continuous change, reliance upon individual resources to navigate the shoals of modernity. And with equal grandeur he employed the first person plural to identify himself with the epic of his ancestors and the epic of America: "In our flight, unattached, we discovered what it was to be an individual, . . . we discovered the unexpected, invigorating effects of recurrent demands upon the imagination, upon all our human capacities." Handlin never failed to note the immigrants' plight, their alienation and suffering, and their desperate embrace of one another in the struggle to survive dislocation. In the end, however, he left little doubt that those immigrants eventually departed from peasant conformism and adopted modern individualism. "America was the land of separated men," he declared, and each immigrant eventually learned to become "an individual alone."[12]

Although Handlin's book became the standard for a whole generation of historians, voices of dissent emerged before long. Many historians discerned flaws in the grand epic and the methods Handlin used to tell it. How could he be so sure about the thoughts, feelings, and attitudes of the people he depicted — did he actually have evidence of such states of mind and feeling? Why had he dispensed with footnotes? Even assuming his evidence was solid, these historians doubted the inferences Handlin drew from that evidence and the sweeping generalizations and unidirectional narrative he

---

[11]Oscar Handlin, *Boston's Immigrants: A Study in Acculturation* (Cambridge, Mass., 1941).

[12]Oscar Handlin, *The Uprooted: The Epic Story of the Great Migrations That Made the American People* (Boston, 1951), 271–73; in a second edition (Boston, 1973), Handlin responded to some of his critics.

imposed on it. Most particularly, they dissented from the thesis that cultural differences dissolved inevitably into a composite American identity. Handlin's critics insisted that ethnic identity was durable, that ethnic pluralism, not assimilation, has been the American norm.[13] In doing so, historians made use of the pluralist theory propounded by philosopher Horace Kallen earlier in the century. Reacting to anti-immigrant Americanizers, Kallen had insisted that group particularism, not assimilation, was the real story of immigrant adjustment to America. In refusing to be melted, immigrants not only preserved the distinctive values of their heritage, but also enriched and strengthened America. A nation of nations, America would be the model of pluralist democracy for the twentieth-century world.

More important than a revival of Kallen's pluralism, new sociological theory encouraged historians in the 1960s to revise their accounts of the assimilation process. In the years just after World War II, Ruby Jo Reeves Kennedy and Will Herberg had proposed that assimilation occurred in a "triple melting pot" defined by religion, rather than in a single process of acculturation. Protestant, Catholic, and Jewish subcultures assimilated diverse coreligionists, but did not melt immigrants into a homogeneous American identity. In the 1960s sociologists further revised the Chicago School account of ethnic assimilation, opening the door to a far more pluralistic theory of ethnicity. Milton Gordon developed a highly complex theory that distinguished cultural assimilation from structural assimilation and marital assimilation.[14] For Gordon, structural assimilation — widespread entrance of outsiders into "cliques, clubs, and institutions" of the dominant group — was the most decisive of the three. From it might proceed marital assimilation, whereby outsiders and insiders amalgamated and dissolved lines of difference between them. However, mere cultural assimilation could occur without entailing the more substantial structural and marital forms of assimilation. Adopting the styles and foodways, the language and habits of the mainstream society — as most immigrants or their children had quite readily done — did not guarantee admission to the circles of influence and hierarchies of power in the society.

In fact, according to Gordon, America was a series of "subsocieties," each with its own "subculture." Some of these subsocieties were based on ethnicity, others on class, and the intersections of the two produced what Gordon dubbed "ethclass."[15] The core subsociety of white, Protestant, middle-class folk had elaborated a core subculture to which outsiders or their children regularly gained access. Nevertheless, Gordon insisted, even such culturally assimilated descendants of immigrants retained vital attachment to the ethnic subculture because they continued to need the subsociety — that is, the institutions and networks and support systems that linked Poles to Poles, Italians to Italians, Jews to Jews, and so forth. Boundary crossing of the triple-

---

[13]One of the first was Rudolph J. Vecoli, "Contadini in Chicago: A Critique of *The Uprooted,*" *Journal of American History* 51 (1964): 404–17.

[14]Milton M. Gordon, *Assimilation in America: The Role of Race, Religion, and National Origins* (New York, 1964).

[15]Ibid., 51–59.

melting-pot sort was occurring, as well as some old-fashioned cleaving to ethnic enclaves, as well as resistance to boundary crossing on the basis of race. The overall picture was one of considerable and increasing cultural assimilation, alongside persistent and only slowly decreasing structural separation. Going even further than Gordon, Michael Novak proposed that ethnicity was "unmeltable." Nathan Glazer and Daniel Patrick Moynihan argued that ethnic boundaries defined political entities whose salience was increasing rather than declining. Glazer and Moynihan saw ethnicity not as constraining but as empowering and insisted that there was no prospect whatever of such an indispensable form of identity melting away.[16]

Historians readily picked up on this more pluralistic social-science theory partly because fellow historians had already been marking the way. As early as 1940, Marcus Lee Hanson had pioneered the argument that immigrants' experiences could not be collapsed into a single, unidirectional theory of assimilation. Over time, he contended, immigrants and their descendants sometimes let go of, and at other times revived or synthesized, versions of ethnicity as historical circumstances demanded. Frank Thistlethwaite in 1960 insisted that immigrants came from many different places, had different motives, goals, and experiences, and interacted in many different ways with transnational labor markets and a variety of host societies. No straight-line theory could comprehend the diversity of experiences within so vast and complex a phenomenon. This more complex view of immigration not only liberated historians from the new man myth and the unidirectional assimilation model, it also allowed scholars to connect studies of immigration to America with the economic and demographic transformations in the wider Atlantic world and beyond.[17]

Beyond the realm of scholarship, in the late 1950s and 1960s the civil rights movement made Americans more conscious of the wide gap between the nation's ideals and its racial practices. Historians responded by producing a host of new studies of slavery and racial conflict in America.[18] But they also uncovered the history of vicious prejudice against foreigners. Thus, John Higham in *Strangers in the Land* traced the cycles of nativist hostility to immigrants from the 1860s to 1920s.[19] With subtlety and amazing thoroughness, Higham made it plain that America was not as welcoming to strangers as the myth of assimilation would have it. At least at times when national confidence waned in the face of economic downturns or other traumas, a

---

[16]Nathan Glazer and Daniel P. Moynihan, *Beyond the Melting Pot: The Negroes, Puerto Ricans, Jews, Italians, and Irish of New York City* (Cambridge, Mass., 1963). In the revised 1970 edition, the authors respond to critics. See also Michael Novak, *The Rise of the Unmeltable Ethnics* (New York, 1971).

[17]Marcus Lee Hanson, *The Atlantic Migration, 1607–1860* (Cambridge, Mass., 1940); Frank Thistlethwaite, "Migration from Europe Overseas in the Nineteenth and Twentieth Centuries," reprinted in Herbert Moller, ed., *Population Movements in Modern European History* (New York, 1964), 73–93; see also Virginia Yans-McLaughlin, ed., *Immigration Reconsidered: History, Sociology, and Politics* (New York, 1990).

[18]See Volume One, Chapters 4 and 9.

[19]John Higham, *Strangers in the Land: Patterns of American Nativism, 1860–1925* (New Brunswick, N.J., 1955). Higham began work on the subject as a graduate student in 1948.

streak of vicious ethnic bigotry was a recurrent thread in the American fabric. This new history coincided with a new ethnicity: just as African Americans were announcing that "black is beautiful," other Americans began reclaiming names such as Pignataro, Lipschutz, and Korzcenowski, which had been Anglicized or abandoned by anxious ancestors. Rather than a fading attachment to tradition, ethnicity increasingly seemed a repository of authentic experience. American "white-bread" culture seemed not just an esthetically featureless wasteland but a machine for homogenizing people, thereby depriving them of an essential form of personal empowerment. For many reasons, therefore, historians in the 1960s plunged into the search for diverse and persistent ethnic experience — and interethnic conflict — in America.

The first of the new pluralist historians to recast Handlin's picture of immigrant assimilation was Rudolph Vecoli. The southern Italian immigrants he studied lived in an ethnic world that excluded not only American identity but even Italian American identity. In tightly bound clusters from specific villages and kinship groups, they had been impelled upon the course of migration by international economic forces and were inured to the requirements of the capitalist market and the rhythms of migratory gang labor. They survived the harrowing ordeal by sticking to what they knew, not by embracing the process of heroic transformation outlined by Handlin. "Amoral familism" not ethnicity shaped their identity; magic not religion haunted their consciousness; persistence not change characterized their behavior over time. Similarly, if less starkly, Virginia Yans-McLaughlin showed how Italian and Polish immigrants adapted quite differently to the challenges of industrial Buffalo, New York. Bringing energy from the growing women's movement and the burgeoning field of women's history to bear on the subject, Yans-McLaughlin was especially insightful about the role of women in regulating the family, and of the family in governing the immigrants' response to a threatening social environment. Like Caroline Golab, who studied Poles in Philadelphia, Yans-McLaughlin painted the picture of women-centered families successfully managing the transition to a new world with a minimum of change and disruption.[20]

Some historians in the 1970s found considerable assimilation, even submergence, of immigrants into the dominant Anglo-American culture, but usually their subjects were English, Scandinavian, or German, or from other northern European countries.[21] More recently, historians have more substan-

---

[20]Vecoli, "Contadini"; Virginia Yans-McLaughlin, *Family and Community: Italian Immigrants in Buffalo, 1880–1930* (Ithaca, N.Y., 1977); Caroline Golab, "The Impact of the Industrial Experience on the Immigrant Family: The Huddled Masses Reconsidered," in Richard L. Ehrlich, ed., *Immigrants in Industrial America, 1850–1920* (Charlottesville, Va., 1977). See also Rudolph J. Vecoli and Suzanne M. Sinke, eds., *A Century of European Migrations, 1830–1930* (Urbana, Ill., 1991).

[21]See, for example, Kathleen Neils Conzen, "Immigrants, Immigrant Neighborhoods, and Ethnic Identity: Historical Issues," *Journal of American History* 66 (December 1979): 603–15. See also the review of this and other questions in Russell A. Kazal, "Revisiting Assimilation: The Rise, Fall, and Reappraisal of a Concept in American Ethnic History," *American Historical Review* 100 (April 1995): 437–71.

tially qualified the picture sketched by Vecoli and other neo-pluralists in the 1960s and 1970s. They contend that neither the ethnic enclave nor American society itself was ever as unitary as both Handlin and his critics had made it seem. Along with considerable ethnic resilience, considerable assimilation can be found in the record because immigrants neither resisted nor accommodated something called America. Rather, they came to terms with local and changing circumstances, over decades and generations, and so their experience requires a tale with multiple plotlines. This tale also frequently portrays ordinary people as agents of their own fate. When immigrants assimilated to American ways they did so not out of cultural self-abandonment or self-hatred but as the result of a reasoned accommodation to a relatively tolerant environment. When that environment proved itself hostile to their interests and sense of dignity, they resisted it, defending their traditions but not abjuring their commitment to assimilation. Thus, Eva Morawska has found considerable cultural adaptation among Slavic immigrants in Pennsylvania, sometimes in the direction of "hyphenated" ethnic identity, sometimes evolving toward working-class Americanism.[22] In her view ethnicity is not a primordial feature of the immigrants' cultural identity but a tool to help them negotiate labor markets, social networks, and political crosscurrents. Neither peasant villagers nor alienated moderns, the immigrants and their children discovered a variety of ways of "becoming American" that rejected repressive versions of Americanization while validating more inclusive forms of American identity.

In the early to mid-1980s, two major synthetic accounts of immigration history appeared, each in its own way striving to recast along more pluralist lines the tale of migration, settlement, and assimilation. Although embracing the findings of the neo-pluralists, however, both Thomas Archdeacon in *Becoming American* and John Bodnar in *The Transplanted* find ample evidence of assimilation along with ethnic, racial, and class divisions in the United States.[23] In their titles both authors announce the intention to set the narrative of immigration on a course more complex than that proposed either by new man myth, or by Chicago School sociology, or by advocates of cultural pluralism. *Becoming* emphasizes the elastic quality of identity-formation, while *transplanted* suggests not alienation from the past but the re-rooting of durable stock in new environments. In both Archdeacon and Bodnar, international capitalism drives the migrants; families and larger groups and institutions, not individuals, are the key historical actors. In both accounts, class, race, and gender shape historical outcomes at least as much as ethnic identity, cultural assimilation, and emerging American national identity.

---

[22]Eva Morawska, "The Internal Status Hierarchy in the Eastern European Immigrant Communities of Johnstown, Pa., 1890–1930s," *Journal of Social History* 16 (Fall 1982): 75–108; also "The Sociology and Historiography of Immigration," in Virginia Yans-McLaughlin, ed., *Immigration Reconsidered: History, Sociology, and Politics* (New York, 1990), 187–238.

[23]Thomas Archdeacon, *Becoming American: An Ethnic History* (New York, 1983); John Bodnar, *The Transplanted: A History of Immigrants in Urban America* (Bloomington, Ind., 1985).

Many historians have contributed to this maturation of immigration history. James R. Barrett emphasized the significance of class in shaping both assimilation and resistance to it by immigrants and their descendants in the first half of the twentieth century. For him, ethnic identity was one among many forms of consciousness developed by people who were also men and women, workers and citizens. Lizabeth Cohen similarly argued that ethnicity was transitional, evolving by the 1930s into a trans-ethnic working-class identity.[24] What both Barrett and Cohen suggest is a working-class melting pot that, like the religious melting pots proposed by Herberg and Kennedy in the 1950s, assimilated immigrants across ethnic lines while falling short of absorption into an undifferentiated American mainstream.

George J. Sanchez shows in the first reading in this chapter that Mexican migrants forged a new identity that drew on all their resources, including Mexican, Anglo-American, and newly synthesized elements, all the while intersecting with the hard realities of class hierarchy in America. As Sanchez sees it, the new ethnicity paradigm that dominated so much of the scholarship in the field of immigration history in the 1970s and 1980s treated ethnicity as "an undifferentiated cultural position." Both old world and American cultures were "depicted largely as static, impermeable, . . . bipolar cultural opposites" by proponents of a highly pluralist view of history. Moreover, by presenting the alternatives as either absorption by the "dominant culture" or courageous preservation of a precious "ethnic identity," pluralists made questions about class and gender divisions within an immigrant community seem almost a form of cultural betrayal.[25]

By the 1980s, a new generation of scholars, many of them feminists and some influenced by postmodernist thought, sought to "de-essentialize" ethnicity. That is, they insisted that ethnic identity was, like race, gender, and other seemingly natural or essential qualities of persons, actually a social construction; that it was unstable and ever-changing in response to circumstances; and that it was a part, not the whole, of anyone's identity. Thus, a lesbian Latina scholar, Gloria Anzaldúa, could find in her Mexican heritage both treasure and dross. Rejecting the homophobia and "cultural tyranny," she gloried especially in the pre-Hispanic Aztec spirituality that had been a submerged element in her upbringing.[26] Aware of such complexity, Sanchez argues "in favor of the possibility of multiple identities and contradictory positions" among immigrants and their descendants. Ethnicity is "a collective identity that emerged from daily experience in the United States," neither "Mexican" nor "American," but an evolving synthesis of elements. Finally, recalling Milton Gordon's assertion that cultural assimilation can occur with-

---

[24] James R. Barrett, "Americanization from the Bottom Up: Immigration and the Remaking of the Working Class in the United States, 1880–1930," *Journal of American History* 79 (December 1992): 996–1020. See also Lizabeth Cohen, *Making a New Deal: Industrial Workers in Chicago, 1919–1939* (Cambridge, Mass., 1990); and Gary Gerstle, *Working-Class Americanism: The Politics of Labor in a Textile City, 1914–1960* (Cambridge, Mass., 1989).

[25] George J. Sanchez, *Becoming Mexican American: Ethnicity, Culture and Identity in Chicano Los Angeles, 1900–1945* (New York, 1993), 6, 8.

[26] Gloria Anzaldúa, *Borderlands/La Frontera: The New Mestiza* (San Francisco, 1987).

out entailing structural assimilation, Sanchez argues that for Mexican Americans, "cultural adaptation occurred without substantial social mobility."[27]

In the last two decades historians have emphasized even further the significance of race as a social category in American history. Some of these scholars make race the crucial factor in shaping American ethnic identity, even as they come to quite different conclusions about it. Many "multiculturalists," inspired by the huge new inflows of immigrants from Asia, Africa, and Latin America, believe that recognizing the diversity of the American population past and present entails a radical pluralism. Thus Ronald Takaki insists that fully acknowledging the history of blacks, Latinos, Asians, and other racial outsiders will finally allow Americans to discard Anglocentric notions and construct a realistic picture of their heterogeneous society. Many commentators see the multilingualism of cities such as New York, Miami, and Los Angeles as evidence of the approach of a radically decentered, postmodern society, which will make it impossible for any "tribe" to dominate the national culture. Ironically, Takaki suggests that acknowledging diversity will lead Americans to an almost mystical unity. He ends his book, *A Different Mirror*, with paeans to "wholeness" and a quote from Whitman: "Of every hue and caste am I, . . . I resist any thing better than my own diversity."[28]

Far from affirming a Whitmanesque note of "America singing," scholars who associate themselves with "whiteness studies" have constructed a grim tale of racial division in America. Most European immigrants, in this reading, learned quickly after arriving that America was free and full of opportunity for those who could win recognition as members of the "white tribe." At one time or another, many of them — Irish, Italians, and Jews, among others — were denied membership, especially during the flush years of racial nationalism in the nineteenth and early twentieth centuries. Still, by virtue of skin color most of these — or at least their children — could aspire to and eventually win a place within the world of whiteness. For Asians, Latinos, and American Indians, the chances were far lower. Historians of the Asian American experience have made especially clear the extent to which racial hatred, racial ideology, and racial hierarchy repeatedly subverted efforts to generate class solidarity or pluralist national identity among working-class Americans in the late nineteenth and early twentieth centuries.[29] Whatever the fate of immigrants, for African Americans racial otherness was an indelible feature of their social identity. White Americans could not allow that crucial dividing line to be breached and still hope to retain the opportunities and privileges that kept them from falling through the cracks of America's competitive economic and social system. The psychic investment that whites — including descendants of immigrants — have made in their whiteness is too valuable to tamper with. Solving America's racial dilemma, then, requires not just good

---

[27]Sanchez, *Becoming Mexican American*, 11, 13.

[28]Ronald Takaki, *A Different Mirror: A History of Multicultural America* (Boston, 1993), 428.

[29]See, for example, Alexander Saxton, *The Indispensable Enemy: Labor and the Anti-Chinese Movement in California* (Berkeley, Calif., 1971); and Roger Daniels, *The Politics of Prejudice: The Anti-Japanese Movement in California and the Struggle for Japanese Exclusion* (Berkeley, Calif., 1962).

will but a readiness on the part of whites to "disinvest" themselves in whiteness and to suffer the material consequences of doing so. It also requires scholars to abandon their fixation on the narrative of inclusion and assimilation and to focus instead on America's racial divide.[30]

Some scholars criticize whiteness studies for resorting to a monocausal and unidirectional narrative that makes the building and maintenance of racial hegemony the master dynamic of American history.[31] Resisting this tendency, the intellectual historian David A. Hollinger has sought to trace a middle way between the narrative of smooth assimilation and that of racial polarization. He insists that "ethnos" neither has nor should dominate American culture, that a "cosmopolitan" alternative exists and has historic roots, and that only by facing class and racial inequalities can Americans give to ethnicity the important but limited place it deserves in their lives.[32] In somewhat different terms, Lawrence H. Fuchs insists that "Americans have gone farther than any other multiethnic nation in developing a humane and decent multiethnic society," and rejects any suggestion that immigrant assimilation depends upon reinforcement of the racial divide. And British scholar Desmond King concludes that, despite the baleful effects of whiteness, America's history of assimilation bodes well not only for its own, but for much of the world's multicultural future.[33] Yet, many historians argue that the rosier possibilities of cosmopolitanism are figments of the liberal imagination; that coercion far more than voluntary embrace has marked the process of adaptation to the American mainstream; that race is not like ethnicity, but is rather a permanent impediment to assimilation of blacks (and possibly others). Moreover, other historians, taking their cue from the post–Cold War devolution of nation states, insist that the very subject of assimilation is given exaggerated emphasis by nationalistic American historians and should be replaced by the study of "transnational" migration flows, "borderlands," "diasporas," and the like.[34]

---

[30]David Roediger, *The Wages of Whiteness: Race and the Making of the American Working Class* (New York, 1991), and *Toward an Abolition of Whiteness: Essays on Race, Politics, and Working Class History* (New York, 1994); see also Alexander Saxton, *The Rise and Fall of the White Republic: Class Politics and Mass Culture in Nineteenth-Century America* (London, 1990), Matthew Frye Jacobson, *Whiteness of a Different Color: European Immigrants and the Alchemy of Race* (Cambridge, Mass., 1998), and Noel Ignatiev, *How the Irish Became White* (New York, 1995).

[31]See Chapter 3 for a discussion of labor historians' critique of whiteness studies.

[32]David A. Hollinger, *Postethnic America: Beyond Multiculturalism* (New York, 1995). Also affirming the continuing power of cosmopolitan liberalism, see John Higham, "Multiculturalism and Universalism: A History and Critique," *American Quarterly* 45 (June 1993): 195–219, as well as critical responses in the same issue. In the realm of cultural studies, see Werner Sollors, *Beyond Ethnicity: Consent and Descent in American Culture* (New York, 1986), and Jacobson, *Whiteness of a Different Color.*

[33]Lawrence H. Fuchs, *The American Kaleidoscope: Race, Ethnicity, and the Civic Culture* (Hanover, N.H., 1995). See also Desmond King, *Making Americans: Immigration, Race, and the Origins of Diverse Democracy* (Cambridge, Mass., 2000).

[34]See the lively debate, "People in Motion, Nation in Question: The Case of Twentieth-Century America," with contributions from Gary Gerstle, David Hollinger, and Donna Gabaccia, in *Journal of American History* 84 (September 1997): 524–80. See also Nicholas De Genova, *Working the Boundaries: Race, Space, and "Illegality" in Mexican Chicago* (Durham, N.C., 2005). For

Historians of Asian American and Latino experience have in recent years cast doubt on assimilation models, however pluralist, and focused rather on racial exclusion.[35] Certainly, the Chinese Exclusion Act (1882) uniquely barred one immigrant group, based solely on its racial otherness, from achieving any of the gains of inclusion or assimilation. Other discriminatory laws excluded Chinese and other Asians from property ownership, access to the justice system, freedom to marry, and many other rights accorded European immigrants and their descendants. Furthermore, racist linguistic conventions penetrated legislative, journalistic, educational, and reform discourses in such a way as to make invisible the fundamentally racist uses of such apparently neutral legal, political, and administrative categories as equality, liberty, property rights, public health, seniority, national security, and a host of others.[36] Similarly, Mexicans faced racialized discrimination since the Mexican-American War, and suffered deportation in the 1930s, even as the descendants of European immigrants were forging a "working-class patriotism" built on CIO unionism and New Deal politics.[37]

In a major reinterpretation of immigration history, Paul Spickard neatly summarizes this approach in the phrase, "Not Assimilation But Race Making."[38] Encompassing four hundred years of racial and ethnic interaction in North America, Spickard criticizes most scholars' focus on European immigrants, on the eastern seaboard (especially New York City), and on questions of ethnic identity and assimilation. He insists that diasporic and transnational approaches are more productive than older immigrant assimilation models, and most importantly that race-making within a wide context of capitalist colonialism clarifies the reality of difference and inequality in the United States (and beyond). In the end, Spickard's synthesis of a vast literature and his survey of different approaches accomplishes more than his sometimes

---

a thoughtful review of history and a plea for a revived, if chastened, form of assimilative civic nationalism, see Noah Pickus, *True Faith and Allegiance: Immigration and American Civic Nationalism* (Princeton, N.J., 2007).

[35]Yen Le Espiritu, *Asian American Panethnicity* (Philadelphia, 1992); Eileen Tamura, *Americanization, Acculturation, and Ethnic Identity: The Nisei Generation in Hawai'i* (Urbana, Ill., 1994); Arnoldo DeLeon, *Racial Frontiers: Africans, Chinese, and Mexicans in Western America, 1848–1890* (Albuquerque, N.M., 2002); Xiaojian Zhao, *Remaking Chinese America: Immigration, Family, and Community, 1940–1965* (New Brunswick, N.J., 2002); Paul Spickard et al., eds., *Pacific Diaspora: Island Peoples in the United States and Across the Pacific* (Honolulu, 2003); Jeanne Pfaelzer, *Driven Out: The Forgotten War against Chinese Americans* (New York, 2007). On a more conventionally progressive and assimilative note, see Iris Chang, *The Chinese in America* (New York, 2003).

[36]On the racial inflection of modern realist literary and liberal reform discourses, see Colleen Lye, *America's Asia: Racial Form and American Literature, 1893–1945* (Princeton, N.J., 2005).

[37]See Sanchez, *Becoming Mexican American.* On anti-Mexican and anti-Indian racial thinking, see Douglas Monroy, "Guilty Pleasures: The Satisfactions of Racial Thinking in Early-Nineteenth-Century California," in Paul Spickard, ed., *Race and Nation: Ethnic Systems in the Modern World* (New York, 2005), 33–52; William Deverell, *Whitewashed Adobe: The Rise of Los Angeles and the Remaking of Its Mexican Past* (Berkeley, Calif., 2004); Claire F. Fox, *The Fence and the River: Culture and Politics at the U.S.-Mexican Border* (Minneapolis, 1999); and essays in Nicholas De Genova, ed., *Racial Transformations: Latinos and Asians Remaking the United States* (Durham, N.C., 2006).

[38]Paul Spickard, *Almost All Aliens: Immigration, Race, and Colonialism in American History and Identity* (New York, 2007).

dismissive attitude toward the "cant" of other approaches and his polemical insistence that good evidence of immigrant assimilation is "Nonsense!"

The issue of assimilation evokes the most tendentious rhetoric within the new histories. For some scholars, there is nothing other than "crude assimilationism." If the adjective in this phrase is redundant, then the complex history of assimilation and the maturation of assimilation theory can be ignored. But in fact, new ways to explain immigrants' engagement with host societies — for example, "segmented assimilation" — have more than kept pace with the broadening of scholars' focus to include race-making, colonialism, and transnationalism.[39] Such scholars take full note of the undeniable evidence that today, as a century ago, immigrants display a range of motivations and behaviors. Some are temporary migrants, intending and accomplishing a return to their homelands; others, unable to anchor their lives in either a homeland or a new land, learn to live in the shifting spaces of the diaspora. Some devote fierce energy to reinforcing homeland culture, or to forging new hybrid versions of "hyphenated" identity in a new environment. Many find a new identity in cross-ethnic class solidarity. Others strive to become Yankees as soon as possible. But most strive for and, at least in the second generation, realize some form of assimilation into the host society. As earlier scholars have made clear, assimilation does not usually mean cultural suicide or cultural treason. The America immigrants embrace or hope to be embraced by presents a variety of fearsome and benign faces. Immigrants play a part in redefining the very social, political, and cultural construction of U.S. national identity.

Today's new immigrants seem sometimes distinctively transnational, in the sense that many of them migrate back and forth more frequently and exhibit dual loyalties. Yet there is good reason to believe that these aspects of migration are not so distinctive. Moreover, the apparently homogeneous enclaves within which the new immigrants live are more similar to past "ghettoes" than some commentators suggest. Like the earlier neighborhood, the new ones are more porous and diverse, the inhabitants more assimilative than appearances indicate. Even the political critique of the American nation-state, which marks the rhetoric of many scholars who insist that assimilation is dead, does not seem so different from the socialist, anarchist, and other sorts of radical criticism mounted by their predecessors. In the end, while distinctive in some ways, the experience of recent immigrants seems as much continuous as discontinuous with that of earlier immigrants, as Nancy Foner argues in the second reading in this chapter. Easier transportation and acceptance of dual citizenship, among other factors, may favor transnationalism in the twenty-first century. Likewise, identifying with international critiques of U.S. imperialism and global capitalism might discline new immigrants to identify with the American nation. Conversely, it might strengthen a progressive politics that resists campaigns for "English only" and against "illegal" immigrants, but

---

[39]See Richard Alba and Victor Nee, "Rethinking Assimilation Theory for a New Era of Immigration," in Marcelo M. Suarez-Orozco et al., eds., *The New Immigration: An Interdisciplinary Reader* (New York, 2005), 35–66; and Nancy Foner, *In a New Land: A Comparative View of Immigration* (New York, 2005).

which embraces more democratic and inclusive versions of "Americanism." Much evidence of second-generation English acquisition and educational achievement, intermarriage, and integration into urban electoral coalitions suggests that newer immigrants are following many of the patterns of older ones in assimilating — to a degree on their own terms — to American society and polity.[40]

What remains undeniable is that white America has persistently subordinated black America. Partial racialization of Jews, Italians, and Slavs gave way over generations to their variable but progressive incorporation into American society. Moreover, strong evidence suggests that many persons of Asian and Latino ancestry have at least begun to take a similar path, and that many middle-class African Americans have benefited from civil rights legislation and affirmative action. But most blacks and many other persons of color still occupy the lowest rungs of the economic ladder and suffer most from social exclusion and cultural denigration. In trying to explain the persistence of racial inequality, most scholars have long given up trying to use assimilation models based on European ethnic experience. As Philip Kasnitz has argued, they should also resist the temptation to impose "race-making" upon the interpretation of immigrants' experience.[41] Whether Europeans or persons of color, such immigrants experience both exclusion *and* inclusion, marginalization *and* assimilation in complex patterns that scholars cannot reduce to unidirectional explanations.

For students of history, recent developments in the study of immigration and ethnicity bear out two conclusions. First, cycles of interpretation recur; and second, even as interpretations recycle, distinctively new elements are added to historical narratives in response to new evidence, new intersections among disciplines, and new social and intellectual influences upon historians. Given the ferment that continues to unsettle the field of immigration studies, as well as the continuing and immense flow of migrants around the globe, it is likely that the history of mass migration will remain in the foreground of historical interest. Moreover, however sharply historians focus on the failures of assimilation in the United States, the long-term incorporation of tens of millions of diverse migrants into a fairly stable democracy will continue to win the attention of scholars, especially in a world where ethnic hatred takes its toll with frightening regularity. And finally, as long as race continues to haunt American dreams of equality, the assimilative possibilities of American society will evince doubt in those who observe — and experience — the burdens of race.

---

[40]See David A. Hollinger, "Amalgamation and Hypodescent: The Question of Ethnoracial Mixture in the History of the United States," and critical responses that follow from Thomas E. Skidmore, Barbara J. Fields, and Henry Yu, *American Historical Review* 108 (December 2003): 1368–414. See also Karin Brulliard, "At Odds Over Immigrant Assimilation: Whether the U.S. Government Should Offer Encouragement Is Debated," *Washington Post*, August 7, 2007. Pickus, *True Faith and Allegiance*, offers a historically supported reaffirmation of the wisdom and efficacy of a moderate form of assimilative civic nationalism.

[41]Philip Kasnitz, "Race, Assimilation, and 'Second Generations,' Past and Present," in Nancy Foner and George M. Fredrickson, eds., *Not Just Black and White: Historical and Contemporary Perspectives on Immigration, Race, and Ethnicity in the United States* (New York, 2004): 278–98.

Geor≥E J. Sanchez

from Becoming Mexican American: Ethnicity,
Culture, and Identity in Chicano Los Angeles,
1900–1945   [1995]

GEORGE J. SANCHEZ (1959–) is professor of American studies, ethnicity, and
history at the University of Southern California.

Just south of Los Angeles' central Plaza lay the area known throughout
the city as the main arena for activities of leisure in the Mexican community
of the 1920s. Sundays were not only a big day for religious practice; they
also were big business days for the area's movie theatres, gambling dens,
and pool halls — all of which dominated the streets to the south. The constant sound of Mexican music — music that ranged from traditional
Mexican ballads to newly recorded *corridos* depicting life in Los Angeles —
was everywhere. A burgeoning Mexican music industry flourished in the
central and eastern sections of the city during the 1920s, largely hidden
from the Anglo majority.

The diminished role of organized religion in the day-to-day life of
Mexican immigrants was coupled with increased participation in secular
activities. In Mexico, most public events in rural villages were organized
by the Catholic Church, with few other opportunities outside the family
for diversion. Los Angeles, however, offered abundant entertainment of
all sorts. These amusements were generally part of a rapidly growing market in leisure which targeted working-class families during the 1920s.
Money spent on leisure-time activities easily outstripped donations to the
Church, revealing much about the cultural changes occurring in the
Mexican immigrant community. Chicano entrepreneurs responded to
the emerging ethnic mass market in cultural forms, even though that
market was often dominated by outside advertising and controlled primarily by non-Mexicans. Still, the presence of a growing ethnic market in
Los Angeles provided room for many traditional practices to continue,
some flourishing in the new environment, but most being transformed in
the process. . . .

Music, specifically the creation of a Spanish-language music industry
and market in Los Angeles, provides one of the best windows for viewing
this nexus of cultural transformation in detail.

The Plaza itself continued to cater to single males, offering pool halls,
dance rooms, bars, and a small red-light district. Protestant reformers,
therefore, consistently viewed Plaza residents as prime targets for moral
rejuvenation. In addition, many small, immigrant-owned eateries were

---

located in the area which catered to a male clientele often unable or unwilling to cook for themselves.

A description of a dancing club frequented by single males during this period indicates the extent of the intermingling between sexes and nationalities in the Plaza, a situation which concerned reformers. Located on Main Street, the club "Latino" . . . was illuminated by red, white, and green lights, the colors of the Mexican flag. Entrance to the club cost 25 cents, and tickets were 10 cents apiece to dance with women. The female employees were mostly immigrant Mexicans or Mexican Americans, although Anglo American, Italian, Filipino, Chinese, and Japanese women also were available. The band, however, was made up of black musicians and played only American pieces. Mexican immigrant men, dressed in working-class garb, danced "Mexican style" to the American songs; a ticket was required for every dance; and the women partners earned 5 cents per dance. In one corner of the dance floor a Mexican woman sold sandwiches, tacos, pastries, and coffee.

As Los Angeles Mexicans moved away from the Plaza and the community became more familial in structure, different diversions predominated. Some customs were carried over to marriage from single life. For example, a federal survey reported that three-quarters of Mexican families in Los Angeles continued to spend an average of $14 a year for tobacco. Almost two-thirds read the newspaper on a regular basis. Increasingly Mexican families began to purchase other forms of entertainment which could be enjoyed by all ages and in the confines of one's home. Over one-third of the families in the Los Angeles study owned radios, often buying the equipment "on time" for an average of $27 a year. . . .

During the 1920s, many American manufacturers and retailers discovered a fairly lucrative market in the local Mexican immigrant community. Despite the clamor for Mexican immigration restrictions, these producers understood that Los Angeles contained a large and growing population of Spanish-speaking immigrants. By 1930, some national products were advertised in the Spanish-language press, and increasingly large distributors sponsored programs in Spanish on the radio. Among products heavily advertised in *La Opinión* during this period were cigarettes, medicinal remedies, and recordings to help immigrants learn the English language.

Even more widespread were appeals to Mexican shoppers by certain downtown department stores. In 1929, for example, the Third Street Store advertised in *La Opinión* by asking, "Why are we the store for Mexicans?" The answer stressed the appeal of special merchandise, prices, and service. Located near the Plaza, offering generous credit, the store had apparently already become a favorite in the Mexican community. . . .

Many of the mass-produced consumer goods in the 1920s were specifically marketed with an appeal to youth. This appeal had profound consequences for Mexican immigrant families. Older children who entered the work force often earned enough to become more autonomous. Adolescents and young adults were often the first to introduce a Mexican family to certain foods, clothing, or activities that were incompatible with traditional

Mexican customs. For example, younger Mexican women began to use cosmetics and wear nylon stockings. Young men were more likely to seek out new leisure-time activities, such as American sports or the movie houses. . . .

Despite some initial reservations, most Mexican parents joined other Americans in the 1920s in a love affair with motion pictures. Ninety percent of all families in the Los Angeles survey spent money on the movies, averaging $22 a year per family. . . .

The movie industry in Los Angeles aided Mexicans in retaining old values, but also played a role in cultural change. On the one hand, films produced in Mexico made their way into the many theatres in the downtown area in the late 1920s catering to the Mexican immigrant population. These supplemented American- and European-made silent films which were aimed by their promoters at an often illiterate immigrant population. Sound was not introduced until 1929, so that throughout the decade of the 1920s, movies stressed visual images and presented few language barriers for the non-English speaker.

Since their inception in the nickelodeons of eastern seaboard cities, American films consistently contained storylines intentionally made for the immigrant masses. Messages tended to be largely populist and democratic in tone. Plots stressed the commonality of all Americans. The children of Mexican immigrants were especially intrigued by the open sexuality depicted on the screen. The experience of sitting alone in a darkened theatre and identifying with screen characters, as Lary May has argued, could feel quite liberating.

What made American-made films even more appealing was the appearance of actors and actresses who were Mexican by nationality. Although Ramón Navarro and Lupe Vélez were introduced to audiences in the early twenties, the arrival of Dolores del Río in 1925 brought Mexican immigrants flocking to the box office. . . . *La Opinión*, for example, the city's leading Spanish-language periodical, regularly followed the Hollywood scene, paying particular attention to the city's rising Latin stars. . . .

While the motion-picture industry displayed one aspect of the impact of consumerism on immigrant cultural adaptation, opportunities for other entrepreneurs to make an ethnic appeal emerged during this period. . . . While huge American corporations consolidated their hold on a national mass market of goods during the 1920s, much room was left for local entrepreneurs to seek sub-markets that catered to the interests and desires of particular groups. . . .

As early as 1916, small Mexican-owned businesses advertised in Spanish-language newspapers. These establishments were generally store-front operations which allegedly provided items that were "typically Mexican." . . .

By 1920, large, well-financed operations dominated the Mexican retail business. Their advertisements regularly appeared in the city's Spanish-language periodicals for the next two decades. Farmacia Hidalgo, run by G. Salazar and located at 362 North Main street, declared that it was the only store "positively of the Mexican community." Farmacia Ruiz was founded by an influential Mexican expatriate and quickly gained much status in the immigrant community. . . . Mauricio Calderon, another emigrant from Mexico, would soon dominate the Spanish-language music industry in Los Angeles. During this decade he established the Repertorio Musical Mexicana, an outlet for phonographs and Spanish-language records, which he claimed was "the only Mexican house of Mexican music for Mexicans." Finally, two theatres, the Teatro Novel and the Teatro Hidalgo, located on Spring and Main streets respectively, were already in operation in 1920, offering both silent films imported from Mexico as well as live entertainment. . . .

In addition, the 1920s witnessed the emergence of Mexican professionals who also targeted their fellow countrymen for patronage. A small, but significant group of doctors, dentists, and lawyers from Mexico set up shop in Los Angeles, and their advertisements stressed that their training had been conducted in the finest Mexican universities.

Mexican entrepreneurs, however, were not the only individuals in Los Angeles who appealed to the Mexican consumer; non-Mexicans also tried to capitalize on the growing ethnic clientele. Leading this effort was the medical profession, particularly women doctors and physicians from other ethnic groups not likely to develop a following within a highly male-dominated, Anglo Protestant profession. Most of these physicians were located near the Plaza area, particularly along Main Street, an area which provided direct access to the immigrant population. Female physicians held special appeal as specialists for women, capitalizing on the sense of propriety among immigrant women. . . . Asian American physicians . . . were the largest group of non-Mexican professionals to appeal to Mexican immigrants, largely stressing their training in herbal medicine, an area not unfamiliar to rural Mexicans. Among them was Dr. Chee, who characterized himself as "Doctor Chino" in 1920, and Dr. Y. Kim, who boasted the combination of a Yale degree and a speciality in Oriental herbal treatments.

The growth and increasing economic stability of the Mexican immigrant community in Los Angeles made these appeals profitable. While the Mexican middle class remained small and relatively insignificant, the large working-class community was quickly developing east of the Los Angeles River. Lack of capital and professional training in the Mexican community made it difficult for most Mexicans to take direct economic advantage of this growth. Yet their cumulative purchasing power did allow for the growth of certain enterprises which catered to the unique backgrounds of Mexican immigrants, while creating new modes of ethnic expression.

One of the most important of these enterprises was music. Although the musical legacies of different regions in Mexico were significant, traditions were both reinforced and transformed in the environment of Los Angeles. As a diverse collection of immigrant musicians arrived from central and northern Mexico, often via south Texas, they stimulated the growth of a recording industry and burgeoning radio network that offered fertile ground for musical innovation.

Of 1,746 Mexican immigrants who began the naturalization procedure, 110 were musicians (6.3% of the total), making them the second largest occupational group in the sample, well behind the category of "common laborer." Although 80 percent of the musicians did not complete the process, their ample presence among those who initiated the naturalization process indicates their willingness to remain in the United States. Unlike working-class musicians of Mexican descent in Texas, it appears that many Los Angeles–based musicians were willing to consider changing their citizenship. If, as Manuel Peña has claimed, musicians do function as "organic intellectuals" for the working class, challenging American cultural hegemony while expressing the frustrations and hopes of their social group, then the experiences of Los Angeles musicians indicate a complex, if not contradictory, relationship with American cultural values.

Compared with the larger sample of Mexican immigrants, musicians were more likely to have been born in the larger cities of the central plateau in Mexico, particularly Guadalajara and Mexico City. . . .

The musical traditions brought to the United States from these locales were varied. The mobility within Mexico caused by economic upheaval and violence related to the revolution had pushed many rural residents, including folk musicians, to seek shelter in towns and cities. There, previously isolated folk music traditions from various locations were brought together, and musicians also encountered the more European musical tastes of the urban upper classes. One study of street musicians in Mexico City during the 1920s, for example, found twelve different regional styles performing simultaneously on the corners and in the marketplaces of the capital. . . .

If there was one particular musical style which stood out from the rest in popularity during this period, it was certainly the *corrido*. A prominent student of this genre has called the *corrido* "an integral part of Mexican life" and the creative period after 1910 its "most glorious epoch." During the Mexican Revolution, almost every important event, and most political leaders and rebels, became the subjects of one or more *corridos*. . . . As these *corridos* made their way into Mexico's urban centers, they were codified and transformed from folk expression to popular songs.

The *corrido*'s continued popularity during the 1920s in areas far away from its folk origins can be explained by particular characteristics of its style which made it appealing as an urban art form. First, the urban *corrido*, like the *canción ranchera*, embodied what was a traditional music style from the countryside, while adapting it to a more commercially oriented atmosphere. It reminded those who had migrated from rural areas of their provincial roots, and gave urban dwellers a connection to the agrarian ideal which was seen as typically Mexican. Second, most *corridos* appealed to a Mexican's nationalist fervor at a time when the pride of Mexican people, places, and events was flourishing. Several observers have identified the period between 1910 and 1940 as one of "national romanticism" in Mexican cultural affairs, extending beyond music to literature and mural painting. *Corridos* produced in the United States often exalted

"Mexicanism" at the expense of American culture, but even those composed within Mexico paid inordinate attention to promoting Mexican cultural identity.

Finally, the *corrido* was an exceptionally flexible musical genre which encouraged adapting composition to new situations and surroundings. Melodies, for the most part, were standardized or based on traditional patterns, while text was expected to be continuously improvised. A vehicle for narration, the *corrido* always intended to tell a story to its listeners, one that would not necessarily be news but rather would "interpret, celebrate, and ultimately dignify events already thoroughly familiar to the *corrido* audience." As such, *corrido* musicians were expected to decipher the new surroundings in which Mexican immigrants found themselves while living in Los Angeles. Its relation to the working-class Mexican immigrant audience in Los Angeles was therefore critical to its continued popularity. . . . This adaptive style was particularly well suited for the rapidly expanding Los Angeles Mexican community of the 1920s and the ever-complex nature of intercultural exchange in the city.

The first commercial recording of *corrido* in the United States was "El Lavaplatos." . . . The *corrido* describes a Mexican immigrant who dreams of making a fortune in the United States but, instead, is beset with economic misfortune. Finally, after being forced to take a job as a dishwasher, the narrator bemoans: "Goodbye dreams of my life, goodbye movie stars, I am going back to my beloved homeland, much poorer than when I came."

Most Mexican composers and musicians had firsthand knowledge of working-class life in Los Angeles; not only were they products of working-class homes, but most continued in some form of blue-collar occupation while struggling to survive as musicians. . . . The vast majority of Mexican musicians never were able to support themselves as full-time artists. . . .

Los Angeles during the 1920s, however, presented more possibilities for earning a livelihood as a musician than any other location outside of Mexico City, or perhaps San Antonio. . . . By 1930 the Chicano population in the city of Los Angeles was larger than any other in the United States. The potential audience for Mexican music was enormous. Since most of these residents were recent migrants from Mexico, they often longed for tunes from their homeland. Others had come from south Texas, where the Spanish-language musical tradition was strong and widespread. In fact, one writer claimed in 1932 that more Mexican music had been composed in the United States than in Mexico.

One stimulus to the Mexican music industry was the explosion of Chicano theatre in Los Angeles during the 1920s. Over thirty Chicano playwrights moved to the city during the decade, producing shows ranging from melodrama to vaudeville. The Spanish-speaking population of the region was able to support five major theatre houses from 1918 until the early 1930s. . . .

A more disparate, yet still lucrative market for Mexican musicians existed among the streets and informal gatherings of Los Angeles. During Mexican patriotic festivals and the Christmas season, musicians had larger audiences, more exposure, and greater potential for earnings. From these "auditions," Mexican groups were often recruited to play for weddings and other ethnic festivities. Moreover, a market for "traditional" Mexican music also existed among some Anglo residents of Los Angeles, often to provide a nostalgic backdrop to the distinctive "Spanish" past of the city. . . .

The emergence of Hollywood as the leading movie-making capital in the United States during the 1920s stimulated a flourishing recording industry in the city that began to rival New York's. Both these developments boded well for Mexican musicians in Los Angeles, although prejudice, union discrimination, and the lack of formal training kept many out of regular employment in the entertainment industries in the western part of town. Still . . . the possibility of such employment — "the dream of a life in Hollywood" — was enough to attract some performers from south of the border.

Thus musicians from Mexico flocked to Los Angeles during the 1920s, becoming a significant segment of the Mexican cultural renaissance of that decade. Unlike the Harlem Renaissance, where black writers and entertainers were often sponsored by white patrons, this Chicano/Mexicano renaissance was largely supported by Mexican immigrants themselves and existed far out of the sight of the majority of Angelinos. The presence of large numbers of Mexican musicians in the city . . . created an environment of cultural experimentation where traditional music was blended with new methods. In short, musicians often served as social interpreters who translated and reflected the cultural adaptations that were taking place among the Mexican immigrant population as a whole. In fact, one astute observer of *corridos* in Los Angeles recognized that this music often served to "sing what they cannot say":

> Mexicans are so intimidated by the government officials, even by social workers, and so timid on account of the language difficulty that it is almost unheard of for a Mexican to express his opinion to an American. Here, however, he is speaking to his own group and an emotional outlet is offered in the writing of *corridos* on the subject so well known to every Mexican.

. . . Already, several large American recording companies such as Vocalion, Okeh (a subsidiary of Columbia), Decca, and Bluebird (RCA) had begun to produce "race" records, featuring black folk music. These companies now realized the potential ethnic market among Mexicans, and sought out Chicano musicians and singers from Texas to California. . . .

To most musicians, the $15 or $20 they earned per record seemed substantial for a few hours' work, especially when compared with the wages they earned as laborers or the limited income from playing on the streets. Yet these tiny sums were a pittance relative to the hundreds or thousands of dollars any single recording could earn, even with records selling for 35 cents apiece. Musicians rarely earned sufficient income to feel secure as recording artists. Offering only "contracts" that were usually verbal agreements consisting of no royalties or other subsidiary rights, the recording companies profited handsomely from this enterprise. . . .

Local ethnic middlemen played an important role in identifying talented musicians and putting them in contact with recording companies. . . .

American laws prohibited the importation of records from Mexico, a fact which greatly stimulated the recording industry in Los Angeles. In addition, Mexican companies were not allowed to record in the United States. These restrictions severely crippled the music industry in Mexico, while creating a vast economic opportunity for American companies and ethnic entrepreneurs. When Mexican recordings were finally admitted during the 1950s, interest in immigrant and native-born Spanish-language talent evaporated quickly. . . .

During the 1920s and 1930s, however, a vibrant environment for Mexican music existed in Los Angeles. Another factor in creating this cultural explosion was the advent of the radio. During the 1920s, commercial radio was still in an experimental era where corporate sponsors and station managers tried to discover how best to make radio broadcasting profitable and enlightening. For most of the decade, the radio was seen as a way of uplifting the masses, of bringing elite American culture into the homes of common laborers. By the end of the decade, however, advertising and corporate economic interests dominated the airwaves. This transformation created a market for Spanish-language broadcasts. . . .

American radio programmers scheduled Spanish-language broadcasts during "dead" airtime — early morning, late night, or weekend periods which had proven to be unprofitable for English programs. Pedro J. González remembers first broadcasting from 4 to 6 a.m. on Station KELW out of Burbank. He often scheduled live music, including many amateur musicians and singers from the community. While Anglo Americans were rarely listening at this hour, many Mexican immigrants tuned into González's broadcasts while they prepared for early morning work shifts. González's daily shows provided day laborers important information about jobs as well as cherished enjoyment to workers who toiled all day.

Corporate radio sponsors in the mid-1920s were quick to understand the profitability of ethnic programs. Large advertisers such as Folgers Coffee used airtime to push their product in the Spanish-speaking market. More often, local businesses appealed to Mexican immigrants to frequent their establishments. In Los Angeles, radio broadcasting soon became a highly competitive industry. By selling blocks of airtime to foreign-language brokers, marginally profitable stations could capture a ready-made market. During the late 1920s, the hours dedicated to Spanish-language broadcasts multiplied. . . . Chicano brokers such as Mauricio Calderón profited handsomely as they negotiated with stations, paying them a flat rate during cheap broadcasting time, which they then sold to businesses advertisements.

Key to the success of Spanish-language broadcasting was its appeal to the thousands of working-class Mexican immigrants within the reach of a station's radio signal. Radio, unlike *La Opinión* and other periodicals, reached Mexican immigrants whether or not they could read. In addition, the content of radio programming focused less on the tastes of the expatriate middle class and more on those of the masses. A 1941 analysis of Spanish-language programming found that over 88 percent of on-air time (outside of advertisements) was dedicated to music, with only 4 percent used for news. Programming was dominated by "traditional" music from the Mexican countryside. . . . "The corrido, the shouts, and all that stuff was popular" with working people, remembered González. Although some bemoaned the commercialization of the *corrido* tradition and its removal from its "folk tradition," most Mexican immigrants found this transformation to their liking because it fit well with their own adaptations to urban living.

The potential power generated by this mass appeal was so substantial that it not only threatened the cultural hegemony of the Mexican middle class in Los Angeles but also worried local Anglo American officials. González himself was the target of District Attorney Buron Fitts, who in 1934 had the musician arrested on trumped-up charges. Earlier, Fitts had attempted to force González off the air by getting federal authorities to rescind his broadcasting license. Along with other government authorities, Fitts believed that only English should be heard on the radio and that only American citizens should have the right to broadcast. As a result, many radio stations curtailed their Spanish-language programs during the early 1930s, often because of the continued harassment directed at ethnic broadcasters and the imposition of more stringent rules for radio licensing.

These restrictions in the United States encouraged the growth of Spanish-language broadcasting in Mexico. Although many American stations continued to reserve Spanish-language blocks, entrepreneurs based just across the border capitalized on the potential market on both sides by constructing powerful radio towers capable of reaching far-flung audiences. Increasingly, individuals unable to be heard on American-based stations moved their operations to Mexico. It proved much harder for American authorities to control the airwaves than the recording industry. . . .

The economic crisis of the 1930s curtailed much of Mexican cultural activity in Los Angeles. First, deportation and repatriation campaigns pushed almost one-third of the Mexican community back to Mexico, effectively restricting the market for Spanish-language advertising campaigns. Second, the enthusiasm of American companies for investing in "experimental" markets that did not insure a steady flow of income understandably cooled. . . .

Movies and other forms of cheap, cross-cultural entertainment continued to thrive in Depression-era Los Angeles. Simply because of the economics of scale, Hollywood was able to continue to produce entertainment accessible to families at every economic level. In addition, the introduction of sound to motion pictures made it more difficult to sustain a steady Spanish-language audience with Mexican imports, since the Mexican film industry had difficulty throughout the transition of the 1930s. English talking-pictures, on the other hand, had a wider, and therefore more secure audience. The advent of sound coincided with the rise of the second generation of Mexicans in this country, more likely to be as fluent in English as in Spanish. Increasingly, changing demographics and limited economic resources stunted the growth of the ethnic market. A new era in Mexican/Chicano cultural activity began.

Although commercial activity was slowed during the Depression, Mexican cultural life did not die out in Los Angeles. Indeed, aspects of cultural life were altered dramatically, reflecting the changing composition and nature of the Mexican/Chicano community. Musical activity, for example, became less dependent on *corrido* story-telling (which required the ability to understand Spanish lyrics) and more concentrated in dance clubs. . . .

Second-generation youth, in particular, flooded the dance clubs during the 1930s. Social commentators of the period commented on the "dance craze" that had seemingly overtaken adolescents and young adults in Mexican American families. One such nineteen-year-old, known only as Alfredo to his interviewer, boastfully explained this "craze":

> I love to dance better than anything else in the world. It is something that gets in your blood. Lots of boys are that way. I go to five dances a week. I can't wait for Saturday night because all the time I am thinking of the dance. It is in my system. I could get a job playing my trumpet in an orchestra but then I couldn't dance. I quit school because I got plenty of everything they teach, but dancing.

This new "dance craze" did not often sit well with Mexican immigrant parents. . . . Increasingly, however, it became difficult for parents to withstand the effect of peer pressure on their children, as evidenced by the words of one mother in the early 1930s:

> Juanita has joined a club and now she wants to learn to dance. That is what comes of these clubs. It is wrong to dance and my Juanita wants to do it because the others do. Because everybody does it does not make it right. I know the things I was taught as a girl and right and wrong cannot change.

Although the vast majority of musicians and clientele in each of these establishments were Mexican, the music demonstrated a wide variety of American and Latin American styles. Cuban music was especially popular in the latter half of the decade, with many orchestras specializing in the mambo. . . . Regular groups that played in these clubs all included Mexican songs in their repertoire. In addition, English-language music increasingly became popular among American-born youth. Many Mexican immigrants bemoaned this turn of events, as evidenced by the comments of one unnamed señora:

> The old Spanish songs are sung only by the old people. The young ones can sing the "Boop-da-oop" like you hear on the radio but they can't sing

more than one verse of *La Cruz*. Do you know *La Cruz*? It is very beautiful. It is about our Lord carrying the cross. It is sad. In Mexico we would all sing for hours while someone played a guitar. But here, there are the drums and the saxophones.

Undoubtedly, a more eclectic and diverse musical life than in former decades emerged among the Mexican/Chicano community in Los Angeles. In fact, Los Angeles probably offered a richer environment for such leisure-time activity than any other city in the American Southwest.

This diversity of choice in musical styles and taste not only created a more experimental environment for musicians themselves but also reflected developments in Chicano culture as a whole. Clearly, the control of the individual over his or her own cultural choices paralleled the growth of an ethnic consumer market. . . . Neither the Mexican elite nor the Anglo American reformers intent on Americanization could completely determine the character of these private decisions. Instead, an unsteady relationship between American corporations, local businesses, Mexican entrepreneurs, and the largely working-class community itself influenced the range of cultural practices and consumer items available in the Spanish-language market. If appeals to Mexican nationalism could be used to sell a product, then so be it. Although barriers to the ethnic market were constructed by local officials, particularly during the Great Depression, change in economic circumstances and in cultural tastes of the population had the most important impact.

Appeal to the tastes of youth also created subtle power shifts within the Chicano community. In Mexico, few outlets were available to young people for influencing cultural practices in an individual village or even one's own family. The American metropolis, on the other hand, gave Mexican youth an opportunity to exercise more cultural prerogatives merely by purchasing certain products or going to the movies. Rebellion against family often went hand in hand with a shift toward more American habits. This pattern was stimulated by the extent to which adolescents and unmarried sons and daughters worked and retained some of their own income. As the second generation came to dominate the Chicano population by the late 1930s, their tastes redefined the community's cultural practices and future directions of cultural adaptation.

Behind the vast American commercial network lay an enterprising group of ethnic entrepreneurs who served as conduits between the Mexican immigrant population and the corporate world. These individuals were often the first to recognize cultural changes and spending patterns among the immigrant population. Individuals such as Mauricio Calderón and Pedro J. González were able to promote Mexican music in entirely new forms in Los Angeles because they had daily contact with ordinary members of the Los Angeles Mexican community. Although they found tangible financial rewards in their efforts, they also served an important role in redefining Mexican culture in an American urban environment.

NANCY FONER

from Transnational Ties   [2000]

NANCY FONER (1945–) is Distinguished Professor of Sociology at Hunter College and the Graduate Center, City University of New York. Her books include *Islands in the City: West Indian Migration to New York* (2001) and *Not Just Black and White: Historical and Contemporary Perspectives on Immigration, Race, and Ethnicity in the United States* (co-edited with George Fredrickson, 2004).

The conception of citizenship itself is rapidly changing and we may have to recognize a sort of world or international citizenship as more logical than the present peripatetic kind, which makes a man an American while here, and an Italian while in Italy. International conferences are not so rare nowadays. Health, the apprehension or exclusion of criminals, financial standards, postage, telegraphs and shipping are today to a great extent, regulated by international action. . . . The old barriers are everywhere breaking down. We may even bring ourselves to the point of recognizing foreign "colonies" in our midst, on our own soil, as entitled to partake in the parliamentary life of their mother country. — Gino Speranza

Sound familiar? This reflection on the globalizing world and the possibility of electoral representation for Italians abroad describes issues that immigration scholars are debating and discussing today. The words were written, however, in 1906 by the secretary of the Society for the Protection of Italian Immigrants. They are a powerful reminder that processes that scholars now call transnational have a long history. Contemporary immigrant New Yorkers are not the first newcomers to live transnational lives. Although immigrants' transnational connections and communities today reflect many new dynamics, there are also significant continuities with the past.

The term transnationalism, . . . refers to processes by which immigrants "forge and sustain multi-stranded social relations that link together their societies of origin and settlement. . . . An essential element . . . is the multiplicity of involvements that transmigrants sustain in both home and host societies." It's not just a question of political ties that span borders of the kind that Gino Speranza had in mind. In a transnational perspective, contemporary immigrants are seen as maintaining familial, economic, cultural, and political ties across international borders, in effect making the home and host society a single arena of social action. Migrants may be living in New York, but, at the same time, they maintain strong involvements in their societies of origin, which, tellingly, they continue to call home.

Nancy Foner, *From Ellis Island to JFK: New York's Two Great Waves of Immigration* (New Haven, Conn., 2000), 169–87. Used with permission of Yale University Press.

In much of what is written on the subject, transnationalism is treated as if it were a new invention; a common assumption is that earlier European immigration cannot be described in transnational terms that apply today. Perhaps, as Nina Glick Schiller notes, the excitement over the "first flurry of discovery of the transnational aspects of contemporary migration" led to a "tendency to declare . . . transnational migration . . . a completely new phenomenon." . . . Recently, Alejandro Portes has argued that present-day transnational communities — dense networks across political borders created by immigrants in their quest for economic advancement and social recognition — possess a distinctive character that justifies coining a new concept to refer to them.

Of course, there have been hints in the literature that modern-day transnationalism is not altogether new — suggestions, for example, that it differs in "range and depth" or "density and significance" from patterns in earlier eras. . . . Historians, too, have been jumping on the transnationalism bandwagon, pointing out that they've been writing about transnational practices and processes all along — they just haven't used the term. . . .

Many transnational patterns often said to be new have been around for a long time — and some of the sources of transnationalism seen as unique today also operated in the past. At the same time, there is no denying that much is distinctive about transnationalism today, not only because earlier patterns have been intensified or become more common but also because new processes and dynamics are involved.

Continuities between Past and Present

Like contemporary immigrants, Russian Jews and Italians in turn-of-the-century New York established and sustained familial, economic, political, and cultural links to their home societies at the same time as they developed ties and connections in their new land. They did so for many of the same reasons that have been advanced to explain transnationalism today. There were relatives left behind and ties of sentiment to home communities and countries. Many immigrants came to America with the notion that they would eventually return. If . . . labor-exporting nations now acknowledge that "members of their diaspora communities are resources that should not and need not be lost to the home country," this was also true of the Italian government in the past. Moreover, lack of economic security and full acceptance in America also plagued the earlier immigrants and may have fostered their continued involvement in and allegiance to their home societies. Of the two groups, Italians best fit the ideal transmigrant described in the contemporary literature; many led the kind of dual lives said to characterize transmigrants today.

. . . What social scientists now call "transnational households," with members scattered across borders, were not uncommon a century ago. Most Italian men — from 1870 to 1910 nearly 80 percent of Italian immigrants to the United States were men — left behind wives, children, and parents; Jewish men, too, were often pioneers who later sent money to pay for the passage of other family members. Those who came to New York sent letters to relatives and friends in the Old World — and significant amounts of money. . . . The New York Post Office sent 12.3 million individual money orders to foreign lands in 1900–1906, half the dollar amount going to Italy, Hungary, and Slavic countries. Gino Speranza claimed that "it was quite probable that 'Little Italy' in New York contributes more to the tax roll of Italy than some of the poorer provinces in Sicily or Calabria."

There were organized kinds of aid, too. Between 1914 and 1924, New York's Jewish *landsmanshaftn*, or home town associations, sent millions of dollars to their war-ravaged home communities. The societies' traditional activities — concerts, balls, banquets, regular meetings, and Sabbath services — all became occasions for raising money. Special mass meetings were held as well. In one week in December 1914 more than twenty rallies took place in New York, raising between seventy-five and fifteen hundred dollars each for the war victims of various towns. After the war, many Jewish immigrant associations sent delegates who actually delivered the money. . . .

Putting away money in New York to buy land or houses in the home country is another long-term habit among immigrants who intend to return. In the last great wave, Italian immigrants were most likely to invest in projects back home. "He who crosses the ocean can buy a house," was a popular refrain celebrating one goal of emigration. An inspector for the port of New York quizzed fifteen entering Italians who had previously been to the United States. "When I asked them what they did with the money they carried over, I think about two-thirds told me they had bought a little place in Italy, a little house and a plot of ground. . . ." It was not unusual for Italians in New York to send funds home with instructions about land purchases. An Italian told of his five years of backbreaking construction work in New York. Each day, he recalled, "I dreamed of the land I would one day buy with my savings. Land anywhere else has no value to me."

Many did more than just dream of going back — they actually returned. Nationwide, return migration rates are actually lower now than they were in the past. In the first two decades of the century, for every one hundred immigrants entering the United States, thirty-six left; between 1971 and 1990, the number had fallen to twenty-three. Return migration, as Glick Schiller observes, should be viewed as part of a broader pattern of transnational connection. Those who have come to America with the notion of going back truly have their "feet in two societies." Organizing a return, Glick Schiller argues, necessitates the maintenance of home ties and entails a continuing commitment to the norms, values, and aspirations of the home society.

Russian Jews in turn-of-the-century New York were unusual for their time in the degree to which they were permanent settlers. Having fled political repression and virulent anti-Semitism, the vast majority came to the New World to stay. Even so there was more return migration than is generally assumed. Between 1880 and 1900, perhaps as many as 15 to 20 percent who came to the United States returned to Europe.

Many Russian Jewish migrants planned to return only temporarily in order to visit their home towns, although "not a few turned out to be one-way visits." Some had aged relatives whom they longed to see; others sought brides, young Jewish women being in short supply in America; still others went home merely to show off, to demonstrate that they had some-how made good; and in a few cases immigrants returned home to study. Some Russian Jews went back, savings in hand, to found businesses. . . . Russian statistics indicate that 12,313 more U.S. citizens entered Russian territory from 1881 to 1914 than left. According to American government investigators, "Plenty of Jews living in Russia held United States passports, the most famous being Cantor Pinchas Minkowsky of Odessa, formerly of New York."

After 1900, however, events in Russia led immigrants in New York to abandon the notion of return. With revolutionary upheaval and the in-creasing intensity of pogroms, the rate of return migration among Russian Jews fell off to about 5 percent. In the post-1900 period there were also few repeat crossers. Of the Jews who entered the United States between 1899 and 1910, only 2 percent had been in the country before, the lowest rate of any immigrant group in the United States in this period.

Many more Italians arrived with the expectation of returning home. They were the quintessential transnational New Yorkers of their time, as much commuters as many contemporary immigrants. Many were "birds of passage" who went back to their villages seasonally or after a few years in America. Italians called the United States "the workshop"; many ar-rived in March, April, and May and returned in October, November, and December, when layoffs were most numerous. For many Italian men, navi-gating freely between their villages and America became a way of life. They flitted "back and forth," writes Mark Wyman, "always trying to get enough for that additional plot, to pay off previous purchases, or to re-move the load of debt from their backs." By the end of the nineteenth century, steamships were bigger, faster, and safer than before; tickets for the sixteen- or seventeen-day passage in steerage from Naples to New York cost fifteen dollars in 1880 and twenty-five in 1907 and could be paid for in installments. Prefiguring terms used today, one early twentieth-century observer of Italian migration wrote of how improved methods of transportation were leading to the "annihilation of time and space." Overall, between the 1880s and World War I, of every ten Italians who left for the United States, five returned. Many of these returnees — *ritornati*, as the Italians called them — remigrated to the United States. According to reports of the United States Immigration Commission, about 15 per-cent of Italian immigrants between 1899 and 1910 had been in the United States before.

If economic insecurity, both at home and abroad, now leads many mi-grants to hedge their bets by participating in two economies, it was also a factor motivating Italians to travel back and forth across the Atlantic. The work Italian men found in New York's docks and construction sites was physically strenuous and often dangerous: the pay was low and the hours long; and the seasonal nature of the building trades meant that laborers had many weeks without any work. During economic downturns, work was scarcer, and, not surprisingly, Italian rates of return went up during the financial depression of 1894 and the panic years of 1904 and 1907. Many Jews in the late nineteenth century, according to Jonathan Sarna, returned to Russia because they could not find decent work in America — owing to "the boom-bust cycle, the miserable working conditions, the loneliness, the insecurity." . . .

Lack of acceptance in America then, as now, probably contributed to a desire to return. Certainly, it fostered a continued identification with the home country or, in the case of Jews, a sense of belonging to a large diaspora population. Because most current immigrants are people of color, it is argued that modern-day racism is an important underpinning of transnationalism; nonwhite immigrants, denied full acceptance in America, maintain and build ties to their communities of origin to have a place they can call home. Unfortunately, . . . rejection of immigrants on the grounds of race has a long history, and, in the days before "white ethnics," Jews and Italians were thought to be racially distinct from — and inferior to — people with origins in northern and western Europe.

Whether because they felt marginalized and insecure in America or maintained ethnic allegiances for other reasons, Italians and Jews then, like many immigrants today, avidly followed news of and remained actively involved in home-country politics. As Matthew Jacobson puts it in his study of the "diasporic imagination" of Irish, Polish, and Jewish immigrants, the homelands did not lose their centrality in "migrants' ideological geographies." Life in the diaspora, he writes, remained in many ways oriented to the politics of the old center. Although the immigrant press was a force for Americanization, equally striking, says Jacobson, "is the tenacity with which many of these journals positioned their readers within the envisaged 'nation' and its worldwide diaspora. . . . In its front-page devotion to Old World news, in its focus upon the ethnic enclave as the locus of U.S. news, in its regular features on the groups' history and literature, in its ethnocentric frame on American affairs, the immigrant journal located the reader in an ideological universe whose very center was Poland, Ireland, or Zion." Continued connections to the homeland influenced immigrants' political orientations and involvements in other ways. According to Michael Topp, the ideas, activities, and strategies of Italian American radicals in the years just before and just after World War I were shaped, at least in part, by communications with unionists and other activists in Italy, their reactions to events in Italy, and their physical movement back and forth between countries.

New York immigrants have also long been tapped by home-country politicians and political parties as a source of financial support. Today, Caribbean politicians regularly come to New York to campaign and raise money; earlier in the century, Irish nationalist politicians made similar pilgrimages to the city. Irish immigrants, who arrived in large numbers in the mid-1800s, were deeply involved in the Irish nationalist cause in the early decades of the twentieth century. In 1918, the Friends of Irish Freedom sponsored a rally in Madison Square Garden attended by fifteen thousand people, and street orators for Irish freedom spoke "every night of the week" in Irish neighborhoods around the city. In 1920, Eamon de Valera traveled to New York seeking support for Sinn Fein and an independent Irish Republic, raising $10 million for his cause.

Moreover, home governments were involved with their citizens abroad. The enormous exodus to America and return wave brought a reaction from the Italian government, which, like many states that send immigrants today, was concerned about the treatment of its dispersed populations — and also saw them as a global resource. The Italian government gave subsidies to a number of organizations in America that offered social services to Italian immigrants and set up an emigration office on Ellis Island to provide the newly arrived with information on employment opportunities in the United States. . . . In 1901, the Italian government passed a law empowering the Banco di Napoli to open branches or deputize intermediaries overseas to receive emigrant savings that could be used for Italian development. Beyond wanting to ensure the flow of remittances and savings homeward, Italy tried to retain the loyalty of emigrants overseas as part of its own nation-building project. A 1913 law addressed the citizenship issue: returnees who had taken foreign citizenship could regain Italian citizenship simply by living two years in Italy; their children were considered Italian citizens even if born elsewhere. Although it never came to pass, there was even discussion of allowing the colonies abroad to have political representation in Italy.

What's New

Clearly transnationalism was alive and well a hundred years ago. But if there are continuities with the past, there is also much that is new. Technological changes have made it possible for immigrants to maintain more frequent and closer contact with their home societies and, in a real sense, have changed the very nature of transnational connections. Today's global economy encourages international business operations; the large number of professional and prosperous immigrants in contemporary America are well positioned to operate in a transnational field. Dual nationality provisions by home governments have, in conjunction with other changes in the political context, added new dimensions to transnational political involvements. Moreover, greater tolerance for ethnic pluralism and multiculturalism in late twentieth-century America, and changed perspectives of immigration scholars themselves, have put transnational connections in a new, more positive light.

Transformations in the technologies of transportation and communication have increased the density, multiplicity, and importance of transnational interconnections. . . . A century ago, the trip back to Italy took about two weeks, and more than a month elapsed between sending a letter home and receiving a reply. Today, immigrants can hop on a plane or make a phone call to check out how things are going at home. . . .

In the jet age, inexpensive air fares mean that immigrants, especially from nearby places in the Caribbean and Central America, can fly home for emergencies, like funerals, or celebrations, like weddings; go back to visit their friends and relatives; and sometimes move back and forth, in the manner of commuters, between New York and their home community. Round-trip fares to the Dominican Republic in 1998 ran as low as $330. . . . A study of New York's Asian Indians notes that despite the distance and cost, they usually take their families back to visit India every year or two. Inexpensive air travel means that relatives from home also often come to New York to visit. . . . Thanks to modern communications and air travel, a group of Mexicans in New York involved in raising money to improve their home community's water supply was able to conduct meetings with the *municipio* via conference call and to fly back to the community for the weekend to confer with contractors and authorities when they learned the new tubing had been delivered.

Now that telephones reach into the far corners of most sending societies, immigrants can hear about news and people from home right away and participate immediately in family discussions on major decisions. . . .

Faxes and videotapes also allow immigrants to keep in close touch with those they left behind. . . . The better-off and better-educated may use e-mail as well. . . . Immigrant cable-television channels, moreover, allow an immediate, and up-close, view of homeland news for many groups; Koreans in Queens can watch the news from Seoul on the twenty-four-hour Korean channel, while Russian émigrés can turn to WMNB-TV for live performances from a Moscow concert hall.

Modern forms of transportation and communications, in combination with new international forms of economic activity in the new global marketplace, have meant that more immigrants today are involved in economic endeavors that span national borders. Certainly, it is much easier today than a hundred years ago for immigrants to manage businesses thousands of miles away, given, among other things, modern telecommunications, information technologies, and instantaneous money transfers. Alejandro Portes and Luis Guarnizo describe how Dominican entrepreneurs in New York reap rewards by using their time in New York to build a base of property, bank accounts, and business contacts and then travel back and forth to take advantage of economic opportunities in both countries. . . .

Many Asian Indian New Yorkers, encouraged by the Indian government's attempt to capture immigrant capital for development, invest in profit-making ventures in India, including buying urban real estate and constructing factories, for-profit hospitals, and medical centers. Often, relatives in India provide on-the-spot help in managing the business there. . . .

The Indian example points to something else that's new about transnationalism today. Compared to the past, a much higher proportion of newcomers today come with advanced education, professional skills, and sometimes substantial amounts of financial capital that facilitate transnational connections — and allow some immigrants to participate, in the manner of modern-day cosmopolitans, in high-level institutions and enterprises here and in their home society. The affluence of Indian New Yorkers, Lessinger argues, makes them one of the most consistently transnational immigrants in behavior and outlook. Indeed, *within* the Asian Indian community, it is the wealthiest and most successful professionals and business people who maintain the closest links with India and for whom "extensive transnationalism is a way of life." They are the ones who invest in India, make numerous phone calls, and fly home frequently, where they mix business with pleasure; such individuals have "a certain influence and standing wherever they go." The Chinese "astronauts" who shuttle back and forth by air between Taiwan or Hong Kong and America are typically well-educated and well-off professionals, executives, and entrepreneurs who move easily in financial, scientific, and business worlds around the globe. . . .

When it comes to transnational political involvements, here, too, technological advances play a role. The newest New Yorkers can hop on a plane to vote in national elections in their home countries, as thousands did in a recent Dominican presidential election. (With new Dominican electoral reforms, due to go into effect in 2002, such trips will be unnecessary, since it will be possible to vote in Dominican elections from polling places in New York.) Politicians from home, in turn, can make quick trips to New York to campaign and raise funds. Candidates for U.S. electoral positions have been known to return to their country of origin for the same reason. Guillermo Linares, for example, during his 1991 campaign for New York's City Council, briefly visited the Dominican Republic, where rallies held in support of his candidacy generated campaign funds and afforded opportunities for photos that were featured in New York newspapers.

Apart from technological advances, there are other new aspects to transnational political practices today. Russian Jews brought with them a notion of belonging to a broader Jewish diaspora community, but they had no interest in being part of the oppressive Russian state they left behind. Italians, coming from a country in the midst of nation-state consolidation, did not arrive with a modern "national identity." Except for a tiny group of political exiles, migrants did not care much about building an Italian state that "would welcome them back, protect them from the need to migrate further, or represent the character and glories of the Italian people." Among other groups in the past, such as the Irish, migration became part of their continuing struggle for national liberation. What's different today is that immigrants are arriving from sovereign countries, with established nationalist ideologies and institutions, and are a potential basis of support for government projects, policies, and leaders in the homeland. As a new way of building support among migrants abroad, former president Jean-Bertrand Aristide of Haiti popularized the notion of overseas Haitians as the Tenth Department in a country that is divided into nine administrative departments and set up a Ministry of Haitians Living Abroad within the Haitian cabinet.

Moreover, today, when the United States plays such a dominant role in the global political system and development strategies depend heavily on U.S. political and economic support, a number of sending states view their migrant populations as potential lobbies. It has been argued that one reason some nations are encouraging their nationals to become United States citizens is their desire to nurture a group of advocates to serve the home country's interests in the American political arena.

Of enormous importance are the dual-nationality provisions that now cover a growing number of New York's immigrants. Early in the century, a new citizen forfeited U.S. citizenship by voting in foreign elections or holding political office in another country. Today, the United States tolerates (though does not formally recognize or encourage) dual nationality — and many countries sending immigrants here have been rushing to allow it. As of December 1996, seven of the ten largest immigrant groups in New York City had the right to be dual nationals. Legislation passed in Mexico in 1998 allows Mexicans, one of the fastest-growing immigrant groups in the city, to hold Mexican nationality as well as U.S. citizenship although, as of this writing, dual nationals cannot vote in Mexican national elections or hold high office there. . . .

A powerful economic incentive is involved in the recognition of dual nationality by various sending countries. In the Dominican Republic, for example, immigrant remittances rank as the most important source of foreign exchange, and there, as elsewhere, the government wants to ensure the flow of money and business investment homeward. The record-breaking naturalization rates in the United States, in large part a response to recent U.S. legislation depriving noncitizens of various public social benefits, may have increased concern about losing the allegiance — and dollars — of emigrants. . . .

Although some scholars and public figures worry about the trend toward dual nationality — it makes citizenship akin to bigamy, says journalist Georgie Anne Geyer, in *Americans No More: The Death of American Citizenship* — by and large transnational connections are viewed in a more favorable light today than they were in the past. Early in the century, return migration inflamed popular opinion. "Immigrants were expected to stay once they arrived," writes historian Walter Nugent. "To leave again implied that the migrant came only for money; was too crass to appreciate America as a noble experiment in democracy; and spurned American good will and helping hands." Another historian notes: "After 1907, there was tremendous hostility . . . toward temporary or return migrants. . . . The inference frequently drawn was that [they] considered the United States good enough to plunder but not to adopt. The result was a high degree of antipathy." Indeed, Randolph Bourne's classic essay "Transnational America," published in 1916, responded to rising anti-immigrant sentiment, arguing that the nation should "accept . . . free and mobile passage of the immigrant between America and his native land. . . . To stigmatize the alien who works in America for a few years and returns to his own land, only perhaps to seek American fortune again, is to think in narrow nationalistic terms."

At the time, a common concern was that the new arrivals were not making serious efforts to become citizens and real Americans. Public schools, settlement houses, and progressive reformers put pressure on immigrants to abandon their old-fashioned customs and languages. A popular guide on becoming American advised immigrant Jews to "forget your past, your customs, and your ideals." The Americanization move-ment's "melting pot" pageants, inspired by Israel Zangwill's play, depicted strangely attired foreigners stepping into a huge pot and emerging as immaculate, well-dressed, accent-free "American-looking" Americans. Expressions of ethnicity were suffocated in New York City's schools, where, in the words of Superintendent Maxwell, the goal was "to train the immigrant child . . . to become a good American citizen." Much of the scholarship concerning the earlier immigration emphasized the way immigrants were assimilating and becoming American; ties to the home society were often interpreted as "evidence for, or against, Americaniza-tion" and, in many accounts, were seen as impeding the assimilation process.

Today, when there's an official commitment to cultural pluralism and cultural diversity, transnational ties are more visible and acceptable — and sometimes even celebrated in public settings. Anti-immigrant sentiment is still with us, and immigrant loyalties are still often questioned, but rates of return are not, as in the past, a key part of immigration debates. . . . Increasingly today, the message is that there is nothing un-American about expressing one's ethnicity. In New York, officials and social service agencies actively promote festivals and events to foster ethnic pride and glorify the city's multiethnic character. Practically every ethnic group has its own festival or parade, the largest being the West Indian American Day parade on Brooklyn's Eastern Parkway, which attracts between one and two million people every Labor Day. Exhibits in local museums and libraries highlight the cultural background of different immigrant groups; special school events feature the foods, music, and costumes of various homelands; and school curricula include material on diverse eth-nic heritages. In the quest for votes, established New York politicians of all stripes recognize the value of visits to immigrant homelands. . . .

Scholars are now more interested in transnational ties and see them in a more positive light than in the past. In emerging transnational perspec-tives, the maintenance of multiple identities and loyalties is viewed as a normal feature of immigrant life; ties to the home society complement — rather than detract from — commitments in this country. At the same time, as immigrants buy property, build houses, start businesses, make marriages, and influence political developments in their home societies, they are also shown to be deeply involved in building lives in New York, where they buy homes, work on block associations and community boards, join unions, run school boards, and set up businesses. Generally, the literature stresses the way transnational relationships and connections benefit immigrants, enhancing the possibility of survival in places full of uncertainty. In an era when globalization is a major subject of scholarly study, it is perhaps not surprising that immigrants are seen as actors who operate in a transnational framework or that commentators in the media are following suit. "Today," writes journalist Roger Rosenblatt, "when every major business enterprise is international, when money is international, when instant international experiences are pictured on T.V., more people think of themselves as world citizens. Why should not immigrants do likewise?"

Obviously, there is much that is new about transnationalism. Modern technology, the new global economy and culture, and new laws and political arrangements have all combined to produce transnational connections that differ in fundamental ways from those maintained by immigrants a century ago. Once ignored or reviled, transnational ties are now a favorite topic at conferences and are sometimes even celebrated in today's multicultural age. Yet the novelty of contemporary conditions should not be exaggerated. . . .

If many academic observers who studied earlier immigrants were guilty of overlooking transnational ties in the quest to document assimilation, there is now a risk of overemphasizing the centrality of transnationalism and minimizing the extent to which contemporary immigrants "become American" and undergo changes in behavior and outlook in response to circumstances in this country. Indeed, as David Hollinger notes, today's immigrants "are more prepared for a measure of assimilation by the worldwide influence of American popular culture; most are more culturally attuned to the United States before they arrive here than were their counterparts a century ago." Moreover, as a recent study of Mexican and Central American migrants points out, transnationalism tends to put too much stress on ephemeral migration circuits and understates the permanency of migrant settlement. Although many, perhaps most, immigrants come with the idea of improving their lot and returning home, as they extend their stay and as more family members join them, they become increasingly involved with life and people in this country. Ties to the homeland seldom disappear, but they often become fewer and thinner over time.

. . . The new immigration, like the old, to quote Hollinger again, is very mixed. "It displays a variety of degrees of engagement with the United States and with prior homelands, and it yields some strong assimilationist impulses alongside vivid expressions of diasporic consciousness." . . .

There is . . . variation *within* groups in the frequency, depth, and range of transnational ties. Just as well-off Asian Indian immigrants have more resources to maintain transnational connections than their poorer counterparts, so, too, this may be true in other immigrant groups. Legal status is likely to affect the types and extent of transnational connections maintained;

undocumented immigrants cannot easily go back and forth, to give one obvious example. Whether migrants came on their own or with their families also must be considered. There are also bound to be differences in the nature and impact of transnational ties between men and women and between the old, young, and middle-aged. And as I've noted, transnational connections may well lose force with the length of stay in America, as suggested by research showing that remittances tend to taper off over time.

Finally, there are the consequences of transnational connections for migrants' lives here. If scholars of turn-of-the-century immigration once tended to blame home-country ties for a host of problems, from poor English skills to lack of interest in naturalizing, today's transnational perspectives often have a celebratory tone. Transnational ties are seen as helping migrants cope with discrimination and prejudice in this country and providing access to a wide range of resources, including business and investment opportunities, political and organizational leadership positions, and assistance with child care. In an insecure world, they allow migrants to keep their options open. . . .

But it is important to bear in mind that modern-day transnationalism has costs as well. Financial obligations to relatives left behind may be a drain on resources. . . . The family separation involved in transnationalism often brings great personal strain. . . . In the realm of politics, involvement in political and organizational affairs of the home country may draw energies and interests away from political engagement and activism on behalf of the immigrant community here. . . .

That scholars are debating the contradictory pressures of transnational ties is a sign of their importance for today's immigrants — and perhaps for their children as well. What is clear is that for the first generation, transnational practices are very much part of the modern scene. It is also clear, to return to the comparison, that they are not just a late twentieth-century phenomenon. Transnationalism has been with us for a long time, although in its modern guise it appears to be more far-reaching and more intense — and may also turn out to be more durable and long-lasting.

The Progressive Movement: Elitist or Democratic?

In the years between the end of the Civil War and the onset of World War I, the United States underwent dramatic social change. That change was accelerated by the Civil War, but it involved a set of interconnected processes that had been underway for decades: the shift from a commercial and agricultural economy to an industrial one; the rapid growth of cities; the diversification of the American population as a result of new immigration; and the development of a more pervasive consumer culture. These economic and social innovations had far-reaching consequences, requiring Americans to reexamine cultural values and political practices that had seemed unchallengeable only a few years earlier.

Among the most central of all those values was individualism. Although the rise of industry was often rationalized as a triumph of "self-made men" of talent, drive, and probity, by the end of the nineteenth century it was becoming more difficult to conceive of industrial progress solely in terms of the achievements of individuals. The growth of a national transportation and communications system, which had led to the rise of a national market, stimulated the formation of huge industrial enterprises. This organizational revolution, to use Kenneth Boulding's phrase,[1] raised profound questions for Americans at the turn of the twentieth century. If individual achievement had produced America's greatness, what would happen as giant corporations limited individual opportunities for self-employment and diminished individual liberty within machinelike and bureaucratic settings? If families and communities unraveled in the face of urbanization and shifting demands for labor, how could healthy individuals be nurtured? Was not the growing disparity between rich and poor introducing an almost European class strife into America's open society? Could democracy survive the diminishment of the individual and the elephantine growth of new structures of domination that one historian has dubbed "the incorporation of America"?[2] In trying to answer these questions, many Americans turned to moral reform and ultimately to politics to restore dignity to the individual and vitality to democracy.

The forces of reform gradually gathered momentum in the last quarter of the nineteenth century, although their roots reached back to antebellum

---

[1]Kenneth E. Boulding, *The Organizational Revolution: A Study in the Ethics of Economic Organization* (New York, 1953).

[2]Alan Trachtenberg, *The Incorporation of America: Culture and Society in the Gilded Age* (New York, 1982). The 25th Anniversary Edition (New York, 2007) includes a new preface and expanded bibliography.

abolitionist, labor, women's rights, public education, and prison reform movements, among others. Reformers could not agree upon a specific diagnosis, let alone remedial measures, but, especially after two sharp depressions in the 1870s and 1880s, their search for solutions increased. Proponents of antitrust measures focused on dissolving or reducing the size of corporations, which would presumably restore market competition and thereby revive rugged individualism. Proponents of civil service reform hoped to insulate public administration from political corruption. Seeking to re-create the solidarity and authority that seemed to be vanishing with the "island community," advocates of the Social Gospel, Populism, socialism, and government regulation contributed to the swelling chorus of reform.

What brought these diverse efforts together and added urgency to the cause of reform was the catastrophic depression that began in 1893 and lasted most of the decade. Outstripping the depressions of the previous two decades in intensity and scope, the crisis of the 1890s produced a precipitous plunge in the value of productive enterprises, a rash of bankruptcies, rural devastation, and mass unemployment. What had happened to the American economy since the Civil War suddenly became apparent to all: the scale of enterprise had vastly expanded; the market had become truly national and even international; the fate of the individual now hinged on the collective fate of corporations, classes, nations. Whatever the efficacy and continuing value of personal, voluntary, and local solutions to problems, few Americans could doubt any longer that the authority and force of government were needed to relieve and prevent such misery. While faith in progress remained strong, and revolutionary thoughts occupied relatively few, there could be little doubt at the turn of the century that political change was inevitable and necessary.

Between 1900 and 1917 formerly discrete reform efforts increasingly found common cause in what came to be known as the Progressive movement. Pluralistic rather than unitary, the Progressive movement was actually a series of loose coalitions — at the local, state, and national levels — made up of quite diverse reformers who sought a variety of goals. Among the symbolic leaders of the movement were Jane Addams, the pioneer of the settlement house and the social work profession, and Frances Willard, leader of the Woman's Christian Temperance Union (WCTU), which fought not only demon rum but a host of social ills, including child labor. Academics such as Richard Ely and John Dewey promoted the professionalization of social science and the application of expert knowledge to the solution of public problems. Reformers included muckraking journalists such as Lincoln Steffens, who exposed urban corruption; Ida Tarbell, who exposed the Standard Oil monopoly; and Upton Sinclair, who exposed the oppressive labor conditions and unsafe health standards of the meat-packing industry. Politicians such as Robert M. La Follette, governor of Wisconsin (1901–1906), taxed corporate wealth and forced railroads to submit to state regulation; Tom L. Johnson, mayor of Cleveland (1901–1909), a businessman turned "municipal socialist," instituted a comprehensive system of public utility regulation. Progressivism came to be associated particularly with two presidents, Theodore

Roosevelt and Woodrow Wilson, who not only revived the moral authority and expanded the role of the presidential office, but signed an extraordinary number of laws that brought to fruition many of the reformers' goals.

Until after World War II, most American historians, influenced by Charles Beard and his Progressive school of history, interpreted these reform movements as popular challenges to the privileged classes. The reformers' goals had been clear and simple: to restore government to the people; to abolish special privilege and ensure equal opportunity for all; and to promote social justice through legislation and sound administration. The reformers, Progressive historians emphasized, were not anticapitalists who wanted to abolish private property or establish a socialist society. On the contrary, they took seriously the American dream and wanted simply to make it attainable. The enemies of that dream — greedy businessmen, dishonest politicians, and "special interests" — threatened the full realization of American democracy. Vernon L. Parrington, one of the best-known Progressive historians, saw Progressivism as a "democratic renaissance" — a movement that roused the public to fight "plutocracy" and purify the "cesspools that were poisoning the national household."[3]

In this view, a continuous struggle between liberalism and conservatism, democracy and aristocracy, equal opportunity and special privilege marked American history. The reformers, regardless of their specific goals or the eras in which they appeared, invariably supported the "people" against their enemies. Such was the position of John D. Hicks, whose textbooks in American history were used by tens of thousands of high school and college students between the 1930s and 1960s. Hicks in 1931 published *The Populist Revolt*, the first major account of Populism based on wide research in the original sources. To Hicks the Populists represented the first organized protest of the mass citizenry against the encroachments of plutocracy. Although the Populist movement failed, it was victorious in the long run, Hicks held, because Progressive reformers enacted much of its program into law during the first two decades of the twentieth century. To a large extent his thesis rested on the assumption that American reformers drew inspiration from the Jeffersonian agrarian tradition that had survived intact among the nation's farmers and rural population.[4]

Beginning in the 1940s, American historians began to change their view of both Progressivism and the Progressive tradition of historiography. Like the post–World War II philosophers and theologians who criticized liberalism for its facile optimism and obtuseness in the face of human tragedy, historians faulted Progressive historians (and liberals, more generally) for underestimating humankind's propensity for evil, overestimating its capacity for good,

---

[3]Vernon L. Parrington, *Main Currents in American Thought*, 3 vols. (New York, 1927–1930), vol. 3, 406.

[4]John D. Hicks, *The Populist Revolt: A History of the Farmers' Alliance and the People's Party* (Minneapolis, 1931); Marxists, too, asserted the link between Progressives and the agrarian past, but found in such nostalgia not democratic promise but petit-capitalist reaction: see John Chamberlain, *Farewell to Reform* (New York, 1932).

and turning history into a simple morality play. The new appreciation for the tragic dimension of human affairs led contemporaneous European historians in radical directions; under the influence of the Cold War, however, it led most Americans toward what came to be called consensus history.

The caricature of consensus historians is that they asserted the unity and homogeneity of America's past, the stability of basic institutions, and the existence of a homogeneous national character. They insisted that social conflict always occurred within a common liberal framework and that the protagonists were never really in disagreement over fundamentals. Moreover, this caricature continues, in a world brutalized by fascism and communism, consensus historians doubted the value of social change and feared mass movements of any kind. In this reading, consensus historians trimmed the sails of history to the anti-Communist winds of the McCarthy era. In fact, as the Introduction to this volume makes clear, those called consensus historians were remarkably diverse, and most were liberals. Some were, indeed, "Cold War liberals," but there was no simple correlation between Cold War defensiveness and anti-Progressive historiography. Arthur M. Schlesinger Jr., who never departed from the Progressive historiographical camp, was the leading Cold War liberal in the history profession.

On the other hand, the distinguished Columbia University historian Richard Hofstadter, who was definitely a critic of Progressive historiography, judged Progressive reform (and liberalism, more generally) insufficiently tough-minded about American social inequality. His critique was a form of self-criticism: he emerged from within the Progressive historiographical tradition and considered himself first a Marxist, later a liberal partisan. Hofstadter was more dismayed than satisfied with the excess of consensus and the absence of conflict he found in American history. In 1948 he published *The American Political Tradition and the Men Who Made It,* which studied the careers of political leaders from Andrew Jackson to Franklin Delano Roosevelt; he followed it in 1955 with *The Age of Reform.* Both argued that nostalgia for an era of self-made men doomed both Populists and Progressives, neither of whom faced up to the fundamental problems of an industrialized and corporate America.

The Populists, Hofstadter argued, "looked backward with longing to the lost agrarian Eden, to the republican America . . . in which there were few millionaires and . . . no beggars, when the laborer had excellent prospects and the farmer had abundance, when statesmen still responded to the mood of the people and there was no such thing as the money power." Having scapegoated Wall Street bankers, Jews, and foreigners, the Populists' provincialism would later manifest itself in national paranoid scares such as McCarthyism in the 1950s. Nor were the Progressives much better. By the end of the nineteenth century, the scions of Anglo-Saxon Protestant families found themselves displaced from traditional positions of leadership by a nouveau-riche plutocracy, on the one hand, and political machines controlled by "alien elements," on the other. In response, these bourgeois reformers launched a moral crusade based on the simple idea that only men of character — the "right sort of people" — should rule. "In the attempts of the

Populists and Progressives to hold on to some of the values of agrarian life, to save personal entrepreneurship and individual opportunity and the character type they engendered, and to maintain a homogeneous Yankee civilization," Hofstadter wrote, "I have found much that was retrograde and delusive, a little that was vicious, and a good deal that was comic."[5] Hofstadter's interpretation revealed few Progressive victories for "the people" in what he saw as a mostly conservative chronicle of consensus.

Hofstadter's interpretation of Progressivism meshed with that of other post–World War II historians, particularly George E. Mowry. Author of a number of important books on Theodore Roosevelt and the Progressive movement, Mowry was one of the first historians to see Progressivism as the effort of middle-class Protestants to restore declining status and recapture a world of individualism and face-to-face community, rather than a serious attempt to tackle fundamental economic reforms.[6] The Mowry-Hofstadter thesis did not go unchallenged by historians who pointed to a serious methodological flaw. To argue that the Progressives' social status shaped their politics requires a demonstration that their political adversaries represented a quite different group. In fact, historians began to find that the social, economic, and ideological characteristics of anti-Progressives were almost identical to those of the Progressives.[7] However damaging to the "status anxiety" thesis, however, this criticism only reinforced Hofstadter's larger argument about the triviality of American reform. Progressives and their adversaries were drawn from the same class; whatever they argued about, it was not class equality or the redistribution of wealth and power. Despite later criticisms, most historians in the 1950s and early 1960s seemed to agree that the older interpretation of Progressivism as a struggle between the people and special interests was oversimplified, if not erroneous.[8]

Even in the 1960s, however, not all historians fell into a uniform interpretive line. John Morton Blum followed the consensus historians in seeing early-twentieth-century reform as essentially conservative, but unlike them he saw that conservatism as a sign of the movement's strength, rather than weakness. For Blum, Theodore Roosevelt was a sort of American Disraeli, that is, a pragmatic conservative who tried to force the privileged classes to

---

[5]Richard Hofstadter, *The Era of Reform* (New York, 1955), 11–12; and *The American Political Tradition and the Men Who Made It* (New York, 1948).

[6]George E. Mowry, "The California Progressive and His Rationale: A Study in Middle Class Politics," *Mississippi Valley Historical Review* 36 (September 1949): 239–50. See also *The California Progressives* (Berkeley, Calif., 1951), and *The Era of Theodore Roosevelt and the Birth of Modern America, 1900–1912* (New York, 1958).

[7]See Richard B. Sherman, "The Status Revolution and Massachusetts Progressive Leadership," *Political Science Quarterly* 78 (March 1963): 59–65; and Jerome M. Clubb and Howard W. Allen, "Collective Biography and the Progressive Movement: The 'Status Revolution' Revisited," *Social Science History* 4 (1977): 518–34.

[8]Louis Hartz, *The Liberal Tradition in America: An Interpretation of American Political Thought since the Revolution* (New York, 1955), famously argued that America had very little class conflict or socialism because nearly everyone had access to a middle-class way of life; similarly, conservatism meant little in America because the only thing to conserve — the only continuous tradition — was liberalism. On Hartz and consensus history, see also the Introduction to this volume.

recognize the need to adapt to change. Among Roosevelt's greatest ambitions was to convince his fellow Republicans and the men they represented that only by expanding the powers of the presidency could they manage an increasingly complex and conflictual society.[9] Conversely, in Blum's reading, Woodrow Wilson's righteous moralism seemed too close to the simpleminded reform tradition that Hofstadter had so discredited. Wilson's "New Freedom" harkened back to a bygone age when all individuals had equal opportunity in the economic sphere. His foreign policies also failed dismally because they emerged out of a moralism that could not appreciate the reality of national interests.[10]

As some historians undermined the Progressive emphasis on class and group conflict, other historians developed a new synthesis based on organizational theory (a species of modernization theory) derived from work in the social and behavioral sciences in the 1950s and 1960s. Organizational historians pictured American society as increasingly dominated by hierarchical and bureaucratic structures and marked by a sharp acceleration in the process of professionalization. Simultaneously, nineteenth-century individualism gave way to the values of order, efficiency, collaboration, and systematic control.[11] Already employed by the business historian Alfred D. Chandler Jr.[12] to explain the emergence of large corporations, the organizational model also reinforced the thesis that Progressives aimed to govern society in accordance with the ideals of scientific management and efficiency.

The conservation movement, for example, no longer seemed a popular struggle against special interests bent on hijacking natural resources and despoiling the landscape. On the contrary, according to Samuel P. Hays, it won support from scientists and corporate managers interested in "rational planning to promote efficient development and use of all natural resources." Conversely, small farmers, cattlemen, and other groups that Progressive historians had portrayed as democratic masses often opposed conservation because it thwarted their hopes of economic advancement through the exploitation of cheap natural resources. "The broader significance of the conservation movement," Hays concluded, "stemmed from the role it played in the transformation of a decentralized, nontechnical, loosely organized society, where waste and inefficiency ran rampant, into a highly organized, technical, and centrally planned and directed social organization which

---

[9] John M. Blum, *The Republican Roosevelt* (Cambridge, Mass., 1954).

[10] John Morton Blum, *Woodrow Wilson and the Politics of Morality* (Boston, 1956). For a critical but more sympathetic interpretation, see Arthur S. Link's two-decade-long engagement with Wilson: *Wilson*, 5 vols. (Princeton, N.J., 1947–1965), in particular *Woodrow Wilson and the Progressive Era, 1910–1917* (New York, 1954; rev. ed., 1963). A study that compares the two presidents is John Milton Cooper Jr., *The Warrior and the Priest* (Cambridge, Mass., 1983).

[11] See Kenneth E. Boulding, *The Organizational Revolution*; Louis Galambos, "The Emerging Organizational Synthesis in Modern American History," *Business History Review* 44 (Autumn 1970): 279–90, as well as his follow-up analysis, "Technology, Political Economy, and Professionalism: Central Themes of the Organizational Synthesis," *Business History Review* 57 (Winter 1983): 471–93.

[12] See Chapter 3.

could meet a complex world with efficiency and purpose."[13] Like other reform efforts it had little or nothing to do with the liberal-conservative categories of the Progressive school of historiography. In a similar vein Hays argued that support for reform in municipal government came from men and women of the business and professional classes. These "cosmopolitans" insisted that the welfare of the city could be served only if city governments were run in a businesslike manner. This meant essentially removing decision making from the hands of corrupt political machines, whose aims were strictly local and political, and relocating it in nonpolitical, centralized administrative structures staffed by people like themselves.

Hays's survey of Progressive reform, *The Response to Industrialism*, captured the essence of the era in the phrase "Organize or Perish."[14] An even more comprehensive version of this approach, *The Search for Order*, by Robert H. Wiebe, remained probably the leading historical synthesis of the Progressive era for thirty years. During most of the nineteenth century, Wiebe argued, the United States was a nation more in name than in fact. Most individuals resided in nearly autonomous island communities where relationships were personal, communication was face-to-face, and the knowledge needed to live successfully was accessible without much recourse to the world outside. By the 1880s, however, technological and economic change had undermined the cohesiveness of such locales, leaving individuals vulnerable to "dislocation and bewilderment." The result, according to Wiebe, was a "search for order." Some of the searchers attempted to restore the local community to a position of significance; others turned to agrarian or monetary reform; still others joined moral crusades against alcohol or prostitution, hoping thereby to buttress traditional values even as traditional structures eroded.

Up to this point, Wiebe sounds much like Hofstadter. But whereas Hofstadter located the origins of Progressivism in the problems of an old and declining middle class, Wiebe identified it with the ambition and professional elan of a new middle class. Whatever anxiety might have troubled older middle-class types such as yeomen farmers, shopkeepers, and small businessmen, their children, who were increasingly college-educated professionals or salaried employees of large institutions, believed they could master the future. In such diverse fields as law, medicine, economics, social work, architecture, business, and engineering, among others, these new middle-class folk emerged with the conviction that their expertise could bring order to a fragmented society. "The heart of progressivism," Wiebe argued, "was the ambition of the new middle class to fulfill its destiny through bureaucratic means."[15] In thus fulfilling its destiny, this middle class helped to modernize the United States and prepare it for the twentieth century.

---

[13]Samuel P. Hays, *Conservation and the Gospel of Efficiency: The Progressive Conservation Movement, 1890–1920* (Cambridge, Mass., 1959), 2, 265; see also his *American Political History as Social Analysis: Essays by Samuel P. Hays* (Knoxville, Tenn., 1980).

[14]Samuel P. Hays, *The Response to Industrialism, 1885–1914* (Chicago, 1957).

[15]Robert H. Wiebe, *The Search for Order, 1877–1920* (New York, 1967), 166.

Both consensus and organizational interpretations of the Progressive movement grew in influence in the late 1950s and 1960s. Ironically, in denying that Progressive reform was very progressive (or liberal or radical), consensus and organizational interpretations had paved the way for the New Left historians. Disillusioned by the continued existence of war, poverty, and racism, New Left scholars tended to write about the shortcomings and failures of American reform, and to argue that only radical changes in the structure of society could establish true justice and equality in America. Consequently, New Left historians adopted their predecessors' awareness of the importance of organizations in twentieth-century America, as well as their view of Progressive reformers as essentially conservative.

One of the leading New Left historians, Gabriel Kolko, whose work is also discussed in Chapter 3, argued that both major political parties shared a common ideology, which Kolko called political capitalism. Political capitalism "redirected the radical potential of mass grievances and aspirations" into the promotion of government regulation of business. Business elites launched the regulatory movement because they wanted government to stabilize markets, and they controlled it because political elites shared their faith in the basic justice of private property. Progressivism, argued Kolko, arose on the assumption that the welfare of the nation was synonymous with the interests of these elites. Since neither the Populist nor the Socialist Party developed a persuasive diagnosis of social injustice, Americans had no viable political alternative to the two business-dominated major parties. "The Progressive Era," concluded Kolko, "was characterized by a paucity of alternatives to the status quo, a vacuum that permitted political capitalism to . . . determine the ground rules for American civilization in the twentieth century, and to set the stage for what was to follow."[16]

The disparagement of the Progressive movement did not convince all historians. Some rejected the radical idea that reformers were either agents or dupes of corporate capitalism. Others questioned the organizational view that reform was nothing more than adjustment to modernization (or the consensus view that it was nothing more than maladjustment). While sharing doubts about the Progressive historians' saga of "the people versus the special interests," and acknowledging the reformers' "search for order," these neo-Progressive scholars continued to see Progressive reform as a serious critique of inequality and injustice. J. Joseph Huthmacher, for example, explicitly rejected the Mowry-Hofstadter idea that Progressivism was a middle-class movement dominated by anxious, small-town Yankee-Protestants. On the contrary, Huthmacher maintained that Progressivism in the city was much more broadly based, incorporating the views and drawing the active participation of workers and other urban lower-class groups. Huthmacher insisted that Progressivism addressed complex dilemmas of an urban-industrial society. Although he clearly rejected the more simplistic formulations of the old

---

[16]Gabriel Kolko, *The Triumph of Conservatism: A Reinterpretation of American History, 1900–1916* (New York, 1963), 2–3, 285, 303. See also James Weinstein, *The Corporate Ideal in the Liberal State, 1900–1918* (Boston, 1968).

Progressive interpretation, he essentially updated the view that the reform movement of 1900–1920 was a continuing phase in the perennial struggle between liberal have-nots and conservative haves.[17]

Nor was Huthmacher alone in reasserting a version of the old interpretation of Progressivism. John C. Burnham, for example, took issue with the view implicit in the organizational interpretation that Progressives were cold experts rather than passionate volunteers in a reform crusade. In fact, he showed, Progressives strove to merge Protestant moral fervor with the hard facts of science and technology. Indeed, Burnham insisted, moral fervor lay at the heart of the movement and contributed to such specific achievements as child-labor legislation and public health reform. Melvin Holli described the reform movement in Detroit as a coalition of the "cool" and the "hot." "Structural" reformers, who resembled Hays's technocrats, sought clean and efficient government; "social" reformers, often with a sense of class grievance and evangelical zeal, sought justice in new municipal benefits for immigrant workers and new restraints on the power of corporations. Sometimes the two sorts of reformers fell out over issues such as taxes and temperance; but often enough they found common cause and succeeded in bringing both a measure of order and a measure of justice to the industrial city.[18]

After Huthmacher and Holli, a number of historians developed the idea of Progressivism as coalition politics to a high point of sophistication. In their hands reform movements revealed themselves to be alliances not just of structural and social reformers, but of a great variety of groups and interests, ranging broadly across the social continuum. They insisted that Progressive politics was *real* politics, not just a shadow-act behind which "political capitalists" or "new middle class" technocrats pulled the strings. On the other hand, they implied that Progressivism was *small* politics — that is, local politics that varied enormously from place to place, interest to interest. This approach, however, could lead to a highly fragmented and incoherent picture of Progressivism. If it was not a coherent movement with a unitary ideology, organizational structure, and social basis, what was it? One historian, Peter G. Filene, decided that it was nothing at all — just a false label superimposed upon a gaggle of unrelated phenomena.[19] But other historians had a better answer.

Progressivism was a series of "shifting coalitions," to use John D. Buenker's phrase, that enabled previously separate groups and causes to form alliances around specific issues. If urban liberals and trade unionists made common cause with the WCTU on labor legislation, they parted company on prohibition. Similarly, as David Thelen showed, if Wisconsin farmers joined the

---

[17] J. Joseph Huthmacher, "Urban Liberalism and the Age of Reform," *Mississippi Valley Historical Review* 44 (September 1962): 231–41.

[18] Melvin G. Holli, *Reform in Detroit: Hazen S. Pingree and Urban Politics* (New York, 1969); Martin J. Schiesl complicated the picture by showing that the two types of reform were less contradictory and more interconnected than Holli suggested: *The Politics of Efficiency: Municipal Administration and Reform in America, 1880–1920* (Berkeley, Calif., 1977).

[19] Peter G. Filene, "An Obituary for 'The Progressive Movement,'" *American Quarterly* 22 (Spring 1970): 20–34.

Milwaukee Chamber of Commerce in promoting railroad regulation, they parted company on tax equalization. Thus, if Progressivism was not a movement of the people against the interests, as the old Progressive historians would have it, neither was it an elite phenomenon. If Hays had exposed the folly of taking all the Progressives' democratic rhetoric at face value, Buenker, Thelen, and others exposed the folly of reducing so complex a movement to a single explanatory rubric, especially one based on so vague a social category as "new middle class" or "cosmopolitans." Progressivism is more fruitfully seen, said Thelen, as a revolt against "corporate arrogance" that inspired working-class, middle-class, and even some upper-class Americans to rally around men like Tom Johnson, Robert La Follette, and Theodore Roosevelt, who promised to take on the bullies in the interest of the general citizenry. "When the progressive characteristically spoke of reform as a fight of 'the people' or the 'public interest' against the 'selfish interests,' he was speaking quite literally of his political coalition because the important fact about Progressivism, at least in Wisconsin, was the degree of cooperation between previously discrete social groups now united under the banner of the 'public interest.' . . . Both conceptually and empirically it would seem safer and more productive to view reformers first as reformers and only secondarily as men who were trying to relieve class and status anxieties."[20]

In uncovering the political astuteness and effectiveness of women reformers, some recent historians have reinforced the notion that, however diverse, Progressivism was in fact animated by a broad critique of inequality and injustice in industrial America. In the first reading in this chapter, Katheryn Kish Sklar argues persuasively that women used the language of "maternalism" to suffuse Progressive reform with a passion to restrain the powerful and promote justice for all. With organized labor relatively weak and socialism branded as alien, middle-class women assumed responsibility for applying moral judgments to market relations, for bringing both Christian charity and modern hygiene to bear upon the problems of the "social household." Denied the vote, women used their nonpolitical status to act as nurturers, teachers, and scolds toward those men who had become morally disoriented by the competitive and unscrupulous world of business and politics.

Generations of experience in church organizations and reform causes from abolitionism to temperance had well prepared women to take on new tasks. They fought, of course, for women's suffrage, sometimes basing it on the claim that they embodied Victorian virtues of restraint, moral sensitivity, and passionlessness that were increasingly needed to calm a diverse and turbulent society. Beyond "women's issues," they fought both the machine

---

[20] John D. Buenker, "The Progressive Era: A Search for a Synthesis," *Mid-America* 51 (1969): 175–93, and *Urban Liberalism and Progressive Reform* (New York, 1973); David P. Thelen, "Social Tensions and the Origins of Progressivism," *Journal of American History* 56 (September 1969): 323–41; *The New Citizenship: Origins of Progressivism in Wisconsin, 1885–1900* (Columbia, Mo., 1972); and *Robert M. La Follette and the Insurgent Spirit* (Boston, 1976). See also John D. Buenker, John C. Burnham, and Robert M. Crunden, *Progressivism* (Cambridge, Mass., 1977).

politicians who failed to provide clean water to immigrant masses, and the businessmen who polluted the water in the first place. They lobbied for minimum-wage, maximum-hour, and child-labor legislation, but often infuriated the same men who were their allies in those campaigns by their crusades to restrict liquor licenses or to enact civil service reforms. Whatever the rationale, the activism of middle-class women in organizations such as the General Federation of Women's Clubs, the YWCA, the Women's Trade Union League, and the National Consumers' League provided the grassroots support for the emerging welfare state that was supplied in Europe by unions and socialist parties. In the United States, Sklar argues, it was women's activism that "served as a surrogate for working-class social-welfare activism."[21]

If Buenker, Thelen, Sklar, and other historians rescued Progressivism from diminishment at the hands of many consensus, organizational, and New Left interpreters, they did not inoculate it from all attacks. A few historians showed that Progressivism in some places and guises was more conservative — and more reprehensible — than even earlier detractors had made it seem. In an analysis of Alabama during the Progressive era, Sheldon Hackney found a few similarities with, but some disturbing differences from, the better-known movements in the Northeast and Midwest. Hackney found Populists to be "primitive rebels." They viewed society in static terms, employed a backward-looking republican rhetoric, and preferred a minimal rather than an activist government. Progressives, by contrast, saw society in dynamic terms and insisted that economic opportunity could come only through greater economic growth stimulated by governmental action. Earnestly interested in bringing southern society into the modern industrial era, Hackney's Progressivism resembled more the urban brand associated with Theodore Roosevelt than the Populist-tinged rural variety associated with William Jennings Bryan.[22]

Whatever their differences, nevertheless, both Populism and Progressivism had sharply negative implications for the status of black Americans. From 1890 to 1910 the pattern of race relations in the South was inconsistent and fluid, which led to racial anxiety among whites. And that anxiety led to an increase in lynching. In Alabama, Hackney showed, lynching, specifically, and social instability, generally, began to decline only when the Constitutional Convention of 1901 in effect eliminated black citizens from political participation. Ironically, reformers who equated restriction of the franchise with "purification" of the body politic championed disfranchisement. Their success helped Progressives create a new coalition from the purged (and less numerous) electorate that owed little to Populist antecedents. Progressivism in Alabama, therefore, rested on the institutionalization of legal and political inequality. Hackney's book certainly made it difficult to characterize

---

[21]Kathryn Kish Sklar, "The Historical Foundations of Women's Power in the Creation of the American Welfare State, 1830–1930," in Seth Koven and Sonya Michel, eds., *Mothers of a New World: Maternalist Politics and the Origins of Welfare States* (New York, 1993), 43–93; quote from 44. See also Linda Gordon, ed., *Women, the State, and Welfare* (Madison, Wis., 1990), and *Pitied But Not Entitled: Single Mothers and the History of Welfare, 1890–1935* (New York, 1994).

[22]Sheldon Hackney, *Populism to Progressivism in Alabama* (Princeton, N.J., 1969). See also C. Vann Woodward, *Origins of the New South, 1877–1913* (Baton Rouge, La., 1951).

Progressivism in the South as a broad-based coalition for "social welfare" or against "corporate arrogance." Whatever was true of Progressivism in other places, in the land of Jim Crow it was a profoundly racist and conservative movement. Finally, Edward Blum's recent study of post-Reconstruction America shows that literary, religious, and political elites across the nation collaborated in grounding Progressive reform in racist and imperialist solidarity among whites.[23]

If Progressivism was bad for blacks, it also had other negative effects. It certainly strengthened the hand of prohibitionists and advocates of immigration restriction. The Progressive years marked a high point in the history of American racism. All non-Nordic people — descendants of Africa, Asia, Latin America, and southern and eastern Europe, among others —became targets of those who considered themselves descendants of "the great race." As John Higham showed, antiforeign, anti-Catholic, anti-Semitic, and antiradical tendencies in American politics came together in the early twentieth century and culminated in the World War I period. Those years saw hysterical assaults upon the liberty of German Americans, the passage of the Alien and Sedition Acts, which sent hundreds of pacifists and critics of the war to jail, the Red Scare, which resulted in the jailing and deportation of hundreds of socialists and anarchists, and finally the Immigration Restriction Act of 1924.[24] Historians disagree as to whether such baneful forms of chauvinism were the fruit of Progressivism or a corruption of it. But certainly Progressivism furthered a newly intense form of nationalism. And it gave political advantage to those Protestant professionals who were best able to organize themselves into special-interest groups, and who were most tempted to explain social instability as a product of alien influences upon *our* country.

As political historians have recently shown, the urge to purify the electoral system produced some of the most antidemocratic results of Progressive reform. Many of the Progressives' favorite structural reforms — for example, primaries, voter registration, city commissions — contributed to a dramatic shrinkage in the electorate. Walter Dean Burnham, a political scientist, identified the period immediately following the depression of the 1890s as a moment of major realignment in American politics that also witnessed a weakening of party loyalty and a massive decline in voting. The decline of party, in turn, magnified the significance of pressure groups of all kinds.[25] In New York state, Richard L. McCormick showed party bosses weakened under attacks from nonpartisan reformers who raised new issues incapable of being resolved by the traditional party technique of distributing favors as widely as possible. McCormick further showed that between 1904 and 1908 the regulatory authority of government increased in precisely the same

---

[23]Edward J. Blum, *Reforging the White Republic: Race, Religion, and American Nationalism, 1865–1898* (Baton Rouge, La., 2005), 200.

[24]John Higham, *Strangers in the Land: Patterns of American Nativism 1860–1925* (New York, 1963). See also Chapter 5.

[25]Walter Dean Burnham, "The Changing Shape of the American Political Universe," *American Political Science Review* 59 (March 1965): 7–28, and *Critical Elections and the Mainsprings of American Politics* (New York, 1970).

period that voter turnout declined, ticket-splitting increased, and organized pressure groups gained power at the expense of party. In discovering that business corrupted politics, Progressive-era Americans created a demand for the regulatory and administrative state. But the rise of that state disempowered lower-class constituents of political machines at the same time that it empowered the organizationally skilled middle classes. Whether men or women, whether more liberal or more conservative, whether structural or social reformers, and whether they intended to or not, these well-to-do Progressive reformers achieved political efficacy at the expense of mass democracy.[26]

In recent years, studies of Progressive-era politics continue to fill out or reinterpret the story limned by the historians discussed above. Michael McGerr's *A Fierce Discontent* insists that Progressivism was both middle-class and radical, especially in its determination to transform lower-class behavior and control corporate power. To accomplish these ends Progressives sought to break up trusts and regulate them, to educate the masses and segregate some of them, to constrain individualism and liberate the individual. McGerr succeeds only partially in gathering all these tendencies under the banner of "the radical middle," but the breadth of his interpretation rivals that of the most serious historians of Progressivism. Maureen Flanagan's *America Reformed* makes plain that several "Progressivisms" flourished at the turn of the century, but focuses on four varieties: "social justice, political, economic, and foreign policy."[27] Although she underplays the role of religion in inspiring (and sometimes thwarting) both reformers and imperialists, Flanagan succeeds in taking continuous account of race and gender in her evaluation of reform, and especially in bringing foreign policy into the center of the story.

Few contributions to the history of Progressivism offer more original or fruitful insight than Daniel Rodgers's *Atlantic Crossings: Social Politics in a Progressive Age*. Magisterial in its scope and its command of varied sources in several languages, Rodgers's book surveys the evolution of "social politics," or "cosmopolitan Progressivism," within the transatlantic world. Stretching from fin de siècle Paris, to Chicago in the Hull House years, to London during the blitz, Rodgers's work will require all future historians of twentieth-century reform to discuss their subject in comparative terms. He has established that, whatever the differences between Europe's social democratic trajectory and America's Progressive and New Deal versions of the regulatory and welfare state, the similarities are just as striking. "The tides of culture were not inflexible," Rodgers notes, "just as they were not neatly contained by nation-states." American reformers in touch with their European counterparts discovered something even more important than the legitimacy of state action to right

---

[26]Richard L. McCormick, *From Realignment to Reform: Political Change in New York State, 1893–1910* (Ithaca, N.Y., 1981), and "The Discovery That Business Corrupts Politics: A Reappraisal of the Origins of Progressivism," *American Historical Review* 86 (April 1981): 247–74.

[27]Michael McGerr, *A Fierce Discontent: The Rise and Fall of the Progressive Movement in America, 1870–1920* (New York, 2003); Maureen A. Flanagan, *America Reformed: Progressives and Progressivisms, 1890s–1920s,* (New York, 2007), vii.

social wrongs, as momentous as this was in the land of laissez-faire. This discovery amounted to nothing less than the end of intellectual "geocentricity." The United States was not the center of the political universe, even though Europeans continued to cherish and learn from America's political democracy. The American conversation about what constitutes a just society and a good government would never again, after the Progressive era, resemble an internal monologue.[28] An excerpt from Rodgers's book appears as the second reading in this chapter.

At a far remove from Rodgers's effort to reconceive Progressivism as the collective project of cosmopolitan intellectuals, Elizabeth Sanders sees agrarian radicalism at the heart of both Populist and Progressive efforts to use state and national legislation to right the wrongs of the unregulated capitalist marketplace. Rejecting the top-down approaches of scholars such as Kolko, Sanders insists that agrarian radicals on the periphery fundamentally shaped legislation and political coalitions by exercising their local and regional power within the electoral system. Capitalist interests at the core fought bitterly first to stop, then to co-opt and moderate that thrust from the periphery, but they never simply imposed their will. By focusing on legislative rather than administrative records, Sanders shows that, in a functioning political democracy, the interests of mobilized grassroots movements played a large part in setting the agenda for what Rodgers calls social politics.[29]

In a very different, though equally significant way, historians attentive to the distinctive power of religion in American political culture have reshaped our understanding of the Progressive era. Michael Kazin's new biography of William Jennings Bryan persuasively argues that Bryan's career embodied many of the most Progressive tendencies of his age and shaped liberal politics for several generations. Arguing that the Social Gospel made Progressive reform possible to a substantial (if not exclusive) extent, Kazin reminds readers of the deeply rooted power and transformative potential of evangelical Christianity at the turn of the twentieth century — and, indeed, into the present. He offers strong support to the proposition that evangelicalism and liberalism are not necessarily, or usually, antagonistic, although here Edward Blum's more cautionary tale of late-nineteenth-century religious complicity in white supremacy should be remembered.[30]

Gaines M. Foster's *Moral Reconstruction* transforms the picture of Gilded Age and Progressive-era politics by placing organized Christian moralism at its very center. The people who eventually brought prohibition to the United States, though sometimes allied with Progressive reformers (and sometimes arrayed against them), entered politics "to outlaw sin, not to promote justice or equality."[31] They inherited the nationalism of the Civil War era but

---

[28]Daniel T. Rodgers, *Atlantic Crossings: Social Politics in a Progressive Age* (Cambridge, Mass., 1998), 366, 1.

[29]Elizabeth Sanders, *Roots of Reform: Farmers, Workers, and the American State, 1877–1917* (Chicago, 1999).

[30]Michael Kazin, *A Godly Hero: The Life of William Jennings Bryan* (New York, 2006).

[31]Gaines M. Foster, *Moral Reconstruction: Christian Lobbyists and Federal Legislation of Morality, 1865–1920* (Chapel Hill, N.C., 2002), 3.

employed it not to pursue a "search for order" devoid of specific content. Rather, they aimed to use the magnified authority of the nation-state to impose Christian morality upon individual "avarice and appetite." Their religiosity was neither a mask for class or ethnic interest, nor a vehicle for women's political empowerment. Instead, it expressed a deeply settled intention to make God's law the law of the land. Far from a momentary "symbolic crusade," or a movement designed to defend or advance middle-class status, or a "response to industrialism" that sought to adjust America to the requirements of a modernizing capitalist society, "moral reconstruction" linked Christian activists in a continually renewing crusade that stretched from abolitionism in the past to "the moral majority" in the future. Foster wisely notes that resistance to Christian moralism in the form of secular civil libertarianism represents no less enduring a political tradition. As David Rabban has made clear in his study of civil libertarianism at the turn of the twentieth century, the Progressive era revealed the future of both American liberalism and American conservatism.[32]

Daniel Rodgers has observed that historians no longer attempt to describe the Progressive era within a unitary political or ideological framework.[33] The roots, forms, and outcomes of Progressivism were diverse and even conflicting. But if Progressives lacked a systematic intellectual system and a coherent politics, they did share a sense — which can only be called modern — that a new scale had come to human affairs; that great enterprises, cities, and organizations, both private and public, would thenceforth shape the destinies of most people in the modern world. Appalled by corporate arrogance and political corruption, and sometimes moved by the sufferings of less-fortunate Americans, these mostly Christian reformers — of upper, middle, and sometimes lower class — sought order or justice or moral coherence, using their new professional skills and their electoral clout. Most of them tried to preserve what they valued in the legacies of individualism, decentralized government, citizen voluntarism, and the like, even as they embraced new forms of government intervention and new forms of solidarity. America changed as a result of Progressivism, but it became neither a Christian commonwealth nor a bureaucratic dystopia. America was always larger and less coherent than any Progressivism imagined or accomplished. Those who rejected Progressive reform in all or large part — proponents of laissez-faire and small government, for example, not to mention champions of Anglo-Saxon or Christian supremacy and patriarchal privilege — would continue to shape American history along with their more progressive fellow citizens. Finally, in the New Deal years a generation of reformers from more diverse ethnic and class origins proposed reforms that went well beyond Progressivism. But in going beyond Progressivism they also revealed its traces. For better or worse, Progressivism shaped the political landscape for subsequent generations of Americans seeking to engage their diverse, unequal, and ever-changing society.

---

[32]David M. Rabban, *Free Speech in Its Forgotten Years* (New York, 1997).
[33]Daniel T. Rodgers, "In Search of Progressivism," *Reviews in American History* 10 (December 1982): 113–32.

KATHRYN KISH SKLAR

from The Historical Foundations of Women's Power in the Creation of the American Welfare State, 1880–1920   [1993]

KATHRYN KISH SKLAR (1939–) is distinguished professor of history at the State University of New York, Binghamton. She is the author of *Catharine Beecher, a Study in American Domesticity* (1973), *Florence Kelley and the Nation's Work: The Rise of Women's Political Culture, 1830–1900* (1995), and *Women's Rights Emerges within the Anti-Slavery Movement, 1830–1870* (2000).

One of the most exciting features of the new stream of scholarship on women and the creation of the American welfare state during what has been called the "watershed" of American history between 1880 and 1920 has been its tendency to draw large conclusions about the relationship between the political activism of white middle-class women and that of other social groups. . . .

This essay examines . . . features of American life that help us explain the power that middle-class women exercised in the white polity between 1890 and 1920 as they channeled the resources of the state in new directions. . . .

Women's activism was crucial because it served as a surrogate for working-class social-welfare activism. For complex historical reasons that derived partly from the political culture of middle-class women, partly from American political culture generally, women were able to provide systematic and sustained grass-roots support for social-welfare programs at a time when the working-class beneficiaries of those programs could lend only sporadic support. . . .

"Welfare" carries quite different connotations today than it did when the word first entered into common usage in the 1920s. Today "welfare" refers primarily to single mothers who receive Aid to Families with Dependent Children through the program that built "mothers' pensions" into the Social Security Act in 1935. . . .

Those who laid the foundations for the "welfare state" between 1880 and 1920 had a different perspective. For them, workers, not mothers, formed the chief focus of social legislation. Contemporary debate about how to alleviate social problems arising from industrialization revolved around wage-earning men, women, and children. "Mothers' pension" plans were one of the least-contested consequences of a larger policy debate about the regulation of the modern workplace and the intervention of the state in relation between capital and labor. Then, as now in the United States, the relatively unregulated workplace produced much higher rates of injuries and deaths than were common elsewhere. In tracing the origins of the American welfare state, feminist scholars have focused on the antecedents of AFDC or "mothers' pensions," but they have often overlooked the larger context within which mothers' pensions emerged — the large population of widows and orphans created by industrial injuries. "Make fewer widows!" one leading woman reformer declared when asked for her opinion on mothers' pensions. Her harsh but realistic reply shows us that there is more to the story of the emerging American welfare state than the "maternalism" that historians have called its chief characteristic. . . .

Opportunities for the expression of women's political activism multiplied after 1870, when traditions of limited government in the United States curbed forces that in England and Europe aided in the creation of welfare legislation. Traditions of limited government had three consequences. They undercut the development of problem-solving governmental agencies and bureaucracies; they promoted the power of professional politicians within the two major political parties; and they invested an uncommon degree of authority in the judiciary branch of government. . . .

Historians once believed that political bosses met the social-welfare needs of urban immigrant constituencies, but recent scholarship challenges that assumption. While municipal governments did dispense most nonfederal state spending before 1940, and hundreds of patronage-based jobs were distributed on the basis of party loyalty, taxes remained low and social services rudimentary. Partly due to a lack of imagination among party bosses, partly due to the restraining influence of the tax-conscious middle-class, urban political machines did not meet their constituencies' needs for positive government. They distributed food at Christmas, and mediated between members of their constituencies and social-service agencies. Sometimes they championed pure-milk campaigns, supported woman suffrage, and welcomed the construction of new schools, but most machine politicians were fiscal conservatives who, except in the business of getting votes, shunned policy innovations. Moreover, machine coalitions reinforced the power of capital by blocking pressures from below that might challenge its hegemony.

Thus policies to help the working poor survive the negative effects of industrialization went against the grain of American political structures, and crucial groups that advanced those policies elsewhere were hobbled in their attempts to do so in the United States. These circumstances created unprecedented opportunities for women reformers. When they moved into the political arena in large numbers in the 1890s, women became crucial catalysts, forming effective coalitions with men and with them constituting a new majority of politically active middle-class people in support of systematic changes in the political status quo. Men in every social group capable of advancing social legislation — lawyers, labor leaders, social scientists, industrialists, party politicians, middle-class male reformers, and even socialists — worked closely with middle-class women and their class-bridging organizations to achieve what men had not been able to accomplish separately. . . .

In the 1870s middle-class northern women propelled autonomous, mass-based women's organizations into the nation's political mainstream. This was the development stage of women's political culture. By far the most important organization, the Woman's Christian Temperance Union (WCTU), formed in 1874, carried women's pan-Protestant voluntarism into a new scale of political activism and a new depth of cultural meaning for its participants. Organizing their locals geographically to coincide with congressional districts, the WCTU endorsed woman suffrage as early as 1879. Through its "do everything" policy the Union became an umbrella organization with thirty-nine departments in 1896, twenty-five of which dealt wholly or mostly with nontemperance issues. . . .

The WCTU created new opportunities for middle-class women's social activism in a social environment that was absorbing massive numbers of recent European immigrants and a political environment where municipal, state, and national governments offered little if any assistance to needy men, women, and children. . . .

At the same time, other changes in American life democratized access to higher education and opened institutions of higher learning to women on an unprecedented scale. By 1880 more than forty thousand women were pursuing higher education, and one out of every three undergraduates was female. The feminization of the teaching profession generated these high statistics. Historically controlled by local rather than state or national governments, public schools vastly increased in number between 1800 and 1880 as the Euro-American population spread across the continent. In the competition among neighboring towns for settlers and other commercial advantages, the number or quality of village schools could define the difference between a potential county seat and a permanent backwater. The feminization of the teaching profession occurred in this context of unprecedented demand for teachers, because women were cheaper (and, many argued, better) than the traditional schoolmaster. . . . When the American welfare state began to emerge in the 1890s, a sizable second generation of college graduates was mobilized for action.

Tens of thousands of urban middle-class women put their education to use in the women's club movement. In 1890 the General Federation of Women's Clubs (GFWC) drew together a vast network of local women's organizations, which since 1869 had emerged as the secular equivalent of the WCTU. Generating an effective intermediate level of organization through state federations, and channeling women's energies into concerted political action, the GFWC became the chief voice of "organized womanhood" after 1900. By 1910 it represented 800,000 women, some of whom could vote in local elections, and most of whom had at least some influence on the male voters in their families. Even more remarkable than their formidable numbers was the impressive range of topics women's clubs explored. By 1890 these extended far beyond what might be expected to be their class-specific or gender-specific interests, or even the issues raised by the National American Woman Suffrage Association. For example, the Chicago Women's Club in the early 1880s, under its motto "Nothing Human can be Alien to Us," discussed such political questions as "Free Trade," "The Eight Hour Day," and "Bismarck and His Policy." They circulated petitions in 1886 for state legislative bills to place the treatment of women in public institutions under the supervision of women and city-council ordinances to add more women to the Board of Education. In response to Eleanor Marx's tour of the United States in 1887, members debated "Socialism and the Home." Two years later a club member spoke on "The Influence and Results of Merely Palliative Measures of Reform."

Opposed to the employment of mothers of young children, the [General] Federation [of Women's Clubs] energetically campaigned for the passage of state mothers' pensions laws. Its rhetoric critiqued industrialization from the perspective of exploited women and children. The Federation's official history in 1912 expressed the moral outrage that regularly aroused hundreds of thousands of women to social action. "Probably the most piteous cry which has reached the ears of the mothers of the nation is that which goes up from the little children whose lives are sacrificed to the greed of manufacture," it noted in a chapter on "Federation Ideals." Although the "advent of machinery" had been a great blessing to some, it also increased "the labor of women and little children." . . .

Politically aware, willing to experiment, and eager to undertake cross-class initiatives, large numbers of middle-class women were not mirror images of their fathers, husbands, and brothers but drawing on common political traditions, structured their own forms of political action.

The gendered components of American social science made it relatively easy for college-trained women to think of themselves as policy experts. By the time Progressive women reformers encountered social science in the 1880s, it was already thoroughly gendered — in a woman-friendly way. . . . Women responded to this congeniality in social science by forming their own social-science organizations as well as by joining those led by men. In New York in the early 1870s they formed the New York City Sociology Club, the Women's Progressive Association, and the Ladies' Social Science Association. By the 1890s women reformers confidently used social-science tools in ways that permitted them to engage in reform activity on an equal basis with men without surrendering the "feminine" qualities that differentiated them from men. Moreover, leading women social scientists, like Florence Kelley and Jane Addams, who were sustained by female institutions like Hull House and undeterred by the repression experienced by their male colleagues in universities, continued throughout their lives to affiliate closely with popular social movements, particularly those dominated by women.

Just as important as education and social science in drawing middle-class women into public activism was the growth of their consciousness as consumers. This consciousness reflected the unprecedented market in consumer goods and the emergence of a consumer culture that linked producers, sellers, and buyers. Waves of immigrants who entered industrial and manufacturing jobs between 1880 and 1900 lifted most northern native-born working-class Americans into white-collar work, creating a large and relatively new group of middle-class consumers. New forms of marketing emerged, visible in the size and number of advertisements in popular magazines and the scale and diversity of department stores. Consumer culture had two striking effects on women within the older, well-established middle class. It made them more conscious of their relatively elite position within emerging middle-class consumer culture; and it highlighted the contrast between their relatively privileged lives and the lives of women who toiled to produce consumer goods. The National Consumers' League and its scores of local branches embodied the new consciousness of middle-class consumers.

Amplifying the trends that deepened and intensified the potential for political activism among middle-class women, a vanguard of talented leaders emerged within the social-settlement movement. Choosing to live in working-class, immigrant neighborhoods, this vanguard acquired potent leadership skills for cross-class cooperation with working-class women, and the ability to speak for the welfare of their entire society, not merely for the needs of women and children, or for the interests of their own class. In the United States the social-settlement movement built on and consummated social trends that had steadily enlarged women's public activism since 1830: religious or moral values that justified women's activism; the gender-specific autonomy of women's organizations and institutions; women's access to higher education; and their use of social science as a reform tool.

A product of the Social Gospel movement, settlements drew on the religious roots of women's justifications of their public power. . . . For hundreds of young women between 1890 and 1920, the question, "After college, what?" was answered with a few years of settlement work before marriage. Moreover, for dozens of talented college graduates like Jane Addams, Florence Kelley, Julia Lathrop, Alice Hamilton, Grace Abbott, and Mary Simkhovitch, settlement life sustained lifelong careers in reform activism. . . .

Nevertheless, the new empowerment of women reformers through the social-settlement movement did not turn women into men. Indeed, the more women acquired power and resources, the more they did so as women. Women and men remained highly differentiated — socially, politically, and economically. Women's very prominence within the American social-settlement movement reflected that difference, since for them settlements served as a substitute for the political, professional, academic, and religious careers from which they were excluded by reason of their gender. . . .

The years between 1900 and 1920 marked the maturation of the political culture of middle-class women. Able to vote in only a few states before 1910, excluded by law from public office in most states, and perceived as outsiders by lawmakers in Congress, and in state and municipal governments, women had to find ways to overcome these gender-specific "disabilities" if they were to affect public policy. They did so by drawing on the most fundamental and enduring features of women's political culture — the strength of its grass-roots organizations, and the power of its moral vision.

Structured representationally, women's organizations, even those with strong national leaders like the National Consumers' League, gave great weight to the views of state and local affiliates. This sparked grass-roots initiative. It also fostered belief in democratic processes and the capacity of large social organizations — like state and federal governments — to respond positively to social needs. Whereas the predominant moral vision of men's political culture tended to regard the state as a potential enemy of human liberty, the moral vision of women's political culture viewed the state as a potential guarantor of social rights. . . .

To a remarkable degree the creation of the American welfare state before 1930 was due to the endorsement these predominantly middle-class women's associations gave to the expansion of governmental responsibility for the welfare of able-bodied wage earners and their families. They lobbied for legislative interventions in the relations between capital and labor to protect those they viewed as the weakest and most exploited by the forces of industrial capitalism. Shorter hours, higher wages, safer work sites would, they thought, create sounder citizens and a better society. Many of these organizations were explicitly class-bridging, such as the Women's Trade Union League, the National Consumers' League, and the YWCA. All invited the influence of the vanguard of reform leadership concentrated in the social-settlement movement. All cooperated closely with a variety of men's groups.

The distinction between white middle-class women's and men's political cultures expressed deeply rooted gender-specific social structures and cultural values. Yet while this distinction maintained firm differences between women's and men's public endeavors, it also established the preconditions for close cooperation between women and men. . . .

Women needed access to the institutional power and positions of public authority that men held, and men needed the grass-roots support that women could mobilize. Thus the National Congress of Mothers drew on the help of juvenile-court judges to launch a successful campaign for state mothers' pensions laws between 1910 and 1915. The National Consumers' League relied on prominent male attorneys to argue their cases before the U.S. Supreme Court. The General Federation of Women's Clubs worked with state superintendents of education and other state and municipal officials in designing and implementing their legislative agendas. . . .

What was it about the combination of women's grass-roots activism and small groups of male experts and leaders that accounted for their success at passing welfare legislation before 1930? What did this partnership accomplish and what does it tell us about the forces that created the American welfare state? The success of these forces was limited. For example, their effort to outlaw child labor through a constitutional amendment failed, as did their attempts to create unemployment insurance nationally — two reforms that became possible only after the devastating depression of the early 1930s — and they failed to establish state-sponsored health care for workers, an issue that continues to bedevil the American polity in the 1990s. But their efforts built a foundation on which it was possible to construct the "New Deal" of the 1930s. . . .

Women's collective action in the Progressive era certainly expressed a maternalist ideology, as historians have frequently pointed out. But it was also sparked by a moral vision of a more equitable distribution of the benefits of industrialization, and the vitality of its relatively decentralized form of organization. Within the political culture of middle-class women, gender consciousness combined with an awareness of class-based injustice, and talented leaders combined with grass-roots activism to produce an impressive force for social, political, and economic change. Issues regarding women and children wage earners captured the imagination of tens of thousands of middle-class women between 1890 and 1920, so much so that gender — women's organizations and female-specific legislation — achieved much that in other industrializing nations was done through, and in the name of, class. Women did what Florence Kelley called "the nation's work" by reaching beyond the betterment of their own class to shape a new social compact for the society as a whole. . . .

Weighing the outcome of women's efforts, the cup can appear half full or half empty, depending on one's perspective. Lacking the power to dominate the American polity, women could not themselves institute a strong welfare state. From this perspective the cup seems half empty. Some historians have viewed the American welfare state as a failure and attributed its shortcomings to the women who did so much to create it, and the gender-specific policies they pursued. Yet, seen from another perspective, the cup appears half full. Women's grass-roots organizations and their network of leaders were responsible for many pathbreaking innovations that men could not achieve. The American Association for Labor Legislation, for example, gave up on its efforts to create state-sponsored programs of workers' health insurance in 1920, but in 1921 a broad coalition of women's organizations succeeded in creating a federally sponsored program for infant and maternity health, the Sheppard-Towner Maternity and Infancy Protection Act, which many state governments sustained after federal funds ceased in 1927. Women's gender-specific and child-specific strategies aimed to aid all working people, not merely the "truly needy." Rather than isolating poor women, activists envisioned a better society in which poverty could be ended. In the 1990s the Children's Defense Fund shows that their strategy remains a necessary if not sufficient surrogate for class-specific action in a polity that remains deeply hostile to class legislation.

Today, as we near the end of the twentieth century, persisting traditions of limited government empower those who discredit social-justice programs, and the lack of class-based politics erodes the power of those who advocate such programs. Today, during the height of deindustrialization, these problems seem even more grave than they were during the height of industrialization, since the nation is losing jobs that seem unlikely to return. Moreover, welfare policies today have become inextricably combined with attitudes toward race and social justice for African Americans. One hundred years ago gender served as a surrogate for class. Today class is still less prominent than gender and race in the minds of those who design American welfare policy.

Between 1890 and 1930 middle-class women changed American public policy, but they could not and did not change the fundamental nature of the state itself, or alter the character of the male-dominated polity. Nevertheless their legacy amounts to more than the policies they embraced. Their example reveals the enduring efficacy of their methods — grass-roots organizations and class-bridging visions — for those who aspire to change American public policy.

DANIEL T. RODGERS

from Atlantic Crossings: Social Politics in a Progressive Age   [1998]

DANIEL T. RODGERS (1942–) is Charles Lea Professor of History at Princeton University and author of *The Work Ethic in Industrial America, 1850–1920* (1978) and *Contested Truths: Key Words in American Politics since Independence* (1987).

Two phenomena of the late nineteenth century made the North Atlantic progressive connection possible. The first was the rapidly convergent economic development of the key nations of the North Atlantic basin. Across the older, intricately varied political and cultural checkerwork of Europe and North America began to appear, in thicker and thicker concentrations, economic institutions instantly recognizable from one end of the North Atlantic region to the other. Nothing was more important for sustained trade in social policies than this dramatic expansion of the social landscapes of industrial capitalism. In a world of nation-states, economic forces were particularly aggressive trespassers and powerful centralizers of experience.

The second phenomenon was less tangible and more fragile than the first, but to the emerging transnational social-political networks it was no less fundamental. This was a new understanding of common histories and vulnerabilities. The new landscapes of fact and the intertwined landscapes of mind had equally indispensable parts to play in the Atlantic progressive connection. For social policies to be borrowable across political boundaries, there must be not only a foundation of common economic and social experience but also a recognition of underlying kinship. The polities in question must be seen to face similar needs and problems, to move within shared historic frames, and to strive toward a commonly imagined future. Relatedness is the core assumption. Where there is only comparison or culturally imagined difference there can be envy or pride in abundance, but there can be no sustained trade in social policy. . . .

In the dominant, "republican" understanding of the relationship between European and American politics, the tyrannies of the Old World were pitted against the freedom of the New World. . . . Through their monopoly on governance, the aristocracies seemed to have hung the state's apparatus on the peoples of Europe like massive millstones. Overtaxed, overgoverned, rent-racked, and impoverished, the European nations groaned under the double weight of political and economic parasitism.

The genius of New World liberty, in contrast, had been to set the people's will and welfare on top. Constitutional government, democratization of office holding and suffrage, and abolition of inherited privilege down to the final, nation-wrenching overthrow of the despotism of slavery: in these Americans imagined that the torch of liberty had been passed westward to the New World republic. In these, the exceptionalist historical promise of America was engraved. . . .

The republican image of Europe was not made wholly out of wish and illusion. . . . One quarter of England and Wales in 1873 was held by only 360 owners; in the same year 350 landowners possessed fully two-thirds of all land in Scotland. . . . Nowhere in late-nineteenth-century Europe, France and Switzerland excepted, did universal male suffrage rule, as it did in theory (and, in practice, for white males) in the United States. At one extreme was Belgium where, until a general strike finally forced the government's hand in 1893, less than a tenth of the adult male population was eligible to vote; even after the reforms of the 1890s, a system of plural votes for property holders and university graduates permitted the wealthiest third of the nation to outvote all the rest in parliamentary elections. Not far behind Belgium in its suffrage restrictions was Sweden, where on the eve of suffrage reform in 1909 barely a third of all adult men met the property tests for Riksdag elections.

In Germany, where Reichstag elections were open to universal male suffrage, local and state elections were hedged in by such extremely high barriers that the Social Democratic Party in 1900, although it could count on a quarter of the popular Reichstag election vote, had yet successfully to elect a single delegate to the Prussian legislature. The most casual visitor to imperial Germany could not miss the massive political presence of the Junkers in the army, the higher ranks of government administration, the Prussian legislature, and the Reichstag. Victorian England was much more effectively democratized than Germany, but even in 1890, in the wake of three major suffrage reform acts, residence and property exclusions still kept four out of every ten adult males off the voting lists. Despite a century of rising bourgeois fortunes, almost half the seats in the turn-of-the-century British cabinet were still occupied by landed aristocrats.

Democratic radicals in nineteenth-century Europe honed these same points of contrast and helped publicize the American promise. . . .

But if the image of their democratic future in the west riveted the imaginations of European democrats in the 1870s and 1880s, it was the Americans who polished the image to perfection. When in the middle years of the century, buoyed by curiosity, cheap steamship travel, and new reserves of disposable wealth, middle- and upper-class American tourists began to descend on Europe, their responses fell quickly into the waiting formulas. Pilgrims in search of proof of their own distinctiveness, Americans in mid-nineteenth-century Europe came back amply sated. . . .

The formulas of the republican encounter with Europe were a lesson in patriotism. The polarities already fixed in the mind's eye of the American travelers bent their attention toward evidence of backwardness and poverty: the wooden clogs of the peasants, the dark country bread, the women toiling in the fields. They brought into relief the pretenses of the European monarchs: the pageants and parades, the imperial profiles . . . stamped on pocket handkerchiefs, embroidered on sofa cushions, carved on tobacco pipe bowls. The standing armies, so unfamiliar to Americans, were a constant affront. . . .

From a Europe so conceived, there was nothing to be learned. The American Federation of Labor's Samuel Gompers, returning to the England of his boyhood for a summer's tour in 1909, reiterated the point. "The Old World is not our world. Its social problems, its economic philosophies, its current political questions are not linked up with America. . . . In the procession [of nations], America is the first."

By the last decades of the nineteenth century these reassuring republican contrasts had begun to jostle more and more frequently in American minds with a rival, "aesthetic" framing of the Old World–New World relationship, whose keys were no longer oppression and liberty but culture, custom, and time. Against the slow, organic forces of Old World growth, they set the New World's raw, competitive unfinishedness. . . .

It was the customs of the grand tour that most forcefully encouraged the aesthetic mood. Seeking out an imagined premodern and apolitical Europe, middle- and upper-class Americans traveling through Europe in the late nineteenth century fell quickly into the terms packaged for them in their commercial guidebooks. Above all, the grand tour was a lesson in time and antiquity. Here was a continent not only dotted with antiquities but also seeming itself to be a museum where nature and artifice blended into a seamless, "organic" whole. . . .

Politically, there was no missing in the aesthetic reappraisal of Europe a sharp deflation of the democratic ideal. The aesthetic travelers let the huddled cottages assume a patina of quaintness and transformed the uniforms of the soldiers into a brilliant wash of color. . . . Where in the early 1870s the anthropologist Lewis Henry Morgan could not think of the Arc de Triomphe except as a monument to despotism, a generation later John Frey thought it part of the handsomest streetscape in the world. Visiting Napoleon's tomb, Frey gave not a whisper of censure. The stages of historical progress, once marked so clearly by constitutionalism, suffrage expansion, and the abolition of slavery, fell into confusion.

Such half-articulated doubts about the older democratic certainties were no mere quirk of the grand tour. Across a broad front in both the United States and fin de siècle Europe, those who . . . had once thought the formal structures of democracy sufficient were not as confident as they had been a quarter century before. Suffrage and constitutionalism, the liberties of trade and person: as a political program bare and alone, these had lost much of their earlier luster. By the end of the century, European radicals, stung by the rapid consolidation of American trusts and monopolies, by the eruption of popular protest in the land of formal democratic promise, and by the unnerving stench of American political corruption, had begun to recant their earlier admiration for the United States. "A quarter of a century ago the American republic was the guiding star of advanced English political thought, [but] it is not so now," William Clarke, the most favorably inclined of the early Fabians toward the United States, wrote in the mid-1890s. Of one thing Clarke was now sure, that "a mere theoretic democracy, unaccompanied by any social changes, was a delusion and a snare." The image of a democratic showcase in the west faded for European radicals. Worrying about the immigrant voter question and backpedaling hard on African-American suffrage, many Americans, too, joined the general retreat from the mid-nineteenth-century democratic verities.

But if this rereading of Europe in organic rather than republican terms could not be separated from dissolution of confidence in formal constitutional democracy, it would be wrong to see in it only conservative and nostalgic political implications. For what was the middle-class American tourists' hunger for an imagined, preindustrial Old World stability except an act of recoil against the disordered, violent camping expedition that was the United States? Europe was "organic" and harmonious, the United States "anarchic"; through the one ran common customs, through the other unrelieved competitive individualism. Pushing out the older political antitheses, the dualities seated themselves at the very core of the aesthetic image of Europe. . . .

Outside the polarities of the nineteenth-century grand tour, beyond the ken of both the republican and the aesthetic tourists, engines of convergence were, in fact, hard at work. On both sides of the Atlantic a new world of coal and iron, factory towns and sprawling urban agglomerations, accumulated capital, massed wage labor, and new forms of misery was swiftly coming into being. . . .

The birthplace of this new world was Britain. From the late eighteenth century forward, with consequences that had all but swept away the social landscape of Scott and Wordsworth by the time late-nineteenth-century American tourists set out to look for it, the forces of industrial capitalism had turned the old agrarian economy upside down. The mills, machinery, and steam pumps of the new economic order were still strange and revolutionary when they burst into William Blake's consciousness in 1790s London, their "cogs tyrannic/Moving by compulsion each other." By the last third of the next century, the output of Britain's mines and factories bestrode the world. In 1870, the United Kingdom produced almost a third of the world's manufactured goods. Britain's mines produced two and a half times as much coal in 1870 as its nearest rival and almost four times as much iron ore: in cotton spindles, Britain's lead was almost five to one. . . .

The nations of the North Atlantic economy vied for markets with fierce intensity, manipulating trade and tariff policies or grabbing for captive colonial markets in an effort to leapfrog past each other in industrial primacy. Still, to focus on the nation-state is to distort the fundamental forces at work. Slipping across national borders with the fluidity of quicksilver, investment capital and management and production techniques diffused through the avenues of North Atlantic trade. By the late nineteenth century, what struck those who traversed the industrial regions of the Old and New Worlds was not their difference but their extraordinary sameness.

Physically, the most important common linkage was coal. Not all the world's industrial regions sat above or close by massive coal deposits in the nineteenth century, but most did. Coal was the critical natural resource of the industrial revolution. . . . The coal regions were furnaces not only of production but also of labor-capital conflict — home to the largest labor unions of the late nineteenth and early twentieth centuries and early sites everywhere of state economic action.

Of the four major manufacturing regions of nineteenth-century Britain, three (the fourth was London) lay atop a landscape of coal. The most important was the great textile mill and factory agglomeration of northern England. In 1901 more than a third of Britain's "great cities" of more than 100,000 persons were to be found there, within a forty-mile radius of Manchester. . . . Coketown, Dickens called the new industrial city in derision. But there were Coketowns everywhere.

They stretched through Belgium and northern France, across a broad seam of mineral deposits from Lille to Liège, copies in every essential regard of their English progenitors. Belgium's mines, factories, and densely packed industrial towns made it the most intensely industrialized nation of continental Europe — a region of strenuously overcrowded workers' dwellings, low wages, intensive child labor, and startlingly high illiteracy rates. Across the French border, the social landscape resumed without a break. The northern departments were the heart of industrial France, the source of most of its coal and cotton textiles, site of many of its large, paternalistic industrial enterprises, cockpit of the radical French labor movement, and, by the century's end, a stronghold of working-class socialism.

To the east, the common landscape resurfaced in the lower Rhineland and the Ruhr. Capital investment came late to the Ruhr, but nowhere in Europe between 1870 and the First World War did industrialization advance at a more furious pace. By the turn of the century the Ruhr and its surrounding ring of industrial cities . . . boasted the continent's largest, most intense concentration of heavy industry. Between 1890 and 1900, German steel production, the heart of it in the Ruhr, vaulted ahead of Britain's and soon helped nose Germany past Britain in shares of world manufacturing output. . . . By 1900 the industrial regions of Germany were in the teeth of an economic transformation swifter even than that of the United States itself.

On the western rim of the Atlantic, tied into the same nexus of trade, primed by infusions of British capital and wholesale borrowings of British technology, the same forces ran. . . . By the second half of the nineteenth century, . . . the "Europeanization" of the industrial landscape was well under way. Pennsylvania, with its massive coal deposits, was the nation's economic heartland. The country's two most important manufacturing cities, New York and Philadelphia, drew on Pennsylvania mines for their swelling energy needs; the Pittsburgh district was the American Ruhr. In the Middle West, the Illinois coal fields fed another massive industrial concentration, stretching from Pittsburgh and Cleveland on the east to Milwaukee and Chicago on the west. . . . The United States had caught up to Britain in steel production by 1880 and in coal production by 1900. In the production of ships and textiles, Britain remained unchallenged, but in the Anglo-German-American race for overall manufacturing output, the primacy of the Americans was a settled fact by the century's end. Alarm at the American penetration of customary European markets fed a steady press diet. The "Americanization" of the world, European journalists called it. It would be fairer to think of it as the Europeanization of America. Better still, to think of it as the manifestation of market processes that sprawled everywhere across the boundary lines neatly marked by statesmen and diplomats.

Coketown was the first defining element of the new world industrial capitalism made. The second was what contemporaries called, with both expansive pride and sweeping nervousness, the "great city." Great cities were not as novel as the new factory towns. Nodal points of trade and capital accumulation, they had played a critical role in the economy of early modern Europe. London had a population of more than a million in 1800, Paris 500,000, Vienna 250,000. But the multiplication of big urban centers in the last decade of the nineteenth century was, nonetheless, a startling phenomenon. From Andrew Mearns's *The Bitter Cry of Outcast London* to Jacob Riis's *How the Other Half Lives* to the strident German outcry against the *Grossstädt*, the growth of the metropolis played hard on the consciousness of turn-of-the-century social reformers throughout the North Atlantic economy.

Of the proliferation of great cities — not mere towns but cities of 100,000 persons or more — the facts left no doubt. In 1871 there were eight cities in the German empire of more than 100,000 persons, accounting in total for about 5 percent of the German Empire's population. Forty years later there were forty-eight *Grossstädte*, one of which, Berlin, had passed the million mark; two in ten Germans now lived in one. There were fifteen great cities in France and forty-one in Britain and Ireland, including the giant of them all, London, swollen now to a population of 7 million. In the United States, where there had been fourteen great cities in 1870, there were fifty in 1910. Notwithstanding the massive, diluting effects of the agrarian West and South, the United States in 1890 was already as urbanized as Belgium, as measured by the percentage of its population in cities of more than 20,000. Of the seven *Millionenstädte* in the North Atlantic economy in 1890, three were located in the United States.

Some of these great cities were heavy-industry complexes. The more common pattern was woven out of trade, finance, and small-scale manufacturing. London's East End, New York's Lower East Side, and their counterparts throughout the North Atlantic economy were centers of production as well as poverty, crowded hives of low-wage, irregular work for the great cities' swelling populations. From their inner commercial cores of banks and fashionable shopping districts, the great cities spread out through their dock districts, warehouses, and rail yards, on into a seemingly endless sea of sweatshops and small factories, corner stores and pawnshops, slums and cheap working-class housing, all in great unplanned confusion. . . .

The great cities' contrasts in fortune were one of their characteristic marks; another was the ceaseless motion of property and populations. . . . Contributing to this instability was the astonishing tide of persons who poured yearly into the cities, scrambling for place and shelter in an environment that never had enough to go around. Berlin, Vienna, Glasgow, and New York all presented particularly acute cases of housing famine, but no great city in the nineteenth and early twentieth centuries could be said to have adequately solved the problem of housing supply. Transportation and public health issues also pressed hard on urban authorities as they struggled to rationalize the crazy quilt of private water contractors, night-soil haulers, and horsecar lines that sprang up to meet the new urban needs. It is little wonder that the great cities should have absorbed so much of the political energy and imagination of turn-of-the-century progressives. Nowhere else was the clash between private property rights and public needs more tangibly and urgently displayed. . . .

But the countryside was no more immune to the market revolution than the cities. Foreign grain began to pour into Europe in the late 1860s and 1870s — from Canada, Russia, and (most importantly) the United States — with devastating consequences for agricultural stability. In

Ireland these pressures fanned long-standing tensions over religion and land-ownership into outright tenant revolt. And if resistance was common, flight was universal. The extreme case was Sweden, where 20 percent of the population emigrated between 1860 and 1910. Everywhere rural depopulation proceeded at a startling rate as the countryside emptied itself into the cities, leaving contemporaries struggling to find new crop mixes and marketing structures for the farm population that remained behind.

By the last quarter of the nineteenth century, there were, in conse-quence, uprooted peasants throughout the North Atlantic economy. The cities of the United States received them in particularly massive numbers, but Europe, beneath the tourists' preoccupation with stasis and custom, was hardly less in flux. In England by the century's end, scarcely more than a quarter of the people lived in the county in which they had been born; in Berlin in 1890, four out of every five male workers between the ages of thirty and sixty had been born outside the city. There were migrants everywhere: transient Irish in English factory towns, Polish miners in the Scottish collieries, Spanish miners in the coal works of southern France, Italian textile mill operatives in the factory towns of Belgium and the Lorraine, and country folks in every city. . . .

Among the most visible consequences of these interlocked changes in markets and labor was a tremendous outpouring of new goods. Real wages rose in the North Atlantic economy over the long course of the late nineteenth and early twentieth centuries. So did the opportunities for education, the supply of books and reading matter, the range of consum-able pleasures, and the avenues of mobility. . . .

But if the economic revolutions of the nineteenth century brought a flood of new goods into being, there could be no denying that they also brought new forms of misery. . . . The pains of rural life had been harsh and recurrent: crop failures, pestilence, disease, accident, childbirth. . . . The pains of industrial capitalism were less predictable, and their human face was less easily disguised. Both mobility and vulnerability increased with the growing commodification of labor. Without the safety of peasant plot, kin, and custom, the collapse of earning capacity in the new wage-labor market could be breathtakingly swift. . . . In these new forms of misery, the hand of human callousness, or calculation, or stupidity, or cheapness loomed at least as large as fate itself. An industrial accident, a landlord's eviction notice, a boss's intransigence over wages: these were all patently social events. Being matters of power and politics, it was hardly surprising that some men and women thought they must have social and political solutions. . . .

As custom receded before the onward march of commodification, the role of human agency became more and more evident. An entire vocabu-lary sprang up around the term "social" — "social economics," "social politics," the "social problem," the "social question" — all in testimony to the growing consciousness of the socially constructed nature of market capitalism. Pain was old, but the pains of the wage-labor market and of great city life were different than before, and less easily accepted under the old formulas.

. . . Whether or not middle-class progressives were right in calling the new age one of outright "industrial warfare," there is no doubt that social classes faced each other more frequently and over more deeply institutionalized hostility than before. Strikes were the most unnerving sign of the new order; bitter and violently fought on both sides, they grew in scope as the era proceeded, pulling the state more and more deeply into the role of policeman, negotiator, or military suppressor. . . . Where private rights ended and public rights began in this simmering conflict between organized labor and organized capital was an item of perpetual debate. . . .

. . . Those who forged the new social politics in the generation before the First World War never shared a common name. Some of them never found a consistent referential language even for themselves. William Beveridge referred to himself variously as a "Tory democrat," a "Labour imperialist," "very nearly" a socialist, and a Liberal. Frederic C. Howe, the American municipal reformer, called himself a single-taxer, a "liberal," a "reformer," and a "radical." Between national political cultures, the confusion of terms was even more pronounced. In France the pioneers of social politics styled themselves radicals, *solidaristes*, economic *interventionistes*, or simply proponents of *la réforme sociale*. In England they went under the name of "new Liberals," "new radicals," Christian socialists, Fabians, or "collectivists." In Germany, a dozen rival socio-political parties and pressure groups constructed themselves around permutations of the core term, *sozial*.

One comes close to a common denominator, however, with "progressive." As a political designation it was English before it was American, born in the heated municipal politics of 1890s London before crossing to the United States in the first decade of the new century. By 1910, in the Progressive People's Party (Fortschrittliche Volkspartei) of Friedrich Naumann, Lujo Brentano, and other younger reform intellectuals, the term "progressive" had acquired social-political overtones in Germany as well. . . .

Radicals and reformers before them had imagined themselves at work at the cutting edge of history, of course, but they had not located the economy as the key sector of change. Since the great eighteenth-century revolutions, their core project had been to restrain not the processes of commodification but the concentrated powers of the monarchical state. . . .

Into the last quarter of the nineteenth century, these projects still framed party politics and political culture. . . . In the United States in 1870, where radicals and reformers were still absorbed in the aftershocks of secession and civil war, the political reconstitution of the nation and the terms on which liberty was to be offered to the former slaves overshadowed every other political consideration.

The progressives of the late nineteenth and early twentieth centuries
were not indifferent to these issues. . . . But whether the shapers of the
new social politics sustained the old democratic radicalism or (more commonly) borrowed selectively from it, hedging the rest round with second
thoughts and qualifications, they shared a conviction that a politics
focused on the redivision of state power could no longer suffice. As the
authority that had once been the prerogative of courts and kings and the
landowning nobility passed to the possessors of capital and captains of
industry, as the key sources of power and pain became economic and
social, the grand legal-political dismantling projects of the radical past
faded before the need to rethink the purposes of society and the state.
This was what H. G. Wells, writing from the United States in 1906, meant
when he insisted that there was more political promise to be found in the
ambitious metropolitan park system being laid out in Boston, or in the
dynamos at Niagara that were just beginning to generate public power for
the province of Ontario, than in Washington, D.C., where the "national
government lies marooned, twisted up into knots, bound with safe guards,
and altogether impotently stranded." This was what progressives everywhere meant when they claimed that the mere negation of power was not
enough. The focus of politics turned from constitutions to administration, from the consequences of aristocratic privilege to the contexts of
everyday life. "The politics of the future," Britain's Joseph Chamberlain
put the point as early as 1883, "are social politics." . . .

The first major raptures in the prevailing frame proceeded opportunistically,
in quick, untheoretic seizures of crises and opportunities. Bismarck, who
had a visceral dislike for state interference in private wage contracts,
backed crabwise into his social insurance program of the 1880s — setting
the sanctity of a factory master's economic "household" aside for the
prospect of disarming the outlawed socialists and rewedding the loyalties
of the German working class to the state and emperor. Gladstone's Irish
land reform act of 1881, abrogating contracts, removing the question
of fair rent to a special state commission, and pledging state aid for a buy-
out of English landlords, was a similar singularity, an emergency breach
of Liberal principles in an attempt to calm the seething anger of Irish
tenants and drive the vexing Irish question, at last, out of politics.

By the 1890s, however, signs of broader, more lasting political realignments could be seen across the North Atlantic economy and in its out-
posts in Australia and New Zealand. The progressive movements of that
decade — Wilhelm II's flirtation with a "social monarchy," the emergent
social radicalism in France, the Liberal-labor alliance in New Zealand,
and the progressive urban coalitions in Britain and the United States —
differed sharply in their origins. . . .

By the first decade of the twentieth century there was no party system
within the North Atlantic economy that had not been profoundly shaken by
the new social politics. In Britain, the Liberal government of 1906–1914
embarked on a flurry of legislation that, a quarter century later, still stuck

in Franklin Roosevelt's mind for its daring. For the aged poor, it inaugurated an old-age pension system borrowed from New Zealand; for the crippling economic effects of sickness, a program of compulsory wage-earners' health insurance borrowed from Germany; for the most exploited of workers, a set of Australian-style wage boards empowered to establish legal minimum wages; for the sake of fiscal justice, progressive land and income taxes; for the unemployed, a German-style network of state-run employment offices; and, for workers in trades of particularly uneven labor demand, an untried experiment in pooling the risks of unemployment through state-administered insurance. The Radical coalitions that governed France between 1899 and 1914, though their failures were greater, proposed no less: progressive income taxation, public medical assistance to the elderly poor, a legally fixed maximum working day, tax subsidies for trade union unemployment benefits, public mediation of labor disputes, and — in a policy reversal that hinted at the international volatility of the new social politics — German-modeled, compulsory, old-age insurance. In timing and content, the prewar progressive movement in American politics fit, as fragment to whole, into this broader North Atlantic pattern.

On both sides of the Atlantic, politicians rode the new issues to power and popularity: David Lloyd George and the young Winston Churchill in Britain, Georges Clemenceau in France, Theodore Roosevelt and Woodrow Wilson in the United States. Parties and pressure groups drew up sweeping social programs. For the rest of the twentieth century, although parties split and polarized over the new issues, no politics could be divorced from social politics. . . .

The progressives' success in remaking the agenda of politics was no guarantee that their solutions would prevail. Everywhere the new policies proceeded in fits and starts, in opportunities seized and opportunities closed off again. Wilhelm II's new course of 1890 was exhausted by 1894; a second wave of social-political legislation in Germany, begun in 1905 was spent by 1911. The British "new Liberals" had depleted most of their political capital well before the First World War. Léon Bourgeois's government of 1895 fell within a year; the reform ambitions of Clemenceau's government of 1906 were quickly consumed in a cascade of labor strikes.

The fragility of prewar progressive politics was partly the result of a plurality of parties competing for the same terrain. In France, social politics was by definition coalition politics, always fragile. In the prewar United States, neither of the major parties successfully cornered the market in progressive issues. In Britain as late as 1905, the Webbs were still busy "permeating" the Conservative Party, certain it was the more promising vehicle than the Liberal Party for their collectivist ambitions. In Germany, where the Social Democratic Party and socialist labor unions remained beyond the pale of imperial legitimacy — tightly policed, their members excluded from all but the most minor administrative offices — social politics at the national level ran fitfully, on one leg alone, as reformers gained the emperor's ear and then lost it to others. Everywhere, the new politics made similar enemies. Property owners' and tax payers' associations, employers' interest groups, and chambers of commerce multiplied apace. . . . The new politics, in short, hardly thrust out the old. But between 1890 and 1914 reform politics was reconstituted in a new key and language.

The new politics was framed not only by the age's economic transformations but also by what progressives everywhere, with nervous delicacy, called the "labor question." The rise of mass working-class organization was a key feature of the times, and, like the new forms of capital, its reach was international. From the American Knights of Labor organizers canvassing for recruits in the English midlands in the 1880s to the British and American fraternal delegates trading places at their respective annual labor union gatherings to the work of Marx's successors at the Second Socialist International, there was no missing the sharply conscious international edge to labor politics. The German and Swedish Social Democratic Parties, the French and Belgian Parties Ouvriers, the English Social Democratic Federation, the American Socialist Labor Party, and the Second International itself were all founded between 1875 and 1889. A quarter of a century later, socialist parties constituted a major political challenge everywhere in the North Atlantic economy. In the United States, the socialists polled almost a million votes in 1912. In France in the last election before the First World War, one in six popular votes went to the socialists; in Germany, one in three. . . .

Beneath the growth of socialist and labor organizations lay a still more widespread, less organized set of resentments, more worrisome in some ways to middle-class progressives in their inchoateness and volatility. Strikes and lockouts, bitterly and often violently fought on both sides, were their most visible manifestation. From the 1880s forward these erupted on a scale unknown before. The Knights of Labor's nationwide eight-hour-day strike of 1886 and the London dockworkers' and Ruhr miners' strikes of 1889 were harbingers of the massive disputes to come. Strike waves shook . . . virtually all the industrialized societies between 1910 and 1913. . . . Union rolls in Germany between the early 1890s and the First World War mushroomed from less than 300,000 to 2.5 million; in Britain, from 1.6 to 4.1 million; in France from 140,000 to over a million; in the United States from 400,000 (in 1897, when reliable estimates begin) to 2.6 million.

In the face of these challenges, governments swung between military repression and the "soft embrace" of social-political concession. Yearning as they did for "social peace," it is not surprising that progressives swung with much the same ambivalence. . . .

It was within all these fields of force — the rapid intensification of market relations, the swelling great city populations, and the rising working-class resentments from below — that the new social politics took shape. The common social landscapes of industrial capitalism helped to knit its national strands together; so did deep, commonly shared anxieties. The internationalization of capital and labor were its preconditions. But progressive politics in the North Atlantic economy possessed its own international dynamics and institutions, and in the reconfiguring of social politics on a transnational frame, these were no less essential.

Within Europe itself, one of the most striking signs of the new transnational social politics was the phenomenon of legislation passed from one nation to another, sometimes despite acute distrust and rivalry. An early example was British-modeled factory legislation, which began to turn up in France, Germany, and elsewhere in the 1870s. A generation later, borrowings of this sort formed a crazy quilt of transnational influences and appropriations. Danish old-age pensions were imported (via New Zealand) to Britain, British industrial liability codes to France, and French subsidarism to Denmark, Holland, and Scandinavia, even as more radical French progressives turned to German-style compulsory state insurance. The noisiest of these appropriations was the British National Insurance Act of 1911, which was cheered on by Lloyd George less than three years before the war as outstripping Germany at its own social-political game.

Beneath and enabling these events lay a web of less prominent connections. One was the international conference of like-minded reformers, whether expert or amateur. Accelerated by the Paris expositions, conference organizing was one of the most striking products of the era. . . .

Another conduit was the public or private inspection visit. England was an early magnet. Since the middle of the nineteenth century, England's freely operating agencies of working-class associationalism (labor unions, cooperatives, and friendly societies) and its broadly institutionalized collective bargaining — all anomalies in mid-nineteenth-century Europe — had drawn the attention of continental reformers. German progressives, hoping to deflect the German labor movement from revolutionary socialism, were particularly eager visitors. . . .

By the turn of the century, a countercurrent of curiosity about Germany was flowing as hard in the other direction, as British progressives struggled to unravel the relationship between Germany's social policy and its striking commercial success. British manufacturers, restless under the regime of free trade, sent workers' commissions . . . to study labor and social conditions in protectionist Germany. Others set out to investigate the social efficiency of German cities, the work of the imperial labor statistics bureau and the social insurance system, or the techniques of German trade and technical education. Other lines of investigation spread farther afield. British agricultural reformers studied Denmark, and Danish reformers Ireland. . . .

In every one of the industrializing countries, finally, there were influential publicists with a keen interest in another nation's social policy. . . . A striking example of the cosmopolitan type was Britain's William Dawson. Sent to Germany as an economic journalist in the 1880s, he had found his way (as did many contemporary Americans) into Adolph Wagner's economics lectures in Berlin, where, with a convert's eagerness, he caught the early stirrings of German social politics. . . . His attempt to found a

British journal dedicated to German-style "state socialism" failed in the early 1890s. But after these false starts, Dawson found his groove in more straightforward reportage. Between 1891 and 1914 he authored nine more books on Germany, translating its social-political developments into closely written, admiring, and influential description. . . . When David Lloyd George needed an expert on German social insurance, Dawson was recruited for the task; he ended his career as principal clerk for the National Health Insurance Commission for England.

Within the shifting, eclectic social-political currents of the day, the single-mindedness of Dawson's absorption with Germany was unusual. But at a lesser intensity his type was critical to the emergent progressive politics. Superimposed on the convergent economic and social forces of the age, brokers of international social politics like Dawson added to the network of ideas, ambitions, and information that made the progressive political connections possible. . . .

Coming from so far, the Americans had no automatic access to the networks and discussions taking shape in Europe. . . . Slowly, however, Americans began to find their way across the barriers of both space and mind.

An early channel was through university study abroad. From a trickle in the mid 1870s to a broad, institutionally established stream in the 1890s, a generation of American students of economics and social science made their way to Germany for graduate study. . . .

A more modest early node of contact was created within the Bureau of Labor. Founded as a sop to the labor vote in 1885, the bureau soon emerged as the key social investigative agency in Washington. Its first international inquiries turned on the question of comparative standards of living, to which it tended (as did parallel inquiries elsewhere) to give the answers that home-country pride demanded. But the bureau's inquiries quickly broadened. In its *Bulletin* one can read closely written, detailed accounts of the workings of Dutch poor relief; British agencies of labor conciliation; French and German company welfare policies; British city-owned public utilities; and pawnbroking, public baths, workmen's compensation legislation, child labor legislation, and factory legislation across the nations of Europe. In 1911, when the Germans recodified their social insurance legislation and the British enacted their National Insurance Act, the bureau printed both documents in full. . . .

An international link of a different kind ran through the social gospel movement. In every corner of the North Atlantic economy, from the early Fabian Society to the German Evangelical Social Congress to the well-placed sprinkling of Protestants in the Musée Social, progressive politics was intricately entangled with social Protestantism. W. T. Stead, who made his mark as a social evangelist and journalist on both sides of the Atlantic, was a prominent figure in the Atlantic social gospel network. Another was the Christian socialist W. D. P. Bliss, sponsor of the first American edition of the *Fabian Essays*. . . . Ties between the American and German social gospel movements were never as close as those between the United States and Britain, but when the University of Chicago's Charles Henderson set out to report on the stirrings of German social Protestantism in the 1890s, the *American Journal of Sociology* made space for his reports.

The settlement house movement was one of transatlantic social Protestantism's most striking productions. Here the innovators were English. From the opening of Toynbee Hall in Whitechapel at the edge of London's East End in 1884, Samuel Barnett's institution was a magnet for American visitors. Jane Addams made visits in 1887, 1888, and 1889. Stanton Coit, whose Neighborhood Guild in the Lower East Side beat Hull House by three years as the first American settlement, had apprenticed as a Toynbee Hall resident. Richard Ely and Margaret Dreier (cofounder of the English-modeled Women's Trade Union League) signed Toynbee Hall's visitors' book in 1889; Gifford Pinchot, set his name down in 1890, one of forty-two American visitors that year. Robert Woods (of Andover House, Boston), Vida Scudder (of the College Settlement in New York), Charles Zueblin (of the Northwestern University Settlement in Chicago), George Hodges (of Kingsley House, Pittsburgh), and Cornelia Foster Bradford (of Whittier House in Jersey City) all visited Toynbee Hall before setting out institutionally on their own. . . .

Sometimes the social Protestant connection yielded less expected results. Robert A. Woods was a young student at Andover Seminary in the late 1880s when William J. Tucker, an early social gospel teacher, picked him out to work up the subject of "social economy." Dispatching him first to New York City to investigate the relationship between socialism and trade unionism, Tucker then sent him on to England in 1890, where he settled into Toynbee Hall for a six-month stay. . . . But the socialists soon interested Woods more than the philanthropists, and the labor movement soon interested him most of all. William Clarke pulled Woods into the discussions of the Fabian Society, then only six years old, joined him on a tour of the northern English factory towns, and helped nurse his growing interest in the new industrial trade unionism. In London, Woods sought out the borough workingmen's clubs and the infant socialist movement. Above all the "new unionism" of unskilled London workers, still fresh from the great dock-workers' victory of 1889, inspired him. . . . Woods's *English Social Movements*, summarizing these discoveries and enthusiasms in 1891, was one of the first descriptions of the "social democracy" stirring beneath the outward complaisance of late-Victorian England.

Woods's lessons at the Fabian Society's hands were to form a type, an event that repetition made expected, even formulaic. Possessed of enormous skills of self-publicity, the Fabians formed something of a transatlantic network of their own. A striking number of them made the crossing themselves in the 1890s. Sidney and Beatrice Webb traversed the United States from New York to San Francisco in 1898. . . .

The Webbs, stunned by the "infantile" character of American politics, never repeated the event, but other Fabians forged lasting transatlantic connections. . . .

Yet another, gradually enlarging node of connection ran through the international conferences. Americans had cut only a minor figure in the French-dominated social economy conferences held in Paris in 1889 and

1900. . . . Over the next years, however, the American presence grew. Ten Americans were reported as attending the International Congress on Unemployment in Paris in 1910; 28 turned up in Vienna that same summer for the International Housing Congress. . . .

Journals of liberal and progressive opinion formed another channel of social-political knowledge and exchange. European letters had long been a familiar genre; it was a rare American with a yen for writing who could not find an outlet for his or her travel impressions in the local newspaper. Prominent political travelers like William Jennings Bryan set out with a journalistic contract in their pocket, returning home to bundle up their dispatches for book publication. Increasingly the genre of travel impressions was joined by specially commissioned investigative pieces. Albert Shaw's *Review of Reviews*, an American offshoot of W. T. Stead's British journal of the same name, was an early, active conduit for news of European social politics. The aptly titled *World's Work* was another. So were the social gospel–linked *Outlook*, . . . the *Chautauquan* (which was running a series entitled "Social Progress in Europe" by 1904–1905), and the social-work journal, the *Survey*.

The muckraking press had its cosmopolitan curiosities. *McClure's* sent Ray Stannard Baker to Germany to see what he could find in 1900. Its rival, *Everybody's Magazine*, sent Charles E. Russell around the world in 1905 in search of the most important examples of social advance. . . . Some journals made a specialty of interest in progressive currents abroad. Benjamin O. Flower's radical *Arena* was filled with reports from what he called our "foreign experiment stations abroad." The *New Republic* was launched with a sense of political kinship with the British *Nation* and shared with it a great number of common writers.

Although curiosity and optimism fueled most of this work, some of the best of it flowed from defeat. Henry D. Lloyd and Frederic C. Howe, the two most able and prolific of the cosmopolitan reform journalists, turned to the task out of a sense of frustration and impasse at home. Lloyd had begun his career as a Chicago editorial writer of conventional economic opinions until the hard times of the 1870s jolted him out of accustomed tracks. He wrote an angry book on labor relations in the Illinois coal fields, made a national name for himself with an indictment of the monopoly practices of Standard Oil, and plunged deeply into Populist and labor politics. By 1896, however, shaken by the degeneration of Populism into mere free-silver politics, Lloyd had had enough. . . . He would be neither theorist nor muckraker but collector — a "salad" maker (as he was soon to put it) of "all the good ideas of Europe and Australasia." . . .

In similar fashion, Frederic C. Howe, who succeeded Lloyd as the leading interpreter of progressive Europe to American audiences, came to his calling when mayor Tom L. Johnson's reform coalition in Cleveland, in which Howe had played a leading part, stumbled in 1909. Adrift, he too set out to discover more successful stories elsewhere. Like Lloyd, Howe turned the world into a kind of lending library of practical, tested reform notions. "I had dreams of social democracy," he remembered long afterward. "What we needed were facts. I would assemble the achievements of Germany, England, Switzerland, and Denmark, and present them as a demonstration of constructive democracy, of the kind of a society we might have if we but saw the state as an agency of service."

By the decade before the First World War, these gathering streams of interest in European social politics were joined by especially commissioned investigations. The National Civic Federation, entering into the heated debate over American municipal streetcar politics in 1906, dispatched a commission of fifteen experts to observe municipal ownership at work in England and Scotland. During the American debate over industrial accident legislation between 1910 and 1913, the American Federation of Labor, the National Association of Manufacturers, and several state governments all organized rival commissions to sort through the experience of Britain and Germany for the lessons they might hold for the United States. Spurred on by the municipal reform crusade, a team of investigators from the Bureau of Municipal Research spent four to five months in Frankfurt gleaning the secrets of efficient municipal administration in 1912. The next summer at least four institutionally sponsored investigations in Europe were under way: George Price's study of European factory inspection methods for the New York garment trades' Joint Board of Sanitary Control; Raymond Fosdick's investigation of European police methods for the Rockefeller-financed Bureau of Social Hygiene; yet another investigation of European social insurance, this one by Katharine Coman for the Progressive Party's information service; and the inquiries of the mammoth, 120-some-person moving caravan of the American Commission on Agricultural Cooperation and Rural Credit in Europe. . . .

We Americans are "Losing Our Scorn for 'Abroad,'" the editors of the *Nation* wrote in summing up these trends in the summer of 1914. "Plainly, we are moving away from the attitude that no Old World idea need apply for employment here." . . .

This evolving web of connections could not erase two enduring peculiarities of the transatlantic progressive relationship. The first was the asymmetry of the exchange. The second was the mediating effects of travel. . . .

Radical and progressive Europeans continued to make American pilgrimages in the decades to come and to carry social political ideas and innovations back home from the United States. Through the 1920s, the Fabian Society's *What to Read?* tracts were stocked with American as well as British titles. . . . Politically, the promise of American-style democracy could still inspire, as the chanting crowds that mobbed Woodrow Wilson's arrival in Europe in late 1918 so dramatically showed.

Lay this list alongside the list of initiatives moving in the other direction, however, and there is no missing the stark trade imbalance on the American side. From settlement houses to zoning ordinances, labor legislation to farm cooperatives, city-owned transit systems to social insurance, the list of social-political experiments drawn westward from the European nations to the United States outstrips by severalfold the corresponding movement in the opposite direction. The transatlantic progressive connection was no one-way street, but in the period from 1870 to 1940 nothing defined it for American participants more than its massive asymmetry.

One of the painful signs of this imbalance was a marked contraction of European progressive interest in American politics. Where American attention to British progressive politics was "coherent and continuous," Kenneth Morgan writes of this period, the influences in the other direction were "intermittent and partial at best." The Marxian disillusionment with American politics is well known. The Webbs' came early. Both were driven hard by theory.

Alfred Zimmern's seven-month pilgrimage in search of progressive America in 1911 and 1912 was more telling and more poignant. Fresh from studying civic republicanism in ancient Athens, Zimmern arrived in the United States fired with ideals of civic political culture, both ancient and modern. He worked hard to locate the centers of political vitality in the New World. . . .

"Lots of new ideas," Zimmern wrote his sister, "which may be applied at home." But from there on, progressive America unraveled for him. The more he talked with Americans, the thinner his confidence wore. The raw, unmitigated capitalism of Chicago unnerved him. The U.S. Steel Corporation's model city, Gary, Indiana, seemed to him a monstrous "fortress." Six months after he began, he wrote home: "I have long ago given up looking at America as the land of progress. The only question left in my mind is how many years it's behind England. I think it's somewhere in the eighties and not going our pace at that."

By the time Zimmern picked it up, the metaphor of American behindhandedness was already a hardened trope among European progressives. . . .

The cumulative weight of judgments like these could not but reinforce the Americans' sense of outsiderness, their place as junior partners in the Atlantic exchange. To that sense of marginality, the second enduring factor of the Atlantic progressive exchange added its weight. That was the physical distance of the American participants from the new social-political network's centers. The Americans had been latecomers at the Paris exposition in 1900, scrambling for place and information. It was inherent in the geography of their relationship that the Americans were repeatedly to encounter European social politics, letters of introduction in hand, as if on a brief surveying expedition into a distant land.

Coming from so far, the Americans rarely saw things in the building stage. The word "finished" runs through their accounts like a thread. They came in search of practical accomplishments, from a polity that often seemed to them full of rag ends and unfinished business. The emphasis on the built rather than the process of building often obscured the politics of European social policy making. Few of the American progressives in Germany had a fully adequate sense of the terrific political tensions within Wilhelmine Germany — or, later, within Weimar politics. . . . The experience of coming to social-political Europe as foragers for tested, usable devices led them to emphasize the advantages of the devices they were keen to bring back, rather than the sorts of coalitions responsible for putting them in place. It accentuated their tendency to think of politics in terms of invention and rational design — a conception that set them up, more than once, for cruel disappointment.

The fact that they came from so far, and were continually surprised at what they found, likewise encouraged in the American social travelers' minds the sense of behindhandedness. . . .

In seizing the metaphor of lag, however, a certain number of Americans began to find, at last, a route past the polar types and exaggerations that had dominated the language of Atlantic contrast. By the decade before the First World War, the new terms had settled deep in the rhetoric and self-consciousness of many American progressives. "Shall we always . . . 'stand by the roadside and see the procession go by?'" Wisconsin's Charles McCarthy wrote after his own first pilgrimage to progressive Europe. . . .

Given the density of connections and influences joining social politics throughout the North Atlantic economy, given the multiple faces of the "social question" and the avenues of approach to it, the notion that the world's polities might be imagined as a long line of runners, strung out, one behind another, in a footrace toward progress was every bit as strained and artificial as the rival metaphors it supplanted. . . .

But the image of a race helped point progress in a clear direction and gave American progressives an added sense of urgency. "The greatest nation on earth slowly crawls into the rear of the humanitarian procession," Charles Henderson charged in a comparison of American and European methods in child welfare. Frederic Howe's Ohio ally Brand Whitlock echoed the formula: while the "new" Old World was learning democracy, "the old new world was and is paltering and hesitating over municipal problems which Europe solved a generation ago." . . . But the sense of being emissaries from a backward land clarified the Americans' task; theirs was to catch up with the "progressive" nations of the world, to borrow, adapt, and bend the work of others to the circumstances of the United States.

The metaphor of laggards and leaders also helped to shield American progressives from the charges of political utopianism their antagonists were poised to hurl at them. It made their idealism hard-headed and practical. "Many persons think that the progressive movement proposes to usher in the millennium by legislation," Benjamin De Witt wrote in 1915. "Nothing could be farther from the minds of the men and women who call themselves progressive. What they propose to do is to bring the United States abreast of Germany and other European countries in the matter of remedial legislation." To catch up to the "civilized" nations of the world was a running progressive theme. Seconding Theodore Roosevelt's nomination at the Progressive Party convention of 1912, Jane Addams made the point official: "The new party has become the American exponent of a world-wide movement toward juster social conditions, a movement which the United States, lagging behind other great nations, has been unaccountably slow to embody in political action." If the rhetoric left its users vulnerable to the accusation that their schemes were un-American, unsuited to the special political genius of the United States, it had its countervailing advantages. Cosmopolitan American progressives took the gulf between Old World and New World political cultures and labored to transform it into a lag in time, a gap to be overcome.

"We are no longer the sole guardians of the Ark of the Covenant," Walter Weyl opened his *The New Democracy* in 1912. "Europe does not learn at our feet the facile lessons of democracy. . . ." He added: "Today the tables are turned. America no longer teaches democracy to an expectant world, but herself goes to school to Europe and Australia. . . . Our students of political and industrial democracy repair to the antipodes, to England, Belgium, France, to semi-feudal Germany. . . . Why has the tortoise Europe outdistanced the hare?"

That sentiment — that momentary emancipation from the "geocentricity" around them — was one of the American progressives' key achievements. . . . Underneath the nationalism of the age, the suspicion that the world might have passed the Americans by was, in its own right, a heroic accomplishment. It shaped American politics through the New Deal in far more ways than historians have yet fathomed. Against the inward-turning counterforces, these nagging doubts about the self-sufficiency of American politics could hardly be expected to win an easy victory. . . . But over the oceanic distance between New World and Old, American progressives began slowly to discern — where kings and cathedrals had once dominated the imaginative landscape — models and allies, reservoirs of potentially usable experience, the unexpected outlines of a progressive Europe.

I t is difficult to narrate the history of the twentieth century without placing the Great Depression and World War II at the heart of the story. And,
certainly for the United States, such placement requires that the person of
Franklin Delano Roosevelt be called to center stage. Roosevelt remains the
most popular and esteemed occupant of the White House in the twentieth
century. For more than twelve years he led the American people through
the worst depression in their history and then through a war that encompassed virtually the entire globe. To his admirers he was a leader of heroic
stature, who preserved free institutions by means of democratic reform rather
than authoritarian or totalitarian methods. To his enemies he was at best
misguided, at worst an immoral demagogue who pretended to save democracy by taking the American people down the road to socialism. Like few
other presidents, Roosevelt had an uncanny ability to arouse strong passions.
His contemporaries either loved or hated him; to this day few remain neutral
or react blandly to his legacy.

Why has Roosevelt aroused such strong passions? Little in his background
or his accomplishments prior to 1933 would have led anyone to predict so
momentous a career. Even those friends and associates who worked closely
with Roosevelt during his dozen years in the White House had difficulty
grasping his many-sided personality or understanding his actions. Frances
Perkins, his longtime secretary of labor, described him as "the most complicated human being I ever knew," a comment echoed by other associates.
Beyond the matter of Roosevelt's imposing and complex personality, the
sheer magnitude of the New Deal's innovations guaranteed that FDR would
remain controversial. The length of Roosevelt's tenure in the White House
has been matched by the quantity of books written about him by friends,
associates, and enemies. According to Alan Brinkley, "'the age of Roosevelt' . . .
has generated a larger literature than any other topic in twentieth-century
American history."[1]

---

[1]Alan Brinkley, "Prosperity, Depression, and War, 1920–1945," in Susan Porter Benson,
Stephen Brier, and Roy Rosenzweig, eds., *The New American History* (Philadelphia, 1990),
reprinted as an American Historical Association pamphlet; the quote is from p. 10 of the lat-
ter. For historiographical overviews, see Alfred B. Rollins Jr., "Was There Really a Man Named
Roosevelt?" in George A. Billias and Gerald N. Grob, eds., *American History: Retrospect and
Prospect* (New York, 1971), 232–70; and the bibliographic essay in Alonzo L. Hamby, ed., *The
New Deal: Analysis and Interpretation* (2nd ed., New York and London, 1981).

Although his victory in 1932 was broad-based, FDR soon alienated many businesspeople and other conservatives who accused him of using centralized government to threaten private enterprise. Even a staunch Democrat such as former presidential candidate Al Smith hotly argued during the campaign of 1936 that Roosevelt had headed down the road to socialism along with Marx, Lenin, and "the rest of that bunch."[2] The attack on Roosevelt's New Deal from the right was matched by fusillades from the left. Radicals claimed that Roosevelt clung to a traditional individualism and can-do pragmatism, both rendered obsolete by industrial and technological advances. One such critic, Rexford G. Tugwell, a professor of economics and an early New Deal "brain truster," argued that America's competitive economy had never worked well, certainly not in the twentieth century, and that minor reforms would prove hopelessly inadequate. Only governmental planning for all aspects of the economic system, he insisted, could prevent future depressions. Much to his disappointment, Roosevelt seemed merely a tinkerer, either unwilling or unable to plan in a rational and systematic manner.[3] To the left of Tugwell stood a growing number of American socialists and communists for whom the New Deal was nothing more than a bandage on the cancer of American capitalism. The only proper approach to the depression, they insisted, was a complete overhaul of America's social and economic system and the establishment of a socialist state.[4]

Reflecting the passions of their age, these critics helped to establish the frame of reference for later writers. The questions raised by contemporary commentators and later historians revolved around the extent to which the New Deal reshaped American society and politics. Was the New Deal simply an extension of the Progressive tradition of piecemeal reform or did it involve a radical departure from the mainstream of American political history? Did it usher in the era of big government and the "imperial presidency," or create an effective and efficient state to handle the needs of a twentieth-century society, or succumb to the traditional centrifugal and localistic forces of American politics? Did it save capitalism or pave the way for an American version of socialism? Did it co-opt workers and other have-nots who struggled for democracy and social equality, or did it confirm the partial triumph of those movements?

Historians of the Progressive school bore little doubt about the basic nature of the New Deal.[5] Viewing America's past in terms of a conflict between liberalism and conservatism, the people versus the interests, they saw the New Deal as a significant advance in the struggle against monopoly and privi-

---

[2]Quoted in William E. Leuchtenburg, *Franklin D. Roosevelt and the New Deal, 1932–1940* (New York, 1963), 178.

[3]See Rexford G. Tugwell, "The New Deal in Retrospect," *Western Political Quarterly* 1 (December 1948): 373–85, and his full-length study of Roosevelt, *The Democratic Roosevelt* (New York, 1957).

[4]See Harvey Klehr, *The Heyday of American Communism: The Depression Decade* (New York, 1984); and Richard Pells, *Radical Visions, American Dreams: Culture and Social Thought in the Depression Years* (New York, 1974).

[5]On Progressive historians, see Chapter 1.

lege. Evolved from Jeffersonian and Jacksonian democracy, Populism, and Progressivism, the New Deal represented the continuing popular struggle to achieve a greater measure of political, economic, and social equality. Thus, in the mid-1940s Louis Hacker referred to the New Deal as the "Third American Revolution." Though he sometimes made actual New Deal programs sound quite unrevolutionary and unoriginal, Hacker still insisted on the New Deal's significance in countering the individualist and laissez-faire traditions of American politics. Always at the center of the New Deal, he wrote, "there existed the thought that the responsibility of public authority for the welfare of the people was clear and that the intervention of the state was justifiable."[6] Henry Steele Commager, the distinguished historian of the American liberal tradition, found the relationship between the New Deal and earlier reform movements obvious. Simply a new deal of old cards, the New Deal appeared radical for two reasons: the rapidity with which Congress enacted its programs into law; and the sharp contrast between its activism and the conservatism of the Harding-Coolidge-Hoover administrations. If compared with the Progressive era rather than the 1920s, Commager maintained, "the contrast would have been less striking than the similarities. . . . [P]recedent for the major part of New Deal legislation was to be found in these earlier periods."[7]

Perhaps the fullest and most eloquent argument for the New Deal's continuity with America's liberal legacy came from Arthur M. Schlesinger Jr., who wrote squarely within the Progressive tradition. A former Harvard professor, public intellectual, prominent liberal anticommunist in the McCarthy era, and later adviser to President John Kennedy, Schlesinger was a shrewd commentator on current affairs. He regularly championed a modified brand of American liberalism whose roots, he believed, went far back into the nation's history. Thus, his Pulitzer Prize–winning *The Age of Jackson* (1945) portrayed Jacksonian democracy as a coalition of urban workers and other democratic groups which, taken together, looked very much like the New Deal coalition of the 1930s. According to Schlesinger, American history evolved cyclically, periods of liberal reform alternating with periods of conservative consolidation. Thus, Jacksonian democracy followed the complacent "era of good feelings," the Progressive era followed the age of the robber barons, the New Deal came after the sterile conservatism of the 1920s, and the New Frontier and Great Society of the 1960s responded to the inaction of the Eisenhower years. The generative force behind this cycle was social conflict, which arose from a constant accumulation of discontent within American society.

Schlesinger spelled out his thesis most fully in *The Age of Roosevelt*, a three-volume study of the New Deal published between 1957 and 1960. He argued that by the 1920s the nation had tired of the Progressive crusade of the prewar years. National disinterest in politics meant that power gravitated

---

[6]Louis M. Hacker, *The Shaping of the American Tradition* (New York, 1947), 1125–26.
[7]Henry Steele Commager, "Twelve Years of Roosevelt," *American Mercury* 40 (April 1945): 391–401.

power gravitated

toward businessmen and other conservative interests. Inevitably, just as Progressivism had given way to 1920s conservatism, the forces of reform gathered their energies. Even without a depression, Schlesinger suggested, the New Deal was bound to have happened in one form or another because workers, poor farmers, ethnic minorities, and others continued to press for political redress of their grievances, mostly on the local and state level. The depression gave the New Deal its particular force and character — an inclusive, national political movement urgently responding to economic collapse. The New Deal, Schlesinger concluded, rejected the dogmatic absolutes posed by communism and fascism, rather assuming that a "managed and modified capitalist order achieved by piecemeal experiment could combine personal freedom and economic growth."[8]

Frank Freidel, author of a multivolume biography of Roosevelt, belonged to the same Progressive historiographical tradition as Schlesinger but posed the discussion differently. To him the New Deal took shape from the work of people who had grown to political maturity during the Progressive era and the First World War and still shared the moral fervor of that era. Fairly conservative, like Roosevelt himself, they sought to save rather than to destroy the free enterprise system. What made them progressive was their willingness to use the machinery and authority of government to improve the lot of the common citizenry.[9] Commager, Schlesinger, and Freidel all identified themselves with the American liberal tradition. Whatever their criticisms of the New Deal, they wrote approvingly of Roosevelt's pragmatism, his faith in democracy and "the common man," and his obvious distaste for totalitarian methods. The alternative to the New Deal, they hinted, might very well have been a dictatorship of the right or left, had the nation continued to drift along as it had under Hoover. If the New Dealers experimented with radical means, they always aimed to preserve a modified version of the existing order of things.

The relatively partisan and Roosevelt-centered approach to the history of the New Deal did not go unchallenged. A few conservative writers followed former president Hoover in accusing FDR of undermining individual freedom, imposing a bloated and expensive form of centralized government on the American people, and disrupting the "natural" self-correcting processes of the marketplace.[10] But the most important critique came from so-called "consensus" historians, in particular Richard Hofstadter. A liberal critic of liberalism, Hofstadter depicted the New Deal as a promising "new departure" from received political values. In the past, he observed, American lib-

---

[8]Arthur M. Schlesinger Jr., *The Crisis of the Old Order, 1919–1933* (Boston, 1957), *The Coming of the New Deal* (Boston, 1958), and *The Politics of Upheaval* (Boston, 1960). Schlesinger revisited and refined this cyclical interpretation in *Cycles of American History* (Boston, 1986).

[9]Frank Freidel, *Franklin D. Roosevelt: The Apprenticeship* (Boston, 1952), *The Ordeal* (Boston, 1954), *The Triumph* (Boston, 1956), and *Launching the New Deal* (Boston, 1973); see also *The New Deal in Historical Perspective* (2nd ed., Washington, D.C., 1965).

[10]Herbert Hoover, *The Challenge to Liberty* (New York, 1934); Edgar Eugene Robinson, *The Roosevelt Leadership, 1933–1945* (Philadelphia, 1955); John T. Flynn, *The Roosevelt Myth* (rev. ed., New York, 1956).

eralism had failed because its moralizing tendencies blinded it to class conflict and structural inequality. Reformers generally operated under the assumption that American society was a big version of the small towns they had grown up in. The reformers' "village mind" could only conceive of social problems as aberrations from a healthy democratic norm; reform meant clearing the way for individual enterprise — smashing illegitimate privilege and monopoly and providing all Americans with an equal opportunity in life. Within this frame of thought the national government appeared a threat to individual success. At best, someone like Herbert Hoover — a village mind with an engineering degree — might use government to harmonize the initiatives of free economic actors and thereby maximize the potential of the marketplace. Even more exuberant Progressive reformers could only imagine solutions to social problems in terms of mild bureaucratic oversight of the marketplace, preferably on the local or state level, by middle-class folks like themselves.

In *The Age of Reform: From Bryan to F.D.R.*, Hofstadter insisted that the New Deal operated initially on entirely different premises. Instead of viewing America as healthy, New Deal reformers saw it as a sick society in need of therapy that could only be administered through federal action. Thus, the New Deal accepted ideas that would have been anathema to old-fashioned Progressives: permanent federal responsibility for the relief of the unemployed, Social Security, the regulation of wages and hours, the construction of vast public works and public housing, and the acceptance of massive deficits to fund such programs. Many of the traditional aims of past reform movements — to restore government to the people and to destroy big business and monopolies — were simply bypassed or ignored by Roosevelt. "The New Deal, and the thinking it engendered," wrote Hofstadter, "represented the triumph of economic emergency and human needs over inherited notions and inhibitions. . . . At the core of the New Deal, then, was not a philosophy (F.D.R. could identify himself philosophically only as a Christian and democrat), but an attitude, suitable for practical politicians, administrators, and technicians, but uncongenial to the moralism that the Progressives had for the most part shared with their opponents."[11] Despite early indications, however, Hofstadter found that New Deal liberalism failed to live up to its promise. FDR and his followers shrank from comprehensive planning and remained content to respond pragmatically to economic and political exigencies; that is, they failed to get much beyond mere Progressivism.

In the end, Hofstadter's most influential contribution to New Deal historiography may have been to detach interpretations of the era from partisan attitudes. He was deeply critical of both liberal reformers and their conservative critics. Regarding the latter, he found right-wing condemnations of the New Deal's piecemeal reforms to be "hollow and cliché-ridden," the sometimes hysterical complaints of a class increasingly cut off from reality. More

---

[11]Richard Hofstadter, *The Age of Reform: From Bryan to F.D.R.* (New York, 1955), 314, 323. In *Encore for Reform: The Old Progressives and the New Deal* (New York, 1967), Hofstadter's student, Otis L. Graham, reaffirmed that old Progressives and New Dealers were birds of quite a different feather.

importantly, Hofstadter criticized Roosevelt and his liberal followers for their political opportunism and superficial approach to the serious problem of social inequality. Political scientist James MacGregor Burns echoed these criticisms. Yet, the stunning first volume of his biography of FDR, while acknowledging the president to be an opportunist of "no fixed convictions," also portrayed him as a leader of masterly instincts. Without FDR's experimental and supremely confident leadership in the midst of crisis, according to Burns, the American political order might not have survived. Nevertheless, Burns concludes by wondering "whether the American political system can meet the crises imposed on it by this exacting century."[12] To another political scientist, Heinz Eulau, the New Deal tendency toward pragmatic and piecemeal reform signaled its strength, not its weakness. Whatever blueprints for social reconstruction some New Dealers had in mind, they neither articulated a utopian faith nor called upon people to join a crusade to remake society. The New Deal represented a mature politics of adjustment and compromise, the triumph not of liberal zeal but of managerial technique.[13]

In the 1960s, admiration for Roosevelt's New Deal dimmed as growing social conflict raised doubts about the effectiveness and significance of liberal reform. New Left historians asked searching questions about America's social and economic order and the possibilities of reform. If the New Deal had modified and humanized American society, why were so many people — blacks, Puerto Ricans, Mexican Americans, blue-collar workers, and middle-class youths — alienated from their society? If the New Deal had truly reined in an unbridled capitalism and made it more responsive to citizens' needs, why did poverty and racism continue to exist? Even before New Left critics delivered their harsher judgments, scholars had begun to build on the work of Hofstadter in narrating a tale of FDR and the New Deal that was less personalized, less partisan, and less positive.

The first sign of this newly critical attitude to New Deal liberalism appeared in William E. Leuchtenburg's mildly revisionist *Franklin D. Roosevelt and the New Deal*.[14] Although Leuchtenburg left no doubt about his positive valuation of both the president and his programs, he also made clear the limitations of both. Although the New Deal brought relief to millions who suffered under the depression, it could not achieve prosperity in peacetime. Although it empowered industrial workers, small farmers, and others who could organize themselves into interest groups, it ignored those less organized and less powerful Americans, especially African Americans, who could not "ante up" for the New Deal. Roosevelt failed to break the hold of southern conservatives on the Democratic Party and thus failed to build a broad-based social democracy that could fight Jim Crow or survive the inevitable backlash of business interests and defenders of traditional values and local prerogatives.

---

[12] James MacGregor Burns, *Roosevelt: The Lion and the Fox, 1882–1940* (New York, 1956), x, 474.
[13] Heinz Eulau, "Neither Ideology Nor Utopia: The New Deal in Retrospect," *Antioch Review* 19 (Winter 1959–1960): 523–37.
[14] William E. Leuchtenburg, *Franklin D. Roosevelt and the New Deal* (New York, 1963).

Still, Leuchtenburg insisted, "however conservative it was," the New Deal was "a radically new departure" for American society and politics.[15] No matter how limited, the New Deal and the man who made it retain immense stature in Leuchtenburg's account. As he argues in the essay reproduced in this chapter, the New Deal achieved myriad and enduring results. They include reconstructing the federal government as an instrument for managing social change and cushioning the weak against the worst consequences of such change; certifying the legitimacy of labor unions and other newly organized interests; building new respect for the public sector; and preparing a diverse people for vast collective endeavors without weakening their respect for cultural differences, civil liberties, and democratic processes. In these ways, Roosevelt and his New Dealers performed as well, and almost certainly better, than any similar political cadre in American history. They transformed America, and mostly for the better.

In a similar though somewhat more revisionist interpretation, Paul K. Conkin's 1967 reassessment of the New Deal praised Roosevelt's political astuteness and charismatic qualities, but judged his intellect too shallow and unfocused even to be called pragmatic. In this, the nation's leader merely reflected its people. "For the historian," noted Conkin in his thoughtful summation, "every judgment, every evaluation of the past has to be tinged with a pinch of compassion, a sense of the beauty and nobility present when honest hopes and humane ideals are frustrated. He sees that the thirties could have brought so much more, but also so much worse, than the New Deal. The limiting context has to be understood — the safeguards and impediments of our political system, Roosevelt's intellectual limitations, and most of all the appalling economic ignorance and philosophic immaturity of the American electorate. . . . The New Deal solved a few problems, ameliorated a few more, obscured many, and created new ones. This is about all our political system can generate, even in crisis."[16]

Relatively conservative historians showed a similar dispassion in their work. In a major study of New Deal economic policy, for example, Ellis W. Hawley echoed Conkin's belief that the New Deal reflected the ambivalences and contradictions within the American people themselves. Those Americans, Hawley noted, shared a commitment to two hardly compatible values. On the one hand they cherished liberty, which implied a competitive economic and social order and broad freedom of personal choice. On the other hand they valued progress, which implied order, rationality, and an imposing economic structure needed to guarantee abundance and a rising standard of living. Yet the latter value posed a potential threat to the former; monopoly negated competition; order threatened, at least in theory, liberty. Much of twentieth-century American history, Hawley observed, revolved around the search for a solution "that would preserve the industrial order, necessarily based upon a high degree of collective organization, and yet would preserve

---

[15]Ibid., 336.
[16]Paul K. Conkin, *FDR and the Origins of the Welfare State* (New York, 1967), 106; also published in paperback under the title *The New Deal* (Arlington Heights., Ill., 1967).

America's democratic heritage at the same time." New Deal economic policy mirrored this basic ambivalence, vacillating between rational planning and antimonopoly measures.[17]

Measured assessments of the limiting context within which Roosevelt and the New Dealers operated shaped the work of revisionist historians throughout the 1970s and 1980s. Albert U. Romasco argued that Roosevelt needed to cooperate with the business community in order to stimulate investment and recovery. However hostile to the "economic royalists," Roosevelt nevertheless had to confront them with a little stick and a big carrot.[18] Charles Trout's study of Boston showed that the localistic orientation of American politics sharply limited the reach and success of New Deal programs.[19] Looking at a very different limit on New Deal activism, Nancy Weiss made perfectly clear that Roosevelt largely ignored the plight of black Americans during the Great Depression. He declined to support antilynching legislation for fear of alienating southern Democrats whom he needed to pass crucial New Deal (and, later, war preparedness) legislation. Blacks benefited economically only because they were included, albeit inconsistently, in New Deal programs designed to assist the poor and the unemployed as a whole. Consequently, blacks embraced the Democratic Party and abandoned the Republican, even though Roosevelt did not directly woo their support.[20]

The sharpest critique of Roosevelt and the New Deal came from younger historians who more fully identified with the New Left. Some of them actively worked in the labor and civil rights movements and hoped that a searching examination of the past could illuminate the present and discover a radical path to the future. Historian Barton J. Bernstein argued that the liberal reforms of the 1930s had not transformed or tamed corporate capitalism or significantly redistributed power in any way. Even its bolder programs had neither extended the beneficence of government beyond better-off groups nor used the wealth of the few for the needs of the many. The New Deal followed essentially conservative goals because it was intended to maintain the American system intact. "The New Deal," Bernstein concluded, "failed to solve the problem of depression, it failed to raise the impoverished, it failed to redistribute income, it failed to extend equality and generally countenanced racial discrimination and segregation. It failed generally to make business more responsible to the social welfare or to threaten business's preeminent political power. . . . In acting to protect the institution of private property and in advancing the interests of corporate capitalism, the New Deal assisted

---

[17]Ellis W. Hawley, *The New Deal and the Problem of Monopoly: A Study in Economic Ambivalence* (Princeton, N.J., 1966), 493.

[18]Albert U. Romasco, *The Politics of Recovery: Roosevelt's New Deal* (New York, 1983). See also Michael A. Bernstein, *The Great Depression: Delayed Recovery and Economic Change in America, 1929–1939* (New York, 1987).

[19]Charles H. Trout, *Boston, the Great Depression, and the New Deal* (New York, 1977).

[20]Nancy J. Weiss, *Farewell to the Party of Lincoln: Black Politics in the Age of FDR* (Princeton, N.J., 1983).

the middle and upper sectors of society. It protected them, sometimes, even at the cost of injuring the lower sectors."[21]

Another New Left historian, Thomas Ferguson, defined the New Deal as the political project of advanced sectors of American industrial and finance capitalism, with support from associated labor interests. They aimed to generate expansion in the capital-intensive, high-consumption, "multinational" sector of the economy, in place of the failed labor-intensive and nationally oriented regime of steel, rail, textiles, and other older industries. For Ferguson, the needs of the "multinational bloc," not the demands of grassroots protest or the pressures of electoral politics, explain the political evolution of the New Deal.[22] Similarly, Christopher L. Tomlins depicted New Deal labor legislation as a triumph of bureaucratic management over grassroots labor insurgency. New Deal labor policy aimed not at justice, but at stabilizing the interests of giant corporations and the state.[23]

In a more nuanced way, labor historians Steve Fraser and Nelson Lichtenstein traced the decline of shop-floor radicals in major CIO unions to the rise of bureaucratic labor managers closely tied to corporate elites and to the Democratic Party.[24] Although this transformation, presided over by the brilliant labor leaders Sidney Hillman and Walter Reuther, consolidated and expanded many of the gains made by industrial workers in the 1930s and 1940s, it also decisively disarmed them as a force for radical change in the future. It certainly confirmed the dividing line between managerial elites who make policy and workers who bargain for better wages and working conditions, but only if they cease trying to determine the larger contours of their economic world. In related but quite distinctive ways, labor historians David Brody and David Montgomery also described the "New Deal Order" as a triumph as much for corporate, labor, and political elites as for the men and women who staged sit-ins at General Motors and fought the company "goons" in the coal towns of West Virginia.[25] Finally, historians of race have found the least to admire in the New Deal. Robin D. G. Kelley showed that in rural Alabama blacks more likely found their way to the Communist than to the Democratic Party; indeed the latter remained the agent of white

---

[21] Barton J. Bernstein, "The New Deal: The Conservative Achievements of Liberal Reform," in Barton J. Bernstein, ed., *Towards a New Past: Dissenting Essays in American History* (New York, 1968), 264, 281–82.

[22] Thomas Ferguson, "Industrial Conflict and the Coming of the New Deal: The Triumph of Multinational Liberalism in America," in Steve Fraser and Gary Gerstle, eds., *The Rise and Fall of the New Deal Order, 1930–1980* (Princeton, N.J., 1989), 3–31.

[23] Christopher L. Tomlins, *The State and the Unions: Labor Relations, Law, and the Organized Labor Movement in America, 1880–1960* (Cambridge, Mass., 1985).

[24] Steve Fraser, *Labor Will Rule: Sidney Hillman and the Rise of American Labor* (New York, 1991); Nelson Lichtenstein, *The Most Dangerous Man in Detroit: Walter Reuther and the Fate of American Labor* (New York, 1995), and also his *Labor's War at Home: The CIO and World War II* (Cambridge, Mass., 1982).

[25] David Brody, *Workers in Industrial America: Essays on the 20th Century Struggle* (New York, 1980; 2nd ed., 1993); David Montgomery, "American Workers and the New Deal Formula," in *Workers' Control in America: Studies in the History of Work, Technology, and Labor Struggles* (Cambridge, Mass., 1979).

supremacy and the implacable enemy of justice for African Americans.[26] More recently, Karen Ferguson has argued that blacks in Atlanta gained much from the New Deal, though elites gained most; in the end, the New Deal was a real but "imperfect catalyst for African American liberation."[27]

One of the pitfalls of some New Left interpretations lies in their tendency to see the New Deal (and, indeed, the entire realm of politics and the state) as a kind of shadow-act behind which the hegemonic force of corporate capitalism works its will. Against this tendency, a powerful new body of scholarship on "state formation," some of it with an explicitly feminist bent, has brought new insights to New Deal history. The political scientist Theda Skocpol and her collaborators argue forcefully that the state is a semiautonomous actor in the great dramas of modern history. Political parties and administrative elites do indeed serve the interests of the most powerful; but they must also demonstrate a capacity to promote stability for a wide range of constituents. Equally important, they also respond to their own interest in reproducing and expanding their power. They exercise, in particular, the significant power to define the very issues of political concern that all actors, even the biggest, must attend to. The state-making perspective allows scholars to acknowledge the New Deal's shortcomings — "frustration," "failure," and "loss," are words that spring from their pages — while acknowledging its real potential for reform.[28]

The historian Linda Gordon has effectively employed the insights of state formation theory to study social welfare policy in the twentieth century. Seeing a range of provisions for single mothers, families, and children as genuine achievements, Gordon notes that the very legitimacy of the welfare state depended on the efforts of the women's movement.[29] At least until the 1930s, recipients of such benefits remained more pitied than entitled. While the New Deal changed things for the better, Gordon argues from a "socialist-feminist" viewpoint that the welfare state has proven incapable of fundamentally correcting gender and class inequality. Still, Gordon believes that the New Deal years offer a partial model for a feminist-labor coalition that can expand to include the interests of racial minorities and other less-powerful Americans and thereby exercise new political leverage over the state.[30] More pessimistically, Suzanne Mettler argues that conservative strengths, more than inherent liberal weaknesses, account for the failure of the New Deal to promote women's equality and other progressive social ends. She notes especially that the federal system and traditions of local control often trumped

[26]Robin D. G. Kelley, *Hammer and Hoe: Alabama Communists during the Great Depression* (Chapel Hill, N.C., 1990).

[27]Karen Ferguson, *Black Politics in New Deal Atlanta* (Chapel Hill, N.C., 2002), 268.

[28]Margaret Weir, Ann Shola Orloff, and Theda Skocpol, eds., *The Politics of Social Policy in the United States* (Princeton, N.J., 1988); Kenneth Finegold and Theda Skocpol, *State and Party in America's New Deal* (Madison, Wis., 1995).

[29]On this point see Kathryn Kish Sklar's essay in Chapter 6.

[30]See Linda Gordon, ed., *Women, the State, and Welfare* (Madison, Wis., 1990), and her *Pitied But Not Entitled: Single Mothers and the History of Welfare, 1890–1935* (New York, 1994). See also Gwendolyn Mink, *The Wages of Motherhood: Inequality in the Welfare State, 1917–1942* (Ithaca, N.Y., 1995); Eileen Boris, *Home to Work: Motherhood and the Politics of Industrial Homework in the United States* (New York, 1994).

other ideological imperatives and that many "efforts to preserve state and local authority had important [conservative] gender [and racial] effects."[31]

As the above discussion suggests, recent historians tend less to portray the New Deal as either a front for socialism or a front for corporate hegemony.[32] In trying to assess the causes, effects, and meaning of the New Deal, they increasingly blend complex explanations derived from the study of electoral politics, social and economic forces, legal and political systems, and the long-term (and comparative) evolution of modern states. In the field of legal history, debate over the "Constitutional Revolution of 1937" has evolved beyond the "internalist vs. externalist" debate of the past. In a 2003 forum, published in the *American Historical Review*, William E. Leuchtenburg and G. Edmund White offer recognizable if chastened versions of the contending sides in this debate. Leuchtenburg insists that the landslide of 1936 and the threat of court-packing convinced reluctant justices to mend their conservative ways; White argues that the slow evolution of legal doctrine, not short-term political pressure, brought the justices to a more expansive view of federal power. Laura Kalman wisely notes that the internalist argument helps to explain how external political and cultural influence finds expression in judicial decisions, that is, by way of evolving legal doctrine.[33] More narrowly, but more provocatively, Ruth O'Brien insists that New Deal labor policy was neither new nor radical. Rather, it hewed to legal and political lines worked out by Progressives and Republicans from 1880 through the 1920s, which aimed to protect individualism and the public interest against threats from corporate or labor power.[34]

In the field of social history, several historians have taken the insights of the New Left historians of the 1960s and reworked them in productive and sometimes startling new ways. Ronald Edsforth showed how the shopfloor radicalism among the autoworkers of Flint, Michigan, evolved into the managed labor peace of the 1950s. Edsforth ascribes this transformation not simply to the defeat or co-optation of workers at the hands of the capital, but also to the social and intellectual world that the workers had themselves made and affirmed. However militant, he argues, labor activists wanted restoration of the high-consumption promises of the 1920s, not the radical remaking of their world.[35] In a different way, Lizabeth Cohen traced the

---

[31]Suzanne Mettler, *Dividing Citizens: Gender and Federalism in New Deal Public Policy* (Ithaca, N.Y., 1998), 20–21.

[32]Of course, polemics continue to fly. Right-wing examples are Gary Dean Best, *The Retreat from Liberalism: Collectivists versus Progressives in the New Deal Years* (Westport, Conn., 2002), and Jim Powell, *FDR's Folly: How Roosevelt and His New Deal Prolonged the Great Depression* (New York, 2003). A partisan but less polemical popular history from the moderate left is Jonathan Alter, *The Defining Moment: FDR's Hundred Days and the Triumph of Hope* (New York, 2006).

[33]"AHR Forum: The Debate over the Constitutional Revolution of 1937," *American Historical Review* 110 (October 2005): 1046–80; the forum is extensively footnoted and also contains a brief introduction by Alan Brinkley. See also Melvin I. Urofsky, "The Roosevelt Court," in William H. Chafe, ed., *The Achievement of American Liberalism: The New Deal and Its Legacies* (New York, 2002), 63–98.

[34]Ruth O'Brien, *Workers' Paradox: The Republican Origins of New Deal Labor Policy, 1886–1935* (Chapel Hill, N.C., 1998).

[35]Ronald Edsforth, *Class Conflict and Cultural Consensus: The Making of a Mass Consumer Society in Flint, Michigan* (New Brunswick, N.J., and London, 1987).

complex making of a new working class in Chicago in the twentieth century. Focused closely on workplace, family, neighborhood, and cultural life over several decades, Cohen discerned a grand mobilization of poor and ethnically diverse people into a momentous political and social force. History would expose the limitations of that achievement, Cohen acknowledged: "The racial conflicts, the ideological divisions, and the centralization of authority that would come to characterize CIO unions [and the New Deal state] . . . have led many postwar labor analysts to minimize the achievements of ordinary workers in the 1930s." But Cohen insists that, "without romanticizing who they were or denying the imperfections in what they achieved," those citizens changed the world they lived in for the good.[36]

Alan Brinkley's study of the careers of Huey Long and Father Charles Coughlin revised historians' understanding of the context within which FDR and the New Deal operated. Insisting that radicals such as Long and Coughlin were neither proto-fascists nor madmen, Brinkley described them as representatives of an "alternative political vision" that he dubbed "localism." With links to the long tradition of American "republicanism," and equipped with a moral critique of the ruthless marketplace and the overbearing state, these radicals and their followers were trying to restore to ordinary people a measure of control over their own lives. At the very least, they were symptoms of a very widespread "ambivalence . . . about the costs of modernization."[37] Looking at working-class politics, Gary Gerstle discerned greater continuity between the 1920s and the 1950s than historians had previously understood. FDR's regime cemented the working-class descendants of immigrants and rural migrants to the New Deal state, but only by generating a new patriotism that had conservative as well as liberal potential. Besides opposition from localistic conservatives and big business, therefore, another limit to the radicalism of the New Deal came from within its most basic constituency, the industrial working class. And thus working-class anticommunism in the 1950s and electoral support for George Wallace in the 1960s and Ronald Reagan in the 1980s seem less anomalous.[38]

Alan Brinkley's later overview of the era, *The End of Reform*, in emphasizing the social, political, and ideological limits of the New Deal, reflects several decades of revisionist scholarship. In this study, political experimentation comes up against structural limitations; liberal, even radical possibilities are partly thwarted by localistic conservatism, especially in the one-party South; proponents of egalitarian policies sometimes impressively overcome but never eliminate countervailing forces.[39] Similarly, in an attempt to construct a grand synthesis of twentieth-century reform from the standpoint of the

---

[36]Lizabeth Cohen, *Making a New Deal: Industrial Workers in Chicago, 1919–1939* (Cambridge, Mass., 1990), 368.

[37]Alan Brinkley, *Voices of Protest: Huey Long, Father Coughlin, and the Great Depression* (New York, 1982), 7; see also his "The New Deal Experiments," in William Chafe, ed., *Achievement of American Liberalism*, 1–20.

[38]Gary Gerstle, *Working-Class Americanism* (New York, 1989).

[39]Alan Brinkley, *The End of Reform: New Deal Liberalism in Recession and War* (New York, 1995).

New Left, historian Alan Dawley assesses the New Deal in a way far more balanced than those of radical historians a few decades earlier. Dawley's New
Deal is a conservative effort to save capitalism from itself, but his story is not
about elites co-opting masses. Rather, his New Deal derived energy from and
helped advance the grassroots struggles for justice launched by workers and
other less powerful people. In the process it "altered the organic relation
between the state and society," took a "quantum leap into the business of
regulating the market," and "enshrined a new set of ruling values keyed to
security, so that the mass of the population . . . felt as if the government
cared about their welfare."[40] Nuanced and qualified in its judgments, Dawley's
assessment, reproduced as the second reading in this chapter, represents a
maturing of historical treatment of the New Deal. If Leuchtenburg moderated the "heroic liberal" interpretation of FDR and the New Deal, then Dawley
moderated the "debunking radical" interpretation. Like Brinkley, each sees
achievements and failures, though in different places and different degrees.[41]

David M. Kennedy's sweeping *Freedom from Fear*, part of the Oxford History
of the United States, puts FDR at the center of history and makes victory
the theme. While the second half of the book addresses victory in war, the
first half defends the New Deal as a triumph of reform. Summing up this
triumph, Kennedy insists that FDR convinced Americans that the national
government bore responsibility for, and possessed the democratic means to
guarantee, their security. Roosevelt's New Deal "erected an institutional
scaffolding designed to provide unprecedented stability and predictability
for the American economy."[42] Those expectations and that structure — not
just the economic surge of the war years — made possible the era of postwar prosperity. Although Kennedy's grand synthesis will probably remain
the standard account for many years, it should be noted that conservative
scholars, such as economist Elliot A. Rosen, reject entirely claims that the
New Deal achieved anything more than temporary relief to the destitute. It
inflicted some longer-term damage to the economy, Rosen contends, and
played no role whatsoever in postwar prosperity. "The fundamentals of economic advance," he asserts, "are best explained by technological development, adaptability of business to new technologies, workforce educational
levels, natural resources, and private and public support for scientific institutions."[43] A far different assessment comes from Sarah T. Phillips, who argues

---

[40]Alan Dawley, *Struggles for Justice: Social Responsibility and the Liberal State* (Cambridge, Mass.,
1991).

[41]Another fine general study is by an Englishman, Anthony J. Badger, *The New Deal: The
Depression Years, 1933–1940* (New York, 1989).

[42]David M. Kennedy, *Freedom from Fear: The American People in Depression and War, 1929–1945*
(New York, 1999), 376; Jason Scott Smith, *Building New Deal Liberalism: The Political Economy of
Public Works, 1933–1956* (New York, 2006), similarly insists that New Deal public works projects built an infrastructure that undergirded prosperity for decades; in Sidney M. Milkis and
Jerome M. Mileur, eds., *The New Deal and the Triumph of Liberalism* (Amherst, Mass., 2002), Morton Keller asserts that we have for decades lived "in a polity best defined as a lengthened
shadow of the New Deal."

[43]Elliot A. Rosen, *Roosevelt, the Great Depression, and the Economics of Recovery* (Charlottesville,
Va., 2005), 7.

that New Deal conservation and resource policies aimed not just at efficiency but at justice. They had some success and long-term influence both in shaping the Democratic Party coalition and setting the stage for rational planning in the interest of the national — and eventually international — environment.[44]

One of the most promising new directions in New Deal history is comparative. More than thirty years ago, John A. Garraty comparatively evaluated the New Deal and Adolf Hitler's government, concluding that the New Deal was by no means unique. To be sure, in great contrast to the Nazi regime, the New Deal functioned within and maintained a commitment to democratic institutions. Yet the economic policies adopted in the United States and Germany did not differ fundamentally. Both combined direct relief for the indigent with public-works programs to create jobs; both created semi-military programs for the young; both experimented with corporatist solutions that sought to enlist capitalists, workers, and farmers in efforts to eliminate competition and restore social order; and both relied on charismatic personalities to promote patriotic unity.[45] Garraty's formulation did not go unchallenged, but it possessed the great virtue of reminding American historians that the New Dealers neither faced unique challenges nor, in addressing them, reached into unique reservoirs of past practice and ideas. Fairly similar experiences of industrialization, state-making, social dislocation, and the rise of mass culture determined the range of means and the possibilities of success in both cases.

Recently, European scholars have taken up Garraty's challenge, mostly reinforcing his conclusions, but adding detail and a longer chronological frame to the comparative task. Kiran Klaus Patel, in an exhaustive comparison of the CCC and Nazi youth-labor organizations, concludes that neither labor service contributed to economic recovery, but both occupied idle young men and sought to discipline them for socially constructive labor. Both succeeded partly in instilling nationalist ideas in their clients, though American individualism made these efforts far less focused and effective than the Nazi organization's compulsory membership, military drill, and intensive "education." Jytte Klausen focuses on the postwar years, but suggests that the New Deal legacy differed from the more expansive, European-style social-democratic state not because of its inherent limitations or America's distinctive political culture, but rather because the United States never had to deal with the problem of scarcity. Turning the old question, "Why is there no socialism in America?" on its head, she asks why Europeans turned toward central planning. She concludes that the Europeans' need to ration resources and goods required a more collectivist psychology that tolerated greater state controls of production and distribution. Thus, she argues, it was not ideology but wartime

---

[44]Sarah T. Phillips, *This Land, This Nation: Conservation, Rural America, and the New Deal* (New York, 2007).

[45]John Garraty, "The New Deal, National Socialism, and the Great Depression," *American Historical Review* 78 (October 1973): 907–44; see also Garraty's book, *The Great Depression* (New York, 1986).

stringencies, combined with a postwar currency crisis, that made the dollar hegemonic in the postwar economy and left Europeans with little option but to ration and plan.[46]

In conclusion, assessment of the New Deal has evolved considerably, even since the heyday of New Left critique in the 1960s and 1970s. Of course, critical judgments still depend to a degree on the historian's prior assumptions about the nature of the American past and the nation's ideals in both the present and future. To scholars of a laissez-faire bent, the New Deal will always seem a movement hostile to traditional values of individualism and competition. By contrast, to those scholars (whether on the political left or right) who value communal or collective obligations above individual rights, the New Deal may appear to be a signal moment in the maturing of American politics. To those who maintain that only a radical restructuring of American society can establish genuine equality, the New Deal appears as a palliative designed to gloss over fundamental defects in the social and economic order. Historians of a liberal bent will probably see the New Deal as a major, if only partial, advance in American efforts to advance social equality. But whatever their assumptions, historians will have to address key questions: Was the New Deal a continuation of America's liberal tradition or was it a repudiation of that tradition in the face of the relentless forces of modernization? Did the New Deal reflect an attempt by corporate capitalism to maintain its power by forging a partnership with the federal government, with the latter in a subordinate position? Or did the New Deal represent a significant shift in power to classes and groups that in the past had been powerless? Rather than political or ideological failings, to what extent did the New Dealers' inconsistencies reflect the ambivalent commitments of Americans to order and progress, on the one hand, and localism and liberty, on the other? Finally, in addressing these questions, the most ambitious scholars will assess the New Deal from a transnational perspective, comparing the ways in which the United States and other industrial societies confronted the Great Depression and mounted political responses to it.

---

[46]Kiran Klaus Patel, *Soldiers of Labor: Labor Service in Nazi Germany and New Deal America, 1933–1945* (New York, 2005); Jytte Klausen, "Did World War II End the New Deal? A Comparative Perspective on Postwar Planning Initiatives," in Milkis and Mileur, eds., *The New Deal and the Triumph of Liberalism*, 193–230.

WILLIAM E. LEUCHTENBURG

from The Achievement of the New Deal   [1985]

WILLIAM E. LEUCHTENBURG (1922–) is professor of history emeritus at the University of North Carolina, at Chapel Hill. His books include *Franklin D. Roosevelt and the New Deal, 1932–1940* (1963), *In the Shadow of FDR: From Harry Truman to Ronald Reagan* (1989), and *The FDR Years: On Roosevelt and His Legacy* (1995).

The fiftieth anniversary of the New Deal, launched on March 4, 1933, comes at a time when it has been going altogether out of fashion. Writers on the left, convinced that the Roosevelt experiment was either worthless or pernicious, have assigned it to the dustbin of history. Commentators on the right, though far less conspicuous, see in the New Deal the origins of the centralized state they seek to dismantle. Indeed, the half-century of the age of Roosevelt is being commemorated in the presidency of Ronald Reagan, who, while never tiring of quoting FDR, insists that the New Deal derived from Italian fascism.

To be sure, the New Deal has always had its critics. In Roosevelt's own day Marxists said that the New Deal had not done anything for agriculture that an earthquake could not have done better at the same time that conservatives were saying that FDR was unprincipled. Hoover even called him "a chameleon on plaid." Most historians have long since accepted the fact that New Deal policies were sometimes inconsistent, that Roosevelt failed to grasp countercyclical fiscal theory, that recovery did not come until armaments orders fueled the economy, that the President was credited with certain reforms like insurance of bank deposits that he, in fact, opposed, that a number of New Deal programs, notably aid for the marginal farmer, were inadequately financed, and that some New Deal agencies discriminated against blacks.

During the 1960s historians not only dressed up these objections as though they were new revelations but carried their disappointment with contemporary liberalism to the point of arguing either that the New Deal was not just inadequate but actually malign or that the New Deal was so negligible as to constitute a meaningless episode. . . . An "antirevolutionary response to a situation that had revolutionary potentialities," the New Deal, it was said, missed opportunities to nationalize the banks and restructure the social order. Even "providing assistance to the needy and . . . rescuing them from starvation" served conservative ends, historians complained, for these efforts "sapped organized radicalism of its waning strength and of its potential constituency among the unorganized and discontented." The Roosevelt Administration, it has been asserted, failed to achieve more than it did not as a result of the strength of conservative opposition but because of the intellectual deficiencies of the New Dealers and because Roosevelt deliberately sought to save "large-scale corporate capitalism." . . .

This emphasis has so permeated writing on the New Deal in the past generation that an instructor who wishes to assign the latest thought on the age of Roosevelt has a wide choice of articles and anthologies that document the errors of the New Deal but no assessment of recent vintage that explores its accomplishments.

The fiftieth anniversary of the New Deal provides the occasion for a modest proposal — that we reintroduce some tension into the argument over the interpretation of the Roosevelt years. If historians are to develop a credible synthesis, it is important to regain a sense of the achievement of the New Deal. As it now stands, we have a dialectic that is all antithesis with no thesis. . . .

As a first step toward a more considered evaluation, one has to remind one's self not only of what the New Deal did not do, but of what it achieved.

Above all, one needs to recognize how markedly the New Deal altered the character of the State in America. Indeed, though for decades past European theorists had been talking about *der Staat*, there can hardly be said to have been a State in America in the full meaning of the term before the New Deal. If you had walked into an American town in 1932, you would have had a hard time detecting any sign of a federal presence, save perhaps for the post office and even many of today's post offices date from the 1930s. Washington rarely affected people's lives directly. There was no national old-age pension system, no federal unemployment compensation, no aid to dependent children, no federal housing, no regulation of the stock market, no withholding tax, no federal school lunch, no farm subsidy, no national minimum wage law, no welfare state. . . . From 1933 to 1938, the government intervened in a myriad of ways from energizing the economy to fostering unionization. . . .

This vast expansion of government led inevitably to the concentration of much greater power in the presidency, whose authority was greatly augmented under FDR. Rexford Tugwell has written of Roosevelt: "No monarch, . . . unless it may have been Elizabeth or her magnificent Tudor father, or maybe Alexander or Augustus Caesar, can have given quite that sense of serene presiding, of gathering up into himself, of really representing, a whole people." The President became, in Sidney Hyman's words, "the chief economic engineer," to whom Congress naturally turned for the setting of economic policy. Roosevelt stimulated interest in public affairs by his fireside chats and freewheeling press conferences, shifted the balance between the White House and Capitol Hill by assuming the role of Chief Legislator, and eluded the routinized traditional departments by creating emergency agencies. In 1939 he established the Executive Office of the President, giving the Chief Executive a central staff office for the first time. "The verdict of history," wrote Clinton Rossiter, "will surely be that he left the Presidency a more splendid instrument of democracy than he found it."

To staff the national agencies, Roosevelt turned to a new class of people: the university-trained experts. . . . During the First Hundred Days, large numbers of professors, encouraged by FDR's reliance on the Brain Trust, flocked to Washington to draft New Deal legislation and to administer New Deal agencies. The radical literary critic Edmund Wilson wrote, "Everywhere in the streets and offices you run into old acquaintances: the editors and writers of the liberal press, the 'progressive' young instructors from the colleges, the intelligent foundation workers, the practical idealists of settlement houses." He added: "The bright boys of the Eastern universities, instead of being obliged to choose, as they were twenty years ago, between business, the bond-selling game and the field or foreign missions, can come on and get jobs in Washington." . . .

Some may doubt today whether it is always an unmitigated good to have "the best and the brightest" in seats of power, but in the 1930s this infusion of talent gave an élan to the national government that had been sorely missing in the past. The *New Republic* commented: "We have in Washington not a soggy and insensitive mass of dough, as in some previous administrations, but a nervous, alert and hard-working group who are doing their level best to effectuate a program." . . .

This corps of administrators made it possible for Roosevelt to carry out a major change in the role of the federal government. Although the New Deal always operated within a capitalist matrix and the government sought to enhance profitmaking, Roosevelt and his lieutenants rejected the traditional view that government was the handmaiden of business or that government and business were coequal sovereigns. As a consequence, they adopted measures to discipline corporations, to require a sharing of authority with government and unions, and to hold businessmen accountable. In the early days of the National Recovery Administration, the novelist Sherwood Anderson wrote:

> I went to several code hearings. No one has quite got their significance. Here for the first time you see these men of business, little ones and big ones, . . . coming up on the platform to give an accounting. It does seem the death knell of the old idea that a man owning a factory, office or store has a right to run it in his own way.
>
> There is at least an effort to relate it now to the whole thing, man's relations with his fellow men etc. Of course it is crude and there will be no end to crookedness, objections, etc. but I do think an entire new principle in American life is being established.

Through a series of edicts and statutes, the administration invaded the realm of the banker by establishing control over the nation's money supply. The government clamped an embargo on gold, took the United States off the gold standard, and nullified the requirement for the payment of gold in private contracts. In 1935 a resentful Supreme Court sustained this authority, although a dissenting justice said that this was Nero at his worst. The Glass-Steagall Banking Act (1933) stripped commercial banks of the privilege of engaging in investment banking, and established federal insurance of bank deposits, an innovation which the leading monetary historians have called "the structural change most conducive to monetary stability since bank notes were taxed out of existence immediately after the Civil War." The Banking Act of 1935 gave the United States what other industrial nations had long had, but America lacked — central banking. . . .

A number of other enactments helped transfer authority from Wall Street to Washington. The Securities Act of 1933 established government supervision of the issue of securities, and made company directors civilly and criminally liable for misinformation on the statements they were required to file with each new issue. The Securities and Exchange Act of 1934 initiated federal supervision of the stock exchanges, which to this day operate under the lens of the Securities and Exchange Commission (SEC). The Holding Company Act of 1935 levelled some of the utility pyramids, dissolving all utility holding companies that were more than twice removed from their operating companies, and increased the regulatory powers of the SEC over public utilities. . . . To be sure, financiers continued to make important policy choices, but they never again operated in the uninhibited universe of the Great Bull Market. . . .

The age of Roosevelt focused attention on Washington, too, by initiatives in fields that had been regarded as exclusively within the private orbit, notably in housing. The Home Owners' Loan Corporation, created in 1933, saved tens of thousands of homes from foreclosure by refinancing mortgages. In 1934 the Federal Housing Administration (FHA) began its program of insuring loans for the construction and renovation of private homes, and over the next generation more than 10 million FHA-financed units were built. Before the New Deal, the national government had never engaged in public housing, except for the World War I emergency, but agencies like the Public Works Administration now broke precedent. The Tennessee Valley Authority laid out the model town of Norris, the Federal Emergency Relief Administration (FERA) experimented with subsistence homesteads, and the Resettlement Administration created greenbelt communities, entirely new towns girdled by green countryside. When in 1937 the Wagner-Steagall Act created the U.S. Housing Authority, it assured public housing a permanent place in American life.

The New Deal profoundly altered industrial relations by throwing the weight of government behind efforts to unionize workers. At the outset of the Great Depression, the American labor movement was "an anachronism in the world," for only a tiny minority of factory workers were unionized. Employers hired and fired and imposed punishments at will, used thugs as strikebreakers and private police, stockpiled industrial munitions, and ran company towns as feudal fiefs. In an astonishingly short

period in the Roosevelt years a very different pattern emerged. Under the
umbrella of Section 7(a) of the National Industrial Recovery Act of 1933
and of the far-reaching Wagner Act of 1935, union organizers gained millions of recruits in such open-shop strongholds as steel, automobiles, and
textiles. Employees won wage rises, reductions in hours, greater job security, freedom from the tyranny of company guards, and protection against
arbitrary punishment. Thanks to the National Recovery Administration
and the Guffey acts, coal miners achieved the outlawing of compulsory
company houses and stores. Steel workers, who in 1920 labored twelve-
hour shifts seven days a week at the blast furnaces, were to become so
powerful that in the postwar era they would win not merely paid vacations
but sabbatical leaves. . . .

Years later, when David E. Lilienthal, the director of the Tennessee
Valley Authority, was being driven to the airport to fly to Roosevelt's funeral,
the TVA driver said to him:

> I won't forget what he did for me. . . . I spent the best years of my life
> working at the Appalachian Mills . . . and they didn't even treat us like
> humans. If you didn't do like they said, they always told you there was
> someone else to take your job. I had my mother and my sister to take care
> of. Sixteen cents an hour was what we got; a fellow can't live on that. . . .
> If you asked to get off on a Sunday, the foreman would say, "All right you
> stay away Sunday, but when you come back Monday someone else will
> have your job." No, sir, I won't forget what he done for us.

. . . The NRA wiped out sweatshops, and removed some 150,000 child
laborers from factories. The Walsh-Healey Act of 1936 and the Fair Labor
Standards Act of 1938 established the principle of a federally imposed
minimal level of working conditions, and added further sanctions against
child labor. If the New Deal did not do enough for the "one-third of a
nation" to whom Roosevelt called attention, it at least made a beginning,
through agencies like the Farm Security Administration, toward helping
sharecroppers, tenant farmers, and migrants like John Steinbeck's Joads.
Most important, it originated a new system of social rights to replace the
dependence on private charity. The Social Security Act of 1935 created
America's first national system of old-age pensions and initiated a federal-
state program of unemployment insurance. It also authorized grants for
the blind, for the incapacitated, and for dependent children, a feature
that would have unimaginable long-range consequences. . . .

Roosevelt himself affirmed the newly assumed attitudes in Washington
in his annual message to Congress in 1938 when he declared: "Government has a final responsibility for the well-being of its citizenship. If private co-operative endeavor fails to provide work for willing hands and
relief for the unfortunate, those suffering hardship from no fault of their
own have a right to call upon the Government for aid; and a government
worthy of its name must make fitting response."

Nothing revealed this approach so well as the New Deal's attention to the plight of the millions of unemployed. During the ten years between 1929 and 1939, one scholar has written, "more progress was made in public welfare and relief than in the three hundred years after this country was first settled." A series of alphabet agencies — the FERA, the CWA, the WPA — provided government work for the jobless, while the National Youth Administration (NYA) employed college students in museums, libraries, and laboratories, enabled high school students to remain in school, and set up a program of apprentice training. In Texas, the twenty-seven-year-old NYA director Lyndon Johnson put penniless young men like John Connally to work building roadside parks, and in North Carolina, the NYA employed, at 35 cents an hour, a Duke University law student, Richard Nixon.

In an address in Los Angeles in 1936, the head of FDR's relief operations, Harry Hopkins, conveyed the attitude of the New Deal toward those who were down and out:

> I am getting sick and tired of these people on the W.P.A. and local relief rolls being called chiselers and cheats. . . . These people . . . are just like the rest of us. They don't drink any more than us, they don't lie any more, they're no lazier than the rest of us — they're pretty much a cross section of the American people. . . . I have never believed that with our capitalistic system people have to be poor. I think it is an outrage that we should permit hundreds and hundreds of thousands of people to be ill clad, to live in miserable homes, not to have enough to eat; not to be able to send their children to school for the only reason that they are poor. I don't believe ever again in America we are going to permit the things to happen that have happened in the past to people.

Under the leadership of men like Hopkins, "Santa Claus incomparable and privy-builder without peer," projects of relief agencies and of the Public Works Administration (PWA) changed the face of the land. The PWA built thoroughfares like the Skyline Drive in Virginia and the Overseas Highway from Miami to Key West, constructed the Medical Center in Jersey City, burrowed Chicago's new subway, and gave Natchez, Mississippi, a new bridge, and Denver a modern water-supply system. Few New Yorkers today realize the long reach of the New Deal. If they cross the Triborough Bridge, they are driving on a bridge the PWA built. If they fly into La Guardia Airport, they are landing at an airfield laid out by the WPA. If they get caught in a traffic jam on the FDR Drive, they are using yet another artery built by the WPA. . . . In New York City alone the WPA employed more people than the entire War Department. . . .

The New Deal showed unusual sensitivity toward jobless white-collar workers, notably those in aesthetic fields. The Public Works of Art Project gave an opportunity to muralists eager for a chance to work in the style of Rivera, Orozco, and Siqueiros. The Federal Art Project fostered the careers of painters like Stuart Davis, Raphael Soyer, Yasuo Kuniyoshi, and Jackson Pollock. Out of the same project came a network of community art centers and the notable *Index of American Design*. . . .

The Federal Writers' Project provided support for scores of talented novelists and poets, editors and literary critics, men like Ralph Ellison and Nelson Algren, John Cheever and Saul Bellow. These writers turned out an exceptional set of state guides, with such features as Conrad Aiken's carefully delineated portrayal of Deerfield, Massachusetts, and special volumes like *These Are Our Lives*, a graphic portfolio of life histories in North Carolina, and *Panorama*, in which Vincent McHugh depicts "the infinite pueblo of the Bronx." Project workers transcribed chain-gang blues songs, recovered folklore that would otherwise have been lost, and collected the narratives of elderly former slaves, an invaluable archive later published in *Lay My Burden Down*. When the magazine *Story* conducted a contest for the best contribution by a Project employee, the prize was won by an unpublished 29-year-old black who had been working on the essay on the Negro for the Illinois guide. With the prize money for his stories, subsequently published as *Uncle Tom's Children*, Richard Wright gained the time to complete his remarkable first novel, *Native Son*.

Some thought it an ill omen that the Federal Theatre Project's first production was Shakespeare's *Comedy of Errors*, but that agency not only gave employment to actors and stage technicians but offered many communities their first glimpse of live drama. . . . If the creation of America's first state theatre was an unusual departure, the New Deal's ventures in documentary films seemed no less surprising. With Resettlement Administration funds, Pare Lorentz produced *The Plow That Broke the Plains* in 1936 and the classic *The River* in 1937. He engaged cameramen like Paul Strand, who had won acclaim for his movie on a fisherman's strike in Mexico; invited the young composer Virgil Thomson, who had just scored Gertrude Stein's *Four Saints in Three Acts*, to compose the background music; and employed Thomas Chalmers, who had sung at the Metropolitan Opera in the era of Caruso, to read the narration. Lorentz's films were eyeopeners. American government documentaries before the New Deal had been limited to short subjects on topics like the love life of the honeybee. *The River*, which won first prize in Venice at the International Exposition of Cinematographic Art in 1938, proved that there was an audience in the United States for well-wrought documentaries. By 1940 it had drawn more than 10 million people, while *The Plow That Broke the Plains*, said one critic, made "the rape of millions of acres . . . more moving than the downfall of a Hollywood blonde."

Lorentz's films suggest the concern of the New Deal for the American land. . . . The Tennessee Valley Authority, which drew admirers from all over the world, put the national government in the business of generating electric power, controlled floods, terraced hillsides, and gave new hope to the people of the valley. In the Pacific Northwest the PWA constructed mammoth dams, Grand Coulee and Bonneville. Roosevelt's "tree army," the Civilian Conservation Corps, planted millions of trees, cleared forest trails, laid out picnic sites and campgrounds, and aided the Forest Service in the vast undertaking of establishing a shelterbelt — a windbreak of trees and shrubs: green ash and Chinese elm, apricot and blackberry, buffalo berry and Osage orange from the Canadian border to the Texas panhandle. Government agencies came to the aid of drought-stricken farmers in the Dust Bowl, and the Soil Conservation Service, another New Deal creation, instructed growers in methods of cultivation to save the land. . . .

These services to farmers represented only a small part of the government's program, for in the New Deal years, the business of agriculture was revolutionized. Roosevelt came to power at a time of mounting desperation for American farmers. Each month in 1932 another 20,000 farmers had lost their land because of inability to meet their debts in a period of collapsing prices. On a single day in May 1932, one-fourth of the state of Mississippi went under the sheriff's hammer. The Farm Credit Administration of 1933 came to the aid of the beleaguered farmer, and within eighteen months, it had refinanced one-fifth of all farm mortgages in the United States. In the Roosevelt years, too, the Rural Electrification Administration literally brought rural America out of darkness. At the beginning of the Roosevelt era, only one farm in nine had electricity; at the end, only one in nine did not have it. But more important than any of these developments was the progression of enactments starting with the first AAA (the Agricultural Adjustment Act) of 1933, which began the process of granting large-scale subsidies to growers. As William Faulkner later said, "Our economy is not agricultural any longer. Our economy is the federal government. We no longer farm in Mississippi cotton fields. We farm now in Washington corridors and Congressional committee rooms."

At the same time that its realm was being expanded under the New Deal, the national government changed the composition of its personnel and of its beneficiaries. Before 1933, the government had paid heed primarily to a single group — white Anglo-Saxon Protestant males. The Roosevelt Administration, however, recruited from a more ethnically diverse group, and the prominence of Catholics and Jews among the President's advisers is suggested by the scintillating team of the Second Hundred Days, Corcoran and Cohen. The Federal Writers' Project turned out books on Italians and Albanians, and the Federal Theatre staged productions in Yiddish and wrote a history of the Chinese stage in Los Angeles. In the 1930s women played a more prominent role in government than they ever had before, as the result of such appointments as that of Frances Perkins as the first female cabinet member, while the influence of Eleanor Roosevelt was pervasive. . . .

Although in some respects the New Deal's performance with regard to blacks added to the sorry record of racial discrimination in America, important gains were also registered in the 1930s. Blacks, who had often been excluded from relief in the past, now received a share of WPA jobs considerably greater than their proportion of the population. Blacks moved into federal housing projects; federal funds went to schools and hospitals in black neighborhoods; and New Deal agencies like the Farm Security Administration (FSA) enabled 50,000 Negro tenant farmers and sharecroppers to become proprietors. "Indeed," one historian has written, "there is a high correlation between the location of extensive FSA operations in the 1930s and the rapidity of political modernization in black communities in the South in the 1960s." Roosevelt appointed a number of blacks, including William Hastie, Mary McLeod Bethune, and Robert Weaver, to high posts in the government. . . . The reign of Jim Crow in Washington offices, which had begun under Roosevelt's Democratic predecessor, Woodrow Wilson, was terminated by Secretary of the Interior Harold Ickes who desegregated cafeterias in his department. Ickes also had a role in the most dramatic episode of the times, for when the Daughters of the American Revolution (DAR) denied the use of their concert hall to the black contralto Marian Anderson, he made it possible for her to sing before thousands from the steps of the Lincoln Memorial; and Mrs. Roosevelt joined in the rebuke to the DAR. Anderson's concert on Easter Sunday 1939 was heard by thousands at the Memorial, and three networks carried her voice to millions more. Blacks delivered their own verdict on the New Deal at the polling places. Committed to the party of Lincoln as late as 1932, when they voted overwhelmingly for Hoover, they shifted in large numbers to the party of FDR during Roosevelt's first term. This was a change of allegiance that many whites were also making in those years.

The Great Depression and the New Deal brought about a significant political realignment of the sort that occurs only rarely in America. The Depression wrenched many lifelong Republican voters from their moorings. In 1928, one couple christened their newborn son "Herbert Hoover Jones." Four years later they petitioned the court, "desiring to relieve the young man from the chagrin and mortification which he is suffering and will suffer," and asked that his name be changed to Franklin D. Roosevelt Jones. In 1932 FDR became the first Democrat to enter the White House with as much as 50 percent of the popular vote in eighty years — since Franklin K. Pierce in 1852. Roosevelt took advantage of this opportunity to mold "the FDR coalition," an alliance centered in the low-income districts of the great cities and, as recently as the 1980 election, the contours of the New Deal coalition could still be discerned. Indeed, over the past half-century, the once overpowering Republicans have won control of Congress only twice, for a total of four years. . . .

Furthermore, the New Deal drastically altered the agenda of American politics. When Arthur Krock of the *New York Times* listed the main programmatic questions before the 1932 Democratic convention, he wrote: "What would be said about the repeal of prohibition that had split the Republicans? What would be said about tariffs?" By 1936, these concerns seemed altogether old fashioned, as campaigners discussed the Tennessee Valley Authority and industrial relations, slum clearance and aid to the jobless. That year, a Little Rock newspaper commented: "Such matters as tax and tariff laws have given way to universally human things, the living problems and opportunities of the average man and the average family."

The Roosevelt years changed the conception of the role of government not just in Washington but in the states, where a series of "Little New Deals" — under governors like Herbert Lehman in New York — added a thick sheaf of social legislation, and in the cities. In Boston, Charles Trout has observed, city council members in 1929 "devoted endless hours to street paving." After the coming of the New Deal, they were absorbed with NRA campaigns, public housing, and WPA allotments. "A year after the crash the council thought 5,000 dollars an excessive appropriation for the municipal employment bureau," but during the 1930s "the unemployed drained Boston's treasury of not less than 100,000,000 dollars in direct benefits, and the federal government spent even more."

In a cluster of pathbreaking decisions in 1937, the Supreme Court legitimized this vast exercise of authority by government at all levels. As late as 1936, the Supreme Court still denied the power of the United States government to regulate agriculture, even though crops were sold in a world market, or coal mining, a vital component of a national economy, and struck down a minimum wage law as beyond the authority of the state of New York. Roosevelt responded with a plan to "pack" the Court with as many as six additional Justices, and in short order the Court, in what has been called "the Constitutional Revolution of 1937," sounded retreat. Before 1937 the Supreme Court stood as a formidable barrier to social reform. Since 1937 not one piece of significant social legislation has been invalidated, and the Court has shifted its docket instead to civil rights and civil liberties.

What then did the New Deal do? It gave far greater amplitude to the national state, expanded the authority of the presidency, recruited university-trained administrators, won control of the money supply, established central banking, imposed regulation on Wall Street, rescued the debt-ridden farmer and homeowner, built model communities, financed the Federal Housing Administration, made federal housing a permanent feature, fostered unionization of the factories, reduced child labor, ended the tyranny of company towns, wiped out many sweatshops, mandated minimal working standards, enabled tenants to buy their own farms, built camps for migrants, introduced the welfare state with old-age pensions, unemployment insurance, and aid for dependent children, provided jobs for millions of unemployed, created a special program for the jobless young and for students, covered the American landscape with new edifices, subsidized painters and novelists, composers and ballet dancers, founded America's first state theater, created documentary films, gave birth to the impressive Tennessee Valley Authority, generated electrical power, sent the Civilian Conservation Corps boys into the forests, initiated the Soil Conservation Service, transformed the economy of agriculture, lighted up rural America, gave women greater recognition, made a start toward breaking the pattern of racial discrimination and segregation, put together a liberal party coalition, changed the agenda of American politics, and brought about a Constitutional Revolution.

But even this summary does not account for the full range of its activities. The New Deal offered the American Indian new opportunities for self-government and established the Indian Arts and Crafts Board, sponsored vaudeville troupes and circuses, taught counterpoint and *solfeggio*, was responsible for the founding of the Buffalo Philharmonic, the Oklahoma Symphony, and the Utah State Symphony, served hot lunches to school children and set up hundreds of nursery schools, sent bookmobiles into isolated communities, and where there were no roads, had books carried in by packhorses. And only a truly merciful and farsighted government could have taken such special pains to find jobs for unemployed historians.

The New Deal accomplished all of this at a critical time, when many were insisting that fascism was the wave of the future and denying that democracy could be effective. For those throughout the world who heard such jeremiads with foreboding, the American experience was enormously inspiriting. A decade after the end of the age of Roosevelt, Sir Isaiah Berlin wrote:

> When I say that some men occupy one's imagination for many years, this is literally true of Mr. Roosevelt and the young men of my own generation in England, and probably in many parts of Europe, and indeed the entire world. If one was young in the thirties, and lived in a democracy, then, whatever one's politics, if one had human feelings at all, the faintest spark of social idealism, or any love of life whatever, one must have felt very much as young men in Continental Europe probably felt after the defeat of Napoleon during the years of the Restoration: that all was dark and quiet, a great reaction was abroad, and little stirred, and nothing resisted.

In these "dark and leaden thirties," Professor Berlin continued, "the only light in the darkness that was left was the administration of Mr. Roosevelt and the New Deal in the United States. At a time of weakness and mounting despair in the democratic world Mr. Roosevelt radiated confidence and strength. . . . Even to-day, upon him alone, of all the statesmen of the thirties, no cloud rested neither on him nor on the New Deal, which to European eyes still looks a bright chapter in the history of mankind."

For the past generation, America has lived off the legacy of the New Deal. Successive administrations extended the provisions of statutes like the Social Security Act, adopted New Deal attitudes toward intervention in the economy to cope with recessions, and put New Deal ideas to modern purposes, as when the Civilian Conservation Corps served as the basis for both the Peace Corps and the VISTA program of the War on Poverty. Harry Truman performed under the shadow of FDR, Lyndon Johnson consciously patterned his administration on Roosevelt's, Jimmy Carter launched his first presidential campaign at Warm Springs, and Ronald

Reagan has manifested an almost obsessive need to summon FDR to his side. Carl Degler has observed:

> Conventionally the end of the New Deal is dated with the enactment of the Wages and Hours Act of 1938. But in a fundamental sense the New Deal did not end then at all. Americans still live in the era of the New Deal, for its achievements are now the base mark below which no conservative government may go and from which all new reform now starts. . . . The reform efforts of the Democratic Truman, Kennedy, and Johnson administrations have been little more than fulfillments of the New Deal.

The British historian David K. Adams has pointed out that the philosophy of the New Frontier has "conscious overtones of the New Deal" and indeed that John Kennedy's "New Frontier" address of 1960 was "almost a paraphrase" of an FDR speech of 1935. Theodore White has commented that both John and Robert Kennedy shared sentences from a Roosevelt address that reporters called the "Dante sequence." When at a loss for words, each was wont to quote a favorite passage from Franklin Roosevelt: "Governments can err, Presidents do make mistakes, but the immortal Dante tells us that Divine Justice weighs the sins of the cold-blooded and the sins of the warm-hearted on a different scale. Better the occasional faults of a government living in the spirit of charity, than the consistent omissions of a government frozen in the ice of its own indifference."

By restoring to the debate over the significance of the New Deal acknowledgment of its achievements, we may hope to produce a more judicious estimate of where it succeeded and where it failed. For it unquestionably did fail in a number of respects. There were experiments of the 1930s which miscarried, opportunities that were fumbled, groups who were neglected, and power that was arrogantly used. Over the whole performance lies the dark cloud of the persistence of hard times. The shortcomings of the New Deal are formidable, and they must be recognized. But I am not persuaded that the New Deal experience was negligible. Indeed, it is hard to think of another period in the whole history of the republic that was so fruitful or of a crisis that was met with as much imagination.

ALAN DAWLEY

from Struggles for Justice   [1991]

ALAN DAWLEY (1943–) is professor of history at the College of New Jersey. He is the author of *Class and Community: The Industrial Revolution in Lynn* (1976), which won a Bancroft prize, and *Struggles for Justice: Social Responsibility and the Liberal State* (1991).

The ink was hardly dry on Roosevelt's recovery program before the New Deal was overtaken by an unexpected development: social movements awakened from their long slumber. From the grimy coal regions of Pennsylvania to the sultry bayous of Louisiana, the sleeping giants of labor, social justice, and populism snapped the cords that had tied them down in the early stages of the depression. As the earth began to shake with the tramp of strikes and rallies, there was a revitalization of radicalism and a resurgence of faith in the common people: Why not? Everything else seemed to have failed. Carl Sandburg captured the new mood in the title of his epic poem, *The People, Yes* (1936).

Ironically, the rebirth of social movements at the grass roots was in part the consequence of elite activities in Washington. The corporate planners and Brain Trusters of the early New Deal had found it necessary to penetrate ever deeper into the daily lives of ordinary Americans. As reported in a summer 1933 issue of the *Literary Digest*, "This central government of ours has now become the almoner to 12,000,000 unemployed and distressed people. It has become the guardian of middle-class investors, of the mortgaged-farm owner, of the mortgaged-home owner, of the bank depositor, and of the railway employee. It has become the partner of industry and of agriculture. And it has even become the friend of the beer maker and the beer drinker."

The last thing New Dealers wanted was to have "distressed people" taking things into their own hands, but that is exactly what happened next. For the more the Roosevelt administration rationalized banking, industry, and agriculture, the more it raised expectations for government aid among workers, retirees, and the unemployed. Roosevelt had stumbled upon the law of unintended consequences, but anyone with a sense of the cunning of history could have seen it coming. Having cultivated the analogy between the depression "emergency" and the war "emergency," Roosevelt should not have been surprised when the people demanded delivery on the government promise of recovery, just as people had demanded that Wilson live up to his promise to "make the world safe for democracy."

Reprinted by permission of the publisher from "Rendezvous with Destiny," in *Struggles for Justice: Social Responsibility and the Liberal State*, by Alan Dawley, pp. 371–74, 377–85, 395, 402–5. Cambridge, Mass.: The Belknap Press of Harvard University Press. Copyright © 1991 by the President and Fellows of Harvard College.

Nothing better illustrated the unwritten law of unintended consequences than the way New Deal labor policy inadvertently mobilized workers. None of Roosevelt's inner circle could be accused of harboring a passion for organized labor, not even Secretary of Labor Frances Perkins, who was more of a progressive reformer than a trade unionist. The president betrayed his own indifference to the labor movement in remarking that he didn't care whether workers paid allegiance to a trade union, the Ahkoond of Swat, or the Royal Geographic Society. The fact that section 7a of the 1933 National Recovery Act piously declared that workers had the right to organize and bargain collectively "through representatives of their own choosing" did not mask any secret desire to rally workers to the union cause. It was simply a political bone thrown to the AFL in hopes of ending its support of a bill mandating a thirty-hour week, which the entire Roosevelt administration opposed.

It took a canny opportunist such as John L. Lewis to ignore all this. The flamboyant autocrat of the United Mine Workers launched a membership drive under the slogan "The President wants you to organize." As tens of thousands of mine workers signed union cards, the spirit soon spread to workers in mass production. Together with the garment workers and a few other industrial unions, Lewis prepared to commit the greatest sin known to the labor movement — dual unionism — by breaking away from the AFL in 1935 to form the Committee (later Congress) of Industrial Organizations. It may have been all a misunderstanding, but by seeming to remove government objections to labor unions, section 7a contributed to the most significant mobilization of wage earners since the war.

A dozen years of labor peace ended with a bang in 1934. From one end of the country to the other, industrial workers rediscovered a long-lost militancy. The textile industry was convulsed by the first nationwide general strike in its history, punctuated by company violence. In San Francisco a longshoremen's strike against the indignities of the "shape-up" (in which foremen hired favorites from men herded together like cattle) escalated into a citywide general strike when police killed strikers. Similarly, teamsters brought truck transport to a halt in the vital entrepôt "of Min-neapolis, and, again, company thugs killed strikers. Communists and Trotskyists, respectively, played vital leadership roles in these strikes. Returning from a sojourn in the Soviet Union, Walter Reuther, future president of the United Auto Workers, was amazed at what he saw: "the NRA and the series of strikes and struggles of labor that followed ushered in a new epoch in America."

Violence accompanied all the major strikes, and the reason was the same as always — business' hatred for unions. Although a handful of companies were prepared to recognize genuine unions, most fought as if there was no tomorrow. Turning section 7a to their own advantage, they set up company unions, or employee representation plans, which success-fully forestalled independent trade unions in a host of places. At the same time, they brought in labor spies, hired thugs, private detectives, and "citi-zen" vigilantes, whose massive violations of civil liberties would soon be

amply documented by a Senate investigating committee under Robert La
Follette. A handful of so-called brass hats such as Tom Girdler of Republic
Steel vowed never to accept collective bargaining. Girdler's intransigence
led to the infamous Memorial Day Massacre of 1937, when ten members
of a crowd of peaceful demonstrators were shot in the back by police.
Although the number of strikes and the level of violence never reached
that of the end of the First World War, industrial warfare was back.

The difference was that this time unionism often came out on the winning side. Whereas the 1919 Seattle general strike had been crushed, the
strikers of San Francisco and Minneapolis could justly claim victory.
Whereas mass production and heavy industry had emerged union free
from the postwar battles, organizing drives were now under way that would
soon bring strong unions to the auto, meatpacking, electrical and steel
industries; in short, to the entire heartland of modern capitalism. Whereas
the craft unions of the AFL had lapsed into a lethargic "business unionism" during the 1920s, now the emerging industrial unions of the CIO
rekindled a crusading spirit that brought in almost 3 million members and
sparked an equivalent expansion in the ranks of the revitalized AFL.

What explains this remarkable mobilization of "labor's new millions"?
Once the trigger effect of the New Deal has been duly acknowledged,
the upsurge should be understood in the context of the evolution of
modern capitalism. Class relations were being reshaped by the impersonal
structures of mass society. In the realm of production, two decades of
technical rationalization and bureaucratic management had homogenized
the labor process so that workers in widely different settings had the sense
that they were all parts of a single whole. By the same token, in the
realm of reproduction, the homogenizing impact of mass culture — from
advertising and chain stores to major league baseball and public schools —
had lifted people out of their parochialism and given them a common
basis of communication across ethnic and religious boundaries. Everybody
could root for the home team, and who didn't love Charlie Chaplin?

Taking these structural conditions as a given, real, flesh-and-blood
human beings brought about the rebirth of labor. Because the working
class spanned so many different cultures, the labor movement could not
count on a common set of values, and in almost every struggle against the
boss, there was a concurrent struggle for leadership within the movement.
In the case of New England textile workers, secular radicals in the tradition of the French Revolution vied with devout Catholic French-Canadians;
and in the case of the electrical workers, Communist fellow travelers competed with Catholic corporatists. The divisions had always been there.
The difference was that now the common struggle against the boss took
precedence and drew these warring factions together. In one of the most
bizarre cases, an alliance arose among New York transit workers between
closet Communists and Irish nationalists in the secret Clan Na Gael.

That atheist lions could lie down with churchgoing lambs reflected the
change in climate in working-class communities. After years of eclipse,
visions of a just society were returning to the forefront. To judge from the

many testaments they left behind, labor organizers were motivated as much by a desire to change society as by a desire for power. Certainly, that was the case for Jewish garment workers, who combined socialist ideals, *Yiddishkeit* (the transplanted culture of eastern European Jews), and a sophisticated pursuit of political power that eventually installed Sidney Hillman of the Amalgamated Clothing Workers as one of President Roosevelt's many righthand men. And in general, the advance of social consciousness helped revitalize the labor movement and thrust it to the center of the historical stage. . . .

The change was registered as populists and progressives became major players in the midterm elections of 1934. Upton Sinclair ran a creditable campaign for governor of California on watered-down socialism and the slogan "End poverty in California." Midwestern voters elected members of the Minnesota Farmer-Labor party, sent progressive Robert La Follette, Jr., to the Senate from Wisconsin, and revived the prairie populist ideas of the Non-Partisan League. Southern populism spoke through Huey Long's Share Our Wealth campaign, and southern progressives such as Hugo Black put aside states' rights and worry about race relations to support federal assistance to the poor. Contrary to the traditional pattern in midterm elections, voters further reduced the Republican contingent in Congress, and many of the new Democrats stood to the left of Roosevelt. For the first time in a decade of reversals, the labor movement actually gained friends in high office. Once the New Deal broke the logjam in American politics, a host of reformers came flooding through.

In some respects, the new dynamic was comparable to the aftermath of the First World War. Then, the largest strike wave in American history, the onrushing women's movement, and the emergence of the New Negro confronted elites with a choice between progressive "reconstruction" that would co-opt these popular forces into a new governing system and top-down repression that would freeze things as they were. Although the Women's Suffrage Amendment was an example of cooptation, for the most part the Wilson and Harding administrations had chosen the path of repression. Nervous about Bolshevik revolution in Europe, they chose to crack down on strikers, incite the Red Scare, and abandon social reform in favor of laissez faire and immigration restriction.

Now, a decade and a half later, as the political initiative shifted from elites to masses, the Roosevelt administration faced a similar choice between repressing popular forces or co-opting them into some yet-undiscovered consensus. In the frame of international comparison, that choice translated into an ominous question of whether liberalism would be sacrificed to save capitalism. The question was posed most cruelly in Germany, where the Nazi seizure of power in 1933 had destroyed all semblance of civil liberties. If Germany could descend into fascism, was it possible that the United States would find its own road to repression?

Given all that was at stake, the choice facing the country in the mid-1930s was full of historical significance. For if the Roosevelt administration continued to take its cues from managerial liberals, and if, as seemed likely, its half-baked experiments in state planning failed to end the depression, then the inevitable protests would be met with troops and anticommunist hysteria. And if the lights of free expression were snuffed out in the land of liberty, how long could they remain lit elsewhere? If, on the other hand, the administration chose to reach out to the grass-roots movements, it would have to chart a new course for American politics. Since there were precious few precedents for incorporating wage earners in state policies, and since the interests of wage earners and capitalists were fundamentally at odds, it would not be easy to find the way.

In the event, the choice was for a new round of experiments in 1935 that became known as the Second New Deal. In what was the truly new part of the New Deal, the Roosevelt administration enacted a set of enduring reforms, including the National Labor Relations Act and the Social Security Act, that somehow reconciled capitalism and social reform, altered forever the relation between state and society in the United States, and stood as a beacon of liberal renewal to the entire world.

The original impetus for reform came not from corporate planners but from the popular movements for social justice and their allies in the administration and Congress. That fact was crystal clear in the more radical pieces of legislation, such as the Works Progress Administration (WPA). Responding to unemployed workers and social reformers, Harry Hopkins, a Chicago social worker in the Jane Addams tradition, devised a vast federal jobs program that spent over $2 billion at its peak in 1939 and had more than 3 million people on payroll doing everything from digging ditches to writing plays. Though ridiculed as "We Poke Along," it made lasting contributions in public works and even in public art through the heroic murals of people's struggle painted by the likes of Diego Rivera. To its supporters, WPA represented a rational system of production-for-use as against the chaos of production-for-profit. Verily, it prefigured the cooperative commonwealth.

No doubt the most annoying burr in the saddle of privilege was the wealth tax. Roosevelt backed the "soak the rich" tax on capital stock, estates, gifts, and excess profits to recapture political ground lost to Long's Share Our Wealth campaign. Once enacted in 1935, the tax did not, in fact, soak the rich; econometric studies attribute most of whatever downward distribution of income occurred after 1929 to market forces or the impact of the Second World War. But nothing did more to provoke fear and loathing of the New Deal and "that man in the White House," and it marked the apogee of Roosevelt's swing toward redistributive ideas. Radicalism was also evident in TVA-style planned economy, WPA production-for-use, and the presence of agrarian reformers in Henry Wallace's Department of Agriculture. Thus for the first time since the border between progressivism and socialism had closed in 1917, Washington was open to influences from the left.

The turn toward reform split the business community into pro- and anti-New Deal factions. A minority of corporate leaders such as Thomas

Watson, head of International Business Machines, recognized the desirability, or at least the inevitability, of some social legislation. Rockefeller interests supported public pensions and unemployment assistance and sponsored a national tour by William Beveridge, who became the father of the British welfare state. When Secretary Perkins picked people associated with the well-connected American Association for Labor Legislation to work with the newly appointed Committee on Economic Security, the corporate-liberal wing of the business community knew it could count on Roosevelt to come up with a "sober" social insurance plan for the unemployed and the elderly. Managerial liberalism was not totally dead.

Most businessmen, however, attacked public welfare as if it flew the red flag of socialism. At the first sign that social-democratic ideas were making headway in Washington, conservatives in the U.S. Chamber of Commerce deposed its pro-New Deal leader. Although the National Association of Manufacturers raised no serious objection to unemployment aid along the lines of the "Wisconsin Plan" (privately controlled employer reserves), it opposed anything that smacked of public control. In the face of 12 million unemployed, NAM commended individual "thrift and self-denial" as the answer to unemployment. NAM's Ohio affiliate denounced the "Ohio Plan" (compulsory group insurance) as "the greatest menace that has ever faced Ohio industry," and the Ohio Chamber of Commerce thundered against this "Bolshevik" proposal. . . .

Beset by these political cross-pressures, Roosevelt was galvanized into launching the Second Hundred Days when the Supreme Court declared the National Recovery Act unconstitutional in the *Schechter* decision of May 1935. Shattering the centerpiece of Roosevelt's recovery program at a time of growing popular discontent, the Court's bombshell threatened to wreck the fragile public confidence that had returned in the preceding two years. Eager to experiment with ideas that might win votes, Roosevelt quickly shifted his labor policy. Having steadfastly ignored Senator Robert Wagner's bill for regulating labor relations, he now thrust it forward as a piece of essential legislation.

With ties to both enlightened corporate leaders and labor progressives in his home state of New York, Senator Wagner espoused an "underconsumption" theory of the Depression and argued that collective bargaining was the route to recovery because it would raise "the purchasing power of wage earners." Wagner's aim was not to redistribute wealth from capital to labor but to rationalize the chaos of competition by smoothing out the peaks and valleys between boom and bust, large and small employers, and high- and low-wage industries. In an attempt to avoid running afoul of the Supreme Court, Wagner's bill employed a bit of legalistic legerdemain in making *individual* rights the legal basis for *collective* bargaining. In fact, the words *trade union* never appeared. All the same, the Wagner Act gave the new National Labor Relations Board power to halt "unfair labor practices," supervise representation elections, and certify duly chosen bargaining agents. Hoping to reap the advantage, the AFL put aside its traditional objections to state intervention and supported the bill, a move AFL leaders regretted when it turned out the CIO would be competing for the same harvest of union members.

For all its labor sympathies, the Wagner Act did not fail to protect elite interests. Using their clout as committee chairmen, southern conservatives weakened the bill by excluding agricultural and casual laborers, thus leaving most of the Afro-American and Hispanic work force unprotected. The largely female occupations of domestic servants and retail clerks were also excluded. The friends of business, for their part, saw to it that the act confined "responsible" unions to a narrow range of bargaining issues, and, most important, it carefully avoided trenching upon the inner sanctum of managerial control over investment, product, and labor process. Freighted with such enfeeblements and exclusions, the bill passed overwhelmingly, with support from a majority of southern Democrats. Even the Supreme Court upheld the Wagner Act, granting its first approval to a major piece of New Deal legislation in the *Jones and Laughlin* decision (1937).

All in all, it was a historic turnabout. The Wagner Act constituted labor as a great estate of the realm, not the peer of business or even agriculture, but in some sense a collective entity with legitimate interests deserving state protection. Although the intent of the framers was to promote recovery, the effect was to install the government as the patron of unionism and, in some measure, to redress the balance of power toward workers. But the beauty of the Second New Deal's expansion of interest-group liberalism was its exquisite compromise between mass interests and elite privileges. . . .

Having already gone into the business of emergency relief, New Dealers were determined to create a permanent and more rational welfare system. From one side, they were buffeted by a host of modern-day Robin Hoods who pushed a cartload of reform — the Lundeen Bill on unemployment, Townsend's revolving pensions, and Long's Share Our Wealth — all of which quite openly aimed at the redistribution of wealth through confiscatory taxes on the rich. From the other side, New Dealers were pummeled by a shrill campaign financed by business against any system of government subsidies to the poor. . . .

Artfully crafted to minimize conservative opposition, the Social Security Act exempted many of the groups that needed help the most. To placate southern planters, agribusinessmen, and economic conservatives in general, it denied protection to farm workers, domestics, and casual laborers, the very people whose low wages and irregular employment made them among the poorest in the land. Likewise, instead of setting a minimum national unemployment benefit, the system bowed to low-wage regions and allowed state officials to set the dollar level of unemployment checks. Thus with the same enfeeblements and exclusions found in the Wagner Act, Social Security easily passed through a Congress eager to show a humane face to the public that had lived through six grinding years of depression. . . .

Sexual inequality was built into every part of the welfare state. Constructed around the nuclear family ideal, the system favored life-long homemakers over working wives and single women. Large groups of the lowest-paid female workers who needed protection the most were systematically excluded, including 3 million domestic servants; almost a third of all working women were thus deprived of unemployment and old-age benefits. In a compounding of women's predicament, divorced women were initially denied survivor's benefits, and young widows had to wait until retirement to collect. No one can say how a vital feminist movement would have changed all this, but it is clear that the absence of the kind of agitation that characterized the 1910s allowed these gender subordinations to go unchallenged.

When it came to labor and capital, the architects of Social Security were quite explicit about their intention to buttress the ladder of wage inequality. Chief Administrator Arthur Altmeyer laid down the "fundamental principle" that benefits were not to exceed 80 percent of former wages. According to Edwin Witte, the main architect of the bill, "Only to a very minor degree does it modify the distribution of wealth and it does not alter at all the fundamentals of our capitalistic and individualistic economy. Nor does it relieve the individual of primary responsibility for his own support and that of his dependents." . . .

Contrary to common mythology, the poor and the working classes were not the only ones to receive welfare. The middle classes were also beneficiaries of massive state aid. For one thing, in the absence of a means test for old-age insurance, salaried white-collar workers were entitled to a federal pension. Although the old middle class of self-employed persons was initially exempt from the system, the fact that the new salaried middle class participated helped guarantee the political survival of Social Security through the thick and thin of successive liberal and conservative administrations in Washington. For another, small property owners also received the largesse of federal insurance on savings deposits and home loans. Tapping a deep vein of American folklore, Franklin Roosevelt proclaimed that "a nation of homeowners, of people who own a real share in their own land, is unconquerable." To stem the tide of mortgage foreclosures, in 1933 and 1934 the Roosevelt administration created the Home Owners Loan Corporation to refinance shaky mortgages, the Federal Savings and Loan Insurance Corporation to prop up wobbly financial institutions, and the Federal Housing Administration (FHA) to underwrite private loans for housing construction. Before long, the federal government held mortgages on fully one-tenth of all owner-occupied nonfarm residences in the United States. Working through Hoover's Home Loan Bank Board, the New Deal largely succeeded in repairing the bonds between middle-class families and capitalist institutions that had been ruptured by the Depression.

The middle-class bias was evident in guidelines for home loans. The Home Owners Loan Corporation devised an invidious, four-tier, color-coded system for ranking neighborhoods in which, predictably, the top-ranked were composed of "American business and professional men" (that is, no Jews, blacks, or recent immigrants), while the bottom — coded red — were crowded slums or any neighborhood with a "rapidly increasing Negro population." This was the beginning of official federal sponsorship of redlining, or disinvestment in poorer urban neighborhoods, which did so much to devastate inner cities in the middle decades of the twentieth century. To its credit, the New Deal also subsidized low-income tenants through public housing, and it was the market, not the federal government, that created the slums. But in smoothing the transition from the productive farms and workshops of the old middle classes to the consumer homes of the new, Washington became the biggest single player in the housing market, and, as such, it did much to preserve the gap between "good" neighborhoods and "bad."

The fact that New Deal reforms preserved social hierarchy does not mean the Wagner Act and Social Security were the result of a conspiracy of the rich or were devoid of humanitarian intent. Certainly, the New Deal had more than its share of humanitarian moments, including the abolition of child labor in the NRA codes and subsequently in the Fair Labor Standards Act of 1938. But even as the New Deal responded to popular demands for social justice, it was careful not to infringe too much upon the privileges of wealth. By the end of the Second New Deal, the Roosevelt administration had crafted a compromise between privileged elites and subordinate groups that restrained liberty in the name of security without upending the social order. . . .

For all its limitations, the fact remains that by the time the New Deal was checkmated at the end of the 1930s, it had already altered the organic relation between the state and society. Responding to the resurgence of popular protest, the New Deal pushed through a social compromise between corporate elites and laboring masses that forever changed the dynamics of American civilization. In institutional terms, the state took a quantum leap into the business of regulating the market, so that virtually everyone from the Wall Street investor dealing with the Securities and Exchange Commission to the Pittsburgh steel-worker voting in a union election supervised by the National Labor Relations Board, felt the power of some arm of the federal bureaucracy. In terms of legitimacy, the New Deal enshrined a new set of ruling values keyed to security, so that the mass of the population, from the small savings depositor trusting in the Federal Deposit Insurance Corporation to the retired couple relying on a pension from Social Security, felt as if the government cared about their welfare.

Although Roosevelt popularized his program with populist rhetoric, the new governing system did not redress the balance of class power or redistribute wealth so much as mediate social antagonisms by creating a new set of bureaucratic institutions. Building on Hoover's initiatives, Roosevelt's New Deal expanded state intervention in the market and launched a welfare state. None of these experiments in Keynesian economics ended the Depression; prosperity would not return until war orders started coming in. But the New Deal did succeed in restoring political balance to a system all out of kilter. The "fourth branch" of government, the New Deal coalition, and the ruling myths of security and pluralism renewed popular faith in the state and narrowed the gap between the state and modern society. Thus did the modern governing system take its place alongside the consumer family and corporate property as the third leg of the stool of political stability. . . .

Taken as a whole, Nazism was the product of a historical conjuncture triggered by humiliating defeat in the First World War and economic anxiety in the Great Depression. The door to fascism was opened by traditional elites who eviscerated liberal democracy but who were themselves incapable of governing modern, capitalist societies. That created the opportunity for counterrevolutionaries to come storming through on the strength of a mass movement whose taproot lay in the lower middle class and whose appeal was built around a set of negations — anticommunism, anticonservatism, antiliberalism, anti-feminism, and anti-Semitism. Invited into power by military and industrial elites who hoped to use the Nazi party as a mass base, the Nazis gave elites more than they had bargained for. Once in power, the Nazis imposed a brutal regime whose leading traits were capitalism by violence, racial nationalism, hypermasculinism, and imperial expansion. Having already conquered Italy under Mussolini, fascism now swept Germany and Austria, gained strength in eastern Europe, and found a close cousin in imperial Japan. Whereas in 1919 and 1920 the question of social revolution had hung over world affairs, the pertinent question after 1932 was whether counterrevolution might spread throughout the globe.

Did that possibility include the United States? That some type of authoritarian regime would emerge in the land of liberty did not seem out of the question at the time. Few could match John Dewey's credentials as an astute observer of the American scene, and in 1932 he was worried: "We have permitted business and financial autocracy to reach such a point that its logical political counterpart is a Mussolini, unless a violent revolution brings forth a Lenin." In fact, there were ominous signs of a corporatist regime in the state capitalism of Hoover and of Roosevelt in his first administration. Pointing to the fusion of capitalist titans and government bureaucrats in the RFC and NRA, Walter Lippmann warned of "the dictatorship of casual oligarchs," while the *New Republic* described the early New Deal as an American-style "corporative state."

In addition, many contemporaries saw militarist glimmerings in General Hugh Johnson's Blue Eagle and the Civilian Conservation Corps. Certainly, state repression was by no means foreign to America, as the labor movement, the Bonus Army, and generations of African Americans could attest. No wonder some imaginations ran wild. Under the ironic title *It Can't Happen Here* (1935), Sinclair Lewis described the fictional seizure of power by an authoritarian regime backed by Wall Street, the Wasp establishment, and the military on the heels of a presidential victory by a bombastic demagogue bearing a strong resemblance to Huey Long.

If a repressive regime was going to develop in the United States, conservative elites would have to link up with a potent, right-wing mass movement. The fact that such a movement failed to emerge does not mean that the ingredients were altogether missing. America was no stranger to the class resentments and ethnic hatreds that fueled the revolt of the little guy in Germany. If anything could have become the basis for an American *Volksgemeinschaft*, it was white racism, and, in fact, the entire repertoire of unreason — racial bigotry, Christian anti-Semitism, nativist paranoia, anticommunism, and antifeminism — was tapped by hate groups such as the Ku Klux Klan and even by the more respectable Rotarians, American Legionnaires, and women's clubbers.

The closest thing to a counterrevolutionary movement in the United States gathered around the figure of Father Charles Coughlin. A magnetic speaker who outdid FDR in the mastery of mass communications, the Detroit "Radio Priest" reached as many as 40 million listeners, and at its peak his National Union for Social Justice attracted perhaps 5 million members. Wrapping patriarchal and corporatist views in a quasi-populist cover, he portrayed an unholy conspiracy of bankers, Communists, and Jews. With the characteristic logic-chopping of the demagogue, he could pronounce that "the most dangerous communist is the wolf in the sheep's clothing of conservatism," and in ever more putrid rhetoric he excoriated "money changers" such as Andrew Mellon and Treasury Secretary Henry Morgenthau with their "Jewish cohorts."

There was nothing unique in Coughlin's anticommunism, anticonservatism, and anti-Semitism, common elements in the underworld of American politics. Likewise, when he warned that birth control and premarital sex led to prostitution and socialism, his antifeminism was in keeping with the sentiments of a long line of purity crusaders. What was peculiar about Coughlin — and what linked him to European fascism — was his antiliberalism. Unlike most American rightists, he called for greater state control of the economy, including nationalization of the banks. Strongly influenced by the corporatist philosophy of social relations in Pope Pius XI's *Quadregesimo Anno* (1931), he urged a national welfare system. Just as the National Socialist party impersonated socialism, so his National Union for Social Justice impersonated social justice reform.

If there was a threat of tyranny, it lay in the possibility that big business would join forces with the kind of mass bigotry represented by Coughlin. Given America's liberal inheritance, there was little likelihood of an all-powerful leviathan state, but there was a good deal of experience with the undemocratic power of business and the tyranny of the majority. In the frenzy of 100 percent Americanism after the First World War, the country got a taste of what a repressive regime might look like in a set of harsh measures ranging from the open shop to immigration restriction. In many ways, the choices confronting the country in the mid-1930s were quite similar. Would the response to popular discontent be social reform or the repression of another Red Scare? With the memory of postwar violations of civil liberties still fresh, the question was not whether fascism would spread to America, but whether the United States would pick up where it had left off in the early 1920s and develop a homegrown, repressive regime of its own.

Comparison with Germany illuminates the reasons why no such regime emerged. Perhaps the starkest contrast between the two countries lay in foreign policy. From the day the Versailles Treaty was signed, Germany was a revisionist power, and the fact that the United States was not goes a long way toward explaining why there was nothing to compare with the German impulse toward militarism. While the Nazis turned resentment over defeat in the First World War into a militarist crusade for *Lebensraum,* the United States was content to reap the harvest of economic exports and corporate diplomacy in the 1920s. Then in the 1930s the United States retreated into its shell. Signs of rising economic nationalism included the Smoot-Hawley Tariff of 1930, Roosevelt's "torpedo" of the 1933 London Economic Conference, and the Neutrality Acts (1935–1937), by which Congress pretended that the United States had no vital interests outside its borders. On the positive side, Roosevelt's Good Neighbor Policy toward Latin America foreswore armed intervention. But on the negative, the United States buried its head in the sand while fascist powers conquered Ethiopia, Spain, and Manchuria, only making the inevitable reckoning that much more devastating when it finally came in September 1939. Be that as it may, the spirit of neutrality allowed little room for the sort of bellicose nationalism that would have fostered a militarist regime in the United States.

On the domestic side, it is necessary, first of all, to credit popular social movements for revitalizing democratic traditions. Undoubtedly, the most important event in this regard was the resurgence of the labor movement as embodied in the newborn Congress of Industrial Organizations. Not only did the CIO seek to give workers a say in industry — that is, to make the Bill of Rights apply inside the factory gate — but CIO organizers were forced to combat ethnic hatred in order to unite the immigrant nationalities among the rank and file. The same pluralist imperative was imposed on political parties. Capitalizing on the popularity of the repeal of Prohibition, the Democrats brought urban ethnics into the New Deal coalition and prepared the way for general acceptance of the idea that the United States was a "nation of nations."

What was especially distinctive about democracy in the 1930s was that it came with a social twist. When social movements spilled over into electoral politics behind southern populists, midwestern progressives, and the occasional leftist, it became advantageous for politicians all the way up to the president to support social-democratic reforms such as the Wagner Act and Social Security. Roosevelt may have saved liberalism; he may have saved capitalism; but grass-roots social movements were the saviors of democracy.

The Cold War and Beyond: Stability, Hegemony, Chaos?

With the collapse of Soviet communism and the dissolution of the USSR by 1991, the Cold War, which had preoccupied American leaders and millions of ordinary Americans for almost half a century, suddenly ended. Whatever tension remained or might recur in relations between the United States and Russia, the future was not likely to be shaped by the same kind of nuclear standoff that had for decades dissuaded the great powers from direct military confrontation, while at the same time spurring ruinous interventions in small countries and terrorizing much of humankind with the prospect of nuclear Armageddon. Nor, it seemed, would the demands of the national security state ever again be so irresistible or unarguable, whether those demands were for the allocation of material resources or the subordination of civil liberties.

Questions of long-term consequences aside, in the United States the *end of* the Cold War was almost universally interpreted as *triumph in* the Cold War. Among contemporary historians, debate is now underway as to how wise or useful it is to let this sort of "triumphalism" or "vindicationism" shape historical accounts of the Cold War. Yet, few historians doubt the benefit of new access to Soviet archives, the fruits of which are already beginning to reshape interpretations. Finally, all historians now have the opportunity to view the Cold War as a whole, a historical phenomenon —like, say, "the Progressive era" or "the Jacksonian era" — with beginning, middle, and end. Even in this regard, however, some historians insist that the strategic, economic, and political roots of the Cold War preceded the World War II era and will therefore continue to generate problems and conflicts into the next millennium. At the very least it can be said that the end of the Cold War has spurred historians to rethink their accounts of the development of that east-west rivalry that so profoundly shaped America and the world in the second half of the twentieth century.

In the wake of the terrorist attacks of September 11, 2001, and of the Iraq War, skepticism about the meaning of the Cold War "victory" has sharpened. On the one hand, historians who laid some blame for the Cold War on the United States saw a reawakening of the simplistic "us versus them" thinking that helped create, intensify, and prolong the Cold War. On the other hand, others saw victory in the last war as reassurance about the possibilities of victory in the next, leading them to a lusty embrace of imperial mission, sometimes in the name of democratic universalism, at other times in the name of strategic stability. Still others saw the emergence of a less polarized world order as an opportunity to reinterpret the Cold War itself as more "pericentric," as one scholar dubbed it. Observing nationalist, religious, and ethnic rivalries in the contemporary world, these authors sought to recover the significance of seemingly peripheral agents in the making and unmaking of the Cold War. More generally, they asserted the limits of great power and the contingency of historical events.

Most accounts of the Cold War begin with the end of World War II. Two consequences of that war established the context within which the Cold War would be waged. One was the toppling of five major nations from the ranks of first-rate powers. America's enemies — Germany, Japan, and Italy — were defeated. Its friends — Britain and France — spent too much blood and treasure ever to regain their prewar military and economic power. This situation left only two superpowers, the United States and the Soviet Union. The second development was the technological revolution in warfare. With the exploding of the atomic bomb in 1945, diplomacy entered upon a new age. From that moment forward every confrontation between great powers portended the destruction of humankind. For Americans, the "age of free security" had come to an end: neither great oceans to the east and west, nor unthreatening neighbors to the north and south, any longer guaranteed the United States immunity from attack.[1] Now long-range bombers, intercontinental ballistic missiles, and nuclear weapons exposed the United States for the first time to the possibility of enormous, even total, destruction. In a sense, the United States had joined the rest of the world, particularly Europe, and even more particularly the Soviet Union, which not only feared but had actually experienced in two world wars levels of destruction that were almost unimaginable. That casualties in the tens of millions and the pulverization of millions of acres of productive terrain might have to be suffered again in the USSR — or for the first time in the United States — drove both superpowers toward obsessive concern with national security, and a spiral of confrontation and arms buildup that fell just short of outright war. One historian likened the U.S.-USSR relationship to that of a scorpion and tarantula together in a bottle, each trying to sting the other.[2]

Since 1945 scholars have disagreed about the causes of the Cold War and the assignment of responsibility for its origination and continuation. American historians have divided into several schools: the orthodox, the revisionist, the realist, and the postrevisionist. The first to appear was the orthodox school. During the immediate postwar years, most scholars, like most Americans, tended to accept the official explanation of events that justified Allied postwar foreign policy. Winston Churchill, speaking at Fulton, Missouri, in the spring of 1946, set forth the basic outline of this interpretation. An "iron curtain," said Churchill, had been lowered across Eastern Europe by the Soviets. No one knew what secret plans for expansion were being hatched

---

[1]This phrase was coined by historian C. Vann Woodward in "The Age of Reinterpretation," *American Historical Review* 66 (1966): 1–19.

[2]Louis Halle, *The Cold War as History* (New York, 1967), xiii.

behind that curtain. Communist ideology, Communist parties, and "fifth column" activities within non-Communist countries increasingly threatened what he called "Christian civilization." President Truman in 1947 echoed similar sentiments when announcing his now-famous Truman Doctrine. Although the United States had made every effort to bring about a peaceful world, he said, the Soviet Union had used "indirect aggression" in Eastern Europe, "extreme pressure" in the Middle East, and intervention by "Communist parties directed from Moscow" into the internal affairs of many other countries. Orthodox scholars traced the start of the Cold War to the announcement of the Truman Doctrine in 1947, which they saw as a necessary response to Soviet aggression.

Although some orthodox scholars focused on traditional Russian imperialism, most argued that Marxist-Leninist ideology required the Soviets to override traditional balance-of-power foreign policies. The USSR consequently violated all its agreements with the Western powers, including the Yalta agreement on the political future of Eastern Europe and its informal accords on the role of China in the postwar world. American foreign policy, according to the orthodox, differed markedly from that of the Soviet Union. Guided by the principles of collective security, American leaders looked to the newborn United Nations to resolve future international conflicts. Faced with Soviet intransigence and aggression, however, the United States reluctantly changed its foreign policy. To thwart the Soviet drive for worldwide domination, the United States committed itself to "containment." The orthodox position appeared in a 1947 article by American diplomat George F. Kennan under the pseudonym "Mr. X." In this historic essay Kennan set the terms for the theory of containment, which would undergird the diplomatic and military policy of the Truman administration and, indeed, of the Western world, for years to come.[3]

While the orthodox school assigned responsibility for the Cold War to the Soviet Union,[4] some of the earliest orthodox scholars, including Kennan and historian Herbert Feis, modified their views with the passage of time, emphasizing somewhat less the perfidy of the Soviets and the earnest good will of the Americans. By the early 1970s, a younger historian, John Lewis Gaddis, tried as even-handedly as possible to update the orthodox interpretation. His first important book argued that neither the Soviet Union nor the United States was solely responsible for the Cold War, even while insisting that Stalin was more responsible than any Western leader for the onset and

---

[3]Mr. X [George F. Kennan], "The Sources of Soviet Conduct," *Foreign Affairs* 25 (July 1947): 566–82. Subsequently, Kennan regretted exaggerating the power of ideology in shaping Soviet behavior and lamented that his article had been misread; in particular, he claimed, Truman had implemented containment in a far more militarily confrontational way than he had intended: George F. Kennan, *Memoirs, 1925–1950* (Boston, 1967).

[4]For a few examples of the orthodox interpretation see Herbert Feis's three books, *The Road to Pearl Harbor* (Princeton, N.J., 1950), *The China Tangle* (Princeton, N.J., 1953), and especially *Roosevelt-Churchill-Stalin* (Princeton, N.J., 1957); William H. McNeill, *America, Britain, and Russia: Their Cooperation and Conflict, 1941–1946* (London, 1953); Norman Graebner, *Cold War Diplomacy: American Foreign Policy, 1945–1960* (Princeton, N.J., 1962); and Andre Fontaine, *History of the Cold War from the October Revolution to the Korean War, 1917–1950*, 2 vols. (New York, 1968).

development of hostile relations. Gaddis's masterpiece, *Strategies of Containment,* published in the early 1980s, went even further in criticizing American policymakers. By succumbing to anti-Communist hysteria, Gaddis charged, they confused essential interests (e.g., in central Europe) with peripheral interests (e.g., in southeast Asia), thereby prolonging and worsening the Cold War. Despite this emphatic acknowledgment of American failings, Gaddis nevertheless reiterated the central orthodox claim that the Cold War would never have taken place in the absence of Stalinist aggression.[5]

Although orthodox scholars never merely parroted an official U.S. line, their views proved remarkably compatible with those of governmental and private sources of research funds, not to mention mainstream politicians and the press. They certainly achieved broader credibility and professional success than those who bucked the orthodox line. Nonetheless, almost from the outset of the Cold War, their views provoked challenges. Henry Wallace, former vice president, sharply questioned President Truman's analysis of Soviet intentions and policies during the immediate postwar years. Running as a presidential candidate of the Progressive Party in 1948, Wallace made his case for a less confrontational policy toward the Russians, but his poor showing marked the end of serious political challenge to the policy of containment until the 1960s. Walter Lippmann, one of the nation's leading journalists, likewise refused to blame the Soviets exclusively for postwar tensions. It was Lippmann who popularized the term *Cold War,* using it in the title of a 1947 book.[6] He argued that America's statesmen, by assaulting Russia's vital interests in Eastern Europe, furnished the Soviet Union with a reason for seeking iron rule over countries on its borders. These U.S. policies also gave Russians grounds to believe what Leninist ideologues had been teaching for years: that a capitalist alliance had organized to surround and destroy them. Lippmann's high standing as a writer and thinker gave his views a measure of credibility, especially among the revisionist-minded. Over the years such revisionists proposed, in a variety of ways and with a variety of voices, that the causes of the Cold War could be located in the interests, ideology, and policies of the United States, at least as much as those of the Soviet Union. They suggested, to put it bluntly, that the Cold War was "our" fault as much as — maybe more than — "theirs."

The revisionist historians were diverse, but most agreed that in 1945 the USSR, having been ravaged by war, was weak, not strong. They then argued that a weak Soviet Union was neither willing nor able to pursue an aggressive foreign policy. Some revisionists maintained that while the Russians feared America's technological superiority and military power, they still viewed the United States as a potential source of monetary aid and trade concessions,

---

[5] John Lewis Gaddis, *The United States and the Origins of the Cold War, 1941–1947* (New York, 1972); *Strategies of Containment* (New York, 1982). See also George C. Herring, *Aid to Russia, 1941–1946: Strategy, Diplomacy, and the Origins of the Cold War* (New York, 1973); and Bruce R. Kuniholm, *The Origins of the Cold War in the Near East: Great Power Conflict and Diplomacy in Iran, Turkey, and Greece* (Princeton, N.J., 1980).

[6] Walter Lippmann, *The Cold War* (New York, 1947). This was a collection of newspaper articles written to counter Kennan's interpretation of the motivation behind Soviet policy.

both of which they desperately needed to recover from the war. Most revisionists further argued that the Soviet Union, despite its ideological bravado, consistently pursued cautious, defensive, and limited foreign policy goals. Thus, a worldwide policy of aggression, which the orthodox claimed to detect in the Soviet Union's behavior, seemed to the revisionists to be entirely out of character and beyond its means.

Revisionists likewise differed from the orthodox on America's strategic motivations. Some claimed that the Truman administration and its allies tried to deny the Soviet Union its rightful gains won in battle and confirmed in the Yalta agreement. What Roosevelt and Churchill had been compelled by circumstances to concede at Yalta — that is, a Soviet sphere of influence in Eastern Europe — Truman and his advisers refused to recognize. Other historians argued that the United States, with a missionary zeal at least as fervid as that of the Soviets, intended to reshape the world to suit what it believed were universal democratic principles. Still other scholars saw economic expansionism as the keynote of American policy, postulating that Cold War foreign policy aimed to capture world markets. The United States, in this reading, used its early monopoly of nuclear weapons and its economic strength to browbeat its allies and other nation-states into submitting to Washington's leadership. As proof of this position, revisionists pointed out that the Marshall Plan had been designed to preclude Soviet participation. And finally, some revisionists saw the demonization of the Soviet Union as a product of American domestic politics. In particular, they discerned a drive by Republicans to regain their traditional control over government and the public agenda by branding the New Deal, the unions, and the left-leaning Democrats as dupes (even agents) of the "international Communist conspiracy," which led to a defensive effort by Democrats to prove their patriotic bona fides.[7]

The most significant challenge to the orthodox position came ironically from a historian whose primary interest lay outside the Cold War era, but who exerted an immense influence on the entire field of U.S. diplomatic history. William Appleman Williams, whose career is discussed at length in Chapter 4, was dubbed America's "preeminent critic of empire."[8] He insisted that U.S. Cold War policies were not just reactions to Soviet aggression, but

---

[7]On the relationship between foreign and domestic policy, still indispensable is Richard M. Freeland, *The Truman Doctrine and the Origins of McCarthyism, 1946–1948* (New York, 1972). On McCarthyism, the literature is vast; especially useful are Robert Griffith, *The Politics of Fear: Joseph R. McCarthy and the Senate* (Amherst, Mass., 1970); Stanley I. Kutler, *American Inquisition: Justice and Injustice in the Cold War* (New York, 1982); and Robert W. Cherny et al., eds., *American Labor and the Cold War: Grassroots Politics and Postwar Political Culture* (New Brunswick, N.J., 2004). A recent update with useful documents is Ellen Schrecker, *The Age of McCarthyism: A Brief History with Documents* (Boston, 1994). An insightful if idiosyncratic interpretation of the impact of the Cold War on American culture is Tom Engelhardt, *The End of Victory Culture: Cold War America and the Disillusioning of a Generation* (2nd ed., Amherst, Mass., 2007); more conventional but no less insightful is Stephen J. Whitfield, *The Culture of the Cold War* (Baltimore, 1991). Recently, a legal scholar has distinguished the legitimate right of nonassociation with Communists from McCarthyite assaults on civil liberty: Martin H. Redish, *The Logic of Persecution: Free Expression and the McCarthy Era* (Stanford, Calif., 2005). See also Chapter 11.

[8]Paul Buhle, "William Appleman Williams: Grassroots against Empire," in Allen Hunter, ed., *Rethinking the Cold War* (Philadelphia, 1998), 289–306.

part of a continuous American "Open Door" policy that was expansionist from its beginnings. Needing ever-expanding markets for its products, the United States first pursued its imperial ambitions in the western regions of the North American continent. By the 1890s, however, with the frontier gone, the search for markets continued overseas. From this perspective, Williams saw U.S. policy after World War II as nothing more than an extension of the Open Door. Pursuing market penetration into Eastern European and "third world" nations, America sought to impose on them governments that would do business with U.S. corporations. Counterrevolution to make the world safe for American capitalism, not containment, was therefore the major motive behind the postwar policies of the United States.[9]

Williams exerted great influence over all those who in the 1960s began to revise prevailing interpretations of the Cold War. Still, revisionists came in many varieties, from moderate to radical, differing over the precise degree to which the United States should be held accountable for the onset of the Cold War. The moderate revisionist Denna F. Fleming in 1961 portrayed President Truman as the crucial precipitator of the Cold War. While Roosevelt had been dedicated to "Wilsonian internationalism," Truman adopted a belligerent policy toward the Russians as soon as he assumed the presidency. In April 1945 he ordered the Soviets to loosen their grip on Poland or else forfeit the economic aid that America had promised. Contrary to the orthodox version, which generally dated the beginning of the Cold War to 1947 with the Truman Doctrine, Fleming believed it began at this moment in 1945.[10]

Gar Alperovitz agreed that Truman started the Cold War in 1945, but blamed "atomic diplomacy" for the breakdown of wartime cooperation. The U.S. monopoly of atomic weapons led Truman to adopt a hard line toward the Soviets, forcing them to either acquiesce in America's postwar hegemony or go it alone. Like most of the moderate revisionists, Alperovitz did acknowledge that Russian actions poisoned the postwar atmosphere. "The cold war cannot be understood simply as an American response to a Soviet challenge" (or vice versa), he wrote, "but rather as an insidious interaction of mutual suspicions, blame for which must be shared by all." Nevertheless, the thrust of Alperovitz's work clearly placed heavier responsibility for the beginnings of the Cold War on American policymakers who not only brandished but twice used atomic weapons.[11]

One of Williams's most accomplished followers, Walter LaFeber, developed and expanded this revisionist view of the Cold War. LaFeber criticized

---

[9] William A. Williams, *The Tragedy of American Diplomacy* (New York, 1959) and *The Contours of American History* (Cleveland, 1961). On fears of economic depression as a major motive of U.S. expansionist foreign policy, see Williams's student Lloyd C. Gardner, *Architects of Illusion: Men and Ideas in American Foreign Policy, 1941–1949* (Chicago, 1970).

[10] Denna F. Fleming, *The Cold War and Its Origins, 1917–1960*, 2 vols. (New York, 1961). See also Athan Theoharis, "Roosevelt and Truman on Yalta: The Origins of the Cold War," *Political Science Quarterly* 87 (June 1972): 210–41.

[11] Gar Alperovitz, *Atomic Diplomacy: Hiroshima and Potsdam* (New York, 1965).

both the United States and the Soviet Union for failing to maintain peace. Focusing on U.S. foreign policy, he concluded that domestic events — not just the long-term pursuit of commercial empire, but short-term events such as presidential campaigns, economic recessions, the hysteria of McCarthyism, and factional power struggles within the government — contributed as much to the making of America's foreign policy as did external events. In Russia the same was true: power struggles within Stalin's and later Khrushchev's Communist Party, regional tensions, and problems of economic recovery, along with traditional Russian imperial ambitions, shaped most foreign policy actions. LaFeber also found that the United States and the Soviet Union showed equal interest in exploiting foreign markets wherever possible. Both nations, he concluded, created their postwar policies with an eye to maintaining freedom of action in those spheres they considered vital to their economic and strategic interests.[12]

However evenhanded, LaFeber concentrated primarily on what had gone wrong with U.S. policy. During the first phase of the Cold War, 1945 to 1953, he argued, the U.S. policy focused on Europe; it sought to preserve a transatlantic capitalist trading sphere, to thwart the leftward drift of European politics, and to convince European powers to line up behind the policy of containing the Soviet Union.[13] Even the Korean War, LaFeber insisted, was fought to preserve America's credibility among the European allies as the bulwark against communism.[14] But in the mid-1950s, when both America and Russia shifted their focus from Europe to the emerging nations of the world, the Cold War entered its second phase. The United States fought and lost the Vietnam War, according to LaFeber, because it sought a military solution to the economic, social, and political problems of an emerging postcolonial nation. Stubbornly applying the Truman Doctrine, which imagined aggression or subversion as the source of disorder, to an anticolonial revolution, U.S. policymakers produced a tragedy of immense proportions.[15]

The work of Williams and these revisionists served as a point of departure for many radical scholars. In 1968 Gabriel Kolko, whose earlier study of the origins of "political capitalism" from 1900 to 1917 had heralded the advent of the New Left school of historical interpretation,[16] made a detailed case for locating the origins of the Cold War in the narrow period of time from

---

[12]Walter LaFeber, *America, Russia, and the Cold War, 1945–2000* (9th ed., Boston, 2000; orig. pub. New York, 1967). See also Chapter 4.

[13]See also Michael Hogan, *The Marshall Plan: America, Britain, and the Reconstruction of Western Europe, 1947–1952* (New York, 1987) and *The Cross of Iron: Harry S. Truman and the Origins of the National Security State* (New York, 1998); and Thomas G. Paterson, *Soviet-American Confrontation: Postwar Reconstruction and the Origins of the Cold War* (Baltimore, 1973).

[14]On Korea, see also Bruce Cummings, *Origins of the Korean War: Liberation and the Emergence of Separate Regimes* (Princeton, N.J., 1981).

[15]See also Christopher Lasch, "The Cold War, Revisited and Re-Visioned," *New York Times*, January 14, 1968. On Vietnam, the place to start is George C. Herring, *America's Longest War: The United States and Vietnam, 1950–1975* (4th ed., New York, 2002); also see Robert McMahon, *The Limits of Empire: The United States and Southeast Asia since World War II* (New York, 1999), and Charles E. Neu, *America's Lost War: Vietnam, 1945–1975* (Wheeling, Ill., 2005).

[16]See Chapter 3.

1943 to 1945. The United States had acted not only to win the war in these years, Kolko argued, but to gain the political and economic leverage needed to extend its influence throughout the postwar world. Like Williams, he depicted the United States as a counterrevolutionary state bent on economic hegemony.[17] Most New Left scholars asserted that the United States, not Russia, was mainly responsible for bringing on the Cold War and for continuing threats to international peace and stability. They further assumed that, because American capitalism depended on ever-expanding foreign markets for survival, that the United States pursued worldwide counterrevolution. And finally, because of these two assumptions, they located the origins of the Cold War in the years preceding the Truman Doctrine: back to World War II, or World War I, or even as early as the beginnings of U.S. continental and overseas empire in the nineteenth century.

The revisionist view of the Cold War could not have emerged with any vigor had it not been for the emergence of the New Left in the 1960s. In this decade, American intellectuals developed sharply critical views of the nation's race relations, its economic inequalities, and its foreign interventions. The escalating war in Vietnam especially led many scholars to scrutinize America's "free world leadership." They uncovered the sorry record of U.S. support for right-wing dictatorships and subversion of popularly elected governments in Latin America and in postcolonial Africa and Asia. Moreover, they feared that American leaders were so obsessed with the "Communist menace" that they saw enemies where none existed. In places as different as Guatemala, the Dominican Republic, the Congo, Indonesia, and, most horrifically, Vietnam, the United States had committed itself to endless intervention, low-level and indirect to begin with, but readily escalating into direct and bloody combat if circumstances or calculations went awry.[18] Moreover, the United States had locked itself into a nuclear arms race that seemed only too well captured in the acronym MAD — mutual assured destruction. That race not only drained immense resources from American taxpayers, but also terrorized every inhabitant of the globe with the prospect that some "brushfire war" might spiral out of control and provoke a nuclear confrontation between the superpowers. The 1962 Cuban missile crisis proved that such a possibility was not so remote.[19] Some orthodox scholars reacted with undisguised anger and contempt toward the revisionist challenge. Robert J. Maddox, for example, accused seven leading revisionist historians of distorting facts to prove their thesis. "Stated briefly," he charged, the "New Left

---

[17]Gabriel Kolko, *The Politics of War: The World and United States Foreign Policy, 1943–1945* (New York, 1968). See also Joyce and Gabriel Kolko, *The Limits of Power: The World and United States Foreign Policy, 1945–1954* (New York, 1972).

[18]See, for example, Walter LaFeber, *Inevitable Revolutions: The United States in Central America* (New York, 1983; 2nd ed. 1993); Richard Barnet, *Intervention and Revolution: The United States in the Third World* (rev. ed., New York, 1972); and *Roots of War: The Men and Institutions behind U.S. Foreign Policy* (New York, 1972).

[19]James G. Blight and David A. Welch, *On the Brink: Americans and Soviets Reexamine the Cuban Missile Crisis* (New York, 1989). For a view of the missile crisis from the Soviet perspective, see Timothy Naftali and Alexandr Fursenko, *One Hell of a Gamble: Khrushchev, Castro and Kennedy, 1958–1964* (New York, 1997).

authors have revised the evidence itself."[20] Many revisionists, of course, had not been gentle in their assaults on orthodoxy. But as orthodox and revisionist scholars faced off in their own little cold war in the 1960s, others followed a distinct alternative line of interpretation that styled itself "realist."

If the orthodox and revisionist interpretations were antithetical, the realist school represented, in some ways, a middle-of-the-road position about the origins of the Cold War. Whereas orthodox historians saw the United States reluctantly containing Soviet aggression, and revisionists saw the United States relentlessly expanding its hegemony, realists saw rival empires doing what empires normally do: defending and, wherever possible, expanding their spheres of influence. Unlike the revisionists, the realists declined to condemn containment, which in their eyes represented a necessary response to Russian expansionism. On the other hand, they also refused to condemn the Soviet Union's pursuit of its legitimate sphere of influence. They criticized orthodox scholarship's moralistic rendering of U.S. benevolence and Soviet perfidy and its tendency to view conflicts of interests through a distorting lens of anti-Communist ideology.

The realists, as their name implies, interpreted foreign relations in terms of *realpolitik* — the play of long-term national interests and the power politics deployed to defend and promote them. They therefore viewed the Cold War as a traditional power conflict, comparable to previous struggles to prevent a single nation from dominating Europe's east-central regions, or more generally to preserve the European (and eventually Asian) balance of power. Predictably, historians of the realist school declined to assign to leaders of the United Sates or USSR moral responsibility for bringing on the Cold War. They preferred to see themselves as dispassionately identifying long-term national interests and pragmatic policy options. They abhorred especially the prospect of "irrational" swings between ideological crusade and isolationist disgust, between missionary fervor and morbid national self-criticism. The policymakers they lauded were (perhaps like themselves?) "wise men": cool-headed, far seeing, not easily distracted, and capable of decisiveness under pressure.[21]

Like the other two schools of Cold War historiography, the realists could trace their origins to the late 1940s and early 1950s. They sought at first to counter strong right-wing criticisms of Roosevelt's foreign policy, which held that Roosevelt's misunderstanding of or weakness toward the Soviets led directly to the Communist subjugation of Eastern Europe. The realists countered that Roosevelt had faced a fait accompli, his diplomatic options severely limited by the powerful Russian armies occupying every nation that was to become part of the eastern bloc. The realists assigned blame for the Cold War either to both sides or, more accurately, to neither. Both had hoped that cooperation among wartime allies would continue — but, as much as possible, on their own terms. Each country had sought limited objectives

---

[20]Robert J. Maddox, *The New Left and the Origins of the Cold War* (Princeton, N.J., 1973), 11.

[21]On American intellectuals and the realist strain in foreign policy thinking, see Bruce Kuklick, *Blind Oracles: Intellectuals and War from Kennan to Kissinger* (Princeton, N.J., 2007).

and expected the other to accept them as such. However, whenever one side pursued its limited objectives, the other misread the act as a threat to its existence and, in reacting accordingly, triggered a countermeasure, which led in turn to increasing escalation. Thus, Russia's determination to stabilize its border by creating satellite states in an unstable Eastern Europe provoked Western European fantasies of Russian tanks peering (like German ones a few years earlier) across the English Channel. And American efforts to secure long-term interests in the Pacific seemed to Russians just another demonstration of the capitalist determination to encircle and strangle the Soviet Union. As a result of these misperceptions, small and otherwise manageable crises led inevitably to a widening Cold War.

No scholar articulated the realist interpretation more eloquently than the political scientist Hans J. Morgenthau. His many publications amounted to a sustained critique of the "legalistic-moralistic" tradition of foreign policy. His *In Defense of the National Interest: A Critical Examination of American Foreign Policy* (1951) surveyed the whole span of America's foreign policies since 1776, condemning as utopian almost all that it surveyed. Only in the years since World War II, he suggested, had Americans more realistically formulated their policy on the basis of power politics and national interest. Yet, even then, irrational anticommunism and the widespread fantasy that U.S. omnipotence would lead to a conflict-free world distorted American policy. In the postwar era, Morgenthau explained, American policymakers failed to see the essential continuity in the expansionist objectives long sought by czars and commissars. They therefore mistook the security goals of a continental empire for the ideological goals of a revolutionary movement. Morgenthau criticized orthodox scholars for reflecting rather than correcting these provincial American misreadings of reality.[22]

While the realist school had emerged to counter a conspiratorial right-wing view of the origins of U.S.-Soviet tensions, it turned its energies against the left-wing revisionists in the 1960s. Realists agreed with revisionists that the United States had used its monopoly of atomic weapons to force other nation-states into submission. They acknowledged that the United States had dropped two atom bombs not just to defeat Japan, but to preclude the Soviet Union from entering the Pacific war. Unlike revisionists, however, realists did not scold American leaders for having made these decisions. America, they wrote, had reason to fear that Moscow might attempt to do in the Far East what it appeared to be doing in Eastern Europe. Even if they partly misread Soviet motives, the Americans' new concern for balance of power in Asia was a mark of growing maturity in thinking about international relations. The realists reacted with even greater disquiet to the more radical New Left revisionists. In his review of Kolko's *The Politics of War*, Morgenthau charged that the radical revisionist interpretation reflected the mood of a generation

---

[22]Hans J. Morgenthau, *Politics among Nations: The Struggle for Power and Peace* (New York, 1948), and *In Defense of the National Interest: A Critical Examination of American Foreign Policy* (New York, 1951). It should be noted that George Kennan's rethinking of his earlier views brought him effectively into the realist school: see footnote 2.

that, having discovered the simplistic error of those elders who blamed the
Soviets for the Cold War, now seemed determined to commit an equally simplistic error, blaming the Cold War entirely on America. In Morgenthau's
view, "revisionism tends to be as moralistic in its critique of American foreign
policy as orthodoxy is in defending it. While the moralistic approach remains,
the moral labels have been reversed: what once was right is now wrong, and
vice versa."[23]

The realists took special aim at the motives of U.S. and Soviet policy. The
political scientist Joseph R. Starobin, a former Communist, insisted that most
American historians — the revisionists in particular — were blind to the
true nature of Soviet calculations. During and after World War II, Starobin
argued, the Soviet Union determined to overcome the ideological diversity
among Communist parties around the world with whatever ruthlessness was
necessary. All Communists had to set their rudders on the course determined by Stalin; all interests would be submerged in the interests of the
Soviet state.[24] Viewed in this light the struggle between the Soviet Union and
the United States was the product of an internal crisis within the former.
Starobin's "realism," that is, was really a kind of "counter-revisionism." As
revisionists found the origins of the Cold War in internal American political
and economic pressures, so Starobin found it in internal Soviet pressures.
Another realist attack on the revisionists came from Robert W. Tucker, who
insisted that New Left revisionism was based on a simple-minded explanatory
mechanism that related all policy decisions to the imperatives of a capitalist
economy.[25] Turning the tables on the revisionists, Tucker argued that if the
Williams school was right about the domestic sources of foreign policy, they
would have to explore cultural, social, and political motives, and not just
economic ones, in explaining the making of Cold War policy.

Most realists strove for an almost Olympian dispassion and evenhanded-
ness. In describing the mutual mystifications that handicapped Americans
and Russians both, Louis Halle stressed the essentially tragic nature of the
conflict. Neither side was really to blame for the Cold War; on both sides
misconceptions reinforced ideological myths. The United States embraced
the myth of a monolithic Communist conspiracy dedicated to global domination. The Communists, from Lenin to Mao, fell under the spell of another
myth: that a world divided between capitalist-imperialists and peasants-
proletarians teetered on the verge of revolution. Such ideological renderings
of a world in crisis promoted confrontational thinking, the hallmark of the
Cold War — and of Cold War history — on both sides.[26] The realist Charles
S. Maier likewise criticized virtually every scholar who had written on the

---

[23]Hans J. Morgenthau, "Historical Justice and the Cold War," *New York Review of Books*, July
10, 1969. See also Lloyd C. Gardner, Arthur M. Schlesinger Jr., and Hans J. Morgenthau, *The
Origins of the Cold War* (Waltham, Mass., 1970), for a fascinating debate among, respectively,
revisionist, orthodox, and realist views.

[24]Joseph R. Starobin, "Origins of the Cold War: The Communist Dimension," *Foreign
Affairs* 47 (July 1969): 681–96.

[25]Robert W. Tucker, *The Radical Left and American Foreign Policy* (Baltimore, 1971).

[26]Halle, *The Cold War as History*.

origins of the Cold War. "Spokesmen for each side," he noted in 1970, "present the reader with a total explanatory system that accounts for all phenomena, eliminates the possibility of disproof, and thus transcends the usual process of historical reasoning. . . . As a result much Cold War historiography has become a confrontation manqué — debatable philosophy taught by dismaying example."[27] The same tendency to avoid extremes of interpretation appears clearly in Martin Sherwin's study of the decision to use the atomic bomb. Rejecting Alperovitz's contention that Truman used the bomb to intimidate the Soviets, Sherwin found that Roosevelt had decided early in the war to drop the bomb on one or another of the enemy. Truman used the bomb (as Roosevelt would have) to win the war against Japan, not to stop the Soviet Union from entering the war in the Far East. If Stalin recognized America's atomic monopoly and adopted a more conciliatory policy as a result, that was a by-product not a goal of wartime nuclear strategy.[28] A similarly evenhanded realism marks the work of Daniel Yergin. Although conceding the brutality of Stalin's regime (an orthodox point), Yergin nevertheless insisted that the "U.S.S.R. behaved as a traditional Great Power" (a realist point), and that American leaders "downplayed the possibilities for diplomacy and accommodation" (a revisionist point).[29]

Events of the last several decades have spurred further convergence among rival interpretations and reconsideration of the history of the last half-century.[30] The collapse of the Soviet empire and the overthrow of communism in Eastern Europe have brought the Cold War effectively to an end. As the contours of the international order have changed radically, the need to justify (or condemn) containment or to fix blame for the advent of the Cold War has diminished, allowing a fundamental reevaluation of American diplomacy. Moreover, the opening of Soviet archives offers scholars the opportunity to test interpretations theretofore based on American (or Western European) sources only, and to uncover a range of Soviet motives and calculations that were unknowable for fifty years. In a paper published in 1983, the orthodox scholar John Lewis Gaddis signaled this new era by suggesting "postrevisionism" as the most accurate description of the new historiographical situation.

For Gaddis postrevisionism meant the rejection of the classic revisionist and orthodox interpretive systems, but the salvaging of important insights from both. Nevertheless, this proposed new interpretation showed strong traces of its orthodox pedigree. While Gaddis credited revisionists with introducing to scholarship a healthy acknowledgment of America's imperial ambitions, he emphasized even more the essentially defensive and sometimes uncertain

---

[27]Charles S. Maier, "Revisionism and the Interpretation of Cold War Origins," *Perspectives in American History* 4 (1970): 311–47.

[28]Martin J. Sherwin, *A World Destroyed: The Atomic Bomb and the Grand Alliance* (New York, 1975). See also Robert L. Messer, *The End of an Alliance: James F. Byrnes, Roosevelt, Truman, and the Origins of the Cold War* (Chapel Hill, N.C., 1982); and Gregg F. Herken, *The Winning Weapon: The Atomic Bomb in the Cold War* (New York, 1981).

[29]Daniel Yergin, *Shattered Peace: The Origins of the Cold War and the National Security State* (Boston, 1977), 11–12.

[30]A brief and very useful overview is Ralph B. Levering, *The Cold War: A Post–Cold War History* (2nd ed., Wheeling, Ill., 2005).

character of American foreign policy. He also insisted that fear of Soviet perfidy, which guided containment diplomacy, had been proven clearly correct by new investigations in Soviet archives; moreover, these fears were hardly an American obsession, but were shared by most Europeans, as well as inhabitants of emerging nations.[31] Gaddis's tentative call for detente with his historiographical adversaries proved less durable than real-world reconciliation among former Cold War enemies. Indeed, in the essay that appears as the first reading in this chapter, Gaddis embodies that "vindicationist" tendency that has emerged strongly in American and Western scholarship in the post–Cold War years.[32] Even the title of the book from which this essay is drawn, *We Now Know*, strikes a clear note of triumph: not only did "we" win the Cold War, but we won because we are better. As one opinion writer for the *New York Times* put it, the Cold War ended because "freedom" conquered "slavery."[33] Even some Russian scholars have joined the chorus of condemnation directed at the entire Soviet experiment, which Lenin conceived and Stalin brought to monstrous fruition.[34] At the very least, it has become clearer than ever that, had Hitler's Holocaust not claimed the ghastly privilege of embodying evil in the modern world, Stalin's Soviet nightmare would have done so.

Despite the strong appeal of this essentially neo-orthodox vindicationism, the revisionist critique of American foreign policy has not disappeared. In a 1990 review of the historical literature on U.S. Cold War diplomacy, Edward Pessen, a nineteenth-century specialist who had never published in the field of diplomatic history, jumped boldly into the debate over the origins of the Cold War. He charged that America's postwar call to arms against the Soviet threat "was either groundless, absurd, false, or known by those making the charges to be false." Questions that policymakers should have asked "went largely unasked." Though Pessen never identified with the New Left, he went beyond even the most extreme revisionist condemnations of American

---

[31] John Lewis Gaddis, "The Emerging Post-Revisionist Synthesis on the Origins of the Cold War," *Diplomatic History* 7 (Summer 1983): 171–91; and responses by a number of prominent historians on this same issue, 191–204. See also Gaddis, *The United States and the End of the Cold War: Implications, Reconsiderations, Provocations* (New York, 1992).

[32] See Arthur Schlesinger Jr., "Some Lessons from the Cold War," *Diplomatic History* 16 (Winter 1992): 47–53.

[33] A. M. Rosenthal, "Victors in the Cold War," *New York Times*, June 10, 1990, quoted in Allen Hunter, ed., *Rethinking the Cold War* (Philadelphia, 1998), 4. For a thorough neo-orthodox or vindicationist review of current historiography see Douglas J. MacDonald, "Communist Bloc Expansion in the Early Cold War," *International Security* (Winter 1995–1996): 152–88. A broader range of views can be found in two parts in *Diplomatic History* 23 (Spring and Summer 1999) under the heading, "The American Century: A Roundtable." The Cold War International History Project, based at the Woodrow Wilson Center in Washington, publishes a *Bulletin* containing documents from Soviet (and Chinese) archives, which support a range of realist and postrevisionist interpretations.

[34] See, for example, Dmitri Volkogonov, *Lenin: A New Biography* (New York, 1994); Vojtech Mastny, *Cold War and Soviet Insecurity: The Stalin Years* (New York, 1996); Vladimir M. Zubok and Constantine Pleshakov, *The Kremlin's Cold War: From Stalin to Khrushchev* (Cambridge, Mass., 1996); more recently, Zubok issued a mixed assessment of Gorbachev, while emphasizing the power of personality to shape history, in "Gorbachev and the End of the Cold War: Perspectives on History and Personality," *Cold War History* 2 (January 2002): 61–100.

diplomacy. "The most rigid relativism," he concluded, "cannot deny that our government's flagrant lies, plans to incinerate much of the world, secret wars, and arbitrary assassinations are unworthy actions."[35]

A more informed and measured defense of revisionist views can be found in the work of Melvyn P. Leffler. Leffler's subtly argued and deeply researched account of the origins of the national security state clearly retains the revisionist insistence that American imperial ambitions, heavily influenced by the interests of major economic and political elites, caused the Cold War every bit as much as the Soviets did. And he shows persuasively how much damage the Cold War did to American society and political culture in the postwar decades.[36] In his newest work, he sounds more like a realist, recalling the wisdom of Kennan and the founders of containment who sought to balance strategic power with multilateral restraint (not to mention the restraint of common sense and decency). Similarly, H. W. Brands acknowledges the realist insight that the Cold War was a real "strategic struggle" and not, as some revisionists had made it seem, just "the latest episode in an ongoing search for enemies." Nevertheless, Brands insists on reasserting the revisionist insight that American elites and broader publics did use "the devil" of Soviet communism to resolve their own internal contradictions and rationalize their own worldly ambitions, thus precipitating and extending the Cold War.[37] Revisionist historians continue to challenge complacent assumptions about the efficacy of nuclear deterrence, the morality of both American and Soviet intentions and actions, the bipolarity of Cold War international relations, and the peacefulness of an era that avoided nuclear holocaust but sacrificed millions of lives in "brush-fire wars" in Latin America, Asia, and Africa.[38]

Beyond the backward-looking debate between vindicationism and chastened revisionism, the immediate post–Cold War period witnessed expressions of hope on almost all sides that a "peace dividend" would make possible what had seemed unachievable only a few years earlier: lowering the national debt, increasing expenditures on useful and popular domestic programs, and investing in institutions of international cooperation — "a new world order" — that might improve the lot of impoverished peoples and ensure a Pax Americana around the world. But such hopes dimmed as the former

---

[35]Edward Pessen, "Appraising American Cold War Policy by Its Means of Implementation," *Reviews in American History* 18 (December 1990): 453–65; and also his *Losing Our Souls: The American Experience in the Cold War* (Chicago, 1993).

[36]Melvyn P. Leffler, *The Specter of Communism: The United States and the Origins of the Cold War, 1917–1953* (New York, 1994). See also his *A Preponderance of Power: National Security, the Truman Administration, and the Cold War* (Stanford, Calif., 1992); his thoughtful reconsideration of one of the most debated questions in this field, "Truman's Decision to Drop the Atomic Bomb," *IHJ Bulletin* 15 (Summer 1995): 1–7; and his masterly overview of the historiography, "The Cold War: What Do 'We Now Know'?" *American Historical Review* (April 1999): 501–24, which takes direct aim at Gaddis's vindicationism. His latest and most distilled insights into the long history of the Cold War and its aftermath bring him closer to Gaddis, especially in assertions of the continuously expansive, unilateral, and preventative impulses in U.S. foreign policy: *For the Soul of Mankind: The United States, the Soviet Union, and the Cold War* (New York, 2007).

[37]H. W. Brands, *The Devil We Knew: Americans and the Cold War* (New York, 1993).

[38]Informed revisionist critiques of vindicationism, as well as bibliographic references to a broad range of recent scholarship, can be found in Hunter, *Rethinking the Cold War*.

Soviet rim devolved into conflict; as the Middle East grew more, not less, violent; as the former Yugoslavia and Rwanda witnessed genocidal ethnic cleansing; and as African states suffered economic decline, coups, invasions, and breakaway regional conflicts, not to mention an equally appalling epidemic of AIDS. Before long the United States found itself drawn into perplexing and expensive engagements. In Kosovo and the Persian Gulf these resulted in limited and successful military action.

But with 9/11, all expectations that the post–Cold War world might be significantly more peaceful or stable than the last half century vanished. After successfully overthrowing the Taliban regime in Afghanistan, an intervention supported by a vast majority of Americans, a considerable number of allies, and even many Muslims around the world, the United States invaded Iraq, overthrew Saddam Hussein, and announced the dawn of democracy in the Middle East. Neoconservatives in the administration, along with many scholars and commentators, frankly embraced the emergence of American hegemony. Among the most thoughtful and persuasive of these, the British political scientist Niall Ferguson called for an unapologetic U.S. assumption of the mantle of the British empire. Only if the United States met its imperial responsibility, he argued, could the world's fractious peoples find a modicum of peace and security. Only by joining in America's benignly liberal imperium could the advanced democracies guarantee the future of their free and abundant societies. According to Michael Ignatieff, a renowned scholar, human rights activist, and Canadian Liberal Party leader, only American assertiveness — including intervention in Iraq — could safeguard the heritage of human rights and extend it beyond the privileged nations of the first world.[39]

After several years in Iraq, however, America's mission, far from accomplished, appears unwise and unachievable, even to many once-bullish neo-imperialists. By 2006, when congressional elections registered widespread disillusionment and anger over the war, Iraq seemed more and more like Vietnam to both scholars and the public: conceived in hubris, justified by deception and sophistry, and implemented with incompetence and cruelty. As the neo-orthodox retreated into analysis of failed means (rather than ends and purposes), revisionist scholars found a new audience for their insistence that, even after the end of the Cold War, domestic economic, political, and ideological impulses still pushed American foreign policy in dangerous directions.[40] Realists once again bemoaned America's faulty grasp of its true interests and its weakness for alternating bouts of isolation and crusade. Post-

---

[39]Niall Ferguson, *Colossus: The Price of America's Empire* (New York, 2004); Michael Ignatieff, *The Lesser Evil: Political Ethics in an Age of Terror* (Princeton, N.J., 2004). In *Warrior Politics: Why Leadership Demands a Pagan Ethos* (New York, 2002), journalist Robert Kaplan offers a cruder and grimmer version of this argument: Cold War or no, peace and civilization require empire; empire requires military force; the United States is the hegemon and so must use its force. A wide-ranging account of the distinctiveness of U.S. imperial tendencies over several centuries is Frank Nincovich, *The United States and Imperialism* (Malden, Mass., 2001).

[40]For example, Fredrik Logevall, "Bernath Lecture: A Critique of Containment," *Diplomatic History* 28 (2004): 473–99; Arnold Offner, "Presidential Address: 'Another Such Victory': President Truman, American Foreign Policy, and the Cold War," *Diplomatic History* 23 (1999):

revisionists pointed to structural requirements for international security in a world that is frustratingly unipolar in some ways, chaotic in others. Several scholars averred that the real diplomatic successes of the Cold War — in European integration, multilateral institutions, and arms control — had left a legacy of law and practice that continues to serve the world well, even (and especially) in the age of terrorism and in the face of an international system that seems less coherent than the bipolar world of the Cold War.[41]

Most imaginatively, a number of scholars have proposed a new history of international relations that better accounts for the agency of smaller states and substate movements and the contingency of historical events. Tony Smith, despite orthodox tendencies, suggests a "pericentric" framework for interpreting the Cold War that synthesizes elements of orthodox, revisionist, realist, and postrevisionist schools of historiography. The end of the bipolar Cold War, he claims, not only freed the world from the threat of Armageddon, but liberated historians to reconsider the efficacy of those small states and movements that appear in many accounts to be merely the pawns of the Cold War principals. From Peking to New Delhi, Tel Aviv to Havana, Paris to Johannesburg, the hills of Afghanistan to the jungle camps of Angola, clients and potential clients cajoled, wooed, and panicked Washington and Moscow into committing themselves to conflicts they might well have avoided. These clients sometimes lessened, but more often increased, the vehemence and intractability of both powers. Though Smith sometimes inflates the role of smaller actors (most especially Fidel Castro, who ends up seeming the whip hand in an improbably large number of bipolar encounters), he convincingly explains how nationalist, ethno-religious, and regional animosities broke through the strategists' fantasies — whether of hegemony or bipolar condominium. Provoking intervention on the part of patrons who hoped to avoid direct confrontation and advance their interests in less costly and risky ways, these smaller actors — some sly democratic politicians, others crude but daring dictators — left their mark on world history.[42]

Odd Arne Westad, in this chapter's second reading, offers similar insights and adds a more comprehensive approach to the history of the Cold War.[43]

127–55. See also a beautifully crafted case study, *American Orientalism: The United States and the Middle East since 1945* (Chapel Hill, N.C., 2002), in which Douglas Little shows that by relying on cultural stereotypes and the dubious maxim, "the enemy of my enemy is my friend," the United States lost the chance to engage secular nationalists and instead helped create the "Frankenstein's monster" of Islamic terrorism. On this subject see also Chalmers A. Johnson, *Blowback: The Costs and Consequences of American Empire* (New York, 2000); and David F. Schmitz, *The United States and Right-Wing Dictatorships* (New York, 2006).

[41] See G. John Ikenberry, *Liberal Order and Imperial Ambition* (Malden, Mass., 2006); Vojtech Mastny, "Diplomacy and the Legacy of the Cold War: Post–11 September," *Cold War History* 2 (April 2002): 15–28.

[42] Tony Smith, "New Bottles for New Wine: A Pericentric Framework for the Study of the Cold War," *Diplomatic History* 24 (Fall 2000): 567–91.

[43] Odd Arne Westad, "Bernath Lecture: The New International History of the Cold War: Three (Possible) Paradigms," *Diplomatic History* 24 (2000): 551–65; and also his fuller exposition in *The Global Cold War: Third World Interventions and the Making of Our Times* (Cambridge and New York, 2005); for a more orthodox version of this story, see Peter W. Rodman, *More Precious Than Peace: The Cold War and the Struggle for the Third World* (New York, 1994).

Suggesting "Three (Possible) Paradigms" for a "New International History of the Cold War," Westad insists that the Cold War was neither just bipolar, nor just about diplomacy, nor just about "interests," however defined. Like orthodox scholars he acknowledges the Soviets' ideological imperatives; like revisionists he judges the U.S. "ideological project" to have been even more responsible for the transformation of U.S.-Soviet rivalry into Cold War. Like some postrevisionist scholars, he sees U.S. flexibility and ideological attractiveness as crucial to the acceptance by Western Europeans and Japanese of America's "invitation to empire."[44] But he also argues that, in organizing and subsidizing postwar multilateral arrangements, the United States aimed not just for stability but for hegemony, a total transformation of politics, culture, and ideology around the "free world." It sought to ensure not only strategic and trade advantages, but an ideologically comprehensive version of "high modernism," that is, a vision of progress (meaning scientific control of nature and the production of abundance). While the Soviets shared the modernist goal of progress, their model emphasized central planning, repression, and "collective sacrifice." In the eyes of Europeans, this package proved less attractive than America's better-subsidized and freer social and political system. If diplomacy, trade, and military treaty structured the alliance between America and its partners in the advanced world, popular culture infused that structure with ideological élan and expanded it to "the third world." In some places, the words, images, and sounds of American culture outraged conservative elites and nationalist leaders.[45] So did Marxist ideology, especially in the Islamic world. In most cases, "modernizing traditionalists" sought to deploy Western technology (and sometimes Soviet-style planning) to build a cordon of security around their traditions, enabling them to compete both economically and "spiritually" with the United States (or with the USSR).[46] Westad concludes that the power of the great rivals was never absolute; especially in the developing world, it did not always determine outcomes:

> With decolonization, . . . one hundred new states emerged, each with
> elites that had their own ideological agendas. . . . Instead of reducing ten-

---

[44]This phrase was coined by Geir Lundestad, "Empire by Invitation? The United States and Western Europe, 1945–1952," *Journal of Peace Research* 23 (1986): 263–77.

[45]On foreign reactions to American culture see Rob Kroes, *If You've Seen One, You've Seen the Mall: Europeans and American Mass Culture* (Urbana, Ill., 1996); Richard Pells, *Not Like Us: How Europeans Have Loved, Hated, and Transformed American Culture since World War II* (New York, 1997); Reinhold Wagnleitner and Elaine Tyler May, eds., *"Here, There, and Everywhere": The Foreign Politics of American Popular Culture* (Hanover, N.H., 2000); Victoria De Grazia, *Irresistible Empire: America's Advance through Twentieth-Century Europe* (Cambridge, Mass., 2005). On the Cold War period in particular, see Giles Scott-Smith and Hans Krabbendam, eds., *The Cultural Cold War in Western Europe, 1945–1960* (London, 2003); see also a number of essays in Michael J. Hogan and Thomas G. Paterson, eds., *Exploring the History of Foreign Relations* (New York, 2004); on antipathy to American cultural exports, see Jessica C. E. Gienow-Hecht, "Shame on US? Academics, Cultural Transfer, and the Cold War — A Critical Review," *Diplomatic History* 24 (Summer 2000): 465–94. A theoretical critique of theories of cultural imperialism can be found in John Tomlinson, *Cultural Imperialism* (Baltimore, 1993).

[46]On the seldom-noted appeal of Soviet planning models, see David C. Engerman, "The Romance of Economic Development and New Histories of the Cold War," *Diplomatic History* 28 (January 2004): 23–54.

sions . . . decolonization . . . often increased them. . . . Had it not been
for the existence of these new states, it is likely that the Cold War conflict
. . . would have petered out sometime in the 1960s. . . . What prolonged
the conflict was its extension into areas in which the Cold War ideological
duality had no relevance . . . but where the U.S. and Soviet leaders convinced themselves that the postcolonial states were theirs to win or lose.[47]

Views of the Cold War that are less bipolar and comprehend more than
just warfare and statecraft help clarify recent international events. Still driven
by powerful ideological commitments to "openness,"[48] the United States moves
outward to incorporate more and more regions of the globe into its democratic, capitalist empire. Rivals respond, sometimes with their own imperial
agendas, or, if less powerful, scrambling to find advantage by accommodating U.S. policy or resisting it to gain the notice of an alternative patron or
partner. Entire populations, increasingly linked by new communications
technology and hoping for some combination of modern abundance, traditional identity, and freedom from the heavy hand of both modernizing and
traditional elites, advance or frustrate on their own terms and in their own
time the schemes of global strategists. In the United States, citizens rarely
attentive to foreign affairs, yet committed to an uncomplicated ideological
agenda of spreading free enterprise and free government, reveal a democratic distaste for long-term, costly commitments to imperial structures.[49] It
is such a world that most recently has trapped the United States in a war it
cannot win, in a place it does not understand, in pursuit of goals it cannot
reconcile or even clearly formulate.

The end of the Cold War has made possible a convergence of views on
several important issues, but it has not settled all questions about its causes
and consequences. Did the Cold War commence at the end of or during
World War II, or did its roots stretch back in time to World War I or even
earlier? Was the Soviet occupation of Eastern Europe the realization of a
centuries-old Russian dream of a sphere of influence, a reaction to the more
recent devastation sustained during the Nazi invasion, or an advance in the
revolutionary strategy of an international Communist movement? Did American policymakers act on the belief that U.S. economic well-being required
ever-expanding foreign markets? Has American diplomacy since the Spanish-
American War pursued global hegemony, global status quo, or global democracy? Was the Cold War "our" fault, "theirs," or a combination of both? Was
it always more "pericentric" than scholars imagined? Has the post–Cold War

---

[47]Westad, "Bernath Lecture," 563. A symposium on "The Global Cold War," in *Cold War History* 6 (August 2006): 353–63, includes appreciative yet critical comments from Jeremi Suri and William Wohlforth, and a reply from Westad.

[48]On the continuity of Open Door ideology in U.S. foreign policy, see Andrew Bacevich, *American Empire: The Realities and Consequences of U.S. Diplomacy* (Cambridge, Mass., 2002).

[49]Note, however, that Robert David Johnson, *Congress and the Cold War* (New York, 2006), shows that neither the citizenry, nor Congress, nor other institutions of the constitutional republic are quite as overmatched by the military-industrial complex and the imperial presidency as some fear.

world been freed of bipolar thinking, or are the roots of "us versus them" policies deeper than statecraft and rival ideologies and interests? Whatever the answers to these questions, today, as in the Vietnam era, Americans have come increasingly, if reluctantly, to recognize the arrogance of power and the illusion of omnipotence that plague both policy elites and citizens searching for safety in a perilous world. Although we regularly remind ourselves that history offers no foolproof lessons, reviewing the international history of the last half century might supply sufficient wisdom for us to avoid the worst disasters.

JOHN LEWIS GADDIS

from We Now Know: Rethinking Cold War History [1997]

JOHN LEWIS GADDIS (1941–) is Robert A. Lovett Professor of History at Yale University. He is the author of *The United States and the Origins of the Cold War, 1941–1947* (1972), *Strategies of Containment* (1982), *The Long Peace* (1987), and *The Cold War: A New History* (2005).

The idea of containment proceeded from the proposition that if there was not to be one world, then there must not be another world war either. It would be necessary to keep the peace while preserving the balance of power: the gap that had developed during the 1930s between the perceived requirements of peace and power was not to happen again. If geopolitical stability could be restored in Europe, time would work against the Soviet Union and in favor of the Western democracies. Authoritarianism need not be the "wave of the future"; sooner or later even Kremlin authoritarians would realize this fact and change their policies. "[T]he Soviet leaders are prepared to recognize *situations*, if not arguments," George F. Kennan wrote in 1948. "If, therefore, situations can be created in which it is clearly not to the advantage of their power to emphasize the elements of conflict in their relations with the outside world, then their actions, and even the tenor of their propaganda to their own people, *can* be modified."

This idea of time being on the side of the West came — at least as far as Kennan was concerned — from studying the history of empires. Edward Gibbon had written in *The Decline and Fall of the Roman Empire* that "there is nothing more contrary to nature than the attempt to hold in obedience distant provinces," and few things Kennan ever read made a greater or more lasting impression on him. He had concluded during the early days of World War II that Hitler's empire could not last, and in the months after the war, he applied similar logic to the empire Stalin was setting out to construct in Eastern Europe. The territorial acquisitions and spheres of influence the Soviet Union had obtained would ultimately become a source of *insecurity* for it, both because of the resistance to Moscow's control that was sure to grow within those regions and because of the outrage the nature of that control was certain to provoke in the rest of the world. "Soviet power, like the capitalist world of its own conception, bears within it the seeds of its own decay," Kennan insisted in the most famous of all Cold War texts, his anonymously published 1947 article on "The Sources of Soviet Conduct." He added, "the sprouting of those seeds is well advanced."

All of this would do the Europeans little good, though, if the new and immediate Soviet presence in their midst should so intimidate them that their own morale collapsed. The danger here came not from the prospect that the Red Army would invade and occupy the rest of the continent, as Hitler had tried to do; rather, its demoralized and exhausted inhabitants might simply vote in communist parties who would then do Moscow's bidding. The initial steps in the strategy of containment — stopgap military and economic aid to Greece and Turkey, the more carefully designed and ambitious Marshall Plan — took place within this context: the idea was to produce instant intangible reassurance as well as eventual tangible reinforcement. Two things had to happen in order for intimidation to occur, Kennan liked to argue: the intimidator had to make the effort, but, equally important, the target of those efforts had to agree to be intimidated. The initiatives of 1947 sought to generate sufficient self-confidence to prevent such acquiescence in intimidation from taking place.

Some historians have asserted that these fears of collapse were exaggerated: that economic recovery on the continent was already underway, and that the Europeans themselves were never as psychologically demoralized as the Americans made them out to be. Others have added that the real crisis at the time was within an American economy that could hardly expect to function hegemonically if Europeans lacked the dollars to purchase its products. Still others have suggested that the Marshall Plan was the means by which American officials sought to project overseas the mutually-beneficial relationship between business, labor, and government they had worked out at home: the point was not to make Wilsonian values a model for the rest of the world, but rather the politics of productivity that had grown out of American corporate capitalism. All of these arguments have merit: at a minimum they have forced historians to place the Marshall Plan in a wider economic, social, and historical context; more broadly they suggest that the American empire had its own distinctive internal roots, and was not solely and simply a response to the Soviet external challenge.

At the same time, though, it is difficult to see how a strategy of containment could have developed — with the Marshall Plan as its centerpiece — had there been nothing to contain. One need only recall the early 1920s, when similar conditions of European demoralization, Anglo-French exhaustion, and American economic predominance had existed; yet no American empire arose as after World War II. The critical difference, of course, was national security: Pearl Harbor created an atmosphere of vulnerability Americans had not known since the earliest days of the republic, and the Soviet Union by 1947 had become the most plausible source of threat. The American empire arose *primarily*, therefore, not from internal causes, as had the Soviet empire, but from a perceived external danger powerful enough to overcome American isolationism.

Washington's wartime vision of a postwar international order had been premised on the concepts of political self-determination and economic integration. It was intended to work by assuming a set of *common* interests that would cause other countries to *want* to be affiliated with it rather than to resist it. The Marshall Plan, to a considerable extent, met those criteria: although it operated on a regional rather than a global scale, it did seek to promote democracy through an economic recovery that would proceed along international and not nationalist lines. Its purpose was to create an American sphere of influence, to be sure, but one that would allow those within it considerable freedom. The principles of democracy and open markets required nothing less, but there were two additional and more practical reasons for encouraging such autonomy. First, the United States itself lacked the capability to administer a large empire; the difficulties of running occupied Germany and Japan were proving daunting enough. Second, the idea of autonomy was implicit in the task of restoring European self-confidence; for who, if not Europeans themselves, was to say when the self-confidence of Europeans had been restored?

Finally, it is worth noting that even though Kennan and the other early architects of containment made use of imperial analogies, they did not see themselves as creating an empire, but rather a restored balance of power. Painfully — perhaps excessively — aware of limited American resources, fearful that the domestic political consensus in favor of inter-nationalism might not hold, they set out to reconstitute *independent* centers of power in Europe and Asia. These would be integrated into the world capitalist system, and as a result they would certainly fall under the influence of its new hegemonic manager, the United States. But there was no intention here of creating satellites in anything like the sense that Stalin understood that term; rather, the idea was that "third forces" would resist Soviet expansionism while preserving as much as possible of the multilateralist agenda American officials had framed during World War II. What the United States really wanted, State Department official John D. Hickerson commented in 1948, was "not merely an extension of US influence but a real European organization strong enough to say 'no' both to the Soviet Union and to the United States, if our actions should seem so to require."

The American empire, therefore, reflected little imperial consciousness or design. An anti-imperial tradition dating back to the American Revolution partially accounted for this: departures from that tradition, as

in the Spanish-American War of 1898 and the Philippine insurrection
that followed, had only reinforced its relevance — outside the Western
hemisphere. So too did a constitutional structure that forced even imperi-
ally minded leaders like Wilson and the two Roosevelts to accommodate
domestic attitudes that discouraged imperial behavior long after national
capabilities had made it possible. And even as those internal constraints
diminished dramatically in World War II — they never entirely dropped
away — Americans still found it difficult to think of themselves as an imperial power. The idea of remaking the international system in such a way as
to transcend empires altogether still lingered, but so too did doubts as to
whether the United States was up to the task. In the end it was again
external circumstances — the manner in which Stalin managed his own
empire and the way in which this pushed Europeans into preferring its
American alternative — that brought the self-confidence necessary to
administer imperial responsibilities into line with Washington's awareness
of their existence. . . .

It is apparent now, even if it was not always at the time, that the Soviet
Union did not manage its empire particularly well. Because of his personality and the structure of government he built around it, Stalin was —
shall we say — less than receptive to the wishes of those nations that fell
within the Soviet sphere. He viewed departures from his instructions with
deep suspicion, but he also objected to manifestations of independent
behavior where instructions had not yet been given. As a result, he put
his European followers in an impossible position: they could satisfy him
only by seeking his approval for whatever he had decided they should
do — even, at times, before he had decided that they should do it. . . .

The Americans' unexpected offer of Marshall Plan aid to the Soviet
Union and Eastern Europe in June 1947 caused even greater difficulties
for Stalin's management of empire — which is precisely what Kennan
hoped for when he recommended making it. In one of the stranger illusions arising from their ideology, Soviet leaders had always anticipated
United States economic assistance in some form. Lenin himself expected
American capitalists, ever in search of foreign markets, to invest eagerly
in the newly formed USSR, despite its official antipathy toward them.
Stalin hoped for a massive American reconstruction loan after World War II,
and even authorized Molotov early in 1945 to offer acceptance of such
assistance in order to help the United States stave off the economic crisis
that Marxist analysis showed must be approaching. When the Marshall
Plan was announced Stalin's first reaction was that the capitalists must be
desperate. He concluded, therefore, that the Soviet Union and its East
European allies should indeed participate in the plan, and quickly dispatched Molotov and a large delegation of economic experts to Paris to
take part in the conference that was to determine the nature and extent
of European needs.

But then Stalin began to reconsider. His ambassador in Washington,
Nikolai Novikov, warned that the American offer to the Soviet Union
could not be sincere: "A careful analysis of the Marshall Plan shows that

ultimately it comes down to forming a West European bloc as a tool of US policy. All the good wishes accompanying the plan are demagogic official propaganda serving as a smokescreen." Soviet intelligence picked up reports — accurate enough — that American Under-Secretary of State William Clayton had been conspiring with British officials on using the Marshall Plan to reintegrate Germany into the West European economy and to deny further reparations shipments to the Soviet Union. This information, together with indications at Paris that the Americans would require a coordinated European response, caused Stalin to change his mind and order his own representatives to walk out. "The Soviet delegation saw those claims as a bid to interfere in the internal affairs of European countries," Molotov explained lamely, "thus making the economies of these countries dependent on US interests." . . .

Unfortunately, the Czechs and the Poles, following the earlier instructions, had already announced their intention to attend. The Poles quickly changed their mind but the Czechs procrastinated, more because of confusion than determined resistance. . . .

. . . Stalin's intentions were now clear to all including himself: there would be no East European participation in the Marshall Plan, or in any other American scheme for the rehabilitation of Europe. "I went to Moscow as the Foreign Minister of an independent sovereign state," Czech Foreign Minister Jan Masaryk commented bitterly. "I returned as a lackey of the Soviet government."

But the Kremlin boss too had shed some illusions. Marxist-Leninist analyses had long predicted, not just a postwar economic collapse in the West, but eventual conflict between the British and the Americans. In a September 1946 report from Washington which Molotov had carefully annotated, Ambassador Novikov had insisted that "the United States regards England as its greatest potential competitor." The Anglo-American relationship, "despite the temporary attainment of agreements on very important questions, [is] plagued with great internal contradictions and cannot be lasting." By early 1947, Stalin was even offering the British a military alliance: as one report to Molotov put it, "Soviet diplomacy has in England practically unlimited possibilities." What the Marshall Plan showed was how wrong these assessments were. Capitalists, it now appeared, could indeed reconcile their differences; they considered the Soviet Union a greater threat to all than each posed to the other; time was not on Moscow's side. Ideology again had led Stalin into romanticism and away from reality. Once he realized this — in Europe at least — he never quite recovered from the shock. . . .

The United States, in contrast, proved surprisingly adept at managing an empire. Having attained their authority through democratic processes, its leaders were experienced — as their counterparts in Moscow were not — in the arts of persuasion, negotiation and compromise. . . .

Americans so often deferred to the wishes of allies during the early Cold War that some historians have seen the Europeans — especially the British — as having managed *them*. . . .

But one can easily make too much of this argument. Truman and his advisers were not babes in the woods. They knew what they were doing at each stage, and did it only because they were convinced their actions would advance American interests. They never left initiatives entirely up to the Europeans: they insisted on an integrated plan for economic recovery and quite forcefully reined in prospective recipients when it appeared that their requests would exceed what Congress would approve. "[I]n the end we would not *ask* them," Kennan noted, "we would just *tell* them, what they would get." The Americans were flexible enough, though, to accept and build upon ideas that came from allies; they also frequently let allies determine the timing of actions taken. As a consequence, the British, French, and other West Europeans came to feel that they had a stake in what Washington was doing, despite the fact that it amounted to their own incorporation within an American sphere of influence.

One might argue, to be sure, that European elites agreed to all of this for their own self-interested reasons; that the European "masses" were never consulted. It is worth remembering, however, that free elections ultimately ratified alignment with the United States in every country where that took place. The newly-formed Central Intelligence Agency, not always confident of such outcomes, did take it upon itself at times to manipulate democratic processes, most conspicuously in the Italian elections of April 1948. But these covert efforts — together with clandestine CIA support for anti-communist labor unions and intellectual organizations — could hardly have succeeded had there not already existed in Europe a widespread predisposition to see the Americans as the lesser of two evils, and perhaps even as a force for good. "I am entirely convinced," the French political theorist Raymond Aron insisted, "that for an anti-Stalinist there is no escape from the acceptance of American leadership." French peasants did not see it all that differently.

The habits of democracy were no less significant when it came to defeated adversaries. . . .

The United States could of course hold out the prospect of economic recovery and the Soviet Union could not: this certainly made the advantages of democracy more evident than they might otherwise have been. But democratization . . . was well under way before there was any assurance that Germans would receive Marshall Plan aid or anything comparable. Authoritarianism, which was all Moscow would or could provide, was by far the less attractive alternative. "Soviet officers bolshevized their zone," Naimark has concluded, "not because there was a plan to do so, but because that was the only way they knew to organize society. . . . By their own actions, the Soviet authorities created enemies out of potential friends." Or, as General Clay recalled years afterwards: "We began to look like angels, not because we were angels, but we looked [like] that in comparison to what was going on in Eastern Europe."

The Americans simply did not find it necessary, in building a sphere of influence, to impose unrepresentative governments or brutal treatment upon the peoples that fell within it. Where repressive regimes already existed, as in Greece, Turkey, and Spain, serious doubts arose in Washington as to whether the United States should be supporting them at all, however useful they might be in containing Soviet expansionism. Nor, having constructed their empire, did Americans follow the ancient imperial practice of "divide and rule." Rather, they used economic leverage to overcome nationalist tendencies, thereby encouraging the Europeans' emergence as a "third force" whose obedience could not always be assumed. It was as if the Americans were projecting abroad a tradition they had long taken for granted at home: that civility made sense; that spontaneity, within a framework of minimal constraint, was the path to political and economic robustness; that to intimidate or to overmanage was to stifle. The contrast to Stalin's methods of imperial administration could hardly have been sharper.

Stalin saw the need, after learning of the Marshall Plan, to improve his methods of imperial management. He therefore called a meeting of the Soviet and East European communist parties, as well as the French and the Italian communists, to be held in Poland in September 1947, ostensibly for the purpose of exchanging ideas on fraternal cooperation. Only after the delegations had assembled did he reveal his real objective, which was to organize a new coordinating agency for the international communist movement. Stalin had abolished the old Comintern as a wartime gesture of reassurance to the Soviet Union's allies in 1943, and the International Department of the Soviet Communist Party, headed by the veteran Comintern leader, the Bulgarian Georgii Dimitrov, had taken over its functions. What had happened during the spring and summer of 1947 make it clear, though, that these arrangements provided insufficient coordination from Stalin's point of view. . . .

The French communist leader Jacques Duclos summed up the new procedures succinctly: "Paris and Rome will be able to submit their proposals, but they shall have to be content with the decisions to be adopted in Belgrade."

Even with the Cominform in place, the momentary independence Czechoslovakia demonstrated must have continued to weigh on Stalin's mind. That country, more than any other in Eastern Europe, had sought to accommodate itself to Soviet hegemony. Embittered by how easily the British and French had betrayed Czech interests at the Munich conference in 1938, President Eduard Benes welcomed the expansion of Soviet influence while reassuring Marxist-Leninists that they had nothing to fear from the democratic system the Czechs hoped to rebuild after the war. "If you play it well," he told Czech Communist Party leaders in Moscow in 1943, "you'll win."

But Benes meant "win" by democratic means. Although the Communists had indeed done well in the May 1946 parliamentary elections, their popularity began to drop sharply after Stalin forbade Czech participation in the Marshall Plan the following year. Convinced by intelligence reports that the West would not intervene, they therefore took advantage of a February 1948 government crisis to stage a *coup d'état* — presumably with

Stalin's approval — that left them in complete control, with no further need to resort to the unpredictabilities of the ballot box. This development came as no surprise in Washington: Kennan had predicted that the Soviet Union would sooner or later crack down on those East European states where communists did not fully dominate the government. Czechoslovakia had figured most prominently on that list. But to an unprepared American and Western European public, the Prague takeover was the most appalling event yet in the emerging Cold War, occurring as it did in the country whose abandonment by the West only ten years earlier had led directly to World War II. There followed shortly thereafter the suicide, or murder, of Masaryk, son of the founder of the country and himself a symbol — now a martyr — to the fragility of Czech liberties.

Because of its dramatic impact, the Czech coup had consequences Stalin could hardly have anticipated. It set off a momentary — and partially manufactured — war scare in Washington. It removed the last Congressional objections to the Marshall Plan, resulting in the final approval of that initiative in April 1948. It accelerated plans by the Americans, the British, and the French to consolidate their occupation zones in Germany and to proceed toward the formation of an independent West German state. And it caused American officials to begin to consider, much more seriously than they had until this point, two ideas Bevin had begun to advance several months earlier: that economic assistance alone would not restore European self-confidence, and that the United States would have to take on direct military responsibilities for defending that portion of the Continent that remained outside Soviet control.

Stalin then chose the late spring of 1948 to attempt a yet further consolidation of the Soviet empire, with even more disastrous results. Reacting to the proposed establishment of a separate West German state, as well as to growing evidence that the East German regime had failed to attract popular support, and to the introduction of a new currency in the American, British, and French sectors of Berlin over which the Russians would have no control, he ordered a progressively tightening blockade around that city, which lay within the Soviet zone. "Let's make a joint effort," he told the East German leaders in March. "Perhaps we can kick them out." Initial indications were that the scheme was working. . . .

But the Soviet leader's plans, by this time, had already begun to backfire. There was now a quite genuine war scare in the West, one that intensified pressures for an American-West European military alliance, accelerated planning for an independent West Germany, further diminished what little support the communists still had outside the Soviet zone, and significantly boosted President Truman's re-election prospects in a contest few at the time thought he could win. Nor did the blockade turn out to be effective. "Clay's attempts to create 'an airlift' connecting Berlin with the western zones have proved futile," Soviet officials in that city prematurely reported to Moscow in April. "The Americans have admitted that the idea would be too expensive." In fact, though, the United States and its allies astonished themselves as well as the Russians by improvising so successful a supply of Berlin by air that there was no need to make concessions. Stalin was left with the choice he had hoped to avoid — capitulation or war — and in May 1949, in one of the most humiliating of all setbacks for Soviet foreign policy, he selected the first alternative by lifting the blockade.

The Berlin crisis demonstrated that Soviet expansionism in Europe had generated sufficient resistance from the United States and its allies to bring that process to a halt. Stalin had never been prepared to risk a military confrontation — at least not in the foreseeable future — and the West's response to the blockade, which included the deployment to British bases of apparently atomic-capable bombers, made it clear that further advances might indeed produce this result. The Soviet leadership, a Red Army general recalled many years later, had not been prepared to commit suicide over Berlin.

There remained, though, the task of consolidating Soviet control over those territories where communists already ruled, and here too 1948 proved to be a turning point, because for the first time this process provoked open resistance. Despite appearances of solidarity, Soviet-Yugoslav relations had become increasingly strained following earlier disagreements over the Red Army's abuse of Yugoslav civilians, plans for a Balkan federation, and support for the Greek communists. The fiercely independent Yugoslavs were finding it difficult to defer to the Soviet Union, whose interests seemed increasingly at odds with those of international communism. Stalin himself alternated between cajoling and bullying their leaders, sometimes including them in lengthy late-night eating and drinking sessions at his dacha, at other times upbraiding them rudely for excessive ideological militance and insufficient attention to Moscow's wishes. Tensions came to a head early in 1948 when the Yugoslavs and the Albanians began considering the possibility of unification. Stalin let it be known that he would not object to Yugoslavia "swallowing" Albania, but this only aroused suspicions among the Yugoslavs, who remembered how the Soviet Union had "swallowed" the Baltic States in 1940 and feared that the precedent might someday apply to them. Their concerns grew when Stalin then reversed course and condemned Belgrade bitterly for sending troops into Albania without consulting Moscow. By June of 1948, these disagreements had become public, and the communist world would never be the same again. . . .

Stalin responded to this insult in a wholly characteristic way: if he could not get at the Yugoslavs themselves, he would get at all other possible Yugoslav sympathizers elsewhere. There followed the East European purge trials, precise replicas of what Stalin had ordered within the Soviet Union a decade earlier when he detected heresy or the prospect of it. By 1949–50, there were few overt Titoists left outside Yugoslavia. But there were also few people left — apart from the party and official bureaucracies who ran it — who believed that they had anything to gain from living within a Soviet sphere of influence: vast numbers of them now became closet Titoists, with results that would make themselves evident periodically over the years in places like East Berlin in 1953, Budapest and Warsaw in 1956, Prague in 1968, and everywhere all at once in 1989.

West Europeans were meanwhile convincing themselves that they had little to lose from living within an American sphere of influence. . . .

Why were allies of the United States willing to give up so much autonomy in order to enhance their own safety? How did the ideas of sovereignty and security, which historically have been difficult to separate, come to be so widely seen as divisible in this situation?

The answer would appear to be that despite a postwar polarization of authority quite at odds, in its stark bilateralism, from what wartime planners had expected, Americans managed to retain the multilateral conception of security they had developed during World War II. They were able to do this because Truman's foreign policy — like Roosevelt's military strategy — reflected the habits of domestic democratic politics. Negotiation, compromise, and consensus-building abroad came naturally to statesmen steeped in the uses of such practices at home: in this sense, the American political tradition served the country better than its realist critics — Kennan definitely among them — believed it did.

Bargains of one kind or another were struck at every step along the way in constructing the American sphere of influence in Western Europe. The Truman administration extended a postwar loan to Great Britain to replace Lend-Lease, but only on the condition that the Labour government dismantle barriers to foreign trade and investment. When the effect proved to be disastrous for the British economy, the Americans moved quickly to relieve the strain by assuming responsibility for economic and military assistance to Greece and Turkey; but at the same time they took advantage of that situation, by way of the Truman Doctrine, to issue a far more sweeping call for containing Soviet expansionism than either Bevin or Attlee had expected. The United States then extended its offer of reconstruction aid to all of Europe under the Marshall Plan, but only on the condition that recipients submerge their old national rivalries and move toward economic and political integration, including Germany in this process.

The West Europeans, unlike the Soviet Union, agreed to this, but soon found a condition of their own to impose upon the Americans. This was the requirement of a formal military alliance with the United States, to which Washington acquiesced — but with the understanding that the British, the French, and their immediate neighbors would in turn agree to the formation of an independent West German state. Confronted with this unpalatable prospect, the French made the best of it by justifying NATO to themselves as an instrument of "double containment," directed against *both* the Soviet Union and the Germans. This made it possible for them to shift from an emphasis on punishing Germany to one directed toward economic cooperation with that country in the form of the Schuman

Plan to create a European Coal and Steel Community, an initiative that surprised but gratified the Americans, who had been seeking the resolution of Franco-German rivalries by pushing integration in the first place.

Meanwhile, a less obvious series of social compromises was going on within Western Europe. The Americans worried about the "tilt" toward the Left that had taken place as a result of the war; at the same time, though, they were cautious about pressuring the Europeans to move toward more centrist politics. A few officials in Washington understood that what they called the "non-communist Left" could itself become a center of resistance against the Soviet Union; there was also a more widespread fear that excessively overt pressure might backfire. The West Europeans, though, also made compromises. The United States did not *have* to pressure the French and the Italians very much to move toward the center because the leftward "tilt" in those countries had never extended so far as a rejection of capitalism in the first place. Their people could easily see that the American assistance and protection they wanted would be more likely if they themselves took the initiative in building centrist political coalitions.

What is significant, then, is not simply that the West Europeans invited the United States to construct a sphere of influence and include them within it; it is also that the Americans encouraged the Europeans to share the responsibility for determining how it would function, and that the Europeans were eager to do this. Washington officials were themselves often genuinely uncertain about what to do, and that provides part of the explanation for this pattern of mutual accommodation. But it also developed because the American vision of national security had become international in character: Franklin D. Roosevelt's most important foreign policy legacy may well have been to convince the nation that its security depended upon that of others elsewhere, not simply on whatever measures it might take on its own. Habits of compromise growing out of domestic politics made it easier than one might have thought for a formerly isolationist nation to adapt itself to this new situation; and those compromises, in turn, allowed West Europeans to define their interests in such a way as to find *common* ground with those of the United States.

It would become fashionable to argue, in the wake of American military intervention in Vietnam, the Soviet invasions of Czechoslovakia and Afghanistan, and growing fears of nuclear confrontation that developed during the early 1980s, that there were no significant differences in the spheres of influence Washington and Moscow had constructed in Europe after World War II: these had been, it was claimed, "morally equivalent," denying autonomy quite impartially to all who lived under them. Students of history must make their own judgments about morality, but even a cursory examination of the historical record will show that these imperial structures could hardly have been more different in their origins, their composition, their tolerance of diversity, and as it turned out their durability. It is important to specify just what these differences were.

First, and most important, the Soviet empire reflected the priorities and the practices of a single individual — a latter-day tsar, in every sense of the word. Just as it would have been impossible to separate the Soviet Union's internal structure from the influence of the man who ran it, so too the Soviet sphere of influence in Eastern Europe took on the characteristics of Stalin himself. The process was not immediate: Stalin did allow a certain amount of spontaneity in the political, economic, and intellectual life of that region for a time after the war, just as he had done inside the Soviet Union itself after he had consolidated his position as Lenin's successor in 1929. But when confronted with even the prospect of dissent, to say nothing of challenges to his authority, Stalin's instinct was to smother spontaneity with a thoroughness unprecedented in the modern age. This is what the purges had accomplished inside the USSR during the mid-1930s, and Eastern Europe underwent a similar process after 1947. There was thus a direct linkage from Stalin's earliest thinking on the nationalities question prior to the Bolshevik Revolution through to his management of empire after World War II: the right of self-determination was fine as long as no one sought to practice it.

The American empire was very different: one would have expected this from a country with no tradition of authoritarian leadership whose constitutional structure had long ago enshrined the practices of negotiation, compromise, and the balancing of interests. What is striking about the sphere of influence the United States established in Europe is that its existence and fundamental design reflected as frequently pressures that came *from those incorporated within it* from the Americans themselves. Washington officials were not at all convinced, at the end of World War II, that their interests would require protecting half the European continent: instead they looked toward a revival of a balance among the Europeans themselves to provide postwar geopolitical stability. Even the Marshall Plan, an unprecedented extension of American assistance, had been conceived with this "third force" principle in mind. It was the Europeans themselves who demanded more: who insisted that their security required a military shield as well as an economic jump-start.

One empire arose, therefore, by invitation, the other by imposition. *Europeans* made this distinction, very much as they had done during the war when they welcomed armies liberating them from the west but feared those that came from the east. They did so because they saw clearly at the time — even if a subsequent generation would not always see — how different American and Soviet empires were likely to be. It is true that the *extent* of the American empire quickly exceeded that of its Soviet counterpart, but this was because *resistance* to expanding American influence was never as great. The American empire may well have become larger, paradoxically, because the American *appetite* for empire was less that of the USSR. The United States had shown, throughout most of its history, that it could survive and even prosper without extending its domination as far as the eye could see. The logic of Lenin's ideological internationalism, as modified by Stalin's Great Russian nationalism and personal paranoia, was that the Soviet Union could not.

The early Cold War in Europe, therefore, cannot be understood by looking at the policies of either the United States or the Soviet Union in isolation. What evolved on the continent was an interactive system in which the actions of each side affected not only the other but also the Europeans; their responses, in turn, shaped further decisions in Washington and Moscow. It quickly became clear — largely because of differences in the domestic institutions of each superpower — that an American empire would accommodate far greater diversity than would one run by the Soviet Union: as a consequence most Europeans accepted and even invited American hegemony, fearing deeply what that of the Russians might entail.

Two paths diverged at the end of World War II. And that, to paraphrase an American poet, really did make all the difference.

ODD ARNE WESTAD

from The New International History of the Cold War: Three (Possible) Paradigms   [2000]

ODD ARNE WESTAD (1960–) is professor of international history at the London School of Economics and author of *The Global Cold War: Third World Interventions in the Making of Our Times* (2005) and (with Sophie Quinn-Judge) *The Third Indochina War: Conflict between China, Vietnam, and Cambodia, 1972–1979* (2000).

The Cold War is not what it once was. Not only has the conflict itself been written about in the past tense for more than a decade, but historians' certainties about the character of the conflict have also begun to blur. The concerns brought on by trends of the past decade — such trifles as globalization, weapons proliferation, and ethnic warfare — have made even old strategy buffs question the degree to which the Cold War ought to be put at the center of the history of the late twentieth century. In this article I will try to show how some people within our field are attempting to meet such queries by reconceptualizing the Cold War as part of contemporary international history. My emphasis will be on issues connecting the Cold War — defined as a political conflict between two power blocs — and some areas of investigation that in my opinion hold much promise for reformulating our views of that conflict, blithely summed up as ideology, technology, and the Third World. . . .

Odd Arne Westad, "Bernath Lecture: The New International History of the Cold War: Three (Possible) Paradigms," *Diplomatic History* 24 (Fall 2000): 551–65. Reprinted by permission of Wiley-Blackwell Publishing, Ltd.

For our purpose, I want to look at paradigms as patterns of interpretation, which may possibly exist side by side, but which each signify a particular approach — an angle of view, if I may — to the complex problems of Cold War history. . . .

I have chosen to discuss three such possible paradigms in this article. They are the ones that seem to me best suited for rapid advances in our understanding of the Cold War as a period or as an international system, and not just as a bilateral conflict or as diplomatic history.

Ideology

Perhaps the most useful — and certainly the most misused — of the paradigms I will be addressing here is that of ideology, understood as a set of fundamental concepts systematically expressed by a large group of individuals. Integrating the study of such fundamental concepts into our approach to international history holds tremendous promise as a method within a field that has often ignored ideas as the basis for human action. Used in ways that are sensitive to historical evidence and consistent in their application, the introduction of ideology as a part of our understanding of motives and broad patterns of action helps us overcome two of the main problems that international historians of the Cold War often face. One is that we are seen to be better at explaining single events than we are at analyzing causes and consequences of larger historical shifts. The other is that we are — rightly, I believe — often seen as using a narrow concept of causality, mostly connected to *interests or state policies.*

Let me use an example. When President John F. Kennedy met with First Secretary of the Communist Party of the Soviet Union (CPSU) Nikita Khrushchev in Vienna in June 1961, both leaders brought with them briefs and position papers that underlined the need to seek common ground on a number of issues, including the threat of nuclear war. Still, their public and private encounters were marked by sharp confrontation . . . culminating in the Cuban missile crisis the following year. Obviously, the policies that the two leaders pursued on most issues prior to their meeting were in conflict. Equally clearly, the personalities of Kennedy and Khrushchev were, to put it mildly, disharmonious. But in order to understand the outcome of the summit, I find that each man's basic ideological perception — his preconceived image of his own role and that of the other leader — is an invaluable tool that can only be discarded at our peril.

For Khrushchev, it was not primarily Kennedy's youth and relative inexperience that made it necessary to go on the offensive over Cuba and Berlin during the summit, or to lecture JFK on communism. It was, as those who came with Khrushchev to Vienna explain, because the Soviet leader was convinced that his society and political thinking were in ascendance, and that Kennedy, as a class representative of the U.S. "monopolists," could be brought to recognize this historical necessity. For John Kennedy, it was exactly this ideological challenge that mattered most, since he perceived his own role as U.S. president as assuring "the survival and success of liberty" on a global scale. With the passing of the torch to a new generation, Kennedy more than anything meant a more vigorous and determined pursuit of U.S. ideological hegemony in the world.

While the Vienna example shows how ideologies can be used to understand both concrete historical events and long-term trends, it is important . . . that our use of the concept does not become determinist or one-sided. One danger is associated with the overreliance on ideologies as a kind of theoretical catchall . . . or the replacement of the historical narrative with the study of ideas per se. In other cases, ideology has been reduced to formal concepts, such as often happened in Cold War era U.S. studies of the Soviet Union, in which Marxism-Leninism . . . kept out more composite and complex views of Soviet ideology. Finally, there is always the danger of making the other side "ideological" — and one's own side only too logical or interest driven. I see this as one of the main post–Cold War fallacies of U.S. international historians — while we have gradually become comfortable with making ideology an integral part of the study of *Soviet* foreign relations, many people in the field find it much more difficult to deal with *U.S.* elite ideology as a meaningful concept.

As Michael Hunt has pointed out . . . the ideology of the U.S. foreign policy elite was *more* pervasive in terms of decision making than was that of Soviet party leaders. In the cases that really mattered — the Marshall Plan, the support for European integration, U.S. occupation policy in Japan — it was a set of key U.S. ideas centered on a specific U.S. responsibility for the global expansion of freedom that made the difference. These ideas, which emphasized freedom of expression, freedom of ownership, and freedom of capitalist exchanges and negated freedom of collective organization, precapitalist values, or revolutionary action, were essential elements in the U.S. transformation of the world after 1945, and in Washington's unwillingness to engage the Soviet Union in the give and take of pre–World War II diplomatic practice.

As will be clear from the above, I to some extent go along with Anders Stephanson's contention that the Cold War may profitably be seen as a U.S. ideological project. . . . It was to a great extent American ideas and their influence that made the Soviet-American conflict into a *Cold War*. While Soviet foreign policy was no less fueled by its key ideas or its understanding of what made the world tick, the crucial difference is that at most times Soviet leaders were acutely aware of their *lack* of international hegemony and the *weakness* (relative to the United States and its allies) of Soviet or Communist power. . . . On the U.S. side, although the general public have been quite regularly visited by elements of paranoia with regard to the outside world, what really needs explanation is the remarkable consistency with which the U.S. foreign policy elite has defined the nation's international purpose over the past three to four generations. That purpose has been the global domination of its ideas — and although military domination has not always been recognized as a necessary companion to this ideological hegemony, it has still been an aim that U.S.

leaders have been willing to intervene to accomplish from World War I to the Kosovo conflict.

For most of the Cold War the majority of Americans did not share their leaders' willingness to spend their resources on extending U.S. ideas abroad. Without help from Stalin and the generation of Soviet leaders he created, it is uncertain whether the Truman and Eisenhower administrations would have been able to keep a strong U.S. involvement in Europe, the Middle East, and East Asia. Stalin believed that by isolating the Soviet Union and the countries it had occupied after the war, he could preserve the Communist dictatorship and build a long-term challenge to U.S. domination. Had it not been for Stalin's inflexibility and his insistence that his "zone" was extraneous to any form of U.S. influence, it would have been much more difficult for the U.S. foreign policy elites to get at least limited acceptance among the general public for substantial and long-term foreign involvements.

What then about the countries that joined with the United States in waging Cold War against communism — first and foremost Western Europe and Japan? The West European elites that issued the "invitations to empire" that Geir Lundestad has emphasized seem to have done so both out of fear of Stalin's intentions and because of the attractiveness of U.S. assistance in sorting out their own domestic problems. What is much more important to understand, though, is how the U.S. response to the "invitations" came to be shaped — not as a rescue operation for besieged (and to a great extent discredited) political leaderships but as conscious and comprehensive attempts at changing Europe (and Japan) in the direction of U.S. ideas and models.

To me, it is the flexibility of U.S. policies and the negotiability of the ideology they were based on that explain both the uniquely successful alliance systems that the United States established with Western Europe and Japan and the rapid political, social, and economic transformation that these countries went through. This, perhaps, was the real revolution of the Cold War: that the United States over a period of fifty years transformed its main capitalist competitors according to its own image. This did not, of course, happen without conflict. But mostly — and in great part because of the Cold War perceptions of an external threat — it was a peaceful transformation. Its peacefulness, however, and the fact that it happened as much as a result of trade, education, and consumer culture as political pressure should not obscure its intrinsicality.

In the novel for which he received the Nobel Prize for literature last year, the German author Günter Grass describes how his country has changed over the past century, with the most basic transformations happening after 1945. It was not just the effects of World War II that changed Germany, Grass seems to argue, it was the postwar presence of the Americans. . . . The changes in policies, social stratification, and economic foundations that the U.S. presence inspired gradually created systems of alliances that were based on similar world views and that could survive conflicts of interest (unlike those of the East). . . .

Technology

In terms of ideologies, one may say that the Cold War was a conflict between two different versions of what anthropologist James C. Scott refers to as high modernism — on the one hand, one that underlined social justice and the role of the industrial proletariat, and, on the other, one that emphasized individuality and the role of the stake-holding middle class. For the world at large, both ideologies were in their ways revolutionary, intent on transforming the world in their image. As with many modernist projects, American and Soviet Cold War ideologies based an important part of their legitimacies on the control of nature, be it human nature or our physical surroundings. They were both attempts at simplifying a complex world through social engineering, massive exploitation of resources, regulation, and technology. Technology was the epitome of both ideologies and of the systems they represented — it symbolized the conquest of nature itself for socialism or for freedom and the use the physical world could be put to in constructing a social system or in confronting its enemies.

At the beginning of the Cold War, nuclear technology stood at the core of the conflict. U.S. possession of the secrets of atomic energy created a push for wider global responsibilities among U.S. political leaders and fueled deep-felt suspicions within the Communist movement about U.S. plans for controlling their countries. The Soviet quest to develop a nuclear capability of its own was — as David Holloway has explained — a key feature in Moscow's establishment of a Cold War world view. The future of socialism depended on the Soviet Union matching the technological achievements of the imperialist states. Without a Soviet bomb, the socialist world would be inherently weak and under constant pressure.

But nuclear technology was not only important for the military aspects of the conflict. In the late 1940s and early 1950s the battle for access to energy resources formed part of the core Cold War competition, and atomic energy was of course a vital part of that battle. Both on the Soviet and the American side degrees of modernity were measured in energy output — it was as if Lenin's adage that "Communism is workers' power plus electricity" held true in both Moscow and Washington. As the Soviet Union dramatically increased its energy output in the 1950s — the first Soviet nuclear power plant became operational in 1954 — there was a widespread sense that Moscow's model of development could eventually overtake that of the United States.

One of the biggest surprises that early Cold Warriors would have been in for, had they still been with us in the 1980s and 1990s, was that it was neither nuclear bombs nor nuclear power that came to decide the Cold War. After Nagasaki, the bombs were never used. After Three Mile Island and Chernobyl, nuclear power lost much of its luster, and some advanced industrial states, such as Sweden, are now closing down their nuclear plants. While nuclear technology therefore defends its place in Cold War history, more attention needs to be paid to other connections and implications of the relationship between the Cold War conflict and the development of science and technology.

As David Reynolds explains in his compelling survey of international trends since World War II, these connections are not difficult to find. Already in October 1945 Secretary of War Robert Patterson noted that "the laboratories of America have now become our first line of defense." Ten years later more than half of all spending, public or private, on industrial research and development in the United States went to defense projects. Crucial areas of technology that were opened up through defense-related funding include navigation systems, space exploration, and even genetics (including the Human Genome Project). But first and foremost, in terms of its short-term implications, the Cold War provided public funding for research in electronics and communications — the two areas of technology, it might be said, that most contributed to the global changes that took place during the Cold War, and to the way the conflict ended.

With regard to the development of global, interconnected communication systems, it has been argued that the Soviet Union collapsed because, in the words of one author, it "did not get the message." In 1985, the Soviet Union had around one-sixth as many telephone connections as the United States, and — as everyone who visited with the Soviets can testify to — those that did exist often did not work very well. By the mid-1970s, however, the Soviets had communications satellites in orbit, as a result of their enormous investments in space technology, that could have been used to connect the Soviet Union to the emerging communication networks and to spread the Soviet message to the world. Why didn't that happen?

There are two meaningful ways of answering that question. The first is that the failure to link up was the result of decades of Soviet isolation — in part self-imposed, in part enforced. On the one hand, there was Moscow's fear that, as one former CPSU leader put it, "with their technology comes their political system and their culture." On the other hand, there was the Western urge to isolate the Soviets, in part so that their political system would suffer from not having access to the newest technology. But there are also more inherent reasons for the Soviet communications failure. Not only did the peoples of Eastern Europe show by the direction of their antennas that they preferred Dallas to Dresden but also the Soviet leadership simply did not want to invest in more elaborate wars of propaganda, since they knew that socialism was winning in the long run. Contrary to the general perception at the time, it was the United States that was the propaganda master of the Cold War, in terms of both effort and resources spent.

The other main technology with an immediate Cold War relevance was, of course, the development of computers. Like advanced communications, the first computers were all for military use in the United States and Britain, and, as a technology, came out of the needs of World War II. In the United States, the history of the development of computers is very much connected to the history of one company, IBM, and one business leader, Thomas J. Watson. In the 1950s over half of IBM's revenues came from the analog guidance computer for the B-52 Bomber and from the SAGE air defense system. As Watson himself put it: "It was the Cold War that helped IBM make itself the king of the computer business."

The Soviet Union, it could be argued, was not far behind the West in computer development in the early 1960s. But then something happened. Even though the U.S. military took 50 percent of the overall production of computer chips as late as 1967, by 1964 the Pentagon procurers had begun to look outside the big companies for some of their needs. It was this increasing flexibility in the U.S. military-industrial-academic complex in the mid-1960s — or, to put it more bluntly, the marriage between easy defense money and Bay Area flower-power — that created the crucial breakthrough, the commercially available personal computer. This was something the Soviet Union would not want to match — its research went into big computers for big purposes.

It was out of the need to link small (but available) computers at different U.S. military research centers that the first long distance computer network, ARPAnet, developed in the 1960s. This union of computer chips and communications — later to be known as the Internet — was perhaps the single most important technological innovation of the Cold War. By the late 1980s it came to define, in a very narrow sense, who was on the inside and who was on the outside. Linking the main capitalist centers more closely together in terms of business, trade, and education, the Internet came to underline exchange of all sorts, and was gradually spreading out of its original centers in North America, Japan, and Western Europe. Communications technology had become an important part of the message of global capitalism. Indeed, it could be argued that the market revolution of the late twentieth century — or *globalization* if one prefers to use that term — would not have been possible without the advances in communications that the Cold War competition brought on.

The Soviet Union and Eastern Europe were cut off from this development by choice as well as by design. The new communications technology made the East Bloc elites feel isolated in a different sense than before. By the late 1980s it seemed as if not just the Soviet Union's Western enemies but substantial parts of the rest of the world — East and Southeast Asia, Latin America, and parts of the Middle East — were moving *away* from interaction with it and toward a higher degree of interaction with each other. The ruling Communist parties, within their own countries, also had to compete with the image of the West as being more advanced, an image that was, in the case of Eastern Europe, projected daily into many people's homes through terrestrial or satellite antennas. In the end, Mikhail Gorbachev's *perestroika* project was about being included into the world that the satellite channels represented while upholding a degree of ideological challenge to the system that had created them. His was no surprising failure, although the consequences of that failure rightly stunned the world.

In the little that has been written so far by historians about the role of technology in the Cold War, their overall relationship has often been reduced to the simple question of which political and social system delivered and which did not. Looking at Cold War technology in the way I have tried to present it here, this is perhaps the wrong question to ask. It is better, I think, to explore the purposes for which technology was developed in its different settings and to discuss the way the military-technological policies on both sides contributed to the direction of science and to the many weapons with which the Cold War was fought — from strategic missiles to satellite transmissions and computer networks.

Against this proposition of making the history of technology a key aspect of the new Cold War history, it is sometimes said that we are confusing categories, that technology is in its essence politically and ideologically neutral. In the strictest sense this is of course true. For individual scientists it is the thrill of discovery that matters, not the specific purposes for which the invention will later be used. But if we want to understand the Cold War in terms not just of diplomacy and warfare but also in terms of social and political development, we need to look more closely at how technology was created, for what purposes it was used, and how some aspects of it came to define, in very concrete terms, the final stages of the Cold War conflict. We need to explore the links between military priorities and technological development and to be open to the suggestion that innovation in some key areas during the past fifty years moved in directions it would not have taken had it not been for the Cold War.

Approached along these lines, I believe that the interplay between technology, politics, and social development forms one of the most useful prisms through which to view the East-West conflict. Such research would not just deal with "technological imperatives" (if there ever was such a thing), but more profoundly, begin to see the Cold War as a conflict of the core concepts of modernity, an essential part of which was what direction technological innovation should take and for what means its products should be used. This conflict took on a particular significance for areas *outside* Europe and North America, since their meeting with modernity, and, eventually, with capitalism, to a great extent happened during the Cold War era. As I will explore in the next section, there is little doubt that these encounters would have been less unhappy and less destructive had it not been for the globalization of the Cold War conflict and the superpower interventions that this produced.

The Third World

The concept of three worlds is often seen as a product of Cold War perceptions: A first (in every sense) world consisting of the main capitalist states; a second (alternative) world made up of the Soviet Union and its allies; and a third (-class) world constituting the rest. Interestingly, this etymology is almost certainly wrong; the term *Tiers monde* was first developed by the French economist and demographer Alfred Sauvy in 1952 to denote a

political parallel to the Third Estate (*Tiers état*) of the French Revolution —
Sauvy's point was to underline the revolutionary potential that the new
countries in Africa, Asia, and Latin America would possess in relation to the
existing bipolar world system. Sauvy and many of those theorists who
adopted the term envisaged a Third World that, like its illustrious predecessor in France, would rise against and overturn the established order(s).

In terms of the Third World's actual fate during the Cold War, Sauvy
could not have been further from the truth. Instead of overturning the
international system, many Third World countries became its main victims through the extension of Cold War tensions to their territories.
Central America, Angola, Afghanistan, Indonesia, Indochina, Korea —
the list of countries that have had their futures wrecked by superpower
involvement is very long indeed, and many of these countries are still not
beginning to come to terms with the consequences of their predicament.

But equally damaging to the new states that were created in the aftermath of World War II was the willingness of Third Word elites themselves
to adopt Cold War ideologies for purposes of domestic development and
mobilization. This wholesale takeover of aerial and divisive ideas by feeble
states caused untold damage not only through warfare but also through
social experiments inspired by both socialist and capitalist versions of
high modernism. From rural resettlement programs in Indonesia and
Thailand and strategic villages in South Vietnam, to collectivization in
Ethiopia and five-year plans in Mozambique and Angola, the social and
human cost of the attempts by Third World elites to force change on
unwilling societies has been frightful. In some cases, such as in South
Vietnam or in Ethiopia, it makes sense to speak of a continuous war
against a peasantry that had to be "transformed" — and fast — if the version of modernity that the regime had bought into should be able to
overcome its rivals.

The main significance of the Cold War for the Third World (and of the
Third World for the Cold War) seems to me to be this: That the ideological
rivalry of the two superpowers came to dominate Third World politics to
such an extent that in some countries it delegitimized the development
of the domestic political discourse that any state needs for its survival.
As a result, the elites in these countries increasingly isolated themselves
from the peasant population and, in the end, sought a superpower ally in
order to wage war on their own people. Guatemala after 1954 and
Ethiopia after 1974 are good cases in point.

Seen from a U.S. perspective during the Cold War, this was, of course,
not quite the way things looked. The United States's Third World allies
were most often seen, by both supporters and critics of U.S. Cold War
policies, as local powerholders who joined with the United States in order
to fight communism and preserve their own privileges. They were "traditionalists" — a term that in the early 1960s quickly made the leap from
modernization theory textbooks to State Department dispatches.

Few general descriptions could, in my opinion, be further from the truth.
When we look at their actions and their beliefs, leaders such as Indonesia's

Suharto and the last Pahlavi shah in Iran were, in their way, revolutionaries, who attempted to create completely new states based on authoritarian high modernist visions of social transformation. Like leaders in Western Europe, their main source of inspiration was the United States, but their societies were much further removed from that ideal in social, ideological, and technological terms. Just as Mao Zedong in the late 1950s spoke about "catapulting" China into socialism, Suharto and the shah wanted to catapult their countries into advanced capitalism. Not surprisingly, since human societies cannot be formed into projectiles aimed at ideological images, none of them had much success.

The civil wars in the Third World during the Cold War era therefore often began as clashes between a center that had adopted one form or the other of high modernist ideology and movements on the periphery that saw themselves as defending their values and customs. Like all wars, however, these conflicts transformed because of the levels of violence, uprooting, and destruction that they created. This transformation was often as much ideological as military or strategic. In many cases, these calamitous wars provided unique opportunities for revolutionary movements to recruit adherents to their beliefs, and thereby transform peasant communities into armies of rebellion. The Chinese Communist Party is a good case in point: In the first phase of the Cold War, radical socialist movements in the Third World often began their march to power by defending local areas against imperialist armies, or "modernizing" states, or simply against encroachments by capitalist practices that, for the peasants, could be as destructive as warfare or forced labor.

The second phase of the Cold War, beginning in the early 1960s, saw an extension of this pattern. With decolonization, within two decades more than one hundred new states emerged, each with elites that had their own ideological agendas, often connected up to the ideals constituted by the superpowers. Instead of reducing tensions in society, decolonization — for the formerly colonized — often increased them, and gave rise to state administrations that were, for the peasants, *more* intrusive and *more* exploitative than the colonial authorities had been. As a result, most of the new states became chronically unstable in both political and social terms.

Had it not been for the existence of these new states, it is likely that the Cold War conflict, in its 1940s and 1950s form, would have petered out sometime in the 1960s, with the stabilization of European borders and the Soviet post-Stalin "normalization." What prolonged the conflict was its extension into areas in which the Cold War ideological duality had no relevance for the majority of the people, but where U.S. and Soviet leaders convinced themselves that the postcolonial states were theirs to win or lose. Local Third World elites were therefore able to attain Great Power allies in their wars against their peoples, and the organizations opposing them could often forge their own foreign links, in some cases based on the most incongruous of ideological alliances, such as U.S. support for radical Islamist parties in Afghanistan. What changed from the early Cold War, however, was the pattern of superpower involvement: During the 1980s, it was as often the Soviet Union as the United States that found itself on the side of the government against the rebels.

In this latter point I think there is an important clue to how we may be changing our understanding of the relationship between the Cold War and developments in Africa, Asia, and Latin America. As seen from within many Third World societies, the United States was as much of a revolutionary force as was the Soviet Union — the two, and those who adopted elements of their ideologies, emphasized standardization, engineering, and planning; the orders that they wanted to establish were distinctly Western, with roots going back to the Enlightenment and the eighteenth century. I was struck by this recently when I attended a series of oral history conferences on the Vietnam wars with former Secretary of Defense Robert McNamara as one of the main participants. As far as I could see, McNamara and his former North Vietnamese enemies still lived in completely different worlds as to their understanding of the war *except* when talking about the social changes that they had attempted to foist on Vietnamese society — McNamara's "villagization" was only a few steps away from the North's collectivization in terms of its effects (unfortunately both intended and real). Like Mao Zedong — perhaps the most destructive utopian of the past century — both sides viewed the peasants as "blank slates, on which the most wonderful texts may be written."

The civil rights movement changed the United States forever and mobilized a generation to activism. News of blacks fighting for equal rights in the segregated South — being attacked by dogs, clubbed, fire hosed by white policemen, and murdered by racists — brought racial oppression to the consciousness of white Americans who had mostly been content to ignore it since Reconstruction. Southern white hatred and resistance outraged northern public sentiment and embarrassed Washington. The movement overturned Jim Crow laws, which had divided the South into white and black, unjustly distributing rewards and services of society, keeping black adults in menial jobs, black children in understaffed and under-equipped schools, and both routinely subject to social humiliation and physical brutality. This movement, with its own historians and historiography, continues to have a massive impact on the study of the history of the United States.

Work on civil rights, which is profuse and growing fast, has led to a much deeper understanding of black protest throughout the twentieth century and thus of American and African American history. Scrutiny of the movement has moved from studies of its leaders during what biographer Taylor Branch has named the King Years (1954–1968) to studies of the unsung participants and their antecedents in protest going back as far as Reconstruction. Early historians were also sometimes participants and, like subsequent historians, always sympathetic with the movement's goals. In this large sense, there has been no central debate about the civil rights movement, although there have been diverse lines of investigation, a remarkable expansion of the historical canvas on which scholars analyze the movement, and controversies about aspects of the movement.

Questions about strategies and mobilization have interested historians eager to understand the huge outpouring of energy and hope that so indelibly marked the 1950s and 1960s. Martin Luther King's extraordinary power to bring people together and generate optimism still fascinates scholars, although many historians are dissatisfied with analyses that stress King's importance. Historians have examined class relations among blacks within the protest tradition and the overlap and tension between liberal-style protests insisting on civil rights and utilizing nonviolent direct action and Black Power protests insisting on economic justice and an end to police violence against blacks and justifying armed self-defense. Historians disagree over the relationship between these two strands of action. Gender relations in the movement, largely unexplored until the 1980s, are an ongoing concern for historians.

Recently, historians have begun exploring the effects of the Cold War and anticolonialism around the globe on the movement. Studies are providing a deeper understanding of the religious roots and influences on the movement, although the religious foundation for much civil rights activism has long been common knowledge.

Although Jim Crow has become a distant memory, affirmative action has proved vulnerable to challenge, black poverty remains disproportionately high, and ever-increasing numbers of black men are being incarcerated and disenfranchised. Impatient with continuing manifestations of racism and with "ongoing conservative efforts to bury the memory of sixties radicalism via the 'culture wars,'" historians have begun asking new questions about the movement and are inspecting the long-term effects of the once-sacrosanct *Brown v. Topeka Board of Education* decision.[1] Among them is Charles Eagles, who, in 2000, criticized the historiography for lacking balance and called for more studies of white resistance and accommodation as well as a more objective stance toward the movement altogether. Some scholars have begun examining white resistance to civil rights, with some seeing it as a direct result of *Brown*. Others are reevaluating the Black Panthers and Black Power. And a continuing stream of local studies, including works on northern communities, have illuminated different approaches to activism, many with important perspectives and insights on the development of the whole movement.[2]

Early historians tended to conceptualize the movement as national with King at its head and its greatest victories in the Supreme Court, Congress, and the White House.[3] These works located the movement's beginning with the *Brown* decision of 1954 and saw its culmination in the 1963 March on Washington, where King delivered his "I Have a Dream" speech, and the Civil Rights Act of 1964. King's arrival in the national consciousness with the *Brown* decision and his assassination in 1968 during the period of militant black resistance helped identify him with the years in which the movement, committed to nonviolence, attracted its most intense popular support. Historians like Harvard Sitkoff identified King's death in 1968 as the end of the movement's effectiveness. Today there is general agreement that after the passage of the Civil Rights Act of 1964 and King's subsequent emphasis on poverty and its relation to the war in Vietnam, the movement began to fragment. However, there is disagreement about the origins, efficacy, and support for the new prominence of Black Power. And many historians see the

---

[1] See, for example, Daryl Scott, *Contempt and Pity: Social Policy and the Image of the Damaged Black Psyche, 1880–1996* (Chapel Hill, N.C., 1997).

[2] Cedric Johnson, *Revolutionaries to Race Leaders: Black Power and the Making of African American Politics* (Minneapolis, 2007), xxxiv; Charles Eagles, "Toward New Histories of the Civil Rights Era," *Journal of Southern History* 66 (2000): 815–48.

[3] For useful essays on civil rights historiography, see Steven F. Lawson, "Freedom Then, Freedom Now: The Historiography of the Civil Rights Movement," *Journal of American History* 96 (April 1991): 456–71. See also Steven F. Lawson, *Civil Rights Crossroads: Nation, Community, and the Black Freedom Struggle* (Lexington, Ky., 2003); Kevern Verney, *The Debate on Black Civil Rights in America* (Manchester, U.K., and New York, 2006); Mark Newman, *The Civil Rights Movement* (Westport, Conn., 2004).

struggle for civil rights continuing into the 1970s, and some to the present day.[4]

Taylor Branch's monumental three-volume study, *America in the King Years*, is among the most detailed and offers the broadest scope of the many works on King.[5] David J. Garrow's *Bearing the Cross: Martin Luther King Jr. and the Southern Christian Leadership Conference* has become the invaluable standard reference on King's life and his organization. Garrow followed this work with an eighteen-volume series, *Martin Luther King and the Civil Rights Movement* (Brooklyn, N.Y., 1989), containing four decades of sources from many disciplines that shed light on King and the movement from the traditional standpoint of civil rights studies. Regarding the movement from King's point of view inevitably emphasizes its national dimension and impact and focuses on the years 1954 to 1968.

Bearing the Cross gives readers an intimate and balanced view of King's development as a man, a theologian, and a national leader. Garrow's study of King is not adulatory, but he manages to communicate King's ability to move audiences, to negotiate with any and all kinds of people, and to keep his heart set on nonviolence even as he witnessed — or experienced — grievous harm. This volume displays King's constant struggle to maintain the semblance of unity among the disparate sectors of the movement, to continue leading despite unceasing threats on his life and that of his family, and to try to keep the movement's momentum going in the face of deadly racist violence, a mostly indifferent and manipulative federal government, and competing desires among activists. Garrow's portrait is the more haunting because he does not spare us King's flaws. King was only too aware of his own shortcomings, and Garrow's delineation of his ruthless self-criticism makes his ability to have articulated and, in some measure, to embody the highest ethical aspirations of the nation all the more powerful. Garrow skillfully places King in a broad intellectual and global context, so that the reader understands the growth of his political agenda and his decision to express openly his opposition to the war in Vietnam and to focus on economic injustice not

---

[4]For a view of civil rights up through Hurricane Katrina in 2006, see Manning Marable, *Race, Reform, and Rebellion: The Second Reconstruction and Beyond in Black America, 1945–2006* (Jackson, Miss., 2007); on Black Power see, for example, Jama Lazerow and Yohuru Williams, eds., *In Search of the Black Panther Party: New Perspectives of a Revolutionary Movement* (Durham, N.C., 2006); Peniel Joseph, ed., *The Black Power Movement: Rethinking the Civil Rights–Black Power Era* (New York, 2006); Peniel Joseph, *Waiting 'Til the Midnight Hour: A Narrative History of Black Power in America* (New York, 2006); Andrew Witt, *The Black Panthers in the Midwest: The Community Programs and Services of the Black Panther Party in Milwaukee, 1966–1977* (New York, 2007); Lance Hill, *The Deacons for Defense: Armed Resistance and the Civil Rights Movement* (Chapel Hill, N.C., 2004); Daniel Matlin, "'Lift Up Yr Self!' Reinterpreting Amiri Baraka (LeRoi Jones), Black Power, and the Uplift Tradition," *Journal of American History* 93 (2006).

[5]Taylor Branch, *Parting the Waters: America in the King Years, 1954–1963, Pillar of Fire: America in the King Years, 1963–1964,* and *At Canaan's Edge: America in the King Years, 1965–1968* (New York, 1988, 1998, 2006); Stephen B. Oates, *Let the Trumpet Sound: A Life of Martin Luther King Jr.* (New York, 1982); David L. Lewis, *King: A Critical Biography* (Baltimore, 1970); David J. Garrow, *Bearing the Cross: Martin Luther King Jr. and the Southern Christian Leadership Conference* (New York, 1986); Stewart Burns, *To the Mountaintop: Martin Luther King Jr.'s Sacred Mission to Save America, 1955–1968* (San Francisco, 2004), is a recent example of King biography.

just civil rights. Above all, Garrow's portrait of King reflects the book's title: we see a man who reluctantly agreed to lead, and who wearied under the strain. As King said on receiving the Nobel Peace Prize, "There would always be 'the temptation of wanting to retreat to a more quiet and serene life' but one could not surrender to it. One must go forward bearing the weight of one's burden, whether one wanted to or not."[6]

Ambitious as Garrow's book is, Taylor Branch sets out to describe an even broader subject: evolving race relations in the King years. Writing with wit and energy, he weaves together gripping stories of high politics, local organizing, social movements like the development of the Nation of Islam, and the sometimes conflicting efforts of CORE (Congress for Racial Equality), the NAACP (National Association for the Advancement of Colored People), and SNCC (Student Nonviolent Coordinating Committee) in addition to King's SCLC (Southern Christian Leadership Conference). The undertow of tragedy tugs at Branch's narrative, as does his admiration for King's unwavering commitment to nonviolence and participatory democracy. "His oratory mined twin doctrines of equal souls and equal votes in the common ground of nonviolence. . . . King himself upheld nonviolence until he was nearly alone among colleagues weary of sacrifice. To the end, he resisted incitements to violence, cynicism, and tribal retreat. He grasped freedom seen and unseen, rooted in ecumenical faith, sustaining patriotism to brighten the heritage of his country for all people. These treasures abide with lasting promise from America in the King years."[7]

However much both authors eschew pieties about King and locate him in the swirling hopes and forces unleashed by World War II and the *Brown* decision, nevertheless understanding civil rights through the lens of King is controversial, and was so even at the time. One SNCC worker complained that King had one foot in the cotton field and the other in the White House.[8] And later historians who have written from various local perspectives have argued that a national view of events was often irrelevant on the ground and served to diminish the significance of the countless grassroots initiatives that accounted for the movement's success. Many have argued that the movement created King and other leaders, not the reverse. Ironically, as Garrow and Branch show, King probably would have agreed with this.

Beginning in the late 1970s, many historians began bringing to bear on civil rights the tools and concerns of social historians who are eager to see how people's uncelebrated decisions and acts give shape to larger events. Scholars studied both individual southern communities and the South as a whole in the process of movement-building. They made the point that charisma was a common characteristic of African American Baptist ministers in the South and was not unique to King. Furthermore, the larger move-

[6]Garrow, *Bearing the Cross*, 365.

[7]Branch, *At Canaan's Edge*, 771.

[8]Adam Fairclough, "The Southern Christian Leadership Conference and the Second Reconstruction, 1957–1973," in David J. Garrow, ed., *We Shall Overcome: Martin Luther King and the Civil Rights Movement*, 3 vols. (Brooklyn, N.Y., 1989), 186.

ment needed a figure with King's qualities. Others would have stepped forward with similar attributes if King had not existed.[9]

Some scholars, like the sociologist Aldon Morris, focused not on King but on the "creativity of the black masses" who, he thought, were too often portrayed as unthinkingly responding to influences beyond their control.[10] His book, *The Origins of the Civil Rights Movement*, begins, pointedly, not in Montgomery, where King was drafted leader of the bus boycott, but the year before in Baton Rouge, where a seven-day boycott ended when city officials put almost all seating on Baton Rouge buses on a first-come, first-served basis. Morris shows what Montgomery learned from Baton Rouge. He also suggests that some of the reasons for King's assumption of leadership had nothing to do with his talents. Instead, his relatively new status in Montgomery meant that he had not accumulated a backlog of obligations or grievances. He was an innocuous choice.[11]

Nathan Huggins offered a middle position in 1987. To view civil rights activism through King's eyes was not succumbing to the Great Man fallacy of history, but provided a uniquely useful lens on a movement that can be difficult to understand. Huggins stressed the difficulty secular people have understanding the religious beliefs of the movement, particularly the belief that "undeserved suffering is redemptive," and that too many historians had failed to look closely at what King said that resonated so deeply with southern blacks.[12]

Another way of approaching the history of the movement has been to study civil rights organizations or the civil rights activities of a particular city or region. Both kinds of studies shift the focus from King, and taken as a whole, give a sense of the remarkably multifaceted nature of the movement as well as its broad, robust base. Community studies began coming out in 1979 and included accounts of Greensboro, North Carolina; Tuskegee, Alabama; St. Augustine, Florida; and Jackson, Mississippi.[13] Historians focusing on particular cities saw the civil rights movement as part of a much longer battle, beginning, in some cases, with economic conflict during the depression, or with the changes in racial relations initiated during World War II. Through their local perspectives and emphases on the long fight, these

---

[9]See, for example, Clayborn Carson, "Martin Luther King, Jr., Charismatic Leadership in a Mass Struggle," *Journal of American History* 74 (September 1987): 448–54; Manning Marable makes this case very persuasively in *Race, Reform, and Rebellion*, 77–81; Aldon Morris discusses the availability of charismatic ministers in *The Origins of the Civil Rights Movement: Black Communities Organizing for Change* (New York, 1984), 7–8.

[10]Morris, *Origins*, v–vi.

[11]Ibid., 17–25.

[12]Nathan Irvin Huggins, "Martin Luther King, Jr., Charisma and Leadership," *Journal of American History* 74 (September 1987): 477–81.

[13]William Chafe, *Civilities and Civil Rights: Greensboro, North Carolina, and the Black Struggle for Freedom* (New York, 1980); David Colburn, *Racial Change and Community Crisis: St. Augustine, Florida, 1877–1980* (New York, 1985); Robert J. Norrell, *Reaping the Whirlwind: The Civil Rights Movement in Tuskegee* (New York, 1985); John Salter, *Jackson, Mississippi: An American Chronicle of Struggle and Schism* (Hicksville, N.Y., 1979).

studies contradicted a common belief about the movement, cultivated by movement participants to stress its spontaneous and indigenous nature: that it had sprung up spontaneously because Rosa Parks had tired feet one day. The truth, they argued, was far more complex, and the effort was much longer and more widespread.

Robert Norrell's *Reaping the Whirlwind*, for example, located the beginning of the civil rights movement in Tuskegee, Alabama, in 1941, but traced its roots as far back as 1870 when white Democrats began their campaign of violence to reverse the gains blacks had achieved in Reconstruction, particularly in holding political office.[14] Norrell began his account in 1941 for two reasons. First, because that is when members of the Tuskegee faculty and Civic Association decided to challenge the procedures that prohibited blacks from registering to vote. (Requirements for whites included either $300 worth of property or literacy, but the white election officials demanded of blacks literacy *and* property and also compelled them to have two white people to vouch for their character.) Second, with America's entry into World War II, Tuskegee became the location of a segregated military base to train black pilots.

Norrell's starting point coincides with the beginning of a local controversy within the black community about whether to accommodate to the segregated world or to engage in the politics of integration. This debate paralleled the old debate between Booker T. Washington and W. E. B. Du Bois over the best way for blacks to make their way in a hostile white society and would have parallels later. Militants in the late 1960s condemned accommodation and self-help, but by the 1970s when blacks had replaced whites in government in Tuskegee, Washington's philosophy had been rediscovered and revalued.[15]

Community studies have proliferated, including studies of Tennessee; Wichita, Kansas; San Francisco; Phoenix; Philadelphia; Michigan; Los Angeles; and New York City. All have brought to light little known activists and events; some also have contributed to an analysis of the dynamics of the whole movement.[16] For example, Adam Fairclough inferred from his work on Louisiana

---

[14]Robert Weisbrot, *Freedom Bound: A History of America's Civil Rights Movement* (New York, 1990), begins his account of the movement in Reconstruction as well, but then skips to Montgomery in 1955, 1–18. Vincent Harding in his introductory section to Clayborne Carson, David J. Garrow, Vincent Harding, and Darlene Clark Hine, eds., *A Reader and Guide to Eyes on the Prize* (New York, 1987), begins with the first slave ships, but then skips to the *Brown* decision.

[15]Norrell, *Reaping the Whirlwind*, 35–50, 203–13.

[16]See, for example, Matthew J. Countryman, *Up South: Civil Rights and Black Power in Philadelphia* (Philadelphia, 2006); Sidney Fine, *Expanding the Frontier of Civil Rights: Michigan, 1948–1968* (Detroit, 2000); Peter B. Levy, *Civil War on Race Street: The Civil Rights Movement in Cambridge, Maryland* (Gainesville, Fla., 2003); Matthew C. Whitaker, *Race Work: The Rise of Civil Rights in the Urban West* (Lincoln, Neb., 2005); Peter F. Lau, *Democracy Rising: South Carolina and the Fight for Black Equality since 1865* (Lexington, Ky., 2006); James Phillips Noble, *Beyond the Burning Bus: The Civil Rights Revolution in a Southern Town* (Montgomery, Ala., 2003); Daniel Crowe, *Prophets of Rage: The Black Freedom Struggle in San Francisco, 1945–1969* (New York, 2000); Bobby Lovett, *The Civil Rights Movement in Tennessee: A Narrative History* (Knoxville, Tenn., 2005); Diane McWhorter, *Carry Me Home, Birmingham, Alabama: The Climactic Battle of the Civil Rights Revolution* (New York, 2001).

that the larger movement occurred in two acts, one beginning in the 1930s and 1940s, led by the NAACP and CORE, that mobilized networks of activists. McCarthyism and accompanying repression stifled this movement between 1947 and 1955. The second act emerged with the Montgomery bus boycott, but grew from earlier activism.[17]

Martha Biondi's thought-provoking 2004 study of New York City located the origins of the civil rights movement and particularly Black Power in New York where African Americans from 1945 to 1955 battled for better jobs, an end to police brutality, access to new housing, more representation in government, access to colleges for black students, and against existing legal racial barriers to blacks' betterment. This movement got the city and the state to pass antidiscrimination laws that became the model for national legislation. The New York movement, which was not for formal civil rights alone but for complete equality, clearly joined the civil rights and Black Power fights as African Americans in New York articulated what would become urban black political demands across the country, including criminal justice reform and affirmative action.[18]

J. Mills Thornton, studying three cities in Alabama, discovered that local political and economic developments determined which southern cities produced powerful movements. Economic growth in selected urban areas encouraged a political revolution of rising expectations among blacks there. This, Thornton contends, explains the difference between dynamic centers like Selma, Birmingham, and Montgomery, for example, and other towns in Alabama where no struggle ensued. In Thornton's view, conventional civil rights histories cannot account for the variations among localities and incorrectly ascribe them to the choices of national movement leaders. But it was local activism and preexisting militancy that attracted the national leadership. In fact, local leaders emerging from ongoing direct action struggles invited SCLC rather than the other way around.[19]

Thornton's story of Selma, Montgomery, and Birmingham, like so many other local studies, de-centers the movement from King and SCLC. It also stresses the lengthy history of black resistance to oppression, which focusing on the "King years" tends to obscure. The scholarship on the main civil rights organizations also shifts the camera away from King. Historical accounts of the four major movement organizations — the NAACP, CORE, SCLC, and SNCC — have greatly enriched our understanding of the movement. Scholars disagree on the relative importance of the groups as did participants at the time, but by describing the diversity of membership, ethos, and strategies of these organizations they have contributed to a complex portrait of the movement.

---

[17]Adam Fairclough, *Race and Democracy: The Civil Rights Struggle in Louisiana, 1915–1972* (Athens, Ga., 1995), xii.

[18]Martha Biondi, *To Stand and Fight: The Struggle for Civil Rights in Postwar New York City* (Cambridge, Mass., 2004).

[19]J. Mills Thornton, *Dividing Lines: Municipal Politics and the Struggle for Civil Rights in Montgomery, Birmingham, and Selma* (Tuscaloosa, Ala., 2002), 9, 11, 17.

For forty years no complete study of the NAACP emerged, but memoirs, biographies, and monographs have raised important questions about the relation of the black masses to the NAACP's emphasis on litigation and civil rights, its elite leadership, and its goals of integration and equal rights — issues which can seem irrelevant to the very poor.[20] In 1962, Louis Lomax criticized the NAACP for stodgy tactics, centralized and unresponsive leadership, and elitism. Like Lomax, frustrated activists had respect for the NAACP's work that culminated in the *Brown* decision, but they had a jaundiced view of the relatively privileged makeup of its members and its on-again-off-again support for direct action.[21]

August Meier, reviewing Lomax's book in 1962, defended the NAACP, although he would later criticize it himself. He argued that it was natural in an organization as old as the NAACP to have a bureaucracy and be less flexible than newer associations like CORE and SNCC but that the NAACP *had* engaged in "direct action," sit-ins, and other demonstrations.[22] Nevertheless, when Meier collaborated with Elliot Rudwick in a 1973 work on CORE, he suggested that the NAACP's victories were not always meaningful because they could not be enforced. For example, in 1947 CORE activists organized the Journey of Reconciliation in which eight black and eight white men left on a bus tour of the Upper South to protest nonviolently segregation on public transportation. They found that although an NAACP legal challenge to a bus company operating in Virginia had already been successful, the bus company had done nothing to change its practices. This suggested to the founders of CORE the need for direct action and the brittle nature of the NAACP's single-minded focus on the law.[23]

Mark Tushnet's *The NAACP's Legal Strategy against Segregated Education, 1925–1950*, considered the NAACP's effectiveness on education. Tushnet, influenced by critical legal theory, saw the law as more than formal decisions and arguments in a social vacuum. He described all litigation as a "social process" in which enforcement of a decision was as important as the decision itself. He argued that the NAACP therefore could not have been very distant from or unresponsive to the communities in which it worked, since it had to rely on local support for its effectiveness.[24] He showed that while NAACP lawyers did often persuade clients that integrated education was the primary goal they should fight for, not, for example, equalizing racially sep-

---

[20]Many books cover NAACP activists and activities like Jack Greenberg, *Crusaders in the Courts* (New York, 1994); Genna Rae McNeil, *Groundwork: Charles Hamilton Houston and the Struggle for Civil Rights* (Philadelphia, 1983); Charles Flint Kellogg, *NAACP* (Baltimore, 1967); Roy Wilkins with Tom Matthews, *Standing Fast* (New York, 1982); Richard Kluger, *Simple Justice* (New York, 1975).

[21]Louis Lomax, *The Negro Revolt* (New York, 1962).

[22]August Meier, Book Review of Louis Lomax, *The Negro Revolt*, in David J. Garrow, ed., *We Shall Overcome*, vol. 2, 729–35.

[23]August Meier and Elliot Rudwick, *CORE: A Study in the Civil Rights Movement, 1942–1968* (New York, 1973), 34.

[24]Mark Tushnet, *The NAACP's Legal Strategy against Segregated Education, 1925–1950* (Chapel Hill, N.C., 1987), 151–53.

arate educational facilities, this strategy could not have played out success-fully without the support and cooperation of the black community. Where such support did not exist — in North Carolina, for example — the NAACP failed to accomplish its objectives.[25]

One study illuminated changing class strategies of the NAACP. Beth Tompkins Bates described the NAACP in 1941 uncharacteristically reach-ing out to working-class African Americans at the moment when unionized blacks had achieved some visibility and leverage in the labor movement. Walter White, head of the NAACP, supported a UAW strike against Ford, consciously hoping to attach the new mass of working-class blacks in Detroit to the NAACP. White called for collective action and publicly associated the labor movement with the NAACP, traditionally composed of elite blacks and dedicated to civil rights, not economic struggles.[26]

Gilbert Jonas published a history of the NAACP in 2005, claiming that it *was* the civil rights movement from its founding in 1909 on. Jonas recounts the organization's legal and political struggles with the justifiable pride of a participant. In his account of the NAACP's struggle against the Communist Party he argues that Truman was the only reliable friend of African Americans in the 1940s, and reveals that Thurgood Marshall cooperated with J. Edgar Hoover in tracking Communists. Jonas portrayed civil rights leader Roy Wilkins with great admiration, arguing that his politics, which some criticized as too moderate, derived from his understanding that blacks were and will be a small minority of the American population and could achieve change only with the support of whites. He described the ambivalence Wilkins felt about the lionization of King, while the NAACP was, in Wilkins's view, always the heart of positive change for African Americans.[27]

The *Brown* decision, won on arguments devised by members of the NAACP, is perhaps the most famous Supreme Court decision of the last cen-tury and has attracted considerable attention from legal scholars, among others, who have been evaluating its status in an era in which there is no con-sensus on the goal of integration in schools nor progress toward it. White flight, private schools, federal and local policies that have increased the pov-erty and furthered the ghettoization of inner cities have discouraged schol-ars about the decision and its aftermath. Furthermore, the country is debating the proper conduct of the Supreme Court. Conservatives, who now dominate the Court, find the Warren Court's "activism" in support of social justice unacceptable, while liberals find laissez-faire jurisprudence equally "activist" and supporting an unjust status quo. Thus, the debate over *Brown* is also about the role of the courts in changing the conditions of social, political, and eco-nomic life.

---

[25]Tushnet, *Legal Strategy*, 138–66.
[26]Beth Tompkins Bates, "The New Crowd Challenges the Agenda of the Old Guard in the NAACP," *American Historical Review* 102 (1997): 340–77.
[27]Gilbert Jonas, *Freedom's Sword: The NAACP and the Struggle against Racism in America, 1909–1969* (New York, 2005), 147–50, 303–56; see also Kenneth Robert Janken, *White: The Biography of Walter White, Mr. NAACP* (New York, 2003); see also Eagles, "Toward New Histories of the Civil Rights Era," 815–16.

Legal scholar Michael Klarman has argued that the decision itself was unimportant and would have been a failure without legislation that followed it, that the political climate was ready to see changes, and that Jim Crow would have dissolved anyway. Klarman also argued that *Brown* catalyzed the extraordinary reaction and backlash in the South that has been at the root of conservatism of the last decades. Mark Tushnet rejected his argument that social change was happening anyway, seeing in it a denial of black agency in pushing on all fronts for equality — in schools and elsewhere. And King biographer David Garrow asserted that *Brown* was directly responsible for the Montgomery bus boycott and much else that followed.[28]

Other scholars have directly taken on the question of the liberal jurisprudence of the 1960s and its place in the civil rights movement. J. Morgan Kousser wrote that *Brown* and surrounding legislation were relatively successful until recently when the counterrevolution of "colorblind justice" undermined both *Brown* and the Fourteenth Amendment by convincing the government to ignore racial discrimination past and present. Kousser likened this to a new conservative redemption, overturning the Second Reconstruction as effectively, but without the bloodshed of the first redemption in 1877.[29]

Others, like Lani Guinier, have argued that *Brown* was flawed. According to her, it was argued on grounds that were too narrow — psychological prejudice — against a target that was too small — school segregation. Without a much more comprehensive understanding of the way racial thinking had grown to control the nation's ideas about status — without a new "racial literacy" — integration could not change the vast economic and power inequalities that upheld and verified the nation's understandings of race.[30] The *Brown* decision is generating interpretive disagreements in an era in which it is eclipsed and in which the role of the Supreme Court is contested.

August Meier and Elliot Rudwick argued in 1973 that CORE, founded in 1942 in Chicago, not the NAACP, was the precursor of civil rights methods and concerns. CORE activists were committed to Gandhian nonviolence, dedicating themselves to loving their enemies and refusing violence no matter what the provocation, even if it meant dying.[31] This philosophical foundation and CORE's flexible direct action approach provided the basis for

---

[28]Michael Klarman, *From Jim Crow to Civil Rights: The Supreme Court and the Struggle for Racial Equality* (New York, 2004); Mark Tushnet, "The Significance of *Brown v. Board of Education,*" *Virginia Law Review* 80 (February 1994): 173–84; David Garrow, "Hopelessly Hollow: Revisionist Devaluing of *Brown v. Board of Education,*" *Virginia Law Review* 80 (February 1994): 151–60.

[29]J. Morgan Kousser, *Colorblind Justice: Minority Voting Rights and the Undoing of the Second Reconstruction* (Chapel Hill, N.C., 1999). See also James T. Patterson, *Brown v. Board of Education: A Civil Rights Milestone and Its Troubled Legacy* (New York, 2001). See also Ken Kersch, *Constructing Civil Liberties: Discontinuities in the Development of American Constitutional Law* (New York, 2004); and Denise C. Morgan, Rachel D. Godsil, and Joy Moses, *Awakening from the Dream: Civil Rights Under Siege and the New Struggle for Equal Justice* (Durham, N.C., 2006).

[30]Lani Guinier, "From Racial Liberalism to Racial Literacy: *Brown v. the Board of Education* and the Interest-Divergent Dilemma," *Journal of American History* 91 (2004): 92–118; see also Daryl Scott, *Contempt and Pity: Social Policy and the Image of the Black Psyche, 1880–1996* (Chapel Hill, N.C., 1997).

[31]Meier and Rudwick, *CORE*, 12.

Meier's and Rudwick's claim that it pioneered the strategies and philosophy of the civil rights activists. In summing up CORE's contribution to the civil rights movement, Meier and Rudwick cautioned readers not to see organizational failure, that is, the subsequent quick decline of CORE as an organization, as the same as the failure of its goals, which were, in many cases, achieved. Ironically, CORE's decline was the result of its success in getting the 1964 Civil Rights Act passed. It also had to cope with the increasing fragmentation of the black movement and with growing rejection of its integrated structure. As a new mass movement, no longer a small, northern, integrated one, CORE moved toward a black nationalist agenda, eschewed nonviolence, and focused on the battles still unwon: the inequities of capitalism that played particular havoc with the lives of black Americans. Raymond Arsenault recently added a valuable perspective on CORE's impact. In his book, *Freedom Riders,* Arsenault narrated the experiences and significance of the roughly 400 activists, many of whom were CORE members, who rode buses and trains in small integrated groups in 1961 to test the new federal legislation against Jim Crow transportation. Arsenault showed that the Freedom Riders' heroism injected vitality and power into CORE and SNCC as a victorious example of direct action. Although the riders themselves embraced and practiced nonviolence, that has not, ironically, been central to their legacy.[32]

The history of SCLC has been tied much more closely than any other organization to perceptions of King. Initially some scholars like August Meier looked at SCLC as organized around King solely to glorify him, raise money, and do his bidding.[33] Later historians have seen it as just one expression of a multifaceted movement. SCLC developed in 1957 in response to the need that national figures, such as Ella Baker, Stanley Levison, and Bayard Rustin, felt for a coordinating organization to give direction to the many local demonstrations that emerged all over the South. According to Aldon Morris, SCLC "was the force that developed the infrastructure of the civil rights movement." SCLC's southern church base was important to its successes and its legitimacy in the South as well as to its failures, such as when the organization went to Chicago and tried to deal with northern racism and poverty.[34]

Despite the feelings of some SNCC members that SCLC tended to take credit for the arduous work SNCC had been doing and its conviction that SCLC was bourgeois and too religious, Adam Fairclough argued that the two organizations maintained fairly good relations. For example, SNCC, unlike the NAACP, approved of King's 1965 announcement that he was against the Vietnam War.[35] Fairclough assessed SCLC as successful in the South, but not in the North. Thomas R. Peake, in *Keeping the Dream Alive,*

---

[32]Meier and Rudwick, *CORE*, 409–31; James Farmer, *Freedom — When?* (New York, 1965), 79; see also Raymond Arsenault, *Freedom Riders, 1961 and the Struggle for Racial Justice* (New York, 2006), 513.

[33]August Meier, quoted in Fairclough, "SCLC," 232.

[34]Morris, *Origins*, 83; Fairclough, "SCLC," in Garrow, ed., *We Shall Overcome*, vol. 1, 231–48.

[35]Fairclough, "SCLC," 240–43.

contended that SCLC had made a creditable start on the enormous problems of the urban North. It had managed to force concessions out of Chicago's wily Mayor Richard Daley even if he reneged on his promises.[36]

SNCC has fascinated scholars from its early days, and many of its members wrote important memoirs describing the group's work and ethos.[37] The group's founding statement from 1960 captures its philosophy. "We affirm the philosophical or religious ideal of nonviolence as the foundation of our purpose, the presupposition of our faith, and the manner of our action. . . . Mutual regard cancels enmity. Justice for all overthrows injustice. The redemptive community supersedes systems of gross social immorality."[38]

Ella Baker, SNCC's originator and guiding spirit, had been thinking about leadership for a long time, and the sexism of SCLC and King went against her most cherished egalitarian ideals.[39] Baker believed that change could only come about when people transformed themselves from passive objects of others' decisions to activists on behalf of social justice for themselves and their communities. SNCC came into being in 1960 after Baker called a "Southwide Student Leadership Conference on Nonviolent Resistance to Segregation" inviting about 600 students to live out her ideas, including the four who had initiated the sit-in in Greensboro, North Carolina.[40]

SNCC worked with rural blacks isolated from schools and services. The vote would be only one of many changes that they would themselves come to demand. SNCC quite self-consciously was, as Clayborne Carson has written, trying "to create new social identities for participants and for all Afro-Americans."[41]

SNCC's increasing militancy after 1964 led some historians to see it as a metaphor for the whole movement. In 1981, Harvard Sitkoff published *The Struggle for Black Equality, 1954–1980* in which he depicted SNCC's turn toward black nationalism and Black Power as the end of the civil rights movement.[42] Political scientist Emily Stoper, instead, attributed SNCC's decline to internal stresses as outsiders entered the "redemptive community" without sharing its moral vision and transformative experiences. The influx of strangers in the "Freedom Summer" of 1964 and SNCC's own inability to deal with everyday politics — that is, compromises and trade-offs — brought the organization to implosion.[43]

---

[36]Thomas R. Peake, *Keeping the Dream Alive: A History of the Southern Christian Leadership Conference from King to the Nineteen Eighties* (New York, 1987).

[37]For example, Anne Moody, *Coming of Age in Mississippi* (New York, 1968); Sara Evans, *Personal Politics: The Roots of the Women's Movement in the Civil Rights Movement and the New Left* (New York, 1979).

[38]Quoted in Robert A. Goldberg, *Grassroots Resistance: Social Movements in Twentieth-Century America* (Prospect Heights, Ill., 1991), 149.

[39]Joanne Grant, *Ella Baker, Freedom Bound* (New York, 1998), 105–25.

[40]Quoted in Goldberg, *Grassroots Resistance*, 149; Richard King, *Civil Rights and the Idea of Freedom* (Athens, Ga., 1996).

[41]Quoted in Lawson, "Freedom Then," 457.

[42]Harvard Sitkoff, *The Struggle for Black Equality, 1954–1980* (New York, 1981), 199–220.

[43]Emily Stoper, "The Student Nonviolent Coordinating Committee, Rise and Fall of a Redemptive Organization," in Garrow, ed., *We Shall Overcome*, 1041–62; Lawson, "Freedom Then," 470–71.

Joanne Grant's biography of Ella Baker traces SNCC's decline to exhaustion and harassment by the FBI. She marks its collapse beginning with what Baker regarded as the rigged election of Stokely Carmichael as chairman. Grant portrays Baker as tolerant of SNCC's turn toward black nationalism and away from nonviolence because she understood the psychological needs of battle-fatigued activists.[44] Recently, Wesley Hogan has argued that the organization changed when activists lost their patience with the slow and difficult labor of creating democratic relations and began to value rhetorical skills over building "freedom [from] the inside."[45]

In 2003, Michael Thelwell published posthumously the political autobiography of Kwame Ture (Stokely Carmichael) who ascended to the chairmanship of SNCC after giving a speech in 1966 in Greenwood, Mississippi, in which he invoked Black Power for the first time. Ture refuted many of the claims that writers had made about a rift between him and King, or between SNCC and King. He wrote that King argued against using the phrase *Black Power* because it would frighten off potential support, particularly in the white world. But he agreed that black communities should address their own issues and articulate their own demands. In retrospect, Ture agreed with King's strategy in the sense that he was surprised by the storm of liberal outrage that the phrase unleashed, before he had even attempted a definition of it and a program for future activism. The NAACP, on the other hand, Ture described as lining up with white liberals and conservatives to denounce Black Power before it had been defined. In Ture's view white liberals led the charge against the slogan they interpreted as racist, separatist, and threatening.[46]

If Ture was surprised about the commotion Black Power evoked, J. Mills Thornton's work commented on the cultural need that Black Power filled. Thornton, writing about the movement in general, not SNCC, insisted that pessimism and low expectations dominated the grass roots until some hard-won breakthrough would momentarily encourage activists. Black self-esteem through Black Power found a ready audience.[47]

In addition to community studies and organizational histories, scholars have expanded the study of the movement by looking at it from the perspectives of gender, class, and labor. Gender openly played a prominent and early role in SNCC's history, unlike that of the other civil rights organizations. This is because of its high percentage of female participants, Ella Baker's leadership, its early ethos of profound egalitarianism and what has been described as a "female style of activism,"[48] and the youth of SNCC participants, some of whom would become active in women's liberation politics. Sara Evans, in *Personal Politics* (1979), famously argued that SNCC women went on to generate the women's liberation movement after experiencing their

---

[44]Grant, *Freedom*, 125–210.
[45]Wesley C. Hogan, *Many Minds, One Heart: SNCC's Dream for a New America* (Chapel Hill, N.C., 2007), 254–55.
[46]Stokely Carmichael with Ekwueme Michael Thelwell, *Ready for Revolution: The Life and Struggles of Stokely Carmichael [Kwame Ture]* (New York, 2003), 501–35.
[47]Thornton, *Dividing Lines*, 7.
[48]Lawson, "Freedom Then," 469.

own leadership capabilities in a nurturing — but still sexist — environment.[49] More recently, a number of SNCC women have written of their experience of power but have largely denied the sexism.[50] In 1988, Mary King remembered the paper she coauthored on gender in 1964 as less protest about sexism than a call for SNCC to return to a more "decentralized and democratic" ethos. "We were asking SNCC, will there be room for us as women to act on our beliefs as we had with the early vision of SNCC with the sit-ins?" Another analysis suggests that white and black women experienced the movement differently, particularly during the summer of 1964 when an influx of northern white students resulted in considerable interracial sex and crosscurrents of social tension new to the group.[51]

Recent memoirs, biographies, and studies of women have continued to reveal their significance to the movement.[52] Elaine Brown's description of her years with the Black Panthers and her slow awakening to feminism is one of many discussions of the unique difficulties black women have experienced in insisting on women's rights in the context of pervasive racism.[53] Deborah Gray White's *Too Heavy a Load* puts the dilemma of African American women in civil rights into a longer perspective while exploring painful class divisions among black women. These divisions, she argues, have inhibited cross-class alliances and repeatedly failed to address the needs of the poor. White reveals the tremendous pressure on women in civil rights organizations to shelve their demands for equality with men in the interests of the struggle for racial equality and particularly singles out the Black Power movement for its misogyny.[54]

Belinda Robnett's *How Long? How Long?* demonstrated how women supplied connective tissue between people in local neighborhoods and the movement leadership. Scholars have studied women's activism in Durham, North Carolina; Jewish women activists joining the movement; women in the Louisiana NAACP; and privileged southern white women's participation. Steve Estes has also studied constructions of masculinity from the civil rights and Black Power eras of the movement to ask questions about gender and the different ways whites and blacks have seen citizenship. A recent investigation of women and religion brings together two growing subfields that prom-

---

[49]Evans, *Personal Politics*, 83–101, 126–55.

[50]Lawson, "Freedom Then," 468–69; Aimee Koch, "The Women of SNCC," unpublished paper, Amherst College, 1999.

[51]Cheryl Lynn Greenberg, ed., *A Circle of Trust: Remembering SNCC* (New Brunswick, N.J., 1998), 130; Lawson, "Freedom Then," 469.

[52]Martha Prescod Norman, "Shining in the Dark," in Ann D. Gordon with Bettye Collier-Thomas, John H. Bracey, Arlene Voski Avakian, Joyce Avrech Berkman, eds., *African American Women and the Vote, 1837–1965* (Amherst, Mass., 1997), 172–99; see especially Kathryn Nasstrom, "Down to Now: Memory, Narrative, and Women's Leadership in the Civil Rights Movement in Atlanta, Georgia," in *Gender and History* 11 (April 1999): 113–44.

[53]Elaine Brown, *A Taste of Power: A Black Woman's Story* (New York, 1992); see also Paula Giddings, *When and Where I Enter: The Impact of Black Women on Race and Sex in America* (New York, 1984); Pauli Murray, *Pauli Murray: The Autobiography of a Black Activist, Feminist, Lawyer, Priest, and Poet* (Knoxville, Tenn., 1987).

[54]Deborah Gray White, *Too Heavy a Load: Black Women in Defense of Themselves, 1894–1994* (New York, 1999), 219; see also Giddings, *When and Where.*

ise much to students of civil rights. Despite the importance of religion to the large majority of civil rights activists, there has been little scholarship on it until recently.[55]

Economic justice is inextricably bound to the struggle for equality, and some historians have focused on the struggle for good jobs and fair wages as a primary aspect of the fight for racial justice. They usually begin such studies in the depression era. In 1978, Harvard Sitkoff argued that the New Deal was a crucial time in which progress generated optimism for further change in the black community. He believed that the depression and the New Deal "constituted a turning point in race relations trends." The most positive results in interracial activity, Sitkoff argued, flowed from the CIO's and, in particular, the United Mine Workers' active promotion of racial equality. These interracial union experiences supported greater black militancy. Although the struggle for civil rights was sidelined during the depression as economic issues were on the nation's mind, interracial labor activism was key in preparing blacks to demand their civil rights in the 1950s.[56]

Robert Korstad and Nelson Lichtenstein, writing in the late 1980s, agreed with Sitkoff that the movement's roots were in the depression and early 1940s. They emphasized the new urban, working-class character of the black masses. The migration of the 1940s and 1950s transported more than 2 million blacks from the rural South to the urban North and another million to southern urban centers. Black voters registered in northern and southern cities in great numbers; they joined both the NAACP and unions. The CIO was the center of the civil rights struggle in the depression and the 1940s. Unionization provided blacks with a link to a government sympathetic to labor, and this opened a window through which black demands could be heard.[57] The expanding economy of the mid-1940s produced a period of high employment, high wages, and a supportive and widely felt federal presence, which helped blacks push for a civil rights–oriented labor movement. However, the end of the war and the onset of the Cold War radically transformed this environment and temporarily put an end to the gains blacks were making.

When blacks began organizing through their churches and stressing nonviolence and Christian fellowship, they were able to develop support in much of the nation for increased civil rights. When, however, the movement's

---

[55]Belinda Robnett, *How Long? How Long?: African American Women in the Struggle for Civil Rights* (New York, 1997); Christina Greene, *Our Separate Ways: Women and the Black Freedom Movement in Durham, North Carolina* (Chapel Hill, N.C., 2005); Debra Schultz, *Going South: Jewish Women in the Civil Rights Movement* (New York, 2001); Bettye Collier-Thomas and V. P. Franklin, *Sisters in the Struggle: African American Women in the Civil Rights–Black Power Movement* (New York, 2001); Lee Sartain, *Invisible Activists: Women of the Louisiana NAACP and the Struggle for Civil Rights, 1915–1945* (Baton Rouge, La., 2007); Gail S. Murray, ed., *Throwing Off the Cloak of Privilege: White Southern Women Activists in the Civil Rights Era* (Gainesville, Fla., 2004).

[56]Harvard Sitkoff, *A New Deal for Blacks: The Emergence of Civil Rights as a National Issue* (New York, 1978), ix.

[57]Robert Korstad and Nelson Lichtenstein, "Opportunities Found and Lost: Labor Radicals, and the Early Civil Rights Movement," *Journal of American History* 75 (1988): 786–811.

focus shifted to poverty and its causes, they were unable to find the same kind of support. They were hampered in this, conclude Korstad and Lichtenstein, because McCarthyism undermined and racially split the integrated labor movement over communism two decades earlier.[58] This was the legacy that prevented widespread mobilization around the economic issues that King and others came to articulate with more and more frequency after 1964.

More pessimistically than these authors, Nikhil Pal Singh argued in *Black Is a Country* in 2004 that unless one sees the civil rights movement in the context of the development of the welfare state, beginning with Franklin D. Roosevelt, it is impossible to understand the nation's long-term commitment to racial exclusion. Looking at the movement in the short term suggests that the Black Power movement created a backlash, ending African American gains, but "willfully ignores historically entrenched opposition to even the most modest civil rights reforms throughout the white South" and even in the North after World War II. In Singh's view, the movement did not produce full citizenship for blacks, which, he says, becomes ever more evident as the value of "formal citizenship depreciates under the pressure of inegalitarian distribution and is remanded under the auspices of excessive policing and punishment."[59]

Two recent scholars of the relation of labor to civil rights have focused on the integration of the textile industry in the South. One looked back to the fights of the 1930s between a white labor force and white management as the source of contemporary successes in integrating textile factories. The other found gains in integrating the industry in the decades from 1960 to 1980 through federal regulations, not labor shortages or other market forces. Nancy MacLean's 2006 study of changes in the workplace, *Freedom Is Not Enough*, showed that there has been a notable shift toward hiring blacks and that minority groups like Hispanics fighting for good jobs follow the lead of African American activists. She also argued that leaving workers and the fight for jobs out of the civil rights story helps to validate the right-wing view that formal equality and civil rights are enough. She has called for more scholarship in this field.[60]

Robin D. G. Kelley in *Hammer and Hoe: Alabama Communists during the Great Depression* demonstrated that civil rights activism in Alabama in the 1960s picked up where Communists had left off at the end of the depression.[61] Building on work like this, many contemporary scholars have explored the

---

[58]Korstad and Lichtenstein, "Opportunities," 801–11; see also John Egerton's *Speak Now against the Day: The Generation before the Civil Rights Movement in the South* (Chapel Hill, N.C., 1994) for an elegiac evocation of the years 1932–1954 in Atlanta and a discussion of anticommunism and its effect on race relations, 553–72.

[59]Nikhil Pal Singh, *Black Is a Country: Race and the Unfinished Struggle for Democracy* (Cambridge, Mass., 2004), 8, 214.

[60]Nancy MacLean, *Freedom Is Not Enough: The Opening of the American Workplace* (Cambridge, Mass., 2006), 342.

[61]Lawson, "Freedom Then," 463; Robin D. G. Kelley, *Hammer and Hoe: Alabama Communists during the Great Depression* (Chapel Hill, N.C., 1990); Karen Sacks, *Caring by the Hour: Women, Work, and Organizing at Duke Medical Center* (Urbana, Ill., 1988).

relationship between the Cold War and the civil rights movement from a wide range of perspectives.

Mary Dudziak, among the first scholars to put the movement into the larger framework of the Cold War, found that the latter provided opportunities to civil rights leaders to use the world's heightened scrutiny of the United States to push for change. On the other hand, leaders also had to rein in the movement's economic agenda for fear of persecution as Communists.[62] Azza S. Layton, a political scientist, gave an account of Truman's progressive program against racism, including integrating the military and pushing a civil rights plank at the 1948 Democratic Party convention because he was afraid that segregation was hindering America's success in the Cold War. She shows how African American leaders petitioned the UN and exposed U.S. racial politics in order to make headway in civil rights.[63] These works emphasize the Cold War dynamic in producing civil rights gains and also put domestic policy into a global context as scholars in other fields are doing.

In an essay evaluating the NAACP's relationship with the Cold War, Manfred Berg argues that it was not a "glorious chapter in the association's history" and that it was opportunistic in picking its way through the McCarthy years. The leadership did not join Americans for Democratic Action, the foremost liberal, anticommunist pressure group, in censuring McCarthy. On the other hand, Berg says it did not conduct witch hunts or purges within its own ranks, while it maintained its legitimacy for the work to come.[64]

Related works discuss African American expatriates in Ghana and the development of a diasporic or not-nationally bounded consciousness among African Americans in the Cold War years. Penny Von Eschen studied African American anticolonial thinkers of the 1940s who argued for equalizing global power relations by empowering emerging nations. These black intellectuals saw race, not nationality, linking 400 million people through their African heritage. Slavery, the global exploitation of people of color, and the development of "racial capitalism" constituted their shared experience.[65] The U.S. government harassed these activists, like Paul Robeson and W. E. B. Du Bois, and marginalized the Council on African Affairs that supported anticolonial movements in Africa.

---

[62]Mary Dudziak, *Cold War Civil Rights: Race and the Image of American Democracy* (Princeton, N.J., 2000), 13–14.

[63]Azza S. Layton, *International Politics and Civil Rights Policies in the U.S., 1941–1960* (New York, 2000); for other takes on this question, see Brenda Gayle Plummer, ed., *Window on Freedom: Race, Civil Rights, and Foreign Affairs, 1945–1988* (Chapel Hill, N.C., 2003) and *Rising Wind: Black Americans and U.S. Foreign Affairs, 1935–1960* (Chapel Hill, N.C., 1996); Manfred Berg, "Black Civil Rights and Liberal Anticommunism: The NAACP in the Early Cold War," *Journal of American History* 94 (2007): 75–96; Jeff Woods, *Black Struggle, Red Scare: Segregation and Anticommunism in the South, 1948–1968* (Baton Rouge, La., 2004); Thomas Borstelmann, *The Cold War and the Color Line: American Race Relations in the Global Arena* (Cambridge, Mass., 2001).

[64]Berg, "Black Civil Rights and Liberal Anticommunism," 95.

[65]Penny Von Eschen, *Race against Empire: Black Americans and Anticolonialism, 1937–1957* (Ithaca, N.Y., 1997), 3–4.

Kevin Gaines's fascinating study of American expatriates in Nkrumah's Ghana explored similar themes, finding a transnational outlook in figures like Malcolm X and W. E. B. Du Bois who shared Nkrumah's anticolonialism but were ultimately disappointed when his desire for rapprochement with the United States pushed him into liberal rather than radical democratic politics. However, Gaines argued that despite the U.S. effort to delegitimize and discourage transnational solidarity among black people, anticolonialism, African decolonization, and the goal of nonalignment, embraced by emerging nations like India, nevertheless powerfully influenced African Americans' political consciousness.[66]

When Charles W. Eagles in 2000 called for balance and objectivity in covering the movement, he pointed to the need for studies of white response.[67] Scholars rose to the challenge. Unsurprisingly, many focused on Mississippi, the most recalcitrant and arguably the most violently racist state of the Deep South. Yasuhiro Katagiri examined the Mississippi State Sovereignty Commission, which was founded in 1956 expressly to resist civil rights and was the most active states' rights and pro-segregation organization in the South. Joseph Crespino's *In Search of Another Country* (2007) investigated how elite white Mississippians permitted just enough accommodation to the new civil rights protocol to stay out of trouble but managed to retain command of the region's economy and political structures. Crespino looked at Mississippi's role in the conservative counterrevolution beginning in 1980, shifting the lens from presidential politics and coded racist language to the economic changes in the South that created a broad pro-corporate, anti-union, antitax consensus. Crespino began with white resistance to *Brown*, but linked support for segregation to broader conservative trends that have mobilized much of rural and suburban America (see Chapter 11). Clive Webb's edition of essays, *Massive Resistance*, detailed the origins of the White Citizens' Council in 1954 in Mississippi, but looked at reaction in many regions: the widespread repression of the NAACP, economic punishments for black citizens who registered and voted, the failure of the federal government to enforce *Brown* and protect blacks, and the erosion of the political center in the South. Dennis A. Deslippe studied resistance in Detroit, illuminating the battle of white policemen against "reverse discrimination" or affirmative action in the 1970s. Such studies underline the unity of the northern and southern civil rights movement, the economic demands that followed the legislation of 1964 and 1965, and the nuclei of reaction developing across all parts of the country.[68]

---

[66]Kevin K. Gaines, *American Africans in Ghana: Black Expatriates in the Civil Rights Era* (Chapel Hill, N.C., 2006), 23, 20, 25.

[67]Eagles, "Toward New Histories."

[68]Yasuhiro Katagiri, *The Mississippi State Sovereignty Commission: Civil Rights and States' Rights* (Jackson, Miss., 2001); Joseph Crespino, *In Search of Another Country: Mississippi and the Conservative Counterrevolution* (Princeton, N.J., 2007); Clive Webb, ed., *Massive Resistance: Southern Opposition to the Second Reconstruction* (New York, 2005); see also J. Todd Moye, *Let the People Decide: Black Freedom and White Resistance Movements in Sunflower County, Mississippi, 1945–1986* (Chapel Hill, N.C., 2004); Dennis A. Deslippe, "'Do Whites Have Rights?'" White Detroit Policemen and "'Reverse Discrimination' Protests in the 1970s," *Journal of American History* 91 (2004): 932–60.

Other scholars have explored how reactions to *Brown* changed over time in places less fiercely reactionary than Mississippi. Matthew D. Lassiter and Andrew B. Lewis documented Virginia's varied replies to school integration as battles between hard-line segregationists and the NAACP resulted in closing the schools. The authors exposed the depth and diversity of the ideas of those in the middle as well as how they maneuvered to get the schools reopened and integrated in 1959.[69]

Just as scholars have begun to study white response and resistance to the movement, so they have begun to study the Black Power movement and the Black Panther Party as important and legitimate developments, not simply counterproductive manifestations of frustration that were opposed to the "real" or "good" civil rights movement. Jane Rhodes has provided a study of the creation and control of the image of the Panthers in the media and in American memory. Jama Lazerow and Yohuru Williams also edited an important volume of essays, and Peniel Joseph has published both an edited collection and a narrative history of the Black Panthers. Black Power activists articulated many of the demands integral to equality for blacks, such as prison reform, jobs, racial justice for the poor, welfare rights, and black studies programs. Martha Biondi's study of New York City exposed the continuity — indeed, the inextricability — of civil rights and Black Power concerns. The anticolonial thinking of Black Power advocates also links them and their thought with the new historiography on the relation of the Cold War to civil rights activism. Scholars working in this field call for a study of the "long Black Power movement" to show its duration, continuity with, and enrichment of the fight for political equality in the South in the late fifties and early sixties. Offering a more critical view, Cedric Johnson's *Revolutionaries to Race Leaders* (2007) looks at the way the generation of radical leaders from the civil rights years came to moderate their goals and focus on race rather than work with people of all races for the more radical goals articulated in the 1960s — those of transforming the economic system and fundamentally redistributing power.[70]

Scholars of the Black Panther Party call it a victim of "egregious" historical neglect. Academics called the first conference on the Black Panthers only in 2004. Jane Rhodes wrote that few outside of specialists even notice such conferences, but "this one met with swift and fierce condemnation."[71]

---

[69]Matthew D. Lassiter and Andrew B. Lewis, *The Moderates' Dilemma: Massive Resistance to School Desegregation in Virginia* (Charlottesville, Va., 1998); Jason Sokol, *There Goes My Everything: White Southerners in the Age of Civil Rights, 1945–1975* (New York, 2006); see also Alexander Leidholdt, *Standing before the Shouting Mob: Lenoir Chambers and Virginia's Massive Resistance to Public School Integration* (Tuscaloosa, Ala., 1997).

[70]Jane Rhodes, *Framing the Black Panthers: The Spectacular Rise of a Black Power Icon* (New York, 2007); Jama Lazerow and Yohuru Williams, *In Search of the Black Panther Party: New Perspectives on a Revolutionary Movement* (Durham, N.C., 2006); Joseph, *Waiting 'Til the Midnight Hour*; Joseph, ed., *The Black Power Movement* (New York, 2006); David Blight, *Race and Reunion: The Civil War in American Memory* (Cambridge, Mass., 2001); David Burner, *Making Peace with the Sixties* (Princeton, N.J., 1996); Matlin, "'Lift Up Yr Self!'"; Cedric Johnson, *Revolutionaries to Race Leaders: Black Power and the Making of African American Politics* (Minneapolis, 2007).

[71]Rhodes, *Framing the Black Panthers*, 10.

Students of the party compare what happened to its history to David Blight's explanation of how northern and southern whites in the decades after the Civil War reunited by "forgetting" that slavery and emancipation were at the center of the war. In "making peace with the sixties," as David Burner titled his study of the period, whites designated a good and a bad civil rights movement, the first successful and completed, the second subversive, violent, and better forgotten. Jane Rhodes's research on the history of twentieth-century media images of black males as violent, dangerous, and angry shows how they overlapped with but altered the Panthers' own projections of their armed resistance to white violence. This produced a memory of threatening black masculinity divorced from its political objectives. The works of Rhodes and others on the Panthers aim to retrieve them from being marginalized as extreme cultural icons of black danger and to recall their political work, including the provision of services like breakfast programs to poor African American communities and their pursuit of participatory democracy through coalitions with left-wing, white people. The political aims of the Black Panthers' legacy have been all but wholly obscured by thirty years of academic neglect, demonization by liberals and the right wing alike, and the media's relentless concentration on their menacing cultural symbolism.

A key aspect to Black Power, as Stokely Carmichael and others articulated it, was armed self-defense. Scholars have studied Robert Williams and the roots of Black Power and self-defense in the South, but the most significant new study, *Deacons for Defense,* by Lance Hill explores the southern working-class movement that provided protection to civil rights workers, had shoot outs with the KKK, and offered an indigenous alternative to nonviolent direct action. The Deacons' frustration with nonviolence, with the NAACP's legal strategies, and the indifference of the white community to the murders and torture of blacks encouraged them to adopt armed self-defense to *avoid* white violence. They worked to create a new consciousness among black southerners, to develop their self-respect, and to fight for their political and economic gains by eliciting fear and respect from whites, not guilt and pity.[72]

As the civil rights movement recedes in time there remains plenty to discover and much to debate in its history. The work of restoring women to the movement is underway, but unfinished. Articulating a legitimate relationship between civil and economic rights becomes more and more crucial at a moment in history when there appears to be no alternative to capitalism. What was the significance of Black Power? What is its relationship to the politics of class? What did it mean to different people within the movement and without? Can all people, as Ella Baker believed, become their own leaders? What would that kind of transformation mean? Is nonviolence a workable strategy in a violent nation? What kinds of political tactics succeed in a conservative era? Manning Marable has referred to the civil rights movement as the Second Reconstruction in order to shine a spotlight on the historical

---

[72]On Robert Williams, see Joseph, ed., *The Black Power Movement,* 7; Lance Hill, *The Deacons for Defense: Armed Resistance and the Civil Rights Movement* (Chapel Hill, N.C., 2004).

relationship between economic and political justice. The failure of the federal government to provide economic security by distributing land to newly enfranchised freed people in the South made it possible for elite whites to deprive blacks of the vote and access to most benefits of society for more than a century. The majority of African American voters in the North and South still do not have the economic power to enforce their political will. Understanding the springs that fed the civil rights movement may help to mobilize other movements. The historical search for the conditions that produce an uncontainable enthusiasm for justice is always vital.

DAVID J. GARROW

from Martin Luther King, Jr., and the Spirit of Leadership   [1987]

DAVID J. GARROW (1953–) is professor of political science at the City College of New York and the City University Graduate Center. His books include *Bearing the Cross: Martin Luther King, Jr., and the Southern Christian Leadership Conference* (1986) and *Atlanta, Georgia, 1960–1961: Sit-Ins and Student Activism* (1989).

Martin Luther King, Jr., began his public career as a reluctant leader who was drafted, without any foreknowledge on his part, by his Montgomery colleagues to serve as president of the newly created Montgomery Improvement Association (MIA). Montgomery's black civic activists had set up the MIA to pursue the boycott of the city's segregated buses called by the Women's Political Council (WPC) immediately after the December 1, 1955, arrest of Rosa Parks.

King was only twenty-six years old and had lived in Montgomery barely fifteen months when he accepted that post on Monday afternoon December 5. Two years later King explained that "I was surprised to be elected . . . both from the standpoint of my age, but more from the fact that I was a newcomer to Montgomery." On December 5, however, King was as much anxious as surprised, for his new post meant that he would have to deliver the major address at that evening's community rally, which had been called to decide whether a fabulously successful one-day boycott would be extended to apply continuing pressure on bus company and city officials to change the bus seating practices. King later explained that he had found himself "possessed by fear" and "obsessed by a feeling of inadequacy" as he pondered his new challenge, but he turned to prayer and delivered a superb oration at a jam-packed meeting that unanimously resolved to continue the protest.

David J. Garrow, "Martin Luther King, Jr., and the Spirit of Leadership," *Journal of American History* 74 (September 1987). Reprinted with the permission of Copyright Clearance Center.

Initially King and his MIA colleagues mistakenly presumed that the boycott would be relatively brief, that white officials would be eager to negotiate a quick solution to the dispute. Indeed, the MIA's three modest demands asked not for the abolition of segregated seating, but only for the elimination of two troubling practices that the WPC had been protesting for several years: black riders never could sit in the ten front "white only" seats on each bus, no matter how crowded with black riders a bus might be, and black riders seated to the rear of the reserved section had to surrender their seats to any newly boarding white riders for whom front seats were not available. Instead, the MIA proposed, blacks would seat themselves from the rear forward, and whites from the front backward, without the two races ever sharing parallel seats. There would be no reserved seats, and no one would have to give up a seat once taken.

Only on Thursday afternoon December 8, after the first negotiating session had ended with the city evincing no willingness to compromise with the MIA's requests, did King and his colleagues begin to realize that the modesty of their demands would not speed white concessions. WPC president Jo Ann Robinson, reflecting back on the white obstinacy, explained that "they feared that anything they gave us would be viewed by us as just a start." The intransigence of the city and bus company officials continued at a second negotiating session and then a third, where King objected strenuously to the addition of a White Citizens Council leader to the city delegation. His objection angered several whites, who accused King himself of acting in bad faith. Still anxious about his leadership role, King was taken aback and left temporarily speechless. "For a moment," he later remembered, "It appeared that I was alone." Then his best friend and MIA partner, Rev. Ralph D. Abernathy, spoke up to rebut the white's claims. Thanks to that crucial assistance, King overcame his first major anxiety crisis since the afternoon of his election.

After that tense session, however, King's doubts about his ability to serve as the boycott's leader increased. He confessed to "a terrible sense of guilt" over the angry exchanges at the meeting, and he became painfully aware that white Montgomery had launched a whispering campaign against him personally. "I almost broke down under the continuing battering," King stated two years later. His MIA colleagues rallied around him, however, and made clear their full support.

By mid-January 1956, as the ongoing boycott received increased press coverage, King became the focal point of substantial public attention. That visibility made King a particular target when Montgomery's city commissioners adopted new, "get tough" tactics against the MIA. On Thursday, January 26, while giving several people a lift as part of the MIA's extremely successful car pool transportation system, King was pulled over by two policemen and carted off to the city jail on the fallacious charge of going thirty miles per hour in a twenty-five-mile-per-hour zone. For the first time since the protest had begun, King feared for his immediate physical safety. Initially, he was uncertain as to where the officers were taking him. "When I was first arrested," he admitted two years later, "I thought I was going to be lynched." Instead, King was fingerprinted and jailed for the first time in his life, thrown into a filthy group cell with a variety of black criminals. In a few moments' time, Abernathy and other MIA colleagues began arriving at the jail, and white officials agreed to King's release. His trial would be Saturday.

That arrest and jailing focused all the personal tensions and anxieties King had been struggling with since the first afternoon of his election. The increased news coverage had brought with it a rising tide of anonymous, threatening phone calls to his home and office, and King had begun to wonder whether his involvement was likely to end up costing him, his wife, Coretta, and their two-month-old daughter, Yolanda, much more than he had initially imagined. The next evening, January 27, King's crisis of confidence peaked. He returned home late, received yet another threatening phone call, and went to bed, but he found himself unable to sleep. He went to the kitchen, made some coffee, and sat down at the kitchen table. "I started thinking about many things," he later explained. He thought about the obstacles the boycott was confronting, and about the increasing threats of physical harm. "I was ready to give up," he remembered. "With my cup of coffee sitting untouched before me I tried to think of a way to move out of the picture without appearing a coward," a way to hand over the leadership of the MIA to someone else. He thought about his life up until that time. "The first twenty-five years of my life were very comfortable years, very happy years," King later recalled.

I didn't have to worry about anything. I have a marvelous mother and father. They went out of their way to provide everything for their children. . . . I went right on through school; I never had to drop out to work or anything. And you know, I was about to conclude that life had been wrapped up for me in a Christmas package.

Now of course I was religious, I grew up in the church. I'm the son of a preacher . . . my grandfather was a preacher, my great grandfather was a preacher . . . my daddy's brother is a preacher, so I didn't have much choice, I guess. But I had grown up in the church, and the church meant something very real to me, but it was a kind of inherited religion and I had never felt an experience with God in the way that you must . . . if you're going to walk the lonely paths of this life.

That night, for the first time in his life, King felt such an experience as he thought about how his leadership of the MIA was fundamentally altering what had until then been an almost completely trouble-free life.

If I had a problem, I could always call Daddy — my earthly father. Things were solved. But one day after finishing school, I was called to a little church down in Montgomery, Alabama, and I started preaching there. Things were going well in that church, it was a marvelous experience. But one day a year later, a lady by the name of Rosa Parks decided that she wasn't going to take it any longer. . . . It was the beginning of a movement,

. . . and the people of Montgomery asked me to serve them as a spokesman, and as the president of the new organization . . . that came into being to lead the boycott. I couldn't say no.

And then we started our struggle together. Things were going well for the first few days, but then, . . . after the white people in Montgomery knew that we meant business, they started doing some nasty things. They started making some nasty telephone calls, and it came to the point that some days more than forty telephone calls would come in, threatening my life, the life of my family, the life of my child. I took it for a while, in a strong manner.

That night, however, in the wake of his arrest and jailing and the continuing telephone threats, King's strength was depleted. Then, in what would forever be, in his mind, the most central and formative event in his life, Martin King's understanding of his role underwent a profound spiritual transformation.

"It was around midnight," he explained years later. "You can have some strange experiences at midnight." That last threatening phone call had gotten to him. "Nigger, we are tired of you and your mess now, and if you aren't out of this town in three days, we're going to blow your brains out and blow up your house."

I sat there and thought about a beautiful little daughter who had just been born. . . . She was the darling of my life. I'd come in night after night and see that little gentle smile. And I sat at that table thinking about that little girl and thinking about the fact that she could be taken from me any minute.

And I started thinking about a dedicated, devoted and loyal wife who was over there asleep. And she could be taken from me, or I could be taken from her. And I got to the point that I couldn't take it any longer. I was weak. Something said to me, you can't call on Daddy now, he's up in Atlanta a hundred and seventy-five miles away. You can't even call on Mama now. You've got to call on that something in that person that your Daddy used to tell you about, that power that can make a way out of no way.

And I discovered then that religion had to become real to me, and I had to know God for myself. And I bowed down over that cup of coffee. I never will forget it. . . . I prayed a prayer, and I prayed out loud that night. I said, "Lord, I'm down here trying to do what's right. I think I'm right. I think the cause that we represent is right. But Lord, I must confess that I'm weak now. I'm faltering. I'm losing my courage. And I can't let the people see me like this because if they see me weak and losing my courage, they will begin to get weak."

Then it happened.

And it seemed at that moment that I could hear an inner voice saying to me, "Martin Luther, stand up for righteousness. Stand up for justice. Stand up for truth. And lo I will be with you, even until the end of the

world." . . . I heard the voice of Jesus saying still to fight on. He promised
never to leave me, never to leave me alone. No never alone, no never
alone. He promised never to leave me, never to leave me alone.

That experience, that encounter in the kitchen, gave King a new strength
and courage to go on. "Almost at once my fears began to go. My uncertainty disappeared."

The vision in the kitchen allowed King to go forward with feelings of
companionship, of self-assurance, and of mission that were vastly greater
spiritual resources than anything he had been able to draw on during the
boycott's first eight weeks. It also allowed him to begin appreciating that
his leadership role was not simply a matter of accident or chance, but was
first and foremost an opportunity for service — not an opportunity King
would have sought, but an opportunity he could not forsake. His new
strength also enabled him to conquer, thoroughly and permanently, the
fear that had so possessed him that Friday night in his kitchen, while
allowing him to appreciate that although his calling might be unique, it
was the calling, and not himself, that was the spiritual centerpiece of his
developing role.

That strength and dedication remained with King throughout the
Montgomery protest, which ended in success, with the integration of the
city's buses just prior to Christmas 1956. In the wake of that achievement,
however, some whites directed repeated acts of violence against the newly
desegregated buses, and in mid-January a series of bombings struck several
black churches and the homes of MIA leaders. The violence weighed
heavily on a very tired King. Then, on Sunday morning January 27 — the
first anniversary of King's kitchen experience — twelve sticks of dynamite,
along with a fuse that had smoldered out, were found on the porch of
King's parsonage.

The murder attempt deeply affected King. In his sermon later that
morning to his Dexter Avenue Baptist Church congregation, he explained
how his experience one year earlier had allowed him to resolve his previous fears about the question of his own role and fate. "I realize that there
were moments when I wanted to give up and I was afraid but You gave me
a vision in the kitchen of my house and I am thankful for it." King told
his listeners how, early in the boycott, "I went to bed many nights scared
to death." Then,

early on a sleepless morning in January 1956, rationality left me. . . .
Almost out of nowhere I heard a voice that morning saying to me,
"Preach the gospel, stand up for truth, stand up for righteousness." Since
that morning I can stand up without fear.

So I'm not afraid of anybody this morning. Tell Montgomery they
can keep shooting and I'm going to stand up to them; tell Montgomery
they can keep bombing and I'm going to stand up to them. If I had to
die tomorrow morning I would die happy because I've been to the mountaintop and I've seen the promised land and it's going to be here in
Montgomery.

Those remarks, uttered in January 1957, and so clearly presaging the very similar comments that King made in Memphis, Tennessee, on the evening of April 3, 1968, bring home a simple but crucial point: that Martin Luther King, Jr.'s mountaintop experience did not occur in April 1968, nor even in August 1963, but took place in the kitchen at 309 South Jackson Street in Montgomery on January 27, 1956. King's understanding of his role, his mission, and his fate was *not* something that developed only or largely in the latter stages of his public career. It was present in a rather complete form as early as the second month of the Montgomery boycott.

Appreciating King's own understanding of his role and responsibilities is really *more* crucial than anything else, I would contend, to comprehending the kind of leadership that Martin Luther King, Jr., gave to the American black freedom struggle of the 1950s and 1960s. By 1963–1964, as that role and those responsibilities grew, King thought increasingly about his own destiny and what he termed "this challenge to be loyal to something that transcends our immediate lives." "We have," he explained to one audience, "a responsibility to set out to discover what we are made for, to discover our life's work, to discover what we are called to do. And after we discover that, we should set out to do it with all of the strength and all of the power that we can muster." As his close confidant Andrew Young later expressed it, "I think that Martin always felt that he had a special purpose in life and that that purpose in life was something that was given to him by God, that he was the son and grandson of Baptist preachers, and he understood, I think, the scriptural notion of men of destiny. That came from his family and his church, and basically the Bible."

The revelation in the kitchen gave King not only the ability to understand his role and destiny, but also the spiritual strength necessary to accept and cope with his personal mission and fate. Its effect was more profoundly an ongoing sense of companionship and reassurance than simply a memory of a onetime sensation. "There are certain spiritual experiences that we continue to have," King stated, "that cannot be explained with materialistic notions." One "knows deep down within there is something in the very structure of the cosmos that will ultimately bring about fulfillment and the triumph of that which is right. And this is the only thing that can keep one going in difficult periods."

King's understanding of his life underwent a significant deepening when he was awarded the 1964 Nobel Peace Prize. The prize signaled the beginning of a fundamental growth in King's own sense of mission and in his willingness to accept a prophetic role. "History has thrust me into this position," he told reporters the day the award was announced. "It would both be immoral and a sign of ingratitude if I did not face my moral responsibility to do what I can in this struggle."

More and more in those years King thought of his own life in terms of the cross. It was an image he invoked repeatedly, beginning as early as his 1960 imprisonment in Georgia's Reidsville State Prison. He focused particularly on it, and on the memory of his experience in the kitchen, at

times of unusual tension and stress. In mid-September 1966, amid a dete-
riorating intramovement debate about the "Black Power" slogan, King
talked about how his sense of mission was increasingly becoming a sense
of burden.

> We are gravely mistaken to think that religion protects us from the pain
> and agony of mortal existence. Life is not a euphoria of unalloyed com-
> fort and untroubled ease. Christianity has always insisted that the cross we
> bear precedes the crown we wear. To be a Christian one must take up his
> cross, with all its difficulties and agonizing and tension-packed content,
> and carry it until that very cross leaves its mark upon us and redeems us
> to that more excellent way which comes only through suffering.

More than anything else, the Vietnam War issue brought King face to
face with what was becoming a consciously self-sacrificial understanding
of his role and fate. He had spoken out publicly against America's conduct of the war as early as March 1965 and had stepped up his comments
during July and August 1965, but he had drawn back in the face of
harsh criticism of his views stimulated by the Johnson administration.
Throughout 1966, King largely had kept his peace, reluctant to reignite a
public debate about the propriety of the nation's leading civil rights
spokesman becoming a head-on critic of the incumbent administration's
uppermost policy. Then, in early 1967, King resolved to take on Lyndon B.
Johnson's war publicly as never before.

King knew full well that his new, aggressive stance on the war would
harm him politically and might well damage the civil rights movement
financially. Those considerations, however, were not enough to shake
King from his resolve. "At times you do things to satisfy your conscience
and they may be altogether unrealistic or wrong but you feel better," King
explained over wiretapped phone lines to his longtime friend and coun-
selor, Stanley Levison. America's involvement in Vietnam was so evil, King
explained, that "I can no longer be cautious about this matter. I feel so
deep in my heart that we are so wrong in this country and the time has
come for a real prophecy and I'm willing to go that road."

King's attacks on the war, and particularly his April 4, 1967, anti-war
speech at New York's Riverside Church, brought down a flood of public
criticism on his head. Even some of King's most trusted advisers, including Levison, reproached him for the tone of that speech. King, however,
rejected the complaints. "I was politically unwise but morally wise. I think
I have a role to play which may be unpopular," he told Levison. "I really
feel that someone of influence has to say that the United States is wrong,
and everybody is afraid to say it."

In late May 1967, King spoke to his aides about how he had come to
see the war issue in terms of his understanding of the cross.

> When I took up the cross, I recognized its meaning. . . . The cross is some-
> thing that you bear and ultimately that you die on. The cross may mean

the death of your popularity. It may mean the death of a foundation
grant. It may cut down your budget a little, but take up your cross, and
just bear it. And that's the way I've decided to go.

No longer did he suffer from any indecision on the question of Vietnam.

I want you to know that my mind is made up. I backed up a little when I
came out in 1965. My name then wouldn't have been written in any book
called *Profiles in Courage*. But now I have decided that I will not be intimidated. I will not be harassed. I will not be silent, and I will be heard.

King's determination to forge ahead in the face of discouraging political circumstances also manifested itself during the late 1967–early 1968
planning of the Poor People's Campaign, Washington protests intended
to be so "dislocative and even disruptive" that the federal government
would launch a full-scale program to eliminate poverty in America. On
March 28 King's determination to pursue the campaign faltered and
turned to despair when a protest march that he had helped lead in
Memphis, Tennessee, ended in widespread violence. The next day a
deeply depressed King poured out his feelings to Levison in a long phone
conversation. Levison refused to accept King's assertions that the Memphis
violence was an all-but-fatal blow to King's public status as a nonviolent
civil rights leader. King demurred. "All I'm saying is that Roy Wilkins, that
Bayard Rustin and that stripe, and there are many of them, and the
Negroes who are influenced by what they read in the newspapers, Adam
Clayton Powell, for another reason . . . their point is, 'I'm right. Martin
Luther King is dead. He's finished. His nonviolence is nothing, no one is
listening to it.' Let's face it, we do have a great public relations setback
where my image and my leadership are concerned." Levison disagreed,
but King insisted that the media reaction would be extremely damaging,
and that he would have to help stage a second, completely successful
Memphis march to overcome the damage from the first one.

King also told Levison that he was deeply pessimistic about the entire
Poor People's Campaign. "I think our Washington campaign is doomed."
Even though he had long been "a symbol of nonviolence" to millions, in
the press coverage of the March 28 violence "everything will come out
weakening the symbol. It will put many Negroes in doubt. It will put
many Negroes in the position of saying, 'Well, that's true, Martin Luther
King is at the end of his rope.'" Levison again responded that King ought
to reject the news media's portrayals. "You can't keep them from imposing it," King answered. "You watch your newspapers. . . . I think it will be
the most negative thing about Martin Luther King that you have ever seen."

King's expectations proved largely correct. The *New York Times*, terming
the Memphis violence "a powerful embarrassment to Dr. King," recommended he call off the Poor People's Campaign since it probably would
prove counterproductive to his cause. King, however, did not give up, and

on Wednesday, April 3, he returned to Memphis to aid in the preparations for a second march. That evening at the cavernous Mason Temple church, before a modest-sized but emotionally enthusiastic crowd, King vowed that both the Memphis movement and the Poor People's Campaign would go forward. Then he turned to an emotional recapitulation of his own involvement in the preceding thirteen years of the black freedom struggle, expressing how happy and thankful he was that he had been given the opportunity to contribute to and to live through its many significant events. Then he closed with the same ending he had used more than eleven years earlier in Montgomery when he had first explained how the vision in the kitchen had given him the strength and the courage to keep going forward.

> I don't know what will happen now. We've got some difficult days ahead. But it really doesn't matter with me now, because I've been to the mountaintop. And I don't mind. Like anybody, I would like to live a long life. Longevity has its place. But I'm not concerned with that now. I just want to do God's will. And he's allowed me to go up to the mountain, and I've looked over, and I've seen the promised land. I may not get there with you. But I want you to know tonight that we, as a people, will get to the promised land. And so I'm happy tonight. I'm not worried about anything. I'm not fearing any men. Mine eyes have seen the glory of the coming of the Lord.

In conclusion, then, I want to reiterate that the key to comprehending Martin King's own understanding of his life, his role, his burden, and his mission lies in that spiritual experience that began for him in his Montgomery kitchen on January 27, 1956. Martin King's awareness that his calling was to devote and ultimately to sacrifice his own individual life in the service of a great and just cause ennobled him as a human being, strengthened him as a leader, and allowed him to accept the symbolic role and accompanying fate that helped propel forward a struggle he rightfully recognized would be never ending.

KWAME TURE (STOKELY CARMICHAEL) AND EKWUEME MICHAEL THELWELL

from We Gotta Make This Our Mississippi   [2003]

EKWUEME MICHAEL THELWELL (1935–), a SNCC worker in the 1960s, has written numerous articles, stories, and screenplays, and, in 1980, published a novel, *The Harder They Come.* He is currently on the faculty at the University of Massachusetts, Amherst. Working with Kwame Ture (Stokely Carmichael) until his death, Thelwell wrote Ture's autobiography, *Ready for Revolution: The Life and Struggles of Stokely Carmichael,* published in 2003.

I mean it's passing strange how just about everything I've read about this march manages to completely miss the point. . . . It started with the press. Now I'm not saying that they printed straight-up lies, or that they outright made up stuff. No. No. No. But they may as well have. It's more what they *didn't* report, what they *couldn't* see, didn't see, or more likely, didn't *want* to see. Or equally what they *were* looking for and what they *wanted* to see. A failure of communication on our part and of understanding and emphasis on theirs. Whatever.

Hey, we read that the Deacons were there with (oh, horrors) *guns.* But not that after Meredith, no one else got shot and nobody was killed on our march. We read that whites were excluded. Not true. The "leaders" weren't invited but quite a few white supporters did march. We read that the numbers were down, meaning that support had "waned," but not that thousands of black folk turned out along the way, and that almost *five thousand* of them registered to vote in Mississippi for the first time. First draft of history, huh? What we miss in nearly all historical accounts is the most important aspect. The incredible spirit of self-reliance, of taking responsibility, of taking courage, which local people demonstrated. That it really had become for all those local people *their* real march against fear. Somehow that got missed? Gimme a break.

What the press saw, or thought it saw and reported stridently, and what has subsequently been recycled in second and third drafts of history, is that young militants turned on a beleaguered Dr. King. That an ideological struggle took place between SCLC and SNCC, between Dr. King and the "young firebrand" Carmichael. Gimme a break. That's not how it went. No way. The only part even remotely true was that SNCC people and SCLC staff jostled considerably. I'll explain that later.

I remember a great deal about that march with great satisfaction and pride. But the one thing that absolutely stands out about that campaign is the way our relationship with Dr. King deepened during the days we spent together on that march. In fact, the fondest memories I cherish of

Dr. King come from that time. We'd always respected him, but this is when I, and a lot of other SNCC folk, came to really know him. I know Cleve, Ralph, Stanley, and others felt that way too.

After that . . . meeting, we set up a planning meeting with our Delta projects. We put together teams for specific tasks, divided up responsibilities for every community along the line of march. Our network of local contacts was activated to mobilize folk for voter registration, handle logistics, find sites to pitch the tents, feed the marchers, and set up the mass meetings. Folks swung into action and in a matter of days we were ready to go.

We had meetings with the Deacons to clarify their responsibilities. No problem at all. They were just splendid. Young brothers, mostly veterans who had trained the others. They were very clear, very disciplined. They would patrol the perimeters of the march and at night guard the campsite. During the day they would also walk the ridges along the highway and investigate any possible ambush sites, beating the bushes and stands of trees along the road, and very politely check out anyone they found loitering there. In fact, the only violence our marchers did experience came at the hands of the so-called law — the Highway Safety Patrol.

Within days we felt ready to set off. We gathered outside Hernando, the place where Meredith was taken down, and formed up. No more than 150 or so marchers met us there. Mostly SNCC staff and young local folk physically able to undertake the walk of nearly 150 miles. I'd say most of them had been students in our freedom schools two years earlier. Also a lot of the young people I'd worked with in Greenwood. It was good to see them again. There was also a contingent of Highway Patrol — about a dozen — ostensibly there for our protection. First crisis.

Man, no sooner had the march started, these men started shouting and bellowing orders at us. They were ordering us off the road surface. This one trooper was just shouting and turning redder. I guess his idea was that we should walk more than a hundred miles over the tufts of grass and overgrown weeds on the roadside. When we didn't leave the roadbed, this big rednecked policeman came charging at us. I saw him coming with his hands stretched to bull-rush us. I was in the middle with Dr. King on my right, Attorney McKissick on the left, our arms linked. Certain he was going to shove me, I tensed up, bracing myself to meet the charge. I was set to ram my chest forward and — nonviolently, at the point of impact — hopefully break his wrists. I stuck out my chest and almost fell. Nothing.

Man, that cop went right by me to slam into Dr. King, knocked him down. I couldn't believe it. I yanked free to go after him, got one arm free, but Dr. King had my right hand and was not letting go. I was fighting to get to that cracker. But Dr. King hung on to my arm shouting, "Get Stokely, somebody, lay on him." People were screaming. A bunch of folks piled on top of me. After they cooled me out, we continued the march. We walked on the highway.

All day SNCC people kept saying, "Man, you really messed up." I said, "Yeah, yeah, I know." That evening there would be a meeting to discuss the day's events and plan for the next day. I expected that folks — especially SCLC — would come after me at that meeting. But none of them did. Because, I think, they'd all seen the cop push Dr. King. So it was left to Dr. King to chastise me:

"You know, Stokely, as we've discussed, you have greater responsibility now. You have to be very, very careful now that you represent SNCC. You can never forget you're now the head of an organization . . . ," etc. He corrected me firmly but gently.

I apologized. "I am sorry, Dr. King. This is the first time I've broken discipline on a nonviolent demonstration. But you, Dr. King, look around this room. We all know each other. I've been in battle with everyone here. You all know me. You all know I've been on the front line and I've never broken nonviolent discipline, right? I've been beaten, knocked unconscious. I've been sent to the hospital. And until today, I've never broken discipline. I'm sorry, Dr. King." Folks were nodding support. When I saw that I got bold. I said, "Dr. King, this is the first time. And the only reason I did was because that cracker charged into you. I know I kinda lost it then, but, Dr. King, you can tell those good white folk out there that, if they want nonviolence to stay alive, they had better not touch you. Better not lay a hand on you. Because, Dr. King, the moment they touch you is the moment nonviolence is finished, done."

Dr. King understood. Everyone understood that that was true. Once they touched Dr. King, nonviolence was dead.

Even with the presence of the Deacons, the debate on self-defense was far from over . . . among us. 'Cause, by day and by night the harassment never stopped, ceaseless. And, of course, the state troopers were a joke. They intervened only when some of our people were about to retaliate.

All day, man, passing pickup trucks and cars would veer over, speed up, and zoom by, inches from where our people were walking. Folks had to jump off the highway. Not once did the troopers issue a ticket or a warning, not once. So you know dudes were talking about bringing out their pieces.

Then at night when we pitched the tents, crowds of armed whites would gather close as they could get and shout insults and threats. The leaders would ask the cops to disperse them or move them back. That never happened. Except once. If memory serves, in Belzoni. Three, four cars full of gunmen drove up, within feet of the tent. The Deacons challenged them and there was a facedown. *Then* the cops intervened and backed them off. So of course there would be folk saying, "What we waiting for, till they kill some of us?" Oh, yeah, the debate went on.

Add to that, every night when the voter registration teams reported in, more harassment. In these little towns they were stoned with rocks, bottles, what have you. They be followed by groups with guns and clubs swearing to kill them. Cars veering over at them, chasing them down the highway. Those teams went through hell, man, yet they registered a lot of folks. But it was nerve-racking and you'd have folks saying the teams should be allowed to carry weapons. Before someone got killed. But the leadership counseled restraint, nonviolent discipline. But the debate went on . . . inside the tents every night.

What brought it out into the open was Philadelphia. After that, the debate boiled to the surface at a rally where the press was present. After that, national headlines: "Movement Divided on Nonviolence." Actually, there was no debate on nonviolence, that was clear. The debate was on self-defense.

See, the march was approaching Yazoo City, near Jackson, on the anniversary of the Neshoba County murders. We had to pay our respects to the memory of the three martyrs, but it was too far for the entire march to go. So we decided that the march leaders would drive over with a group of marchers, hook up with the local folks, and have a public memorial service. Dr. King would conduct the service in front of the courthouse after we marched from the black section.

Wow. We gits there and the local folk tell us that a mob has been gathering at the courthouse from early morning. They said that *[Deputy Sheriff]* Cecil Price and a few of the cops on duty at the court had been indicted for the murders. As were some others in the crowd. We discussed, but those local Neshoba County people were clear: "Ain't nothing to discuss, we going." So we set out. It wasn't a long march, but I wasn't sure we'd make it. Every block there'd be an attack. First came the rocks, bottles, and firecrackers. Followed by small gangs with fists and clubs. Cars swerving into the marchers. Only when a fight broke out would the cops do anything. Dr. King's presence and constant calls for discipline kept most marchers nonviolent. But even Dr. King was hit by a bottle.

We get to the courthouse only to find a screaming mob, at least a thousand white men. I really wasn't sure we'd even get to complete the service, much less make it out with everyone alive. But somehow we did. Dr. King was just steadfast. That night, after we left, the Klan drove into the black community shooting. The community fired back seriously. I hear they peppered those night-rider cars. So they took off, only made one pass.

That night at the usual rally the debate flared up. Dr. King was hot. *[Press reports call it "one of the angriest speeches of his life."]* He talked about the state of Mississippi and its vicious racism. Said that Philadelphia was the worst situation by far, the most violent that he had ever faced. But, he said, the only reason no one was killed was because the march had maintained order and discipline. McKissick supported that. But others took a different position. Willie Ricks said nobody was killed because we showed them that we could defend ourselves when attacked. I think this was the first rally where the brother from the Deacons *[Ernest Thomas]* shared the platform with the leaders. Among other things, he issued a warning to the white folks between here and Jackson. Anyone who messes with this march be putting their life on the line. The brother sounded serious too. That was what triggered the headlines. But I do seem to recall that we got to Jackson without further incident.

But the Mississippi police were a constant provocation, all march. The next time they nearly caused a riot was in Greenwood. Early on there'd

been a slight confrontation over the Deacons. But since it was legal to
carry loaded weapons as long as they were not concealed, they had to
back off. Not happily now, but they backed off and withdrew most of the
troopers, leaving only four. That was fine with us. But when we got to
Greenwood, they were back in force.

Greenwood was like a homecoming for me. Everyone in the community
knew me. Even the whites. I'd been in jail so much even the police chief
knew me. The African community really turned out. There was going
to be a huge rally in the Brant Street park in front of the black high
school that June Johnson and her friends attended. We were to pitch the
tent there. A lot of our people, hundreds, were gathering in the park.
The march was gathering momentum. I could see it was going to be our
largest rally.

Local leaders were becoming really involved. Even Charles Evers (who
had replaced his brother Medgar as head of the Jackson NAACP) had
come to Greenwood for the rally. I guess he must not have heard or didn't
care about the organizational "hand-washing" from on high.

And there Bro Evers was, talking loudly about his feelings on being in
Greenwood, a place he'd vowed never to set foot in, because it was the
hometown of Byron De La Beckwith, his brother Medgar's murderer.
Medgar's killer, armed and deputized, was rumored to have been seen
among the groups of armed whites and cops patrolling the area. Which,
naturally, created some serious undercurrents of anger in the people.
And I knew that some elements in the Greenwood community had been
ripe for a confrontation with the vigilantes ever since Freedom Summer.
SNCC had managed to avert that then, but now?

About then, June Johnson, my little sister, came rushing up. She was
visibly angry and agitated, and she'd been looking for me all over.

"Stokely, I gotta talk to you. Now. In private." I'd never seen June so
emotional. She had tears in her eyes. But she had reason.

Turns out she'd recognized one of the state troopers. He was the white
cop who had directed the beatings of June, Annell, and Mrs. Hamer in
the Winona jail the night Medgar Evers was murdered. The one who'd
taken the blackjack from the prisoner and brutalized Mrs. Hamer. *Oy*,
trouble, blues and trouble, Jack. June was one of the most popular and
admired teenagers in the community. Once that news got out, nobody but
nobody could stop some brothers from going home after their guns. And
who could blame them? But the human and political consequences. . . .
All the anger I'd felt when the beating went down came rushing back.

June was absolutely certain and offered to point the sick bastard out. I
didn't trust myself to be in his presence. "I'll handle it, babe, be cool."

I found the Safety Patrol commander; maybe it was Birdsong, I don't
recall. But I told him, "You leave that sick, twisted, sadistic [expletive
deleted] out here and it's going to be on you. *On you.* My people find out
who that bastard is — and what he did — and this mess is over. You
understand you got about ten minutes, if that." Of course the news got

out to some of the brothers, but by that time that trooper was nowhere to be found. Birdsong got him out of there. Another crisis narrowly averted.

After talking to the commander, I was called over to the school. The local Greenwood cops were trying to prevent the workers from raising the tent. The school board had given us permission and stood their ground. It was their school so it was an issue of community control, black power if you will. I told the workers to put up the tent unless the local community leaders stopped them. Words were exchanged and I was dragged off to jail. But the tent went up.

By the time I got out of jail, I was in no mood to compromise with racist arrogance. The rally had started. It was huge. The spirit of self-assertion and defiance was palpable. I looked over that crowd, that valiant embattled community of old friends and fellow strugglers. I told them what they knew, that they could depend only on themselves, their own organized collective strength. Register and vote. The only rights they were likely to get were the ones they took for themselves. I raised the call for Black Power again. It was nothing new, we'd been talking about nothing else in the Delta for years. The only difference was that this time the national media were there. And most of them had never experienced the passion and fervor of a mass meeting before. That was the only difference. As I passed Mukasa *[Willie Ricks]*, he said, "Drop it now. The people are ready. Drop it now."

[Cleve Sellers remembers:

"Stokely, who'd been released from jail just minutes before the rally began, was the last speaker. He was preceded by McKissick, Dr. King, and Willie Ricks. Like the rest of us, they were angry about Stokely's unnecessary arrest. Their speeches were particularly militant. When Stokely moved forward to speak, the crowd greeted him with a huge roar. He acknowledged his reception with a raised arm and clenched fist.

"Realizing that he was in his element, with his people, Stokely let it all hang out. 'This is the twenty-seventh time I have been arrested — and I ain't going to jail no more!' The crowd exploded into cheers and clapping.

"'The only way we gonna stop them white men from whuppin' us is to take over. We been saying freedom for six years and we ain't got nothin'. What we gonna start saying now is Black Power!'

"The crowd was right with him. They picked up his thoughts immediately.

"'BLACK POWER!' they roared in unison.

"Willie Ricks, who is as good at orchestrating the emotions of a crowd as anyone I have ever seen, sprang into action. Jumping to the platform with Stokely, he yelled to the crowd, 'What do you want?'

"'BLACK POWER!'

"'What do you want?'

"'BLACK POWER!'

"'What do you want?'

"'BLACK POWER!! BLACK POWER!!! BLACK POWER!!!!'

"Everything that happened afterward was a response to that moment.

*More than anything, it assured that the Meredith March Against Fear would go
down in history as one of the major turning points in the black liberation struggle."
— Sellers,* The River of No Return*]*

We left Greenwood with more new black voters on the rolls in two days
than we'd been able to accomplish in four arduous and bloody years. On
the march, the crowds remained large and enthusiastic. Local leadership
was praised, brought forward, and encouraged to run for local office.
Gathering strength all the way, we came down out of the Delta and got to
Canton, not far from Jackson. Canton was the home of Mrs. Annie
Devine (peace be unto her wise spirit), one of the FDP candidates in the
Congressional Challenge.

After Greenwood, the troopers' behavior had become — if you can
imagine this — even more surly and provocative. I guess not having succeeded in provoking a riot, they decided to riot themselves. So on this
night they rioted. The same issue as Greenwood. Again, we had permission from the black community to put up our tent in their school yard.
Only difference is that by the time we got into Canton, night had fallen.
We had to work in darkness. At first we did not know that they had surrounded the school in large numbers. Could not have been less than a
hundred of them. It was nothing but a planned, vicious ambush,
designed, I imagine, to demonstrate white power at its most brutal. We
are working by flashlight, trying to erect the tent. Tired, hungry people
are milling around. Suddenly the scene is lit up by searchlights out of the
surrounding darkness. A bright, white, blinding light. A voice amplified
by a bullhorn commands us to disperse. It was dark. We had no place for
150 marchers to go, and they knew that.

I told the voice that we had permission and nowhere else to put the
people. I told the people to stand their ground. Next to me, and clearly
illuminated by the lights, Dr. King made an anguished appeal for calm
and reason. "I am tired, so tired of violence," he said.

"Dr. King," I cried. "Please get down. You're too good a target here."

Some SCLC folks had started to pull him down and to encircle him
with their bodies when the cops fired in the tear gas.

I took a direct hit in the chest from a canister and was knocked to the
ground. Semiconscious and unable to breathe; my eyes tearing. My ribs
felt as though crushed. Gas in my lungs was always my weakness. It felt
like Cambridge, Maryland, all over again. Choking for breath, I could
hear screams, shouts, and Dr. King calling on people to remain calm
amid the sickening thud of blows. They were kicking and clubbing people
lying on the ground to escape the gas. Men, women, children, it made no
difference. Then they were gone, leaving us to tend the wounded and
raise the tent. So obviously it had simply been a demonstration of naked
brute force for its own sake.

[June Johnson:

*"It was awful. Worst thing I ever saw. People was choking everywhere. They
gassed Dr. King. Nearly killed Stokely. Whupped on every black head they could
find. The only blacks that didn't take a beating that night was the Deacons."]*

First draft again? According to the press — God bless 'em — Greenwood was when SNCC first issued the call for Black Power and changed the character and direction of the movement. Also, according to those accounts, this was when the "ideological struggle" between SCLC and SNCC, or between Dr. King and me, became public. A struggle expressed as a battle between shouted slogans, "Black Power" versus "Freedom Now." Wrong on both counts, wrong, wrong, wrong, and worse, trivial: as though Dr. King and I were high school cheerleaders. They sure do have a habit of reducing the black community and our issues to absurdity.

First of all, SNCC had been talking about political change and self-determination for years. The entire march was predicated on that. So nothing was new there. Given the history and the prevailing tension in Greenwood — the school yard confrontation, De La Beckwith's rumored presence, the sadistic cop, etc., etc., it may have been somewhat more emotional, that's all. But, as usual, the press saw what they could see and heard what they could hear.

[Arlie Schardt, Time *magazine:*

"The media coverage of the march was interesting because there was a tendency, I thought, to overplay it. There were a couple of reasons for that. One is that there were a lot of reporters who were new to this beat who were coming in from a lot of papers around the country as the march began to pick up momentum and as this Black Power theme began to get some publicity. The second reason was that the theme was never really clearly articulated. Or at least what it meant was never clearly defined. And so it was open to very broad interpretations. There were some whites, for their own reasons, who wanted to take this as a signal of real black hostility and enmity, and there were others who simply didn't know how to read what was being said. Therefore it was left open to the idea that this was a dramatic change in the civil rights movement in which blacks were telling the whites, 'Get out and forget it. We're on our own,' and that it was anti-white. But there was a lot of confusion because there was no unanimity about this." — Voices of Freedom]

Now, as for the "struggle" between Dr. King and I on the march? Utter, utter nonsense. In fact, it was exactly the reverse. The fondest memories I have of Dr. King come from that march, and I'd say that, despite the very present danger, the happiest, or at least the most relaxed, I'd ever seen him was on those Delta highways. It was the first real time he'd spent with us or us with him. I know that a lot of us in SNCC ended up seeing him in a very different light. During those sweltering Delta days Dr. King became to many of us no longer a symbol or an icon, but a warm, funny, likable, unpretentious human being who shared many of our values. Dr. King had a great, mischievous sense of humor. Most people don't know that. . . .

See, of all the "adult" leaders, Dr. King had always best understood and supported SNCC's work and approach. Back when we most needed support, he had praised the Summer Project as one of the "most creative projects" of the movement. Well, there were reasons for that. True, he'd never spent time in the field with us, but Dr. King understood and really loved our people's culture. Hey, he was deep down — in one large part of him-self — a product of that culture. And Dr. King had undying love for our people, undying love. On the march, that side of him came out beautifully. Especially in those night meetings in those little churches. You could just see him respond to the people's singing, to the eloquent little speeches, to the preaching, to their spirit. You could see how he enjoyed being among his people.

Another thing people forget is that Dr. King was only about ten years older than most of us. He used to remind me that he was just about my own age when he was first called to lead the Montgomery bus boycott. Remember, he was thirty-nine — same age as Malcolm — when they killed him. So he really understood us better, more sympathetically, and was much closer to us in spirit than people think. Much closer.

The main thing is that I got the strong impression that being out there on the road with us, and with his people, was almost like a holiday for Dr. King. That being away from the office — the phone calls from advisers, supporters, the internal politics of even his own staff, from the constant pressures, often from his own government, and the demands and con-straints of leaderships — was a great relief to him. As if he were out of a straitjacket. We sensed that this was the aspect of the movement that he liked best, where he was most free to be himself. And that out here, marching, talking, sleeping in the tent, he was relishing that freedom.

Another thing people tend to forget about Dr. King is his courage. You hear some ignorant types talking that because Dr. King was nonviolent, he was somehow, y'know, wishy-washy. That's so stupid.

Before I got to know him, when I'd see him in meetings, etc., when he wasn't speaking, he'd sometimes seemed to me somehow strained, under pressure, vaguely distracted. Certainly not happy. Well, as we've since dis-covered, he was under tremendous pressure. Think about it. Since his late twenties, during his entire public life, that brother had lived in the awareness of his impending death. Dr. King knew he wasn't going to sur-vive the movement. It began back in Montgomery when he received an average of forty death threats per week. For the rest of his life — fourteen years — that never stopped. Never stopped. Never stopped. Every Klan and Nazi group had a bounty on his head. Martin Luther King was the number one target for every racist with a rifle, shotgun, or stick of dyna-mite. Being the prime symbol of black aspirations meant being the prime target of white hatred. The brother lived with that.

Now he never said it to me, but I've heard that he said he did not expect to live to see forty. And he didn't. That's the pressure Dr. King lived with all his public life, yet he never backed down and he never backed off. I mean, there he was with us, out on those exposed highways, with the only security he could trust being the Deacons, looking more relaxed than I'd ever seen him. Appearing to enjoy himself. And then to see him with the people. Amazing, incredible, inspiring.

Women's history became a legitimate field of study in the wake of Second Wave feminism, the political movement that appeared in about 1961 and lasted until the demise of the Equal Rights Amendment in 1982 (more or less, depending on who tells the story). That social movement, the largest in our history and perhaps in the world, has penetrated more deeply into the details of everyday American life than any other. As two Second Wave activists wrote, before the movement, "The prevailing assumption of the inferiority of women was the starting point from which one planned one's moves and shaped one's life — whether acquiescent or angry."[1] The movement affected education, the legal system, the medical profession, marriage and divorce, the distribution of work in the home, child rearing, art, and literature, to name only a few areas. The women's movement combated — with mixed success — discrimination in the workplace, quickly equalized the gender composition of professional schools (50 percent of medical students are now women), brought women into amateur and professional sports in a significant way, and began a transformation in the way the nation discusses and responds to sexual violence. It radically broadened the possibilities that life offers girls and heightened many of their aspirations, and, for some men and women, loosened the hold of old, rigid, and humanly wasteful gender roles.

Given all of this, historians have given surprisingly little historical attention to the movement. Unlike the civil rights movement, which has intrigued countless scholars, the women's movement has had relatively few chroniclers, many of them participants. Suspicious of strong leadership and leaders, the movement produced a few spokespeople like Betty Friedan and Gloria Steinem, but no Martin Luther King–like figure. Again, unlike the civil rights movement, there was no NAACP, no SNCC, CORE, or SCLC to focus studies. The National Women's Party (NWP) that had pushed for the Equal Rights Amendment after the achievement of woman suffrage in 1920 was a small, elite, conservative, and sometimes racist group that attracted relatively little study.[2] The National Organization for Women (NOW), founded

---

[1] Rachel Blau DuPlessis and Ann Snitow, *The Feminist Memoir Project: Voices from Women's Liberation* (New York, 1998), 4.

[2] For the NWP see Leila Rupp and Verta Taylor, *Survival in the Doldrums: The American Women's Rights Movement, 1945 to the 1960s* (New York, 1987); on the racism of some NWP members see Dorothy Sue Cobble, *The Other Women's Movement: Workplace Justice and Social Rights in Modern America* (Princeton, N. J., 2004), 175–76; for its marginal impact, see Ruth Rosen, *The World Split Open: How the Modern Women's Movement Changed America* (New York, 2000), 27.

to combat discrimination in employment and later broadened in its agenda to include issues like reproductive rights, has been studied but in the context of the larger movement. In part, neglect of the field has come from the dispersed, fluid, and self-consciously antihierarchical movement that consisted of thousands of local groups, loosely structured, leaving few documents, and working on hundreds of different fronts not easy to summarize. Feminists wrought broad changes in family life and national discourse not only through legislation and collective pressure, but through countless intimate transformations difficult for historians to chronicle.

However, as Linda Gordon and Rosalyn Baxandall have written, the movement has been neglected or misrepresented for "more fundamental reasons" than its elusive tactics and private victories. Portrayed as a social movement concerned largely with matters of sex, women's political goals and activism have been obscured. Students for a Democratic Society (SDS) is remembered for its antiwar work and its promotion of democracy, but the radical feminists who saw gender as the central category of oppression and the socialist feminists who viewed capitalism as the root of the problem of women's subordination have received little recognition for their work toward increased democracy; rather, they have been portrayed as a kind of "special interest group."[3] Organized opposition to the women's movement, developed initially under the leadership of Phyllis Schlafly, found support in the press, grown tired of feminist agitation by the late 1970s. Part of the powerful move to the right, opponents of feminists portrayed them as "bra burners" and "women's libbers," who were "angry" and "shrill." And right-wing talk radio host Rush Limbaugh memorably gave us "femi-nazis."[4]

Like the first wave of feminism, Second Wave feminism grew out of a movement to improve the condition of African Americans. As such, it had a crucial and complex relationship with the civil rights movement. A central theme running through the historiography has been and continues to be the movement's ability to include issues and people representing points of view beyond those of white middle-class women.[5] The prevailing interpretation since the earliest accounts of the movement that began emerging in the 1970s has been that women's rights activists were largely white and that their issues were largely middle class. The years of maximum solidarity were the late 1960s and early 1970s after which the movement began to fragment. This is a surprising and disappointing assessment of a movement that was partially born in the civil rights movement and claimed in its early days to speak for all women. Eerily, the outlines of the story repeat the history of the First Wave of feminists, who emerged in 1848 out of the struggle for abolition. The most radical (or anyway, those most focused on gender above all) among those in that First Wave refused to support the rights of

---

[3]Rosalyn Baxandall and Linda Gordon, "Second-Wave Soundings," *The Nation*, July 3, 2000; see Gloria Steinem, "Women Are Never Front Runners," *New York Times*, January 5, 2008, on women as a special interest.

[4]See Rosen, *The World Split Open*, 331–40.

[5]Baxandall and Gordon, "Second-Wave Soundings."

African Americans to vote when women were not included in the Fifteenth Amendment. They split the movement into two and, in the eyes of many, stained feminism with racism.

Apart from tainting the women's movement with prejudice, this perceived weakness in contemporary feminism has the effect of placing the struggles for gender equality and racial equality in competition with each other, forcing activists to choose between them. It also suggests that black women are not, in some important way, women. Sojourner Truth, the legendary black activist of the First Wave, drew attention to this problem of inclusion in her famous speech for suffrage in which she insisted on her womanhood despite the fact that she had had to work like a man all her life.[6] It also links the movement's focus to middle-class issues as the majority of black women embrace a feminism that recognizes issues of economic need. Historians of the women's movement have wrestled with the movement's inclusiveness over the last forty years.

Since the 1990s, some scholars have argued against the movement's white makeup and middle-class focus, finding evidence of its roots among black and white working-class women and women influenced by the Old Left. They have also painted a broad movement constituted by activism among working-class women, Chicanas, African Americans, Asian Americans, and Native Americans, and influenced by lesbians. The newer view sees these groups influencing one another, disagreeing with one another, working in small groups and occasionally in concert, learning from feminists in other countries — a ferment that did not achieve its greatest coherence and effectiveness until the 1980s and 1990s and that continues today. As a recent scholar has described it, "it was a grassroots movement that, if coherent, was certainly not unified: it was a movement made of coalition and conflict, exuberant experimentation and reactionary doctrine, contradiction and transformation; a movement both visionary in its impulse toward democratic participation, and unwitting — and at times intentional — in its practices of exclusions . . . a movement that changed the world and yet fell short; a movement that despite backlash continues to emerge in ever new forms."[7]

Ellen Levine and Judith Hole published the first historical treatment of Second Wave feminism in 1971, while it was still gearing up.[8] As they wrote, "women's issues were not yet viewed as serious by most traditional political analysts, right, left, or center." The authors identified two streams merging to form the movement: one, a group of older, largely educated, professional and union women in the women's rights tradition who went on to found the National Organization for Women (NOW) in 1966, and the other, a group of younger women coming out of civil rights and the New Left who tended to be more radical than their elders. Although the first group included a few African American women, the historians reported that most activists

---

[6] bell hooks, *Ain't I a Woman: Black Women and Feminism* (Boston, 1981), 3–4.

[7] Anne Enke, *Finding the Movement: Sexuality, Contested Space, and Feminist Activism* (Durham, N.C., 2007), 22.

[8] Judith Hole and Ellen Levine, *Rebirth of Feminism* (New York, 1971).

viewed black women's participation in the Second Wave as "limited" because "for the most part activist minority women have defined the elimination of racism as their primary concern." In Hole and Levine's account, white feminists rejected the accusation of racism and said that black women were not interested in participating,[9] suggesting that women had to choose which oppression to fight. By default these authors tended to define movement women as white.

Jo Freeman, writing in 1975, agreed that Hole and Levine had identified correctly the composition of the movement and argued that the composition of "both branches" tended "to be predominantly white, middle class, and college educated." Freeman pointed to the older group's embrace of the "egalitarian ethos," which derived in part from the nineteenth-century feminists who believed that when women were politically and economically equal to men, discrimination and injustice would be resolved. They took on formal problems of equity, approached them legislatively and judicially, and largely ignored more intimate issues of sexuality and family. The younger stream, however, influenced by their understanding of racial subordination, predicted that if women became the equal to men they would take on the inherent male prerogative of dominating others. They offered a "liberation ethic" for both sexes to free them from gender stereotypes and insure that future generations would not reproduce gender hierarchies.[10] "Liberation" signified an internal transformation that would initiate larger social transformations.

In 1977, historian William Chafe provided a long view of feminist activity. He studied the Second Wave in the context of two previous intervals of feminist activism: one gathering in the mid-nineteenth century and working in the post–Civil War years for a variety of legal reforms including suffrage, and a second focused largely on suffrage, active during the Progressive Era. Chafe, looking for the factors that gave the Second Wave its relative potency, saw the earliest feminists as prescient and dedicated, but extremely isolated. The Progressive Era feminists achieved suffrage, but by addressing only a single issue, the mobilized base of their movement lapsed with the passage of the Nineteenth Amendment. In contrast, large and significant social and economic transformations underlay the mass-based women's movement of the 1960s and 1970s, including dramatically increased employment rates among married women with children, changing values about sexuality dating from the 1960s and accelerated by the availability of the birth control pill, the declining birth rate, and the rising age at which women were marrying. Chafe pointed out that these enormous transformations had already changed women's behavior, but that the movement was crucial to supplying the feminist ideology to protest traditional constraints on women and define new, positive roles for them.[11]

---

[9]Ibid., xv, 149.

[10]Jo Freeman, "The Women's Liberation Movement: Its Origins, Structures, Impact, and Ideas," in Jo Freeman, ed., *Women: A Feminist Perspective* (Palo Alto, Calif., 1975), 448, 459; see also Jo Freeman and Victoria Johnson, *Waves of Protest: Social Movements since the Sixties* (New York, 1999).

[11]William Chafe, *Women and Equality: Changing Patterns in American Culture* (New York, 1977), 142.

Chafe observed that the majority of members of the Second Wave were white and middle class although less exclusively so than their nineteenth-century counterparts had been. He noted that black activists had founded the National Black Feminist Organization (NBFO) in 1973 and that it had 2,000 members by 1974. He also was among the first to observe that women from organized labor participated in the movement, indicating some reach beyond the white middle class.[12] But in an article in 2000, Chafe reemphasized forcefully what he saw as the limited nature of the movement: "The one glaring flaw that should have concerned all women activists, was feminism's failure to escape its narrow class and race boundaries. Despite the ambitions and aspirations of socialist feminists for a cross-class, cross race coalition, most feminist activists were white, middle-class, and college-educated. . . . Both the language and the programs of feminist groups seemed to reflect a white, middle class approach."[13] An excerpt from Chafe's 2000 essay is included as the first reading in this chapter.

The National Black Feminist Organization that Chafe had written about established itself in 1973 and announced in its statement of purpose the importance of feminism to black and third world women. The next year a Boston chapter of NBFO transformed itself into the Combahee River Collective, named for the river in South Carolina where Harriet Tubman had fought during the Civil War to free 750 slaves. Barbara Smith, along with two other members of the group of African American lesbians in "A Black Feminist Statement," emphasized the overlapping goals of liberation for women. These goals included an end to homophobia — articulated most infamously by Betty Friedan of NOW as "the Lavender menace" that threatened the reputation of mainstream women's rights — and an understanding of what has come to be called "intersectionality" or the synergy that makes racism and sexism together more than the sum of their parts. They asserted that they had gone further in their analysis of oppression than white feminists had by including in their deliberations race, class, "compulsory heterosexuality," as well as sexism.[14]

Two years after Chafe's portrait of a movement confined by its origins, historian Sara Evans, a participant in the civil rights movement and a member of one of the earliest (1967) women's liberation groups, published *Personal Politics* about the relationship between the two movements. Evans delineated the evolution of white southern women's experience in the civil rights movement and why these women, long socialized to compliance and deference, were the first to articulate a politics not just of equality, but also of liberation. Her influential exploration argued that women were finding the stress points of their lives not so much in their economically productive activities as in the heavy strains that these produced on them at home. Evans argued that while

---

[12]Ibid., 124.

[13]William H. Chafe, "The Road to Equality, 1962–Today," in Nancy Cott, *No Small Courage: A History of Women in the United States* (New York, 2000), 561.

[14]Beverly Guy-Sheftall, *Words of Fire: An Anthology of African American Feminist Thought* (New York, 1995), 231; The Combahee River Collective, in Guy-Sheftall, *Words,* 234–35; on the homophobia of NOW and the response of gay women see Rosen, *The World Split Open,* 164–75.

the older generation of feminists battled legal and economic inequalities besetting women, they were not interested in or willing to examine the contradictions and tensions in their domestic lives. "The pressures on most women were building up not on the level of public discussion but at the juncture of public and private, of job and home, where older structures and identities no longer sufficed but could not simply be discarded either. . . . A new movement would have to transform the privacy and subjectivity of personal life into a political issue."[15]

Evans documented the early discontent of southern white, female, SNCC (Student Nonviolent Coordinating Committee) workers at being treated as an oppressed caste, just as they had observed blacks being treated. As white women, they were hesitant to speak of the discrimination they felt as SNCC was increasingly leaning toward Black Power and moving toward becoming an all-black organization. Evans saw that white southern women had come to feel like second-class citizens within SNCC. Their dissatisfaction grew during the 1964 Freedom Summer with its massive influx of white students from the North and the ensuing increase in interracial sexual relations that made white women feel exploited and black women activists feel overlooked. In the wake of that summer, SNCC workers Mary King and Casey Hayden wrote a famous memo directed to the black women in SNCC describing their position as analogous to that of blacks and wishing to explore together this kind of discrimination. But, Evans wrote, "The black women who received it were on a different historical trajectory. They would fight some of the same battles as women, but in a different context and in their own way."[16] Mary King later said that "'From our black women friends . . . [n]ot one responded.'"[17] When in 1966 SNCC rejected integration as a goal and became an all-black organization, white activists found places for themselves in the New Left, particularly within SDS, where they encountered gross sexism and a fierce unwillingness on the part of activist men even to discuss gender. In 1967, in a number of cities, women began to form all-women groups to discuss their problems, adapting movement discussion techniques to produce the kinds of personal/political conversations known as consciousness-raising that would be such a powerful tool among Second Wave participants.

Although some movement participants would dispute details of Evans's story, her careful political analysis remains very influential. On the question of the racial makeup of the Second Wave, she painted a picture of a segregated movement, citing the National Black Feminist Organization as the preferred response of African American women to sex discrimination.[18]

African American activist and scholar Paula Giddings confirmed the view of a bifurcated women's movement. In 1984, she quoted the distinguished lawyer Eleanor Holmes Norton's response to the founding of the National

---

[15]Sara Evans, *Personal Politics: The Roots of Women's Liberation in the Civil Rights Movements and the New Left* (New York, 1979), 21.
[16]Ibid., 100.
[17]Quoted in Rosen, *The World Split Open*, 114.
[18]Evans, *Personal Politics*, 227.

Black Feminist Organization: "It took us some time to realize that we had nothing to fear from feminism, but we could not have emerged amidst the confusion of five or six years ago."[19] One historian has since argued that it would have been unlikely for this organization to emerge had it not been for Second Wave feminist analysis, suggesting the dialogue between black and white feminists.[20] At the same time, as theorists like bell hooks and the members of the Combahee River Collective were arguing, black women had long been upset at white feminists' "insistence that race and sex were two separate issues." Numerous white feminists insisted on the primacy of sexism over other kinds of oppression, a view that alienated minority women and working-class women.[21]

Alice Echols, whose 1989 *Daring to Be Bad* has become an important political and social history of the Second Wave, thoughtfully analyzed the ways in which developments in the civil rights movement affected developments in SDS and the New Left in general and how, in turn, these influenced women's organizing.[22] She concurred with Evans that black women initially were not in sympathy with white women raising the issue of sexism. They felt, she argued, that white women were trying to acquire the autonomy and competence that black women had always been forced to cultivate because racism had made it impossible for black men to support them as white men supported white women. They also resented male black activists' sexual attention to white SNCC volunteers. White feminists looking for a home in the New Left found SDS no longer willing to consider varieties of oppression and had shifted back toward an Old Left emphasis on economic injustice as the engine of oppression. Some feminists, infuriated by the sexism of SDS, adapted the Black Power principle in their organizing and began establishing all-women groups.[23] *Daring to Be Bad* concludes with Echols's stating her disappointment that in an increasingly conservative political time, a women's political movement took a cultural turn, celebrating the "feminine," adopting an essentialist point of view — that is, that certain (good) qualities inhere naturally in women — and rejecting the struggles of the New Left. Echols's study located white feminists at the core of the movement.

Narrowing the focus from the grassroots of liberation, Cynthia Harrison's study of the period from the end of World War II to 1968 described high politics. It began with the struggle of liberal Democrats like Esther Peterson, head of the Women's Bureau under JFK, who had worked for many years

---

[19]Quoted in Steven Buechler, *Women's Movements in the United States: Woman Suffrage, Equal Rights, and Beyond* (New Brunswick, N. J., 1990), 156.

[20]Ibid., 156.

[21]hooks, *Ain't I a Woman*, 12; on the original nature of sexism, see Gerda Lerner, *The Creation of Patriarchy* (New York, 1986); others like Shulamith Firestone had made the case long before but not as historians — see Shulamith Firestone, *The Dialectic of Sex: The Case for Feminist Revolution* (New York, 1971).

[22]Alice Echols, *Daring to Be Bad: Radical Feminism in America, 1967–1975* (Minneapolis, 1989).

[23]Alice Echols, "White Women and the Origins of the Women's Liberation Movement," in Mary B. Norton and Ruth M. Alexander, eds., *Major Problems in Women's American History* (Lexington, Mass., 1996), 464–72.

to pass legislation protecting working women, and their fight against the National Women's Party that had pushed since 1920 for the Equal Rights Amendment that would prohibit treating women differently from men. This legislation would wipe out protective legislation based on women's differences from men, but presumably ensure nondiscrimination against women in the legal, economic, and political spheres.[24]

Harrison chronicled Kennedy's appointment of the Presidential Commission on the Status of Women, the passage of the Equal Pay Act of 1963, and the backhanded way that women were included in the 1964 Civil Rights Act. When the newly formed Equal Employment Opportunity Commission (EEOC) let it be known that it would enforce the Civil Rights Act's antidiscrimination policy based on race but not on sex, several former members of the Presidential Commission founded NOW to pressure the EEOC to act fairly. Harrison's study shows how the EEOC used preserving protective legislation as a shield against enforcing the Civil Rights Act, and that its recalcitrance encouraged more and more women to see the ERA as a legitimate tool and much protective legislation as no longer relevant to working women's needs.[25]

Harrison's study focused almost exclusively on white women. It extended the origins of the movement back to the post–World War II period and suggested that it was formal political activity that prepared the way for the mass movement that gathered force in the late 1960s and early 1970s. And once again, it spotlighted the tight but unpredictable links between the women's movement and the civil rights movement. Women were only added to the 1964 Civil Rights Act because an anti–civil rights southern member of Congress hoped in so doing to derail the legislation completely. The act passed because of an unlikely and brief alliance of liberals voting for justice, southern conservatives voting to defeat civil rights, and other conservatives voting to make sure that the new measure did not give black women preferential treatment over white women.[26]

Leila Rupp and Verta Taylor came out at more or less the same time with a study to show that although feminist activity diminished, it was not extinguished in the post–World War II years. They found that the National Women's Party, as well as a sample of activists they studied in Ohio, pushed to mobilize support for the Equal Rights Amendment, for women's history programs, and for federal appointments for women. Rupp and Taylor studied only white women and limited their definition of feminist politics to passage of the ERA.[27]

Picking up themes of bell hooks and others concerned with the absence of black women from significant feminist theorizing, philosopher Elizabeth Spelman published *Inessential Woman: Problems of Exclusion in Feminist Thought*

---

[24]Cynthia Harrison, *On Account of Sex: The Politics of Women's Issues, 1945–1968* (Berkeley, Calif., 1988). See pages 3–38 in Harrison for the background of this debate.
[25]Ibid., 181–96, 207–8.
[26]Ibid., 181.
[27]Rupp and Taylor, *Survival in the Doldrums.*

in 1988. This influential book criticized important theorists of gender like sociologist Nancy Chodorow, author of *The Reproduction of Mothering: Psychoanalysis and the Sociology of Gender*, who tried to show how gender was constructed through women's exclusive involvement in early child rearing.[28] Spelman pointed out that while Chodorow's study of gender was persuasive, she omitted any mention of the ways that class and race get constructed. Similarly, she criticized feminist theorists like Kate Millett and Shulamith Firestone for arguing that sexism precedes racism and is the more powerful.[29] In what has become a basic understanding among feminists today, Spelman, Barbara Smith, and others of the NBFO argued that sexism and racism were not just the sum of two kinds of oppression, but that they were interlocked. White women could and did participate in racism. Black women were positioned differently from white women in society and did not necessarily feel oppressed as housewives, as Betty Friedan argued in *The Feminine Mystique*, but oppressed because they had not been able to be housewives. Thus, the social and economic positions of women would shape their feminism.[30]

Steven Buechler's 1990 study of the first and second women's movements noted that over the last 150 years white middle-class women have been most likely to participate in feminist activities, but that this has not meant that feminism has had no relevance to minority women. Buechler argued that working-class and African American women both had found in feminist ideology "crystallized long-standing grievances over sexual discrimination, segregation, harassment" as well as "historic patterns of male domination and machismo." The founding of the National Black Feminist Organization, according to Buechler, offered women a chance to organize against the forces of racism and sexism in their lives.

Buechler (like Rupp and Taylor) observed that white feminists had become more aware of their own racism throughout the 1980s, through self-critiques and soliciting the criticism and participation of minority women. Nevertheless, NOW did not support many issues of concern to women of color and poor women, and its slant on reproduction illustrates the point. Rather than a focus on preventing the involuntary sterilization of women of color and the poor, NOW concentrated predominantly on trying to insure women's access to abortions, an issue of great importance to the white middle class.[31] Buechler's study saw unconscious racism at work in the contemporary women's movement, producing suspicion and a sense of exploitation among minority women. However, he also asserted that the women's movement has, among all social movements, been the most responsive and self-critical about its lack of diversity.

---

[28]Elizabeth V. Spelman, *Inessential Woman: Problems of Exclusion in Feminist Thought* (Boston, 1988), 80–113; Nancy Chodorow, *The Reproduction of Mothering: Psychoanalysis and the Sociology of Gender* (Berkeley, Calif., 1978).

[29]Firestone, *Dialectic*; and Kate Millett, *Sexual Politics* (New York, 1970).

[30]Spelman, *Inessential*, 114–25; Betty Friedan, *The Feminine Mystique* (New York, 1963).

[31]Buechler, *Women's Movements*, 154–56.

In 1991, Flora Davis published a comprehensive study of the movement, describing it as primarily white and middle class, but covering in her lengthy study many activist groups that she described as being "within the feminist movement," including Mexican Americans, African Americans, Asian Americans, and Native Americans. She also noted that black feminists had been working for feminist goals before the advent of the white women's movement. She thus laid out the diversity of feminism, with which later historians would challenge the notion that the movement was largely white. But she did not articulate a challenge to the view of white, middle-class women as ascendant.[32]

In 1998, Rachel Blau DuPlessis and Ann Snitow edited *The Feminist Memoir Project: Voices from Women's Liberation*, a collection of writings from activists. The editors grappled with the membership and aims of the movement in their introduction. They noted that Jo Freeman remembered the grief many white women felt at being pushed out of the civil rights movement. At the same time, black activists remembered that many of these same women "unified unself-consciously around their whiteness."[33]

"So was the women's movement white?" they ask. "Yes and no" is their answer, holding that "a feminist analysis was formulated in many ethnic groups. All were looking for their own precise point of oppression around which to organize."[34] They also argue that from the beginning, women of color had been critical that they were included in the movement but excluded from shaping feminist analysis and feminist goals. For DuPlessis and Snitow, the early movement cohesion could not endure as some women were oppressing others; the early insistence on sisterhood had to give way to more sophisticated understandings of the implication of differences among women.[35]

In 2000, Ruth Rosen published the most complete history of the women's movement to date. Presenting the movement as sometimes contradictory, paranoid, but extraordinarily far-reaching, Rosen's account contributed to our understanding of early African American feminism. Her evidence showed that it predated the establishment of the National Black Feminist Organization and focused on different issues than those of white feminists, like the prevention of sterilization and improving the lot of children and mothers. *The World Split Open* also portrayed a wide assortment of feminisms proliferating among different ethnic groups, especially visible at the National Women's Conference in Houston in 1977. Her approach still located the cohesion of the movement in the 1960s and 1970s, and while her account is broadly inclusive, it portrays African Americans and others going their separate ways without trying to integrate the perspectives of African Americans or working-class women or to identify their effects on the larger movement.[36]

---

[32]Flora Davis, *Moving the Mountain: The Women's Movement in America since 1960* (New York, 1991), 356, 372–73.

[33]DuPlessis and Snitow, *The Feminist Memoir Project*, 8–9.

[34]Ibid., 9.

[35]Ibid., 16, 17.

[36]Rosen, *The World Split Open*, 263–94; see Baxandall and Gordon, "Second-Wave Soundings."

In that same year, Myra Marx Ferree and Beth B. Hess, sociologists, were among the first to put American feminism into a global context. Since the 1990s, more and more women activists have taken a global perspective on women's issues. This has, in part, been a response to the rise of strong movements in developing nations where most of the world's women produce most of their families' food, suffer the majority of sexual violence, and increasingly are the first to confront the effects of environmental degradation. Ferree and Hess sketched the history of international feminism, but paid particular attention to its central role in the consciousness and issues of North American feminists.[37]

They also supplied a careful political analysis of the early growth of the Second Wave using social movement theory. They used this theory to explain as well the "biases in mobilization," which initially recruited predominantly white, educated women, especially into the liberationist wing. The NOW wing, as many historians had pointed out, had African American activists like Pauli Murray and Aileen Hernandez already within its ranks. Ferree and Hess added that the movement responded to the criticisms of exclusivity and that it became much broader over time, as feminists understood that race, class, and gender cannot be separated.[38]

Alice Kessler-Harris's *In Pursuit of Equity* in 2001 constituted one of the most insightful analyses of the relation between the politics of civil rights and the emergence of the women's movement.[39] She viewed the inclusion of the word "sex" in Title VII of the Civil Rights Act of 1964 as opening up a "new meaning for sex discrimination" among reformers. In the wake of that act, those concerned with discrimination against women would use the fight for racial equality as their model. "The Civil Rights Act helped to create a self-conscious women's movement. This not only placed gender at the center of an impassioned national conversation around equality but reconfigured the debate around the meaning of equality itself."[40] The conflict over who the EEOC would protect against discrimination and why revealed that the commission's assumptions (and the assumptions of most in power) about how women should fulfill their responsibilities as wives and mothers trumped their willingness to enforce their equality. As the equality model gained ground, supported by NOW and white middle-class women in general, it also became clear that poor and/or black women would need — but not get — special assistance to compete in the job market. Thus, the women's movement's embrace of equality and the ERA, rather than difference in economic matters, would help white educated women compete with men for jobs that required education and training, but disadvantage women already disadvantaged by poor education and an inability to pay for child care.[41]

---

[37]Myra Marx Ferree and Beth B. Hess, *Controversy and Coalition: The New Feminist Movement across Four Decades of Change* (New York, 2000), ix–xii.
[38]Ibid., 91–99.
[39]Alice Kessler-Harris, *In Pursuit of Equity: Women, Men, and the Quest for Economic Citizenship in 20th-Century America* (New York, 2001).
[40]Ibid., 246.
[41]Ibid., 274–75.

In the same year as Kessler-Harris's important volume appeared, Rosalyn Baxandall challenged the long-held belief that "the women's liberation movement [was] middle class, bourgeois, and white." She quoted Alice Echols: "Most politically active black women, even if they criticized the black movement for sexism, chose not to become involved in the feminist struggle." Baxandall argued to the contrary that "the early formations . . . were primarily composed of Black and poor women and members of Black nationalists or Old Left groups."[42] Baxandall's research documented the presence of many early groups of feminists, most made up of poor black and white women and a number that had women from the Old Left, especially members of the Socialist Workers Party (the term *male chauvinism* derives from the Old Left). These groups did not invoke the "liberation" standard, in part because so many of them originated before 1967, but also because their analysis of problems centered on their economic and family circumstances and protecting their children. Members tended to focus much more on their roles as mothers than later white, middle-class groups. (Shulamith Firestone, who wished to rescue women from the "barbarity" of child rearing, recommended rejecting men altogether and substituting technological childbirth for women's labor and delivery.) The earlier women's groups, by contrast, worked to provide day care, free schools, nonsexist curricula, and to reach out to black men who were staggering under the burdens of racism.[43]

Baxandall speculated that perhaps these early feminists have been forgotten because they were black, and they left few records. Perhaps those influenced by the Old Left tried to hide that connection out of fear of McCarthyism. The author urged historians to broaden their definitions of feminism to include "self-help and neighborhood action" and in this way recover more accurately their own history while making it more inclusive.[44] Her essay is included as the second reading in this chapter.

Picking up this challenge, Becky Thompson's article "Multiracial Feminism: Recasting the Chronology of Second Wave Feminism" lays out a history of the Second Wave that does not start with *The Feminine Mystique*, but with an array of initiatives from white, black, Latina, Asian, Native American, and Puerto Rican women. Thompson argues that the women's movement was influenced not only (or primarily) by the civil rights movement, but by the Black Power movement. Women of color did not see sexism as primary, but one of many symptoms of an oppressive society. The focus on a feminism that is about more than gender marks the 1980s as the era that brought together women committed to an "expansive notion of feminisms" and substitutes it for the 1960s and 1970s as the most coherent period of the movement.[45]

---

[42]Rosalyn Baxandall, "Re-Visioning the Women's Liberation Movement's Narrative: Early Second Wave African American Feminists," *Feminist Studies* 27 (Spring 2001): 225–45, 228.

[43]Ibid., 239.

[44]Ibid., 240–41.

[45]Quoted in Becky Thompson, "Multiracial Feminism: Recasting the Chronology of Second Wave Feminism," *Feminist Studies* 28 (Summer 2002): 337–61, 343.

Dorothy Cobble's *The Other Women's Movement* (2004) fills a gaping void in the literature with a detailed and thoughtful account of working women's search for equity over the last six or seven decades. Historians of the Second Wave have given some attention to working women, particularly Alice Kessler-Harris, but there has been no in-depth study of their relationship — sometimes harmonious, sometimes at odds — with the women's movement. Cobble lays out the ways in which working women were initially opposed to NOW's support of the ERA and alienated by the middle-class bias of the newly prominent women's group. She shows how working women lobbied hard for child care in the late 1960s and early 1970s while NOW took a relatively inactive role in this struggle. (Their failure means poor and welfare mothers have to work and to care for their children as best they can while wealthier mothers can "opt out.") Cobble details the largely unsuccessful efforts of the mostly black household workers to acquire benefits like other employees and the organizing of stewardesses to get fairer and more dignified job conditions from their employers. These and other struggles bring a welcome working-class perspective to the story of feminism, underlining the economic issues, often neglected by middle-class reformers, that were central to many, probably the majority, of women's concerns.[46]

Of similar significance is Benita Roth's *Separate Roads to Feminism,* a unique, comparative study of parallel Chicana, black, and white "feminisms," their origins, and differences. Roth, like Ferree and Hess, uses social movement theory to explain how these activists mobilized. Black and Chicana women already had prior loyalties to racial/ethnic liberation movements. Their feminisms aimed at eliminating more than just the oppression of gender, and, invoking "intersectionality," they argued that the combinations of gender and race and class inequities were uniquely powerful. White women, on the other hand, deliberately separated themselves from the New Left (and were no longer welcome in the civil rights movement). Thus unencumbered by men, they articulated a universal theory of gender and evoked universal sisterhood that was useful for mobilizing other white women but which alienated women of color. It did mean that white women made ideological feminist advances earlier than feminists of color who continued to work within coeducational organizations, unlike white feminists. Roth's comparative approach results in new insights about the timing and content of the feminisms developed by three groups of women differently situated. And by showing the connections among these movements it arrests the whitewashing of feminism of which she and others have long complained.[47]

Inclusive studies of particular branches of the movement emerge and illuminate the whole, like Jennifer Nelson's *Women of Color and the Reproductive Rights Movement*, which looks at how women of color and white women came into conflict but later joined together to define reproductive rights more

---

[46]Cobble, *The Other Women's Movement,* 195–200, 206–13.
[47]Benita Roth, *Separate Roads to Feminism: Black, Chicana, and White Feminist Movements in America's Second Wave* (New York, 2004), 1–23, 178–95.

broadly than either group did individually.[48] Anne Enke's *Finding the Movement* looks at conflicts over public space to show how a wide variety of women stumbled on feminism serendipitously and then, as feminists, struggled with each other over its meanings. She is particularly attentive to the activism of minority women and of lesbian women who are often marginalized in mainstream accounts of the movement.[49]

The literature on the movement, while small compared to that on the civil rights movement, is nevertheless growing in complexity as feminism and its history continue to evolve. Feminism is becoming more focused on strengthening the position of women in the great, global issues of our time, such as climate change, disaster management (the majority of victims of any catastrophe like Hurricane Katrina are women), work conditions, the feminization of poverty, and the prevention of sexual violence, to name only a few. Meanwhile, scholars are rising to Baxandall's challenge to synthesize the multitude of early contributions to the women's movement. Inclusive histories of the Second Wave are of value not only to historians but also to participants in the Third.

---

[48] Jennifer Nelson, *Women of Color and the Reproductive Rights Movement* (New York, 2003).
[49] Enke, *Finding the Movement.*

WILLIAM H. CHAFE

from The Road to Equality, 1962–Today   **[2000]**

WILLIAM H. CHAFE (1942–) is the Alice Mary Baldwin Professor of History at Duke University. He is the author of *Women and Equality: Changing Patterns in American Culture* (1977), *Civilities and Equality* (1980), and *The Paradox of Change: American Women in the Twentieth Century* (1991).

If a group of journalists had gathered around a table in 1962, they would not have been likely to select changes in women's lives as one of the major emerging stories. After all, politics as defined by John Kennedy was still a "macho" game dominated by the Cold War. Events such as the Cuban Missile Crisis were its real testing points. Even civil rights was more a showdown between male rivals than a searching inquiry into how issues such as race could shape and control a society.

Yet by the start of the 1970s few issues would have more prominence or significance than the feminist revolution and the changes taking place in the everyday lives of countless women. It all happened because of the flowering of criticism and reform that came with a new generation. Women's issues could not be ignored once young people started rebelling against

---

William H. Chafe, "The Road to Equality, 1962–Today," in Nancy Cott, ed., *No Small Courage: A History of Women in the United States* (New York: Oxford University Press, 2000), 29–86. Used by permission of Oxford University Press.

social norms, students began challenging discrimination based on race (why not sex as well?), and antipoverty crusaders started examining the roots of economic oppression. Questions of gender and sexual politics may not have been the headlines that seized popular attention in 1962, but they were just below the surface, ready to become the news story that helped define an era.

No dramatic social change occurs for a single reason or springs from one group of people alone. But any effort to understand the transforming power of feminism in the late 1960s and 1970s must begin with the young people who were attending college when John Kennedy was inaugurated. Those college students already reflected a dramatic shift in life patterns. Twenty years earlier, when their parents were their age, only 15 percent of American youth had gone to college. But then had come World War II, the emergence of a fast-paced economy fueled by consumer purchases, a housing boom and technological innovation, and a corresponding explosion of economic and educational opportunities.

The "affluent society" meant more than a mass migration of young families to suburbia, the spread of sprawling shopping malls, and huge growth in automobile ownership and highway construction. It also necessitated a system of higher education that mass-produced the scientists, managers, and technological experts to sustain and expand the gains that had been made. America had become a "knowledge" society, and the university and its residents were a central part of the nation's nervous system. By 1965 45 percent of young people attended college — three times the proportion of a quarter century earlier. Reflecting the vital connection between education and the affluent society, 75 percent of these college students came from families with incomes above the national median. . . .

Yet the experience of having grown up in such comfort also gave young people a different perspective from which to consider their lifetime goals and priorities. Their parents had been raised during the hardships of the Great Depression in the 1930s and the uncertainties of war in the 1940s. They had struggled to win economic security and then prosperity in the postwar era. For the younger generation, material comfort was taken for granted, not a distant prize to be won or an elusive goal that gave life meaning. . . .

When they got to college, moreover, many of these students found an environment that encouraged them to be skeptical and critical of the social standards and practices that prevailed in the middle class. . . .

A second place to look for the reasons why feminism and women's issues became so visible by the end of the decade is in the civil rights movement. No struggle shaped the 1960s generation as much as that of black Americans to secure full equality and justice. Nor did any other movement capture so completely the desire to create a better world. If white students were ready to criticize the world they inherited, racial discrimination offered them a powerful weapon; if they wished to act on their ideals and religious faith to show they could "make a difference," civil rights offered an ethical case to demonstrate their commitment; and if they hoped to find through their activism a real-life alternative to the world they were now questioning, there was no more inspiring model than that of the "beloved community" where blacks and whites, living and working together, could make peace and love and justice a reality. . . .

Many of the most important leaders in the civil rights movement were women. Rosa Parks had long been a mainstay of the National Association for the Advancement of Colored People (NAACP) in Montgomery. Jo Ann Robinson and the Women's Political Council had played a key role in organizing the bus boycott there. Ella Baker was in many ways the mother of the civil rights movement. In addition to being one of the NAACP's chief organizers in the South, she also served as the acting executive director of Dr. King's Southern Christian Leadership Conference at the end of the 1950s (male ministers, she found, were more comfortable making her "acting" director rather than director). . . .

As some white students came to join blacks in SNCC during the early 1960s, they found black women playing pivotal roles in the movement, roles that demonstrated a new possibility for women's activism, one not usually associated with the roles social convention prescribed for women. Along with the civil rights movement itself, and the growing criticism of societal norms that was emerging in the new generation, this experience of women's leadership would contribute to the gradual emergence of a feminist agenda.

In the meantime, other less visible changes had made the legal and economic status of women a significant concern for policymakers. During the twentieth century the proportion of women in the labor force had been increasing. Before World War II most of these women were young, single, and poor. They worked almost exclusively in sex-segregated jobs, such as domestic service and clerical positions. Where they did occupy jobs similar to those held by men, they were paid only a fraction of the male wage. A disproportionate number of women workers came from immigrant backgrounds or were African Americans or Latinas. Although over time more married women joined the labor force, especially during the Depression when survival required that everyone earn money if possible, society still expected that all but the poorest women should concentrate on homemaking once they married and started to have children.

World War II did not alter this expectation overnight, but it accelerated some long-term trends in women's employment and changed the cultural dynamics affecting women's work. More than six million women took jobs during the labor crisis created by the war — an increase in the female labor force of more than 50 percent. Most important, 75 percent of these women were married and 60 percent were over the age of thirty-five. The end of the war brought a massive propaganda campaign to force women to return to the home, but some effects of the wartime experience remained. The proportion of married women in the labor force had increased from 15 percent in 1940 to almost 25 percent in 1950. The average age of women workers had increased. And more and more women who were middle class and educated were taking jobs.

The aftermath of World War II produced a kind of cultural division in attitudes toward women. On the one hand, psychologists, family "experts," the media, advertisers, and public opinion leaders celebrated domesticity, portraying mothers and housewives as "daily content in a world of bedroom, kitchen, sex, babies and home." Yet at the same time, many women were acting in ways that seemed to contradict the experts' advice. All during the suburban bliss of the 1950s, women were taking jobs at a rate four times faster than men. Frequently, these were not full-time jobs. Rarely were they in fields that offered promotion or high pay. Nor did there appear to be any "feminist" motivation driving women to the work force. In fact, women were taking jobs in order to help the family move one rung higher on the middle-class ladder, afford an addition to the suburban tract house they had just bought, set money aside for a college fund for the kids, or buy a new car. It was part of becoming a member of the affluent society.

Moreover, women — especially middle-class women — were developing a pattern of seeking jobs that had its own clear cultural logic. The greatest increase in employment among women took place among those over thirty-five whose children were in school. The proportion of women at work in that category leaped from 25 percent in 1950 to 39 percent in 1960. Thus young mothers were still staying at home, to do what the magazines said they should do, but once their children started school they were taking jobs on the reasoning that, with another income, the family as a whole could enjoy a better life. . . .

Against this backdrop President Kennedy appointed his national Commission on the Status of Women in 1961. In part he was paying off a political debt to Esther Peterson, a longtime supporter who for years had worked in the halls of Congress as a lobbyist for garment workers and other labor union women, and whom Kennedy now appointed head of the Women's Bureau of the U.S. Department of Labor. Kennedy also hoped to solidify his position with liberals by making Eleanor Roosevelt the honorary chair of the commission. Hardly a bold or risky maneuver from Kennedy's point of view, examining the status of women seemed an ideal way to signal recognition of an important constituency and support mobilizing the full resources of the country to win the Cold War.

The commission fulfilled Kennedy's hopes, completing in 1963 a comprehensive, balanced, and careful analysis of women's situation. It covered some important new ground on women's issues. For example, it emphasized the critical importance of child care facilities to full utilization of women's resources, recommended paid maternity leave, and supported giving unemployment and minimum-wage benefits to large numbers of women previously not covered. Perhaps most important, it focused attention on the pervasive inequities women experienced on the job, preparing the way for the Equal Pay Act of 1963. This act mandated that where women and men did exactly the same job, they should receive exactly the same wage. . . .

Yet the commission's most important contribution was not what it said or failed to say, but the fact that it existed. It formally acknowledged the fact that women's rights and opportunities were of critical national importance. . . .

A network had been established. Pivotal to that network were a series of state commissions on the status of women. These commissions were created throughout the country to pursue on a local level the same work being done by the national commission. Starting in 1964, the state commissions gathered annually in Washington, D.C., to assess the progress that had been made on women's agenda of change and to generate strategies for the next step. Such a gathering in 1966 would lead to a result that Kennedy could never have anticipated in 1961 — the creation of the National Organization for Women (NOW), which would become the civil rights vanguard of a reborn and revitalized feminism. . . .

The overpowering irony of the idea of a woman's movement was that women were everywhere, constituting 51 percent of the population, members of all classes and of all ethnic, religious, political, and economic groups. If, as some argued, women were oppressed like minorities, they surely did not all share the same material circumstances, suffer the same degree of discrimination, or live together in the same run-down neighborhoods as some African Americans did on Chicago's South Side or as Mexican Americans did in the Los Angeles barrios. What, then, did it mean to share an identity? Did a rich, white, college-educated woman who ran the local Junior League have more in common with her Latina maid who had never gone to high school than with her rich, white, college-educated husband? What defined the bonds of gender? And could they be as strong as the bonds of class or ethnicity or religion? . . .

Pauli Murray, a black lawyer who had pioneered the effort to get blacks admitted to Southern law schools in the 1930s, zeroed in on the connection between racial and sexual equality in her work for the Kennedy Commission on the Status of Women. Like black civil rights activists, she declared, women should prosecute their case for freedom by going to court and demanding equal protection under the laws, a right conferred by the 14th Amendment. This amendment, added to the Constitution in 1868, sought to ensure the legal standing of the newly freed slaves by defining their citizenship rights. At the time Congress had inserted the word "male" in front of "citizen," caving in to those who still wanted to exclude women from fundamental rights, such as voting. But the 19th Amendment had altered that by recognizing women's right to vote, and now, Murray argued, women should insist on carrying their case forward on the basis of the civil rights they enjoyed with all citizens under the clause of the 14th Amendment that declared, "No State shall . . . deny to any person within its jurisdiction the equal protection of the laws."

Betty Friedan referred to parallels between racial and sexual equality in her 1963 book, *The Feminine Mystique*, but, more centrally, reached out to galvanize the consciousness of millions of American women by giving a label to "the problem that has no name." The dominant institutions of

American culture, Friedan charged, had tried to treat women like children by enclosing them in "comfortable concentration camps" where they were told they must be happy because they were women, not individuals. Assigned a set of responsibilities solely on the basis of their sex, women had been denied the chance to cultivate their individual talents or assert their personal rights.

"I've tried everything women are supposed to do," one young mother wrote Friedan, "hobbies, gardening, pickling, canning, and being very social with my neighbors. . . . But I'm desperate. I begin to feel that I have no personality. I'm a server of food and putter-on of pants and a bedmaker, somebody who can be called on when you want something. But who am I?" . . .

With the formation of NOW in the fall of 1966, America's women's rights activists had an organization comparable to the NAACP, ready to fight through the media, the courts, and the Congress for the same rights for women that the NAACP sought for blacks. NOW focused on an "equal partnership of the sexes" in job opportunities, education, household responsibilities, and government. Friedan and her allies pressured Kennedy's successor, President Lyndon B. Johnson, to include women in his affirmative action policies, which were designed to speed the movement of minorities to decent jobs, and to appoint feminists to administrative and judicial offices. NOW endorsed the Equal Rights Amendment and made reform of abortion laws a national priority.

Even before NOW formed, a younger generation of women were gaining a new sense of themselves in the civil rights movement. Most of the younger activists joined the Student Non-Violent Coordinating Committee (SNCC), which created an atmosphere in which independent thinking and social criticism could flourish. The majority were black, but a significant minority were white, many of them women, including . . . Mary King, daughter of a Protestant minister. A new sense of empowerment infused the women and men alike. "If you are spending your time [doing] community organization, . . . opening people's awareness to their own power in themselves," Mary King noted, "it inevitably strengthens your own conceptions, your own ability." As women took their turn risking life and limb to make the movement happen, they were transformed in their own sense of who they were and what they could do. "I learned a lot of respect for myself for having gone through all of that," one said.

White women were impressed by the black women they met. Some of the black women were older; black minister Charles Sherrod, the organizer of SNCC's project in southwest Georgia, called them the "mommas" of the movement. "She is usually a militant woman in the community," Sherrod defined such a woman, "outspoken, understanding, and willing to catch hell, having already caught her share." Fannie Lou Hamer of Mississippi was one. Evicted from her land for daring to register to vote, then horribly beaten by a white sheriff, she refused to give in to hate or fear. "Black and white together," she would sing out at civil rights rallies. "We are not afraid." Observing the effect Hamer had on people, the white volunteer Sally Belfrage observed that "a sort of joy began to grow in every face. . . . For just that second, no one is afraid, because they are free."

Younger black women exhibited some of the same strength and determination. Diane Nash was a Fisk University beauty queen, but what struck her colleagues in the movement was her quiet courage as she insisted on continuing the 1961 Freedom Rides through the South. . . .

But some of the women also detected a typical male paternalism in the movement. . . . Women in SNCC saw it when they were treated as though it was natural that they should do the typing and clerical work, or make the coffee, or take notes at meetings. One volunteer said, "The . . . general attitude toward the inferiority and 'proper place' of women is disgusting."

These sentiments were held mainly by white women. The movement — including the prominent role played by black women — had heightened their awareness and consciousness about being treated as less than equal. Because the ideals of the "beloved community" were so high, any failure to measure up to those ideals became a crushing blow. Most black women in the movement seemed not to have the same response. They were already a part of the black community, they assumed their leadership roles in a natural and unforced manner, and they had other priorities. White women, less sure of their identity within the movement, were potentially more critical. . . .

The final ingredient for the rebirth of feminism came from the rapidly expanding student movement in America. That movement was not a unified crusade. . . .

Some generalizations, however, are valid. Most of the participants in the student movement were white and from middle- or upper-class backgrounds. . . . By the mid-1960s, when the student movement started to grow with explosive force, more and more young people began to question the very basis for their society. The Vietnam War radicalized youthful protestors, male and female alike. . . .

As student radicals set out to turn America around from its foreign policy in Vietnam, few constants emerged from the tactics and philosophies of various protest groups. But with virtually no exceptions, the men in the movements treated women as inferiors. "Macho" radicalism seemed the wave of the future — except that the women of the various movements would have none of it.

Some of the paternalism of the student movement reflected classic unconscious assumptions. "We regard *men* as infinitely precious and possessed of unfulfilled capacities for reason, freedom and love," the Port Huron statement had said — as if from the Declaration of Independence in 1776 to the present day nothing had happened to alter the presumption that citizens were men. At other times, though, men in the movement seemed to intentionally regard women as inferior. . . .

Throughout the entire antiwar movement, a . . . condescension and disregard prevailed, symbolized by the antiwar slogan, "Girls say yes to guys [not boys] who say no." Always happy to accept the part of the sexual revolution that allegedly made women more ready to share their affection, male radicals displayed no comparable willingness to share their own authority as part of a larger revolution. Women's equality was not part of the new politics any more than it had been part of the old. . . .

As the women's liberation movement spread from campus to campus and city to city, so too did consciousness-raising groups, the new instrument for mobilizing, then institutionalizing, a sense of collective self. If male values and organizations were the source of the problem with the larger society, women would have to create their own institutions, their own values, and their own way of making decisions and relating to each other. Through this intimate process of self-disclosure and self-discovery women's liberation quickly developed its most famous insight: that the personal is political. Church-activist-turned-radical-feminist Charlotte Bunch declared, "[T]here is no private domain of a person's life that is not political and there is no political issue that is not ultimately personal."

The women in these groups came to understand that they were not responsible for the pain and dissatisfaction of their relationships with men; rather, these problems reflected the whole system of hierarchy and power of a male-dominated system designed to oppress women. To turn the world upside down, women had to begin by creating true democracy in their relationships with each other, then carry those values and ways of making decisions into the public arena and transform it as well.

None of this could happen through traditional institutions with their hierarchies and male values. Women had to occupy their own social space, develop their own definition of who they were, and form their own agenda. This was perhaps the most revolutionary idea of all — taking control of their own lives and refusing to be subservient to what someone else said was their "proper place."

By the end of the 1960s, the foundation had been created for a widespread assault on traditional attitudes and values regarding sex roles in America. The issues could not be summarized easily or quickly. They involved more than questions of equal pay and the chance to compete one-on-one with men for a law partnership or medical residency. The issues were inclusive and varied in nature, ranging from abolishing sexist language like "chick" or "girl" to preserving and protecting woman's reproductive freedom of choice, eliminating sexist stereotypes from children's books, and defending a person's sexual orientation. Some women chose to organize feminist political caucuses, others created committees on the status of women in the professions, and still others organized a woman's legal defense fund to fight in court for women's rights. Countless women joined the battle to heighten public consciousness about rape and domestic violence against women.

Because the issues were so varied, they affected thousands of different groups and virtually every aspect of American life. For the same reason, however, this was no monolithic movement with a single director, program, or credo. The advantage was that women could enter into the movement in many places and feel comfortable. The disadvantage was that at times energies seemed divided, and disagreement rather than consensus prevailed over what needed to be done. . . .

Which Road to Travel

. . . From the time the women's rights movement started in the United States in the 1840s, there had always been a division between those who believed fundamentally that women were *individuals* and should be treated exactly the same as men and those who believed women were different, biologically and psychologically, and should be allowed to act *collectively* to implement their distinctive mission. The division of opinion shaped the arguments made for the 19th Amendment, which granted woman suffrage. Some said women should have the vote because it was their natural right as individual citizens to participate in the electoral process; others insisted that women needed the vote so that they could fulfill their special task of overseeing the national family's moral and spiritual health.

This distinction continued to shape divergent approaches to feminism. It helps explain the difference in goals and tactics between liberal feminism, with its focus on individual rights, and radical feminism, with its concern for group advancement and activities. The liberal National Organization for Women became the premiere civil rights group fighting for individual advancement for women. NOW used court cases, lobbied with Congress, and pressured the President to lower barriers against women. One of NOW's central demands was ratification of the Equal Rights Amendment (ERA) — a measure that would abolish sex as a category for treating women and men differently under the law. The ERA represented an individualist approach to equality: Its goal was a society in which women and men had identical status as individual human beings.

This approach accepted as basically sound the existing structure of the society, including the values underlying social and economic institutions. The plan was to secure women's acceptance as individuals within those institutions on the principle of equal opportunity. Women should be granted the same opportunity as men to become chief executives and board members of corporations. NOW concentrated on destroying obstacles that defined women as different in rights or abilities from men. It forced the *New York Times*, for example, to do away with classified ads that specified "Male Only" or "Female Only" jobs. It also integrated bars and restaurants that in the past had excluded women. But at no time did NOW question corporate domination of American culture or the existing two-party political system. Integration, not separation, and reform, not revolution, were its goals.

Radical feminists, by contrast, wanted to change society by acting collectively to attack the roots of women's oppression. For most women who called themselves radical feminists, the problem was the system of patriarchy — social, economic, and cultural institutions that supported male supremacy. As long as women were trained by patriarchal institutions such as schools and churches to defer to men and suppress their own desires, they could not be free.

This approach treated women as an oppressed political "class." Their oppressor, in turn, was "the class of men, or the male role," as one radical feminist put it. One class remained in control of the other by dividing and conquering its victims, or even worse, persuading its victims that they deserved to be subordinate. "The key to maintaining the oppressor role," New York feminist Ti-Grace Atkinson wrote, "is to prevent the oppressed from uniting." In a patriarchy men did this to women by socializing them to believe in "love," using romantic relationships to convince women to accept their own oppression, and creating such institutions as marriage and the family to reinforce their bondage. Other institutions such as corporations, schools, churches, and government echoed this class relationship, creating the equivalent of a closed system in which women, the majority of the world's population, were fooled into accepting an inferior and powerless role.

Radical feminists called for women to unite to throw off their oppression — and to exclude men from the movement. "We need not only separate groups, but a separate movement," one radical feminist wrote. Coalition with men would lead only to a new version of women's subservience and defeat. Women had to fight for themselves. They had different values and concerns than men had. What they needed was not acceptance as individuals into patriarchal institutions, but the kind of class solidarity as women that would permit their distinctive values to flower and triumph. If male-dominated institutions and values were the problem, women must develop their own institutions — reflecting their own values — and make these the cornerstone of independence.

Radical feminists thus devoted much of their energy to building woman-defined and woman-run structures. Some were cultural, such as publishing houses, journals, and newsletters. Others were health-related — women-run clinics, for example, or centers for women seeking abortions or needing counseling or assistance in the face of domestic abuse from men.

Lesbians participated in all forms of the women's liberation movement, but during the 1970s, following the emergence of a distinctive "gay liberation" movement, there developed among some lesbians a much clearer sense of the need for a separate movement devoted to lesbian issues and concerns. By their commitment to women as well as their rejection of sexual ties with men, lesbian feminists demonstrated their determination to be independent of patriarchal controls. . . .

Whatever the importance of these internal differences, most radical feminists were more similar to each other than to liberal feminists. They might eventually want to be equal with men as individuals, but first they sought to be independent from men and to celebrate their collective identity as a class, nourishing those values and attitudes that emphasized their differences rather than their similarity to men.

. . . Socialist-feminists also focused on the need for revolution rather than reform. Only for them, the class to be overthrown was capitalism,

not men, and the means to secure that end was by uniting with all other
oppressed groups of the world. Socialist-feminists believed in solidarity
but did not support separatism among women. They would continue to
protest against the sexism displayed by men who were oppressed, but they
would do so in the context of recognizing that the ultimate source of
women's inequality was not men but rather the power of a capitalist class
that included women as well as men. The fact that top executives at
General Motors might include women did not make GM any less exploitative. "Women's liberation does not mean equality with men," one writer
observed, "[because] equality in an unjust society is meaningless." . . .

The one glaring flaw that should have concerned all women activists,
whatever their ideological persuasion, was feminism's failure to escape its
narrow class and race boundaries. Despite the ambitious aspirations of
socialist feminists for a cross-class, cross-race coalition, most feminist
activists were white, middle class, and college-educated. There were occasional black feminist groups, such as the National Black Feminist
Organization, and each feminist organization boasted some participation
by African-American or Latina women. Yet on balance, the numbers were
infinitesimally small. Both the language and the programs of feminist
groups seemed to reflect a white middle-class approach. Until women of
all classes and backgrounds felt attracted to and welcomed by feminist
groups, there was little likelihood that the promise of a universal sisterhood could become a reality.

The Persistence of Differences

By the middle of the 1980s two generalizations could be made about
women's lives in the United States. First, no group in society had experienced as much change as women had over the preceding three decades.
Second, the changes that had occurred affected women in dramatically
different ways, depending on whether they were white or nonwhite, rich
or poor, married or divorced. Ethnicity, class, and marital status continued to determine what happened to women. . . .

Employment patterns made the transformations in women's roles
material. In 1960 approximately 30 percent of women worked; four
decades later the figure was 75 percent, including 60 percent of mothers
whose children were not yet of school age, the category of women least
likely to take employment in the past. Women not only constituted half
the entering classes of law schools and medical schools, but they made up
nearly half of the entire labor force. Yet these statistics hid the degree to
which gender remained a source of inequality. . . .

Work continued to be allocated, designed, and valued differently
according to whether women or men performed it. . . .

The impact of race and ethnicity was clear in the feminization of
poverty. Through the decades after 1960, the number of female-headed
households skyrocketed, driven both by divorce and by lower marriage

rates. One-fifth of family-based households among whites were female-headed by the 1990s; among Latino families it was almost one-third, and among African-Americans, almost three-fifths. During these years poverty climbed upward among ethnic minorities, even as it fell overall among whites. In 1998 28.8 percent of white, single mother households with children lived below poverty level, as compared to 47.5 percent for blacks and 52.2 percent for hispanics. The correlation between being a female head of a household with children and being poor was dramatic.

Behind all the stories about a revolution in women's status was a complicated, tortured, and often contradictory reality. Because race and class interacted with gender, some women benefited enormously from the gains that had been won by feminists, while countless others saw no change at all in their lives, and the situation for many worsened rather than improving. To a poor woman struggling to make ends meet while holding down a minimum-wage job at the local fast-food outlet, the promises of women's liberation seemed like a slap in the face. Economic resources and education seemed to be the most important variables. A young college-educated woman from an economically secure background had a world open to her that was strikingly different from her mother's or grandmother's opportunities. If these earlier generations worked outside the home, they were likely to be secretaries, salesclerks, nurses, or teachers. Even then, they were likely to stop work when they married and had a child. The woman with a college degree in the year 2000, on the other hand, could go to law school or get a master's degree in business administration. She might then enter a large corporate firm and make a six-figure salary, doing the same kind of work for the same pay as the brightest young man. If she married, it was probable that her husband would be someone with a comparable background. And if they had a baby, they were likely to pay a child-care worker or a day-care center to take care of the child while continuing to pursue their careers.

A young Latina woman born in the South Bronx, on the other hand, faced a very different situation. If she was like half the young people in New York City's public schools, she would drop out before graduating from high school. There was a good chance she would have a child while still in her teenage years, but would not get married. With no job skills, she could find work only at low-paying service establishments. By the time she was twenty she would be locked into a cycle of work and family responsibilities that seemed to offer little opportunity for improvement. Not only was the life of the South Bronx woman no better than her mother's or grandmother's, but it might even be worse.

There were other possibilities, of course. A white (or black) high school graduate who worked as a secretary for an insurance agency or as a factory operative at General Motors might well find her life better than that of her mother — for which the feminist movement deserved some credit. Greater attention to sexual harassment in the workplace might discourage unwanted advances from male bosses or coworkers. Legal advances for women's rights contributed to higher wages and the opening of some jobs that previously had been restricted to men. If the woman had an unwanted pregnancy, she now could consider terminating it legally.

One of the major problems with feminist advances was that they operated differentially. Their benefits were largely limited to women already in a position to be able to take advantage of the new rights that had been won. Nor did the differential decrease over time. When *Roe v. Wade* became the law of the land, for example, poor women as well as rich women had access to an abortion. But by 1978, Congress had prohibited federal funds from being used to pay for abortions for poor women. Then additional restrictions were enacted to circumscribe women's abortion rights, including a twenty-four-hour waiting period and the requirement that teenagers notify their parents and get their permission. Because of threats to their funding and security, abortion providers dwindled in number. Well-off women had little difficulty coping with these restrictions. But women from culturally conservative and economically disadvantaged backgrounds found the restrictions almost impassable. What had once seemed like a feminist victory for all women had come to have a distinctly middle- and upper-class tinge.

Similarly, government programs designed to force companies and universities to open doors to women had little impact on those clustered in sex-segregated, low-paying jobs. Affirmative action occasionally worked well as a means of giving women lawyers access to jobs at law firms that previously hired only white men, or of giving women professors opportunities to be hired in departments that had never considered women scholars. But affirmative action meant little to women who were data processors working side by side with other women in a giant computer pool (unless it meant that some men were hired), or to operatives at a textile mill who had neither the education nor the training to qualify for a management-level opening. In short, affirmative action — and other equal opportunity programs — tended to benefit those with preexisting credentials that enabled them to move forward. They did less to open new possibilities for people stuck in sex-segregated and low-paying positions.

Programs that might have been of greater value to the mass of women in the workplace either were not implemented or were rejected. Working-class and minority women had no need greater than adequate child care for their young children — child care that would not only permit them to hold decent jobs, but would also give their children the medical care, nutrition, and educational stimulation that might break the cycle of poverty and improve the children's chances for a better life. Congress enacted such a program in 1972. Called the Comprehensive Child Development Act, it would have created day-care centers throughout the country, with places available to all children regardless of ability to pay. But President Nixon vetoed the measure on the grounds that it would undermine the strength of the nuclear family. Well-off people, of course, could afford to pay for their own child care. But poor women did not have that option, and most were forced to rely on makeshift arrangements.

"Comparable worth" was another idea that, if enacted and upheld by the courts, might have significantly improved the economic status of millions of women workers. Equal pay legislation in the past had focused on securing equal compensation for women who performed the same work as men. Yet such laws failed to address the underlying problem of job segmentation — the fact that most women worked with other women and did not hold the same jobs as men. On the other hand, if the skills required for a job could be measured and compared with skills needed for other jobs, it might be possible to arrive at a reliable standard that would lead to people with comparable skills being paid comparable wages. In San Jose, California, for example, job investigators found that the skills and training needed by a nurse were approximately comparable to those required for a fire-truck mechanic. Yet the nurse, a woman, earned nine thousand dollars less than the mechanic, a man. Clearly, given the number of women in skilled positions, whether nurses, secretaries, or data processors, a wage scale adjusted to compensate for comparable worth might bring substantial improvement in wages.

In some cities, such as Minneapolis and Seattle, where comparable worth policies were implemented, it made a significant difference. Yet many government officials criticized the idea as unworkable and a violation of the free market system, and courts were inconsistent in upholding comparable worth laws. What the opponents ignored, of course, was that the so-called free market system was in fact based on old ideas that women should be confined to "women's work" that paid only a "woman's wage."

Poor, working class, and minority women had ample reason to feel that feminism reflected middle-class priorities and values. To be sure, feminist groups from NOW to Redstockings (a radical feminist group) included attention to working-class issues in their literature and did what they could to press for measures that would help the poor as much as the rich. Yet in the end the feminist aims that were achieved seemed to be concentrated in areas designed to promote *individual* rights for those in a position to take advantage of them, rather than on issues that might bring *collective* advancement for women of all classes and races. Justifiably or unjustifiably, "feminism" became associated in the public eye with well-groomed, highly articulate women in business suits who sat around boardroom tables or frequented centers of power. It was not publicly linked to programs that an Irish-Catholic mother of four who worked in a shoe factory, or a black single mother who was a high school dropout, could identify with. Some groups tried to bridge that chasm, and black and Hispanic women occupied prominent positions in feminist organizations. Nevertheless, it was hard to escape the conclusion that impoverished minority women's experiences after 1960 had little in common with those of well-educated middle- and upper-class women; ethnicity and class remained powerful obstacles to women's solidarity.

ROSALYN BAXANDALL

from Re-Visioning the Women's Liberation Movement's Narrative   [2001]

ROSALYN BAXANDALL (1939–) is chair of the American Studies Department and distinguished teaching professor specializing in women's history at the State University of New York at Old Westbury. Among her noteworthy publications are *Words of Fire: The Life and Writing of Elizabeth Gurley Flynn* (1987) and, with her colleague Elizabeth Ewen, *Picture Windows: How the Suburbs Happened* (2000).

Context

There are very few historical studies of the women's liberation movement, the largest mass movement in the United States, and, some Latin American and South Asian Indian women claim, in the world. There is more scholarship on contemporary feminism in sociology, political science, and psychology, but most of these studies focus on liberal organizations, like the National Organization for Women (NOW). Liberal feminism has been especially well documented in large cities because those records are available and the participants were professional women who left a trail of minutes and published writings. In writing about the women's liberation movement, I refer to the loose affiliation of groups, most with radical agendas, not the more formal and liberal membership organizations like NOW. The two movements were not discrete entities, however. Some members of New York NOW, such as Kate Millett, Lucinda Cisler, Ti-Grace Atkinson, and Anselm Dell'Olio, went to meetings of both groups in the early years. Although NOW's goals and tactics were quite different from those of the women's liberation movement, the groups often dovetailed on issues. NOW usually followed Roberts Rules of Order, but after 1971 some chapters adopted consciousness raising, the major new organizational form, theory of knowledge, and research tool of the women's movement.

Because the women's liberation movement was so decentralized, finding information often requires interviewing participants and digging into personal papers and local libraries. Not only were there no national, regional, or state organizations, but in very few cities were there even citywide groups (such as Bread and Roses in Boston or the Chicago Women's Liberation Union). A few cities like Gainesville, Florida, had a citywide meeting once a month. More importantly, perhaps, were the unofficial, spontaneous interchanges between women in different cities, which were

Rosalyn Baxandall, "Re-Visioning the Women's Liberation Movement's Narrative: Early Second Wave African American Feminists," was originally published in *Feminist Studies* 27, no. 1 (Spring 2001): 225–45, by permission of the publisher, Feminist Studies, Inc..

made possible by cheap airfares, hitchhiking, and frequent visiting among activists.

Membership in the women's liberation movement was informal, and most individuals participated by attending events, consciousness raising groups, and demonstrations, rather than general business meetings. Dues were seldom collected and members touted equality while disparaging leadership, although everyone generally knew who the leaders of a group were. Vast numbers of the publications were not signed or dated, perhaps because we lacked a sense of our own history and importance, lived in the present, felt all property (even intellectual property) was theft, and desired all or no one to be stars. What did it matter? In those early days, no one received financial benefit or needed the citation for a vita.

Groups frequently sprang up without formal connections to others; and the circulation of leaflets, position papers, pamphlets, posters, songs, T-shirts, and buttons provided a major source of common culture and intellectual connection. This was one of the last movements before computers; many pamphlets and leaflets were mimeographed on both sides and by now some of the paper has yellowed and the ink has bled — a historian's nightmare. When the movement started, many of us were just out of college and living in tiny nonpermanent quarters. We moved often, and valuable papers were frequently left behind or discarded.

In 1969–71, I was an active radical feminist in New York City — the media center, money capital, and landing place of many adventurous feminists. My participation in New York Radical Women, Redstockings, and WITCH in the cosmopolitan center probably colors my perspective in a Big Apple, New York hue. But I had contact through the various methods noted above to ideas and networks across the country. In 1972, for instance, I hitched from New York City to San Francisco with my five-year-old son, Phineas — stopping in several cities, visiting feminists, and putting Phineas in various daycare centers. Activists often flew at inexpensive rates securing false identification papers that claimed we were less than twenty-one years old.

These experiences must now be made part of the historical record. Linda Gordon and I edited *Dear Sister: Dispatches from the Women's Liberation Movement,* a collection of documents and ephemera covering the years 1965 to 1977. The original plan was for this to be a scholarly collection, two to four volumes intended for libraries. Our collection was to have four functions: preservation, publication, scholarly analysis, and interpretation. The goal was to make available, for the first time, significant literature from all parts of the country: leaflets, position papers, interviews, songs, and posters. This required a systematic search, in large part because no library or archive in the United States contains a broad collection of women's liberation materials. The Schlesinger Library of Radcliffe, the Wisconsin State Historical Society, and Duke University have significant collections; but they have evolved randomly rather than systematically, accepting materials that are donated rather than trying to be thorough.

These libraries, like most others, primarily represent their own regions. The situation will only worsen as public funds for historical preservation diminish, so preservation and publication seemed critical to ensuring the possibility for later analyses and interpretations.

The Origins

A social movement is not like a symphony with an opening and a grand finale. How then does one decide on the notes that form the overture? Unlike a war, there are no shots fired which precipitate the beginning skirmishes. The opening moves take place in streets, living rooms, churches, and conference halls. Only after a movement has been stamped and signified a historic occurrence do origins become relevant; then the digging begins. In excavating the ancestry, we calculate backwards. We weave a cloth of causality, multiple strands, manifold causes. So we come to rely on a convenient birthplace, which then becomes myth, more real than history, and we seldom dig for other ancestors.

The historical, sociological, and popular wisdom places the memo, "Sex and Caste," written in November 1965 by Casey Hayden and Mary King (two white activists in the Student Non-violent Coordinating Committee, known as SNCC) as the well-spring of the modern women's liberation movement. As Sara Evans stated in *Personal Politics: The Roots of Women's Liberation in the Civil Rights Movement and the New Left*, and nearly everyone has echoed since, "It is not surprising that the issues were defined and confronted first by southern women, whose consciousness developed in a context that inextricably and paradoxically linked the fate of women and black people." Evans claimed, "It was from this network of southern women, whose involvement dated from the beginning of SNCC and who understood their commitment in theological formulas of ultimate commitment (Casey quit her job as church secretary to join SNCC), that the earliest feminist response emerged." Hayden was a key organizer and far better known in the civil rights movement than Tom Hayden, her husband at the time. The young civil rights activists, who Evans calls the modern equivalents of the devout Quaker abolitionists Sarah and Angelina Grimke, made a neat parallel between abolition and civil rights as midwives of women's rights movements.

Hayden and King were not aware that their notes to other women in the peace and freedom movements, an internal memo, would years later be considered the founding document of women's liberation. They even say at the end of their memo, which was published by *Liberation*, a small, leftist, peace magazine, in April 1966, that "Objectively, the chances seem nil that we could start a movement based on anything as distant to general American thought as a sex-caste system. Therefore most of us will probably want to work full time on problems such as war, poverty, race." They go on to note that dialogue within radical and liberal groups on the deep human problems of women are rarely taken seriously and usually seen as private matters. Hayden and King were hesitant to make their insights public, but through their participation in the civil rights movement, they had gained the knowledge, self-confidence, and courage to articulate their grievances. Still, neither Mary King nor Casey Hayden became active participants in the women's liberation movement.

The unwillingness of men to take women seriously and the lack of opportunity and equality in the workplace and among activists reverberated for many middle-class white women, both inside and outside the New Left and civil rights movements. No group directly came out of the "Sex and Caste" memo. But there is no doubt that in cities throughout the United States, women from the civil rights movement were among the initiators in forming women's liberation cells. Many of these SNCC activists were also active in Students for a Democratic Society (SDS) and other anti-Vietnam War groups. The Hayden and King memo drew attention to the lack of freedom and equality of women in the society as a whole. Their memo was influential because it hit a nerve, expressing not only what many women in SNCC felt, but also the views of women in SDS, Vietnam Summer, the National Conference for a New Politics, and other New Left groups. Later it also resonated with those who were not New Left activists.

By 1967 women in these networks — particularly white women — started meeting and forming women's liberation groups, first in Chicago, and then in New York City, Seattle, Gainesville, Detroit, and Toronto. The women's liberation movement spread like wildfire. Many early groups were not equipped to accommodate all the women begging to join. In 1968, I was on *The David Susskind Show* which was televised all over the United States. I gave out my own home address, as our group, New York Radical Women (NYRW), did not have a formal mailing address at that time. NYRW received thousands of letters from individuals asking to join a group. We didn't have the womanpower, funds, or even a Xerox machine to respond. Many women, unable to find a group in their community, started one themselves. The media, pamphlets, and radical press kept us all in touch. There were only two national conferences: a small one in August 1968 held in Sandy Springs, Maryland, and a larger one that same year, over Thanksgiving weekend, in Lake Villa, outside Chicago, attended by over 200 women from thirty cities. *The Voice of the Women's Liberation Movement*, edited largely by Jo Freeman, was the only nationwide newsletter publishing from March 1968 to March 1969. The movement was local, and many groups were inconspicuous, often with no listed phone or address.

Black feminism developed as well, notably in large urban centers, but it captured far less media attention. In fact, African American women have historically had a stronger tradition of honoring women's independence, often due to necessity, than have white women. Surveys done in the early 1970s show that, in general, Black women were more feminist than white women in their attitudes toward specific issues such as daycare, equal pay, equal work, and equality in relationships. As Elizabeth Toledo, NOW vice-president of action and organizer of the February 20–22, 1998, Women of Color and Allies Summit, proclaimed, "Women of color have shaped the feminist movement from its inception in this country, yet the public face of feminism is often seen as white." The majority of feminists, journalists, and scholars, Black and white, continue to view early feminism as white. Even so critical and concerned a scholar as Barbara Smith has failed to recognize any Black women's groups before 1973, when largely middle-class and professional African American women formed the National Black Feminist Organization. The history written so far by white and Black scholars largely obliterates individuals such as Cellestine Ware, Florynce Kennedy, Patricia Robinson, Barbara Omolade, Daphne Busby, Safiya Bandele, and Frances Beale — Black activists who wrote about feminism before 1973, as well as Black women's groups such as Mothers Alone Working, a Mount Vernon/New Rochelle group, and the Third World Women's Alliance (which edited a newspaper, *Triple Jeopardy*).

In collecting research for our original multivolume history, we visited libraries throughout the United States; wrote to many activists soliciting their papers; and found other events, organizations, and persons who might equally qualify as forerunners of the Second Wave of feminism. Contrary to many recent claims about the women's liberation movement being middle class, bourgeois, and white, the early formations we uncovered were primarily comprised of Black and poor women and members of Black nationalist or Old Left groups. The Sisterhood of Black Single Mothers, for example, founded by Daphne Busby in Brooklyn, sometime before 1972 and lasting to the late 1970s, published a monthly newsletter, operated home daycare, out-of-home children's activities, a big-sister program for pregnant single women, and an exchange for clothes and books. According to Black feminist/nationalist Barbara Omolade, their focus on support for single-mother families "challenged patriarchal, middle-class, and even cultural nationalist assumptions of women's roles and the family by affirming their [Black women's] completeness and strengths. . . . The Sisterhood creatively and powerfully reflected the complicated intertwining of race and gender, family and women's power."

Mothers Alone Working (MAW), a self-help group in San Francisco composed of 200 Black and white poor women, began in 1965 before most women's liberation groups — their first anniversary was reported in the *San Francisco Examiner and Chronicle* in September 1966. MAW organized summer camps, daycare, and sports days, pairing university students and the children of single mothers for sports events. The group hosted speakers on women's organizing and talks on "What Can You Deduct from Your Income Tax?" as well as on preventive medical services, job training, and food stamps. They developed a referral service for single working mothers, as their members were mainly self-supporting low-income women with dependent children. They also had a Granny Corps and, together with the Office of Economic Opportunity, trained thirty women over fifty-five to be emergency baby sitters, thus allowing mothers to work when a child was sick or a baby-sitting arrangement fell through. It's not clear how successful they were in their daycare campaign, but eleven churches expressed interest. Several children were apparently sent to free summer camps through MAW's intervention. MAW was a service organization, but it also lobbied the Board of Education for expanded daycare at reasonable rates for single parents. Baby-sitting as well as refreshments were provided at their meetings.

MAW was structured formally with officers — president, vice-president, secretary, treasurer, and an executive committee — elected each year. In contrast, most white women's liberation movement groups were informal, believing in participatory democracy and suspicious of hierarchy and organization, including designated officers, although after a few years of loose spontaneous organization, some groups such as the Chicago Women's Union and other socialist feminist groups in Ohio and North Carolina changed to a more formal structure of elected officers. Unlike many women's liberation movement groups that relied on word of mouth or informal networks, MAW made efforts to actively recruit new members. Although most of the officers seemed to live in San Francisco, the meetings were held in Black Oakland churches.

Joan Jordan seemed to have been responsible for organizing MAW. She was a white working-class woman and member of the Socialist Workers' Party (SWP). Radical organizations, such as the SWP, active in the mid-twentieth-century United States, based their political programs on the ideas of Karl Marx, Leon Trotsky, V. I. Lenin, and other socialist and communist revolutionaries. These hierarchical parties became known as the Old Left after the emergence of the more spontaneous New Left, civil rights, and antiwar groups of the 1960s. White men generally dominated both the Old Left and the New Left. Most, however, including the SWP, actively recruited African Americans and, to a lesser extent, white women. Jordan participated in the SWP, a Trotskyist group, until 1966 when she and other feminists were expelled for prioritizing women's issues, along with other charges. Jordan with a few other women then joined another Trotskyite group, the Freedom Socialist Party. She published articles and letters in a number of leftist newspapers and magazines, such as *The Militant, The Guardian,* and *Radical America,* often using the pen name "Vilma Sanchez," perhaps wanting to convey a Latin heritage. Years later, Jordan donated her letters — including a few articles, membership lists, and letters from MAW — to the University of Wisconsin Historical Society archives. A biography that accompanies the collection makes no mention, however, of her Old Left affiliations.

Movement activists who were former or current members of socialist and communist parties often downplayed Old Left connections during this period. The need to hide their socialist/communist affiliations had its roots in the McCarthy era of the 1950s, when to be a Communist Party member meant losing a job, or friends, or even going to prison. Therefore, it is difficult to estimate the Old Left's influence on the New Left or the women's liberation movement. But from the late 1960s well into the 1970s, SWP members, at least in New York City, Boston, and San Francisco, attended women's liberation meetings and functions and often copied our slogans or buttons, acting as if they were their own. Of all the Marxist

and socialist groups, the SWP seemed the most interested in women's liberation and the New Left. It was very active in taking over the abortion
repeal movement, although it watered down the original demands.
Several women's liberation groups like Cell 16 in Boston were almost
taken over by the SWP. Others, like the Chicago Women's Liberation
Union, eventually prevented SWP members from attending meetings.
Certainly Joan Jordan and other feminists brought ideas learned in the
SWP into the women's liberation movement even though the two movements were often in competition with each other.

Can MAW be considered feminist? The members defined themselves as
mothers alone, not women's liberation, but then no group was called
"women's liberation" until 1967–68. They did read and respond to feminist literature. On November 4, 1968, three of the members wrote a letter
to Margaret Benston, the Canadian author of the influential women's
liberation movement pamphlet, "The Political Economy of Women's
Liberation," that took Marxists to task for ignoring women in their analyses of class structure and excluding housework from productive labor.
MAW probably read and discussed this, as did hundreds of feminist and
other women's liberation groups. Some of the members were moved
enough by the piece to communicate with "Miss Benston," as they addressed
her, giving her permission to publish their letter. In this handwritten letter,
they state: "We poor women have known that you cannot move the men,
so we have given ourselves to the children and each other. We have gone
through the process of being honest and finding ourselves. It was a slow
process but we have learned thru experience that we must help each
other, by love and understanding." Might their process of finding themselves through honesty have been akin to consciousness raising, a technique pioneered by New York Radical Women in 1967 and based on the
Chinese Speak Pain to Recall Bitterness Campaigns and on the Tell It
Like It Is organizing testimonials employed by civil rights activists? Or was
this merely a political group-therapy approach popular at the time with
some of the Left? The poor women writing the letter went on to explain:

> The middle class, as you must know, have too many damn hang-ups and
> always puts the male in the forefront. This is positively wrong. The male is
> not going to move in any direction, but the one, where he is going to
> benefit. We feel they will more or less take care of each other. The pimps,
> winos, and hustlers, and men that love themselves more than they love
> women and children, will straighten up or be destroyed by their sons, and
> daughters and younger brothers and sisters, so we are not too concerned
> about them.

However they also remark, "But in this society the men are also afraid. . . ."

MAW focused on children, urging women to take better care of their
daughters and sons because children were the future. Some groups of
largely white feminists with small children focused on children as well,
but much of our impetus was on freeing ourselves from full-time child-

care and constructing nonsexist curricula. Women's movement members made the demand for daycare persistently, and daycare was provided at most feminist functions. In the late 1960s, New York women's liberation movement activists set up feminist daycare centers, wrote about daycare, formed tristate daycare coalitions, and created nonsexist curricula. The Feminist Press and Lollipop Power (Chapel Hill, North Carolina) published nonsexist children's books, some of them still in print today. However, our daycare and prochildren's activities are often erased from the historical record. It has become a cliché to brush off the women's movement as antifamily and antichild. Some groups, mainly separatists who advocated a total separation from patriarchal institutions, were hostile to mothers and children, especially male children; but this was far from the norm. As the women who wrote to Margaret Benston explained,

> We are more or less concentrating on the children. We have found that working with children has proven to be most gratifying because they haven't been entrenched in the American Dream and are able to grasp the truth as it is presented. We believe that it is very important for us to reach the younger children, by this we mean from Elementary thru High School age. If this is done children can reflect through the parents. And this way it will be more far reaching.

Was it because the group was made up of poor Black and white women in San Francisco with Old Left connections that it has dropped off the feminist map? Was it because the members didn't write a public feminist statement that could be passed around and discussed and debated? Or was it because children and service were the focus of their activities?

The Mount Vernon/New Rochelle women's group, sometimes referred to as the Pat Robinson Group or the Damned, was made up of African American women and began even earlier, in 1960. Could it also be christened an architect of the women's liberation movement? Patricia Robinson, a leftist Malcolm X follower and correspondent for Afro-American newspapers, was born in 1926. A social worker and private psychotherapist with three children, she volunteered for Planned Parenthood in Mount Vernon, New York. She started the group in 1960, to address teenage pregnancy, and the group attracted Black women ranging from grandmothers to teenagers, including domestic workers, factory workers, and welfare recipients. They discussed their experiences in a way that would later be called consciousness raising. Earlier, Robinson had used political consciousness raising in tutoring and found this method worked better than the more formal teacher-student relationships offered by the public school. The kids learned better when treated like peers. The students were considered the experts on their lives, and the teachers learned from the students as students learned from the teachers. Children were often present at the Mount Vernon/New Rochelle meetings. Childcare and politics meshed by necessity because mothers did not want to leave their children and often did not have the option to leave them with some man.

Some of the women lived with husbands or boyfriends, but many lived in extended family groupings. Although poor they were assisted with childcare by a female network of neighbors, friends, and relatives, some of them not mothers.

The group operated a Freedom School for neighborhood children on Saturday afternoons, and in the early 1970s went on to agitate for welfare rights and decent housing, basic needs for their children and themselves. The group advocated birth control and specifically the use of oral contraceptives, a method that had the advantage of being controlled by women and not visible to men. However, the group's position ran counter to the growing Black nationalist condemnation of birth control as a white conspiracy to commit genocide against African Americans — a condemnation that also expressed men's anxiety about their loss of control over women. In responding to this attack, the Mount Vernon group wrote a statement, which did not deny "Whitey's committing genocide on black people," but argued powerfully for Black women's self-determination. The group was attacked by the Black Unity Party of Peekskill, New York, whose statement began, "The Brothers are calling on the Sisters not to take the pill" and went on to say, "When we produce children, we are aiding the REVOLUTION in the form of NATION BUILDING." The Mount Vernon sisters responded in no uncertain terms: "Poor Black sisters decide for themselves whether to have a baby or not to have a baby." Furthermore, they criticized Black men for failing to help them raise kids. These women defined the problem as having too many kids rather than having children per se. "Poor black women would be fools," they wrote, "to sit up in the house with a whole lot of children and eventually go crazy, sick, heartbroken, no place to go, no sign of affection — nothing. Middle-class white men have always done this to their women — only more sophisticated like."

The Mount Vernon/New Rochelle group was clearly feminist and wrote many articles that were widely reprinted in feminist collections. Quoted earlier, the letter that members wrote to the *National Guardian,* a leftist weekly, in November 1967, was republished in many places as "The Sisters Reply." It appeared as "Statement on Birth Control" in Robin Morgan's 1970 anthology, *Sisterhood Is Powerful: An Anthology of Writings from the Women's Liberation Movement.* The letter written by Patricia Haden (although unsigned), a welfare recipient; Sue Randolph, a housewife; Joyce Hoyt, a domestic; Rita Van Lew, a welfare recipient; Catherine Hoyt, a grandmother; and Patricia Robinson, a housewife and psychotherapist, endorses birth control. It declares, "Having too many babies stops us from supporting our children, teaching them the truth, or stopping the brainwashing, as you say, and from fighting black men who still want to use and exploit us."

In 1968, "Poor Black Women" by Pat Robinson and Group was published and distributed by the New England Free Press, a large distributor for movement materials, and later included in *The Black Woman: An*

Anthology, edited by Toni Cade. The article analyzed the class structure from the point of view of the poor Black woman, the lowest rung in a hierarchy with white men on top, white women underneath them and Black men below them. Robinson pointed out that Black women in their domestic servant role had diluted and shouldered much of the actual oppression of the white female by the white male. The article stated: "With the help of the Black woman, the white woman had free time from mother and housewife responsibilities and could escape her domestic prison overseen by the white male." And, it continued: "Historically, the myth in the Black world is that there are only two free people in the United States, the white man and the Black woman." But proceeding to debunk this myth, they noted that the oppression of Black women is both economic and psychological. Robinson et al. pointed out that

> The oppressor must have the cooperation of the oppressed, of those he must feel better than. The oppressed and the damned are placed in an inferior position by force of arms, physical strength, and later by threats of such force. But the long-time maintenance of power over others is secured by psychological manipulation and seduction.

They observed that

> the oppressed begin to believe in their own inferiority and are left with two general choices, to identify with the oppressor (imitate him) or to rebel against him. However, no rebellion is possible, as long as the oppressed hold themselves to be inferior, and their oppressors innately superior.

Robinson et al. saw that "for real change to happen Black women must ally themselves with the have-nots of the world and their revolutionary struggles and withdraw her children from male dominance and educate and support them herself." The analysis took an international, revolutionary, child centered approach — stressing female self-sufficiency and independence.

Robinson and Group said that in a capitalist society all power is in male hands. "Western religious gods are all male. . . . All domestic and international political and economic decisions are made by men and enforced by males and their symbolic extensions — guns. Women have become the largest oppressed group in a dominant, male, aggressive, capitalist culture." Their militantly feminist analysis condemned both Black and white capitalism for its exploitative power.

Toni Cade also published an essay by Pat Robinson and Group, "A Historical and Critical Essay for Black Women in the Cities, June 1969," and a "Letter to a North Vietnamese Sister from an Afro-American Woman — September 1968." This second letter gave a brief history of Black struggle in America, praising Malcolm X but criticizing Black Power for implying that the poor Blacks can achieve a more comfortable life through the leadership of elite Blacks who will gain for them better housing, education, medical care, and jobs through the manipulation of the white capitalists. Consequently, they threaten to be the new puppet exploiters, moving out the present white-skinned small businessmen, educators and professionals and installing themselves.

Robinson et al. further informed their Vietnamese sister that American women were revolting against their male oppressors and a male warfare state gone mad.

Calling themselves "the Damned," the Robinson group wrote a book, *Lessons from the Damned: Class Struggle in the Black Community*, published in 1973 by Times Change Press. The book is a collection of theory, short poems, reflections, plays, raps, self-criticism, word definitions, and testimonies from the young — ages eleven to eighteen. The book, a lesson plan, offers an alternative education proceeding from awareness to conflict and struggle. Like MAW, the focus of liberation was on youth.

Patricia Haden, a twenty-two-year-old on welfare; Donna Middleton, a sixteen-year-old from a petit bourgeois family (her description); and Patricia Robinson, all members of this Mount Vernon group, also wrote "A Historical and Critical Essay for Black Women." The essay is included in many of the early women liberation anthologies — Edith Hoshino Albach's *From Liberation Feminism* and Leslie Tanner's 1970 *Voices from Women's Liberation* — and a similar essay is found in Toni Cade's *The Black Woman*. The article was a call to the Black woman, "the most pressed down of us all," to "Rise Up . . . Tell the truth . . . and look at herself not just individually and collectively but historically, if she is to avoid sabotaging and delaying the black revolution." The article ends:

> It is important for black women to remind themselves occasionally that no black man gets born unless we permit it — even after we open our legs. That is the first simple step to understanding the power we have. The second is that all children belong to the women because only we know who the mother is. As to the father's — well, we can decide that, too — any man we choose to say it is, and that neither the child nor MAN was made by God. Third we are going to put ourselves back to school, do our own research and analysis. We are going to have to argue with and teach one another. There are a lot of black chicks, field niggers wanting to be house niggers, who will fight very hard to keep this decaying system because of the few petty privileges it gives them over poor black women. . . . Finally we are going to have to give the brothers a helping hand here and there because they will be "uptight," not only with the "enemy" but with us. But at the same time we've got to do our own thing and get our own minds together.

Certainly with so many publications and a complex well-conceived Black feminist leftist analysis, the group should have been visible to the women's liberation community. In New York City, Redstockings contacted Pat Robinson, sent her articles, and invited her to meetings. Perhaps other feminist groups were in touch with the Mount Vernon group as well. Yet despite this early recognition of the group's work, it has disappeared from recent studies of the women's movement.

The Black women in groups like MAW and Mount Vernon/New Rochelle were far more centered around their role as mothers and the responsibility and power that goes along with motherhood than their counterparts in predominantly white women's liberation groups. The latter largely consisted of young, child-free women, who nevertheless often offered childcare at major functions and campaigned for free twenty-four hour daycare as part of their future needs. The women of color groups generally defined motherhood more broadly than white groups. Motherhood for them encompassed caring for all the children of their community as a way of fighting for the future of their community and themselves.

The public perception of white feminism is that it was antimother, antiman, antimarriage, and procareer and focused on abortion rather than childbirth. Many white feminist groups and individuals were concerned with children but were often painfully torn between the time and responsibility required for raising kids and the desire to make a political contribution themselves. Some decided that childrearing was too difficult, given the current conditions. Other feminists were indifferent. But because white feminists dared to expose the labor-intensive, unnerving nature of childrearing, especially when men and society did not share it, the media was able to present feminists as unnatural women who hated children and men. Much of the feminist writing on children stressed the burdens, which many men were reluctant to share, rather than the joys. The joys, which were already being stated quite loudly by almost every woman's magazine and pulpit, as well as by most sociologists, needed a counterbalance. Many of us also sought not to repeat the lives of women, like some of our mothers, who devoted themselves to their children and then felt cheated, and communicated this to us.

In *The Dialectic of Sex: The Case for Feminist Revolution* published in 1970, Shulamith Firestone, a white feminist, recommended freeing women from the "barbarity" of childbearing through reproductive technology. Her book was well received by radical feminists, but many disagreed with her solution — childbirth through technology and without men — surely the most controversial part of the book. In contrast, the predominantly Black groups accepted motherhood as a given and did not see it in opposition to activism or careers.

Both MAW and the Mount Vernon/New Rochelle group were autonomous women's groups of mixed age and class that focused on mothers and children but were concerned as well about Black men. Unlike most white groups, they wrote about men as weak, rather than as fierce and powerful, needing to be pulled along, willingly or screaming. It is white men who possess the power. The view of Black men needing the support of Black women goes back to slavery and Reconstruction, when Black

men were not allowed to assume their patriarchal family role, and continues today with a high percentage of Black men unemployed and in
prison due to racist hiring policies and a racist legal system. Pat Robinson
and her group of poor, working-class, and welfare women highlighted
class as well as race and gender; the three oppressions were interwoven in
all their writings. By the mid-1960s, they had developed a sophisticated
analysis of race, class, and sex oppression. The Mount Vernon/New
Rochelle group lasted until the late 1970s, longer than many early
women's liberation movement groups.

Some mixed-race and Black feminist groups came out of the civil rights
movement, but there were other branches of feminist activism in the
African American community. MAW and the Robinson group continued a
long tradition of Black women's nationalist and self-help and service
organizations, growing out of segregation and the Garvey movement. The
Mount Vernon/New Rochelle group arose also from reproductive rights
concerns initiated by Patricia Robinson, a leftist, nationalist, feminist
activist. The group is largely forgotten by those who write about the
women's movement, although they left an impressive published record.

The expunging of this group's work is especially apparent in the analyses
of reproductive rights. Abortion repeal was a giant victory for Second
Wave feminism, and the Robinson group made a significant contribution
to that struggle especially in the Black community. Only a few feminists,
however, including Riva Polatnick and Jessie Rodrique, acknowledge this
contribution. Most accounts of the abortion victory leave out the contributions of Black feminists, many of whom left no written records.

Perhaps MAW and the Robinson group are largely invisible because
there has been an underestimation of the contributions to the women's
liberation movement by the Old Left, poor, and working-class women of
all races, and by African Americans engaged in neighborhood or nationalist struggles. Most of the Old Left, including the Communist Party and
Trotskyist and socialist groups, used the term "male chauvinism" and were
more aware of women's discrimination than the mainstream Democratic
or Republican parties. Some of the early feminists were children of communists, "red diaper" babies like myself. But we didn't become aware of
each other until the end of the 1970s. We were all part of the New Left
and perhaps did not want to recall our parents' party affiliations. Also,
many of our parents had recently severed their Old Left connections. As
children we were taught that revealing these ties was dangerous. Were the
Second Wave feminist "red diaper" babies influenced by their parents'
awareness of what the Communist Party called "the woman problem"?
Why has this communist influence on their feminism been largely neglected? Does McCarthyism still prevail? Certainly these feminists did not
wave the Bolshevik flag, and some even went out of their way to obscure
their Communist Party roots. But did their communism nevertheless
inform their feminism? I think many of us learned from the Old Left and
were inspired by lives committed to social justice. We also learned how
autocratic and stifling a strong party organization could be and the pit-

falls of ideology coming from above. Perhaps that is why we feared organization and preferred loose networks.

MAW and the Robinson group also had important Old Left connections,
and they, too, were important in promulgating early feminist thought.
The Robinson group's essays were reprinted in many influential collections, but most feminist scholars have underplayed this seminal group.
Only Rivka Polatnick, who included them in her thesis in the 1980s, has
published articles about them. Alice Echols in her thorough study of radical feminism granted, "Of course, from the early days of the movement
there were black women like Florynce Kennedy, Frances Beale, Cel(l)estine
Ware, and Patricia Robinson who tried to show the connections between
racism and male dominance. But most politically active black women,
even if they criticized the black movement for sexism, chose not to
become involved in the feminist struggle." Perhaps if scholars expanded
their definitions of feminism to include women engaged in self-help and
neighborhood action, MAW and the Mount Vernon/New Rochelle
women would be considered among the pantheon of feminist foremoth-
ers. Are the groups a continuation of the Black women's club tradition?
Did they consider themselves feminist, part of the women's liberation
movement, or the Black liberation movement? Are they ignored by so
many writers and other media because they were largely poor and mostly
Black and lived in Mount Vernon and New Rochelle and Oakland rather
than in New York City? Is it because they don't fit the image of the young,
white, college-educated feminists who flocked to the women's movement
in the late 1960s and 1970s? We certainly need more research about Black
Second Wave women's groups comprised both of African Americans
exclusively and Black and white poor and working-class women in order
to combat racism and fight sexism.

The New Right: Rise . . . and Fall?

The year 1968 appeared to many contemporaries and to some historians as a turning point in the course of American politics. The assassinations of Robert F. Kennedy and Martin Luther King Jr., and the riots that followed the latter, seemed to mark the end of "gradualism" and "liberal reform" and to usher in an era of Weathermen, Black Panthers, "bra-burners," Yippies, and a leftward turn in American politics. In retrospect, however, 1968 seems more the beginning — and 1980 the culmination — of a rightward turn. Whatever was happening on the margins of social protest in 1968, majorities of voters and survey respondents were telling whoever would listen that they were sick of turmoil and wanted law, order, and a reaffirmation of traditional values. They were more likely to congratulate than to condemn the Chicago police for bashing demonstrators at the Democratic National Convention. They were likely to believe that *Reader's Digest* better reflected what was important in America than did *Rolling Stone*. They felt far more threatened by widespread drug use and sexual promiscuity than by "bourgeois conformity" or "suburban tackiness." The fundamental truths of religion seemed to them in need of restating not debunking. The stars and stripes evoked in them a rush of patriotic reverence, not a shiver of embarrassment or contempt.

Such views were not just passively held; increasingly vocal, angry, and well-financed conservative organizations sprouted in many corners of the United States. Evangelical churches began organizing congregants to campaign for conservative candidates who supported "family values." The Catholic hierarchy recruited tens of thousands of parishioners to fight the legalization of abortion and, after *Roe v. Wade*, to turn back the tide of abortion rights. Antitax groups in many locales canvassed door-to-door, wrote for local weekly newspapers, found statewide business allies, successfully resisted tax increases, and eventually pushed through tax-lowering measures. Parents who had never organized any sort of political campaign — including many who had always loyally pulled the Democratic voting lever and thought of themselves as liberals — threw themselves into efforts to stop school busing.

Such grassroots activism was matched by a massive infusion of big money into conservative causes. Some of America's richest families — with names such as Mellon, Scaife, Bradley, Coors, and Olin — heavily financed (or created) organizations designed to combat what they saw as the cause of America's national decline: liberal judicial precedents, liberal special interest groups, liberal academic authority, and liberal media. Whatever their domestic concerns, many of these conservatives brought something else to the New Right cause: an intense anticommunism and a sense of millennial danger that transcended ordinary political calculations. The Cuban missile crisis, the war in Vietnam, and revolutionary (often anti-American) movements around the world, provided conservatives with evidence enough that a relentless enemy was stalking the "free world." What they now feared was that "moral rot" in America had suddenly shifted the odds in favor of the stalkers. Not unlike the radicals and counterculturalists who predicted "the dawning of the age of Aquarius" or "the final crisis of capitalism," these conservative millennialists contributed to a general sense of crisis in the United States in the late 1960s. More positively, the rise of Margaret Thatcher in Britain and the growing European disenchantment with the social-democratic state led many American conservatives to believe that they were on the crest of a historic turn toward traditional political and cultural values.

The combination of grassroots activism, infusions of big money, and a sense of momentum had significant electoral effect. George Wallace, the segregationist former governor of Alabama, scored surprisingly well in the 1964 Democratic primaries, including in the midwestern states of Wisconsin and Indiana. Running as an independent in 1968, he again ran well outside of the South, and pulled 13 percent of the national vote. He appealed to voters angry about African Americans' attempts to enter into jobs, unions, and neighborhoods that had once been white preserves. He also won the votes of those who resented "pointy-headed liberal" bureaucrats telling them how to run their businesses, dispose of their garbage, educate their children, and generally live their lives. And, in promising to run over any hairy protester who lay down in front of *his* car, he tapped a cultural rage that few other politicians had been willing to exploit so openly.[1] Richard Nixon, who narrowly won the 1968 presidential race, used language that was more veiled, if no less threatening, to communicate to receptive voters a simple message: "those people" — war protesters, Black Panthers, snobs who look down on your middle-class lifestyle, and experts who try to engineer your social behavior — would no longer be tolerated. In 1980 Ronald Reagan even more effectively — and with a smile — reassured voters that he could wage the Cold War more fiercely while magically defending the nation against nuclear attack, cut taxes without exploding the deficit, and clamp down on radicals, pornographers, and welfare cheats without damaging the Bill of Rights or the social fabric.

The Democrats who managed to win the White House after the 1960s — Jimmy Carter and Bill Clinton — were both moderate-to-conservative southern governors who had difficulty holding together the splintering New Deal–Great Society coalition. In the four decades since 1968, historians have seen a process of "disaggregation" of coalitions, and "disalignment" (if not

---

[1]Marshall Frady, *Wallace* (New York, 1986); Dan T. Carter, *The Politics of Rage: George Wallace, the Origins of the New Conservatism, and the Transformation of American Politics* (New York, 1995).

"realignment") of political parties.[2] Southern whites who had once been "yellow dog Democrats" became loyal Republican voters; descendants of immigrants whose political hero was Franklin Roosevelt now cast Republican votes with some frequency; once vibrant Democratic organizations in western states shriveled in the face of a conservative ascendancy that brought Republicans and even Libertarians into state offices. These realignments occurred because the Democratic Party came to be associated with the cause of black rights, but also with high taxes and countercultural movements that seemed to threaten the interests and values of white, middle-class Americans. It is within this context that the New Right emerged as a political force and a subject of historical interpretation.

At the turn of the new millennium, the conservative surge seems less coherent or unstoppable. Like the New Left, the New Right contains disparate elements whose incompatibilities have resurfaced in the wake of the Iraq War, the chaos following Hurricane Katrina, and President Bush's precipitous downward slide in the polls. Conservative pundits now accuse the president, his party, and one another of all manner of bad faith and stunted vision. Democrats seem resurgent and liberal commentators bold enough to predict a reorientation of American politics toward "progressive" policies of equal rights, civil liberties, environmentalism, military restraint, and an activist welfare and regulatory state. Since conservatism so significantly shaped American politics at the end of the twentieth century, this chapter addresses first the grassroots organization and electoral success of the New Right. At the end, it addresses the most recent developments — the declining success and solidarity of conservative movements and the resurgence of liberalism.

Although political leanings color historians' treatment of political movements probably less than some conservative pundits or postmodernist critics imagine, it is no doubt true that most historians bend toward the political left and write critically of the New Right, and that most conservatives, in or out of the academy, see the New Left as either fatuous or dangerous. Beyond partisan leanings, one difference among interpreters has to do with whether they see political movements as top-down or bottom-up. A second difference centers on the question of rationality: are activists pursuing their rational interests, or are they driven by irrational anxieties and fantasies? Thus, some writers interpret the New Left as a grassroots movement for social justice, while others see only pampered baby boomers dangerously aping the bad habits of an antisocial underclass. Likewise, while some commentators see the New Right as a "backlash" engineered by elites who scare lower-class dupes into waging culture wars, others cast these movements as insurgencies of a "silent majority" determined to take their country back from distant and arrogant elites.[3]

---

[2]See Walter Dean Burnham, *Critical Elections and the Mainsprings of American Politics* (New York, 1970), especially Chapters 5, 6, and 7; and "The 1980 Earthquake: Realignment, Reaction, or What?" in Thomas Ferguson and Joel Rogers, eds., *The Hidden Election: Politics and Economics in the 1980 Presidential Campaign* (New York, 1981), 98–140.

[3]The classic statement of this view is Kevin P. Phillips, *The Emerging Republican Majority* (New Rochelle, N.Y., 1969).

Increasingly, however, historians have complicated the story. In recent accounts, left and right movements respond to both top-down and bottom-up dynamics, interweave tendencies that are progressive and reactionary, racist and egalitarian, rational and irrational. Historians now write more insightfully about the motives of grassroots activists and constituents and more critically about the targets of their rage. Equally important, they have begun to correct a major historiographical oversight: the tendency to ignore or deny the power of conservatism, especially religious conservatism, in the American past. Perhaps after witnessing for decades the conservative tide in American politics, historians can no longer explain their society without paying closer attention to the conservative forces that have long contributed to shaping it.

Contemporary historians describe the remarkably mainstream and adaptable character of conservative values and political preferences. They connect conservatism to the republican tradition of virtue and community, showing its influence on phenomena as diverse as the women's movement, Progressive reform, the Ku Klux Klan, immigration restriction, anticommunism, the civil rights movement, and contemporary "communitarianism." Finally, historians are noting the great diversity of conservative types — from patricians to blue-collar ethnics, from Pentecostals to Catholics, from libertarians to "moral majoritarians," from Yankee tax protesters to Sunbelt immigration restrictionists, from single-issue pragmatists to ideological crusaders. Telling the history of the New Right, therefore, has become part of an important reassessment of politics and group conflict in modern America.[4] Most recently, as conservatism has hit a bump in the road — or a lethal landmine — historians and pundits are reassessing the standard narrative: liberal demise, conservative ascendancy.[5] Rather, some suggest that the last half of the twentieth century witnessed the disaggregation of voters into blocs smaller than parties and less clearly defined than ideological labels suggest. These blocs coalesce and separate unpredictably, tutored by a range of religious and special-interest groups, and helped along most recently by new forms of mass media and Internet communications.

The first historian to take the political right seriously was Richard Hofstadter. Surprised by the ascendance of Barry Goldwater and his supporters within the Republican Party in 1964, liberal politicians and commentators seemed at a loss to explain who these people were and what they wanted. Hofstadter found an answer to these questions in what he called the "pseudo-conservative revolt" and its "paranoid style."[6] Hofstadter's thesis has come in

---

[4]See Michael Kazin's review essay, "The Grass-Roots Right: New Histories of U.S. Conservatism," *American Historical Review* 97 (February 1992): 136–55; and Alan Brinkley, "The Problem of American Conservatism," *American Historical Review* 99 (April 1994): 409–29, with responses from several historians and a reply by Brinkley on pp. 430–52.

[5]A recent example is David A. Kirkpatrick, "The Evangelical Crackup," *New York Times Magazine*, October 28, 2007.

[6]See the essays in Part I of Richard Hofstadter, *The Paranoid Style in American Politics and Other Essays* (New York, 1967); and also his *Anti-intellectualism in American Life* (New York, 1963). See also David S. Brown, *Richard Hofstadter: An Intellectual Biography* (Chicago, 2006), 152–60.

for much fruitful criticism and revision in the last three decades, but its power needs to be recognized. Hofstadter insisted that the Goldwater phenomenon was not a flash in the pan. Rather, it was connected with both long-term and short-term developments in modern American — and world — history. First, he hypothesized, the two-hundred-year cycle of exploration, conquest, economic, and demographic expansion that shaped American politics and culture had come to a close. The "automatic built-in status elevator" no longer operated so effectively; as a result many frustrated Americans experienced status resentment or status anxiety. Second, the rise of mass media plunged most Americans into a state of almost continuous excitation; their "private emotions" were now "readily projected" onto a public screen where they were subject to political and commercial manipulation. Third, the intrusion of both the media and the administrative state into once sovereign regions of personal and communal life created a widespread sense of "powerlessness and victimization," which would indefinitely feed strong resentments against politicians, bureaucrats, intellectuals, and other "experts." Fourth, the United States' irreversible plunge into military and diplomatic contestation on the world stage meant that fear of war and even catastrophic destruction would continuously fuel a level of public panic that could only play into conservative politics of loyalty and national security. And, finally, the growth of new wealth in what would later be called the Sunbelt, and the growth of evangelical denominations in the same region, guaranteed well-financed and organized movements against liberalism for the foreseeable future.[7]

These factors, Hofstadter believed, had energized the Klan, prohibitionism, antievolutionism, and other forms of anti-intellectualism, nativism, and extreme anticommunism. This last phenomenon, in the form of McCarthyism, impressed itself powerfully on Hofstadter's consciousness in the 1950s, seeming to be a version of the same irrationalism that had swept up Germans and other Europeans into the fascist maelstrom of the 1930s. As a result, Hofstadter clearly misjudged the extent to which McCarthy had succeeded in seducing former working-class liberals (evidence shows mostly old-line conservative voters rallying to McCarthy's cause), and allowed his fear of such quasi-fascist tendencies in the populace to discredit all Populist or mass political movements. Historians eventually discredited his treatment of the late-nineteenth-century Populist movement, finding not so much paranoia as a rational effort to address class injustice. And they corrected his tendency to see status anxiety in almost every form of protest in American history. Indeed, by the mid-1960s, New Left historians had largely rejected Hofstadter's interpretation and in the process swept off the historical stage almost entirely the conservatives whom Hofstadter had tried, however imperfectly, to understand.

In the 1960s, social conflict became the subject of American history to an extent not seen since Charles Beard and his Progressive school of history had first emerged in the early twentieth century. Where consensus historians saw broad agreement in the mainstream and extremism on the margins

---

[7]Hofstadter, "The Pseudo-Conservative Revolt — 1954," *Anti-intellectualism*, 63–64.

of American society, those who came to be called New Left historians saw conflict at the center of American history. But they defined that conflict in altered terms: it was between "market liberals" and "republicans," especially in the colonial and early national eras, and between "corporate liberals" and "radicals" (or "populists") in the industrial era.[8] They claimed that the "establishment" was itself liberal or that liberalism's progressive tendencies had been submerged in its marriage to professional, bureaucratic, and corporate systems of control. Even worse, the marketplace had transmuted liberalism into mindless consumerism. Energies that once fueled great campaigns for suffrage and free speech had degenerated into nervous demands for immediate gratification of appetites: the right to be entertained, the need for self-expression. Liberal individualism therefore now played a reactionary role in modern society: distracting people from their true interests, which were bound up with the collective interests of classes and communities; blinding them to the true goods of a good society — not material things but justice, dignity, and human connection.[9]

Animated by such beliefs, New Left historians in the 1960s and 1970s turned the interpretation of numerous groups and events in American history upside down.[10] On the one hand, historians such as Gabriel Kolko and Christopher Lasch pictured Progressivism as the installation of top-down control — by corporate managers, technical experts, pragmatic politicians, and therapeutic professionals — over a turbulent society with radical tendencies. For New Left historians, true democratic radicals represented the antithesis of the Progressive spirit. Their heroes included the socialist unionist and political candidate Eugene V. Debs, the anarchist feminist Emma Goldman, the black activist and scholar W. E. B. Du Bois, and even the immigrant "bosses" who tried to make life bearable for the "huddled masses."[11] Lawrence Goodwyn persuasively recast the Populists in light of the civil rights movement of the late twentieth century.[12] Like the racial egalitarians of the 1950s and 1960s, Goodwyn's Populists were grassroots

---

[8] On classic republicanism, see Volume One, Chapters 5 and 6. On corporate liberalism, progressivism, and populism, see this volume, Chapters 3 and 6.

[9] The study of "consumer culture" has become a major field in American history. A few landmark works are David Potter, *People of Plenty: Economic Abundance and the American Character* (Chicago, 1954); Warren Susman, *Culture as History: The Transformation of American Society in the Twentieth Century* (New York, 1985); Richard Wightman Fox and T. J. Jackson Lears, eds., *The Culture of Consumption: Critical Essays in American History, 1880–1980* (New York, 1983); Lawrence W. Levine, *Highbrow/Lowbrow: The Emergence of Cultural Hierarchy in America* (Cambridge, Mass., 1988). A sometimes strained New Left critique of consumerism is found in Christopher Lasch, *The Culture of Narcissism: American Life in an Age of Diminishing Expectations* (New York, 1979), and Stuart Ewen, *Captains of Consciousness: Advertising and the Social Roots of Consumer Culture* (New York, 1976). Peerless in balance and subtlety are Daniel Horowitz's *The Morality of Spending: Attitudes toward the Consumer Society in America, 1875–1940* (Baltimore, 1985) and *Anxieties of Affluence: Critiques of American Consumer Culture, 1939–1979* (Amherst, Mass., 2004).

[10] On New Left historians, see the introduction to this volume.

[11] See, for example, Nick Salvatore, *Eugene V. Debs: Citizen and Socialist* (Urbana, Ill., 1982); Richard Drinnon, *Rebel in Paradise: A Biography of Emma Goldman* (New York, 1961); Elliott W. Rudwick, *W. E. B. Du Bois: A Study in Minority Group Leadership* (Philadelphia, 1960).

[12] Lawrence Goodwyn, *The Populist Moment: A Short History of the Agrarian Revolt in America* (New York, 1978).

democrats bent on saving America from its worst sins: structural inequality and cultural arrogance. A social-justice movement with its own "movement culture," Populism was anything but the pathetic lashing-out against modernity that Hofstadter had made it seem. Thus, as Populists and other radicals battled for justice against an establishment that was labeled "corporate liberal," conservatives seemed to have dropped out of the picture.

Other historians found some conservatives to be perceptive critics of liberal society. Eugene Genovese, although he never turned slaveholders into heroes, did make them seem oddly admirable in their refusal to accommodate themselves to market liberalism and industrial capitalism.[13] Ronald P. Formisano interpreted antimasonic and nativist movements in the decades before the Civil War, despite their fantastic or irrational elements, as democratic expressions of "antiparty populism" and egalitarianism.[14] Similarly, new treatments of the Ku Klux Klan in the 1920s and of depression-era right-wingers such as Father Charles Coughlin, while in no sense complimentary, accentuated the community-centered values of ordinary followers.[15] Religious fundamentalists also came in for reevaluation. Having once embodied benighted reaction,[16] they began to seem defenders of local community and antimaterialist values against the juggernaut of the expansive market, the expansive state, and the ideology of rootless individualism.[17] Michael Kazin restored William Jennings Bryan to the stature of Progressive icon and Edward Larson recreated brilliantly the contexts within which Bryan and his faithful followers perceived the Scopes trial as a vindication not only of Christianity, but also of democratic community and humane public policy.[18] Other historians showed that the evangelical credentials of nineteenth-century abolitionists and feminists had been impeccable; some found similar credentials among civil rights activists in the 1950s and 1960s.[19] A number of cul-

---

[13]See Volume One, Chapter 4.

[14]Ronald P. Formisano, *The Transformation of Political Culture: Massachusetts Parties, 1790s–1840s* (New York, 1983); his forthcoming major study of populist movements over 200 years of American history is eagerly awaited.

[15]Alan Brinkley, *Voices of Protest: Huey Long, Father Coughlin and the Great Depression* (New York, 1982); recent work on the Klan includes Richard K. Tucker, *The Dragon and the Cross: The Rise and Fall of the Ku Klux Klan in Middle America* (Hamden, Conn., 1991); Leonard Joseph Moore, *Citizen Klansmen: The Ku Klux Klan in Indiana, 1921–1928* (Chapel Hill, N.C., 1991); Nancy MacLean, *Behind the Mask of Chivalry: The Making of the Second Ku Klux Klan* (New York, 1994).

[16]See, for example, William E. Leuchtenburg, *The Perils of Prosperity, 1914–1932* (Chicago, 1958), Chapter 11.

[17]See George M. Marsden, *Fundamentalism and American Culture: The Shaping of Twentieth-Century Evangelicalism, 1970–1925* (New York, 1980; 2nd ed., 2006), and Martin E. Marty and R. Scott Appleby, *Fundamentalism Observed* (Chicago, 1991).

[18]Michael Kazin, *Godly Hero: The Life of William Jennings Bryan* (New York, 2006); Edward J. Larson, *Summer of the Gods: The Scopes Trial and America's Continuing Debate over Science and Religion* (Cambridge, 1997); see also Garry Wills, *Under God: Religion and American Politics* (New York, 1990). A superb social history of the region within which Scopes and the fundamentalists faced off is Jeanette Keith, *Country People in the New South: Tennessee's Upper Cumberland* (Chapel Hill, N.C., 1995).

[19]Taylor Branch, *Parting the Waters: America in the King Years, 1954–1963* (New York, 1988); see also Sara M. Evans, *Journeys That Opened Up the World: Women, Student Christian Movements, and Social Justice, 1955–1975* (New Brunswick, N.J., 2003). On civil rights see Chapter 9; on antebellum reformers see Volume One, Chapter 8.

tural historians found in seemingly backward-looking cultural phenomena, such as the arts-and-crafts movement and the Gothic revival, surprisingly subversive critiques of prevailing values. Promoters of these movements counterpoised traditions of artisan labor and communal piety against the tyranny of a consumerism predicated on the myth of individual "free choice."[20]

In the context of such reevaluations, scholars began to reassess the meaning and character of conservative political movements of the recent past. Political scientists Thomas Ferguson and Joel Rogers explained the election of Ronald Reagan in 1980 as the result of "extensive elite regrouping triggered by changes in the world economy" and by the weakening of labor and other liberal groups in the United States.[21] Sociologist Jerome Himmelstein and political scientist John Saloma revealed the enormous investment made by America's richest families in conservative think tanks, foundations, and political action committees.[22] There was nothing spontaneous in the surge of neoconservatism in the 1970s and 1980s, they argued. These new activists were neither Hofstadter's "paranoids" nor his critics' "populists." They were "fat-cats" and their direct-mail functionaries. In the New Right surge, the dominant classes in the United States essentially got what they paid for: congenial kinds of academic expertise and media attention, and increasingly conservative politicians responsive to expensively orchestrated pressure-group campaigns. In injecting such huge quantities of money into politics, these authors conclude, the New Right financiers altered the political landscape decisively. Business historian David Vogel narrated the "political resurgence of business" in the late 1970s and 1980s in more cyclical terms. Vogel characterized business as determined to regain the political initiative it lost for two decades to a variety of "public interest" movements. As in their reaction to Progressivism and the New Deal earlier in the century, businessmen entered this third cycle of political mobilization in order to forestall new government regulations and taxes and, even more ambitiously, to turn them back.[23]

If some scholars focused on elite patrons of the New Right movements, others took on the task of understanding the interaction of grassroots clients with both liberal and conservative elites. Even in the 1960s and 1970s, some left-leaning commentators had begun to chastise mainstream liberals for ignoring the continuing class grievances of blue-collar Americans. Sociologist Herbert Gans showed convincingly that white working-class folks felt abandoned by the Democratic Party: liberal mayors, governors, and legislators in Boston bulldozed blue-collar neighborhoods to build freeways for middle-class suburbanites.[24] The same politicians supported desegregation

---

[20]For example, see T. J. Jackson Lears, *No Place of Grace: Antimodernism and the Transformation of American Culture, 1880–1920* (New York, 1981).

[21]Thomas Ferguson and Joel Rogers, "The Reagan Victory: Corporate Coalitions in the 1980 Campaign," in their edited collection, *The Hidden Election*, 3–64.

[22]John Saloma, *Ominous Politics: The New Conservative Labyrinth* (New York, 1984); Jerome L. Himmelstein, *To the Right: The Transformation of American Conservatism* (Berkeley, Calif., 1990).

[23]David Vogel, *Fluctuating Fortunes: The Political Power of Business in America* (New York, 1989).

[24]Herbert J. Gans, *The Urban Villagers: Group and Class in the Life of Italian Americans* (New York, 1965; expanded ed., 1982).

plans that subjected lower-class white children to hours of school busing every day, while the children of those very decision makers attended suburban public and private schools undisturbed by court-imposed desegregation. Ronald Formisano, echoing his reassessment of nineteenth-century antimasons and nativists, found that most of the enraged parents who fought busing in Boston saw themselves as victims of class injustice.[25] Racism undoubtedly played its part in those mobilizations in Boston, as Thomas Sugrue makes plain it did in Detroit.[26] Still, Formisano shows that most of the grassroots opponents of busing in Boston employed with absolute sincerity the language and tactics of the civil rights movement. Far earlier than middle-class Americans — and, ironically, with an insight matched only by African Americans and other minority citizens — they felt the decline in real wages and employment opportunities that commentators later called "de-industrialization." They also felt the unfair consequences of transfers of the tax burden from rich to poor, and of government resources from cities to suburbs. What added insufferable insult to these injuries was the self-righteous condemnation they felt aimed at them. The weight of America's racial sins, having once been laid at the feet of white southerners, suddenly seemed to have been shifted onto them. Reacting angrily to such charges, these voters — sometimes called "blue-collar ethnics," later "Reagan Democrats" — were spurred on by conservative politicians who sensed quickly the political value of their rage. These upsurges of "reactionary populism" — to use Formisano's term — inherited not just American racism, but also the venerable republican tradition of communal resistance to political and business elites.

Recently, historians have recovered the grassroots history of tax resistance and antistatism that has shaped both Democratic and Republican constituencies in the New Deal and post–New Deal years. Julian Zelizer acknowledges that many liberal Democrats were also moderate fiscal conservatives. From FDR to Bill Clinton, they believed that foisting debt onto future generations was morally indefensible. More important, perhaps, they needed to accommodate the power of businessmen and southern conservatives. Finally, they had to take account of the American electorate's long-term, widespread, and cross-class distrust of centralized government and taxation. Since these politicians wanted to guarantee the durability of the active state, they had to protect it from the outraged reaction that would flow from failure to limit its costs.[27] The liberal journalists Thomas and Mary Edsall offer a related

---

[25]Ronald P. Formisano, *Boston against Busing: Race, Class, and Ethnicity in the 1960s and 1970s* (Chapel Hill, N.C., 1991). See also J. Anthony Lukas, *Common Ground: A Turbulent Decade in the Lives of Three American Families* (New York, 1986).

[26]Thomas J. Sugrue, "Crabgrass-Roots Politics: Race, Rights, and the Reaction against Liberalism in the Urban North, 1940–1964," *Journal of American History* 82 (September 1995): 551–86.

[27]Julian E. Zelizer, "The Uneasy Relationship: Democracy, Taxation, and State Building since the New Deal," in Meg Jacobs, William J. Novak, and Julian Zelizer, eds., *The Democratic Experiment: New Directions in American Political History* (Princeton, N.J., 2003), 279; also his "The Forgotten Legacy of the New Deal: Fiscal Conservatism and the Roosevelt Administration, 1933–1938," *Presidential Studies Quarterly* 30 (June 2000): 331–58. See also H. W. Brands, *The Strange Death of American Liberalism* (New Haven, Conn., 2001).

interpretation of the late-twentieth-century tax revolt, which they interweave with a complex of issues to produce a general critique of Democratic Party elites, who failed to understand the people they claimed to represent. The Edsalls condemn the Republican Party for exploiting racial backlash. But, while they applaud the Democratic Party for championing black equality, they excoriate it for refusing to face the costs and traumas that resulted from its policies. "The Democratic party, once it was committed to the long-range goal of black equality," they argue, "had no alternative but to participate in imposing burdens and costs; the central failure of the party was its refusal to acknowledge those burdens and costs and, consequently, its refusal to make adequate efforts to minimize those costs and to distribute them more equitably."[28]

While the Edsalls' analysis of Democratic failure echoes certain conservative criticisms of liberalism, comparing it with the account of the Nixon and Reagan years offered by conservative historian Alonzo L. Hamby makes the differences clear. For Hamby, liberalism is not just errant but "exhausted." Neoconservatives came to define the American political mainstream not just because they took advantage of Democratic missteps but because they more accurately reflected the interests and values of the American people as a whole. According to Hamby, Nixon and especially Reagan won great victories by promising to rescue Americans from extremists on the left, not to deliver them to extremists on the right. Thus for Hamby, the Republican ascendance was a setting-right of American politics after an era of liberal excess.[29] In sharp contrast to Hamby, both Formisano and the Edsalls, while they castigate liberal leaders for ignoring and alienating ordinary white folk, insist that those folk, by virtue of their class interests, should be the liberals' natural constituents.

Other interpreters of the New Right focus even less on elections and tactics and more on endemic patterns of prejudice and principle, of identity and antipathy within the American people. Thus, according to James Davison Hunter, contemporary "culture wars" are not the product of clever stage managers "wagging the dog" of Americans' fears of ethnic difference. Those fears are based in different "living traditions," subcultures with distinctive worldviews. Conflict among them is normal, not pathological; it cannot be avoided, but can be managed. Here leadership is important, but the heavy lifting must, in this view, be done by ordinary citizens in town meetings, churches, school boards, and the like.[30] Hunter's measured optimism about

---

[28]Thomas Byrne Edsall and Mary D. Edsall, *Chain Reaction: The Impact of Race, Rights, and Taxes on American Politics* (New York, 1992), 282.

[29]Alonzo L. Hamby, *Liberalism and Its Challengers: From F.D.R. to Bush* (2nd ed., New York, 1992).

[30]James Davison Hunter, *Culture Wars: The Struggle to Define America* (New York, 1991). Christian Smith, *Christian America? What Evangelicals Really Want* (Berkeley, Calif., 2002), sees evangelicals as less aggressive in these wars than usually portrayed, espousing mainstream views on most (though not all) "hot-button" issues; Todd Gitlin, *The Twilight of Common Dreams: Why America Is Wracked by Culture Wars* (New York, 1995), sees the battle as fierce and an armistice possible only if liberals abandon the fragmentation of identity politics and take back "the commons," that is, civic patriotism founded on individual freedom and equality.

the possibilities of improved dialogue among culture warriors is not shared by other historians.

Thomas Sugrue has made plain, for example, the deep commitment of blue-collar white voters in Detroit to the practices and policies of racial separation. Before Americans ever heard the words *Vietnam* or *Great Society*, and well before either New Left or New Right movements had emerged, post–World War II white homeowners were mobilizing against liberal policies of open housing and school desegregation. Liberal trade union leaders, liberal mayors, and liberal opinion-makers failed (some after battling courageously, others after the briefest moment of resistance) to convince their constituents that racial equality was in their interests. "The local politics of race and housing in the aftermath of World War II fostered a grassroots rebellion against liberalism" that led directly to the New Right surge in the 1970s and 1980s.[31] What is remarkable in this view is that the New Deal coalition hung together for as long as it did. Given the long-term causes of the decline of liberalism, solutions will require more than improved dialogue or clever definitions of common ground. Facing both their material interest in and their psychic attachment to whiteness will require from most white American voters more than they have for half a century been willing to give.[32]

One fact about the Republican ascendancy that has seemed uncontroversial is the triumph of the "Southern Strategy." Indeed, for more than a decade its author, Kevin Phillips, has been atoning for the success of the strategy he now repudiates. Nevertheless, historian Matthew Lassiter turns conventional wisdom on its ear, arguing that the Republican Solid South is not, like the earlier Democratic one, founded on a distinctively regional form of white supremacy. Not race but class interests and ideological commitments primarily bound white southerners to the Republican Party. Closely analyzing voting statistics, Lassiter insists that new migrants who filled the suburbs of Atlanta and Charlotte were neither old-line racists nor very different from their counterparts in Long Island, southern California, or the northwest suburbs of Chicago. Homeowners focused on property values, parents focused on schools, and citizens focused on local control of their political fate, they could think in race-neutral ways about law and politics because a segregated nationwide structure of metropolitan development allowed them to. Convergence not divergence marked northern and southern political development in the post-1960s years. Therefore, Lassiter declares flatly, "The 'Southern Strategy' explanation of the political transformation of the modern South is wrong."[33] The first reading in this chapter presents Lassiter's conclusions.

---

[31]Thomas J. Sugrue, "Crabgrass-Roots Politics: Race, Rights, and the Reaction against Liberalism in the Urban North, 1940–1964," *Journal of American History* 82 (September 1995): 552.

[32]See also Thomas J. Sugrue, *The Origins of the Urban Crisis: Race and Inequality in Postwar Detroit* (Princeton, N.J., 1996); and Lisa McGirr, *Suburban Warriors: The Origins of the New Right* (Princeton, N.J., 2000).

[33]Matthew D. Lassiter, *The Silent Majority: Suburban Politics in the Sunbelt South* (Princeton, N.J., 2006), 5.

In linking the story of moderate conservatism in the suburban South to Sugrue's tale of homeowner resistance to open housing in Detroit, Formisano's story of Boston's antibusing "reactionary populists," and Lisa McGirr's description of "suburban warriors" in Orange County, California, Lassiter performs a major service. But his dismissal of the Southern Strategy (and of "racial backlash") is not entirely convincing, especially in light of recent political trends. First, other scholarship, including Kevin Kruse's on Atlanta, shows that seemingly neutral talk of low taxes and small government served as coded racial talk. Such coded talk appeared almost everywhere, but in the North it had to compete with a still vibrant liberal rhetoric of ethnic pluralism. The sometimes shopworn talk about tolerance and inclusiveness — "we are all immigrants," and so on — had political resonance in the North, but it never played well among more ethnically homogeneous white Southerners, who inherited the starker antinomies of race. Conversely, however much Northerners adopted their own rhetoric of "whiteness," they never clung to it as strongly as did southerners. Nor in the North did the spectacles of lynching and the assassinations of civil rights workers ever comparably summon up deeply held notions of honor and community. Social history, not virtue, accounts for regional differences: the North experienced greater ethnic and religious diversity; much higher rates of unionization; and slow but steady incorporation of blacks, along with immigrants, into political coalitions.

Today, when Lassiter recommends abandoning regional thinking altogether, it remains the case that the South sustains higher levels of black poverty, black imprisonment and felon disfranchisement, black execution, and racially polarized electoral behavior. Moreover, a 1999 poll revealed that 56 percent of whites in the South expressed unqualified support for integration, a major gain over the 1950s, but much lower than the 71 percent of northerners; four years later a poll showed 59 percent of whites in the South accepting interracial dating, as compared to 78 percent in the North.[34] The undeniable convergence among suburban voters across the country, therefore, should not occlude the persistent salience of regionalism in American politics. The media's "red-blue" mapping of electoral support advances a deplorably simplistic notion of regional voting blocs, but it is not altogether meaningless. In fact, the distinctiveness of the South seems more obvious as Republican political fortunes ebb. Once again, the South stands solid, now in the Republican column. If suburban convergence explains as much as Lassiter claims, it remains hard to understand why suburbanites in the East, West, Midwest, and increasingly Southwest seem so often to vote differently from their counterparts in the old Confederacy.

If long-term racial politics and latter-day suburban Sunbelt politics both help to explain the rise of the New Right, so does long-term sexual politics. Historians John D'Emilio and Estelle Freedman, in this chapter's second

---

[34]Polls cited in James C. Cobb, *A Way Down South: A History of Southern Identity* (New York, 2005), 321, which is generally enlightening on the question of continuity (despite change) in southern regional culture.

reading, note that fear of pornography, homosexuality, abortion, and sex education have for at least two centuries played a part in generating "moral panics" in America and, more broadly, in the Western world.[35] Such fears became inextricably entwined with the New Right cause in the years from the late 1960s through the 1990s, shaping presidential campaigns and school-board elections, injecting contentiousness into public library book selection committees and congressional debates over foreign aid, United Nations dues, and AIDS research funding. However salient were tax revolts and other disputes over "rational" interests, D'Emilio and Freedman show that fears of sexual chaos played at least as powerful a part as racial antagonisms in shaping the New Right. Disputes over taxes and spending can almost always be negotiated, but compromises are harder to reach when the banner under which one campaigns reads "Save Our Children" or "Abortion Is Murder." Parents may worry about the media, the educational bureaucracy, or the medical establishment intruding into their children's upbringing, but when the subject is their children's sexuality and sexual expressiveness, worry may turn into panic. This kind of anxiety fed the conservative movements of the post-1960s era. Because "sexuality has become central to our economy, our psyches, and our politics," D'Emilio and Freedman conclude, "it is likely to stay vulnerable to manipulation as a symbol of social problems and the subject of efforts to maintain social hierarchies."[36]

While D'Emilio and Freedman do not simply reinstate Hofstadter's theory of the rise of the "paranoid" right, from one angle they seem to close the historiographical circle. For, in a sense, in their story sexual anxiety does take the place of status anxiety in explaining the irrational basis of right-wing mobilizations. Those revisionist historians who succeeded Hofstadter almost always insisted that their subjects were rational actors. The Edsalls' tax revolters and Formisano's antibusing folk were not simply pathetic or deluded, nostalgic or reactionary. Though sometimes infected by racism or some other political virus, they pursued their interests and even, sometimes, embodied the American republican tradition. That tradition offered a rationally coherent and morally profound critique of market values and individualist culture, and a defense of virtue and communal values as the indispensable underpinnings of a good society. Without this populist critique of capitalism, most critics of liberalism imply, liberal politics is capable only of reasserting the individual's right to more goods and services or, worse, to more "self-expression." Lassiter's suburban southerners seem less republican than Republican, less communitarians than individualistic property owners, but they behave as rational actors, weighing interests and affirming middle-class values, not just succumbing to prejudices. Nevertheless, historians of sex and sexuality, like historians of race and racism, cannot entirely banish the irrational from their accounts of the rise of the New Left or the New Right.

---

[35] John D'Emilio and Estelle B. Freedman, *Intimate Matters: A History of Sexuality in America* (New York, 1988). On "moral panic," see also Nicola Beisel, *Imperiled Innocents: Anthony Comstock and Family Reproduction in Victorian America* (Princeton, N.J., 1997).

[36] D'Emilio and Freedman, *Intimate Matters*, 360.

They insist that sexual fears and fantasies, like "tribal" fears and imperial fantasies, are not easily translated into the pursuit of rational interests. Although readily manipulated by elites and influenced by considerations of material advantage, such fears originate in regions that are socially and psychically far deeper. Even some writers of a conservative bent do not ignore the darker implications of those fears.[37]

As might be expected, conservative historians cast a far more positive light on campaigns for "moral rearmament" and the restoration of "family values." Donald Critchlow's biography of Phyllis Schlafly argues that grassroots activists caused the surge of conservative politics in the post-1960s era, and not vice versa. He takes special note of two aspects of Schlafly's campaign: its religious temper and its mobilization of women. In some ways a perfect embodiment of the Old Right, Schlafly nonetheless tapped into two developments in twentieth-century U.S. history that might, on first glance, appear to have liberal implications: feminism and religious ecumenism. Graduating from Washington University in St. Louis, she proceeded to earn a master's degree in political science at Harvard, then worked as campaign manager for a St. Louis congressman and as publicist for a bank. In the latter capacity she displayed some of that conservative feminism that marked the rest of her life, advising women to educate themselves about finance, taxes, and investments. "When women have been able to get adequate information and experience in investing," she asserted, "they have done as well as men."[38]

After marrying a wealthy lawyer (and equally devout Catholic), Schlafly raised six children, while also becoming an activist in the Daughters of the American Revolution and, with her husband, in local Republican politics. Indeed, in 1952 she beat an established politician in the Republican congressional primary. Although she lost the general election, she won the financial support of Texas oil tycoon H. L. Hunt and of her Alton neighbors, John M. and Spencer T. Olin, who would become major benefactors of conservative causes in the post-1960s era. After the campaign, she became a favorite speaker at Illinois Republican Party events, at which she espoused an especially uncompromising anti-Communist line. For her, communism was a threat not only to private property but to the cornerstones of civilization, religion, and family, and, therefore, the necessary target of any politically responsible woman. To unite women across divisive social and political lines, Schlafly used not just anticommunism but also religious ecumenism. Since the nineteenth century, evangelicals crossed Protestant denominational lines to pursue temperance and suffrage, but treated Catholics as alien enemies of moral reform. Schlafly expanded the reach of "moral republicanism," forging unity among all Christian and Jewish women who embraced family values. Throughout her lifelong speaking and publishing campaigns against abortion, the

---

[37]See Kevin P. Phillips, *Boiling Point: Republicans, Democrats, and the Decline of Middle-Class Prosperity* (New York, 1993), and *Arrogant Capital: Washington, Wall Street, and the Frustration of American Politics* (Boston, 1994); and also Andrew Sullivan, *Virtually Normal: An Argument about Homosexuality* (New York, 1995).

[38]Donald T. Critchlow, *Phyllis Schlafly and Grassroots Conservatism: A Woman's Crusade* (Princeton, N.J., 2005), 30.

Equal Rights Amendment, and "every evil that threatened our children," as one friendly member of Congress put it, Schlafly revealed both the continuities between the Old and New Right, and the opportunity available to assertive women with ecumenical attitudes to build a mass movement.[39]

As recent historical studies of the rise of the New Right characterize its leaders as smart and attuned to grassroots concerns, and as they reassess the realignment that gave the Republican Party majority status (and trends that may be adjusting voter loyalties once again), they also attend to the question: What effect has foreign policy, and specifically the Cold War and its aftermath, had on American politics? After the "Communist Menace" vanished, neither big money, nor racial and sexual anxieties, nor religious fervor, nor tax protest, nor suburban or Sunbelt realignment, proved sufficient to sustain the New Right surge. The "peace dividend" and condemnations of entitlements seemed thin (or unhealthy) gruel for a movement once dedicated to saving America and the world from tyranny. Certainly, opposition to abortion and homosexual rights still elicited passion, but only among a minority that was static or shrinking and insufficient to guarantee electoral success. New external threats — international drug cartels, a resurgent Russia, an ascendant China, the "invasion" of illegal aliens — have vied to occupy the place of communism in the conservative imagination. But after the terrorist attacks of September 11, 2001, there can be no question that national security fears have escalated dramatically and that they focus on the Muslim world.

Chapter 8 assesses these questions more fully. At this point it is sufficient to note that both multilateralist and unilateralist versions of internationalism since the 1930s have been fueled by a sense of threat emanating simultaneously from alien enemies and domestic dupes or collaborators. "Fifthcolumnists," "isolationists," "pinkos," "the China lobby," "the oil lobby," "the Jewish lobby," unassimilated and untrustworthy Asians or Muslims, "fanatical" evangelicals or "cultural traitors" on the secular left — these and other internal enemies always show up in campaigns to mobilize the national defense. In an era of heightened terrorism and imperial frustration, they will again. And these issues will be intertwined with myriad assessments of interest and cultural values. Historians will continue to explore the causes of the grassroots movements of left and right, the decline in Democratic voters, the increase in Republican ones, and the uncertain adjustments and realignments that appear to be shifting the political landscape once again in the early twenty-first century. Most important, they will continue to analyze the racial, class, gender, regional, religious, and ideological currents that underlay such shifts and that may offer clues to future political developments.

---

[39]Ibid., 286.

MATTHEW D. LASSITER

from The Silent Majority: Suburban Politics in the Sunbelt South   [2006]

MATTHEW D. LASSITER (1957–) is associate professor of history and urban and regional planning at the University of Michigan and author of *The Silent Majority: Suburban Politics in the Sunbelt South* (2006).

Middle Americans

At the end of 1969, Time magazine recognized the middle-class victims and suburban heroes of the Silent Majority as "Man and Woman of the Year: The Middle Americans." The editors of Time defined this amorphous yet formidable group in the language of whiteness and populism, rather than partisan ideology or social class: a broad cross-section that firmly occupied the political center, marked by a "contradictory mixture of liberal and conservative impulses." Neither wealthy nor poor, the ordinary men and women in the no-longer Silent Majority "feared that they were beginning to lose their grip on the country . . . [but] still want to believe in America and the American dream." Half of the nation's population fell within these boundaries of Middle America, which apparently included teenagers who watched football and John Wayne films, mothers who worried about rising crime rates and declining moral standards, the National Confederation of American Ethnic Groups, Apollo astronaut Neil Armstrong, the working-class policemen who beat antiwar protesters at the Chicago convention, the evangelical Protestants who followed the Reverend Billy Graham, and the executive director of the Atlanta Chamber of Commerce. From the sprawling suburbs of the Sunbelt South to the ethnic enclaves of the urban North, Time discovered an aggressively but anxiously patriotic mixture of white-collar professionals and blue-collar hard hats that culminated in President Nixon himself — "the embodiment of Middle America." In the most perceptive passages of the article, Time observed that the White House "was pursuing not so much a 'Southern strategy' as a Middle American strategy" and concluded that Nixon "is riding the crest of the huge wave called Middle America, but he is reacting to it rather than leading it."

The unprecedented award given to an estimated 100 million citizens validated a political rediscovery of the Silent Majority shaped by Nixon's appeals to the Forgotten Americans in the 1968 election and confirmed by the grassroots revolts ranging from the law-and-order backlash in blue-collar urban neighborhoods to the antibusing movements in white-collar

Matthew D. Lassiter, *The Silent Majority: Suburban Politics in the Sunbelt South* (Princeton, N.J.: Princeton University Press, 2006), 301–23. Reprinted by permission of Princeton University Press.

suburban subdivisions. *Newsweek*'s lengthy 1969 examination of the "Troubled American" discovered a similar "vast white middle-class majority" from the tract homes outside Atlanta and Los Angeles to the industrial suburbs of the Midwest, in full-scale revolt against the redistributive agenda of racial liberalism. Millions of Middle Americans who had lost faith in the future of their country now embraced an ethos of victimization in the face of urban riots, campus demonstrations, rising inflation, and a general sense of breakdown in traditional moral values. . . . The *Newsweek* report concluded with individual portraits of Middle Americans who believed that their tax dollars subsidized both the rich and the poor and who denounced the liberal elites and the welfare cheats with equal fervor.

As the theme of the radical center moved to the forefront of political analysis, the most perceptive investigations of Middle America placed the unrest and uncertainty among middle-income families within a broader story of the structural limitations of Great Society liberalism and the class-based inequality that animated reactionary populism. In an article called "The Forgotten American," published in the August 1969 edition of *Harper's Magazine*, Peter Schrag warned of the growing anger and alienation among the 80 million white citizens who resided in the psychological and geographical spaces found in between the impoverished ghettoes and the affluent suburbs. Instead of glossing over the socioeconomic differences within a so-called Silent Majority, Schrag identified a more specific revolt of the white lower-middle class, whose transparent racism on social issues and genuine progressivism on economic issues formed a volatile combination unfavorably disposed toward both limousine liberals in their lily-white suburbs and corporate conservatives with their country-club populism. In late 1969, Hubert Humphrey offered a similar assessment when interviewed by *U.S. News and World Report* for an otherwise conventional cover story titled the "Revolt of the Middle Class." The former vice president criticized the disdain for Middle Americans expressed by many affluent liberals, and he warned that the Democratic party must address the perception among blue-collar white families that the government had singled out their schools and neighborhoods for racial integration while their hard-earned tax payments subsidized the lifestyles of the rich and the poor.

The dominant backlash narrative that emerged from the late 1960s and early 1970s glossed over the spatial and socioeconomic disparities among Middle Americans at the grassroots level by condensing the retreat from Great Society liberalism to a strictly racialized phenomenon encompassing the "vast white middle-class majority." This mainstream validation of the populist formulations of the Nixon administration has obscured some basic political facts about the elusive Silent Majority and about American suburbia more generally: white-collar professionals and blue-collar laborers do not have the same class interests, do not generally live in the same neighborhoods, and have never realigned into a permanent electoral coalition. . . .

The recurring fixation on working-class backlash and the resilient framework of the Southern Strategy have operated in parallel fashion to present a distorted story of political transformation in modern America.

Explanatory models of working-class prejudice have consistently overshadowed the persistent insulation of affluent neighborhoods from the reach of civil rights reform, while the durable narrative of southern exceptionalism has long served to reaffirm the de facto racial innocence that is central to the national mythology of American Exceptionalism. In the mid-1970s, as busing battles polarized the urban North and suburban sprawl destabilized the metropolitan South, one of the shrewdest chroniclers of the region observed that "the South and the nation are not exchanging strengths as much as they are exchanging sins." Liberal journalist John Egerton captured the convergence of southern and national politics in his assessment that the dominant trends in both regions included "deep divisions along race and class lines, an obsession with growth and acquisition and consumption, a headlong rush to the cities and suburbs, diminution and waste of natural resources, . . . and a steady erosion of the sense of place, of community, of belonging." The suburbanization of the New South had produced a Sunbelt Synthesis that managed to transcend the region's history by avoiding an ethical reckoning with the past, a political culture of white innocence and collective amnesia firmly grounded in the ideology of American Exceptionalism. "For good and ill," Egerton concluded, "the South is just about over as a separate and distinct place."

The United States became a definitively suburban nation during the final decades of the twentieth century, with the regional convergence of metropolitan trends and the reconfiguration of national politics around programs to protect the consumer privileges of affluent white neighborhoods and policies to reproduce the postindustrial economy of the corporate Sunbelt. Since the rediscovery of Middle America during the Nixon era, the suburban orientation of the bipartisan battle for the political center has remained persistently unreceptive to civil rights initiatives designed to address the structural disadvantages facing central cities and impoverished communities. Despite the ritual declarations that the federal courts would not permit public opposition to influence the enforcement of constitutional principles, the historical fate of collective integration remedies for educational and residential segregation demonstrated the responsiveness of the judicial and policymaking branches to the grassroots protests of affluent suburban families. The color-blind and class-driven discourse popularized in the Sunbelt South helped create a suburban blueprint that ultimately resonated from the "conservative" subdivisions of southern California to the "liberal" townships of New England: a bipartisan political language of private property values, individual taxpayer rights, children's educational privileges, family residential security, and white racial innocence.

"Forced Integration of the Suburbs"

The Kerner Report of 1968 urged the United States to choose the path of residential integration as formal public policy in order to reverse the movement of the nation "toward two societies, one black, one white — separate and unequal." Despite the explosive impact of court-ordered busing, the transportation remedy addressed only the symptoms and not the causes of school segregation in metropolitan regions: the public policies that simultaneously constructed the white suburbs and the urban ghettoes. In the early 1970s, the black freedom struggle launched a multifaceted assault on suburban exclusion as "the next frontier of the civil rights movement," from schools to housing to employment. But federal civil rights policy never seriously addressed the structural forces undergirding residential segregation, and the enduring suburban resistance to "forced busing" and "forced housing integration" has spanned regional boundaries and partisan affiliations. By the middle of the decade, the national insurgency embodied in the Silent Majority successfully pushed all three branches of the federal government to adopt explicit policies of suburban protection that rejected metropolitan remedies for metropolitan inequities and reimagined state-sponsored residential segregation as de facto "economic segregation" beyond the reach of constitutional law. If Kerner represented the last gasp of the progressive impulse during the era of the Great Society, the ensuing decades have demonstrated the inability and the unwillingness of a broad and bipartisan spectrum of political institutions to confront the spatial and socioeconomic boundaries placed on the reach of race-conscious liberalism by the grassroots revolt of the Silent Majority.

For a brief period during the late 1960s and early 1970s, the "Open Communities" initiative of the Department of Housing and Urban Development contemplated the withholding of federal highway funds and infrastructure subsidies from suburban jurisdictions that employed exclusionary zoning policies to ban low-income housing and maintain residential segregation. HUD Secretary George Romney, a liberal Republican from Michigan, warned of the "ominous trend toward stratification of our society by race and by income" and pushed a suburban integration agenda that would give genuine meaning to the affirmative action requirements of the Fair Housing Act of 1968. As leverage for the extremely unpopular program, Romney threatened financial consequences "if the suburbanites refuse to see their obligations, their opportunity," by adopting open-housing policies and rezoning for low-income developments. In 1970, HUD negotiated an agreement to scatter fourteen thousand units of public housing throughout the five predominantly white suburban counties surrounding Dayton, Ohio. Using this Dayton Plan as a model, HUD asked Congress to pass legislation making highway and sewer funding for the suburbs contingent on open-housing policies and acceptance of a fair share of low-income projects. The Open Communities agenda prompted scorn and dismay from the president and his top political advisers, and one journalist remarked that the HUD secretary appeared to operate in "an orbit all his own" within the administration. Romney "keeps loudly talking about it [suburban integration] in spite of our efforts to shut him up," domestic policy adviser John Ehrlichman wrote in a memorandum to Nixon, who responded with a blunt comment in the margin: "Stop this one."

The official federal retreat from affirmative action to integrate suburban housing came in response to a grassroots homeowners rebellion that
spread throughout metropolitan Detroit. In the spring of 1970, the working-
class suburb of Warren, which included only 28 black families in a population of 180,000, chose to forfeit $20 million in federal urban renewal
funds rather than adopt a fair housing ordinance mandated by HUD.
That summer, the *Detroit News* ran an explosive weeklong series charging
that the "federal government intends to use its vast power to force integration of America's white suburbs — and it is using the Detroit suburbs
as a key starting point." The immediate targets would be Warren and
Dearborn, "blatant offenders" of the Fair Housing Act because each suburban municipality included tens of thousands of black workers employed
in automobile factories but remained almost completely segregated in
residential patterns. Under fire from within the administration, Romney
traveled to Michigan to reassure the mayors of thirty-nine communities
outside Detroit that while the law required "affirmative action to prevent
discrimination," HUD did not have a policy of "forced integration of the
suburbs." Hostile white residents jeered their former governor during the
visit and waved signs recommending the construction of low-income
housing in Bloomfield Hills, the elite suburb where the Romneys lived. As
the backlash intensified, Kevin Phillips issued a strident warning in his
syndicated column that HUD liberals planned to "produce a racial balance
in America's suburbs." When asked to clarify administration policy during
a press conference, President Nixon replied that "forced integration of
the suburbs is not in the national interest."

In June 1971, the White House released a major statement on "equal
housing opportunity" that sharply distinguished between illegal racial discrimination resulting from private action and legal class segregation produced by natural market forces. After a paean to the frontier mythology
of suburbia — "through the ages, men have fought to defend their homes;
they have struggled and often dared the wilderness" — the president
promised prosecution of individual violations of open-housing laws. But
Nixon also pledged that the federal government "will not seek to impose
economic integration" or destabilize suburban neighborhoods "with a
flood of low-income families." The policy statement observed that "quite
apart from racial considerations, residents of outlying areas may and
often do object to the building in their communities of subsidized housing which they fear may have the effect of lowering property values and
bringing in . . . a contagion of crime, violence, drugs, and other conditions." Nixon did suggest that suburban communities might voluntarily
choose to provide housing options for low-income families, but he informed
Americans that "we cannot be free, and at the same time be required to
fit our lives into prescribed places on a racial grid — whether segregated
or integrated and whether by some mathematical formula or by automatic
assignment." . . .

The Nixon administration's redefinition of structural racism in suburban
housing as the market-based outcome of benign economic segregation

drew a sharp rebuke from civil rights organizations. The National Coalition against Discrimination in Housing accused the White House of pursuing a national "suburban strategy" and condemned the effort to distinguish between de jure and de facto segregation as "a meaningless charade." . . . The Civil Rights Commission rebuked HUD's retreat from its own Open Communities program, and declared that "racial integration cannot be achieved unless economic integration is also achieved." Later in 1971, during an appearance in Detroit, the president reiterated his opposition to "a forced housing policy" and instead envisioned the end of residential segregation "on a voluntary basis by having an open housing program in which any individual who has the opportunity can move where he wants." Two years later, . . . the Nixon administration announced a moratorium on the construction of federally subsidized projects and impounded almost $13 billion in congressionally authorized funding. The president also fired Romney and instructed his replacement at HUD to curtail programs that challenged exclusionary zoning in suburbia.

The civil rights movement responded by launching a concerted legal assault against exclusionary zoning policies that enforced racial and class segregation in suburban housing markets. At the next NAACP convention, delegates ratified a drive to open up the suburbs by scattering low-income housing throughout the metropolis. Executive director Roy Wilkins declared that the national commitment to racial integration hung in the balance because "the big question for the 1970s is where shall the Negro live? Will he live in the suburbs?" The Supreme Court's rejection of metropolitan remedies came through a series of decisions that extended constitutional protection to municipal housing discrimination on the basis of class and approved exclusionary zoning in the suburbs as long as the policies remained ostensibly race-neutral. In *James v. Valtierra* (1971), the Court upheld a California law that empowered localities to veto low-income housing by voter referendum because the policy did not depend upon "distinctions based on race" but instead banned all poor people in color-blind fashion. The dissent by Justice Thurgood Marshall argued that the equal protection clause of the Fourteenth Amendment covered low-income citizens and therefore any "explicit classification on the basis of poverty" should represent a constitutional violation. Four years later, in *Worth v. Seldin* (1975), the Supreme Court found that although the exclusionary zoning policies of a Rochester suburb intentionally "excluded persons of low and moderate income," the failure of the plaintiffs to obtain housing resulted from the race-neutral "consequence of the economics of the area housing market." The convoluted decision, issued by a majority dominated by Nixon appointees, effectively eliminated the standing of civil rights plaintiffs to bring federal class-action litigation against residential segregation in suburban municipalities.

"A New American Majority"

. . . Busing escalated from a regional issue to a full-blown national controversy in 1971, after black parents filed class-action lawsuits in San Francisco and Los Angeles, and NAACP litigation alleged de jure segregation in New York City, Denver, and Detroit. Public support for federal policies that promoted school integration declined throughout the nation but began to plummet among white families outside the South. In the spring, a bipartisan coalition in the U.S. Senate rejected proposals by Abraham Ribicoff of Connecticut to mandate the construction of low-income housing in the suburbs and to achieve integration through consolidation of all school districts in metropolitan regions. Ribicoff . . . informed liberal politicians that they "can no longer be hypocritical and tell the South how to achieve desegregation and do nothing about the North." When the Supreme Court issued the *Swann* opinion, Richard Nixon clarified the stance of his administration: "Where it [segregation] is de jure, we comply with the Court; where it is de facto, . . . I do not believe that busing to achieve racial balance is in the interests of better education." In the summer, Nixon announced that the administration would "hold busing to the minimum required by law" and directed HEW to jettison its own plan for two-way integration in Austin, Texas. Since almost all smaller southern districts had implemented full desegregation a year earlier, the minimal busing policy effectively targeted the largest cities in the South and their counterparts in the North and West. As another tense academic year began, racial extremists bombed ten school buses in Pontiac, Michigan, the site of the first court-ordered busing program outside the South, and working-class white mothers in the factory town launched NAG (National Action Group against Busing).

The most explosive development came in Detroit, when District Judge Stephen J. Roth ruled that "governmental actions and inaction at all levels, federal, state, and local, have combined with those of private organizations . . . to establish and to maintain the pattern of residential segregation throughout the Detroit metropolitan area." . . . Roth ordered the state of Michigan to devise a metropolitan remedy as the only way to achieve meaningful integration in the majority-black city system. . . . Resistance movements immediately mobilized throughout Detroit's overwhelmingly white suburbs. . . . All five of the white liberal Democrats who represented metropolitan Detroit promptly reversed their previous stances and voted for antibusing legislation hurriedly passed by the U.S. House of Representatives. In mid-1972, Judge Roth ordered the most expansive busing program in the history of desegregation case law, a three-county formula that involved fifty-four independent school districts and nearly 800,000 students. If confirmed on appeal, the consolidation plan would employ two-way busing to integrate every school in a rough approximation of the 80-20 white-black ratio of the metropolitan region.

The grassroots backlash spreading across the nation turned "forced busing" into one of the central issues of the 1972 presidential election. George Wallace fired the opening shots of his campaign for the Democratic nomination by accusing Nixon of "trying to stand forthrightly on both sides of the issue." Although the president "just keeps saying he's against busing," Wallace charged, "our children keep on getting bused." The Alabama governor selected the Florida primary to begin his populist crusade to take the Democratic party back from the "intellectual snobs who feel that big government should control the lives of American citizens from the cradle to the grave." With the slogan "Send Them a Message," Wallace predicted that "if the people of Florida vote for me, Mr. Nixon . . . will end busing" within two months. Among the other Democratic candidates, Hubert Humphrey expressed opposition to "forced busing" and "quota systems," and Senator Henry Jackson of Washington proposed a constitutional amendment to protect neighborhood schools. In mid-March, three-fourths of Florida voters ratified a nonbinding resolution to ban court-ordered busing, and Wallace dominated a crowded field with 42 percent of the ballots. The governor won with the support of working-class men and rural north Floridians, and he promised that the victory marked the beginning of a national movement that would reach Washington.

Two days after the Florida primary, President Nixon appeared on national television and asked Congress to impose a moratorium that would "call an immediate halt to all new busing orders by federal courts," a gambit of dubious constitutionality that eclipsed his former pledge to enforce *Swann.* The White House began devising its latest suburban strategy after the consolidation decrees in the Detroit and Richmond cases, but the timing of the presidential address appeared to validate the impact of the Wallace victory. To counterbalance the moratorium, the president proposed a multibillion dollar commitment to improve inner-city schools "so that the children who go there will have just as good a chance to get quality education as do the children who go to school in the suburbs." The administration promise to uplift urban education as a substitute for integration resembled the emerging stance of many northern liberal politicians who were touting the equalization of funding among school districts as an alternative to metropolitan busing plans in Detroit and elsewhere. . . .

The grassroots anger of the Silent Majority fused with the civil rights retreat of leading politicians in both parties during the spring of 1972. The crucial showdown came once again in Michigan, where the Democratic contenders competed to demonstrate their opposition to the metropolitan busing plan. . . . From the left, Senator George McGovern initially denounced the president for caving in to the extremism of George Wallace and observed that Middle Americans who supported the Alabama governor were "deeply frustrated and disgusted with the way their government is ignoring their concerns and interest." The South Dakotan received unpleasant confirmation of the depth of blue-collar resentment during an appearance at an automobile plant in suburban Detroit, when a factory worker shouted "get out of here, McGovern! You're in Wallace country now!" In the days before the primary, McGovern suggested that the federal courts had gone "too far" and expressed sympathy for parents in the suburbs "who are concerned about their children being sent to inferior schools." . . . Riding a populist backlash against busing and welfare, Wallace won the Michigan primary with a resounding 51 percent of the vote, including a heavy turnout in blue-collar precincts and substantial crossover support from Republicans in the white-collar suburbs.

The presidential campaign matched Nixon against McGovern, who secured the Democratic nomination on a platform of immediate withdrawal
from Vietnam combined with renewed dedication to "justice and jobs" at
home. Wallace won primaries in three additional states dominated by the
busing backlash — Maryland, North Carolina, and Tennessee — but severe
wounds suffered during an assassination attempt in May prevented him
from mounting another third-party challenge. Soon after the Michigan
contest, President Nixon singled out Detroit as "the most flagrant example"
of busing plans that sacrificed quality education for racial balance, and he
warned that if Congress did not enact his moratorium scheme then "we
will have no choice but to seek a constitutional amendment." . . . The
White House also released a list of metropolitan school districts in the
South that might be allowed to return to neighborhood schools under
the administration's proposed antibusing legislation. During the fall campaign, Nixon straddled the political center of a nation in upheaval as he
leveled a barrage of populist attacks against McGovern as the candidate of
income redistribution, higher taxes, racial quotas, forced busing, runaway
crime, permissive morality, and weak national defense. Casting the election as a showdown between "the work ethic and the welfare ethic," a
choice between the Republican belief in color-blind equality and the liberal doctrine of reverse racism, Nixon appealed to "those millions who
have been driven out of their home in the Democratic Party . . . to join us
as members of a new American majority."

Nixon won forty-nine states in the 1972 election and received 60.7 percent of the popular vote. About one-third of Democrats nationwide
defected to the Republican ticket, which also attracted a large majority of
the Wallace supporters from 1968. The GOP reconstructed a solid South
for the first time since World War II, winning 71 percent of the ballots in
the region. But interpretations of the Republican landslide that revolve
around a rehashed version of the Southern Strategy rely on a fundamental
misperception of the full-scale repudiation of race-based and rights-based
liberalism by the white electorate throughout the nation. McGovern did
not even compete in most southern states, marking the advent of a dubious strategem by the national party, and many moderate Democrats in
the region followed Governor Edwin Edwards of Louisiana in renouncing
the nominee as the representative of the "non-American left-wing fringe."
Richard Nixon did not always tell the truth in his political career, but he
spoke with accuracy a few weeks before the election to an audience of
southern Republican leaders in the Sunbelt metropolis of Atlanta. After
half a million people watched the presidential motorcade down Peach-
tree Street, Nixon told the crowd that southern issues and national issues
were identical: parents from Georgia to Michigan opposed the busing of
their children away from neighborhood schools, and all members of the
Silent Majority wanted peace with honor, decent jobs, law and order, justice for all citizens, and preservation of traditional moral values. "It has
been suggested that . . . I have a so-called Southern strategy," Nixon
observed. "It is not a Southern strategy; it is an American strategy. . . .

That is what the South believes in and that is what America believes in. . . .
We seek what I call a new American majority."

Separate and Unequal

The suburban strategy of the Nixon administration dovetailed with the
reconstitution of the Supreme Court in the early 1970s, as the executive
and judicial branches jointly rejected metropolitan remedies for racial
segregation in public schools and residential segregation in suburban
housing. In the fall of 1971, the president appeared on national television
to announce two Supreme Court nominations, Richmond corporate
lawyer Lewis F. Powell, Jr., and Assistant Attorney General William H.
Rehnquist. Nixon praised both men as constitutional conservatives who
would help reorient the federal judiciary away from the liberal activism of
the Warren era. The Senate easily approved Powell, a moderate Democrat
who had personally signed a brief urging the Supreme Court to grant
Richmond a reprieve from busing orders. The nomination of Rehnquist
proved more controversial because the Goldwater Republican had left a
lengthy paper trail of hostility toward racial integration, including states'
rights arguments against the *Brown* decision and the Civil Rights Act of
1964. Just one year earlier, Rehnquist authored a memorandum urging
the administration to introduce a constitutional amendment that would
outlaw busing and protect neighborhood schools. The confirmation of
the two nominees, combined with the previous appointments of Warren
Burger and Harry Blackmun, meant that Nixon had named four members of the Supreme Court in a single term of office. When the president
elected by the Silent Majority decisively altered the ideological direction
of the Supreme Court, the political and legal resistance against affirmative action to integrate the suburbs converged.

The judicial evolution of the de jure/de facto debate ultimately overturned the long-standing distinction between southern-style segregation
and its northern counterpart but confined the remedy within urban
school districts. . . .

In 1974, in the landmark case *Milliken v. Bradley,* a narrow majority on
the Burger Court rejected the civil rights drive for metropolitan remedies
through the consolidation of city and suburban school districts. Two
decades after *Brown,* it was less ironic than fitting that the NAACP's devastating legal defeat came in a Rust Belt metropolis whose racial politics —
like the nation's — changed forever as a result of the Great Migration of
black southerners to the North. The majority opinion by Warren Burger
elided the clear evidence that a history of pervasive state-sponsored housing
segregation had shaped the landscapes of metropolitan Detroit and sar-
castically mischaracterized the suburban remedy as the personal preference of judges who worried that a city-only plan "would not produce the
racial balance which they perceived as desirable." The chief justice
declared that "no single tradition in public education is more deeply
rooted than local control over the operation of schools," rejecting the

trial court's finding that "district lines are simply matters of political convenience and may not be used to deny constitutional rights." *Milliken* reversed the consolidation decree and restricted the desegregation remedy to the city of Detroit, based on the absence of rigorous proof that suburban policies had directly caused "a significant segregative effect" in the urban schools. . . .

From Richmond to Detroit, from Atlanta to Los Angeles, the interplay between the political revolt of the Silent Majority and the judicial accommodation of suburban resistance transformed state-sponsored residential segregation into a historical wrong without a constitutional antidote. . . .

Milliken immunized most suburbs throughout the nation from the burdens and opportunities of meaningful integration and sentenced most minority students who lived in urban centers to attend public schools hypersegregated by a fusion of race and family income. Piecemeal desegregation plans applied within the largest urban districts of the North and West imposed the requirements of social change on working-class families and accelerated residential flight from cities that had already experienced massive white out-migration long before the advent of busing. During the 1970s, New York and Los Angeles each lost more than 200,000 white students, and by decade's end most major cities throughout the nation operated school systems that contained a substantial majority of African-American and Latino pupils. Although the consolidated districts of the Sunbelt South demonstrated that expansive metropolitan remedies could overcome suburban opposition and mitigate white flight, by the mid-1970s a powerful mythology had emerged that court-ordered busing caused the decline of urban schools. This political consensus ignored the necessity of metropolitan approaches to stabilize racial integration and misapplied the lessons of cities such as Boston, where secure suburban spectators watched as struggling white communities fought reassignment to poor black neighborhoods. "To understand reactionary populism," a scholar of the Boston saga concluded, "we must recognize the role of class and its consequences in the formation of public policy, particularly policies designed to alleviate racial injustice. If class is ignored, as it was in Boston and consistently tends to be in dealing with desegregation, then those policies have little chance of success."

Forty-six percent of black students in the South attended majority-white schools at the time of the *Milliken* decision, in contrast with only 28 percent in the rest of the nation. By the end of the 1970s, only 23 percent of southern black students attended racially isolated schools, with 48.7 percent of African-American pupils in the Northeast and 43.6 percent in the Midwest enrolled in intensely segregated institutions. . . .

In the absence of a federal commitment to tackle metropolitan structures of "economic segregation" and residential inequality, civil rights organizations and low-income plaintiffs increasingly turned to state courts to challenge discriminatory features in suburban zoning policies and school funding formulas. In the *Mount Laurel* case that began in the 1970s, the New Jersey Supreme Court found that "economic discrimination" enforced by exclusionary zoning violated the equal protection clause of the state constitution and ordered suburban municipalities to provide a "fair share" affordable housing remedy. The immediate political backlash included grassroots resistance by affluent homeowners, obstructionist tactics by the legislature, and a powerful wedge issue for the suburban Republicans who gained control of state government. While developers in New Jersey eventually built numerous affordable housing units, the litigation has lasted for decades and barely dented the prevailing patterns of residential segregation. A concurrent class-action lawsuit securing court-ordered equalization of school funding galvanized fierce opposition by residents of New Jersey's wealthy suburbs, which systematically delayed legal compliance and denied any obligation even to achieve "separate but equal" educational opportunity. The chastened Democrats regained power only through reinvention as a culturally liberal party that would hold the line on property taxes and defend suburban quality of life at all costs. As New Jersey began moving away from the GOP in the 1990s, it was not incidental but intrinsic to the Democrats' suburban strategy that it represented one of the most racially segregated and income-stratified states in the nation.

In the campaign for school funding equalization, the elusiveness of good-faith compliance with judicial decrees recalls the stratagems of the southern era of "all deliberate speed" without the violence. In 1971, the California Supreme Court invalidated the system of financing public schools through local property taxes, followed by similar action in six other states. . . . Two years later, in *San Antonio v. Rodriguez* (1973), the Burger Court overturned a Texas ruling that massive funding disparities between urban and suburban school systems violated the Fourteenth Amendment. The five-to-four decision formalized the doctrine that federal equal protection guarantees did not forbid state-sponsored "wealth discrimination" and found that public education did not constitute a fundamental right of national citizenship. The school reform movement at the grassroots level proved more successful through litigation that paired the equal protection and public education guarantees found in most state constitutions. Courts in twenty states ranging from Alabama to Massachusetts overturned property tax formulas between 1971 and 2001, but as a general rule the grudging legislative responses increased funding contributions to poorer districts without achieving actual equalization. . . .

The Volatile Center

The grassroots revolt of the Silent Majority reshaped national politics and established durable spatial constraints on civil rights remedies for racial inequality, but the white electorate's repudiation of Great Society liberalism did not translate into a cohesive conservative majority or an enduring Republican realignment. The power of the populist vocabulary that dominated the Nixon era — Middle America, the Forgotten Americans, the Silent Majority, the New American Majority — arose from its ability to transcend the substantial divisions between working-class and upper-middle-class-voters, but never more than temporarily. During the three decades following the national disintegration of the New Deal Order, both political parties have grappled with an unstable class dynamic at the center of their electoral strategies. The Republicans have depended upon the upward mobility facilitated by suburban expansion and Sunbelt development, and they have capitalized on the blue-collar revolts against liberal "special interests" evident in the McGovern disaster of 1972, the Reagan ascendance during the 1980s, and the Gingrich surprise of 1994. The Democrats have won back working-class defectors during periods of economic turmoil — most notably the Carter election in 1976, the Reagan recession of 1982, and the Clinton triumph a decade later — and the party's migration to the center has increasingly attracted white-collar professionals and suburban swing voters who dislike the social conservatism of the Religious Right. Neither party has proved capable of maintaining the allegiance of the broad but elusive group that Richard Nixon (mis)labeled the Silent Majority. Since the 1970s, the bipartisan battle for the volatile center has increasingly revolved around the pursuit of shifting groups of Middle American swing voters in the sprawling metropolises of a self-consciously suburban nation.

The casual analysis that the Solid South simply shifted from the Democratic to the Republican column in direct backlash against the civil rights movement underestimates the ideological breadth and Sunbelt base of the New Right and overlooks the resilience of the interracial tradition of moderate New South Democrats. . . . The overwhelming white support for Nixon's reelection transcended partisan lines but provided almost no coattails for the GOP's southern wing, which suffered a steady decline in office holders for the rest of the decade, from the U.S. Senate down to the state legislatures. Economic divisions reemerged in the 1976 election, when Gerald Ford received the support of the white-collar suburbs and native son Jimmy Carter won back the Wallace faction and swept every southern state except Virginia with a coalition of black voters and the white working class. Kevin Phillips lamented the GOP's inability to maintain the allegiance of blue-collar Democrats and predicted that "the Republican party does not have a long-term future." But the inventor of the Sunbelt label should have had more confidence in the most compelling insight of his realignment manual, the long-term demographic trends that forecast Republican power in the middle-class suburbs and the high-growth Sunbelt states of the South and West. The rejuvenation of the southern Republicans in the 1980s mirrored the national triumph of the Reagan coalition, including the tax revolts in the white-collar suburbs, the grass-roots mobilization of the Religious Right, and the conservative populism that encouraged downwardly mobile voters to blame the government and not the market for the collapse of the middle-class social contract.

As population growth and electoral power shifted to the South and West, the dominant wing of each political party emerged from the political culture of the Sunbelt, the booming region from Virginia to California that produced every American president elected between 1964 and 2004. The Reagan ascendance within the Republican party moved the priorities of Sunbelt corporations to the center of the national agenda and rewarded the upper-middle-class suburbs that strongly supported the fiscal conservatism of the GOP, from Orange County in California to Cobb County outside Atlanta, from Bergen County in New Jersey to Fairfield County in Connecticut. The rise of the Religious Right revealed the grassroots impact of evangelical Protestants whose organizational base rested in Sunbelt "edge cities" such as Colorado Springs and Virginia Beach, and the GOP's social conservatism accompanied the takeover of the party apparatus in many states by the offshoots of the Moral Majority and the Christian Coalition. Reagan's reelection in 1984 with an electoral coalition of forty-nine states exposed the national crisis of identity facing the Democratic party, especially the blue-collar revolt against liberalism in the Catholic suburbs of the Midwest and the working-class precincts of the South. But despite a defeatist tendency among liberals to lament as permanent the loss of the "Reagan Democrats" and (mis)read a new Solid Republican South into specific presidential election cycles, lower-middle-class white voters and southern swing states proved to be critical constituencies in the reinvigoration of the Democratic party in the 1990s. Building on his foundation in the interracial New South politics of the seventies, Bill Clinton launched a populist "third way" drive for the White House with an unattributed homage to the Nixon era and the Silent Majority: a "campaign for the future, for the forgotten hard-working middle-class families of America."

The reinvention of the "New Democrats" as the champions of quality-of-life issues in suburban swing districts and the fiscally responsible managers of the high-tech economy revitalized the competitiveness of the center in a postliberal political order. The ideological transformation of the party engineered by the Democratic Leadership Council (DLC) identified the suburbs and the South as key political battlegrounds and then "triangulated" the difference between the New Right agenda of the GOP and the fading remnants of Great Society liberalism. "The way to win the South," counseled DLC founder Al From, is "by changing the center of political gravity within the party. The South is very much where the mainstream of the country is." Clinton's victory in the 1992 election, the first in which suburban voters represented an outright majority of the electorate, won back crucial states in the South and Midwest while maintaining Democratic strength in the Northeast and on the West Coast. The Democratic agenda during the 1990s revolved around an operational suburban strategy that included targeted entitlement programs for "soccer moms" and working women, an ethic of tolerance for upscale moderates alienated by the culture wars of the Christian Right, probusiness management of the high-tech economy shaped by the Sunbelt boom, and fiscal policies selected for their acceptability in middle-class focus groups. Throughout the decade, DLC strategists reminded the party that "sprawl is where the voters are" and touted the politics of moderation as key to "staying competitive in suburban areas." The new century ushers in an "emerging Democratic majority" in American politics, at least according to the manifesto of the New Democratic movement, because the party understands that "America's future lies in places like Silicon Valley and North Carolina's Research Triangle." But the Republicans have countered with their own time-tested suburban strategy, including sophisticated voter mobilization campaigns targeting the white families moving to the exurban fringes in key battleground states such as Florida and Ohio.

In the South, the ardent conservatism of the overwhelmingly white Republican party and the determination of the New Democrats to occupy the center with a coalition of black voters and white moderates means that regional politics have remained competitive in the aftermath of the civil rights era and the explosive growth of the metropolitan Sunbelt. "The old solid Democratic South has vanished," the leading analysts of regional political trends observed in 2002. "A comparably solid Republican South has not developed. Nor is one likely to emerge." The Republican decision to forfeit the substantial black vote, combined with the rapid expansion of the Latino population and the swing function performed at different times by suburban moderates and working-class populists, effectively guarantees that the GOP cannot reproduce a Solid South on a permanent and grassroots basis. Electoral reapportionment and the racial gerrymandering of congressional districts helped polarize the region's delegation to the House of Representatives, with national consequences during the Republican surge of 1994. But the politics of moderation still resonate in statewide contests — every southern state elected at least one Democratic governor between 1989 and 1999 — and the Democrats can also be competitive in the region during presidential elections, when they actually try. George W. Bush's embrace of "compassionate conservatism" during the 2000 campaign represented nothing so much as an updated version of Richard Nixon's color-blind appeals to the Silent Majority, an inclusive rhetorical device aimed at suburban swing voters in the South and across the nation turned off by the politics of racial extremism and religious intolerance. The genuine political realignment in contemporary America — beyond the fallacy of "red state/blue state" national polarization, symbolized by the corporate conservatism of the Republicans and the suburban moderation of the New Democrats — is the disappearance of a party that represents the interests of the working class and champions the plight of the poor. . . .

The dominant ethos of American suburbia has always idealized the present and celebrated the future at the expense of any critical reflection on the past. For more than three decades, from the grassroots revolt of the Silent Majority in the 1970s to the bipartisan pursuit of middle-class swing voters in the 1990s and beyond, suburban homeowners and their political and judicial champions have naturalized residential segregation and defended metropolitan inequality through a powerful discourse of socioeconomic privilege and free-market meritocracy. For just as long, civil rights activists and progressive scholars have challenged the foundational mythology of suburban racial innocence and the color-blind ideology of middle-class individualism by exposing the de jure roots of almost all cases of allegedly de facto segregation — a historical verdict based on overwhelming evidence that has proved to be singularly unpersuasive in the political and legal arenas. The population shift to the middle-class suburbs and the power shift to the Sunbelt economy requires a new metropolitan framework for political history and public policy that transcends the urban-suburban dichotomy and confronts instead of obscures the pervasive politics of class in the suburban strategies of the volatile center. Surely an honest assessment of the nation's collective responsibility in creating the contemporary metropolitan landscape remains an essential prerequisite for grappling with the spatial fusion of racial and class politics that ultimately produced an underlying suburban consensus in the electoral arena. If "the problem of the color line" represented the fundamental crisis of the twentieth century, the foremost challenge of the twenty-first has evolved into the suburban synthesis of racial inequality and class segregation at the heart of what may or may not be the New American Dilemma.

John D'Emilio and Estelle B. Freedman

from Intimate Matters: A History of Sexuality in America   [1988]

ESTELLE FREEDMAN (1947–) is Edgar E. Robinson Professor of History at Stanford University. Her books include *Their Sisters' Keepers: Women's Prison Reform in America: 1830–1930* (1981), *Maternal Justice: Miriam van Waters and the Female Reform Tradition* (1996), and *No Turning Back: The History of Feminism and the Future of Women* (2002).

JOHN D'EMILIO (1948–) is professor of history and women and gender studies at the University of Illinois at Chicago. He has written *Sexual Politics, Sexual Communities: The Making of a Homosexual Minority in the U.S., 1940–1970* (1983), *Making Trouble: Essays on Gay History, Politics, and the University* (1992), and *Lost Prophet: The Life and Times of Bayard Rustin* (2005).

For political commentators accustomed to following the byways of post–World War II presidential politics, the 1984 campaign offered an interesting spectacle. Certainly many time-tested issues made their appearance in the course of the year — the strength of the military establishment; the struggle against Communism; taxes and the economy;

the continuing fight for racial equality. But there were new dimensions, too. The day before the Democratic convention opened in San Francisco, tens of thousands of homosexuals and lesbians marched through the city to the convention site, with several dozen openly gay delegates to the convention leading the way. When the party adopted its platform later in the week, it condemned the "violent acts of bigotry, hatred, and extremism" aimed at gay men and lesbians, a phenomenon the platform labeled "alarmingly common." Another plank put the party on record as recognizing "reproductive freedom as a fundamental human right." It opposed "government interference in the reproductive decisions of Americans" and declared that "a woman has a right to choose whether and when to have a child." Though the platform avoided any mention of abortion, Geraldine Ferraro, the Democratic nominee for vice president, spent much of the campaign verbally dueling with the Roman Catholic hierarchy which condemned her defense of women's right to have abortion as an option.

Meanwhile, Ronald Reagan, who was running for reelection, returned to issues of sexuality again and again. During the spring primary season, he told the National Association of Evangelicals that America was losing "her religious and moral bearings." Pornography, once hidden, was now available "in virtually every drugstore in the land." Liberals, he charged, "viewed promiscuity as acceptable, even stylish. Indeed, the word itself was replaced by the term 'sexually active.'" In the liberal-dominated media, sex was everywhere. What was once "a sacred expression of love" had now become "casual and cheap." Reagan and the Republicans returned to these themes again and again. In August, he assured the publisher of the *Presidential Biblical Scorecard* that he would "resist the efforts of some to obtain government endorsement of homosexuality," and identified the sex act as "the means by which husband and wife participate with God in the creation of a new human life." As if to affirm these views, and in order to position itself against the Democratic call for reproductive freedom, the Republican party adopted a platform plank opposing abortion and endorsing legislation to make clear that "the 14th Amendment's protections apply to unborn children."

For any who doubted, the 1984 presidential season made clear that whatever consensus existed in the mid-twentieth century about sexuality had dissolved by the 1980s. The debates about sex, rather than remaining the province of feminists and gay liberationists, were polarizing the nation's politics. . . .

Sexual Politics and the New Right

The rapid pace of change and the dissolution of the liberal consensus about sexuality encouraged a political response from the right. As the 1970s ended, the latest in a long line of purity movements took shape. Reacting to the gains of both feminism and gay liberation, and distressed by the visibility of the erotic in American culture, sexual conservatives sought the restoration of "traditional" values. In its rhetoric, this contemporary breed of purity advocates echoed its predecessors by attributing to sex the power to corrupt, even to weaken fatally, American society. But in other important ways, its efforts departed from the past. It plunged directly into politics, as religious fundamentalists joined forces with political conservatives to make the Republican party the vehicle for a powerful moral crusade. Availing themselves of modern technology, these New Right proponents used computerized mailing lists, direct-mail fundraising, and telephone banks to reach deeply into the population and mobilize a constituency. By the early 1980s, journalists and political analysts were giving them credit for the turn to conservatism in American life.

Although feminism and gay liberation seemed to spark the resurgence of the purity impulse, the conservative sexual politics of the 1950s had never fully died. Placed on the defensive by the decisions of the liberal Warren Court, groups such as Citizens for Decent Literature struggled on. In the 1960s, much of the battle focused on the issue of sex education in the public schools. Distressed by the court-decreed elimination of school prayer, some conservatives banded together in an effort to draw the line at sex instruction. Toward the end of the decade, the John Birch Society began targeting Mary Calderone, the renowned sex educator. In Racine, Wisconsin; Anaheim, California; Minneapolis, and other places, parents fought to keep discussions of sex out of the classroom. Ronald Reagan, then governor of California, pushed legislation prohibiting required attendance in sex education classes. . . .

Since the early 1970s, an important item on the gay movement's agenda had been the extension of civil rights statutes to include provisions prohibiting discrimination on the basis of sexual orientation. Activists devoted much of their energy to securing passage of municipal and county ordinances as a foundation for later efforts at the state and national level. By 1977, they had achieved upward of three dozen victories, of which the law in populous Dade County was one. But, for the first time, they encountered an outspoken opposition, ready to fight back, in Florida. Anita Bryant, who led the campaign to repeal the law, was a foe to reckon with. A former Miss Oklahoma and a popular singer in middle America, she remained in the public eye through her commercials for Minute Maid orange juice, where she projected an attractive, motherly wholesomeness. Bryant was outraged that local legislators had seemed to endorse the lifestyle of homosexuals, whom she described as "human garbage." With the aid of her business-manager husband, she formed Save Our Children, Inc., and succeeded in placing a repeal initiative on the ballot. . . .

In a foreshadowing of the direction the purity movement would take, Protestant fundamentalist ministers assumed a highly visible role. A local evangelist told reporters that "homosexuality is a sin so rotten, so low, so dirty that even cats and dogs don't practice it." Jerry Falwell, a Baptist preacher from Lynchburg, Virginia, and soon to become a national figure, flew in to help the repeal forces. "So-called gay folks," he intoned, would "just as soon kill you as look at you." Backed by the Catholic hierarchy, conservative rabbis, and Miami's daily newspapers, the Bryant campaign won a resounding victory as voters rejected the ordinance by a two-to-one majority.

The media publicity that the Dade County battle received guaranteed that its influence would extend beyond its locale. Over the next year, conservatives mounted similar campaigns in St. Paul, Wichita, and Eugene, Oregon; in each case, citizens defeated gay rights in overwhelming proportions. In California, lesbians and gay men faced an even more serious threat. There, inspired by Bryant's success, an ultraconservative state senator from the Los Angeles suburbs, John Briggs, succeeded in placing an anti-gay measure on the state ballot. The Briggs initiative authorized school systems to fire gay employees, as well as anyone who publicly or privately advocated or encouraged homosexual conduct. Throughout 1978, the gay communities in San Francisco, Los Angeles, and other cities put together a well-organized grass-roots campaign against the measure. Winning the support of labor unions protective of their members' jobs, large-circulation newspapers in the state, and even conservative politicians like Ronald Reagan, who objected to the constraints on free speech, gay activists succeeded in defeating the initiative. . . .

Meanwhile, a movement to curtail the right of women to choose abortion was developing. For Americans who objected to abortion, the Supreme Court's *Roe* decision in 1973 had appeared as a "bolt from the blue," catching them off-guard and unprepared. Though local anti-abortion groups formed almost immediately, the Court's ruling seemed clear and incontrovertible, leaving little room for action. Then, in 1976, Representative Henry Hyde of Illinois succeeded in attaching a rider to an appropriations bill, prohibiting the use of federal dollars to fund abortions. The next year, the Supreme Court ruled that government had the authority to bar the financing of abortion with tax dollars. Congress responded with alacrity, and by 1978, the number of federally funded abortions had fallen from 295,000 to 3,000. States, too, cut back on their coverage; by the summer of 1979, only nine states still paid for abortions. Though the constitutional right to abortion remained intact, anti-abortion forces had succeeded in sharply restricting the access that poor women had to it.

The victory over funding also spurred the movement forward. Local groups became part of national organizations such as March for Life and the National Right-to-Life Committee. They registered voters and made abortion the litmus test of political acceptability, campaigning against candidates based on the single issue of abortion. As Nellie Grey, of March for Life, explained, "on a fundamental issue, you can't strike a bargain. You are either for killing babies or you're not. You can't be for a little bit of killing babies." . . . By the end of the 1970s, clinics performing abortions were being torched and bombed across the country.

The involvement of purity advocates in politics, whether to defeat gay rights, restrict abortion, or curtail the spread of pornography, held an irresistible allure for traditional conservatives. During the 1970s, a new set of right-wing organizations came into existence, determined to turn back

the liberal social-welfare policies of the 1960s and to reverse the retrenchment of America's role in the world. Groups such as the Conservative
Caucus, headed by Howard Phillips, the Committee for the Survival of a
Free Congress, led by Paul Weyrich, and the National Conservative
Political Action Committee, chaired by Terry Dolan, saw the discontent
spawned by sexual issues as a force that could propel their politics into
power. In commenting on the potential of the alliance, Richard Viguerie,
the editor of the *Conservative Digest* and a pioneer in direct-mail fundraising techniques, noted that "if abortion remains an issue, and we keep
picking liberals off, this movement could completely change the face of
Congress." Paul Weyrich, too, saw issues of sexuality and family life as "the
Achilles' heel of the liberal Democrats." In 1979, Phillips and Weyrich
helped persuade Jerry Falwell, whose television program *The Old Time
Gospel Hour* reached 18 million viewers weekly, to form the Moral Majority
as a vehicle to mobilize the fundamentalist population. They also established the Religious Roundtable to bring together conservative politicians
and influential television preachers such as Falwell, Pat Robertson, Jim
Bakker, James Robison, and others.

    This religion-based New Right exploded into the nation's consciousness
during the 1980 presidential campaign. While Jimmy Carter, a self-avowed
born-again Christian, remained aloof from it, Ronald Reagan actively
courted the fundamentalist vote, and appeared openly sympathetic to the
New Right's position on abortion, school prayer, and pornography. His
fervid Cold War rhetoric also appealed to preachers who feared a "god-
less" Communism. Reagan addressed a national convention of religious
broadcasters. In return, evangelists appealed to their congregations and
their television viewers to vote for righteousness. Falwell, whose Moral
Majority had already enrolled seventy-two thousand ministers and four
million lay members, castigated the "minority of secular humanists and
amoralists [who] are running this country and taking it straight to hell."
. . . After Reagan won by a landslide and Republicans captured control of
the Senate, many political commentators were quick to attribute an
almost invincible power to the moralistic politics of the New Right.

    When the new Congress reconvened in 1981, the assessment of the
media and the worst fears of feminists and gay liberationists seemed ready
to be confirmed. Despite their rhetorical opposition to big government,
conservatives were prepared to sanction state intervention in issues of
sexual morality and family life. In short order, Senator Jesse Helms of
North Carolina and Representative Hyde introduced a bill that defined
life as beginning at conception, and hence made abortion equivalent to
murder. Another anti-abortion politician, Representative Robert Dornan
of California, presented to the House a constitutional amendment that
identified life as beginning when the sperm fertilizes the ovum, thus
including the birth control pill and the IUD as potential abortifacients.
Republican conservatives also resurrected the Family Protection Act,
which had died an unceremonious death during the Carter presidency.
Its thirty-six provisions included one that prohibited federal funds for

schools whose curriculum "would tend to denigrate, diminish or deny the role differences between the sexes as they have been historically understood in the United States," and another that denied government benefits, including social security, to anyone who presented homosexuality "as an acceptable alternative life style or suggests that it can be an acceptable life style." Meanwhile, religious leaders kept up the impassioned rhetoric. Falwell aroused his supporters by declaring, "we are fighting a holy war and this time we are going to win." His frequent appeals for funds — by 1981 he was raising over a million dollars a week — enticed contributions with questions such as, "Do you approve of known practicing homosexuals teaching in public schools?" . . .

Despite their apparent power, the purity crusaders of the 1980s made only limited gains at the national level. Although abortion debates proved rancorous, consuming much of the time of Congress, no further restrictions were passed into law. Issues such as abortion or school prayer were too unpredictable, and too threatening to Republican unity, for the Reagan administration to pay much more than lip service to them. Instead, Reagan devoted his energy to expanding the nation's military establishment and dismantling liberal social-welfare programs. Some sops were thrown to the New Right. In 1985, Attorney General Edwin Meese established a commission on pornography that toured the country intent on exposing the social harm allegedly caused by explicit sexual materials. . . . Of greater significance, Reagan also tended to appoint to the federal judiciary men and women sympathetic to the New Right. The five-to-four 1986 Supreme Court decision in *Bowers v. Hardwick* that sustained the constitutionality of sodomy laws directed against homosexuals was, perhaps, a harbinger of things to come.

On a local level, meanwhile, purity crusaders more easily flexed their political muscles. School districts throughout the nation faced increasing surveillance from parents angry over sex education classes or the novels that students were asked to read. In Chicago in 1986, the actions of the Roman Catholic hierarchy succeeded in defeating a gay rights ordinance, the passage of which had seemed certain until church leaders spoke up. An Atlanta campaign against adult theaters and bookstores reduced the numbers of such establishments from forty-four in the late seventies to a mere handful by 1981. North Carolina legislators enacted a new, tougher pornography law that allowed police to seize materials and make arrests without a prior order from the courts. . . .

The effort to contain pornography reveals how complex the alignments over sexual issues had become. A major focus of feminist energy in the 1970s had been efforts to combat sexual violence — rape, harassment, wife battering, and incest. Whether these phenomena had increased in scope, or feminist campaigns had simply brought them to light, is impossible to determine. But, the eruption of pornographic imagery into the public sphere seemed like the last straw for activists who daily encountered the victims of violence. . . . Organizations such as Women Against Pornography put together slide shows aimed at exposing the brutalizing fantasies that some hard-core materials purveyed, and their members conducted tours of the porn districts that had sprung up in the early 1970s. Anti-porn feminists subscribed to the dictum "pornography is the theory, rape is the practice." . . . By the early 1980s Andrea Dworkin and feminist lawyer Catharine MacKinnon were drafting their own model obscenity statutes, which defined pornography as a violation of women's civil rights, and they found themselves in political alliance with the New Right in Indianapolis and Suffolk County, New York, and other places where the anti-pornography impulse was strong. Some anti-porn feminists were also witnesses before the Meese commission, urging it to take a tough stand against sexually explicit materials.

Other feminists, meanwhile, bristled at the potential for censorship contained in the anti-porn movement and at the dangers that this unexpected alliance posed to women's exploration of the erotic. Ellen Willis, who had helped launch women's liberation in New York City, acknowledged that pornography could be a "psychic assault," but that "for women as for men it can also be a source of erotic pleasure." For a woman to enjoy pornography, she wrote, "is less to collaborate in her oppression than to defy it, to insist on an aspect of her sexuality that has been defined as a male preserve. . . . [I]n rejecting sexual repression and hypocrisy — which have inflicted even more damage on women than on men — [pornography] expresses a radical impulse." Willis attacked the "goody-goody" concept of sexuality that anti-porn activists espoused as "not feminist but feminine." It preserved, she argued, the old "good girl–bad girl" dichotomy that denied most women access to erotic pleasure and adventure. . . .

Despite the strange alliance over pornography, most ideologues of the Christian-based purity crusade identified feminism and gay liberation as the evils they were organizing against. Yet the reasons for the New Right's rapid growth was both more and less than the existence of radical movements for sexual liberation. . . . Especially for some women — those for whom mothering was a central task, who did not work for wages, and who remained religiously devout — the values of the post-liberal era seemed to attack the very source of their self-worth. At times, New Right leaders acknowledged that they were attacking not merely a clearly delineated opposition such as gay liberation, but something more amorphous and widespread. Falwell, for instance, in lambasting pornography, called network television "the greatest vehicle being used to indoctrinate us slowly to accept a pornographic view of life. Pornography is more than a nudey magazine," he said. "It is a prevailing atmosphere of sexual license." In an era when much of mainstream culture was promoting the erotic, little wonder that moral conservatives responded with fury.

At the same time, the New Right also had its own well-defined symbolic concern that brought its diffuse anxieties together. Whatever the issue — abortion or the Equal Rights Amendment, gay liberation or pornography, sex education or the lyrics of rock music — the sexuality of youth served as the unifying element in its campaigns. . . . Its attacks on pornography, for instance, first took shape around the issue of "kiddie-porn," which easily became the object of new legislation. In mobilizing their forces, Anita Bryant and other gay rights antagonists repeatedly raised the phantom of child recruitment. Faced with an epidemic of pregnant teenagers, parents targeted the schools, not because of a failure to provide the instruction that might allow the young to have sex safely, but because the schools were allegedly giving adolescents too much information. Even issues such as abortion and the ERA, so central to the feminist agenda for women's equality, resonated with concerns about the young. A right-to-life activist in California, for example, saw abortion as one part of a larger problem of youthful sexual expression:

> I don't think we would have as many sexually active teenagers, first of all, if contraception weren't readily available and acceptable. . . . There's more of a temptation to participate in sex than we had when we were young . . . because you just knew that if you were sexually active you might well get pregnant.

A leader of the anti-ERA forces in New York State also turned to the young in explaining her involvement in politics. "For one thing, it would allow gays to marry and adopt children," she said. "If anything ever happened to me, I don't want to think that gays could adopt my children."

Fears about the sexual behavior of youth give the contemporary purity crusade the historical specificity one would expect to find in a social movement. For of all the changes in sexual mores that occurred in the 1960s and 1970s, the spread of sexual activity among the young marked the sharpest break with the past. . . . Youth engaged not just in occasional experimentation, nor did they have sex only in the context of a marriage-oriented relationship. The erotic became incorporated as a regular, ongoing feature of their maturation. The visibility of sex in American culture gave them a familiarity with sex and an interest in it regardless of their parents' wishes. The lyrics of the songs they listened to and danced to — "Let's spend the night together" or "I want a man with a slow hand," to name just two — incited desire as well as suggested possibilities. That many of them would not marry until well into their twenties, and that cohabitation was an acceptable option, made the marriage-oriented ethic of sexual liberalism increasingly irrelevant to their lives. It was the ability and willingness of youth to explore the erotic that most signaled the passing of sexual liberalism. It also imparted emotional power to a purity crusade that attacked all the manifestations of the post-liberal era and that sought the restoration of a marriage-based sexual system replete with gendered and reproductive meanings.

The AIDS Crisis

While the New Right vigorously pursued political solutions to the new sexual permissiveness, an argument for retrenchment came from another, unexpected quarter. In 1980 and 1981, a few doctors in Los Angeles, San Francisco, and New York began encountering puzzling medical phenomena. Young homosexual men in the prime of life were dying suddenly from a rare pneumonia, pneumocystis carinii, or wasting away from an unusual cancer, Kaposi's sarcoma, that normally attacked older men of Mediterranean ancestry who recovered from the disease. By the summer of 1981 it became clear to these doctors, as well as to the Centers for Disease Control in Atlanta, that a devastating new disease syndrome had entered the annals of medicine. Acquired Immune Deficiency Syndrome (AIDS), as it was labeled, destroyed the body's natural defenses against infection, making the victim susceptible to a host of opportunistic infections which the body seemed incapable of resisting. Unlike other recent new illnesses, such as Legionnaire's Disease or Toxic Shock Syndrome, from which most patients recovered, AIDS had no cure. The immune system did not return to normal, and the mortality rate was frighteningly high. Moreover, the case load grew at an alarming pace: 225 at the end of 1981, 1,400 by the spring of 1983, 15,000 in the summer of 1985, and 40,000 two years later.

AIDS revealed how tenuous the progress of gay liberation had been. Because the initial victims in the United States were gay men, and because a majority of the total cases remained within the male homosexual population, AIDS gave those who were hostile, or even ambivalent, toward homosexuality the opportunity to vent their spleen. The New Right quickly recognized AIDS as a vehicle to whip up hysteria and move its political agenda forward. . . . The military imposed mandatory testing for the presence of antibodies to the virus believed to induce AIDS, while Congress enacted legislation requiring the test for all immigrants. Both measures involved areas where gay activists had sought relief from discriminatory policies, and thus they transformed the disease into a new weapon to preserve inequality. . . .

As the medical establishment searched for explanations, some of the mystery dissolved. In France in 1983, and in the United States soon thereafter, researchers isolated a virus that was apparently the culprit. AIDS was infectious rather than contagious. The virus could not be transmitted casually, but seemed to require the exchange of bodily fluids — blood or semen — between one person and another. Rather than a "homosexual disease," it was apparently a quirk that in the United States AIDS first manifested itself among gay men. But once present in that population, it could be passed from partner to partner through anal or oral sex, with the dense web of sexual relationships in the gay male subculture allowing for its rapid spread. Moreover it soon became clear that gay men were not the only high-risk group. Intravenous drug users, whose sharing of needles allowed blood to pass from one to another, accounted for a significant minority of AIDS cases. The virus could also be transmitted through sexual contact from men to women, and from pregnant mothers infected with the virus to their newborn infants. Indeed, by 1986, much media coverage focused on the alleged dangers of the disease spreading quickly through the heterosexual population.

For the gay male community, AIDS provoked fear, anguish, and soul-searching, as well as an upsurge of organization and political involvement. . . . Gay men woke in the morning to check their bodies for the appearance of lesions that signaled Kaposi's sarcoma. The common cold or flu triggered worries about the onset of pneumonia. For some, the fact of AIDS called into question the viability of a nonmonogamous gay male life. As one person with AIDS ruefully commented, "the belief that was handed to me was that sex was liberating and more sex was more liberating." AIDS seemed to be a cruel outcome of the freedom that gay liberation promised. It also shook the pride and confidence that the 1970s had gradually built. "The psychological impact of AIDS on the gay community is tremendous," said Richard Failla, an openly gay judge in New York City. "It has done more to undermine the feelings of self-esteem than anything Anita Bryant could have ever done. Some people are saying 'Maybe we *are* wrong — maybe this is a punishment.'" . . .

On the other hand, the gay community also responded to the AIDS crisis with an enormous outpouring of energy and determination. In New York City, the Gay Men's Health Crisis formed in 1981, at the very start of the epidemic. It drew in thousands of volunteers to help care for the sick and dying, raised millions of dollars for education and research, and lobbied for state and federal research money to unravel the mystery of the disease and find a cure. In city after city where cases appeared, the gay community mounted similar efforts. . . . AIDS organizations widely publicized "safe-sex" guidelines to cut the risk of transmission. In New York and San Francisco, where AIDS hit first and ravaged the community most severely, the impact of the campaigns in reshaping gay male sexuality could be seen in the large decline in the incidence of other sexually transmitted diseases such as syphilis and gonorrhea. Men used condoms for anal sex, reduced sharply the number of sexual partners they had, and learned to enjoy practices such as mutual masturbation. Business at gay bathhouses that did remain open fell dramatically. Observers within the community pointed to a new emphasis on dating, romance, and monogamous relationships. One study of urban gay males found that between 1984 and 1987 the proportion who were celibate rose from two to twelve percent, while those in a monogamous partnership jumped from twelve to twenty-eight percent. The group in the population that had most symbolized the new sexual contours of the post-liberal era was cutting another path.

By the mid-1980s it was also evident that the fear of AIDS was beginning to reach into the heterosexual population. For a generation raised with penicillin and antibiotics, the long historical association of sexual promiscuity with disease had faded as an inhibitor of behavior. Then, at the start of the 1980s, the media gave play to the prevalence of genital herpes. AIDS added a lethal dimension to the disease problem. Especially as it became clear that AIDS could be transmitted through heterosexual intercourse, and after the death of Rock Hudson made AIDS a household word, many heterosexuals took stock of their own sexual habits. On college campuses, health administrators made AIDS a prime focus of their educational efforts. The director of the health service at the University of Southern California thought that students seemed "less willing to have casual encounters than they were four or five years ago." Many universities reported a sharp decline in the cases of venereal disease on campus. Trust and intimacy loomed larger as factors in a sexual relationship, particularly perhaps for women. As one female graduate student phrased her concerns, "it is no longer a question of just you yourself. It's now a question of the commitment of the person with whom you're involved. If he switch-hits, or if he ever has in the last three or four years, it could be a real problem." . . .

The Reagan administration, led by Secretary of Education William Bennett, latched onto the crisis as an opportunity to promulgate a new chastity message among the nation's youth. One federally financed pamphlet, *Sex Respect*, encouraged teenagers to "just say no." But Reagan's Surgeon General, Everett Koop, who a few years earlier had been a prominent anti-abortion activist, dissented vigorously and urged comprehensive sex education in the schools, including the information that condoms were effective in forestalling the spread of the virus. Organizations working on the issue of teenage pregnancy found that AIDS was opening doors previously closed to them. Marian Wright Edelman, founder and president of the Children's Defense Fund, reported that the new sense of urgency created by the epidemic was accomplishing "what one million teenage pregnancies couldn't do: get us talking about sex. . . . People who were tongue-tied realize that they must address something that is lethal." On some campuses students campaigned to have condom vending machines installed in dormitories. Remaining taboos in the media fell. Some network affiliates began accepting ads for condoms, prime-time series addressed the issues of birth control and "safe sex," and news anchors found themselves speaking of anal intercourse before millions of viewers.

Although the political activity of the New Right and the threat of AIDS seemed to augur a retrenchment in the behavior of many Americans, as the 1980s drew to a close it was not at all clear what the future would bring. Certainly the outcome of current controversies about sex would have to build upon the complicated set of sexual meanings that had evolved over generations. For instance, in seeking a restoration of sexuality to marriage, replete with reproductive consequences, advocates of the new chastity had to contend with the permeation of the erotic throughout American culture, the expansive and varied roles available to American women, and a contraceptive technology that sustained the nonprocreative meanings of sexual behavior. A new sexual system that harkened back to a vanished world could not simply be wished into existence. . . .

For almost two centuries sexuality had been moving into the market-place. . . . Not only did modern capitalism sell sexual fantasies and pleasures as commodities, but the dynamics of a consumer-oriented economy had also packaged many products in sexual wrappings. The commercialization of sex and the sexualization of commerce placed the weight of capitalist institutions on the side of a visible public presence for the erotic. Political movements based on sexual issues alone, whether of the right or the left, faced huge obstacles in their efforts to alter this trend, unless they tackled other issues as well. Sex was too deeply embedded in the fabric of economic life for a purity movement to reshape its meaning in fundamental ways. Exploitable as it was for profit, sex had become resistant to efforts at containment that failed to address this larger economic matrix. And, for movements such as feminism and gay liberation that attacked the manipulation of sexuality to sustain social inequality, systems of gender relations as well as economic structures required revision if activists were to achieve their goals.

The contemporary debates over sex also highlight the continuing efforts of Americans to define a place for sex in their lives. . . . Spiritual union, emotional satisfaction, individual identity: these and other definitions have competed for hegemony. For much of the nineteenth and twentieth centuries, the values of the white, native-born urban middle class placed a premium on sexual expression within the context of marriage, even as working-class youth, blacks, an emergent gay community, and others pursued alternative sexual ethics. As the dominant middle-class culture has come to attach more value to sexual fulfillment and pleasure, preserving marriage as a privileged site for sexual expression has proven more difficult. Then, too, the easy availability of effective methods of birth control has removed much of the danger that once attached to nonmarital heterosexuality. And, as women have moved out of the home and into the labor market, their interest in keeping sex within a marital context has declined. . . .

Though not free of agencies of regulation, the individual has more autonomy than ever before to make choices about "personal life." And the range of choices is wider than in the past. A permanent monogamous partnership is one, but so is serial monogamy, homosexual identity, singles life, cohabitation, and unmarried motherhood. Were the choices not so varied, the possibility of AIDS spreading through the population would be too remote to evoke such deep concern.

Contemporary events also illustrate the continuing power of sex as a symbol capable of arousing deep, irrational fears. In the nineteenth and early twentieth centuries, female purity most often served as the symbol that mobilized social anxieties, as campaigns against prostitution and the hysteria over white slavery demonstrated. In the South it combined with fears about racial amalgamation to maintain a rigid caste system of race relations. Today, female purity has lost much of its symbolic force. But the response to AIDS certainly proves the ease with which sexual issues can unleash the irrational. . . .

Finally, the AIDS epidemic and the politics it spawned emphasize the persistence of sexuality as a vehicle for social control. The mythology about blacks propagated by slave owners, the nineteenth-century medical campaigns against abortion, the nativist implications of the white slavery scare, the wave of lynchings in the South, the Cold War preoccupation with homosexuality: these and other episodes demonstrate how commonly sexuality has fostered the maintenance of social hierarchies. The response to AIDS continued this long historical tradition. Gay activists attacked the slow response of the Reagan administration as a sign of how little value it placed on gay lives. The reluctance of government agencies to fund safe-sex campaigns and to provide intravenous drug users with sterilized needles as parts of a comprehensive prevention program allowed the disease to keep spreading not only through the gay male community but also among inner-city black and Hispanic populations where drug use is a serious problem. As in the past, state legislatures targeted prostitutes rather than male customers even though female-to-male transmission of AIDS is much less likely than the reverse. The unwillingness of conservative moralists to make birth control and safe-sex information available to sexually active youth not only perpetuated teenage pregnancy but now threatened the lives of some of the young. Power over sex is the power to affect the life and death of Americans. . . .

Women's role in the family and the public realm has altered so profoundly that a gender-based system resting on female purity is not likely to be resurrected. The capitalist seizure of sexuality has destroyed the division between public reticence and private actions that the nineteenth-century middle class sought to maintain. Perhaps what the study of America's history allows us to say with assurance is that sexuality has become central to our economy, our psyches, and our politics. For this reason, it is likely to stay vulnerable to manipulation as a symbol of social problems and the subject of efforts to maintain social hierarchies. As in the past, sex will remain a source of both deep personal meaning and heated political controversy.

Index